The Horn Book

The Horn Book

STUDIES IN EROTIC FOLKLORE
AND BIBLIOGRAPHY

By G. LEGMAN

UNIVERSITY BOOKS INC.
NEW HYDE PARK, NEW YORK

First Printing February 1964
Second Printing January 1966

CONTENTS

I

STUDIES IN EROTIC BIBLIOGRAPHY

> Those who know
> do not say,
> and those who say
> do not know.
>
> LAO-TZE

THE BIBLIOGRAPHY
OF PROHIBITED BOOKS
"PISANUS FRAXI"

I

THE RANDOM bibliographical articles of which the present volume is composed, sampling and describing at length some of the more typical but elusive masterpieces of erotic literature in various languages, were never intended by the writer as a *World-history of Erotic Literature* in the German sense, a task which is evidently too large for anyone but journalists to presume to undertake. Dr. Paul Englisch, in several handsome volumes published in Germany during the late 1920's, has done as much as can honestly be done in the way of a large-scale survey of erotic literature, without falling into the ignorant and pretentious smattering that is the hallmark of what passes nowadays for literary scholarship, and perhaps always did. This sort of superficiality has also its counter-vice, actually identical but passing itself off instead as erudition: an excessive and finicking concern with unimportant details of literary form or vehicle, to the exclusion of the real matter and meaning; with the piddling minutiæ of line-endings, water-marks, and title-page variants, and altogether with a sort of biblio-coprolitic residue not worth considering at all — the sort of drivel endlessly and solemnly macerated in learned articles and Ph.D. dissertations submitted to, and accepted by, faculties of Literature and Arts, with *apparatus criticus,* notes, variants, stemma, and thematic index invariably as enormously large as the subject-matter is microscopically small.

So far, we have not yet arrived at the biblio-coprolitic or pseudo-scientific approach to the study of erotic literature, attempting to discern the soul of an author, and the meaning of his book, through the watermark of the paper on which it is printed and a Hollerith machine tabulation of its typographical errors. We are, rather, as far as erotic literature is concerned, still largely under the reign of Sunday supplement vulgarizations and the half-

9

baked men's magazine approach, what has so aptly been described as 'the creeping mental slobbism of our times.' It would of course be invidious to single out any one specimen among the many recent assembly-line jobs on the history of erotica, priced from 35¢ to six guineas *au choix* (depending only on the number of nude female illustrations in color), and presented to the palpitating public of England, Denmark, and the United States, with at least three more announced in manuscript as forthcoming. I rather think, however, that no one would refuse the palm to a curious item of less than one hundred pages of text, in large, more-than-readable type, plentifully ventilated with blank chapter-heads and irrelevant poetry, vanity-published — and very well publicized — in New York, 1958, by its author, a Mr. Ralph Ginzburg, at that time 'junior editor' on the staff of *Esquire* magazine, and entitled in purest doublethink, *An Unhurried View of Erotica,* evidently a typographical error for "An *Unheard-of View* . . . ," which sets the all-time, highwater mark for total and grotesque ignorance of this very difficult subject, combined with a delicious and insouciant journalistic retailing of historic lies, twice-told tales, phoney rumors, original nonsense, and agglomerated *dreck.* The present writer cannot compete, and would not try to compete, with these champions.

Bibliography is the poor man's book-collecting. The rich, who collect books — a minority, nowadays — do not in general write bibliographies, though they do sometimes hire librarians to do this work for them. The resulting bibliographies, or rather collection-catalogues, are a harmless ostentation on the part of rich collectors, and an honorable one. More than that, they are almost always useful bibliographical tools, being essentially more or less complete subject catalogues of the collectors' interests. As such, they form a partial key to these subjects, when the collections have been dispersed forever at public sale or auction — for the benefit of poverty-stricken heirs, down to the defunct's last million — or, which is almost as bad, have been spread out irrecoverably among the over-large holdings of modern public and university libraries, many of which, as in Great Britain, have no satisfactory subject-catalogues and seem unaware that these are an indispensable tool.

Erotic literature is one of the few exceptions to this danger of dispersion, when it is preserved at all. It should be noted, however, that most private collections of erotica do not survive their collectors. Though seldom burnt nowadays, as was once almost the rule, they are generally sold off immediately to trusted book-

dealers — in whom, as in the heirs, the lure of profit is somehow
stronger than the hope of heaven — and do not even appear in the
auction catalogue, if any. But in the exceptional cases, where erotic
collections are frankly made part of a posthumous gift to a great
public or university library, the usual prudery will assist in preserving such collections intact, rather than dispersing them
among the general library stock. They still commonly take their
place among the other 'hell' books, or secret collection of erotica
and sexualia, in the repository libraries (not one of which, so far
as I know, puts any similar restriction on books about murder);
and somewhere, one hopes, a catalogue of them continues to exist.
Though not always. One of the largest libraries in the United
States is at the present time under so close a moral surveillance
by its trustees, that no catalogue whatsoever of erotic accessions
is said to be kept, and these are smuggled helter-skelter into a
private room (after having been announced formally as 'destroyed'), in the hope that they — or what will be left of them —
can perhaps be brought out and at least catalogued a century from
now! This is not even unusual, and is also the case in one of the
largest libraries of Great Britain, though there only in connection
with books actually condemned by trial, of which even the library
assistants are not allowed access to the summary catalogue. The
"Enfer" of the Bibliothèque Nationale in Paris, which is the only
great library that straightforwardly lists its erotic holdings in the
printed catalogue, was itself only separately catalogued for the
first time in 1913, *more* than a century after the creation of this
collection, for the deposit of seized and prohibited books, by
Napoleon, the cataloguing having begun about 1880.

Almost invariably, the catalogues of the libraries' erotica are
also kept secret, thus making the books themselves practically impossible to consult, in all these variously-titled "Private Cases"
and "Cherry Cabinets," these "Librarians' Offices" and "Special
Reserves," these Greek-lettered *Delta's, Zeta's,* and punning *Phi's*
and *Scruple's;* these *Double-S* and *Three Star* secret-of-secrets and
unholy of holies, from which doubly and triply barred literary
harems, however, the prize beauties have, nevertheless, an embarrassing habit of being regularly stolen: by the trusted readers
or trusted library-staff, one or the other. All in all, and in spite
of the periodically announced 'new freedom' — for literature, as
for life — any collector who has the courage, or perhaps the folly,
to collect erotic books, is well-advised, if he really wants to make
some contribution to literary history, to arrange to publish him-

self a catalogue of at least this part of his collection, during his
lifetime, with whatever limitation of printing and audience that
discretion seems to warrant; rather than trust to the tender mercies
and bibliographical care of heirs, auctioneers, bookdealers, and
repository librarians, after his death. There is the love that laughs
at locksmiths, and this is the love of books that laughs at locks,
at censors, at cupidity, and at death itself.

In the history of erotic book collecting, only a handful of collectors has been found to see the wisdom of this course. What little
we know of collections and collectors outside this handful comes
to us sparsely, and often with dubious correctness, from the few
auction catalogues, mostly of the 19th century, in which erotic
books have exceptionally been allowed to figure. One of the first
of these was the *Verzeichniss einer Sammlung, &c.* of C. G. Guenther (Dresden, 1834; reprinted in 1862 for its bibliographical interest), largely composed of erotic and 'sotadic' books — so called
after Sotades, the earliest Greek author of erotica of whom any
record (though none of his writings but a handful of poetic fragments) still exists. The section of *facetiæ* in these exceptional
auction catalogues, and in those of specialist bookdealers (now always styled *curiosa* in France), still represents the best source of
bibliographical information, if not on actual erotica, at least on
those marginal elements of unexpurgated literature such as jestbooks and balladry, works on (and against) women and love, facetious treatises in prose and in verse, and the hinterland of
scatologica. One of the richest such collections, in England, was
that of George Daniel, auctioned off by Sotheby in London, 1864,
of which the printed catalogue includes such unique items as,
no. 607, *Peregrine Penis, New Frisky Songster* (1794), and a whole
group of poetic 'garlands' of folk-verse. Two other unusually frank
auction-catalogues of the period were those of the George Holliday
library, sold by Bouton, in New York, 1870; and the *Bibliotheca
Curiosa,* or library of Andrew Odell, sold by Bangs, 1878; upon
both of which the "Fraxi" work draws usefully for its listing of
19th century American semi-erotica (*Catena*, p. 199–237).

Among the last such catalogues published in France was the
Catalogue . . . composant le cabinet de M. L. C. (*i.e.* Constantin),
1876, 70 pages, 8vo, which has been described as 'Une des collections érotiques les plus complètes et les mieux choisies de Paris,'
though it will hardly compare to the *Catalogue du cabinet secret
du Prince G**** (*i.e.* Galitzin), Bruxelles, 1887, of which the indelicacy of splashing the noble collector's title and easily-divined

initial at the top of every leaf, resulted in the sale being stopped after only the first half of the alphabet, *A-L* (192 pages, 8vo) had been published, an irreparable loss to erotic bibliography. Few or no such wholly erotic sales catalogues have ever been published since, and almost no private collection catalogues except the recent *Bibliothèque "La Léonina," III. Curiosa* (Monte Carlo, 1955), prepared for the collector, M. Arpad Plesch, by M. Jacques Pley. It was on the basis of such listings, public and private, of great collections about to be broken up by sale or auction, that the first published bibliography of erotic and facetious literature was undertaken, in the 1860's, as *Bibliographie des ouvrages relatifs à l'amour,* by "le Comte d'I***" (actually the publisher of erotica, Jules Gay), with the help of many collectors; a work later enlarged to four heavy volumes by J. Lemonnyer, 1894–1900, which remains the principal bibliography of French and Italian erotica. This is not the place to discuss at length the history of erotic bibliography, nor to assess the value of the various works in many languages, from German to Japanese, which cover this literature up to a certain date. It is worth mentioning, however, that no bibliography has ever yet been published wholly devoted to the erotic literature of the English language — the only major language of which this is true. The present writer has been collecting materials for such a bibliography over the last twenty-five years, but it has not yet been possible to find a publisher who will undertake so large a work.

II

THE "Notes on Curious and Uncommon Books" of the author calling himself Pisanus Fraxi, printed originally in private quarto editions, in red and black, under the elegant disguise of forbidding Latin titles to the three volumes: *Index Librorum Prohibitorum* (1877), *Centuria Librorum Absconditorum* (1879), and *Catena Librorum Tacendorum* (1885), a set recently reprinted twice — if not three times! — by photo-facsimile (London, 1960, and New York, 1962) are a principal exception to the modern rule of journalistic smattering and superficiality on the one hand, and bibliological over-precision and futilitarianism on the other. Henry Spencer Ashbee — to call "Pisanus Fraxi" by his real name — set out to do only a very limited thing, but in a thorough and profound way. He proposed simply to describe, and copiously to quote, some of the many hundreds of erotic books in various languages that had passed through his hands, and through the hands of some of his friends, during a long and assiduous career as a collector, precisely, of erotica. His striking success, as opposed to the abysmal failure of most of his imitators, rises clearly from the limitations within which he was satisfied to work, without any megalomaniacal vaunting and flaunting of his interests and his evident erudition to cover everything in the world in a pretended 'system' or history.

This is the exact opposite of the hack items to which we are now being treated increasingly by catch-quarter and snag-guinea authors and their publishers, out to cash in on the recent relative freedom to discuss, if not openly to publish, erotic books. Almost the only honorable exception among all the current critical and historical works — which also happens to be one of the least expensive and most unassuming — is *Pornography and the Law* (New York, 1959) by the Drs. Eberhard & Phyllis Kronhausen, which takes a psychological approach covering only a limited area, but there succeeds in digging unexpectedly deep. The same authors give a further analysis of the subject, as "The Psychology of Pornography," in *The Encyclopedia of Sexual Behavior* edited by Drs. Albert Ellis & Abarbanel (New York, 1961, II. 848–59), with an excellent short bibliographical list.

Ashbee's work is modeled on three main annotated bibliographies of the early 19th century, which are the masterpieces of the form: Charles Nodier's *Mélanges tirés d'une petite bibliothèque* (Paris, 1829; importantly supplemented in the catalogue of the Nodier auction, *Description raisonnée, &c.*, 1844), of which the title politely mocks the "Mélanges tirés d'une *grande* bibliothèque" of a predecessor; likewise the *Analectabiblion, ou Extraits critiques de divers livres rares, oubliés ou peu connus*, by the Marquis D. R.*** (*i.e.* Du Roure; 2 volumes, Paris, 1836–37; also supplemented in his auction catalogue, under the initials M. L. M. D. R., Paris: Jannet, 1848), and in particular, the *Medical Bibliography: A. and B.*, of James Atkinson (London, 1834), which, being delayed until the author's seventy-fifth year, never proceeded beyond the first two letters of the alphabet, but which is a truly remarkable production, to which Ashbee gives full appreciation (*Centuria*, p. 502–3), and of which the offset reissue has recently been announced in England.

What is so exceptional about all these works — in particular those of Nodier and Atkinson — is their *personalness* of approach, and fullness of quotation, at a time when bibliography was already turning into what it has almost entirely become today: a soulless and endless cataloguing of titles, publishers, dates, and (sometimes) paginations, and nothing more, owing to the pressure of increasingly enormous international book-production, requiring at the very least this cold and meagre indexing; and even of this, for that matter, English literature is still some two centuries in arrears. Nodier and Atkinson — and Ashbee like them — do not hesitate to devote ten or a score of pages to a single work that they consider to be typical or crucial. All of them work on the unspoken principle of the discoverers of dinosaurs' bones in Chinese pharmacy-shops: *Ab uno disce omnes,* from this *one* guess all the rest. (Virgil, *Æneid,* ii. 65.) Ashbee in particular quotes lavishly from the texts before him, partly because he was a rich man publishing his bibliographies himself, and could afford to quote as he pleased, but also clearly because he was aware that he was dealing with books of exceptional rarity, far more so than the merely medical rarities or bibliographical curios under the attention of Atkinson and Nodier. In very many cases nothing more is known today, or will probably ever be known, of certain works quoted by Ashbee, than the passages he quotes; the books themselves having disappeared since.

It is not well known, and is worth underlining here, that *most erotic books of earlier centuries have disappeared almost completely, or are in the process of doing so.* An extraordinarily large number of erotica, in all languages, are known only by their titles or else by an occasional and very often unique printed copy — a reprint of some later century, as often as not — preserved by accident in some great public or university library. Any collection of erotica (or, for that matter, of any other type of literary ephemera, such as joke books, song books, or humorous magazines) composed of materials published even so recently as the 1900's or 1930's, will invariably contain an astonishing proportion of absolutely unique items, unknown in any other collection after even so short a time as twenty years. Gutenberg Bibles and other incunabula are not rare, and Shakespeare folios even less so; anyone who cares to put up the money can buy one today. But of so famous or infamous an erotic chapbook as the *Sonetti lussuriosi* of Aretino (if their original title was not, more likely, *La Corona di Cazzi*), with woodcut illustrations after the drawings by Giulio Romano, printed in Venice, possibly for Francesco Marcolini, in 1527, not a single copy has been recorded in over four hundred years; and this slender pamphlet was utterly despaired of as lost forever, until, by an incredible stroke of good luck, a unique copy containing fourteen of the original sixteen woodcuts was discovered only a few years back, in Milan. But this is a story too long and too fantastic to tell here. The present writer is preparing an extended study of this unique copy of Aretino's *Sonnets,* its poetic text — in part never reprinted anywhere since 1527 — and the mystery of its famous illustrations, of which all printed 'copies' without exception, circulated since the 18th century, are either unrelated imitations or impudent fakes.

The social historian of the 18th and early 19th centuries in England will, in particular, have much to thank Ashbee for. The only such large-scale social history as yet written, *Englische Sittengeschichte* (2nd ed., 1912, in two volumes; the English translation in the 1930's is much abridged), was, in fact, written by one of Ashbee's co-collectors, and his main biographer, Iwan Bloch — writing under the pseudonym of "Eugen Duehren" — who was given access to Ashbee's library, but whose own collection of modern Spanish erotica and other unique materials was broken up by public sale after his death, with several of the further collections into which it went being seized and destroyed by the Nazis. There is still a great deal to be mined, both in Ashbee's bibliographies and in that part of the collection described which has been preserved in the British Museum, especially in connection with the period from 1700 to about 1860, the period of Dr. William King's *The Toast* (see *Centuria,* p. 301–25), of Wilkes' and Potter's *Essay on Woman* (see *Index,* p. 198–236, and *Centuria,* p. xiv–xv), and, to be sure, of John Cleland's *Memoirs of a Woman of Pleasure* better known as *Fanny Hill* (see *Catena,* p. 60–95). This is the period which is now becoming the principal and most desperately hasty area of library collecting, now that most of the desirable books in English, of earlier centuries, have been thoroughly bought up, locked up, and docketed in the *Short-Title Catalogue* (to 1640, of which a revised edition is now announced in preparation), and its continuation to 1700 by Mr. Donald G. Wing, the indefatigable associate-librarian of Yale University. Unfortunately, the only *subject*-indexing to all this enormous mass of books, from 1475 to 1700, so far attempted, is the magnificent but evidently insufficient *Cambridge Bibliography of English Literature* (5 volumes, 1940–55), and it goes without saying that little will be learned from the *C.B.E.L.,* or from its collateral textvolumes, the *Cambridge History of English Literature,* as to even the English-language erotica.

Ashbee remains — with a few recent minor works, such as Ralph Straus' biography of the erotica-publisher Curll (of whose books one of the best collections, that made by the late Peter Murray Hill, is now in the University of Kansas Library), and the bibliographies by Case and Bond of poetic miscellanies and burlesque verse of the 18th century — remains, I say, the principal guidebook and source work for the future moral historian of England in the 18th century, and has a great deal to tell any similar historian of England and the rest of Europe, as well as America, to nearly the end of the 19th century as well. A number of attempts at such a social history have appeared since the 1920's. All of them almost without exception have the curious feature — a hallmark of modern hurry-up research, and a clear result of the gross inadequacy of modern subject-indexing of published books — of being written in total ignorance of the existence of their predecessors, and they naturally limp badly as a result of this superficiality. The best, after the work by Iwan Bloch cited above, is probably that of Victor F. Calverton (George Goetz) in the 1920's; along with the more recent works — principally on the Victorian age — by Maurice Quinlan, Clarence R. Decker, and, in England, Cyril Pearl (a mere journalist,) and G. Rattray Taylor; of which latter only the volumes by Quinlan and Taylor are anchored, with any real erudition or perception, in the subterranean literature to which Ashbee is still the principal key.

III

THE FEW KNOWN facts of Ashbee's public life are simply the stiff British externals. These are fully reviewed by Iwan Bloch, in *Englische Sittengeschichte* (1912) II. 498–510, following an exceedingly valuable chapter on English publishers and collectors of erotica, and with a long appreciation, well worth consulting, of Ashbee's bibliographical method and achievements. The biographical materials are again presented briefly, by Dr. Paul Englisch, with a handsome ex-libris portrait of Ashbee ('ein auffallend schöner Mann,' as Bloch says, II. 502; 'mit einem sehr sympathischen Gesicht'), in the finest, and only illustrated, erotic bibliography in existence, volumes II and IV of the fabulous *Bilder-Lexikon der Erotik* (Vienna, 1928–31), now announced for republication in Hamburg with a new and important supplement. Almost nothing had earlier been divulged, other than Ashbee's pseudonym of "Pisanus Fraxi," in the excessively discreet notice of his death appearing in the *Annuaire de la Société des Amis des Livres* (Paris, 1901) XXII. 45–52, a society of which Ashbee had been the principal foreign member, and whose secretary was Alfred Bégis — part-author with Duponchel and Hankey of *L'École des biches* (1868) — whose private library of erotica had been added, by police seizure, to the Enfer of the Bibliothèque Nationale, and is still there. (The twentieth volume of the *Annuaire*, 1899, is entirely devoted to Bégis "Revendication," unsuccessfully attempting to regain possession of his books; and the whole story, including that of *L'École des biches,* will be found in English in the article *"The Horn Book,* And Other Bibliographical Problems," here following.

To state very briefly what is known: Henry Spencer Ashbee was born in April 1834. He was a businessman by profession, becoming head of the international firm of Charles Lavy & Co., Coleman Street, London, dealers in 'essential oils' according to one source. His library was, until 1895, shelved in his London home, at 53 Bedford Square, where he was always willing generously to display its treasures to visiting European book-collectors and bibliographers, by all of whom he was extremely well-liked and respected. Ashbee traveled extensively, everywhere in the world — Asia, Africa, America, China and Japan (this in an age long before airplanes) — and his book *Travels in Tunisia* is still of value. He spent most of his winters in Spain, where he accumulated one of the world's best private collections of editions of Cervantes' *Don Quixote,* of which more will be said in a moment, and of which he published an elegant catalogue. More importantly, Ashbee also made, and continued with its collecting right up to the last month of his life, what is still the finest private collection of erotic books in all European languages; though his three volumes of erotic bibliography under the pseudonym "Pisanus Fraxi," now reprinted, are *not* the catalogue of that collection, a point well worth underscoring. On a final voyage to Spain and Morocco, at the age of sixty-seven, Ashbee had a serious heart-attack while at Burgos, following a case of influenza (a winter disease still sub-epidemic in France, Spain, and southwestern Europe generally), but managed to regain England, where he died at his country-estate, Fowlers, in Hawkhurst, Kent, on the 29th of July, 1900. These are evidently only the bare bones of biography. The man is not there.

A good deal more could probably be said about the personal biography of Ashbee, but, for reasons that will soon appear, this is left for a later section of the present essay. Writing of Ashbee's friendship with the other famous, but highly eccentric British collector of erotica, Frederick Hankey, in Apollinaire, Fleuret, and Perceau's *L'Enfer de la Bibliothèque Nationale* (1913) at no. 21, *L'École des biches,* in a discussion of Hankey's extravagant collection, the Paris erotica-publisher Hirsch tells the end of the story, which, though not in accordance with Ashbee's rule of quoting authorities in their original text and language (see his delicious doggerel poem on this, in *Catena,* p. 488, "On Quoting Authorities"), is given here in translation:

> Hankey's erotic library was ceded in part, by private sale (*à l'amiable*), to Mr. Ashbee, a rich London businessman, better known under the pseudonym of Pisanus Fraxi, with which he signed his three celebrated works on sotadic bibliography. The erotic library of Mr. Ashbee, who died a few years ago, was given to the British Museum, which at first considered refusing the gift, but finally accepted it because Mr. Ashbee, who had similarly bequeathed his collection of all the editions and translations of *Don Quixote,* had made it a condition of this bequest, that the British Museum also conserve his erotic library. It will be found there today.

The Asbee Bequest forms, in fact, the nucleus of the Private Case, or "Enfer," of the British Museum, to this day, with an important group of manuscript bibliographies of erotica (in particular those of James Campbell Reddie and of Bérard) and similar works — among them Hankey's copy, or Lord Houghton's, of Coleman's *The Rodiad,* fantastically bound — kept separately in the Department of Manuscripts. As opposed to the Enfer of the Bibliothèque Nationale in Paris, of which the full contents are described in their alphabetical place in the general printed catalogue; the Private Case books of the British Museum are still rigidly excluded from the printed catalogue of that institution, and the only available key to them is the *Registrum Librorum Eroticorum* (1936) of Alfred Rose, published posthumously under the anagram of "Rolf S. Reade."

A final word of warning will not be out of place here as to the Ashbee Bequest in the Private Case of the British Museum. The present three volumes have long been misunderstood as the *catalogue* of Ashbee's own collection, with the further erroneous

belief that the books here described will be found *in toto* in the
British Museum. This is unfortunately not the case. The present
volumes constitute simply, though superbly, a select and annotated
bibliography of erotic works in many languages, on the basis of
notes taken from the books themselves in almost all cases. That
is a very different thing from being the catalogue of an existing
collection, and this point is again insisted upon here, to help other
researchers avoid the intense disappointment that awaited the
present writer when he made a special voyage to England, with the
expectation of finding all the books described in the present three
volumes neatly preserved — under lock & key, to be sure — in the
British Museum. They are not there, not half. The explanation of
this contretemps is, in part, as follows: Ashbee's bibliographies
were inspired by his receiving from his dying friend, James Campbell Reddie (whose biography is given in *Catena*, p. xlvii, with
portrait facing in the original edition — the New York reprint
unfortunately omits all the fascinating frontispieces and plates,
throughout the set), an exceedingly full and fine manuscript
bibliography of erotic works that had passed through Reddie's
hands, but which, not being as rich as Ashbee, he had not always
been able to buy, but had preserved only in the form of bibliographical notes and excerpts, later quoted — without actual access
to the books themselves — in Ashbee's three printed volumes.
Campbell Reddie's "Bibliographical Notes," as the manuscript is
called (fully described in *Catena*, pp. xlviii–xlix, and 493–4), are
well worth separate publication, and the present writer has obtained — not without excessive difficulty — a microfilm copy of the
manuscript, with the hope eventually of finding a publisher for it.

To give one striking example of the misconceptions these notes
in Ashbee, of books not actually in his collection, can lead to:
there will be found in his first volume (*Index Librorum Prohibitorum*, p. 133–37), a list of nearly fifty bawdy 'songsters and
reciters' published in London during the 'coal-hole and cider-
cellar' period of the early and mid-19th century, when the singing
of such songs was a principal feature of the early music-halls, as
described by Ashbee. The titles of these songsters are apparently
among the materials supplied to Ashbee by Reddie. Far from all
fifty of these priceless chapbook songsters being preserved, at present, in Ashbee's collection in the British Museum, only *four* will
there be found, bound up in to a single volumelet as a curiosity,
perhaps (under the call-mark P.C. 31 g 20, and including *The
Cuckold's Nest of Choice Songs*, among others). Among these four

is not even included *The Blowen's Cabinet of Choice Songs,* of which the amusing full title is transcribed to the tune of twenty lines, by Ashbee, *Index,* p. 133. As to the others, no one knows; though a further group of such songsters — probably rather extensive — is still preserved in the important Harding collection of song-books of all kinds, originally made by Sir John Stainer and now in Chicago. (Another such item, *The Bang-Up Reciter,* probably dating from the 1870's or '80's, but not mentioned by Ashbee, is in my own collection; its full title is given in my article, "The Bawdy Song . . . in Fact and in Print," in this volume.)

Since these lines were written, the unerring bibliographical flair of David Foxon, Esq; whose series of articles on lost and early English erotica, presently appearing in *The Book Collector,* London, pile discovery upon flabbergasting discovery, has turned up no less than fifty further bawdy songsters of the period — all in the same 24to size, but entirely different from Ashbee's untraceable fifty except for two items — slumbering peacefully for the last thirty years in the British Museum, under the call-mark C. 116 a 6–55, not ten feet across the aisle from the "Private Case" incorporating Ashbee's collection, but not included even in its secret catalogue. Let it be understood, therefore, that Ashbee's three great bibliographical volumes are strictly a bibliography, not a collection-catalogue, and must be accepted as such — the poor man's book-collecting, as the reader has already been warned.

IV

THE HIDDEN WORLD of erotic literature offers the most difficult of challenges to the bibliographer, far more difficult than the incunabula of the fifteenth century and the secret publications of religious and political controversy. All of these share to some degree the same curious anonymity, appearing originally without any printed place or date of publication — or with place and date fantastically disguised and falsified — and without any satisfactory indication of the real names of the authors, publishers, and printers. But with this difference: the early incunabula, and the religious and political tracts, can generally be identified by the internal typographical evidence of printing types and styles, or when, eventually, the authors and publishers of the polemic tracts win the day and come out of hiding, to sign their later productions and even to brag of the earlier. The authors and publishers of erotic literature have never come out of hiding, so far as the Western civilizations are concerned, until barely yesterday, and only the accident of a brush with the police and law-courts ever serves to bring them even briefly into the open.

The last erotic writings — actually only good-natured folk facetiæ — ever published openly in the West, without the slightest thought on anyone's part that they might be considered morally 'wrong,' were the jestbooks in all European countries, beginning with Poggio's *Facetiarum liber* (written in 1451, as noted at its no. 240; first published about 1470, and first translated into English for Liseux, Paris, 1879); and a semi-folkloristic work, the *Origine delle volgari proverbi* of Cynthio degli Fabritii, published by Bernardino Vitali in Venice, 1526, in-folio, with the author's and publisher's names plainly given, along with a dedication to Pope Clement VII. (A brief analysis of Cynthio's forty-five proverbs will be found in the introduction by "Philomneste Junior," *i.e.* Gustave Brunet, to Aretino's *Sept petites nouvelles,* Paris: Jules Gay, 1861, p. 52–68.) Exception was unfortunately taken by the Catholic hierarchy of the Inquisition — particularly by the Franciscans, satirized in some of Cynthio's proverbial 'explanations' — to the unexpurgated tone of his work, especially in view of its being dedicated to the Pope, whose 'privilege' it bore, as well as that of the Seigneurie of Venice for ten years. The work was seized and destroyed in large part, and the licensing and censoring of books, both before and after publication, was undertaken as of that year, 1526 (Old Style), in Italy, by the following deliberation of the Council of Ten (Consiglio dei Dieci) of Venice, the printing capital, on 29 January 1527:

> That from this day onward there may not be printed, nor, after having been printed, be published any work or book newly composed and not formerly printed . . . unless there has first been obtained the permission of the heads of this Council, by a *termination* signed by their hand. (Italian text quoted by Giuseppe Fumagalli, *Dictionnaire géographique d'Italie,* pour servir à l'histoire de l'imprimerie dans ce pays; Florence, Olschki, 1905, chap. XIII, p. 494. See also G. I. Arneudo, *Dizionario esegetico per le arti grafiche,* p. 2123, under Vitali; both these references from an unpublished article on Aretino by Albini & Toscanini.)

Behind the pretext of Cynthio's "Proverbs in Jest," there was, to be sure, the real alarm of the church concerning the rapidly-spreading doctrines of Luther, which would probably never have converted half of Europe had it not been for the assistance of the printing press. The real intention behind the new censorship is made clear by the fact that the Venetian edict of 29 January 1527 was applied rigorously only against works of an anti-religious or anti-governmental tone, leaving quite free the bawdy satire of Aretino's *Ragionamenti* and those of his school of secretaries, Franco and Veniero, as well as the fabulous bawdry of the burlesque academicians such as Vignale, appearing with tacit permission under obviously false rubrics of publication (such as 'Lugano'), and false predatings. With the organization of the Inquisition, in Spain, showing the way, in repressive religious control, this led immediately, on the one hand, to the modern laws of printers' 'privilege' and copyright; and on the other hand to the institution of the thus easily-operated Roman Catholic censorship and its *Index Librorum Prohibitorum* (1559) — whose title Ashbee has here appropriated, in delicate jest — several decades later.

The open publication of erotic and facetious works having become forbidden, their secret publication immediately began, within a year, in the *Sonetti lussuriosi* of Pietro Aretino, written to fit the sixteen earlier engravings by Marc-Antonio Raimondi of Giulio Romano's drawings, a set of engravings already prohibited and almost entirely destroyed. The secret publisher of Aretino's *Sonnets* in 1527 was perhaps Marcolini, if not Bindoni & Pasini, or even the same Vitali whose open publication of Cynthio's work had been reprimanded the year before; but now neither printer's name nor that of the author appeared anywhere on the book, which was sold surreptitiously (according to a contemporary libel on Aretino, probably by his disaffected secretary, Niccolò Franco, under the name of Fr. Berni) to passers-by on the Rialto bridge, the most public place in Venice. There, as though with a hot iron, the whole pattern of erotic authorship and publication — and suppression — since that time, is struck.

By the early 1530's, the secret and occasionally the semi-open printing of erotic and facetious prose and verse had become a matter of course: by Aretino and his imitators, in particular Niccolò Franco (who set out to double Aretino's sixteen 'postures' in the *Sonnets* to the now classic thirty-two, in the prose *Puttana errante* — the first work described in Ashbee's first volume — which he cannily signed with Aretino's name!) as also by the tellers of erotic folktales in the style of Boccaccio and the *Arabian Nights*, centuries before; and by the burlesque academicians of Siena and elsewhere, among whom Antonio Vignale, in his *Cazzaria* (1531), or "Book of the Prick," stands out as the most astonishing collector of erotic folk-beliefs and just-so stories in the literature of the world. (A manuscript translation into English, by the late Samuel Putnam, discussed by the translator in *Encyclopædia Sexualis,* 1936, is in my possession, but has never yet been printed.) Since the time of the débacle brought on by Raimondi's 'posture' engravings and Cynthio's "Origin of Vulgar Proverbs," the writers of erotica, their publishers and their artists, have always been a hunted crew, and have learned to disguise themselves.

Only one real help exists for the bibliographer of erotic literature, and that is the raw necessity for the publishers of erotica to advertise their wares, usually by the publication of semi-erotic, sexual scientific, or merely gallant works (nowadays called in French slang the *officiel,* or cover-up, of the publisher), intended as window-dressing, or for open display to prospective customers, and also to explain to the authorities, if necessary, the publisher's otherwise inexplicable activity. There is a whole chapter on this subject, with very amusing facsimiles, in Michael Sadleir's *Forlorn Sunset* (London, 1947) p. 412–20. These semi-erotic or "official" wares naturally give the publishers' real names and addresses, often very conspicuously displayed, and by the study of the distinctive typographical *style* of this sort of signed and dated merchandise, it is generally not too difficult to distinguish, to place, and to date the secret publications of the same publishers, operating simultaneously *sous le manteau,* as — to take a group of publishers now all safely dead — Poulet-Malassis, Gay (father and son), Vital-Puissant, and Kistemaeckers, toward the end of the 19th century in Brussels; and by Carrington, Hirsch, Fort, the brothers Briffaut, and later Duflou, Seheur, Pia, and many others, at the beginning of the twentieth century in Paris. The matching group of modern publishers, particularly in the United States during the economic depression of the 1930's and since, obviously cannot be discussed here, such revelations being premature.

A few erotic books escape even the method of identification by typographical style. These are, in particular, the erotic autobiographies and private poetic ejaculations of amateurs, which are printed privately by or for the authors themselves, usually in very small editions — as opposed to the only pretendedly small editions, fraudulently 'numbered,' of many erotica and other *faux-luxe* publications. Such amateur works are seldom paralleled by any typographically similar group of openly-published gallantiana, intended as advertising, and only by the discovery of indiscreetly inscribed presentation copies, or by the chance divulgations of contemporary collectors, bibliographers, and friends — and sometimes of enemies — can the authors and origins of such works be determined at all. Ashbee's bibliographies are of extraordinary value here, as he seldom hesitated, except in the case of living authors and publishers, to divulge what he knew (which was just about everything) of the hidden literary history of his time.

In France, the literary reputations of great authors such as Alfred de Musset, Théophile Gautier, Henry Monnier, Maupassant, Verlaine, Pierre Louÿs, and many others, has never really been seriously prejudiced, among readers of any pretention to culture, by the knowledge that the erotic romances, playlets, sketches, and poems circulated privately and in very limited editions under these famous names are, in all probability, the authentic juvenilia, or bagatelles of later hours of distraction, of these writers famous for more serious work. To the contrary, the *collectionneurs enragés* of the works of these writers are most particularly famished to come into possession of the original (or all!) editions of precisely these erotic works in which their favorite authors show themselves, for once, as complete men, without the customary plaster figleaf adorning their academic statues and publicly published utterances.

In the Anglo-Saxon countries the opposite is true: any identification with erotic literature would invariably have spelled total disaster for any famous writer, or person in public or professional life, until the advent recently of James Joyce, D. H. Lawrence, and Henry Miller; all of whom, in any case, suffered every sort of indignity for the "obscenity" of their work. The classic case is that of the English liberal Parliamentarian in the 18th century, John Wilkes, whose enemies planned to ruin him by reading before the Houses of Parliament the *Essay on Woman* — written, in fact, by Thomas Potter, the son of an archbishop, as an erotic parody of Pope's flatulent *Essay on Man* — which had been printed on Wilkes' private press. (See the whole story, in Ashbee's *Index Librorum Prohibitorum*, p. 202–10.) A bit, but not much more, leeway is allowed to humorists, such as Mark Twain and Eugene Field, and no one makes much secret any more of the bawdy skits and erotic poems that both these writers were pleased to issue privately for the delectation of their friends, for instance Twain's "1601," and Field's many poems (printed in *Immortalia*, 1927) and *Only a Boy*. In their lifetimes, however, no such open jesting could be permitted, as is shown by the famous case of the first edition of Twain's *Huckleberry Finn,* with the phallic addition to one of the illustrations (surreptitiously engraved on the cut by a disgruntled printer's assistant), which is removed and replaced with a properly sedate illustration in almost all copies.

It is hardly to be wondered at, therefore, that the principal erotic autobiographies and autobiographical fantasies in English have been published only in the most restricted editions, and are already among the most difficult books to procure in this language. The only exceptions are the "Tropics" of Henry Miller, and their various and apparently endless sequels printed openly in France, of which the first and only important volume, *Tropic of Cancer,* has only now, in 1961, for the first time, been openly published in the United States. (A private edition in 1940, under the rubric 'México: Medvsa,' actually printed in New York, was seized, and a large part of this first American edition destroyed.) The original editions of the few other such autobiographies in English are absolutely no longer to be found, by even the most diligent search: Frank Harris' *My Life and Loves* (Germany 1922–27, in four volumes); *The Confessions of Nemesis Hunt* (1902–03, three volumes, apparently written by an Englishwoman connected with the theatre); *Surburban Souls* (1901, three volumes, probably a mere work of fiction); and, above all, *My Secret Life,* in eleven volumes, of which hardly more than the three opening volumes have ever been reprinted or translated.

V

LET IT BE frankly stated, before going further, that everything connected with the mysterious *My Secret Life* is based on supposition and deduction, and on hearsay testimony, such as that of the interested publisher Carrington, with the exception of the purely bibliographical descriptions taken from the printed volumes themselves. The first reference ever made to *My Secret Life* appears in Carrington's most ambitious catalogue, for 1902, issued anonymously under the transparent disguise of being the catalogue of a private library, and grotesquely aping the great erotic bibliographies of "Pisanus Fraxi," under the title *Forbidden Books: Notes and Gossip on Tabooed Literature,* by An Old Bibliophile, Paris: For the Author and his Friends, 1902. There is a copy of the original in the Bibliothèque Nationale, in Paris, catalogued as 8° Q. 4665; and an ill-printed counterfeit

of 227 pages also exists, made in New York about 1929, intended
to be passed off as the Carrington original. (The footnotes and
headlines of the original are, in the reprint, ignorantly set in
the middle of the page. See, for instance, its page 37.)

My Secret Life is the fifth work described, and it is evident,
from Carrington's way of puffing it, that he had come into possession of the remainder of the edition, and was trying to sell it
off at £60 sterling per set, an astronomical sum at that time. Here
is the opening of his notice, on which all the legends connected
with this work are based:

My Secret Life. Amsterdam (n.d.) Not for publication. —
11 vols. crown 8vo, of 378, 373, 379, 380, 388, 384, 369,
383, 396, 376, and 394 pp. (The first volume contains an
introduction, a preface, and a second preface. The last
volume has only 255 pp. of text, and the rest to page 394
is made up of an exhaustive alphabetical index.

About the year 1888, a well-known bookseller and publisher of Amsterdam, whose specialty was literature of
an incandescent kind [*i.e.* Auguste Brancart?] was sum-
moned to London by one of his customers, a rich old
Englishman, who desired to have privately printed for
his own enjoyment an enormous MSS., containing in the
fullest detail all the secret venereal thoughts of his existence. He defrayed all costs of printing, on condition
that no more than six copies should be struck off. A few
years afterwards, this eccentric amateur shuffled off the
mortal coil; and a few copies of the extraordinary work
made a timid appearance on the market, being quoted at the
high figure of £100! It is evident that many more than the
half-dozen copies stipulated must have been printed — let us
say about twenty-five or so — as I have unfrequently seen
a complete series, and I should say that at the time I am
writing, the book may be obtained by carefully searching,
for about £60 to £75 according to the condition.

In July, 1894, the publisher issued a volume without
any title save the words: *My Secret Life, Contents,* on the
half-title, and this was simply the index to the chapters,
the introduction and prefaces, and the alphabetical index
from the eleventh volume. This was evidently to whet the
curiosity of collectors and serve as a kind of prospectus. . . .

The first six chapters of the first volume have been

recently reprinted under the title of *The Dawn of Sensuality*, Lutetia (Brussels), 1901, small 8vo, 170 pp., 200
copies on Dutch paper, and gives the autobiography of
the writer and his sensual freaks up to the age of seventeen.

The remainder of Carrington's notice consists of an excerpt
from the remarkable alphabetical index to *My Secret Life* and
a long quotation, of about sixteen pages, which has never been
reprinted elsewhere (intended, as he says, 'to whet the curiosity
of collectors'), giving one of the author's affairs 'differing entirely
from any other in all the eleven volumes.' This is the story of
a French woman — told in her own words to the author — who,
while visiting her sister in Italy in 1859, is gang-raped by twelve
Austrian soldiers, in the course of a single *hour*, on the eve of
the Battle of Solferino. When she attempts to struggle she is
told by the Austrians: 'If you're not quiet we'll fuck you and
your sister too, then kill you both, and set fire to the house —
they will think the French did it.' Another soldier adds, even
more cynically, that she is lucky to be raped by Austrian soldiers
and not by the French, because 'If the French catch you, they
will bugger you, as well as fuck you, and certainly cut your throats
afterwards.' The whole scene, and its emotional aftermath, is
described with unusual incisiveness and depth, from the woman's
point of view, and is clearly authentic. It may be compared to
many similar passages in the erotic autobiography of a prostitute
in World War II, *Marie-Thérèse* (English translation as *I'm for
hire*, Paris, 1955), a remarkable work. It also contrasts very
strikingly with the parallel scene of wartime rape, described in
Robert Merle's *Week-end à Zuydcoote* (Prix Goncourt, 1949)
from the point of view of the well-meaning soldier carried away
by his sexual needs, and without, of course, any erotic details.

My Secret Life is unusual among erotic autobiographies in
many ways, of which not the least is the didactic tone into which
the author falls on occasion, actually giving in one place a short
but complete treatise on the art of sexual intercourse, which
makes rather absurd any pretense that he is writing without the
hope of an audience, or of any audience further than six other
erotica collectors (who would presumably know something about
the art of intercourse already). The most unusual aspect of *My
Secret Life*, among erotic autobiographies, is that it is concerned
almost exclusively with the author's physical erotic experiences,
and purposely omits any discussion of his emotional relationships.

He maintains throughout a gallant British reserve about every woman he really loved, and in particular about his own wife. His elegant reserve here compares in an edifying way with Henry Miller's fantastic soiling and degrading of his first wife in public, in his theoretically autobiographical pornographic series, *Sexus, Nexus, Plexus,* and *Drexus* (in preparation). The style of *My Secret Life* is undistinguished and matter-of-fact, yet in a way which authenticates even further the self-evident intention of the author to tell the simple autobiographical truth about his hidden sexual history, 'a plain narrative of facts,' as he puts it, 'and not a psychological analysis.' His work is therefore, in almost every way — and not solely on the question of literal truth — the exact opposite of the *Mémoires* of Casanova, now for the first time, in 1960–62, published by Brockhaus, in Wiesbaden and Paris, from the original manuscript in Casanova's racy and idiomatic French, to replace the high-falutin' and academic expurgated text (by a university professor) in which Casanova has hitherto been known.

Even in his own words, however, Casanova is eternally concerned not with his sexual activity, but with his emotions about it; with his ideas of self-importance, with what he thought about his women and what they seemed to think of him, etc. etc. . . . the typical Latin egocentrism, even in the midst of the emotion of love, which is supposed to be — as Stendhal indicates — an enormous over-evaluation and crystallization of the virtues of the *other* person. This emphasis on himself is also very much heightened by Casanova's clear need for emotional reassurance, obviously difficult for him to find anywhere else in his miserable career as an international adventurer and swindler, as a failed dramatist (he collaborated with DaPonte on Mozart's *Don Juan,* surely never imagining for an instant that history would identify him with this hero), also as card-sharp and spy; who finally managed to get himself thrown out of his beloved Venice forever by 'revealing' in *Ne' amori, ne' donne,* in 1782 (written as a work of revenge, after having apparently been caught cheating at cards), that he was the illegitimate son of the nobleman, Michel Grimani, and as such the rightful heir of the Grimani fortune!

The author of *My Secret Life* writes, per contra, from a completely assured social position, and does not concern himself in the slightest with any such attempts to bolster up his self-esteem, which is clearly under no strain whatever. He does not seek women, as does Casanova, to love them briefly and abandon them promptly; but rather for the simple and direct purpose of sexual pleasure. When he finds this pleasure with a woman — and everyone is aware that this is by no means so simple or so common as the anatomy of the matter would lead one to believe — he makes every effort to continue the pleasant relationship as long as possible, and to renew it whenever he can. This again is the precise opposite of the character of Casanova, who spends half his time travelling; that is to say, getting away from his last sexual failure, and on to his next 'victory,' and whose real emotions seem never to be involved with any woman whatsoever except in the one profoundly masochistic affair with La Charpillon. This is the incident on which, as is well known, Pierre Louÿs based *La Femme et le pantin* (translated as *Woman and Puppet*) as also his erotic rewriting of the same theme, under the title *Trois filles de leur mère,* the most extraordinary work of erotic fiction in modern French; with a liberal dose taken from Mérimée's *Carmen,* or, rather, from Halévy's operatic revision of her character — to Bizet's passionate music — dramatically heightening all the sado-masochistic overtones of the original story.

VI

IT WOULD evidently be of great interest to discover the name of the author of *My Secret Life.* I have a theory on this subject, which is bound up closely with the later bibliographical history of the book, and in particular with the publisher calling himself "Charles Carrington." This Paris erotica-and-flagellantiana dealer, who dominated the English-language field from about 1895 to 1917, was, in fact, a Portuguese of the real name of Paul Ferdinando, to which he returned only once in his long career, so far as I know, on the title-page of an eccentric work on the so-called Shakespeare controversy, vanity-published for one Célestin Demblon, and entitled *Lord Rutland* EST *Shakespeare* (1912), which — though telling us precious little worth knowing about Shakespeare — does give at least the publisher's identity in full, in the imprint: 'Paul Ferdinando, libraire-éditeur, Ancienne Maison Charles Carrington, 11, rue de Châteaudun.' This was his real address and main store, under his true name; the official 'Maison d'Éditions Scientifiques' under the Carrington name, at 13 Faubourg Montmartre — the address continually mentioned in the transcripts of title-pages in *Forbidden Books,* as a help to prospective customers — was only a cover-address or front, where his 'Medical, Folklore and Historical Works,' or official cover-items, were displayed.

Further details as to Carrington's career, from his beginnings
with a barrow-load of cheapjack books in the street markets of
London, to his repellent end, will be found in the new and enlarged edition of *The Banned Books of England* (London, 1962)
by Alec Craig, the principal fighter for and historian of the
'limited freedom of speech and press' one can hope for, at best, in
Britain. Mr. Craig notes, p. 74, that the minutes of the Joint
Select Committee on Lotteries and Indecent Advertisements of
1908, in England, contain 'evidence about the trade in pornography going on at the time, including details of the activities of
"Roland de Villiers" [the original publisher of Havelock Ellis'
Studies in the Psychology of Sex] and Charles Carrington.' These
details, however, are not quoted in Mr. Craig's work, and I have
not been able to have access to the minutes of this Committee.
Of Carrington's personal career the following details were supplied to Craig, p. 71, by Vernon Symonds. It will be observed
that Carrington's real name and Portuguese origin or descent
are not mentioned, and that the principal part and period of
his activity — his pornographic and semi-pornographic publications from 1895 to 1917 — are hardly noted at all:

Carrington started life as an errand boy, vanboy, and
then lavatory attendant. At sixteen he was keeping a
book barrow in Farringdon Market. By reading his wares
he graduated into the company of men like Dowson,
Beardsley, and Wilde. In the Paris of the early twenties
he was a pathetic figure not without a little dignity of
tragedy. Blind as the result of syphilis, he was no match
for his predatory mistress and was helpless before the follies
of his five children. They and their hangers-on swarmed
over his house and stole his books. A shop was even opened
specially to dispose of the thefts. He endured five years of
this misery before perishing in a lunatic asylum at the age
of sixty-five. His mistress provided a magnificent funeral
and his tortured body was consigned to earth by the
Catholic Church. The moral edification to be derived
from his story must be balanced by the fact that Isidore
Liseux lived to a ripe and contented old age and died
happily.

Alas, but it is not true. Isidore Liseux, who never published
pornography, but only the great landmarks of the erotic literature

of earlier centuries, in French and Italian — his only even dubious
items being those published in English for the tourist trade —
was always a poor man, hounded for money by the printers of
the truly beautiful books he produced right up to the end.
Whereas, the crude money-grubbers and porno-peddlers who
erroneously thought of themselves as his imitators, such as
Kistemaeckers in Brussels and Carrington in Paris, simply rolled
in money for decades, as the preceding account of Carrington's
valuable library stock stolen before his blind eyes leaves plainly
to be understood. (There are profitable little gobbets of it still
being advertised by shady dealers in Paris, Copenhagen, and
Mexico.) As to Liseux' 'ripe and contented old age' and happy
death, his story is really even more of an 'orrible warning' against
publishing sex-books than Carrington's. The truth is that Isidore
Liseux was found dead of starvation and cold in his last little
bookshop on the rue Bonaparte, in Paris, 11 January 1894, at
the age of fifty-eight, as is plainly reported by Apollinaire,
Fleuret, and Perceau in *L'Enfer de la Bibliothèque Nationale*,
1913, no. 96, adding: 'Il fut enterré dans la fosse commune et sa
sépulture fut détruite en 1899.' The event was also commented
upon at the time, as the latest booktrade gossip, in an auction-
sale catalogue, *Quelques-uns des livres contemporains* (March
1894), a vanity sale of a few fancy bindings and similar bibelots
belonging to the successful literary fop and journalist, Octave
Uzanne. This is an excessively fruity item, limited to 125 super
de luxe copies, with engraved title-page portrait, in the fantastic
style of Robida, of the otherwise anonymous bibliophile-owner,
and is printed on (translated directly, as any paraphrase would
be misconstrued as satire) 'Mauve vellum paper, watermarked
with garlands of periwinkles and numbered.' From the heights
of this self-adulatory pile of 'bibliophile' corn and crap, Uzanne
reaches down a gloved hand to toss one faded mauve periwinkle,
p. 2-3, on the grave of Liseux, found dead 'avec dix-neuf sous
pour toute fortune dans sa poche!'

A very striking description of Carrington is given, somewhat
resembling a drug-addicted satyr surging up out of one of his
own publications, in Gaston LeRouge's *Verlainiens et décadents*
(Paris, Marcel Seheur, 1928), in connection with the writer
Hugues Rebell who, having lost all his money, lived by writing
works on erotic flagellation for Carrington, in particular a curious
novel on the background of the American Civil War and slavery,
The Memoirs of Dolly Morton, of which the 'cover-item' —

omitting all the erotic passages, but retaining the perfectly legal
sadistic flagellation! — is entitled *En Virginie,* and is signed "Jean
de Villiot." (The erotic form of the French text, entitled *Dolly
Morton,* which is unknown to Perceau's bibliography of erotica,
gives as author "Donovan Kipps," at least on the prospectus.)
A *bibliographie raisonnée* of other works on erotic flagellation,
pages 187–343, takes up nearly half of Rebell's and Carrington's
'cover' -volume, to replace the missing erotic passages.

Obviously one cannot give much credence to any tale told
by this chameleon-like publisher, particularly not as to the
identity of his stable of pseudonymous authors. Yet, in the case
of *My Secret Life,* the only hint we have comes, in the first instance, from Carrington, and the whole logic of the situation
points to its being probably true. One thing is sure: he did not
originally publish the work himself, though he just as surely did
handle the remainder. Its whole typographical style is entirely
different from that of any of Carrington's publications, whether
cover-items or under-cover items, but does answer precisely to the
Dutch and Belgian pornography-printing style of the 1880's and
'90's, in both English and French. (It might also be mentioned
that the original issue was apparently in a somewhat unimaginative
cloth binding, whereas the remainder copies handled by Carrington were bound only in paper wrappers.) As the imprint given,
of Amsterdam, is possibly a blind, and as Carrington was in close
relations at the turn of the century with the Dutch master-printer
Thieme, in Nimeguen, who printed his two finest books: Rosenbaum's *Plague of Lust . . . in Classical Antiquity* (1898–1901, a
cover-item, recently reprinted by offset in New York), and
Forberg's *Manual of Classical Erotology,* 'Manchester, 1884'
(really 1899, the under-cover item); it is just possible that this
was the printer of *My Secret Life,* and the source or the lead to
the source of the remainder of the edition turned over eventually
to Carrington, who was, of course, the publisher of the prospectus-
volume *The Dawn of Sensuality* in 1901, and probably of the
original prospectus-volume of 1894 as well, at the very beginning
of his career.

In a circular issued by Carrington, probably about 1905,
preserved in an extensive and very remarkable collection of
erotic prospectuses acquired in 1962 for the Private Case of the
British Museum, in an album marked "No. 7," the statement is
made — obviously by someone getting his information from either
the original printer or the publisher — that *My Secret Life* had

cost £1100 to print (*i.e.* £100 per 380-page volume for each of the eleven volumes: those were the days!) and took seven years to complete; suggesting that the publication had continued right on from 1888 to 1894, when the "Contents" prospectus, earlier mentioned, appeared.

Having gone blind, reportedly from syphilis, toward the end of his life, Carrington turned over his business in France in the early 1920's to two young assistants, both of whom are still operating — one in Mexico — and his large clientèle abroad to a delightful old roué, glorying in the name of St. George Best, and long since gone to his reward. It was Best's job to smuggle Carrington's pornographica into America, through Cuba and Mexico, and deliver them safely to paying customers and fashionable bookdealers in the United States. By the 1930's, with Carrington dead since 1922, and the supply of his under-cover publications badly dried up, Best's real job had become the finding of the books, rather than the finding of customers — of whom he already had more than he could satisfy. He addressed himself to me in connection with a set of the already very rare *My Secret Life*, which he erroneously believed I would sell him, to turn over to some more fortunate customer. As it happened, I did not own the original edition, but only a reprint of the first three volumes (made by Smith, in New York, about 1932), the publication of the following volumes having been halted by a police seizure; and also of a further volume — volume four being unfindable by the publishers — reprinted under the typical 'porno' title of *Marital Frolics* by another publisher, also in New York, about 1934.

Observing that Carrington implies, in *Forbidden Books,* that he had access to some twenty-five sets, at least, and that he states directly that the wily Dutch publisher had 'struck off' far more copies than the author had specified, I tried to find out from Best how many sets of the original edition he himself had actually handled for Carrington. This I could never learn, but it is clear that even in admitting that the presumed original six copies printed were in fact at least twenty-five, Carrington was nevertheless trying to keep the printing figure low and the sales-price high. Six sets have since been independently traced, of which four are at present in the United States — one in the Kinsey Institute, and another reported at Yale. (The set reported at Yale does not appear to be the original edition, in eleven volumes, but merely the American reprint of volumes 1–3.) The fifth complete set is currently languishing on a dealer's shelves in Paris, being ruthlessly overpriced; while the sixth is in a particularly fine private collection in England, willed eventually to the British Museum. As to the others . . . ?

Best did tell me two very interesting things about *My Secret Life*. One was that an enormous supplement had been written to it by an American writer and researcher, named R.T., under a rather similar title, and nearly as long as the original's some 4200 pages. This supplement, or imitation, was sold *in manuscript,* volume by volume as it was written, to an old oil-millionaire in Ardmore, Oklahoma, who already had 'all' the printed erotica in English in his collection, which he kept in steel filing-cabinets in his business office, as his wife would not allow them in their home! This gentleman, with whom I later corresponded, was unable to read any language but English, and explained frankly that his 'imagination was excited only once' by any one book, and that he could therefore never return to it 'usefully' until he had forgotten it completely: the identical problem of the readers of murder-mysteries, a similar literary substitute for immoral experience in many ways. He therefore had arranged to have two new erotic manuscripts written to order for him every week — rejecting, as does *My Secret Life*, any scene of flagellation or sadism, for which all honor to him.

The manuscripts were written by impecunious authors, tracked down and invited to the work by a Hollywood literary agent and a private bookseller in New York, and by their sub-agents, each of whom got a sizeable cut of the price paid by the millionaire. The authors received, for their part, as little as $50 to $100 for each 100-page manuscript, depending in part on their literary reputation, but mostly on how good a fight they could put up with the sub-agents or 'bagmen.' Jack Hanley has amusingly described such an encounter, in an article published under the pseudonym of "Gene Harvey," in the American men's-magazine *For Men Only* in the 1930's.

Actually, there is nothing unusual about the combine here described, except that the customer was a private collector. The organization of the affair was patterned precisely on the method used for procuring erotic manuscripts, by publishers, in all countries, at least since the 17th century. I have had in my hands, at one time or another, over fifty of these manuscripts, by various writers, intended for the Oklahoma millionaire, but in carbon copies surreptitiously made for and retained by the agents, for publication later when the millionaire would be dead. Several of these have now been published. This is almost identical with the trick played on the author of *My Secret Life,* as described with complete sang-froid in Carrington's notice. Though the continuations of *My Secret Life* were, in part, among the manuscript copies I saw, their derived and spurious nature was perfectly self-evident and I did not bother to examine them at any length.

Another group of pornographic parodies or continuations of this sort were modeled on Henry Miller's "Tropics," and do not, in fact, read very dissimilarly from the masterpieces in the genre that Miller has gone on since to publish under his own name. However, as the Miller parodies were supplied to the millionaire as coming 'indirectly' from Miller, and are still being circulated under this same bogus provenance — several of them have actually been printed — it should be stated flatly here that they are all spurious. Most of them were written about 1940 by a talented young American, exceptionally gifted at pastiche, named R.S., who is also the author of *The Oxford Professor* (described and quoted at some length in the Kronhausens' *Pornography and the Law,* 1959, p. 42, 177, &c.), and of *The Devil's Advocate,* both of which were mimeographed in New York, about 1942. The latter, an extremely well-written erotic novel, is ascribed on its title-page to "Wood C. Lamont," in order to cast the onus of authorship on the late American poet and littérateur, Clement Wood, who had earlier hacked numerous manuscripts for the same organization — but not this one! That is the way these things are done, and that is how spurious tales of authorship are set forever in circulation.

VII

IT WILL EASILY be understood that I accepted with every possible reserve the other revelation made by Best, as to *My Secret Life,* namely that he had always been told by Carrington that the author was the great bibliographer of erotica "Pisanus Fraxi," otherwise known as H. Spencer Ashbee. (As is common among bookdealers, Best always referred to Ashbee by his pseudonym, as "Fraxi," thus avoiding the embarrassment of the forename, which seems always to come out scatologically whether pronounced with the accent on the first syllable or the second. The same problem has been observed by philologists as to the planet Uranus.) This attribution of *My Secret Life* to Ashbee has occasionally been heard since, from bookdealers, but I assume that in all cases the proximate source must have been St. George Best, who 'drummed' the better booksellers of England and America year after year. The attribution carries with it, however, a striking air of verisimilitude, as Ashbee fits perfectly into every portion of the picture of the rich old English amateur described in *Forbidden Books,* which is, as noted, itself only a parody of Ashbee's three great bibliographical volumes.

The most singular feature of Ashbee's erotic bibliographies must surely be the enormous "Alphabetical and Analytical Index," appended to each volume and printed in five different kinds of type, mercilessly subdividing to infinity every subject touched upon, even in passing (with, for instance, nine full columns of page-references to the *general* subject of "Bibliography" in the first volume only), on the stated principle that 'A good book cannot be too concise — a good index can hardly be too prolix.' (*Index,* p. 478.) This is of course nonsense, and would end in putting Cruden's *Concordance* above the Bible, not to mention Shakespeare and his indexers; but it is the principle on which Ashbee was pleased to work.

The resultant indexes have a striking stylistic similarity, particularly as to the subject of "Copulation," to the extraordinary subject-index appended to *My Secret Life,* which is surely the only autobiography — erotic or otherwise — ever to have such an index printed for it at the author's expense, let alone one extending to a total of eighty-seven pages (XI. 307–94), in addition to a detailed 46-page Table of Contents for all the eleven volumes preceding (XI. 257–303). One almost suspects that the purpose of such an index is not to be useful to the reader, but to allow the aging author to turn over and classify his erotic materials and writing in a long-drawn-out *delectatio morbosa.* The matching concentration in both the bibliographies and the autobiography on the equally protracted foreplay of prefaces, introductions, epigraphs, and the like (see, in particular, Ashbee's opening volume), is perhaps to be discounted as only the literary formulæ of the time. But there is something more than that in the similarity of the indexes, which are certainly not the result of any formula. Even Wheatley's edition of Pepys' *Diary* — and Wheatley one of the principal index-enthusiasts of his time (see *Centuria,* p. 520) — does not go to any such extreme.

Here, in parallel columns, are the first and last few subject-listings under the head of "Copulation" from both works. The full listing, from *My Secret Life,* will be found in *Forbidden Books* (six columns!) with the pious note that 'The common, vulgar word is used in the original.'

INDEX LIBRORUM PROHIBITORUM	MY SECRET LIFE
Copulation —	Copulating and Copulative Organs.
The two most natural modes are the best.	— Essay on.
A woman may be enjoyed by two men at the same time.	— the nature of.
	— described fully.
The woman should not be quite naked.	— æsthetic aspects of.
	— is not obscene or filthy.
The woman has more pleasure than the man . . .	— in obedience to the Divine command "Increase and multiply."
Pleasures of rape.
Time when a virgin should be enjoyed . . .	(ending:) Eccentric postures.
	— against field gates.
Preliminaries described.	— against railings.
Various postures enumerated.	— against trees.
	— against windows.
Monotony condemned.	— against a bed.
	— against a kitchen dresser.

This is hardly more than a sample. The full indexing in *My Secret Life* must be seen, to be savored as it deserves.

One must imagine Ashbee sitting down to write his erotic memoirs — if that is what *My Secret Life* may correctly be considered to be — after having finished his more scholarly erotic life-work with the publication of *Catena Librorum Tacendorum* ('of books about which one is silent') in 1885. Or, rather, simply indexing and arranging then for publication, with a second preface and a second disguising of names and places undertaken, a sort of erotic diary much more frequently kept by Don Juans of all three sexes than is commonly realized, especially not by their conquests. Judged by its typography, *My Secret Life* was visibly and certainly printed somewhere about the time of the last of Ashbee's main bibliographical volumes. The date that Carrington gives, 1888, could of course be extended to about 1894 to finish the eleven volumes; and we are told — again by Carrington — that the first prospectus, by the original publisher (if not by Carrington himself) attempting to sell off the surreptitious copies, was issued in July 1894. In the only bibliographical work which gives a correct notice of it, *Registrum Librorum Eroticorum* (London, 1936) by "Rolf S. Reade," *i.e.* Alfred Rose, at no. 3136, *My Secret Life* is dated as circa 1890.

It is to be observed that Carrington's prospectus-volume *The Dawn of Sensuality* in 1901, and *Forbidden Books* in 1902, followed almost immediately after Ashbee's death in 1900; offering *My Secret Life* for sale at the 'bargain' price of £60, instead of the Dutch dealer's £100. Ashbee's correspondence, and his collection of booksellers' catalogues and prospectuses, if he made such a collection, have not survived (his article, "The Distributor of Prospectuses" appears in *Paris qui crie*), but he would clearly have been acquainted with Carrington's early publications. As the most important collector in the erotic field, Ashbee was certainly not a man for Carrington to offend, and it would hardly have been diplomatic to discuss *My Secret Life,* if it stemmed in any way from Ashbee, until after his death. This is, of course, arguing from a negative ('Wireless telegraphy must have been invented in ancient Greece, since *no* telegraph wires have been excavated there'), but I believe it has a certain force. In any case, the ignorant and impertinent parody of his bibliographical masterpiece that *Forbidden Book*s itself constitutes, would certainly not have been appreciated by Ashbee.

I would be less than candid were I to omit the evidence, or at least the contra-indications that seem to oppose this theory — it is only a theory — ascribing *My Secret Life* to Ashbee. In a never-cited and utterly unknown, yet highly informative catalogue list of erotic books for sale, during the most open period of Paris erotica publishing, about 1910, not only are Carrington's remainder copies of this work offered publicly for sale, over a period of two years, but the author is also identified by his presumed initial, and that initial is not 'A.' This list appeared serially as "Bibliographie galante," covering ten to twenty pages at the end of each annual issue, 1908–1913, of *Paris-Galant,* an illustrated yearbook specializing in gallant and humorous illustrations of the 18th and 19th centuries, and issued by the Paris bookseller and publisher, specializing in semi-erotic works, H. Daragon. It was apparently edited, in continuation of an earlier gallant almanac of 1906–07, *Rire et Galanterie,* by John Grand-Carteret, the Franco-Swiss picture editor whose very successful formula of '*tout par l'image*' so signally influenced modern magazine, and now book, publication, in the new anti-cultural return to precisely that pre-literary pictorialism the world has been struggling out of since the cave-drawings, the *Biblia Pauperum* before Gutenberg, and the grossly colored *imagerie populaire* since; only to find itself now slid completely back to the even more total illiteracy of the picture magazines, glossy 'art'-books and other pop-culch, and the even grosser coloring of the comics.

The so-called "Bibliographie galante" of *Paris-Galant* is of course only a catalogue of highly erotic and flagellational books offered for sale, at marked prices, by Daragon. It is particularly strong in other publishers' ends-of-stocks and remainders, often with their dates of publication, as far back as the 1870's, frankly stated. It is the only such publicly-issued catalogue known to exist, until recently in certain Mexican towns on the U.S. border; all others — from that day to this — being available only 'in plain sealed wrapper, client must be above 18 years of age' (&c.), mailed from drop addresses in Paris, Germany, Spain, and formerly Cuba. In the issues for 1910 and 1912, only, *Paris-Galant* made the following offer, in its alphabetical place, reprinted literally here:

MY SECRET LIFE, or the Modern Casanova
Memoirs of the well. Knonn celebrates Colonel W. Eleven, volumes of 358 pages each.
printed on dutch paper . . . . 2.500 fr.
   *Ouvrage de la plus grande rareté tiré seu-
lement à 40 ex. pour l'auteur et ses amis.
Les exemplaires qui restaient dans sa bibliothèque lors de sa mort ont été* DÉTRUITS.

As repeated in 1912, with all the same typographical errors, except that Colonel W. has been sorted out from the 'Eleven, volumes' (which are now down to 10, in figures, at the same enormous price), the interesting statement as to the destruction of the copies found in the author's library at his death is abbreviated, and the bold puff is added that the work is an 'Excellent bargain at this price.' (2,500 pre-War francs were worth a great deal more than their translation as $500 would imply. Compare the printing of a whole book on rag paper, the entire edition, for so little as £100, at that period, noted above.) Whether or not the 'well. Knonn cele-brates Colonel W.' was intended to point to some British celebrity then in the news, but now unidentifiable, or was simply a name taken by the bookseller out of the air, *à la bonne heure,* to make the mystery more piquant, it is impossible to say. At any rate, and for what it is worth, this is the only other ascription of authorship ever made as to *My Secret Life.*

The principal opponent of the ascription of authorship to Ash-bee is Dr. E. J. Dingwall, whose opinion on such matters is of particular weight, not only as the biographer, in his *Very Peculiar People* [1949] of one of the most curious erotico-mystic eccentrics of all time, Adriaan Beverland (to whom the 'heresy' is credited identifying the Original Sin of Adam & Eve as sexual intercourse, and the serpent as the penis), but also as Honorary Curator of the Private Case of the British Museum, and the one person in the world best acquainted with the Ashbee Bequest as it stands today. Dr. Dingwall has also generously and courageously instituted a testamentary fund for the purchase of appropriate works for the Private Case of the British Museum, which is otherwise able only with difficulty so to allocate funds.

In a letter of 14 August 1962, Dr. Dingwall makes the considerable point 'that Ashbee would have had a copy [of *My Secret Life*] himself, and would have had it passed on as he did with the extra illustrated and annotated copies of two of his great bibliographies.' That is to say, would have had this passed on to the British Museum which, in fact, did not receive any such copy with the Ashbee Bequest. At first sight the idea seems very probable, yet on reflexion, it is exactly what no erotic autobiographer *would* have done, after having gone to so much trouble, as that visible in *My Secret Life,* to disguise himself from any personal recognition or connection with the autobiographical truth there told, along with every other real personal and perhaps even place-name given. There is also the author's attempted restriction of the number of copies to the fantastic few which, even though tripled or quadrupled surely by the wily publisher into whose hands he fell, has always been, in truth, sufficiently small to make *My Secret Life* the highest priced of all erotic books actually available for sale. (The price at which the last copy sold is known to have gone, $1000, is piddlingly small compared with the inflated figures reached by certain well-touted modern rarities in the auction rooms, actually nowhere near as rare.) The really suspicious point is precisely its *absence* from Ashbee's great contemporary collection.

Whoever the author may have been, if he did actually extra-illustrate and annotate his own copy — one can imagine with what mementos! — this would in all probability have been the one erotic book in his collection (and such an autobiographer would certainly have had some such collection) that he would have forced himself back, a dying man, from Burgos in Spain, were he to have been stricken there, to get to his library *and burn!* This is implicit in the whole search for anonymity, struggling ambivalently against the desire for sexual publicity and immortality, in the secret publication of such a work. One may interestingly compare Sir Richard Burton's last effort on his death-bed to complete his homosexually-oriented edition or 'translation' of the *Perfumed Garden* of al-Nafzawi, in the same decade; and Lady Burton's burning the manuscript, for the same reason, before her husband's body was cold.

'Again,' Dr. Dingwall concludes, 'I hardly think that Ashbee was the sort of person to engage in these manifold activities either in London or abroad, and if we put it down to fantasy I don't think Ashbee had that much imagination.' Discounting the last part of this statement, which the examination of Ashbee's bibliographies shows to be only too true, there is a profound insight expressed here, from the point of view of a specialist, as to the *distance* between erotic literature and erotic life. Ashbee, certainly the greatest erotic collector of all time, is hardly to be thought 'the sort of person' to engage in the 'manifold activities' — even the normal and utterly non-sadistic ones of *My Secret Life* — that are the principal matter of precisely the collection of books he left behind. And yet. . . .

VIII

WHAT THERE is left to tell of the story has taken place in France. The *Bibliographie du roman érotique* (1930) of Louis Perceau, II. 154–5, quotes a French bookseller's cataloguing of the original edition in English — the price demanded being 800 pre-War francs, still a sizeable sum — with the remark that the author 'gives the description of the morals, the habits, and the customs of 2500 women of all the countries of the world (except Lapland), whom he had known, and with whom he had sexual relations.' This squares in a striking fashion with the known fact of Ashbee's lifetime of travel, everywhere in the world. Unfortunately, the author's care in disguising dates and places in *My Secret Life* makes it difficult to work out any parallels of chronology or itinerary in the life of Ashbee (on which see further the 'official' life in the *Dictionary of National Biography, Supplement,* 1903, I. 79). One wonders what was the matter with Lapland.

Perceau's *Bibliographie du roman érotique*, at this same item no. 322, notes the original edition of a translation into French: *Ma Vie Secrète* (My Secret Life). *Mon enfance et mon adolescence amoureuses.* Traduit pour la première fois de l'anglais sur l'un des 10 exemplaires [*sic*] de l'édition originale et unique. Paris:

Collection de l'Académie des Dames, 1923, two volumes, 12mo, of 183 and 175 pages. The only copy that Perceau notes is his own, but its present location is not certain, owing to the following unfortunate, and only too typical, contretemps. Perceau states, in the "Avertissement" prefacing his *Bibliographie* (I. 17), concerning his own 'collection, perhaps unique, and which it would certainly be impossible to reconstitute now . . . It is my desire to see it united one day to that of the Bibliothèque Nationale.' His wish, however, has not been followed, and the collection has continued to remain in the possession of his family since Perceau's death at the end of World War II. For the last ten years the present writer has attempted, without success, to organize a fund among French and foreign bibliophiles, to buy this irreplaceable collection *en-bloc* for the Bibliothèque Nationale, before it is accidentally broken up, owing to the continual monetary temptations set before the legatees of such collections by egoistic booksellers. So far, it has not been possible to make the bibliophiles understand the clear necessity, the historical value, and the evident correctness of this very inexpensive gesture, which would not cost any of them more than the price of one moderately well-bound erotic work, each.

In the interim, it may be noted that a copy of Perceau's no. 322, the original edition of this translation, *Ma Vie Secrète,* is given by Rose's *Registrum Librorum Eroticorum,* no. 4730, as then in the library of the Guildhall Annex, London. (The erotic holdings of this library have been transferred, since the War, to the British Museum). At no. 4731, Rose notes a further edition of the same translation, of 405 pages, in three small volumes, with the false imprint 'Londres, 1885.' This reprint is identified, in the most recent erotic collection-catalogue published, *Bibliothèque "La Léonina,"* III. *Curiosa* (Monte-Carlo, 1955), by M. Jacques Pley, at pages 61-2, as having really been issued in Paris, about 1930, by Marcel Seheur, whose 'cover-item' discussing his predecessor, Carrington, is mentioned above, and about whose private publications a good deal can be learned from the notes in the *Léonina* catalogue, anonymously supplied by M. René Bonnel.

The Seheur reprint is ornamented with a '*suite libre*' of twenty-six erotic plates in color, and forty head- and tailpieces in sanguine, also erotic, attributed to Berthommé Saint-André, in which all the actors are charmingly dressed in the clothing of the 1880's. Seheur's edition is in the small square format and pink paper wrappers that are the typographical 'key' to many of his clandestine publications, as for instance *Eveline* ('Londres, 1911,' also published about 1930, on which see Pley, p. 59), which is likewise translated from the English, with an extremely spirited *suite libre* in color. Identical in format is the Seheur reprint of *Alcibiade enfant à l'école* — a classic of homosexual literature of which the oldest existing edition is that of 'Oranges, Juann Wart,' 1652 — in the translation first published by Poulet-Malassis in 1866; with cover-imprint giving at least the correct date, 'Amsterdam et Paris, 1936,' and a suite of five (?) homosexual illustrations, almost the only such existing in modern French erotica except for editions of Verlaine's *Hombres,* written in 1891 and first published by Messein in 1904.

Attempting to complicate even worse the already tangled problem of the *Alcibiade,* Seheur's title-page gives his usual false date, in the imprint 'Amsterdam, chez l'ancien Pierre Marteau, 1862,' and credits the work to Ferrante Pallavicino, as is invariably done in all erotic bibliographies, including Ashbee's *Index,* p. 23–9. This work is important enough, in the history of literature and morals, to correct this invariable but erroneous ascription of authorship. Two contemporary letters have been discovered, from Gian-Francesco Loredano, founder of the Accademia degli Incogniti, to the paradoxal Father Angelico Aprosio ("Scipio Glareano," author of *La Grillaia curiosità erudite,* Napoli, 1668), now preserved in the library of the University of Genoa (Cod. E.V. 19), indicating that the real author of *Alcibiade fanciullo a scola,* D.P.A. (*i.e.* 'di Pietro Aretino,' the inevitable false ascription on the title-page) was not Pallavicino but a somewhat older contemporary of his, Antonio Rocco, professor of philosophy at Venice; and further that the original edition — now lost — was published in Venice by Ginammi early in 1651, from a manuscript that had been in Loredano's possession for some twenty years; that is, since about 1630. This puts Pallavicino, who had made the mistake of writing an attack on the Pope, and was executed in 1644 at the age of twenty-six, and who was thus only about twelve years old in 1630 when Loredano received the manuscript, quite out of the question. (I am indebted to Mr. Joseph Wallfield for this clarification, and for reference to the articles by the historian Achille Neri, in the *Giornale storico della letteratura Italiana,* 1888, XII. 219–27; and in the *Bolletino storico piacentino,* 1918, XIII. 25–9, first making this corrected attribution, now accepted by Giorgio Spini in his *Ricerca dei libertini,* Roma, 1950, p. 155–7.)

Perceau observes that further volumes of the French translation of *Ma Vie Secrète* were intended to be translated from the English, as a sequel to the 1923 edition, but that 'the sequel never appeared.' This is a pity, since the existing French translation, which is the most easily available text, gives hardly more than a tenth of the 4200 pages of the English original. The same translation has recently been published openly, for the first time (Paris: Cercle du Livre Précieux, 1961), with an abridgment of the closing sections of the present essay serving as preface. Perceau adds: 'I was able to obtain certain details as to this translation. It had first been made — for the only two volumes published — with very definite attenuations, by a professor of letters. The publisher demanded of another writer to review this translation, made *currente calamo,* and to give it body [!] by restoring the crude words that had been replaced by more decent terms.' This is the same fate, more or less, that overtook Casanova's *Mémoires,* 'professor of letters' and all. Whether the writer entrusted with the revision of *My Secret Life* worked with the English text before him, or simply after his own fancy, we are not told.

It is to be hoped that a complete translation — and, for that matter, a complete reprint — of the original English text will someday soon be undertaken. *My Secret Life* is admittedly electrifyingly frank, and utterly outside the usual line of expurgated autobiographical ditherings. Now that Joyce's *Ulysses,* D. H. Lawrence's *Lady Chatterley's Lover,* and Miller's *Tropic of Cancer* have openly appeared in America without the utter collapse of public morality once hysterically foretold by the Comstocks, the Sumners, and other bluenoses, if 'such things' were to see the open light of day, it does not seem beyond the limits of probability that the eleven volumes of *My Secret Life* might also be reprinted. They are a document that is worth the try. The evolution of the world to an adult sexual sensibility is not going to be achieved on the basis of fictitious autobiographies — whether sexually expurgated or bragging — and other balderdash and lies. Very few authentic erotic autobiographies have ever been published. With the possible exception of Casanova's *Mémoires,* now at last available as he wrote them (though not yet so translated into English), and the *Confessions* of Jean-Jacques Bouchard, written in 1630 but only first printed in 1881 by the erudite ex-priest and bibliophile, Isidore Liseux; *My Secret Life* may be the only one. As far as the attribution of authorship to Henry Spencer Ashbee is concerned, *se non è vero, è ben trovato.* A more likely candidate will not easily be found.

THE HORN BOOK
And Other Bibliographical Problems

Erotic LITERATURE is fortunate in having excellent bibliographies in almost every major language but English. For French there are the Gay & Lemonnyer *Bibliographie des ouvrages relatifs à l'amour* (1894–1900), the Apollinaire-Fleuret-Perceau *Enfer de la Bibliothèque Nationale* (1913) — meticulously describing the holdings of the "Enfer" of the French national library — and Perceau's own *Bibliographie du roman érotique au XIXe siècle* (1930). For German the field is dominated by the *Bibliotheca Germanorum Erotica et Curiosa* by Hayn, Gotendorf, and Englisch (1912–29) in nine heavy volumes, though there is a great deal of further information on the erotic literature and art of Germany and other countries in the second and fourth volumes of the *Bilder-Lexikon der Erotik* (1928–31), edited by Leo Schidrowitz, and now being reprinted in Hamburg with a supplement under the editorship of Dr. Hans Giese announced.

For English there is basically only the splendid set by "Pisanus Fraxi" (Henry Spencer Ashbee), fully discussed above, but beyond Ashbee there is at present nothing in English of any importance. It is a question whether such purely popular recent meringues as J. J. Kilpatrick's *The Smut Peddlers* (1960), Monroe Fry's *Sex, Vice and Business* (1959), and the insufferable once-over-lightly of David Loth's *The Erotic in Literature* (1961, stated on its title-page to be 'A historical survey of pornography as delightful as it is indiscreet') do more than confuse the matter, meanwhile giving the authors the delightful and profitable feeling of being deeply in the know, and leaving the reader with the same feeling, equally erroneously. The far better work, by the Drs. Kronhausen, and that — incredibly worse — entitled *An Unhurried* [!] *View of Erotica,* have already been noted in the preceding essay. Not one of these supplies more than a bit of the raw materials for the long-needed bibliography of erotic and expurgated literature in English since 1477.

There is an abridgment of Ashbee — adding a few extraneous works — under the title *Bibliotheca Arcana* (London, 1885) anonymously edited by Sir William Laird Clowes, with a Preface by "Speculator Morum" (the Rev. John B. McClellan); and a checklist, *Registrum Librorum Eroticorum* (London, 1936) combining the titles in Ashbee, Clowes, the "Private Case" of the British Museum and the "Enfer" of the Bibliothèque Nationale, compiled by Alfred Rose under the anagram "Rolf S. Reade," and ruinously botched together for the press by W. J. Stanislas after Rose's death on the eve of publication. There is also the *imitation* of Ashbee by the erotica publisher, Charles Carrington, entitled *Forbidden Books* 'by An Old Bibliophile' (Paris, 1902; reprinted New York, 1929), actually Carrington's catalogue of books for sale, with his street address very prominent in the transcripts of titles of his own publications. There are, finally, a number of excellent works, touching only slightly on the field, such as William Hart's unfinished *Index Expurgatorius Anglicanus* (London, 1872–78), Theodore Schroeder's *Free Speech Bibliography* (1922), Roger Goodland's *Bibliography of Sex Rites and Customs* (1931), and Ralph Straus' *The Unspeakable Curll* (1927), a biography and checklist of the principal erotica publisher of the early 1700's in London.

I have been engaged for a number of years in compiling a bibliography of the entire erotic and suppressed or expurgated literature in English, and of works translated from or into English, from and before Shakespeare's *Venus and Adonis* in 1593 — the first book frankly merchandised as erotica in England, with thirteen editions by 1636 — up to and including the last wholesale pornography publishing period, in the 1930's depression in America, and since. (Why it had to be during a depression will be discussed later.) The materials are not arranged in the usual *omnium gatherum* under authors or titles, but by subjects, which seems to me historically a good deal more useful. The particular subject on which I have spent most time is sex technique, which I conceive to be — as opposed, say, to the literature of homosexuality or flagellation — of great importance to the greatest possible number of people. As it happens, the principal work in English on sex technique is an ill-written little volume called *The Horn Book* (1899), whose bibliographical history poses a number of quite difficult problems which I propose now to trace, and perhaps to solve. It is hoped that the reader will care to follow, not merely through the unimportant technical confusion of sizes, pages, and illustrations, but into the maze of hidden facts, unknown actors, and falsified dates, persons, and places that makes up the world of erotica.

In 1899 there was published, probably in Paris or Brussels, but under the rubric, 'Printed for the Erotica Biblion Society of London and New-York,' an almost-square little sextodecimo (5½ x 7") entitled *The Horn Book: A Girl's Guide to the Knowledge of Good and Evil,* and with the subtitle (at the head): "How to Raise Love, or Modern Studies in the Science of Stroking." The title-page is printed in red and black, and carries Gay & Mlle. Doucé's insignia of a piping Pan, but with the punning motto-scroll *'Gai et doux c'est'* partly obliterated. All eight preliminary pages, the 153 text pages, and three supplementary blank pages are enclosed in a double wavy frame printed in red.

There are at least five reprints, the first dated 1901, with text printed all in black in a particularly bold type-face similar to what is now called Cochin, and with twenty illustrations furnished on demand (I take this on Rose's authority: I have never seen the illustrations); and another reprint, dated 1906, of 208 pages, octavo. The original edition was reprinted by photo-offset (without the red frames, and with title-page insignia of two cherubs warming their hands at a fire), dated Paris, 1923; and this was re-photographed and republished in New York about 1932, with the Paris title-page unchanged. There is also a Cuban pamphlet reprint, with cover-title: *'The Horn Book.* Price: Two Dollar. English Book Company, Liverpool, 1937,' of 90 pages (the first 18 prefixed by the somewhat un-Liverpudlian term 'Página') with twelve illustrations, of which half are ordinary erotic photographs and the other half erotic drawings of men and women in Hispanic hairdress and clothing.

The word 'Horn Book' originally referred to a sort of kindergarten battledore on which was tacked a slip of paper with the alphabet and the Lord's Prayer printed on it, and covered with a strip of transparent horn to protect the print from children's grimy hands. By extension the term has come to mean any primer, in this case a primer — actually a quite advanced handbook — of sex technique, with a pun on the word 'horn.'

Oversupplied with subtitles as the volume is, there is still another: "Entrance to the Temple," preceding the text and at the head of the Table of Contents, as though other sections — after entering the Temple — were contemplated. However, no further sections are present. There is a short Introduction, presenting the protagonists of the dialogues to follow: 'Charlie, twenty-eight years

HOW TO RAISE LOVE
OR
MODERN STUDIES IN THE SCIENCE OF STROKING

THE HORN BOOK

A GIRL'S GUIDE

TO THE

KNOWLEDGE OF GOOD AND EVIL

PRINTED FOR
THE EROTICA BIBLION SOCIETY
OF
LONDON AND NEW-YORK
—
1899

The Horn Book

PRICE: TWO DOLLAR

ENGLISH BOOK COMPANY

LIVERPOOL

1937

HOW TO RAISE LOVE
OR
MODERN STUDIES IN THE SCIENCE OF STROKING

THE HORN BOOK

A GIRL'S GUIDE

TO THE

KNOWLEDGE OF GOOD AND EVIL

PRINTED FOR
THE EROTICA BIBLION SOCIETY
OF
LONDON AND NEW-YORK
—
1901

LOVE AND SAFETY

OR

LOVE AND LASCIVIOUSNESS
WITH SAFETY AND SECRECY

A LECTURE, DELIVERED WITH
PRACTICAL ILLUSTRATIONS

BY

THE EMPRESS OF ASTURIA
(THE MODERN SAPPHO);

ASSISTED BY HER FAVOURITE LIZETTE
AND OTHERS,

*To many Ladies, from Youngest to Oldest,
and Dedicated by her to all
Women and Girls,
who long for Love of every kind,
but with Secrecy and Safety.*

———◦◦◦———

THE EROTICA BIBLION SOCIETY
OF
LONDON AND NEW-YORK

of age, brilliantly healthy, enjoying a moderate income,' and 'his mistress, Maud . . . twenty-four . . . the wife of a worthy fellow whose icy temperament formed too great a contrast with that of his better half.' There then follow five Dialogues — actually monologues by 'Charlie' — the first on the conformation of the genital parts in both sexes; the second on 'solitary masturbation,' sodomy and tribady (which we nowadays would call by the psychological state, and not the act, homosexuality and Lesbianism); the third and fourth — the main part of the book — describing sixty-three postures for sexual intercourse, each with a mnemonic title such as "Dog-Fashion Sideways," " 'T' Upside Down," or "Waste Not, Want Not;" the fifth dialogue on sodomy with women, nonvaginal methods of coitus generally, and oragenital acts; and a final section called "Love and Security," on birth-control methods. That is the book.

When one turns to the existing bibliographies of erotica for information on the most obvious point of interest — the anonymous author's name — nothing is to be learned. The date is too late for Ashbee or Clowes to include; Rose gives only the 1901 reprint, under *Horn Book*, saying that it was published in New York (which seems unlikely); and the work is quite unknown to Gay-Lemonnyer, Perceau, and Hayn; while the *Bilder-Lexikon*, vol. 4, gives only the 1906 edition, from a copy in the collection of the sexologist, Iwan Bloch.

On returning to the book itself and examining it more closely, hoping for some lead, perhaps from the internal evidence of style, one is led almost to the conclusion that this is a thoroughly English original, and for that reason practically unknown to foreign bibliographers. So English is it, in fact, that there is even a quite uncalled-for excursus (in Dialogue II, "Sodomy, or Man With Man," p. 43) on the curious Cockney rhyming-slang, in which *sodomite* is not only shortened to 'sod' but further transmogrified into 'Tommy Dodd;' syphilis ('the pox') into 'Jack-in-the-box,' gonorrhea ('the clap') into 'Horse and Trap,' and so on, ending with a little didactic exemplum or joke, using one's new-found lore, in which one 'Tommy' (still shorter for 'Tommy Dodd') says to another, in the act: ' "You know, I've got the 'Horse and Trap'." "Have you?" says the other, "well I've got the 'Jack!' " '

Looking further, one finds similar signs of philological interests in the author in various places in *The Horn Book;* for instance in Dialogue I, on the conformation of the genital organ in man, which is described as having, aside from its commonest slang synonyms, 'a thousand other suggestive [*i.e.* allusive] titles, such as: thing, lance, dagger, spear, dart, perforator, pego, tool, John Thomas, piercer, etc.' At this point, it would appear, the author has been discovered. Only one person writing in English in 1899 or thereabouts is known to have interested himself in English sexual slang — and particularly in sexual synonymies — and to have had contacts with erotica printed abroad, and that was John Stephen Farmer, compiler, with the poet William Ernest Henley, of *Slang and Its Analogues* (1890–1904) in seven quarto volumes.

Henley had entered the work at the second volume, and a revised volume I appeared in 1903–09, presumably incorporating his, as well as Farmer's additions to the 1890 original (for instance, half a page of quotations under 'arse' in 1890, become four full pages in 1903). As a poet's, however, Henley's style could hardly have stumbled so often as does that of *The Horn Book*. In any case, the synonymies of *Slang and Its Analogues* had begun in the first volume, before Henley's collaboration, with a five-page list of synonyms for prostitute at the word *barrack-hack* (four of the pages are of French 'analogues'), a list later enlarged to seven pages under *tart*. Similar synonymies for the male genitals occur under *cream-stick* and *prick*; for the female genitals under *monosyllable;* and for sexual intercourse under *greens* and *ride*. Although there are many other lists of synonyms throughout — as at *bum, bury a Quaker, Mrs. Jones, mutton-monger,* etc. — none even approach the extensiveness of these sexual ones, except those for drunkenness (under *lush-crib, lushington,* and *screwed*) and for stealing, under *prig*. As the principal human problems — or, rather, the principal human escapes — sex, liquor, and crime are also the centers around which slang coinage gravitates.

Farmer's first volume was printed in London by one Thomas Poulter, but Poulter drew the line at volume 2 — containing the letter *C* — and, when sued for breach of contract, won a counter-claim of £114 against Farmer! One assumes the case was judged on moral, rather than legal grounds. At any rate, volumes 2 and 3 were printed instead by Harrison & Sons, 'Printers in Ordinary to Her Majesty the Queen,' as the colophon of volume 2 pointedly mentions. Later volumes were printed abroad, first by H. C. A. Thieme in Nimeguen, Holland, and finally in Scotland. It was in 1896, during his period abroad, that Farmer may be assumed to have come into contact with the practical world of erotica publishing, then operating principally out of Holland, Belgium, and France.

His troubles with printers had given the dictionary project quite a setback, and from 1896 to 1902 only scattered parts appeared. Instead, Farmer turned his attention to publishing scholarly pot-boilers, first a collection of bawdy folksongs in English entitled *Merry, Facetious, and Witty Songs and Ballads* (1895), enlarged to five volumes in 1897; then a collection of slang songs, *Musa Pedestris* (1896); and finally an English translation of the erotic French dictionaries of 'Louis de Landes' (Auguste Scheler) and Alfred Delvau, under the title *Vocabula Amatoria* (1896). Some copies of this, as well as some copies of volume 4 of *Slang and Its Analogues,* published in the same year, have special title-pages substituted, beginning "A Supplemental Glossary . . . etc.," and the last wrap-around sheet of *Vocabula Amatoria* is reset, with all erotic terms omitted from the English, apparently to assist in getting the volume through the English customs inspection. By 1897 Farmer had succumbed temporarily to his troubles, and control of the dictionary project passed out of his hands, the set being issued privately by commercial publishers in London, first Gibbings & Co., then Routledge. It is at this point that one can imagine Farmer setting to work on *The Horn Book* (or digging up the manuscript if it was written earlier), probably for the erotica publisher Carrington, whose best-printed volume, Rosenbaum's *The Plague of Lust . . . in Classical Antiquity,* was also printed by Farmer's printer, Thieme, in Holland in 1898, though not issued till 1901.

One fact, discovered by accident, disproves a part of the above theory, but strengthens the rest. The fact is that *The Horn Book* is a translation from the French, and Farmer could therefore only have been, at most, the translator — interpolating his philological interests — as with the erotic dictionaries of Scheler and Delvau. The orginal of *The Horn Book* is a rare, and itself rather mysterious work (it is unknown to Perceau) entitled *Instruction libertine, ou Dialogues entre Charles et Justine sur la théorie physique de l'amour et les diverses manières de s'en procurer les plaisirs matériels.* The imprint given is 'Sadopolis, 1860,' but the book was actually published in Brussels by Jean-Pierre Blanche in 1870. The entire book (143 pages, octavo) is reproduced by lithography from a calligraphic text probably made — as will be seen — by the artist Ulm. The book is of the greatest rarity, as only fifty copies were produced, but Rose fortunately notes one in the Private Case of the British Museum. Another was evidently under the eyes of the translator of *The Horn Book,* though the relation between this and *Instruction libertine* has apparently not before been observed.

Again, who is the author? Gay, who notes a more complete manuscript (*n.b.*) with not merely 63 postures 'in one series, but nearly a hundred in the various series,' adds that the author is supposed to be one 'Benoît, a former lawyer,' but that this is probably a pseudonym. No more than this can be learned from the long notice of *Instruction libertine* by the Viennese collector, Gustav Gugitz, in the *Bilder-Lexikon,* and further clarification has seemed impossible. Recently, however, through the assistance of a very good friend, I was able to examine an equally rare book, *L'École des Biches* ('Paris, 1863,' actually Brussels: Blanche, 1868), in which the key to the question of the authorship of both books will be found.

L'École des Biches bears in every part a striking resemblance to *Instruction libertine.* Both were published by Jean-Pierre Blanche in Brussels about 1870 with false predatings. Both were printed in a very small number of copies — *L'École des Biches* in an edition of only 64 copies, from a calligraphic manuscript by Ulm. Both texts are in the form of dialogues, and both are preceded by the formal introduction of the actors, with their ages and background. The Introduction to *The Horn Book* (*Instruction libertine*) has been quoted above. *L'École des Biches* begins, in translation: 'Count Henri de Sarsalle. Twenty-five years old. Only son of an opulent Southern family . . . etc.' Most important of all, at the end of Part I, Dialogue xiv (original, p. 218, and reprint, Brussels: Gay & Doucé, 1880, p. 179) a long note introduces the manuscript of *Instruction libertine,* describing it as 'emanating from the pen and leisure hours of Monsieur B . . . . t, a former magistrate, who died in Paris in 1863.' Earlier, a footnote to the fifth Dialogue of *L'École des Biches,* referring to the use of a sponge in birth-control, also says shortly: 'Voir *Instruction libertine.*' It is beyond question that both are the work of the same hands, but whose hands?

In his calm and elevated way, Ashbee answers the question in a notice of *L'École des Biches* appearing in his *Index Librorum Prohibitorum* (1879) p. 194–8, though accidentally omitted from the index. 'It is the joint production of three gentlemen who "ont rempli les principaux rôles," and who, at the opening of the book, give sketches of themselves, as well as of the four "petites dames" . . . by whom they were assisted. In the book the author-actors are known as "Le Comte Henri de Sarsalle, Martin Duvernet, rentier, Adrien Lebel, artiste peintre;" but they have further favoured us [*i.e.* Ashbee] with the following pseudonyms: CHAPUYS, BOKEL, D'ENGHIEN, which contain the exact letters of their real names. The chief of the trio was the late Edmond Duponchel; the other two gentlemen are still alive, and I leave their names veiled.'

This is, of course, a challenge, but, before taking it up, here is Ashbee's short biographical sketch of the principal, if not, in fact, the only, author of *L'École des Biches,* and therefore, of *The Horn Book (Instruction libertine)*:

Edmond Duponchel was born at Paris about 1795, and died in April 1868. In early life he studied architecture, and afterwards went to England to learn the goldsmith's craft, in which he became a proficient, and executed the bas reliefs of the "Minerva" of Simart. In 1835 Duponchel was appointed Director of the Opéra at Paris in place of Véron. This post he carried on single handed until May, 1840, when he obtained the assistance of Léon Pillet, royal commissionaire at the theatre since 1838; after eighteen months of co-administration Duponchel resigned his office in favour of Pillet. Pillet's reign lasted till 1847, when he was replaced by Duponchel and Roqueplan.

With that background, one is hardly surprised at Ashbee's next divulgation (in *Catena Librorum Tacendorum,* 1885, p. 422) that 'The ladies were well known actresses, whose names it would be easy to give, were the disclosure not premature.' Meanwhile, another of the collaborators having died, Ashbee adds: 'I have already named the actual author of the work, at whose dictation it was written, for the most part in the apartments of Mr. F. Hankey, and by the fair hand of one of the ladies who figure in the voluptuous scenes described. Hankey and another gentleman still alive offered suggestions; but M. Baroche, although his collaboration has been affirmed (F. Drujon, *Catalogue des Ouvrages Supprimés,* 1879, p. 134) had nothing whatever to do with the work.'

Frederick Hankey, here introduced, is one of the strangest figures in erotic bibliophily, and opinions about him naturally differ. Ashbee (*Catena,* Preliminary Remarks, p. L) gives the most temperate and friendly:

If ever there was a bibliomaniac in the fullest sense of the word it was Frederick Hankey. His collection was small, but most choice, and comprised objects and books, exclusively erotic. The former do not fall within the scope of the present work. (Among others may be mentioned what he was pleased to call the sign of his house, *viz.* a most spirited marble by Pradier representing two tribades; he had also a beautiful bronze of a satyr caressing a woman, where caresses with the tongue are not usually bestowed; a *ceinture de chastété,* an ivory dildo, &c.) Nor did Hankey attach the same importance to them as he did to his books, which consisted of illustrated MS., the best editions and exceptional copies of the most esteemed erotic works, frequently embellished with original drawings, and clothed by the great French binders . . . and he designed himself appropriate toolings wherewith to embellish them . . . Hankey was in every respect an original; he never rose until after mid-day, and his hours of reception were after 10 o'clock at night, when he was to be found among his books. He had fair hair, blue eyes, and an almost feminine expression, and answered in many respects to the descriptions which have reached us of the Marquis de Sade, his favourite author . . . He had a curious habit of repeating himself, which at times rendered his conversation tedious. In 1878 appeared a sketch, from the facile pen of M. Octave Uzanne (*Caprices d'un Bibliophile,* p. 127) of an *Eroto-Bibliomane* named *le Chevalier Kerhany,* which was generally thought to be intended for Hankey, but this was not [?] the case as at that date M. Uzanne had not seen the well known "riche amateur anglais." (Ashbee adds in a note that it was he who finally introduced them, hardly three months before Hankey's death in 1882.)

The erotica publisher, Hirsch, is quoted in Apollinaire, Fleuret, and Perceau's *Enfer de la Bibliothèque Nationale* (1913) p. 21, as being somewhat less taken by the 'rich English dilettante' — his father was Sir Frederick Hankey, resident governor of the Ionian Islands, his mother a lady of Greek extraction — who 'lived in Paris during the Second Empire, where he used to go on the town with the Prince of Wales, Grammont Caderousse, etc. He was so thin and deformed that he could hardly hold himself up, and walked on crutches. He had altogether 200 books, all very select . . . Part of this library of erotica he kindly left to Mr. Ashbee.'

It is hard to decide whether Ashbee's politeness is, then, mere gratitude, or Hirsch's coolness mere chauvinism. Ashbee's last word on Hankey was to defend him, apparently in all sincerity (*Catena*, p. 523), from the open contempt of Henri Béraldi's *Mes Estampes* (1884) p. 77, where Hankey is called: 'a curious type; the sort of collector that Cohen (in his *Guide de l'amateur*) always qualifies with the euphemistic epithet, "special" (read: superlatively obscene). H . . . .'s only excuse, if he can be excused at all, is that he had the taste of a real bibliophile, and that what he collected had nothing in common with vulgar smut . . . He was a man of fifty, bald, bent, his face glabrous, his speech halting and broken. Being gouty, he often went out wearing one shoe and one bedroom slipper, which hardly seemed proper. His shoes were remarkably pointed and gave him a rather diabolical appearance, and I know one lady bookseller who believed he had a cloven hoof . . . Booksellers welcomed him without enthusiasm, and found him *tacky* . . .' The last time Béraldi saw Hankey, the latter thanked him for having written about some of his books, and wished the note had been longer. 'I escaped,' Béraldi finishes, 'by assuring him that I would repair this deplorable omission when the occasion arose. I have done so now.'

This is of course mere spite. Discounting the excessively moral tone, since a number of the engravings in Béraldi's own collection might also, as Ashbee notes, be called 'superlatively obscene,' it is really hard lines to damn a man for his looks. Which of us would escape? Hankey's fame was in his collection of books. His stammer and gout, his bent body and crutches — he was obviously a dying man by then — even his bald head and alleged cloven hoof, seem somewhat irrelevant. One wonders what Béraldi would have thought of a man like Swinburne who, in spite of red hair, scrawny neck, short stature, a truly horrifying stammer, and his unfortunate penchants for flagellomania, alliteration, and falling into an all-to-bepissed epileptic fit in company, nevertheless wrote splendid poetry and some of the most magnificent invective prose (invariably on the wrong side of every question) in the annals of English literature.

There remains now only the third co-author of *L'École des Biches* to find. Striking out the letters of the two known names, Duponchel and Hankey, from the anagram given by Ashbee: CHAPUYS, BOKEL, D'ENGHIEN, only the five letters SBGIE remain. Since Drujon's *Catalogue des Ouvrages Supprimés,* cited above by Ashbee, makes the statement (quoted from Gay) that the authors were 'quelques hommes du monde, MM. Baroche, fils de l'ancien ministre de la justice [*this was a mistake*], Hankey, riche amateur anglais, bien connu à Paris, Dup . . . ., B . . . ., et autres,' one knows that the missing author's name began with a B. Perhaps that was how the false attribution to Baroche, son of the former Minister of Justice (!) happened to be made. Since openings with BS or BG are out of the question, one has merely to put down the twelve possible permutations beginning with BI and BE, and hope for a familiar name.

BISGE	BESGI
BISEG	BESIG
BIGES	BEGIS
BIGSE	BEGSI
BIESG	BEISG
BIEGS	BEIGS

Most of these are obviously not names. Of the two that might be — Biges and Begis — one *is* familiar. Bégis. In the cheap reprint of the Apollinaire-Fleuret-Perceau *Enfer,* made from plates in 1919 on execrable post-war paper (I couldn't afford the first edition), there is a new Preface, the only new matter in the reprint, and this Preface has only one footnote: '*L'Enfer de la Bibliothèque Nationale, Revendication de M. Alfred Bégis, Débats judiciaires.* Paris, Conquet, Société des Amis des Livres, 1899.' There he is.

ALFRED BÉGIS and his 'revindication' — an action at French law for the recovery of seized property — are themselves quite a story. Here it is, as translated from Fleuret and Perceau's new Preface (Apollinaire being dead) to the 1919 edition of *L'Enfer de la Bibliothèque Nationale.*

'On the 22nd of June, 1866, the Printing and Bookselling Division of the Ministry of the Interior was informed that two suspected packages were about to be delivered to the bookseller Rouquette, 25 rue de Choiseul. At this period, the Imperial Police were on the lookout for political publications coming from abroad, concerning the First and Second Empires. As can be understood, it was very difficult to evade the police-informers, and late readers of Rochefort's *Lanterne* can well remember how they were able to read it, generally, only by means of subterfuges as amusing as they were ingenious. Briefly, however, on the 23rd of June, a special agent who had received orders to seize the packages, was informed by the bookseller that their contents were intended for Monsieur Alfred Bégis, who would probably buy them. Alfred Bégis was by profession an official bankruptcy trustee, and something of a historian. He had published, notably, a biography of Louis XVII, another on the revolutionary, Billaud-Varenne, and a *Registre d'écrou de la Bastille, de 1782 à 1789;* but his most recent publications, and the political opinions expressed, far from suggesting clemency, went against him in quite the opposite direction. An examining magistrate, M. de Gonnet, was named, and on the 5th of July handed down a rogatory commission to M. Berillon, a police agent, "to wit, that he transport himself without delay to the domicile of Monsieur Bégis, 29 boulevard Sebastopol, for the purpose of making a search, and, if the case warrants, to seize every obscene or suspected book, etc. . . ."

'The agent, according to the record, turned upside-down in the course of twelve hours a library of 10,000 volumes of every kind, and finished by picking out several hundred books, most of them *political,* and a few gallant or licentious. Most of these dated from the 18th century, and were ornamented with valuable bindings and enriched with illustrations; the whole representing a value of 30,000 francs, which was a great deal of money for books in those days when only ballet-dancers had incomes. M. Bégis appeared before the examining magistrate, and was told the decision handed down from on high: either he must resign from his official position as bankruptcy trustee, or he must consent to the destruction of the books seized. M. Bégis, who was no hero of bibliophily — doubtless because the subject is not mentioned by Plutarch — decided to sign the order for the destruction of his books. However, he insisted on a reservation in favor of the album by Giulio Romano (Aretino's postures), and a collection of tracings made from these prints. The court consented, and the bankruptcy trustee was "left to live with his sorrow . . ."

'Immediately, and as though by accident, it was somehow learned by the director of the Imperial Library that 30,000 francs' worth of books — and what books! — were about to be reduced to pulp. He obtained permission, by urgent means, it is said, for the Library to take its choice among the books. And so, on the 17th of October, M. Bégis was invited by M. Moignon, the imperial procurator and himself a distinguished bibliophile — such was the exquisite politeness of the government toward M. Bégis — to be shown two crates of books, one for him and one for the Imperial Library. M. Moignon, the bibliophile, then demanded of M.

Bégis, biblio-martyr, that he place his signature, as donor, on the registry of the Library, in consideration of which the books would then be entered permanently in the "Enfer." M. Bégis refused, insensible of the honor offered, before him, only to Michelet, and, in our day, to M. Georges Vicaire. Finally, M. Bégis was allowed to carry away the box so generously surrendered to him, which he found to contain a file of the *Journal Officiel.*

'Several days later, the public prosecutor of the Seine district officially transmitted to the Library the books it had chosen, namely: 154 printed volumes, and 23 engravings, which were duly entered on the register with their accession numbers and mention of their provenance. *Mention of their provenance!* . . . What Bégis counted on, wise in the ways of bankruptcy, was the imminent fall of the Second Empire, at which time he would regain his property. He waited five years, till the Empire fell, and the peace was signed. Then, redoubling his prudent astuteness, he waited even longer, in fact until his retirement in 1882! He then addressed a polite reclaimer to the Minister of Public Instruction, who showed himself favorable in principle, to the restitution of this forced gift. However, on the 6th of December, 1882, the Minister, who had meanwhile consulted the Library — the Bibliothèque *Nationale* this time — turned upon M. Bégis so clouded a countenance, that the former trustee decided to take matters to court.

'Setting aside an adverse judgment handed down in 1885, on the 13th of December, 1892, the Civil Tribunal emitted a judgment that brought back his youth to the bibliophile now aging in hope. But the Bibliothèque Nationale, or rather the "Enfer," would not give up its prey . . . Instead of the usual line from Dante, *Abandon all hope, ye who enter here,* they cited to our appellant Article 2279: *Possession is nine points of the law.* And like an artful debater striking out with an argument long held in reserve — a good argument, the best, the argument of *provenance* — His Honour M. Cléry broke it this way: There had been no gift, since the appellant had refused to sign the register; there remained, therefore, only a list of books obtained by judicial seizures . . .

' "Well then," retorted M. Bégis' lawyer, "has not the Tribunal annulled the seizure? . . ."

' "Very true," replied His Honour M. Cléry, "but observe that *judicial seizures* is in the plural, in the plural! . . . Can you provide a detailed list of your books — minutely detailed so as to distinguish them from all other books of 'anonymous provenance' mixed together on the entry-register under the heading of *judicial seizures* . . . in the plural? If you can, the Library will accord you satisfaction."

'M. Bégis gave up after an embarrassed description of a *Vie de Marie-Antoinette* and the *Portier des Chartreux,* his memory balking at the demanded one hundred and seventy-five detailed descriptions. All that he could do was to take his revenge peacefully, bibliophilically — that is to say, by publishing his misfortunes (*L'Enfer de la Bibliothèque Nationale, Revendication de M. Alfred Bégis, Débats judiciaires.* Paris, Conquet, Société des Amis des Livres, 1899), due on the one hand to the abuse of power by an imperial procurator, and, on the other hand, to the immortal Article 2279!'

It will not have escaped the reader, beneath the confusion of the too-exact dates above, that Bégis' part in *L'École des Biches* — both the enacting and the writing in Hankey's apartment — had taken place at just about the time of the judicial seizure of 1866, possibly in 1863 if the rubric-date of the published edition may be taken as emanating in any way from the manuscript.

Several years after solving the little biblio-cryptographical problem demonstrating Bégis' part, I learned — again by accident — that Jules Gay had, in a sense, made fools of us all. Unknown perhaps to Ashbee, and in any case a year before the British bibliographer proposed to leave 'veiled' the names of the still-living Hankey and Bégis, Gay had published in his *Analectes du Bibliophile* (1876) pt. 3: p. 22, in a charming, if useless, bibliographical *olla podrida* entitled "Liste de livres à titres singuliers et bizarres," by the French bibliographer, Gustave Brunet, writing under the pseudonym "Philomneste junior," the following plain and full notice on *L'École des Biches:* 'Cet ouvrage, dû à quelques hommes du monde (MM. Baroche, fils, de l'ancien ministre de la justice [!], Frédéric Hankey; Duponchel, fils [?] du directeur de l'Opéra, et Alfred Bégis), est aujourd'hui à peu près introuvable.' One can only assume that the unanimity of later bibliographers in concealing Bégis' name was — if not out of ignorance — in respect of the famous seizure, to avoid prejudicing his case.

FLEURET AND PERCEAU pass over, in a few lines and some scattered italics at the beginning of their notice, the peculiar connection that has long existed between political upheaval and erotic literature. As usually stated, this is described simply as a moral stalking-horse, or cynical pretence of suppressing obscenity, behind which political suppressions and imprisonments have so often been made. But this is only half the story. The fact is that a real relation very often does exist, though by no means of the vulgar and direct sort that censors, post-office stooges, and police-spies contemplate. The principal periods of erotic publishing have, historically, almost always preceded and followed revolutions, depressions, protracted wars, and similar upheavals. This has been strikingly evident in both French and English history.

In France the three principal modern periods of erotic publishing were just before and particularly during the French Revolution of 1789; the ten years before and after the Franco-Prussian War and the Commune of 1871 (the period here under discussion, and on which see in particular the records of the Sacré-Duquesne and Poulet-Malassis affairs, in Drujon, *Catalogue des Ouvrages Supprimés*, 1879, p. 49 and 298–99); and the decades preceding and following World War I. (Likewise in Germany.)

In England, erotic publishing began seriously with the first rumblings of the English Revolution in 1640 and did not even stop for breath for a century. Shakespeare's *Sonnets* were immediately republished as his *Poems* in 1640, with the homosexual element expurgated by means of female pronouns replacing male; and an endless profusion of anti-Puritan poetical miscellanies and bawdy 'drolleries' appeared from the Royalist poets and presses. (See Arthur E. Case, *A Bibliography of English Poetical Miscellanies*, 1935, no. 92 to the end, oddly omitting the most famous: Playford & D'Urfey's *Wit and Mirth, or Pills to Purge Melancholy*.) These were followed by the famously unrepressed Restoration drama, which was not actually halted until the advent of the elegant prudery of Richardson and Lillo (and the immediately subterranean eroticism of Cleland's *Fanny Hill*) in the 1740's. During the American and French Revolutions and the Napoleonic aftermath, which had England reeling, both public and publishing morals in England were of the greatest possible freedom, all of which came suddenly to an end with the quashing of the revolution brewing in 1832, of which the birth-control propagandist, Francis Place, was to have been the head.

After backing the wrong horse in the American Civil War, and repealing the Paper Tax, England again saw erotic publishing in the 1860's and '70's (concomitant with the same period in France) in the open Holywell Street period, which has been made the sub-

ject of a novel, *Forlorn Sunset* (1946) by Michael Sadleir. After
the death in 1873 of John Camden Hotten, who had one foot in
both respectable and sub-rosa publishing, and the withdrawal
from the field by 'Cameron,' to whom the erotic magazine *The
Pearl* (1879–80, and sequels) is due, very little of an erotic nature
was published in England, most of its needs being supplied from
France. Meanwhile, in America, a remarkable period of erotic
publishing had shortly preceded and run concurrent with the
Civil War, some of the openly-sold New Orleans pocket volumes
of about 1850 to 1860 being of the most startling eroticism. The
economic ferment in both England and America — to say nothing
of the Continent — in the 1890's and 1900's went quite parallel
to the supply of English-language erotica being rolled off the
presses in Holland and France to supply the demand. (*The Horn
Book* was just a chip on that ocean.) Finally, in America, after a
lead-up of classical and folk erotica beginning in 1927, during the
worst four years of the depression (centering around 1932) an
unparalleled amount of erotic literature appeared privately, while
the semi-erotic public press — *Broadway Brevities* and its tabloid
imitators in particular — remains, although it is already excessively
rare, as the astonishment of the decade.

The explanation is by no means that erotica publishers — or
buyers — are radicals. With certain notable historical exceptions,
such as De Sade, Place, and Bégis (if the latter's mild political
anti-Imperialism can by any stretch be called radical), sex and
politics are seldom seriously combined on the literary level. As a
personal testimony, I have met most of the principal erotica publishers of the 1930's in America, and with two exceptions all of
them were either non-radical or anti-radical, one of them violently
so. The actual connection is somewhat more tenuous, and is seen
most clearly in the sudden spurt of sexual freedom in publishing
immediately following the English Revolution of the 1640's.
When repressive political powers begin to crack, owing to the
internal stress of depression or social change, or to such outside
accidents as losing a war, and when the authoritarian figureheads
of kings and kaisers are deposed, usually in the throes of the upheavals just noted, the sexual repression of even the least revolutionary segments of the public (*e.g.* the pre-Revolutionary aristocracy in France) breaks down. A whole book has been written on
just this point by a gentleman whose later work unfortunately
tapers off into eccentricity: *The Mass Psychology of Fascism*, by
Wilhelm Reich (1933, chapters I through VIII), to which the interested reader is referred, with caution.

THE VARIOUS milieux in which and out of which *The Horn Book* rose should now be rather clear. Nor is its subject, sex technique, to be wondered at. The first and most elementary breakdown in sexual repression is usually the one against sexual experimentation — with tabooed positions, organs, apertures, persons, beasts, bugs, inanimate objects, and even Professor Kinsey. The literature on this subject in English is the sparsest in any major language, as befits the sexually repressed nations that speak it, and it is not surprising that the high-point of this literature in English, *The Horn Book,* had to be brought over from the French. 'Felix Wildmay' in *Anybody's Fanny* ('Quaker Haven,' 1929; reprinted in *American Aphrodite,* 1951, no. 2: p. 21) dismisses *The Horn Book* as 'a journey to the gutter . . . designed as solace for illiterate hucksters,' but he is wrong. Its style, in English, does leave a great deal to be desired, but its postures are well thought out and intelligently varied. It is, of course, no *ne plus ultra* of the coital art. France itself has produced a much superior work of the same sort, apparently a conscious imitation, subtitles and all, in "Doctor A.-S. Lagail's" (actually Alphonse Gallais') *Les Paradis Charnels, ou Le Divin bréviaire des amants: Art de jouir purement des 136 extases de volupté* ('Priapeville: Imprimerie Galante, An III du XXe Siècle Foutatif'), in which the ancient and famous "Basket Trick" and the less well known, but even more spectacular, "Judgment of Solomon" take their place as numbers 130 ("En Panier") and 136*b* in the final section of "Clowneries charnelles." The recent French avant-garde writer, Isidore Isou — name fatality, perhaps, on the assonance with Liseux? — has produced a number of similar eroto-didactic works, one of which, *Isou, ou La Mécanique des Femmes* ('Aux Escaliers de Lausanne,' about 1950), was seized and condemned, the author's curious insistence on his own name in the title also causing him certain *ennuis* with the law. A more recent similar work, *Les 32 Positions* (about 1958, not to be confused with earlier fake works of the same title, but of non-erotic catchpenny contents), which has also been attributed to Isou, is even more closely in the style of Gallais' *Paradis Charnels,* probably in direct imitation.

In the monomania of *positions,* Germany has of course excelled, that particular problem being more mathematical and permutational than really imaginative. In *Das Goldene Buch der Liebe, oder Die Renaissance im Geschlechtsleben; ein Eros-Kodex für beide Geschlechter* — those sub-titles again — presumably the work of a 'Dr. L. van der Weck-Erlen' but actually by a gymnasium professor, Dr. Josef Weckerle (1858–1921), and published by C. W. Stern in Vienna in 1907, the entire second volume (in limp-bound burlap, decorated with *art nouveau* hearts!) is devoted to a "Gymnoplastik der Liebe, oder Das erotische Riesensystem," which gives the astounding total of five hundred and thirty-one (531) different coital positions, all carefully described, numbered, classified, and mnemonically titled. Duponchel and Gallais, not to mention the *Kama Sutra* and *Perfumed Garden*, are left gasping behind, if one is to judge by sheer numbers. The first two hundred of Weckerle's postures have been translated into English under the title *Kinesthesia of Love* 'by T. Van de Velder, M.D.' — a later printing returns to the original pseudonym — in two booklets with imprint 'Bombay: The Times of India Press' (really New York), 1937–38. The first hundred positions have illustrations supplied on bits of superimposable cardboard (female) and transparent plastic (male). With this sort of hopeless erotic doodling is to be compared what is perhaps the finest modern erotic manual, also in German, *Die Weisheiten der Aspasia* by 'Fritz Thurn' (Dr. Fritz Foregger von Greiffenthurn), published in Vienna in 1923, a magnificent volume both as to typographical format and sensitive and intelligent content.

It was noted before, that Gay refers to a more complete manuscript of *Instruction libertine*, the French original of *The Horn Book*, and, in the search for the presumably unpublished portion, I believe the answer to the final question — that of the publisher of *The Horn Book* — will be found. Says Gay, in translation: 'We have seen a manuscript of this work in which are described not merely 40 ways of making love [*the classic number*], but 63 for one series and nearly 100 for the various series. Certainly the author of this work was no ordinary man; but what would he have said if he knew that a modern artist of the — how shall we say — pornographic or pornognostic sort, has collected 3000 groups and postures? — The manuscript of which we speak had 300 pages, and the author is said to be M. Benoît, a former advocate, now deceased. We presume this is a pseudonym.'

One notices that Gay gets away fast from the '3000 groups and postures,' which sound more like a collection of drawings or photographs than anything else, doubtless with all sorts of unsystematic duplication. The soul of poor, great, compulsive Weckerle can surely rest, gymnastically, in peace.

Now what about the rest of the manuscript? As to the French original which Gay describes, that seems to have quite disappeared. No lucky accident has yet turned up any printed work in French answering to its description. If a hunch which will be discussed at the end of this article should prove correct, it may very well be that the manuscript fell into the hands of the editor of *The Pearl* and that a translation was made directly from that. For what is clearly an English translation of the missing part does exist, and has been published under the inordinately long title: '*Love and Safety,* or Love and Lasciviousness with safety and secrecy. A lecture, delivered with practical illustrations by The Empress of Asturia (The Modern Sappho); assisted by her favourite Lizette and others, to many Ladies, from Youngest to Oldest, and Dedicated by her to all Women and Girls, who long for Love of every kind, but with Secrecy and Safety. The Erotica Biblion Society of London and New-York.' No date is given, but for reasons that will appear shortly, it can be dated with some certainty between 1899 and 1904, probably closer to _899. It is unquestionably the production of the same publisher and translator as *The Horn Book,* which it exactly resembles typographically except for the lack of red frames around the eight preliminary and 139 text pages (small sextodecimo). The translation is also filled with philological asides, as on the various anti-national names for the condom ('French Letter' in England, 'Russian Thimble' in Germany, etc.) A reprint exists, dated 1908, followed by Eugene Field's *Only a Boy.* The self-evident relationship between *Love and Safety* and *The Horn Book* has been noted by another writer, in a gallant little anthology of erotic songs called *Folk Poems and Ballads* ('Mexico City: The Cruciform Press, 1945,' actually U.S. 1948) p. 121, with the suggestion, in which I cannot entirely concur, that their free circulation in America would cut down the 'percentage of insane and neurotic people.'

John S. Farmer's hand would appear to be present in *Love and Safety* beginning on the verso of the title-page, where two burlesque dictionary-style quotations in the special SMALL CAPITAL style of *Slang and Its Analogues* are given to support the title: '"Out of the nettle DANGER to pluck the flower safety." — Poem by THINGUMY. "Thou shalt not be FOUND OUT." — XIth Commandment, Old Test., rəv. vər.' (the two *e*'s of the last two abbreviations turned upside-down to suit). The text takes up where *The Horn Book* leaves off. We are now, no doubt, inside 'the Temple' to which that was just the 'Entrance.' Aside from a postscript of directions for birth-control and some prescriptions for aphrodisiacs, all that is to be found in this holy of holies — as one might have suspected from the strong Lesbian penchant of *L'École des*

Biches (the 'Biches' of the title) and from the authoress' cognomen of "The Modern Sappho" — is the physical technique of Lesbianism.

This unfortunate psychological malady had its heyday in France after the breakdown of patriarchal authority in the Revolution, reaching its height from the 1830's of "George Sand" to the Lesbian-worshipping 1860's of Baudelaire, Verlaine, and Swinburne, and, of course, of Duponchel and associates. It may be observed in all periods of history where patriarchy collapses, that the predominantly male homosexual and female masochist characters — in the life of the culture, as in its literature and art — rapidly disappear, and are replaced by the similarly matching female homosexual and male masochistic characters. Examples of the latter in English literature, from Herrick on through Keats and Swinburne, are the rule rather than the exception. One may also see signs of another such period close at hand, as noted in my pamphlets *On the Cause of Homosexuality* (1950) p. 31, and *Love & Death* (1949) p. 78-9.

There is reason to believe that the publisher of *Love and Safety* was — if not Édouard Maheu, in Brussels — Charles Carrington, in Paris, who in 1904 issued a work of suspiciously similar title, namely: *Love Without Danger: A Study in social science,* the text printed in brown borders (*n.b.*) There is a copy in the Library of the New York Academy of Medicine, reserve collection, but the book is hardly worth consulting. Its subject is birth control, and the title has been taken over in recent years for an openly published, in fact pocket-reprinted work on the same subject by a British physician, Eustace Chesser. (There was also *Love and Debauch in Paris: Extraordinary Lustful Scenes.* Nice-London, 1905. 176 p., octavo. A series seems to have been intended, and it is nice to think that a series with the word 'Love' in the title was expected to sell — an idea no longer current.) *Love Without Danger* has all the earmarks of being what is known in the trade as a cover-item: to be shown innocently to the authorities if and when objection is made concerning the under-cover item, in this case evidently *Love and Safety*. A more recent example of the same dodge is *Nova Venus*, an album of drawings by the American artist, Mahlon Blaine, issued in New York, 1938, to 'cover' the re-issue at the same time of the same artist's earlier and more graphic series, *Venus Sardonica* (1929), which is, to date, the only important erotic art album ever issued in America.

Carrington's principal competitor for the English market in

erotica happened to be one of the only other possible candidates for the position of translator or publisher of *The Horn Book*. His name was Leonard Smithers, and he had his small fame as the collaborator with Sir Richard Burton (whose fraudulent 'translation' of *The Arabian Nights* is actually a bold-faced paraphrase of John Payne's translation, and whose exposure is long overdue), and as the publisher of Aubrey Beardsley. Smithers not only collaborated with Burton; he also made a business of publishing their joint productions privately in the industrial town of Sheffield. This was the so-called 'Erotika Biblion Society of Athens,' whose name Carrington or Maheu plagiarized for the 'Erotica Biblion Society of London and New-York.' Carrington never missed an opportunity of needling Smithers, who was taking far greater risks, on English soil, and publishing what were actually far more important, if quite unpretentious little books. It was Smithers who published the first English translation of Forberg's *Manual of Classical Erotology* (from the French) in 1887, and Swinburne's anonymous *Whippingham Papers* in 1888. These Carrington grandiosely topped with a new and better translation of Forberg, with the Latin text facing (he complains in *Forbidden Books* that he lost money on it), actually published in Brussels in 1899, but pre-dated — as the crowning touch — three years earlier than Smithers' edition, under the rubric: 'Manchester: Printed for Viscount Julian Smithson, M.A. and Friends, 1884.' This was coming damned close to home for the safety of Smithers' skin. In the same way, in 1885, at what must have been the very beginning of Smithers' *sub rosa* publications in Sheffield, the Brussels erotica publishers Gay & Mlle. Doucé (or more probably Kistemaeckers) had attempted to attract attention to this new competitor, and thus frighten him or throw him into the hands of the police, by the almost identical imprint — on a collection of 18th century contes-en-vers, *Pornophile: Contes saugrenus* — 'Sur l'imprimé de Bassora, 1789. Samuel-Isaac-Josédiah Smithson, libraire à Jersey, Friend's Bench Road, 92.'

Carrington's activities, be it observed, zigzagged cautiously from Paris to Holland, Belgium, and even England, depending on where the official heat was least, and it is this that makes it difficult to *place* exactly any of his covert publications. His center of operations was principally Paris. The Tijuana Bookshop's Catalog R-5 of *Rare Unusual Books* (1948), p. 4, "The Story of Charles Carrington," states that his 'real name was Paul Ferdinand, of Portuguese descent,' which may be as it may be; that he

died in 1922, which is correct; and that he got into trouble and
had to leave France not for his erotica and flagellantiana (many
of which latter he wrote himself under a variety of pseudonyms),
but for publishing some of the scandals of the French nobility in
Cabanès' *Curious By-Paths of History,* which is the cream of the
jest. One wonders what sort of run-in he had with Smithers, as
the spitefulness of Carrington's thrusts is somehow beyond what
one expects of mere business competitors.

Smithers himself was an altogether improbable person, with a
rough upcountry accent, and an excellent knowledge of Latin
and Greek. He might well be thought the translator and publisher
of *The Horn Book* except for two things. First, the typographical
style — that is to say, the printed book itself, which is always the
paramount item of evidence in placing and dating erotic literature — is wholly different from that of any of Smithers' publications, and smacks clearly of foreign provenance, as, for instance,
in its typographical errors. Just as telling, if not more so, is the
following. One of the best books Smithers had published 'under
the rose,' and, in fact, one of the most charming erotic books in
any language, is *Les Tableaux Vivants,* of complicated bibliographical history, but actually written by Paul Perret and first
published in Paris in 1870. (A recent adaptation of Smithers'
translation, to suit the times, was published in New York, in
mimeographed form, 106 leaves, quarto, with the title *The
Amusements of a Fortnight,* 'by Pierre Louÿs,' and a burlesque
Critical Appreciation 'by Prof. Saintsbury,' under the rubric 'New
Orleans,' 1943.) Smithers published at least three editions of his
translation, one in 1888 (copy in the Enfer), and two in 1889, of
which Rose cites one in the Private Case, B.M., while I have seen
the other, which has 174 pages in all, narrow 16mo (none preliminary). Smithers' editions were intended to replace the spirited,
and essentially far better adaptation into 'sporting' English, ac-
credited to 'A "Masher,"' and published under the title *The
Kaleidoscope of Vice* ('London: Berkeley Square,' 1884, of which
fuller details are given by Ashbee, *Catena,* p. xxxi). *Love and
Safety,* however, in quoting *Les Tableaux Vivants,* refers (page
130) to the *Kaleidoscope* translation, with a ten-line quotation
from it. This immediately removes Smithers from the field as a
possible translator or publisher.

It would be too much to ask that all the problems raised by
The Horn Book and *Love and Safety* be completely solved. One
remaining difficulty must be stated frankly. There are a number

of references in *Love and Safety* to Cameron's *The Pearl* and its 'annuals' (page 29), and a long quotation (pages 127–33) from its sequel for 1882, *The Erotic Casket Gift Book*. There are also a number of interpolated bits of poetry in *Love and Safety*, very much like, and introduced similarly to, those in *The Pearl*. One poem in particular, a birth-control novelty called "The Fruits of Philosophy Condensed" (pages 90–91) gives four verses of a poem of which only three verses appear in *The Pearl* no. 9, for March 1880, some twenty years before. There is also the element of literary style, always difficult but here quite unmistakable, stringing together at least *Love and Safety* (and therefore *The Horn Book* too), the 'A "Masher"' translation of Perret's *Tableaux Vivants*, and parts of *The Pearl*. As good, or better, a case might be made out for "Cameron," the editor of *The Pearl*, as the translator of *The Horn Book* and the rest, as for John S. Farmer. One possible solution of the difficulty is that they might both be one and the same person! I know this sounds like Mark Twain's theory that Shakespeare was written by *another man of the same name*, but there's no help for it.

Absolutely nothing is known of Farmer but his name. As to "D. Cameron," even the name is false, the *Enfer* specifically underlining the joke by calling it 'borrowed' (page 125). I have spent years writing and searching, sending requests to *Notes & Queries*, etc. etc., vainly trying to find out something about John Stephen Farmer. The biographies of Henley, with whom he collaborated for the last ten or more years of the poet's life, hardly more than mention Farmer. Aside from the bare titles of his publications up to about 1915, when he must have died, all that I ever learned — from a man who got it from a clergyman who lived in the same town in England as Farmer — was that 'he was very peculiar, believed in the occult, never had any money, and lived with a woman to whom he was not married.' As biography, that will hardly do.

Farmer knew French well, and was interested in its erotic literature and slang, as witness the long and intensely erotic quotations in *Vocabula Amatoria*, picked up from Scheler and Delvau. Also, he did not compile *Slang and Its Analogues* in a day. To have had the first volume ready for publication in 1890, with its pages of French (mostly) and English synonyms for 'prostitute,' he must have worked on it, and worked hard, all through the 1880's, while publishing his lesser occult works, his dictionary of American slang, etc. The 1880's were 'Cameron's' period too. As my subtitle should have forewarned the reader, I must end, therefore, with a problem. As to the problem of erotic literature in general, I can only say, as Charles Nodier has said (in his *Catalogue*, 1844, no. 565): 'Books of this sort, . . . and spintrian designs, are perhaps not quite suitable to the education of young persons, but one would be sorry, and with reason, not to find them preserved nevertheless in museums. I say this in all the sincerity of a profound personal disinterest, for I have never read an erotic book; but I frankly admit I have often consulted them with profit.'

GREAT COLLECTORS OF EROTICA

I

LET'S STRIP off another layer, and get behind the usual discreet jokes and prepared positions, and see if we can't get a little closer than usual to truth. I once found, in an old book of about the time of Balzac or Théophile Gautier, a yellowed clipping marked — without any other reference — 'From the French : A Book-Collector is like a sultan in his harem, surrounded with more beauties than he can enjoy. The librarian is his eunuch, the book-seller his pimp. The lover, whom he dreads, is the fool who wanders into the harem, strips back the covers from one of the beauties — and reads!' Observe the word 'fool.' Whether this is really from the French, or from one of the old character-books, I don't suppose there's anyone who wouldn't agree that a woman and a book are not the same thing, even though you can sometimes take both of them to bed. Under the circumstances, it's almost hard to understand why men would collect *erotic* books — or even read them — considering that women do exist. As art is long, and time fleeting, and a stick of type very difficult to get into print these days unless it's a lie from start to finish, let me take this unusual opportunity of telling the truth about the collecting of erotica . . . to tell the truth.

Erotic literature exists because it serves an important need. This need is twofold: the education of the inexperienced young, and the excitation of the impotent or old. Few collectors of erotica exist between these limits, though those who do exist there, as will be seen, are generally the most successful. Nevertheless, these two main groups, of the inexperienced young at one end, and the old and impotent at the other, are the principal searchers after and the main buyers of erotic literature, however much anyone may deplore this fact, particularly as to the young. But in a deeper sense — and it's time to try to dig deep — the idea of deploring the sexual education of the young, by whatever real or merely

71

literary methods the young may attempt to get it, is itself simply a curious and temporary perversion of western civilization, a civilization covered with similar perversions, most of them rising from this *one*. More intelligent civilizations in the past, and doubtless in the future, and even a number of current or now-dying civilized groups in the western Pacific, might consider and do consider that the sexual training of the young is too important a matter to leave to the chance divulgations of equally ignorant playmates, or the tardy and embarrassed efforts of shame-faced elders; and certainly not to the fetichistic aberrations and sadistic contaminations of the kind of people who generally write erotic books, at least in English and German. Such civilizations would and do proceed in a very direct and sensible fashion to *show* the young of both sexes, by the visible example of their elders, and by their own encouraged experiments with each other — just as children are now taught ball-room dancing, hula-hooping and the twist — how to engage correctly and pleasurably in what is called 'the' sexual act, and in all the charming preludes and bye-ways of this act, which, like many another main dish, is sometimes not really as good as the appetizer.

In civilizations which simply have not got, or have somehow lost, the plain horse-sense to engage in the sexual education of their young in this direct and forthright fashion, or which save it for well beyond the last possible minute, in the public ordeal of the 'bachelor's dinner' orgy, or the helpless crying-jag of the presumed innocent bride being-given-the-Word-by-mother (and sometimes, in the more intensely balled-up families, by father), it is hardly to be wondered at that children — really children, beginning often near the age of ten, at what the Freudian school considers the crucial period of repression of the child's nascent sexual impulses — set about, in their own way, learning what they can. They learn from each other, from children sometimes slightly older, from little bawdy rhymes they chant, and long and detailed doggerel poems called "The Wedding Night" or similar, which they hand-copy and circulate secretly to each other under the desk; and finally from those unbelievable pornographic pamphlets, heavily thumb-worn and folded in half, and regularly swiped (or let us say confiscated) from both boys and girls alike of public-school age, by horrified school-teachers, generally female; pamphlets inevitably forming the secret Chamber of Horrors of the 'Anti-Pornography drives' of well-meaning small towns, and small-town minds that somehow get to Congress.

These children, with their hopeless pornographic pamphlets, grotesquely illustrated as often as not with smeary photographs of old-time pimps and whores in pointy shoes and torn stockings, are not so much filling in the gaps in their education, as they hope, as they are being exposed to a whole series of fetichistic perversions, beginning with the stockings, probably on the part of the anonymous photographer. (All photographers are at the very least voyeurs, some of them offensively so.) The illustrations are, of course, more than matched by the literary contents of these 50¢ and $1 pamphlets — a higher price, it will be observed, than would ever be demanded by the local bad girl of twelve to go under the porch or down in the cellar: the imitations of art already replacing the real experience of life, which is perhaps the worst perversion of them all. And this whole construct of substitution, abnormality and perversion is somehow fobbed off on the child collectors of erotica — to call them by their right name, as one would if they were child collectors of cancelled postage-stamps — as being in some way a representation of meaningful or even desirable sexual acts, and to be learnt and imitated as such.

One can sympathize in all sincerity with the local chiefs-of-police, crying out in outraged parenthood, far more than policehood, with the thought of their own kids clearly in mind: 'Sure we believe in sex education, but do we want 'em educated to *that?!*' Here flashing an illustrated booklet called, perhaps, *Chinatown Orgies,* beginning: ' "Eat the chocolate, you bitch!" snarled the whip-slashing Countess La Fanghoul.' With an irrelevant photo-illustration facing, showing a fat 1890's female in striped stockings, or a Spanish whore in a torn brassière, spreadeagled full-face, in a manner of speaking, like some particularly hairy spider, on the lap of a bored-looking and rather adenoidal young man (obviously a jock-strap model, but here displaying garters and shoes), against a peeling photo-backdrop showing — somewhat unexpectedly, for *Chinatown Orgies* — the S.S. Pinafore under full sail off Penzance! Or, more modernly, and usually therefore more expensively, two ultra-jazzy young goons, of whom the crop-haired girl looks more like an angry boy, with tits, and the sallow-faced boy looks more like a dirty girl, in positions to match.

Well no, of course not. That's not the 'education' anybody wanted. But that's the way it is, and that is what is supplied and will continue to be supplied, no matter what the legal penalties are set at, until some better sex education, and one that is sincere and equally *graphic,* is undertaken. Striped stockings, torn brassière, or no, that poor fat girl, giving her Anatomical All in the 1890's (or whenever the photo was made), is at the very least indicating in an utterly unmistakable fashion to the youthful inquirer, what sex is all about. She may even for that matter closely resemble the mother — the male model would hardly do for the father — who somehow overlooked the clear and pressing parental duty, here being achieved by these photographic stand-ins, not to let the child flounder in all but perhaps verbal ignorance of what is, after all, as Havelock Ellis has said, the central mystery and the central reality of life.

Until something better is offered — and the weak-kneed approximations of 'marriage counselling' are never going to get there, and too late anyhow, on the eve of marriage — the principal collectors of erotica, in the countries where erotica are to be had, are forever going to remain the adolescent and pre-adolescent kids searching for the plain and practical knowledge of sex that is being denied them by cowardly and culturally-neuroticized parents, but which their developing glands are telegraphing imperatively to them that they are *very soon* going to need. It will be observed that anyone who wants to teach his ten-year-old son how to go fishing, will today, in all fifty states of the Union and parts abroad, still unembarrassedly go about showing him by example how to spear a wiggling worm onto a barbed hook, with more or less sangfroid, while the damn thing's guts ooze out; teasing the frightened kid meanwhile, as unmanly, if the mere sight makes him sick to his stummick. But which parent — including you — has taken, or would ever take, the same plain and practical approach to explaining, *graphically and by example,* to even a fifteen or twenty year old son, how to be 'manly' with the girls. . . . as well as fishworms? Or, if he did so, in which state are such demonstrations legal?

The young, as stated, are therefore the principal group of erotica collectors in the western world, when erotica can be collected at all, and do not let anybody tell you otherwise. They are the principal group, both in tonnage of literature sopped up, and in the number of 'collectors' involved. All the rest of the collectors of erotica, of any other age, including the impotent old; and probably all the other collectors of any age *since as long as erotica have existed,* could not possibly bulk as large in number altogether as the pre-adolescent kids and teen-agers slipping each other today their laborious and pathetic hand-copies of "The Adventures of a French Stenographer" (but French!) in doggerel rhyme, and searching nervously in their out-of-school hours, in dubious slum shops and tonsorial establishments, from crippled tailors and drippy-eyed razor blade vendors, for the further adventures, as promised on page thirty-two (Printed in Havana — read Jersey City — 'Price Ten Dollars,' but cut-rate to you, kiddo, for two bucks), of the whip-slashing Countess La Fanghoul.

II

THERE EXISTS a whole other erotic literature, and a whole other audience, than that. The point has just been raised, in passing, as to how long erotic literature has existed at all. Curiously enough, in the sense of being fictional prose accounts of erotic adventures, erotic literature is of very recent invention. The prose novel itself, after all, is of quite recent popularity — when you consider how long the world has been going on — having arrived in Europe only with *Amadis de Gaul* in 1508, the prototype of the overblown romances of chivalry that Cervantes' *Don Quixote* set out to make fun of, a century later. Of course, the novel form had been invented over a thousand years before, in *Daphnis and Chloë,* in the *Golden Ass* of Apuleius and the *Satyricon* of Petronius, but these models were not then widely imitated, owing to the greater popularity of the less self-conscious forms out of which they themselves had developed: the telling of folktales, and the early folktale collections on the style of the *Arabian Nights.* All of these works, and all these folk-forms, never considered it necessary to expurgate out the sexual element; but they are not therefore erotica. Erotica came into existence only when all the *non*-sexual parts were expurgated out. This is just as much a form of censorship, and a literary conventionalism, as any other; but it could only have come into being when the moral tone of the cultural milieu, out of which literature is produced, brought an excessive interest to focus on the sexual parts — of literature, as of the human body — by attempting to censor these off the open stage of literature and of life altogether.

Erotic literature is therefore a response to the attempt to create a *non*-erotic literature, at least in fiction. It is absurd and unthinkable that fiction should concern itself with every other part of life but the part everybody cares about most: like a boardwalk beauty-contest where the girls show everything *except* the parts that everyone wants to see. They then get ribbons and prizes for that, just as people get prizes for expurgated fiction: big prizes too, much bigger than anyone ever got for writing an erotic book. As you can't make bricks without straw, or novels without action and passion, the expurgation of normal actions and passions inevitably requires the substitution of abnormal actions. That is how it happens that three out of every four lines of fiction printed today — and a great deal of the presumed non-fiction, as in newspapers and 'true' magazines — are concerned with murder and death, very exactly described, while never daring to describe exactly the opposite acts of sexual intercourse and life, for fear of being called pornography and going to jail. All this is extremely obvious; I even wrote a book about it once, called *Love & Death,* but it didn't seem to change anything, any more than books ever do, though there have been at least four plagiarisms of it to date, one of them from as far into the hinterlands as the University of Arschloch, Montana, by the local curator of weak verbs.

The readers and collectors of erotica, as a group, are therefore no different from the readers and collectors of murder-mysteries and other non-erotica, except that the erotica collectors are normal people interested in normal things, and the murder-mystery collectors — and there are millions of them — are perverts. Of course, there are perverted erotica too. Let's get rid of them: all the flagellation books, all the homosexual books, fetichism, coprophily, and so on. Well, unfortunately, those are the ones that are legal, as long as they don't unveil the sexual parts. Publishers of erotica, like the famous or infamous Carrington, in Paris, and one of his successors in the same city today (who doesn't need any plug here), keep a side-string of flagellation books going, which they demonstrate to the police as the *extenuating circumstance* — the cover-up or front — of their publishing activity. This activity is therefore allowed to continue, where it would be stopped at once were the police to discover that, instead of the books stripping the girl naked and then 'merely' beating her to death, they strip her naked and then fuck her till her ears fly off.

It is usually stated, and may therefore safely be considered to be false, that the first erotic novel was John Cleland's *Fanny Hill,* in England, in 1749. Other than the name of the author, which is correct — though generally pronounced wrongly in America — every part of the above statement is false. That isn't the book's correct title, which is *Memoirs of a Woman of Pleasure (Fanny Hill* was the expurgated or cover-up text, issued by the same publisher, Griffiths, about 1750); that isn't the date when the book was first circulated, as it was being read aloud, from the manuscript, a good ten years earlier than the date given, before the Beggar's Benison Society — a sexual initiation and penis-measuring club in Anstruther, Scotland: what would nowadays be called a college fraternity — and, finally, erotic novels are nearly a century older than Cleland, and assuredly did not start in England (or even in Scotland) nor in the English language.

The real origin of the erotic novel, and therefore of its collectors, is implicit in the question as to what *preceded* it, to satisfy the same need. What preceded the novel in general? Narrative poetry — spoken or sung — folktales like Boccaccio's, and jokes. It is therefore in narrative poetry, folksongs, folktales, and jokes, but those of persistently erotic theme, and with all the other, non-erotic elements blocked out, that the origins of erotic literature will be found. There also will be found the earliest 'erotica' collectors of whom there is any record.

The point is worth underlining again that no such straining or blocking out of the non-erotic elements would ever have been conceivable — neither in literature nor in life — except as a clear, and in fact a perfectly manly and rebellious reaction to the moralistic attempt, preceding, to drive out all the normal erotic elements. An absurd attempt, one which would lead immediately, if successful, to the end of the human race, and which could only have seemed desirable to the crippled imaginations of early and surviving monastic groups, vowed to perpetual chastity as far as women were concerned, but devoting themselves to perpetual pederasty in fact.

As to the further expurgations into which this exceptional and abnormal idea of morality has inevitably led, both in literature and in life: the expurgation of normality into abnormality, of natural sex into unnatural murder and the cult of death (once restricted to a small and obviously insane religious group in India), of the 'repulsive' semen into the somehow not-at-all repulsive blood — though both, surely, are equally the stuff of life, and composed of the same materials — little more seems worth insisting upon here. When the world blows itself up, on some elaborate 'miss' at the stalking-horse target of the moon, it will be found (if anyone remains to think it over) that the people who will have blown it up are people who have gone crazy because of the profound mental and moral contradiction involved here, in the forbidden sex that becomes the permitted lust for death, and not people who have gone insane over any economic or political rivalry.

As might have been expected, the attempted expurgation of the literature and art of Europe was a direct result of the Protestant Reformation begun by Luther, though Luther himself had little to do with it, except to undertake the writing of 'sacred counterfeits' of folksongs, making them over into hymns on the stated grounds, as John Wesley later put it, that the Devil ought not to have all the good tunes. This is a point that will be returned to later. When, in the mid-1520's, only a few years after the beginning of the Protestant crusade against the corruption of the Catholic Church (I am still quoting Luther), the Roman hierarchy decided to make a big showy cleanup, as a counter measure, they also began by attacking folklore and folk-art. They naturally did not begin with what had been the principal focus of satire and attack for centuries, the monasteries and nunneries, which were left for Henry VIII, a decade later, to unveil forever to the world. Instead, casting about for some unimportant scapegoats, for whom no one would dare to say a good word, they picked as victims the folk-humorist Cynthio degli Fabritii, author of a mock-serious work on the *Origin of Vulgar Proverbs* that had handled the Franciscans somewhat irreverently; and, more particularly, the artist Marcantonio Raimondi, who had engraved on copper a series of sixteen or more drawings by Giulio Romano, the foremost student of the great Raphael (who was rumored to have planned the series originally), showing sixteen positions of men and women in sexual intercourse, magnificently designed and engraved. This is the first great monument of Western erotic art, comparable in any way to the erotic sculptures of the love-temples of India, and was ruthlessly and forever suppressed.

No one, even today, would attempt openly to justify or publicly to print the Raimondi engravings — assuming they could be found — which are still presumably beyond the pale, as far as the West is concerned, simply because they show sixteen positions of human sexual intercourse; though it may be assumed that surely sixteen *million* acts of human intercourse (in most of the same positions) have since taken place, in exactly the same countries where the Raimondi engravings were hounded into the ground and destroyed forever. Nothing remains today but one engraving, and some mannered copies in the stiff and glossy style of the school of Proudhon and David, made by the artist-adventurer, Count Waldeck, in the mid-19th century in France, the last person known to have seen the actual engravings. No one would publicly print these again today, even if they could be found. No one, that is, except two courageous Danes, Ove Brusendorff and Poul Henning-sen, in their astonishing and unexpurgated four-volume work, *Love's Picture Book* (Copenhagen, 1959–61), published in both Danish and English, a worthy successor to, and with an even more interesting text than Eduard Fuchs' standard German series in nine illustrated volumes, several decades earlier, on the history of erotic art, history of morals, and — his rarest work, having been destroyed by Hitler — *Grossen Meister der Erotik*. Doing the best they could, with the materials still to be found, both Fuchs and Brusendorff & Henningsen (1. 96) have printed several of Count Waldeck's tracings of the lost Raimondi posture-engravings, in which European erotic art really began.

Let us pass on by observing that no one has ever yet made any objection to, or any private auto-da-fé of, the equally powerful engravings, of almost the same period, by Tempesta, for the *Tortures and Torments of the Christian Martyrs* of Father Gallonio, a stomach-turning item of pious and didactic intent (it says here); nor to Foxe's Protestant *Book of Martyrs,* matching, and the further Catholic rejoinder, exactly similar but less well engraved, the *Theatre of the Cruelties of the Heretics,* that is to say, of the Protestants. Both sides of the religious controversy of the Reformation went in heavily for this type of sacred sadism, in pictorial form as well as text, by way of protecting their profits and prerogatives, in simple self-preservation. And no one has ever had a hard word for their method, then or now. An American literary critic, a few years ago, even wrote a hundred-page 'appreciation' of Foxe's ferocious prose. No, all the horror and reprobation — religious as well as critical — are reserved for art masterpieces like Raimondi's magnificent illustrations of men and women, who are *not* killing each other with mallets and clubs, *not* hacking off each other's hands and feet, *not* twisting out each other's guts with broomsticks, as in all the pious picture-books just mentioned; but who are beautifully and passionately entwined in the act of love, as have been all lovers, all married people, and quite a few un-married, since the world began.

It is at this point that the first collectors of printed erotica appear in history. The first thing they seem to have been collecting, needless to say, were the Romano-Raimondi posture engravings, when they could get hold of them. As these proved difficult to find, several lesser Italian artists, such as Caracci, began to produce imitation sets, immediately trailing off into the baroque research for exotic and fantastic positions, such as the "Whirling Basket," which appears first in one of these early imitation sets. The original artist himself, Giulio Romano, was invited to do a series of similar drawings, life size, for the Duke of Mantua, with the Duchess Giulia Gonzaga, 'the most beautiful woman of Italy,' apparently serving as model. A copy of one of these drawings still exists, reproduced with the mythological posture-engraving of Mars and Venus made from it, in the *Bilder-Lexikon der Erotik* (1929, II. 449), from a copy in the collection of the Albertina Museum, Vienna. The drawing, with the old nurse peeping through the half-open door — a typical Arab-Italianate touch — is almost identical with one of the original engravings of the lost set.

The striking similarity here to the method of the architect-monarchs of India, for whom the tremendous art masterpieces of the erotically decorated love-temples of Konarak and Elephanta were created, under a formalized religious pretext, a thousand years before, is too clear to miss. It is evident, in fact, that the earliest patrons and collectors of erotic art were these. Or — turning to the present rather than the past — change the names from India, or from Mantua and Gonzaga (as Hamlet remarks, III. ii. 240), and it all could have taken place yesterday in Chicago; 'most beautiful woman of Italy' and all. If you substitute color-photography for copper-engraving, it probably did.

III

ARETINO, the 'Scourge of Princes,' as he liked to be called, had written his erotic *Sonnets,* in 1527, the first actually erotic book of the Western world, to vindicate Raimondi's engravings, and to defy the harassing of the artist by Gian-Matteo Giberti, the papal chancellor, from whose prisons Raimondi was saved only by Aretino's intercession with the Pope. Various more-and-more bawdy folkloristic works followed after Cynthio degli Fabritii's *Origin of Vulgar Proverbs,* the work that had precipitated the press-censorship the year before; in particular the strange and spontaneous homosexual facetiæ of Antonio Vignale and his Academy of the Intronati ('Dunderheads') in Siena, by then published carefully under cover; but these did not start any vogue, as Aretino did. Keyed by Aretino's erotic poems, and satires in dialogue form, and those of his imitators, this humorous and poetic reaction against the new censorship of both the Catholic and Protestant hierarchies combined, swept up out of Italy in the 1530's into England and France, and remained for over two centuries almost the only sort of erotic literature of broad popular appeal.

The early collectors of erotic literature were all, therefore, collectors of erotic and satyrical poetry. Only a few exceptional collectors — whom the poetry group thought of as inartistic and old-fashioned — still clung to the gathering of bawdy jokes 'from the mouth of the people,' in the style of Poggio and Bebel, a century earlier, both of whom had translated their collected jokes from Italian and German into Latin, not to expurgate them, but rather to make them internationally available, for the entertainment of scholars all over Europe, in what was then the learned Esperanto.

A curious point. The modern adulation of Shakespeare has taken an entirely different turn from what might have been expected from his reputation among his contemporaries. As far as writers for the theatre were concerned, Shakespeare was by no means the most famous or the most popular of his time, nor is there the slightest reason to believe that the audiences of his time understood (anymore than do modern television audiences) the superiority of his plays over the far more popular blood-dramas of Marlowe and Kyd — which are, in any case, still about a thousand miles above television wrestling. Shakespeare was famous in his own period primarily as an erotic poet, as the author of *Venus and Adonis* and the *Rape of Lucrece*. His *Sonnets* were published only much later, probably through the connivance of the rival poet Chapman, with the clear intention of disgracing Shakespeare, and had no popularity, the sonnet-fad being by then out of date. Homosexual or not, as is often claimed, there is certainly something abnormal about Shakespeare's *Sonnets* — an accusation which can hardly be made against those of Aretino! It is a fact that the first known references to the actual collection of erotic literature will be found in the *Shakespeare Allusion-Book,* in the pious exhortations of puritan moralists and the sardonic thrusts of contemporary satirists, as to the inevitable furnishing of the 'private cabinets' of the young ladies of the time with these terribly bawdy poetry-books by Shakespeare.

Collections of erotic poetry of this kind, in book form, were at least as old in England as *The Court of Venus* (or *Boke of Balettes,* of which the earliest known fragment is in the University of Texas Library), and Tottell's Miscellany, *Songes and Sonnettes,* by the Earl of Surrey and others. Both of these were published, and had been attacked as immoral by one Thomas Bryce, a reverend jackass, in his *Against filthy writing, and such like delighting,* before Shakespeare was born. Nor was this by any means the first attack; the Italian poets had already come in for their share in Baptiste of Mantua's *Elegies against the Lascivious Poets.*

Harking back to the oldest love poet of them all — except perhaps King Solomon, who collected women instead of books, and was therefore wiser than most of the erotica collectors since — the playwright Marlowe's translation into English of *All Ovid's Elegies* was published secretly abroad, in Middelburg, Holland, in 1598, but was seized on being smuggled into England. It was condemned by the Archbishop of Canterbury and Bishop of London (probably on account of Davies' satirical poems, published with it), almost all known copies being burnt. This is one of the earliest examples outside Italy of the publication of 'erotica' in the clandestine fashion reserved otherwise, almost exclusively at that time, to works of religious controversy.

The case of the most famous of similar collections in France, two decades later, the *Parnasse Satyrique* of Théophile de Viau, for which the presumed compiler was burnt in effigy and later died as the result of his 'questioning' under torture, proved crucial in the history of censorship in Europe, the same legal precedents later of course being applied in America. Théophile's work is still, to this day, prohibited from being openly published in France, and has never been so published; though American sailors, tourists, and other bibliophiles are freely able to buy the so-called Marquis de Sade's nauseating and repellent catalogue of tortures, *The Hundred and Twenty Days of Sodom,* in the best bookstores of Paris, in either English or French, depending only on the depth of their bibliophily.

The position of the poetic and satirical collections of the earlier centuries, as *the* erotica of their times, implies behind it not only an expected sale and a group of waiting buyers (and anybody who buys three books is a book-collector, after all), but also the existence of whole schools of poets, poets' friends, and poetry fanciers, all of them *collecting* 'secret cabinets' of manuscript poetry years before: collections sometimes never delivered over to printed publication until decades later, if at all. When the Puritan Revolution came, in England in the mid-seventeenth century, the Royalist wits — in particular those grouped around the curious character, Dr. James Smith — issued collection after collection of bawdy and satirical miscellaneous verse, much of its doggerel written or rewritten on the spur of troubled times, to serve the patriotic purpose of mocking the Puritan soldiers and divines caught short in Parliament House, or in shameful intercourse with a serving-wench, a dog, or even a mare. This last is the celebrated "News from Colchester, or The Four-Legged Quaker," in *The Rump,* of 1660, the accusation being unproved of course.

The number of such collectors of erotic poetry and humor cannot easily be calculated. Scores of their collections were printed in England and abroad, and many of the most important collections of the century have never been published at all, not even at the freest period of the Restoration. These range from the magnificent Rochester manuscript (including Butler's *Dildoides* and much other verse), which is still preserved, unpublished, in the oldest American university, and which is too handsomely indited to have been prepared for anyone but a rich or noble collector; to modest little collections of immodest verse, such as the Harleian manuscript of Fearegod Barebone, a Quaker of Daventry in Northampton, who, on the flyleaf, as Jack Lindsay remarks, hypocritically pleads that he, 'beinge at many times idle, and wanting imployment, bestoed his time with his penn and incke wrighting thease sonnets, songes, and epigrames, thinknge that it weare better so to do for the mendinge of his hand in wrighting, then worse to bestow his time.' The collection, says Lindsay, is most bawdry.

With similar pawkiness, one of the greatest early book-and-ballad collectors in England, the diarist Samuel Pepys, records in a guarded entry in his *Diary* — an entry never yet published complete, though it soon will be — how he had got hold, after some tergiversation with his soul, of the latest erotic book from France, *L'Escole des Filles* of Millot, first published in 1655, which is not a novel but a manual of erotic technique cast in the form of a dialogue between two young women, in the style of Aretino. This book, obviously in French and just imported, as it had apparently not yet been translated into English, Pepys carefully studied through for the purpose of enlarging his wisdom of the world, as he tells us, or some such buncombe; after which (and a few as-yet unfilled blanks) he burnt the little book so that it might not be found in his library, to his disgrace, after his death. His moral cowardice he did not consider was any disgrace at all, particularly since nobody was supposed to find out about it, as his *Diary* is written in code. Millot's *Escole des Filles* is certainly not now to be found in Pepys' library, which is preserved integrally — actually mummified, since no one is allowed to use it — at Magdalene College, Cambridge; though a brief manuscript collection of bawdy poems will be found there, on the end-papers of another volume.

IV

OBVIOUSLY, if everyone who ever bought a bawdy book were to burn it after reading it, like Pepys, not only it would be impossible to find out anything about erotica collectors — except through the bragging of their booksellers — but, which is more serious, the erotic books themselves would all soon disappear. This is largely what has already happened. *Most of the erotic books of earlier centuries have almost entirely disappeared,* a fact worth underscoring again. Many are known only through unique copies, often of some later edition or reprint, and even more are known only through tantalizing references to their raw titles in old and manuscript bibliographies, or in the legal records of the condemnation of their publishers: a good place to look. If good books of earlier centuries are rare, 'bad' books of the same centuries are ten or a hundred times as rare, owing to their continuous destruction, as much by their readers (and their readers' widows) as by legal seizure.

That is the main reason why the collecting of erotica has now become increasingly difficult and unlimitedly expensive. Nowadays, almost no one but the very rich can afford to collect anything in this field but the large and quasi-scientific illustrated tomes in German, that are a great bore; and the miserable current output of pornography, which few persons of taste care to collect at all. The result has been that of even so recent a period as the depression 1930's in the United States, during the first five years of which a very large number of erotica were published, mostly in New York, only some forty or fifty physical volumes are now known still to exist, anywhere in the country, of all this output. Omitting duplicates, this means only perhaps two dozen 'titles' still extant, a mere thirty years later, of a hundred or more known to have been published in editions of two thousand or more copies each! Five, perhaps ten more, of the others will doubtless turn up when a few of the older collectors die — if the widows can be prevented, by mere cupidity and at the urging of the booksellers who gather over a dead collector's coffin like vultures, from burning the erotica found in the collections. The rest will never been seen again. The same thing has demonstrably happened, in the last century, when a Scottish collector, James Campbell Reddie, kept a manuscript catalogue of all the English erotica published during the notorious "Holywell Street" period, from about 1830 to 1870; but he could not afford to buy even one copy each, of all the erotica then being published, and no one has seen most of them since, or ever will. Century after century the same thing has been regularly happening since the time of Aretino's *Sonnets* in 1527, a book of which not a single copy of the original edition, with the woodcut illustrations of the Romano-Raimondi 'postures,' was ever recorded again for over four hundred years.

From the standpoint of human history, and literary history, the loss of so much of the earlier erotic literature is a very serious drawback to the study of the moral development — or perhaps decay — of any civilization. The moral history of Europe and America is therefore being continuously written and rewritten, in the lack of the essential documents, from such ice-cold and external relics, written by unsympathetic outsiders to say the least, as police regulations of the hours of opening and closing brothels (and playhouses), or religious exposés of the number of infant skeletons found in the privies of disbanded nunneries. Materials like that may suit the sort of minds that would study sex with an I.B.M. machine, since such minds and such machines are perfectly geared to deal 'scientifically' with whore-house time-charts and nunnery skeleton-counts, not to mention the depth-gauging and vertical measuring of women and men's sexual organs, à la Dickinson and Kinsey, if that can be called science. But such cold and meaningless stuff, which is openly anti-sexual and profoundly anti-human, will not satisfy any real historian, in the tradition of the great French historians and passionate stylists, who created the art of *dis*passionate history by having some real emotions about it: historians like Henri Estienne in the sixteenth century, La Monnoye and Peter Bayle in the seventeenth and eighteenth, and Jules Michelet in the nineteenth, all of whose work — and particularly that of Michelet — comes like an unveiling and a sunburst, and a falling-away of the usual blindfold from the eyes of any English or American reader, and is the model on which the one greatest historian of our own language, Carlyle, fashioned himself.

The real progenitor of erotica-collecting in the West was precisely one of these great French literary and moral historians, Bernard de La Monnoye, who set out determinedly to save, from the already threatened total loss and destruction, some of the priceless and passionate erotic testimonies of the past. La Monnoye expressed his interest perfectly openly, and published his materials without any disguise; not in any Pepysian cipher-code or furtiveness, but in a clear and dignified way; defying, as it were, any small-minded moralistic criticism of his interest in the sexual life of men and women, and in the real and unexpurgated literature of their sexual relations. In the same way, not a hundred years ago, the Library of Congress in Washington, D.C. — unique among the libraries of the world — dedicated on its balcony, in a series of panels devoted to History, Science, and the like, a panel inscribed in candid simplicity: *Erotica*. One trusts this has not yet been painted over, in fluorescent pink, to read *Nuclear Physics* (alias the Atom Bomb), in order to avoid upsetting translator-teams desperately at work dragging over into English foreign encyclopedias now thirty years out-of-date, in which, one may be certain, the secret of how to get to the moon will not be found.

Far from burning himself out at an early age, in the presumed debauchery of those interested in erotica, Bernard de La Monnoye lived to the green old age of eighty-seven, writing some of his best poetry at the age of eighty-five, and died covered with the highest honors of European scholarship, as linguist, folklorist, and literary historian. La Monnoye's collections were not made for any private delectation in his 'secret cabinet,' but for the purpose of furthering human knowledge, and did so further it. He was the first to undertake scholarly and serious editions of all the old jestbooks and facetious French writers, such as Rabelais and the *Moyen de Parvenir* of Béroalde de Verville — a mixture of the serious and facetious that narrower scholars, without La Monnoye's humanistic breadth, have always proved incapable of navigating, owing perhaps to the apparent contradiction in terms. In addition to half a dozen such editions, based evidently on his own collections of both the basic texts and a whole library of collateral works on humor, facetiæ, atheism, and the like; La Monnoye translated into modern French, annotated, and published in the original patois, the 'impious' folk-carols of his native Burgundy, probably written by his life-long friend, the folk-poet Aimé Piron, father of the erotic poet, Alexis Piron. This publication came at a crucial period in the study of folksongs in western Europe, in 1700, and sparked the whole modern field, though it was undertaken at a time when other antiquarians — as folklorists were then called — were still loath to deal with anything so 'vulgar' let alone impious, for fear of being burnt at the stake as heretics, or, in the modern equivalent already operating then, losing their prebendaries or cushy university jobs.

The only real setback of La Monnoye's career, aside from losing all his money on the John Law India Bubble (but what of that!) was in connection with the original edition of Aretino's *Sonnets*, with the woodcut 'posture' illustrations after Raimondi's engravings. This work, violently repressed from 1527 on, was already so rare that, after a lifetime of vainly searching for even a sight of it, La Monnoye was almost ready to imply, in his edition of the *Ménagiana*, in 1715, IV. 60, that it had never really existed at all! He made a manuscript copy of the best text he could find of the *Sonnets* themselves — unfortunately from a later and falsified text, by some imitator of Aretino, as is now known — beautifully handcopying at the same time several other excessively rare Italian *facetiæ* in prose and verse, in particular the *Cazzaria* or 'Book of the Prick' of Vignale. He then translated what he hoped were Aretino's *Sonnets* into elegant Latin distichs, and let it go at that. As it happens, his despair was unfounded. The Aretino *Sonnets*, illustrated with woodcuts, did indeed exist, though the only copy that has ever been recorded in the four hundred years since they were printed, and the more than two hundred years since La Monnoye was ready to give them up as lost, came to light at last only a few years ago, covered with the dust of unknown decades, and apparently fallen behind the shelf of a little bookshop in Milan — a *'winkel,'* as its discoverer, the bibliographer Max Sander, called it. But that is another story.

V

LA MONNOYE left behind, at his death, his manuscript collection of Italian erotic poetry, and *facetiæ* of Aretino's school, made with a wise concern for the disappearing past, when all other French and English poetry fanciers were amusing themselves with collecting only the current poetic satires of their day. La Monnoye's Italian collection was first printed, along with a group of similar French *contes-en-vers*, seven years after his death, on the private press of the Duc d'Aiguillon, set up on his estates at Vérets in Touraine, in an edition of only about twelve copies, under the title of *Recueil de pièces choisies, rassemblées par les soins du Cosmopolite,* in 1735, under the editorship of Paradis de Moncrif and the Abbé Grécourt. None of these names appear on the book itself, of course, which gives only a facetious imprint punning on phallic and yonijic pseudonyms ('A Anconne, chez Uriel Bandant, à l'enseigne de la Liberté'), as is very common in erotic books. The only real name that appears is that of La Monnoye, now safely dead, on his translation of the "Burgundian Noëls," printed for the first time at the end of the volume as a *bonne-bouche*.

One of the most interesting parts of this extraordinary book, of which only three of the presumed twelve copies are known to have survived, is the identity of the "Cosmopolite" for whom it was printed. This does not appear to have been the pseudonym of any one person, as might be thought, but to refer to an orgiastic group of noblemen and women, who met and engaged in what at the period used to be referred to as devil-worship (nowadays 'sex magic,') on the Duc d'Aiguillon's estate and under his protection. This was not by any means the only such orgiast group, of either that century or this, neither in the Old World nor in the New, and was closely imitated by similar orgy groups somewhat later in both England and France. Their history — and their relation with the remnants of an older worship, brilliantly discerned, 'as through a torn curtain,' by Michelet, in *La Sorcière* — remains to be written. Of all these secret societies, the "Cosmopolite" is the one that left the most remarkable private publications, similar in a way — though worlds superior, of course, in their luxurious typography! — to a type of publication still surviving in the secret mimeographed collections of bawdy poems and songs nowadays issued, in more or less the same restricted editions, by college fraternities and private drinking-clubs of the universities and the wartime airforces.

The "Cosmopolite" did not overlook to publish its own songbook as well, also probably edited by Moncrif and Grécourt, the year before the latter's death. What is clearly a matching collection of bawdy folksongs, on the style of La Monnoye's earlier collection of art poems, the *Recueil du Cosmopolite,* was issued as *Les Muses en belle Humeur,* at 'Ville Franche,' 1742, in typography almost identical with the earlier volume, and in an edition also perhaps limited to twelve copies — possibly one for each member of the group. The title-page is illustrated with an engraving showing a band of nymphs and satyrs dancing naked around a phallic statue, which may be an allusion to the activities of the group. Not half a dozen copies of this work appear to have survived, of which only one is known to have appeared at public sale in the last half-century. (In my own collection.) *Les Muses en belle Humeur* is historically important as the first songbook ever published, in any language, of consciously erotic songs; that is to say, with the tacit admission, here in the fictitious imprint, that these could no longer be openly printed at that date. These "Muses in Good Humor" — not identical with an English imitation of the same title in 1751 — mark, in a striking fashion, the end, anywhere in the Western world, of the unashamed public acceptance of folk-poetry and song.

What appears most clearly from the relations of La Monnoye and the D'Aiguillon group, is that the real importance of the rich collector types of the eighteenth century, and their magnificently bound collections, is viable and visible only when, which was not often, they had the largeness of spirit to will, or even to sell, their collections *en bloc* to the royal and national or university libraries of their respective countries. As very few of them ever did so (Pepys, paradoxically, was one who did), most of these great libraries were sold off immediately after the collectors' deaths, the collections of a lifetime — sometimes several lifetimes — being broken up forever in a few hours under the hammer of a public auctioneer, moving on imperturbably, as often as not, from books to bibelots, from Aldine incunabula to a Napoleonic *cagadou* with a winking eye painted at the bottom, as though there were no difference in the world between them but the auction-prices 'realized.'

The main surviving historical importance of the rich and noble collectors of that period is therefore solely in the private presses which it became the style, at the time of the Duc d'Aiguillon, and in part due to his influence, for the rich and noble to affect. That the bagatelles struck off on these presses would tend to be either pointless froth, pure typographical ostentation, or improper literary entertainments, is implicit in the whole format of the private press, always more or less clandestine. But only seldom have such presses justified their existence in either a literary sense or, patriotically, as part of the underground press in wartime. The Royalist drollery printers in England, nearly a century before, who created the form, are a prime exception.

In the improper area, the "Cosmopolite" had all the *primeurs,* the whole fun and spontaneity of the idea being then still new and alive, 'à l'enseigne de la Liberté,' and not painfully and laboriously pumped up, as is now often the case in similar enterprises. In an untranslatable anecdote given on a suppressed page of the Pixerécourt auction-catalogue, *Autographes et Manuscrits* (1840) no. 7, and much improved in the telling as repeated in the *Enfer de la Bibliothèque Nationale* (1913) at no. 924, from a different manuscript, we are told how the young Duchess d'Aiguillon (or perhaps only her butler's wife) was put to work setting type for the *Recueil du Cosmopolite,* and called upstairs from the composing-room improvised on a staircase landing to ask if there ought to be two *R*'s (hours) in *foutre*. 'There should indeed,' the Duke gravely replied, 'but in general one gives it only one.' Apocryphal or not, that is the only way to run a private press.

The classic case in England, which rather put a crimp in the impropriety of private presses ever after, in that country, was of course that of John Wilkes and *The Essay on Woman,* which, though he was not its author, had been printed on Wilkes' private press. Contrariwise, the principal English exemplar, in the same century, of the non-improper or pure-froth type of private press snob, was of course Horace Walpole, Earl of Orford. This repulsive pederast, and toady of all the other rich and noble (whose non-existent 'literary abilities' he wrote an enormous book trying to prove), has been made, as is well known, the object of a sort of library-museum, or private cult, in the eastern United States in recent years. A desperately adulatory article on the matter has even appeared in one of our more cultured comic-books, covering every aspect of this singular and surely undemocratic hobby, except its *reason* for being. Walpole appears, really, to have been important for nothing at all in the history of literature except his responsibility for the wanton death of the boy-poet Chatterton, who had doubtless rejected his overtures. The intransigeant sexual normality of poor Chatterton is, on his side, only too thoroughly demonstrated in his violently erotic *The Letter Paraphras'd,* courageously edited some years back by Professor Mabbott, and fittingly issued from the private press of Charles Heartman, in Metuchen, New Jersey.

Later on in the same century, when the end was approaching for the aristocracy of noble birth, and the simpler aristocracy of raw wealth was forging ahead, the rich and noble French amateurs found the printing even of erotica too much like hard work, on their private presses, in the same way that they found it preferable to turn over the hard labor of making love to their own wives to stableboys and abbés-in-attendance — while they watched, of course. It was then also found preferable simply to *pay* some master-printer in Paris to strike off a handsome, and excessively limited edition, on paper so thick that you have to bend it with your foot (but which, *entre nous,* costs very little more than plain paper), naturally of some erotic masterpiece.

Of these there was by then no dearth. Aretino's *Ragionamenti,* or Dialogues of the Prostitutes, imitated from Lucian's *Dialogues of the Hetairai* a thousand years before (as Pierre Louÿs was to imitate them again, centuries later, in both public and private forms of varyingly erotic text), had themselves been imitated with great success, probably by Aretino's disaffected secretary, Niccolò Franco, in *The Wandering Whore,* of which the only known text, much posterior, is cannily signed with Aretino's name. In this prose work — there is another of the same name, but in verse, by Lorenzo Veniero, another of Aretino's secretaries — the author attempts to double Giulio Romano's and Aretino's sixteen 'postures' to the now classic thirty-two (or forty), each with some such humorous and mnemonic name, intended to tickle the reader's memory and risibilities at the same time, such as "The Donkey-Ride", "The Christmas Candle," and so on: a Hindu and Arabic idea, originally, as seen in the much more ancient *Kama Sutra* of Vatsyayana (and particularly in its commentaries, such as the *Jayamangala* of Yasodhara), and in the *Perfumed Garden* of the Sheik al-Nafzawi, hardly a century earlier than Aretino.

It was this prose imitation, *La Puttana Errante,* rather than Aretino's own dialogues, that had been the model of Millot's *Escole des Filles* in 1655, the first erotic work in French, for which the author was burnt in effigy on the Isle du Palais in Paris, along with all copies of his book that could be found, most of them having been seized in the form of unbound sheets at the printer's. No copy of the original edition has ever been recorded since, though at least one must have escaped the police, since a reprint of it later appeared in Holland, from which all modern editions have in turn been reprinted. Taking caution from the fate of Millot's work, a Grenoble lawyer, Nicolas Chorier, two or three years later, cast in the more discreet Latin language his *Dialogues of Aloisia Sigea,* pretending only to have translated them from a presumed Spanish original. The name of the devout Spanish 'authoress' chosen, was evidently intended — though this similarity has curiously been overlooked — to imply a hardly-veiled connection with the one great French woman-poet of the preceding century, Louize Labé of Lyon (Aloÿsa Labæa). Again, however, the work was in the dialogue form, and was not intended, except indirectly, as a manual of sex technique in the style of the works of Franco and Millot.

Only twenty years later did there finally appear, in Holland in 1676, the first erotic work in French actually in the novel form: Blessebois' *Le Rut, ou La Pudeur éteinte,* a work of revenge, and the form was immediately taken over for the uses of equally violent religious satire, in Chavigny's *Venus in the Cloister, or The*

Nun in her Smock, and in the later and more refined anti-Jesuit
pornographicum, Boyer d'Argens' *Philosophical Theresa.* This
was a satire on the Girard-Cadière scandal of 1731, a scandal that
kept the clandestine presses of Europe busy for forty years with
satires of this kind, and lay at the root of the ultimate abolition of
the Jesuit Order by Pope Clement XIV (since which time no
Pope has ever cared to take the name of Clement).

All these erotic works, except Millot's, had been translated
into English almost immediately upon their publication abroad.
The first erotic novels in England — fifty or more years before
Cleland's *Memoirs of a Woman of Pleasure,* or *Fanny Hill* — were
translations of *Venus in the Cloister* (now lost, and known only
through the court-case against the printer), and Chorier's *Dialogues of Luisa Sigea,* translated under the title *Aloisia,* as discovered only recently by D. Foxon, Esq. By the time of the French
Revolution, hundreds of erotic novels existed in French, though
most of those that existed simultaneously in English were still
simply translations.

The French luxury printers, and the noblemen who angeled
their publications and bought the books similarly produced for
other noblemen, had therefore endless possibilities as to texts to
reprint. The editions produced in this way, by the finest printers
of the period such as Barbou, Grangé, and Didot, circulated mostly
around the by-then standard erotic and semi-erotic texts such as
the *Decameron* of Boccaccio, the *Tales and Novels* of La Fontaine
(this is the hopelessly overstuffed and overpriced 'Farmers-Gen-
eral' edition), the *Dialogues of Luisa Sigea,* and *Fanny Hill* in
French translation, almost the only original English text so hon-
ored. Even Baskerville, the greatest printer in England, is supposed to have struck off a *de luxe* edition of *Luisa Sigea* — in Latin
of course — marked 'From the Printing-Office of Nobody.'

It will be observed that all this vanity-publishing activity, in
which the rich collectors had, as it were, seized the means of production in their own hands, was forced to concern itself strictly
with reprints. Masterpieces *worth* reprinting cannot be written
to order, no matter how much money the rich and noble backers
might offer; and — despite Walpole's *Royal and Noble Authors*
— they somehow cannot produce masterpieces themselves. They
found it necessary, therefore, to disguise (at least from themselves)
the secondary and reprint nature of the editions they were producing, and to put all their visible effort into trying to make these
productions seem desirable 'items' nonetheless, by means of over-

large type faces, puffy paper, broad margins, fancy bindings, gilt boxes double-lined with cramoisie — whatever that may be — and all the rest of the tasteless gingerbread that such *de luxe,* or rather *faux-luxe* editions have concerned themselves with ever since, to the exclusion of any actual literary element.

The pre-Revolutionary rich amateurs and collectors also had the one most disappointing and ridiculous of all theoretically aphrodisiacal tabasco sauces to pepper their publications with: those monumentally over-bloated engravings by the most florid artists of the French roccoco, which were then considered very elegant indeed and blisteringly erotic. From the vantage point of the century and a half now elapsed, one dares now to admit the truth. These elephantine circus-posters — of which four copies in four alternating tints of nipple-pink and goose-turd green are generally bound *seriatim* into any one volume — with the hard-working hero, or shepherd, helplessly lost in the impasse of rib-bons and fluff decorating his shepherdess' pantie-leg (also some-times getting mixed up with the sheep), and, in addition, the extravagantly bovine features of whichever king's mistress it was that had the job tied up of modelling for these supercolossal productions in déshabille, are, and must forever remain, wholly without erotic effect on anybody. Produced simply as items of vanity and ostentation for the more tasteless collectors of their day, they remain simply objects of speculation for the businessmen-collectors of the present. The so-called 'market' for these mon-strosities is entirely a fake, being supported only by the purposely inflated prices and auction-bids of book- and art-dealers solely intent on driving prices upward, precisely as with the even worse monstrosities of self-styled 'modern art.' The suckers — I mean to say, the customers — pay; not the dealers, and with the auction-house percentage tacked on as the *coup-de-bambou.* These points will be returned to in a later series of these essays, under the title "The Bawdy Book Business: Its History, Mystery, and Art."

VI

ENGLAND AND AMERICA have bulked very small in what has gone before, for the obvious reasons that England was far too moral, at least ostensibly, throughout the eighteenth century, for collectors of erotica to flourish openly there, while the United States of America had not yet come into being. This is perhaps the moment to deny and dispel, or at least to challenge, the fake rumors that

George Washington and/or Thomas Jefferson collected erotic
books, and that Jefferson also planned to include a college
brothel, for the benefit of the students, on the premises of the
University of Virginia: to be staffed with Negro prostitutes, the
legend adds gratuitously, these being theoretically more expert
and erotic than the white.

Sexual allegations and folklore of this kind gravitate about
all famous persons and many famous libraries, particularly the
Vatican, which has *no* really erotic books, and positively no erotic
pictures, despite the priceless allegation in Ginzburg's *Unhurried
View,* p. 103, that the Vatican's erotica include '25,000 volumes
and some 100,000 prints,' which is exactitude indeed. Ginzburg
also reports, p. 107–8, that, at the Library of Congress, erotic
works are issued 'to anyone over sixteen years of age, though an
armed guard will be assigned to stand over the reader's shoulder,
ready to shoot if the book is mutilated.' This is a damn good
idea, but unfortunately is not true. Why couldn't it be engineered
electronically right into the erotic books themselves, on the mag-
netic tape principle, with an atomic charge that would eject the
reader into the street at the first touch of his slimy little razor
blade to the colored plates? (They already have this in the
Vatican.)

As opposed to the rigorously scientific statements just quoted,
the usual sexual legends and folklore are, in general, based on
no documents or research of any kind, and simply represent a sort
of wishful intrusion into theoretical history of the things that the
people retailing or inventing such rumors *wish* were true. This
is occasionally a conscious straight-faced joke, taken seriously by
gullible listeners, and retailed by them later as pure fact: their
use, in this way, as 'plants' for the story, being exactly what the
inventor is counting on. Yet one is often actually faced with a
sort of paranoid certainty, on the part of the inventors themselves,
of such tales, that there positively is some hidden sexual scandal
about the rich and famous persons, institutions, or other authority-
figures libelled, and that if they only make up enough lies they
will eventually somehow hit upon the truth! This is the way a
great deal of formal history, both sacred and profane, has evidently
come into existence, and been formalized after centuries of acceptance as gospel truth; and it is, in a way, very edifying to watch
the smaller lies and smaller liars of sexual folklore doing their
work.

The lies and legends that used to be circulated about the sex life of the late President F. D. Roosevelt — turning cruelly and specifically on his infantile paralysis — were enough to turn anyone's stomach. In the same way, the fake-exposé press, which has had a long tradition in the western United States since the 1870's, and still in uranium-rush Canada, is similarly based three-quarters on wishful fantasies and lies. This makes particularly convenient the real activity of such journals, which is blackmail, and shakedowns of various kinds under threat of publication; since a person accused of *what he is guilty of* has sometimes an extenuating circumstance to plead, but is practically helpless in the face of a total lie. This is the 'Great Lie' principle, which was the main lesson of the Dreyfus Case to a certain kind of mind, and was later developed into a conscious rule of practice by Hitler, its success more than attested by the fortunes of the crude forgery at the turn of the century, *The Protocols of the Elders of Zion,* written in fact by two Russian Secret Police (Okhrana) spies in Paris, Ratchkovsky and General Golovinsky. As to the so-called exposé press, a more than sufficient sample is given, from the most successful such newssheet — if I've spelled that right — Robert Harrison's *Confidential,* in the illustrated *Hollywood-Babylone* (Paris, 1959) p. 191–209, by Kenneth Anger, who considers *Confidential* the 'key' to the 1950's in America. He means, of course, the key to the john.

A wonderful and chastening example, of sexual folklore 'planted' on the innocent retailer, will be found in a serious legalistic work, *Obscenity and the Law* (London, 1956), by a young British barrister, Norman St.John-Stevas, who, after prefacing his book with the statement that he had interested himself in the subject for all of two years, and going on to technical discussions of such legal matters as "Evidence" and "Presumption of Fact," also managing somehow on the way to pepper up his work with quotations from Anglo-Saxon bawdy riddles and Rochester's homosexual playlet, *Sodom* (pp. 4, 16), which he carefully notes is only 'credited' to Rochester; finally brings down with a crash the reader's confidence in any real difference between "Evidence" and "Presumption," with the absolutely unhedged statement, opening his final chapter of conclusions as to "Obscenity, Law and Society," p. 189n:

> Obscenity is not confined to literature, sculpture or painting, but sometimes occurs in music . . . Gilbert and Sullivan wrote an obscene opera, *The Sod's Opera.* Characters included Count Tostoff, The Brothers Bollox, a pair of

hangers on, and Scrotum, a wrinkled old retainer. For many years a copy of the opera was kept in the guard room at St. James's Palace.

As Humpty-Dumpty says, 'There's glory for you!' Mr. St.John-Stevas' asseveration is repeated, in utter confidence, a few years later, by Mr. Ginzburg, *ut supra*, p. 83, with the addition of only a few airs & graces, not forgetting Scrotum, the 'wrinkled old retainer;' after which the reader is pointedly reminded that 'Sir Arthur Sullivan, it will be remembered, also composed dozens of Christianity's most passionate hymns, including *Onward Christian Soldiers*,' which nobody can deny.

As it happens, there is no such work in existence as *The Sod's Opera,* and never was, though it is surely not beyond the limits of probability that someone (even in the guard-room at St. James's Palace) *may* have had a copy of George Augustus Sala's bawdy farce in the style of *Sodom,* the 'New and Gorgeous Pantomime' *Harlequin Prince Cherrytop* (privately reprinted for Smithers' Erotika Biblion Society, 1905), in which the Russian ambassador to the Kingdom of Rogeria is, in truth, Baron Tossisselfoff, and a few of the lines of the presumed 'opera,' as I have heard it quoted, are identical. More likely, however, there is no other fire behind this smoke than the derivative British army recitation, or guard-room obscœnum, "The King of the God-damn Isles," concerning who but the Brothers Bollox, a pair of hangers on; Scrotum, the wrinkled old retainer; and, for that matter, 'four separate and distinct packages of W.D. & H.O. Wills' Gold Flake cigarettes (the *only* brand),' balanced amazingly on the shipwrecked sailor-hero's penis, when cast away on the cannibal island of Bungholia, &c. As to Gilbert and Sullivan's part in its composition: *Onward Christian Soldiers* to the contrary notwithstanding, I move that the case is unproved.

As anybody can make a mistake (as the hedgehog said when he got down off the hairbrush), I think I ought to follow the above example of sexual folklore with another, in the bibliographical line, which inspired a young and inexperienced bibliographer — closely related to me — at the beginning of his career, some twenty years ago, to nearly a decade of fruitlessly searching for a 'rare, privately-printed book,' about which he had been told by a bookdealer friend, this book having the curious title of *The Art of the Tongue.* The book was drawn to his attention, by this friend, on the publication of the bibliographer's own first book, which he had boldly hoped was the first book ever published in the history of the world on its subject, *Oragenitalism* — a work which is itself now very rare, as most of the copies were seized and destroyed at its publication in 1940 under the anagrammatic pseudonym, "Roger-Maxe de La Glannège." It is not difficult to imagine how crestfallen he was, on being informed by so knowledgeable a book-dealer and so intimate a friend that, far from his maiden effort being the first book on this indeed unusual subject, it was only the second — with the not-very hidden implication that it would probably also prove to be nowhere near as good as *The Art of the Tongue,* which had appeared privately, as he was told, about fifteen years earlier, 'a small, vest-pocket sized book, in red covers,' if he could only find it.

The details are very exact, are they not? Well, this book does not exist either. The friend, who began by simply wanting to tease the pretentious young author, and perhaps chasten his impudence, ended up being convinced himself. He now firmly believes in the existence of this non-existent book, and will doubtless live and die in the certainty that he once even saw it — fleetingly — with his own eyes. What is perhaps worse, all the repository librarians, to whom our gullible young bibliographer wrote, asking about this 'rare' work, also probably by now believe that it exists. Were any of them to write a bibliographical study of erotica (and just about everybody seems to be writing such studies nowadays — one wonders *where* they are getting to see all the books), this ghost-volumelet, *The Art of the Tongue,* would no doubt appear therein. Yet it does not exist, and never did. One is almost tempted to *write* such a book (easy, there!) and print it with the pre-dating of 'Baltimore, 1925,' as alleged; which would doubtless solve the whole problem. Half a dozen other such 'ghost' titles could be cited, in the erotica field alone, all very seriously outfitted with phoney authors and imprints, such as 'Heger and Dunkirk's *Lexicon of Lechery,* Hawthorn Press, 1913,' which is possibly just an honest blunder for Farmer and Henley's *Slang and its Analogues,* as pirated under the title *The Slang of Venery* by a Chicago newspaperman, Henry N. Cary, in 1916. These 'ghosts' rapidly enter into circulation, and become part of the sexual and bibliographical folklore of their times. The reader is warned that there are more than a few, similar.

The 'erotica collections' of George Washington and Thomas Jefferson would very likely turn out to be equally flimsy, or entirely mythical, were anyone to succeed in tracking down the source of the rumors. It has been suggested that they were simply and consciously cut from the whole cloth, as figments of the lively imagination of some such wily bookdealer as the late A. S. W. Rosenbach, who cornered the market in both real and ostensible book-rarities during the early part of this century, and who — according to his recent exposé biography, by two apparently disgruntled or unconscious employees — was never above throwing an 'enthusiastic' line to gullible millionaire customers, to make some backwoods grammar or horse-farrier's expense book for 1787 look like a Vital Document in the History of the World (at prices to match.)

The English and American book-collectors, right up to the time of the Civil War, were mainly of a very sedate variety, and little will be found today in even the richest private catalogues of the eighteenth century, as for instance those of the Harley and Douce collections, that goes beyond what may properly be called 'facetiæ,' in the way of broad jestbooks, a few sardonic biographies of fashionable prostitutes, actresses, and the like. Moral as it may have been in this sexual sense, the whole book-collecting field in England was otherwise faked to a fare-thee-well and scandalously racketeerized, early in the last century, largely owing to the influence of a journalistic enthusiast named Thomas Frognall Dibdin, cut from precisely the same cloth as the later 'bibliophile' dealers, T. J. Wise in England, and Rosenbach in the United States. T. J. Wise has now been thoroughly exposed as not only not a real collector at all — and simply a dealer passing himself off among the snob collectors, who were his customers, as one of themselves — but a crooked dealer to boot, whose secret stock consisted of forged and fabricated 'pre-first' editions, printed privately for him with false pre-datings, and plugged in his elaborate author-bibliographies of the authors whom he had principally faked.

This is perhaps not the place to discuss, at any further length, the fooltraps for the unwary set before the feet of collectors by dealers of this kind; all the really worst fooltraps being, of course, reserved for collectors of erotica, who are presumably fair game since they seldom care to complain publicly or to the police. A whole guidebook remains to be written, as promised earlier, of *"Hints to Erotica Collectors."* It will be sufficient to point out here that the racketeer dealer — who is generally far better-dressed, better-educated, and smoother altogether than his client — gets his basic foothold, and main leverage, through the snobbery and pretentiousness of his more-or-less amateur clients. It was such clients' pleasure, and still is, to bask in the presumed glory of paying $19,000 for $100 books, which persons of the T. J. Wise type helpfully advise them are worth the higher figure, owing to the fact that the collector-dealer just happens to have an *extra* copy — it's always an extra, of this 'uniquely' scarce book! — which he is willing to cede, out of pure friendship, at the mere pittance of $19,000 as aforesaid. Or he may even go so far as to cede to the favored client his one and only copy, *the only copy known to exist* (here mentally calculating how many dozen are still left on the pile of two hundred down in the cellar, left over from the forged printing). To round things off perfectly, the said unique copy also happens to be bound in the pale-blue skin of wild Nigerian jackasses, hand-tooled by Ravenscroft of London — never by Pincus of Slobodka, though, who was good enough for the Czar — a fact which, basically, would seem to have little real relation to the scarcity value of any book, and none whatsoever to any value above $500, since the finest binding in the world is only *worth,* at maximum, the latter figure, and can thus hardly add more to the value of the book, though easily impressed book collectors pay a great deal more every day.

The typical sucker for this Dibdin type of 'bibliomania,' a mania assiduously peddled to rich collectors for over a century now, when they do not have the simple sense just to shrug it off (as they would similar sales-talk in the field where they are really making their money), was the eccentric British collector, Richard Heber, in the early nineteenth century, to whom Dibdin astutely dedicated his puff-job frankly entitled *Bibliomania.* Heber was the only collector in history ever to have assembled as many books — or perhaps more — than the library of seventy-six thousand volumes collected by and for the Duc de la Vallière, soon to be discussed. But with what a difference! Heber may, certainly, have known how to read, but he does not appear to have spent much time doing so, any more than do most dyed-in-the-wool book collectors, who, once collecting has really become a *mania* with them, seldom read anything but sale-catalogues. Heber's activity consisted mainly of simple-mindedly piling up house after house in England and abroad, full to the gunwales with assorted books and bibelots, until the house could hold no more; whereupon he would lock the place up, buy another house, and start all over. (I sometimes have the feeling, after ten years abroad, that I am doing the same thing myself.)

This is the classic symptom of the anxiety-type of collector, the 'perennial student' satirized by Chekhov, who is driven by the idea that KNOWLEDGE IS POWER, and that only by outfitting himself with a plethora of the books presumably containing this knowledge will he achieve the power and virility he so desperately needs and wants, and without which he feels helplessly ignorant and weak. Compare the legend of Prometheus, driven heavenward to steal the knowledge and the strength of the father-gods. But since, after the buying — or even the reading — of each separate book, or even stack of books, he *still* somehow finds himself without the desired secret or power, and not much knowledge either (owing to having rushed through every book too fast to digest anything, in his anxiety to get on to the next and the next and the next), there is no help for it: he must obviously rush out and buy or read more.

This is exactly similiar to the Don Juan or Casanova complex, where a man or woman reels headlong — to phrase it politely — from the hundredth or thousandth sexual and emotional failure with another human being, onward to that thousand-and-first 'conquest,' without ever noticing that just as much time or more is being spent fleeing from the last failure and disappointment as is being spent searching for, or even enjoying, the next. That this is precisely the problem in 'bibliomania' is more than clear. The underlying insecurity and uncertainty of the Don Juan, male or female, as to whether he or she is orgastically potent, or even a normal heterosexual person at all, is never and can never be assuaged in this way. The same is more than true of book-buying, and the search for the knowledge that is only presumably power, but that is just as often knowledge gone wrong, as in the other side of the legend of Prometheus, the story of the Sorcerer's Apprentice.

Heber was the Don Juan, or anxiety-type of collector to perfection, and when he died his heirs immediately sold off all his houses full of books and trash at auction, not overlooking to search out specially, and piously burn, the few erotic books that had fallen into the net of his collecting. The most famous erotic work in the Heber collection, so destroyed, was in particular the only surviving copy of the Earl of Rochester's *Sodom,* probably printed in London with the false imprint 'Antwerp' in 1684, a roaring satire on the homosexual court of King James I of England, and his minions Carr, Buckingham, and a dozen others. *Sodom* has only been reprinted therefore since that time (in vol. IX of

Kryptádia, and further reprints of this) from defective manuscript copies, such as that probably made by the equally eccentric Adriaan Beverland, and preserved at Hamburg and The Hague. There are far better manuscripts of *Sodom,* in the Harleian MSS., British Museum, and at Princeton, as well as several others, and it now at last has been possible to obtain permission to publish these.

All the English collectors, from the time of Heber on — with only a few elegant exceptions — seem touched with eccentricity or sexual abnormality. To avoid seeming hipped on the subject, I will not mention Heber's own main abnormality, but refer the interested reader to Ashbee's *Index Librorum Prohibitorum,* p. 340, in a list of other such 'cases which have come prominently before the public.' Other eccentric collectors have been far more abnormal sexually, many having a pronounced penchant for sadistic flagellation and the collecting of books on this subject, which is the one and only special contribution of the English language to 'erotic' literature.

VII

WE ARRIVE HERE at the other main group of erotica collectors, the old and impotent, who are searching in books or pictures for the reviving of their drooping sexuality. It can hardly be held that this is wrong, and even the usual hypocrisy about 'protecting the young' — from the knowledge they so very much need — is obviously not applicable here. In any case, no one has ever objected to the collecting (often by the same collectors) of books and illustrations about fox-hunting, pig-sticking, and the slaughtering of bison, elephants, and so forth, with cannon-sized guns; nor, for that matter, to these unpleasant entertainments themselves. Perhaps if the dark and dirty secret were told, that this type of wanton animal murder is also mainly engaged in by the sexually impotent, to excite their flagging virility, there would be a good chance of getting both the fact *and* the literature of 'blood sports' banned as well. But one suspects that would be too much to hope for.

As sex is only a part of life, just as cream is only a part of milk — though the best part! — few book collectors of taste and intelligence are solely collectors of erotica. The erotica form part of a larger collection of books, and there properly take a rightful place, as in life. The most discriminating French collectors, in both the eighteenth and nineteenth centuries, were elevated scholars in the tradition of the great La Monnoye, or, at the very least, solid amateurs who either had a good deal of taste themselves, or had the wit to hire librarians capable of supplying whatever the collectors may have lacked in the way of special bibliographical knowledge and flair.

There are far too many such collectors to do more than list some of the more outstanding names: bibliophiles like Charles Nodier and Count Scipion du Roure; the architect Viollet-Leduc (who restored the Notre Dame cathedral), the playwright Guilbert de Pixerécourt; the remarkable collectors Solar, Veinant, Yemeniz, Cigongne, and a dozen others; above all the antiquarian C. Leber, whose great folklore library was ultimately acquired *en-bloc* by the city of Rouen. In all these French collectors' libraries, as seen in their private or posthumous auction catalogues, there will invariably be found richly-furnished sections of fine classical erotica and facetiæ, and a goodly selection, as well, of the violently obscene satirical pamphlets of the French Revolution, directed against Marie-Antoinette, the Cardinal Rohan (of the Necklace Affair), and particularly against the Duchess de Polignac, allegedly the Queen's lesbian mistress.

Much or most of this sort of sexual scandal is, of course, merely part of the sexual folklore referred to above. Consider, for instance, that the one most famous accusation against Marie-Antoinette, the remark that turned the peasantry against her and probably cost her her head — 'Let them eat cake!' — will, as a matter of fact, be found in the old German jestbook of Martin Montanus, centuries before Marie-Antoinette was born, where it is known to folklorists as the standard Aarne-Thompson Tale-Type No. 1446. It has also a long history, preceding, in Estonia, Russia, and India. Yet Marie-Antoinette, probably, and the Duchess de Polignac, certainly, lost their lives on the basis of sexual folklore very possibly just as bogus; the body of poor Polignac being publicly torn to bits after she was dead, and the sexual parts shamefully displayed, strictly on the idea that the lesbian scandals about herself and the Queen were somehow true, though they were obviously nullified by the simultaneous scandals about the Queen and the Cardinal Rohan and various other presumed male lovers.

The primary historical documents, as to the whole Revolutionary period and ferment, are precisely these ephemeral and scandalous pamphlets, which, as the English antiquarian John Selden put it, are like straws in the wind, showing the true temper of the times, where heavier books fall to the ground. The pamphlets of the Puritan Revolution in England, to which

Selden was referring, were fortunately preserved by a wise collector, Thomason, who bought them day-by-day as they appeared. The Thomason collection is now in the British Museum, but another such collection, equally rich, of a slightly later period, that made by Narcissus Luttrell, has long since been ruthlessly broken up, and peddled in separate bits, by British booksellers. The main such collections, for the French Revolution, are those of Leber, still preserved in Rouen; and of Guilbert de Pixerécourt. The irreplaceable revolutionary section of Pixerécourt's library, thrown on sale when one of his theatrical ventures failed and he was forced to sell his books in order to recoup, was fortunately bought, complete, for the library of the French Senate, where it remains to this day, but not without some humiliating public appeals for its preservation by the greatest bibliophiles of the day, Nodier and Paul Lacroix. No one knows exactly what is meant, yet no one can miss the bitter implication, of the engraved *ex libris* Pixerécourt printed on the presentation copies of his sale-catalogue, with the motto: 'UN LIVRE EST UN AMI QUI NE CHANGE JAMAIS.'

Collectors of this stature never hesitated to set on their shelves, and to allow to figure in their catalogues, early and fine editions of the classical erotica of earlier periods: Chorier's *Dialogues of Luisa Sigea*, the various anti-clerical pornographica such as *The Philosophical Theresa* and *The Nun in her Smock*, and the entire and very remarkable facetious literature of Italy and France, in which the origins of almost all the Western European and American erotic folklore must be sought, or cannot be found. The French collectors did not, however, limit themselves to such works, nor did the erotica and facetiæ ever appear to have formed the main bulk of their real libraries — as differentiated from the 'libraries' of unread Bibles, Shakespeares, Racines, sporting-books, and so on, often bought by secret erotica collectors nowadays, simply as window-dressing or show.

The principal collector of the century preceding, in all fields of literature, actually, but with a decided bent for the erotic, was the Duc de la Vallière, whose collection had been enlarged by leaps and bounds, through the buying of other collections *en-bloc*, and mainly through the activity of his brilliant and curmudgeonly librarian, the Abbé J.-J. Rive, who was really responsible for creating the La Vallière collection, simply using the noble duke to pay the bills. Anyone interested in this remarkable library, and its even more remarkable librarian, is recommended to turn to the *Miscellanées Bibliographiques* of Édouard Rouveyre, for 1880, in which the whole story is laid open in two capital articles. As is usual in learned journals, the authors take no moral position whatever, and pass over with hardly a word — obviously to avoid irritating the patrician sensibilities of the titled collectors of their own day — the cultural atrocity of the breaking up of this stupendous and unparalleled collection, at auction, immediately after La Vallière's death.

According to Paul Lacroix ("le Bibliophile Jacob"), ending his Preface to the great Félix Solar sale-catalogue in 1860, and obviously hoping and hinting for the same fate for Solar's books; when La Vallière's library went on sale, seventy-six years earlier, 'The administration of the King's Library [now Bibliothèque Nationale] obtained from the government of Louis XVI, though the State finances were already pretty sick, an unlimited credit for the buying, at that memorable sale, of everything lacking in the great national library.' Lacroix' preface is altogether wellworth reading, especially today, as the best expression of the climate of opinion, among the real booklovers of his century, as to the plain cultural crime of the dispersion of superb libraries like these under the auctioneer's hammer, for the profit — and sometimes merely for the vain ostentation — of rich collectors. Lacroix himself, though more notable often for his bibliographical blunders (such as the attribution of Cantenac's poem on impotence, "L'Occasion perdue, recouverte," to Corneille!) than for his valid discoveries, was in truth the booklover his pseudonym implies, and did save from oblivion many of the charming facetiæ which he proposed to Gay for reprinting, and for which he wrote introductory notes. A dapper figure at all the great auctions of his period, with his square monocle à la Disraeli; his own very modest means are observable to this day in the inexpensive but very neat cloth bindings, mostly signed by Pierson, in which erotic and bibliographical works from his library — dispersed like all the others — are still sometimes to be found.

The Duc de la Vallière may be considered the model of the then relatively new, but now standard, type of wholesale collector, or collector-by-inheritance, of a sort that became increasingly prominent with the replacement of the titled nobility by the nobility of hard cash, during the eighteenth century. This is nowadays the prevailing form, and the accessions methods of the great public and university libraries of our own day are also clearly modelled on the same pattern, whether for good or for ill only time will tell. The original methods of this sort of collecting are excessively simple: the widows and heirs of real, but less rich, collectors, are decoyed or seduced into parting with the whole library of the defunct collector, by means of crushing lump-sums of cash flung at their heads, generally before the collector's body is even cool enough to bury. This is a bit ghoulish, of course, on the model of the classic anti-woman libel of the Widow of Ephesus folktale, but it is considered by all concerned to be preferable to letting the best books get away at the eventual public auction, in which, as a result, only the sweepings now generally remain to be sold.

In this way, the results of several lifetimes spent in literary study and meaningful collecting can be, and are, dropped into the lap of the rich or noble cash-collectors, in exactly the time it takes to make out a check in the widow's name. As many such collectors, nowadays, are too busy playing golf or seducing each other's wives, to go around comforting the weeping widows of dead bibliophiles by means of spot cash; this work is now generally entrusted to buying agents or self-styled librarians — miles different from the Abbé Rive! — who can, at any rate, be trusted to distinguish the Gutenberg Bibles from the Tarzan paperbacks and murder-mysteries, which the rich collector is not always sure he can do without putting his foot in it. The rest of the new-style private librarian's time — aside from cataloguing the swag, and going out snagging options from other dying scholars' wives — is spent sticking the new collector's heavily gilt leather *ex libris* in the front of each book thus obtained. As often as not, no one knows why, the *ex libris* is also pasted right smack-dab on top of that of the real, but now dead, scholar. This is not hard work; the trick is simply to swing it. There are jobs of this kind in almost all the fancier private, public, and university libraries of the world today. Being homosexual seems to be one of the principal qualifications (*n.b.*) for the work. And abandon all love of books, ye who enter here.

By whatever method it was collected, the La Vallière collection was glorious indeed, though the noble collector did not even stop short of 'borrowing' rare books, by means of his influence at court, from the Sainte-Geneviève Library, and then flatly refusing to return them. As seen by the traces left in the printed volumes of the auction of his collection, prepared by De Bure, the La Vallière library was notably strong in the erotic poetry, the unexpurgated facetiæ, and the new genre of the erotic novel, which had sprung up in the seventeenth century. La Vallière, or, more probably, his librarian the Abbé Rive, had clearly concentrated on these, and was also able to afford any price to get them — which was then, and still is, an essential point. That it was more likely the Abbé Rive than La Vallière, is suggested by the manuscript bibliography the good abbé left after his death, called *A Library of Sotadic, Pornographic, and Infernal Books,* so-called after Sotades, a Greek erotic poet; Pornogros, his horse; and Infernus, the hell where they presumably have gone to search for their proper reward. This manuscript is regularly 'discovered' by débutants in the field of erotic bibliography, who imagine it to be a published work, which they then unsuccessfully search for in the British Museum and the university libraries of Kansas and Moscow — Moscow, Idaho, that is — and other centers of culture.

The tail end of the La Vallière library: 26,500 of its 76,000 books, all catalogued and prepared for final dissolution by auction, did fortunately find a rich enough collector to buy the whole thing, complete; a collector with the munificence of spirit, as well, to present this part, at least, of the once-superb library, to the French nation. Today, the glory of that part of the La Vallière collection so saved, and known by the name of its erudite and generous donor as the collection of the Marquis de Paulmy, is still to be seen in the library of the Arsenal in Paris, of which it forms the base. As to the erotica, that bulked so handsomely in both the La Vallière and the Nyon-Paulmy catalogues . . . well, the sad and paradoxical end of the story is this. Those of the erotica of the La Vallière library that were saved from dispersal at auction, by the Marquis de Paulmy, were added by him frankly to the treasures of the French national libraries, where they were grouped as Nos. 6059 through 6141 of his manuscript catalogue, including such rarities as *two* of the very few known copies of the first edition of Cleland's *Memoirs of a Woman of Pleasure* (1749). Being thus easily available to hand, they were routed out after the French Revolution, by a later abbé of the Restoration, of the new and highly moral type of the nineteenth century, a certain chaplain of the Tuileries given power of life and death over the treasures of the library of the Arsenal, and they were burnt.

The rest of the La Vallière erotica, wantonly dissipated at auction, as all right-minded researchers must deplore, along with the rest of his books, for the benefit of his widow and daughter, to whom he also left several million gold *louis* in cash; these, however — and this is the paradox — may and perhaps do still exist somewhere. The most famous erotic book in his collection, as will be seen, certainly still exists. It may be observed, in passing, that the very first action of his widow and daughter, the moment La Vallière was dead, was to kick into the street his savant librarian, the Abbé Rive, *who had received no salary from the excellent duke for the preceding thirteen years,* during which period, however, an unknown number of millions in gold had been spent not only on the buying of books (not to mention real-estate and furniture) but also on their being magnificently caparisoned in full crushed levant morocco, with an occasional ornately gilt calf by way of contrasting simplicity. One gets the impression that the librarian was presumed to be getting his salary strictly by means of secret discounts and kick-backs from the booksellers, a practice certainly not unknown. Compare the extraordinarily frank passage, in Edwin Wolf & John Fleming's *Rosenbach: A Biography* (1960) p. 207, as to a plain cash bribe of $1000 paid for concealing from the great American collector, Henry Huntington, the actual prices paid for books sold him at unknown mark-ups.

What was certainly the most famous piece, among the erotica of the La Vallière collection, was the unique copy of Crébillon's *Tableaux des Mœurs du temps,* illustrated with colored miniatures by Carême or Chardin, showing the rich financier, La Popelinière, for whom the manuscript had been prepared (and who also pretended to have written it), in the process of making love to the wives of various nobles of the realm and other persons, to whom he had lent money to pay their gambling debts and so on, with interest being demanded and paid in the form of the sexual services of their wives. The 'farmer-general' La Popelinière, being only a *nouveau-riche* arriviste, as is plain to see, had either the bad taste or the grotesque sense of humor, to hide his staff portrait-artist behind the screen of his bedchamber (if he had to hide), there to sketch the ladies thus blackmailed into his bed, *in puris naturalibus,* and in a variety of extravagant positions.

Except for the inevitable presence of the ugly little farmer-general in the resulting miniatures, this set might well have taken its place with the 'postures' of Giulio Romano, and the accompanying *Sonnets* of Aretino — its clear inspiration — as one of the masterpieces of the world's erotic art. As it is, it is instead only a masterpiece of ungallantry, and ungentlemanly bad taste. For instead of the ladies' identities being disguised, as one might have expected, their faces were carefully drawn and colored by the artist, so as to indicate in the most unmistakable fashion their real identity, and the disgrace of their husbands under the power

of La Popelinière's cash. This is evidently the exact opposite of
Balzac's folktale, retold in the *Contes Drolatiques,* of the gallant
who thoughtfully put a pillow-case over the lady's head and valiantly denied everything, when her suspicious husband broke into
his bedchamber, but was fortunately unable to recognize his wife's
uncovered end.

The Duc de la Vallière, by means of influence with the deeply
moral King Louis XV — who kept a harem of underage girls and
noblemen's wives, called the "Deer Park" — had this manuscript
forcibly seized from La Popelinière's heirs in 1762, by the min-
ister-of-state Saint-Florentin, 'to prevent the publication of so
pornographic a work.' At La Vallière's own death, it did not appear in either the De Bure catalogue or that of Nyon and Paulmy,
but was sold off immediately by his daughter, the Duchess of
Chatillon, who clearly preferred the cash it would net, to the
place in heaven she might perhaps have earned by burning it. The
unique *Tableaux des Mœurs du temps* passed, for a paltry twenty-
five *louis d'or,* to an unknown collector (possibly an agent, really
buying it back for the Duchess, to evade taxes?) and was then
smuggled to England at the outbreak of the French Revolution.
There it was bought by the Russian collector, Prince Galitzin,
who later brought it back to France, where it still is. Its further
peregrinations are traced in the Gay-Lemonnyer *Bibliographie
des ouvrages relatifs à l'amour,* III. 1172–3. This identical copy
was only recently offered for sale to an important bookdealer on
the Rive Gauche, in Paris. It now, unfortunately, lacks one of the
most amusing of its colored miniatures, the one in which an elephant figures, complete with palanquin. This has apparently been
torn out to save the shame of the descendants of one of the partici-
pants in the orgy depicted, doubtless the descendants of the elephant, the only family involved which is still authentically extant
after two Revolutions.

VIII

It is with the English and American collectors of the middle nineteenth century that there appears for the first time the type of
erotica collector, who is *a collector of erotica and nothing else.*
However many sporting-books and Shakespeares he may pile up,
on his *un*locked shelves, to disguise his real activity from everyone
but his bookseller; such a collector is self-evidently not a lover
of books at all, and has no particular literary tastes, which erotic

literature in English would seldom satisfy anyhow, as most of it is excessively crudely and badly written unless it has been translated from the French. One would even go so far as to suspect that, were other aphrodisiacal products really available, to do the same job that erotic books are intended to do for such collectors, no recourse to the printed word would be bothered with at all. The collectors would simply swallow down these pharmaceutical aphrodisiacs in the more convenient pill form, or rub them, in the form of a peppery paste perhaps, on their bald heads (or wherever seemed most useful). Lamentably enough, this crude physical approach almost invariably does not work.

The idea of the real existence of chemical aphrodisiacs — once the lowly but then-new and mysterious potatoes and tomatoes ('love-apples'), just as now the equally fallacious Spanish fly and yohimbin — is simply part of the standard sexual folklore of humanity. It is very significant that at least two of the three main works on the subject of aphrodisiacs have been written by proudly-practising and even proselytizing homosexuals, Magnus Hirschfeld (*Liebesmittel,* 1929), and Norman Douglas (*Paneros,* 1930). Douglas also returned to the subject again in his final work, *Venus in the Kitchen* (1952), published posthumously though written at about the same time. Curiously enough, the third main work on the subject, Alan Hull Walton's *Love Recipes, Old and New:* "A Study of Aphrodisiacs throughout the ages, with sections on glandular extracts, hormone stimulation and rejuvenation" (London, 1956), manages somehow, despite the modern gland-and-hormone jargon of its title, and a fourteen-page "Bibliography for the Advanced and Professional Reader," to overlook completely *both* Hirschfeld and Douglas, the two main writers on the subject, and all their works. Mr. Walton now announces for publication a multi-volume bibliographical study of erotica (on the style of Ashbee), also of all times & climes, but, one trusts, just a little better researched; or perhaps, to phrase it more truly, with a little less unconscious resistance to admitting the existence of his predecessors.

One could hardly suggest that Hirschfeld and Douglas lacked culture, or the ability to read the books they collected — Hirschfeld's famous library and sexological collection in Berlin, as is well known, were burned by Hitler. It is to be assumed, rather, that the abnormality driving them toward their own sex, instead of the biologically-determined opposite sex, finally proved insufficient to provoke the desired erection, and recourse was in the end found necessary to chemical and mechanical means rather than to literature, or perhaps in addition. That, in the absence of any skewing abnormality, or impotence, such chemical and mechanical and even literary methods work far less well than the simple presence of the opposite sex, is also very clear. The secret of homo-sexuality (here clearly to be seen) is the *animosity* toward the same sex, seldom very well hidden under the ostensible love, and inevitably therefore veering into sado-masochism; but that is not the subject here.

The reason why chemical and mechanical aphrodisiacs seldom work, except via the user's belief in them, thus acting really on the imagination and not on the physique, is identical with the reason why the impotent generally achieve better results with erotica than with these: The deep-seated mystery of phallic erection in the male, throughout the mammalian order, is not controlled basically by any physical manipulation or secretion that can be imitated by direct application externally or internally to the body of the male. Erection is caused, under normal circumstances, by a combination of visual, tactile, sensory and odoriferous responses to the bodily presence (or even to the thought) of the person who is the sexual object, bound together by what can only be called — even in the case of animals other than man — the imagination. That this is even more true of women than of men is indubitable. None of this is any higher or secret knowledge of some newer psychology, but is a primary recognition gaily expressed in the ancient folk-riddle known in half a dozen languages: 'What is the lightest thing in the world? — John Thursday: even a *thought* will raise him.'

It becomes clear, therefore, that erotica exist not only to satisfy the imaginations of normal men in the natural process of becom-ing old, but also of the relatively abnormal; that is, those whose sexual necessities are not accepted as the public norm. By this I do not in any way mean to refer to, or even to defend, anything perverted; but to such simple — though theoretically immoral or illegal — tastes as the adolescent desire to be the 'husband of all the women in the world.' This particular overcompensatory dream seems to have its most fervent devotees precisely among men of an age when they are least able physically to satisfy it. Though many such men could easily afford, and do sometimes try to have, all the women money can buy; more often they realize they must calm down in the end, and satisfy their harem-dream in the merely visual and literary sexuality of erotic books and pictures. This has been going on a long time, and will continue for a long time, perhaps forever, so long as the imagination plays its integral part in human sexual potency. The laws as to 'obscenity' and so forth, are therefore perfectly irrelevant, and completely unenforceable, though one cannot hope for their total disappearance without the disappearance also, or at least the desuetude, of anti-sexual Western religion. As is understood, this is precisely what has been coming to pass over the last century, as religious leaders are the first to bemoan.

The same reasoning is equally true of many if not most normal men, still sufficiently virile, who nevertheless find themselves less excited by the accustomed charms of a well-beloved wife in her mid-forties than once they were, and who are constrained to search for a much-needed 'variety' in sexual image, in the imaginary replacements available in literature and art. Whatever one may say of the theoretical infidelity of their imaginations, it is evident that they are actually trying, in this way, to preserve — on a physical basis at least — their monogamic marriage of love. As is well known, many women do precisely the same thing, without even bothering with recourse to books; and lie in moments of passion conjuring up behind closed eyes the image of the latest pelvic-crooner — usually named Buddy Goorhackle or something equally non-erotic, you would think — or, among more cultured women, some dark-haired movie idol or silver-tongued Ethical Society lecturer in vogue. Again, who is there to say that this is wrong? Or, assuming that one would be so foolish as to object, how would you go about making the objection stick?

And who is there to say that other, even more unfortunate persons, fetichized in early youth on some such sexual 'partialisms' as frilly underwear or female hair — generally the hair of the head, by the way, and in long tresses — or tiny feet, Chinese fashion, or excessively large and motherly bosoms (the standard American fetich, we are led to believe, by all of t.v. and most of the ads), are not better served with the childish fetiches they require, for the achievement of their virile duty, in the special literary compartment that exists for them, quite aside from television and the public prints. They are certainly not doing anyone any harm. When and if the Anglo-Saxon legal codes finally catch up with the Code Napoléon (which is already a century and a half in successful operation in Europe), and will refrain from concerning itself with the private sexual activities of a non-sadistic kind of adult and consenting parties — no matter what their marital status or specific sexual bent — such very minor deviations as those above noted will simply disappear as subjects of public interest, newspaper scandal, blackmail, &c. Legal groups in both England and America are already attempting to prepare this long-delayed modernization of the sexual law, particularly in regard to homosexuality, as with the earlier and essentially propagandistic work of Hirschfeld and Kinsey. It remains to be seen how far they will get.

It is necessary to admit frankly and at once that the private sexual liberty of the imagination, above discussed, is sometimes taken to most undesirable limits by certain gravely neurotic persons. There exists, and has existed for over a century now, a small but very active group of collectors of self-styled erotica, especially prevalent in the sexually repressed Anglo-Saxon countries such as Germany and England, whose preferred 'erotic' literature and art turn out to be, when examined — preferably with tongs — a snake-pit of vile imaginings, filled with tortures, blood (in red ink), whippings, and gruesome murders, lusciously imagined up and with specially-designed illustrations to match. Except for the unpublished and, one would have thought, unpublishable manuscripts of the Marquis de Sade (who wrote the worst of them in a mad-house), and of certain of his imitators since the 1860's, such books have never before existed in the history of the world, except in the diseased imaginings of the very pious illustrated martyrologies mentioned earlier. Persons of this bent seldom restrained themselves, in the past, to the 'weak' and illusory pleasures of literature and the imagination, but went out and got jobs — who else wants them? — as hangmen, inquisitors, and, more recently, concentration-camp *kommandos:* professions in which, as the Nuremberg Trials have now forever proved, the most evil imaginings of such literature are carefully and systematically turned into hideous fact. Since the inquisitors and *kommandos* commonly brag of their possession of sadistic literature, the inquisitors having been in fact required to possess it, in the form of *Witches' Hammers* and similar manuals of torture over the centuries, the interplay and imitation of literature by life, and the inspiration and formulation of evil-in-fact by evil-in-print, need not be argued. It is proved.

It ought also to be observed how the publication of Sade's work has been systematically funded and undertaken by perverted and presumably *avant-garde* groups in recent times; a special club and publishing company even being set up in Paris in the late 1920's, under the name of 'Stendhal & Cie.', at the expense of a number of rich and aristocratic 'bibliophiles,' specifically for the purpose of issuing homosexual literature, such as the apologetic works of Meier (from Ersch & Gruber's *Encyclopädie,* 1837), and Saikaku Ibara; culminating in an ultra-luxurious edition of the *120 Journées de Sodome* of the Marquis de Sade, of which the manuscript was 'patriotically' brought back from Germany, where the first edition had been printed by Iwan Bloch at the turn of the century.

Nothing more need really be said about sadistic literature, except that it is *legal* in all countries as long as the sexual parts of the victims are not displayed; nor about its collectors, except that they really form only a very tiny group. As with homosexuals, a similar and in fact a largely overlapping group, the noise they make is all out of proportion to their numerical incidence — despite the faked and weighted figures of the late Professor Kinsey, pretending to prove the opposite — and rises solely from the assiduity of their propagandizing and proselytizing activity. The sado-homosexual group is basically similar to the equally small group of devotees of the Grand Guignol in Paris, a back-alley theatre of the perverse which, however, can seat hardly more than one hundred 'special clients' a night. Compare this figure with the millions of average Joes, and their wives, who can and do get to watch and participate in the dubious pleasures of blonde-wig wrestling and horror-movies at midnight over t.v.; that is to say in exactly similar perversions, broadcast nation-wide and internationally by means of the latest technological advances of instantaneous publication *en masse.* The luxurious publications intended for a hundred rich French and British homosexuals, along with the total audience for the Grand Guignol and its ketchupy cuisine, are obviously nowhere by comparison. Don't let's lose track of the forest, in the view of this one twisted stump.

Sadistic literature is extremely repugnant to normal erotica collectors, many of whom specially indicate to their booksellers that books of this kind should not even accidentally be brought to their attention, and who sometimes ask to be reassured that there are no flagellational scenes in the books they are buying, as such scenes immediately destroy for them the aphrodisiacal effect of the rest. Not only any thought of eroticism is ruined for them, by any sadistic admixture, but their stomachs are simply and literally turned by books and spectacles of this kind, as also by the exactly similar murder-mysteries (and the movies and t.v. serials made from them) of the Mickey Spillane and 'Hank Janson' variety, beloved of kings and presidents — in foreign countries. More than one erotica collector has been horrified to find, in Rétif de la Bretonne's *Anti-Justine,* a book which, from its title and *apologia* one would expect to be opposed utterly to Sade and sadism, a necrophilic or cannibalistic chapter just as gruesome, if not more so, than anything Sade ever wrote. How is that to be explained? I have seen, and appreciated the pathos of a copy of the *Anti-Justine* in English, bought by a collector for the purpose of having it read aloud to him by his much younger mistress in bed (the way Mr. & Mrs. Joe watch wrestling on t.v.), with the sadistic chapter carefully quarantined by being pasted shut with gummed paper-tape all around, for fear that the book might fall open there by accident in her hands. This is the exact opposite, of course, of the activity of Dr. Bowdler as to Shakespeare. It is now widely recognized that Dr. Bowdler was in the wrong. Human history may very well decide someday that — far from a 'total liberty' of expression being the real *desideratum* — the collector just referred to was in the right.

The point has already been made that, so far as literature is concerned, the perverted books of perverted collectors, such as sadists, masochists, coprophiles, and so on, do not actually represent the libraries of these persons at all, any more than the aforementioned adventures of the Countess La Fanghoul, published originally *only* for this audience and no one else, represent literary art. Such books are merely a part of the perverted armamentarium of their owners, intended to work on their tangled neuroses and jaded imaginations in the same way that their hollow-balloon whips and rubber-toothed currycombs are intended to work on their hardened posteriors. The literary devices are for the head end; the other devices are for the other end. This has evidently nothing whatsoever to do with literature. As suggested above, were an authentic chemical aphrodisiac really discoverable, which would do the same job for these subvirile unfortunates as do the illustrated horror-books which they collect — and which they call synthetically into existence by their patronage, and the money they offer — this type of literature would cease overnight to be be published, for lack of buyers.

The type forever of the perverted collector of sadistic erotica was Frederick Hankey, about whom the unvaryingly bad opinion of the booksellers who dealt with him has been recorded in an earlier chapter here. With the possible exception of Ashbee (who later got most of his library, and may be assumed to have put up with him for that reason), everybody hated Hankey. The man did not have a friend. His perversion was his brag, and stank. The abnormal part of Hankey's collection, in particular the flagellational books and the works of his favorite author, Sade, which Ashbee apparently did not want; seem to have been ceded to Lord Houghton, the evil genius who had perverted Swinburne and destroyed his art in the special flagellation-brothels of the period. (See Georges Lafourcade's *La Jeunesse de Swinburne,* 1928, a masterly work.) It would also appear that, when Hankey's money and books were both gone, he continued clumping about Paris on crutches, like a superannuated procuress, buying further sadistic erotica for Houghton on a percentage basis. Almost the only thing for which one can really sympathize with him was the indignity (which he unquestionably enjoyed) of being turned into journalistic 'copy,' sight unseen, by the self-styled bibliophile journalist, Octave Uzanne, a sort of French Dibdin but even fruitier. In his *Caprices d'un Bibliophile,* in 1878, Uzanne swept together all the rumors about Hankey to make him into the subject of an imaginary portrait of an "Eroto-Bibliomaniac" and his books, under the transparent pseudonym or anagram of the "Chevalier Kerhany." Though this was published in 1878, Ashbee calmly records that Uzanne never actually *met* Hankey, or saw a single book in his library, until Ashbee introduced them in 1882, only a few months before Hankey's death.

Any critic would indeed have more nerve than brains to try to describe or discuss Hankey, when, as is now known since the integral publication of the *Journal* of Edmond and Jules de Goncourt, these two great critical stylists of their century — or one of them at least — actually did meet Hankey at what was still his prime, on April 7th, 1862, and left a really striking portrait of the man and of his books:

'Today I saw a type, a madman, a monster. One of those human beings confined to the abyss, who admit in their excesses all the evil instincts of humanity. Through him, as through a torn curtain, I could vaguely see one of the abominable lower depths of man, a frightful aspect of the blasé aristocracy of money, the British aristocracy: a ferocity in love, a libertinism that has its pleasure only in the sight of suffering . . .' Hankey is described at length, his background, his fortune, his pleasures, his going to see hangings with prostitutes in attendance, and to brothels of under-age girls, to torture them with pins, along with Monckton Milnes (Lord Houghton). Goncourt is led through his apartment, shown Hankey's erotic statuary, his erotic and sadistic books, his special bindings showing crossed whips and bleeding bottoms, that he corrupted the best binder of Paris into binding for him by offering triple or quintuple price. 'The man does not look at you; he looks at his fingernails. We looked at him as one would look at De Sade. "I'm waiting for a skin," he said. "For a binding. The skin of a young girl. One of my friends is supposed to get it for me . . . They tan it, you know . . . It takes six months to tan it . . . Really you need two, from two women . . . I have a friend, Dr. Barth, you know . . . He travels in Africa. He's promised to get me a real skin, during one of the massacres . . . Something really fine . . ." ' Goncourt ends: 'I left that man's house as one leaves a nightmare, crumpled; my stomach upside-down, as though after drinking; my head empty.' For those whose system can stand the details, the entire passage, which is pages long, is perhaps worth looking up. There are few to compare with it in all the five thousand pages of the Goncourts' *Journal*.

IX

THE TWENTIETH CENTURY is the most important century in the history of the world, since the Renaissance, but in exactly the opposite sense. Western civilization turned upward at the Renaissance, from a thousand-year-long sleep under the dead hand of religious repression, owing to the liberating influence of the ancient arts and sciences of Egypt and Greece, brought to Europe by contact with the Arab vestiges of these arts and sciences during the Crusades. After rising — more or less — for five centuries, as a result of this inspiration, Western civilization has now turned down again, in the twentieth century, and seems to want nothing better than to take the rest of the world down with it. Naturally one does not hear it said that this is the worst of centuries — it is the best, the most progressive, and so forth, owing principally to its pointless little mechanical gimmicks. That human beings cannot endure this best, and this 'progress,' and are being stifled and destroyed by these gimmicks, most of which are hardly sixty years old and the world managed far better for sixty thousand years without them, is no importance. Conform or die. We die.

Private revolt is difficult to express, and even more difficult to make convincing: as having an effect, even on the *révolté* individual. It has also the problem of maintaining its equilibrium, and not diving overboard into every current apparently contrary to that of the evilly rushing social stream, simply because these currents appear to be contrary. The error, in this way, of the presumably *avant-garde* groups who nowadays whoop it up for the Marquis de Sade, while imagining themselves in opposition to the Atom Bomb — which is really just De Sade on a government grant — has already been discussed. Most of the current false revolts, and false-revolt groups and fads of the intelligentsia, similarly make the mistake of embracing precisely the evil, and the evil ethic, they imagine themselves to be fighting. There is almost no way out for the individual, nor, for that matter, is individual action or private revolt likely to succeed. The world is treading water in the West, waiting either to plunge under the surface forever, or to rise, in some new and unexpected avatar, like the prehistoric fish that became a bird: a transmutation that, to the fish, is only another kind of death.

One of the most signal areas of agreement between the literary *avant-garde* and the most reactionary political groups of this century, is the ferocious anti-humanism and anti-intellectualism that has become the banner of both. The old-style humanistic mind simply cannot accept this shitting upon everything that the human intellect has achieved, and its replacement with the bankrupt intuitions of nationalistic superpatriotism and religion — whether under the name of the new intellectuality or the new anti-intellectuality — and simply retires, to die with a certain dignity, in quiet personal communion with the records of the far greater past, and of that rapidly diminishing part of the present, such as authentic folklore, where there is still some tiny margin for the individual. Reading, and the collecting of books, remain one of those areas of private escape, for those who can afford it either through the protection of a university teaching-berth or some otherhow. Since the turn of the twentieth century, however, even the collecting of books has become almost untenable for the individual and individualistic collector, owing to the importation into the field of exactly that type of mass-handling, and the big-business or mathematical and 'percentage yield' methods of attack and conquest, which have already made all the other fields impossible for the individual.

Books now flow — old books and new — by the tens of thousands per month, into the processing and acquisition departments of national and university libraries all over the world, without any seriously comparable organization of, or concern with, the question of who can or will read and use the particular books bought. Books, that is to say old books, are becoming 'scarce,' and must therefore be swept up wholesale, no matter what language they are in. If one library or university cannot afford them, another university will. At any rate, it's a better way of spending money than building football stadia, though of course the universities all built their football stadia first. Furthermore, all the one hundred thousand new books now being published every year, in all the world's languages, must also be bought as well, so far as possible, whether or not there is a single person in the library or university involved who can read the language the books are in. This may seem overstated, but does not tell the half of it.

Since World War II this development has become absolutely maniacal, beginning with government seizures (by more than one government) of entire foreign libraries and literatures as prizes of war; turned over to, and sat upon by, minuscule cataloguing-staffs of sometimes as few as three persons per one hundred thousand books, who are capable of reading the languages in which the books are printed, and unable to catch up in a decade with even the cataloguing of the bare titles of the books seized. The activity is purely that of collectomania. These tons of books are being hoarded together, whether by purchase or seizure, the way lemmings are said to jump into the sea, as an act of faith, with the hope that history will perhaps justify their accumulation — no one knows when. As a matter of probability, the way the world is going, history is far more likely to blow up or burn the entire accumulation, and at a date not too distant, as being simply waste paper. As a matter of fact, if no one reads the books, that is all they are.

That the handwriting is on the wall, for the small or scholarly collector, in the face of this massive collecting activity on millionaire and government funds, has long since been seen, as touched upon, in passing, in connection with the methods of the Duc de la Vallière in the eighteenth century. In an earlier chapter, I have outlined the career of the greatest of erotica collectors, H. Spencer Ashbee, as an individual. It must not be lost sight of, however, that Ashbee was also a member of a numerically rather small group — the rich — and that his success as a collector is strictly assimilable to his private fortune, without which all the special knowledge and assiduity in the world could not have created his collection. This is plainly shown by the more particularly bibliographical, rather than collecting, activity of Ashbee's less fortunate friend and predecessor in the field, James Campbell Reddie, on whose materials the Ashbee collection and sumptuously-printed bibliographies so importantly drew, as Ashbee gratefully acknowledges. I have tried to express this as a joke: that 'Bibliography is the poor man's book-collecting.' But it is not a joke. The day of the little collector is nearly over.

Ashbee's wholesale, or money-implemented, approach is far more visible in the 'gallantiana' he collected than in his erotica, though the former have not been retained as a separate group in his bequest to the British Museum. Ashbee had, however, 'everything' in the gallant or semi-erotic field, as the shelf-lists (the so-called '4th copy cards') of certain of the B.M. presses, quite other than the Private Case, will show. For example, Presses 1080–81, 1093–94, and 1102 — and probably others, not traced — and Tables 603–604–605, principally concentrating on eighteenth century semi-erotic works in English and French. Wholesale sweepings-up of this kind, of entire slices of literature (except for the most inexpensive kinds of colportage literature, such as jest books), can no longer be undertaken by private individuals other than millionaires, as the amounts of money necessary to be spent can easily and very rapidly pass what is, in effect, the interest on more than several million dollars per year.

At an average of even so little as $20 per book, five thousand books bought involve the expenditure now of $100,000. Compare with these figures such one-man collections as the sixty or more thousand books of La Vallière, Heber, and more recently the Field Collection (now at Harvard). When collecting not ordinary books but exceptional items, the amount of money involved — which now comes to more like $100,000 for *five* books, rather than five thousand — makes any attempted buying by the small private collector or scholar perfectly ludicrous, and exposes him to the embarrassment of the UNWELCOME sign, painfully visible in the more successful bookdealers' eyes when the '*bibliophile fauché*,' or private scholar of small means, walks in. The buying of really fine single pieces, of an erotic nature, whether books or albums of illustrations, has risen monetarily quite out of such small collectors' reach or ken (to avoid causing everyone pain, the kinder booksellers will not even *show* such pieces to them anymore!) and has been doing so systematically since the late 1890's, when Ashbee's collecting ended.

It is understood that the mercantile aspect of book collecting — not here really under discussion — makes inevitable the continuous scaling upward of prices, in any field of collection, directly in proportion to the amounts of money made available to the dealers by their richest clients, private or institutional, not by their poorest. This is as true of erotica as of any other type of literature. The biography of the commercially most successful American rare-book dealer, *Rosenbach* (1960), which has been quoted before and will be quoted again, puts the position very plainly in the direct quotation from Rosenbach, in a letter to Dr. Harvey Cushing, p. 236: 'I do not consider 400% a large profit, or 10,000% large. We place a price on the volume based on what we consider its worth, regardless of its cost.' The 'good Doctor' sings a bit smaller, however, on p. 272, when a millionaire customer being curried, Eldridge Johnson, flatly called the turn on Rosenbach, stating that he did not complain as to one hundred percent profits, but 'when it comes to four, five, or six hundred per cent I simply cannot follow you . . . I am perfectly willing that you should make a good profit, as that is your business; but, as Mutt said to Jeff, "Be reasonable!" ' To this Rosenbach replied with the mollifying statement — *somewhat* different from that quoted above — that the average profit on his gross business 'was only 12½% per cent after expenses.' (The poor chap should really have gone into the new-book business instead, where bookdealers can at least hope for 33% discount, and sometimes more.) The perfect expression of the whole situation, so far as it is being discussed here, is the artless *obiter dictum* by the two ex-Rosenbach employees writing his biography, p. 461: 'Dr. Rosenbach, for all his politeness to scholars and modest collectors, could not put his heart into any attempt to enlarge his clientele of hundred-dollar-a-book buyers.' Any 'scholar or modest collector' (with or without a hundred dollars to spend *per* book) who can't understand that one, will have a picture drawn for him free of charge.

The real scholar or bibliophile who cannot compete on this raw monetary basis, has only one possibility left open to him: to *create* new areas of collecting, by means of his superiority in the real knowledge of — as opposed to the snobbish pose of conversance with — literary and bibliographical history. One of the finest private libraries, and not only of erotica, ever put together in the twentieth century, was that of the French poet and novelist, Pierre Louÿs, whose passionate erotic output and self-defeating life will form the subject of a later essay. It is here sufficient to indicate the superb auction catalogue of what was simply the cream of his library, seven hundred volumes intended to be sold to raise desperately-needed money during the War years in 1918. The announced sale did not take place, the whole collection being bought *en bloc* by a generous friend, who left the books in Louÿs' possession until the poet's death, blind, hardly seven years later.

The friend's act having been entirely one of philanthropy, and not bibliophily, even that part of the Louÿs collection that had thus been saved from dispersion was again thrown on sale at public auction in 1930 and was dispersed. The rest of Louÿs' books had already been sold off, shortly after his death, for the benefit of his second wife and her second husband — one of Louÿs' former secretaries. One can almost *smell* the story there, needless to say. In the margins of the same sale, all of Louÿs' erotic MSS. — not one of which had ever yet been printed — were also disposed of privately, to an outright pornography dealer, 'Dr.' (they're all Doctors!) Edmond Bernard. A number of these MSS. have since been published, in both poetry and prose, but by no means all. Further, the hundreds or thousands of bibliographical and lexicographical manuscript *'fiches'* that Louÿs had prepared, of erotic literature and speech in many languages, were wantonly dispersed, and odd lots have been offered only recently for sale. A few of these have accidentally come into my possession — the accident being that I could afford to bid for them — but the location of the majority of them remains unknown.

Obviously, it is not given to all of us to create new areas of collecting, and so to gather choice and coherent collections in competition with far richer collectors, as Louÿs was able to do. Even so, his expense was not small, and, as the reader will have observed, having no income other than that from his writing, he was ruined financially by 1918. The new areas of collecting being advanced today — for example, the dishonest and grotesque fad now being pushed for the horribly ugly 'cathedral' bindings of the 1820's and thereabouts — do not represent any discovery or real taste of book-collectors at all, but simply the commercial desperation of clever bookdealers who, having now sold and resold several times over all the really beautiful books easily to be found, and having lost them at last to the public and university libraries from which they will not, this time, return at the collectors' death; are now down to peddling truly ugly books, instead, meanwhile extasiating in the most embarrassing fashion, for the benefit of their dumber (and richer) customers, over the 'ravishing examples' of the *binder's* art — not even the printer's art, let alone the author's! — that these horrors are pretended to be. Prices rising of course. That is not what I mean by creating new areas of collecting.

Nor do I mean what listeners of the slightest ethical sense must have been electrified to hear stated to them in utter candour, in the Presidential Address to the British Bibliographical Society, 1953, under the title *"Religio Bibliographici,"* by Sir Geoffrey Keynes, surgeon, book-collector, and bibliographer of Blake and others, as printed in the same Society's journal, *The Library* (1953) series 5, VIII. 73:

> for the amateur [bibliographer] there can be no better way to work than by acquiring his basic knowledge as a collector. I do not wish to enlarge on the advantages his special knowledge gives him in the open market, but they can be spectacular. In the end, of course, when his knowledge is published in a printed book the trend is in the other direction, but by then he already has most of the books he wants, and can be content to see the others, the latecomers, scramble for what remains.

This compares very interestingly with the statement, a bit earlier in the same address, that 'ten to sixteen years' was the speaker's 'normal period of gestation' for his bibliographies, before — as it is implied — he could bring himself to drop the 'spectacular' advantages accruing to him by withholding from publication his 'special knowledge' of the real rarities. One is reminded of the folk translation of the British royal motto, '*Dieu et mon droict,*' sometimes politely phrased: 'Shove off the boat, Jack, I've got mine!' There is also a less polite form.

X

IT WOULD BE premature, and evidently indiscreet, to discuss the main erotic collections made in the present century by living collectors. A number of the principal collectors, when asked, have almost unanimously stated that they would prefer not to be named, as this could result only in exposing them to undesired correspondence with bumptious and neurotic youngsters, débutants in the field, and possibly to difficulties with the law. The present history must therefore close with note of a few of the major twentieth-century collectors now dead. It is commonly reported that the elder J. P. Morgan included erotic books in his magnificent library, and, as opposed to the usual sexual folklore of the kind discussed earlier, this appears to be true. However, the younger and more recent Morgan — continuing with collection through the elder Morgan's famous woman librarian — did not sympathize with this area of his father's collecting, and the principal part of the Morgan erotica returned to France, reportedly entering there the superb Victor Cousin collection, and, in part, the Antoine collection in Bordeaux. Practically nothing of this kind except for one Latin dictionary, by Blondeau, which seems to have escaped this *auto da fé* owing to its use of a learned language, will now be found in the Morgan Library in New York, along with the unique first edition of the pseudo-Byron *Leon to Annabella* (a pendant to *Don Leon*).

It should be mentioned that most of the principal collectors of erotic books are still in France, for the obvious reason that most of the really fine erotic books worth collecting are published in that country, or, rather, were published there until about 1948. The majority of the erotic books printed in France since World War II, and in very great number, are principally crude colportage pornographica in both English and French. Some are even illustrated with smeary erotic photographs, of a low order, in the typical German and American style. Only an occasional work, of the really beautiful kind that French erotica once generally were, is still being published today, such as the *Florilège* (1962?) of erotic poetry attributed to A. t'Serstevens, whose earlier similar collection, *Jeux et desduits* (1946) was one of the last of the really beautiful French erotic press-books, till this one. The post-War renaissance in France collapsed during the 1950 decade, and the making of books of the beauty and freedom of these two collections has been followed only by palpably vulgar *faux-luxe* attempts to imitate the genre. Books of this kind will not often be seen again.

Where there is nothing to collect, the collectors disappear. In this case they reappear in other countries with less long and less handsome a tradition of erotic publication and collection. There are today quite a number or very active erotica collectors, not only in England and America, but also in Italy and in the Scandinavian countries, particularly in Sweden and Denmark, where there seems to be no active anti-sexual censorship, as demonstrated by the open publication of the illustrated *Love's Picture Book,* by Brusendorff & Henningsen, in both English and Danish. As to the disappearance of the books, and therefore of the collectors, as L. Derome remarked consolingly in his *Le Luxe des Livres,* in the 1880's, in a closing essay well worth re-reading today, "S'il est vrai qu'il n'y aura bientôt plus des livres rares à recueillir" (this in the 1880's!), in reply to Paul Lacroix, the "Bibliophile Jacob's," dire and very correct predictions to this effect: 'Que son émotion se calme : quand il n'y en aura plus, il y en aura encore.' But . . . with what a difference!

In the opposite direction from the passage of the Morgan erotica from America back to Europe, there is also the case of the

Roederer erotica, now in the famous Kinsey collection at Indiana University. The story is told, in Wolf & Fleming's *Rosenbach: A Biography* (1960) pp. 166 and 585. The Roederer collection of rare books and art works, the treasure of a well-known champagne-producing family of Reims, had been packed hastily, during the German invasion and the shelling of the famous cathedral city in 1914, 'in empty barrels and champagne cases' and rushed to Paris, wholly without loss or damage to the fragile bindings and the rest. A few days later, 'during a bombardment, the château was hit, and the richly paneled room in which the library had been shelved was totally destroyed.' Left in storage for years, the whole Roederer collection was eventually bought, *en bloc,* for resale, by Rosenbach. As to its erotica, these did not reappear till almost the end of Rosenbach's career when,

> Poking around one day, Wolf [the author speaks] came upon two cases full of French pornography which had come with the Roederer collection and had been relegated to the Rosenbach inferno. Rosenbachs never had sold and would not sell pornography. But Wolf had an idea that he could get rid of it respectably . . . he wrote to the famous Dr. Alfred C. Kinsey . . . and offered the collection to him for his scientific library at Indiana University. Dr. Kinsey answered quite scornfully that, with a collection of sex books second only to that of the Vatican, he doubted if there were anything in the lot he did not already have . . .

Why bother with the rest of the quotation? The reference to the 'Vatican' collection tells the tale. In the end, however, and despite Prof. Kinsey's 'scornful' doubts, '$2250 from the royalties of *Sexual Behavior in the Human Male* went for several large cartons of rare French pornography.' Observe the 'several large cartons.' This suggests, and it is a fact, that the books involved were sold off extraordinarily cheaply by the dying Rosenbach, who never did care to deal in erotic books, of which the price-level has never been high enough to absorb the Rosenbach type of ruthless mark-up percentages.

Difficult as it was to make Prof. Kinsey see that he was getting incredible bargains right and left (I was his original bibliographer, and had a small hand in unearthing for him some of the early and basic treasures of his collection, including the now only-known copy of Swinburne's *Whippingham Papers;* the Wise copy, left to the British Museum, having disappeared), Kinsey's activity did have the effect not only of accumulating a very large basic collection, but also of alerting other university libraries in the United States to the possibility of collecting erotic books in a dignified and unashamed way. A few such libraries, mainly the greatest, have now rather diffidently begun. Unfortunately they are a little late to hope for the sort of bargains Kinsey got. Kinsey's great advantage was the ceding to him, owing to the wide publicity he purposely sought and achieved, of many private collections of erotic books, seldom at any high price, and often without any payment at all. Erotic books have a way of becoming an embarrassment to their owners, and Kinsey's willingness to *accept* the books was often all that was needed to bring some remarkable works into his net.

In Kenneth Anger's *Hollywood-Babylone* (Paris, 1959), p. 124, the rather typical example is given of the Hollywood director Josef von Sternberg, whose many films starring Marlene Dietrich were, as Anger puts it, 'pendant un lustre les plus insidieusement raffinées qu'ait jamais connues Hollywood,' who, no longer able to accept the arbitrary business-office interference with the movie work he took seriously, 'could find nothing else to do . . . but to close down his château in San Fernando Valley, sell (to Dr. Kinsey) his very complete erotic library, and pack his bags.' This is not quite correct. As far as his books were concerned, I can think of at least three dealers in California who would certainly have given Sternberg a much better price, and surely without half as much haggling as was Prof. Kinsey's wont. On the other hand, one is glad indeed that the books are now preserved in the comparative safety of a university library, and no longer subject to the usual perils of the book trade and private collecting, especially as regards books of this kind.

It should be observed that Kinsey's real activity has been generally misunderstood, owing to the cloud of statistical hokum and tendentiously 'weighted' population-samplings in which the propagandistic purpose of his first, and only influential work, on the 'Human Male' was disguised. The later and far more trustworthy volume on the 'Human Female,' in collaboration with an enlarged staff, was, unfortunately, nowhere near as successful, and has had no real influence. Kinsey's not-very-secret intention was to 're-spectabilize' homosexuality and certain sexual perversions, in the same way that Hirschfeld attempted to do the same thing in pre-Hitler Germany (where the 'Hirschfeld Law' finally allowed homosexuals to marry each other!) Kinsey did not hesitate to extrapolate his utterly inadequate and inconclusive samplings — mostly of Eastern U.S. white college boys, who do not, after all, comprise the

'Human Male' in its entirety — to the whole population of the
United States, not to say the world, in many of his specified cate-
gories several million times as large. This is pure propaganda,
and is ridiculously far from the mathematical or statistical science pretended. Kinsey's first sensational volume was roundly
damned by almost all the major statisticians in America, assembled
to examine his work, many of them far less prudish than Kinsey
ambivalently was. This naturally had no effect on the public,
which cannot be expected to concern itself with the journal reports of statistical congresses; and Kinsey's "Reports" were and are
accepted as a sort of abstruse mathematical gospel that 'validates,'
as normal human acts and states, the specific abnormality of homosexuality, and a whole theory of wildcat pansexuality of entirely
anti-social effect.

A curious circular of the Cercle du Livre Précieux in Paris —
which might be called the Erotica Book-of-the-Month Club of
France, and is affectionately known to some of its members as the
'Cercle (du Livre) Vicieux' — sent to subscribers to celebrate the
first day of Spring, 1963, announces the work of a purported
'Lausanne sexologist,' formerly of the 'Psychological Research
Center [?] de X. aux U.S.A.,' delivering himself of his lifelong
secret after forty-three years of enforced professional 'mendacity'
and silence, under the title Traité de l'Amour Physique; of which
the main import, in among the erotic postures imitated from Forberg's Manual of Classical Erotology, is simply a cheap and completely irresponsible rewording of the Kinseyist message or fantasy
that 'sexual perversions do not exist,' and that 'every person can
and should allow himself everything in the sexual field.' (The
similar ideas of the French jurist and propagandist, René Guyon,
are only too well known.) The whole presentation of this new message of sexual anarchy as that of a parody or mythical Kinsey of
an American 'Psychological Research Center' is perhaps its most
striking feature, and makes obvious what Kinsey's propaganda
actually meant to the public at large. It seems already rather clear
than Kinsey's real historical contribution of a constructive nature
will, in the end, prove simply to have been that of the first open
American collector of erotica. The manuscript collections of erotic
folklore in the library of the Kinsey Institute, and the similar collections in the folklore archives of the same Indiana University,
are likewise the most considerable in America, in an area of erotic
collection probably even more important than that of printed
books. My own folklore collections, which are perhaps equally
large, are willed to the same library.

The operation of the cultural law is well known, whereby books and art-treasures flow from countries of unstable and inflationary economy to 'hard-currency' countries, based on advancing economic production, such as England during the French Revolution, and the United States today. Not all European dealers, however, are blindly devoted to the principle humorously ascribed to the wine-tasters of France and Italy when they run into some particularly unpalatable mess: 'SEND IT TO AMERICA!' Certain dealers, in fact, out of pure *esprit de corps*, are very reluctant to sell rare books or art-work to public and university libraries and galleries in any country, in the realization that such works can never again return profitably into the book and art trades, at the collectors' death. Some of the best European dealers, who love and themselves often collect books (a dark secret!) are particularly reluctant to send important *illustrated* erotica, which are by far the most expensive and generally the most interesting, through the United States Customs, which have been notorious for nearly a century now for the destruction of such works, begining with the fabulous barbarity of destroying the erotic murals made by François Boucher for the French king's palace in the eighteenth century. Removed by a later French ruler's command: 'Make these indecencies disappear!' Boucher's mural paintings were *sent to America* (as above), but were seized on entering, and were burnt by the U.S. Customs. Fortunately, photographs had been taken before putting the murals on board. Several of these have thus been reproduced in the standard works on erotic art of Fuchs and of Karwath, and more recently by Brusendorff & Henningsen, in *Love's Picture Book*, I. 141–6.

It has been stated, and may very well be true, that Kinsey's own life was shortened by the continuing activities, in our own time, of the U.S. Customs; though it is probably not medically correct that he actually 'died of vexation' over the Customs' holding up for a number of years erotic materials sent to Kinsey's Institute for Sex Research from abroad. After protracted litigation these materials were finally liberated, by a decision of Judge Edmund L. Palmieri, of the U.S. Court, Southern District of New York, 31 October 1957. (Materials similarly seized from the private home of a Washington collector and student, Mr. Lawrence Gichner, were also eventually liberated, but on condition that they be willed to the Kinsey Institute.) 'The gist of the decision,' according to Alec Craig's *Banned Books* (1962) p. 153–4, 'was that the material, although unquestionably obscene were it in the hands of the general public, was not obscene in the hands of scientists . . . The Customs did not appeal and announced that they would base their future policy on the decision.' This may perhaps be true, and suggests a relative liberty — or at least a point of legal argument — for public institutions and libraries in the United States. However, it will take more than one judge's decision to make such liberty law.

The American private collectors, and public and university libraries, now slowly beginning their collecting of erotica, on Kinsey's lead, and very late in the day, cannot expect to find very much except by the *en-bloc* accession of earlier collectors' libraries. For the little they are able to find in booksellers' and auctioneers' catalogues (where the more erotic items are seldom publicly announced at all), they know they will have to pay high. The private collectors, except for the richest, will inevitably find themselves far outpriced, owing to the open avidity of certain of the biggest dealers, who have all the best books, for the coarse Hollywood sugar they imagine to be endlessly available on the 'American market.' It is to the interest of everyone in the book-collecting field, as it is to the interest of scholars and researchers in particular, that the gross cupidity of book- and art-dealers of this kind should not be allowed to empty the field, and at inflated prices, by setting all possible buyers to competing with one another.

If an object lesson is needed, the Wolf & Fleming biography, *Rosenbach,* already cited, is certainly all of that. I would not go so far as to suggest that librarians and collectors have not already examined this adulating business-biography of the principal American rare book dealer of the half-century, who 'created' the swashbuckling methods that other dealers have certainly no thought of abandoning. I would recommend, however, that collectors and librarians (especially those *not* mentioned therein) should study this work very carefully again, especially as to the system of prices paid — and demanded. It is a lesson for those who will take a lesson, if only from its stupefyingly candid details in cheerful profusion, such as that, p. 500, on the throwing of the great bookdealer's ex-mistress into the street with the aid of three policemen, and those, pp. 386 and 416, of Rosenbach's acquisition from one maiden lady, at a ludicrous price, of the rarissime *Bay Psalm Book;* and his giving another maiden lady in Massachusetts less than $20 for a copy of Harrison's *English and Low-Dutch School-Master,* assessed at $3000, which she had sent him on faith. Anybody can get rich that way. Nobody can get rich this way. *A bon entendeur, salut!*

II

THE REDISCOVERY OF BURNS' *MERRY MUSES OF CALEDONIA*

But deevil damn the lousy loun,
    Denies the bairn he got !
Or lea's the merry a--e he loe'd
    To wear a ragged coat !

      "WHA'LL MOW ME NOW?"

THE CUNNINGHAM MANUSCRIPT

I

Of ALL BURNS' editors, none has been so roundly damned as Allan Cunningham. And probably the worst of Cunningham's editorial crimes was the forging of insipid imitations of a number of Burns' songs, after originals in a manuscript to which he alone had access, for the second 'Aldine' edition of Burns' *Poetical Works*, edited by Sir Harris Nicolas, London, 1839, vol. II: pages 155–60, where they have lain for over a century and where every responsible editor since has let them lie.

Cunningham apologizes, *via* Nicolas, in the following terms for what he evidently felt was necessary to do: 'The following fragments occur in Burns' Common Place Book. Mr. Allan Cunningham says, "The Prose portion has been copied from Currie and from Cromek, with some slight additions, and the verses are from another source." He adds, "In several places small but necessary liberties have been taken with the language. It would have been unwise to omit verses so characteristic, and they would have offended many had they appeared as they stand in the original".' There follow rewritten and expurgated versions of "YE HAE LIEN A' WRANG, LASSIE," "O GIE MY LOVE BROSE, BROSE," "LASS, WHEN YOUR MITHER IS FRAE HAME," and ten other pieces. The first, and several others, have recently been printed from authentic texts in the latest, and by far the best edition of *The Merry Muses of Caledonia*, Edinburgh, 1959. A few more, such as "O CAN YE LABOUR LEA, YOUNG MAN" and "THERE CAM' A CADGER OUT O' FIFE," have always been available to other than the easily-offended many feared by Cunningham, in the various editions — there have been nearly thirty — of *The Merry Muses* since 1800, particularly as reprinted from the original edition, more or less incorrectly, in the five volumes of John S. Farmer's *Merry Songs and Ballads*, 1895–97, and in the Burns Federation edition of *The Merry Muses*, 1911, edited under the signature "Vindex" by Duncan McNaught.

Finally, certain of the *vers de circonstance,* epitaphs, and the like, which Cunningham falsified, are printed in Henley & Henderson's 'Centenary' edition of Burns' *Poetry,* 1896–97, which will remain the standard text until the announced new edition, as far as possible from Burns' own MSS., being prepared by Prof. James Kinsley for the Clarendon Press. As to the rest of the originals of Cunningham's forged texts, nothing has been known from that day to this, and the editors of the new *Merry Muses,* Prof. De Lancey Ferguson and Mr. Sydney Goodsir Smith, can refer only in a general way to the spoor left concerning them in the second 'Aldine' edition.

That the British Museum — *in æternum floreat!* — does catalogue its books, it would be idle to deny. (I am stealing a line here from Dorothy Sayers' *Gaudy Night.*) But that anyone, even members of the staff, can necessarily find any specific book in that catalogue is quite another matter. Being a combination of printed and pasted columns, it is not and cannot be kept in alphabetical order; it is often arranged, as to anonyma, under the most unexpected and occasionally infelicitous of words in the title (or English translations thereof), and — most astonishing of all — it is almost entirely without subject-index for books earlier than 1880. What serves even less well the requirements of certain research is that the catalogue of the Private Case, containing the Museum's erotica, is not available to the public (the same is true of the two largest public libraries in America), while part of it — the so-called S.S. collection — is not available even to the library staff. It is obvious that this is contrary to the interests of scholarship, and that the tenuous line between preserving books in a library and interring them in a museum is here being overstepped. That the fault lies, as much or more, in public prudery as in library policy, is equally clear.

It was only by the luckiest of accidents, therefore, in the spring of 1959 — four months after the publication of the Ferguson & Smith edition of the *Muses* — that I stumbled upon Cunningham's own manuscript copy of the original Burns songs here under discussion, where it has long been forgotten, in the British Museum, bound at the end of the only-known copy of an early edition of *The Merry Muses.* This edition is, in fact, the earliest under the abbreviated form of the title; the '*of Caledonia*' being dropped in respect of the presumably Hibernian origin of the work, which bears the imprint, 'Dublin: Printed for the Booksellers. Price Three Shillings.' It is a duodecimo of 126 pages, without date, but published — probably in Scotland — about 1820–25, as the typography and the MS. date '1826' on p. 128n demonstrate. This volume is pressmarked Private Case 31 e 20, and forms part of the superb collection of erotic books in all languages left to the British Museum by H. Spencer Ashbee at his death in 1900, and which, being indissolubly joined to his equally fine collection of editions of *Don Quixote,* the Museum did not feel justified in rejecting on moral grounds, and accessioned in 1915.

Facing the title-page is a worn sheet of paper, mounted, stating in a mid-19th century hand (not Ashbee's): 'This very pretious copy was given to me by Peter Cunningham, son of Allan Cunningham, the editor of Burns works, who has transcribed, from the original manuscript of the Scott's [sic] poet, the free songs at the end of this volume, songs which have never been printed, on account of their indecency.' Pasted to this is Ashbee's rebus book-label (of an ash-tree and bee) dated 1895. Aside from some marginal corrections and notes in the printed volume itself, which will be discussed later, and extended transcripts of Burns' *vers de circonstance* not necessary to print here as they have already been printed, with certain exceptions, by Henley & Henderson in the 'Centenary' edition, vol. II, the principal contents of the Cunningham MS. now follow, including his editorial remarks, which are, as is well known, sometimes colored by his imagination. NOTE: *Only the materials, in verse or prose, printed within double quotation-marks are to be understood as copied from Burns' own manuscripts.* Up to and including "WHIRLIE-WHA," the manuscript used is described thus by Cunningham, p. 140:

'These Songs were copied from a M.S. belonging to Mr. I. Gracie, on about 19th Oct. 1815. Those which follow were coll'd [?] from other sources. The M.S. above alluded to was presented to Mr. Gracie's father by Burns himself.'

The recipient of the original MS., 'Mr. Gracie's father,' was James Gracie, banker, of the village of Thornhill, about fourteen miles from Dumfries, where he was director of the Bank of Scotland's office, who died in 1814. To him the dying Burns had written on 13 July 1796: "I shall not need your kind offer, *this week* . . . God bless you!" (*Letters,* ed. Ferguson, 1931, II. 329), and their relationship will be discussed further at the end of the present essay. That such a manuscript might be presented to a friend or benefactor, at date unknown, is not out of keeping with Burns' habits in connection with his 'high-kilted' songs, both those he collected and, in particular, those he composed. See his letters, offering a sight of his collection and enclosing samples, to James Hoy, 6 Nov. 1787; to Robert Maxwell, 20 Dec. 1789; to Robert Cleghorn, Oct. 1793, and at other dates; to John M'Murdo, probably in February 1792 (*Letters*, 1931, II. 222, with an important correction announced in David Daiches' *Robert Burns*, N.Y. 1950, p. 311, and in *Modern Language Notes*, 1951, LXVI. 471–3); and especially the letter to George Thomson, 26 Jan. 1793, quoted later, promising a complete copy of the collection to Capt. Andrew Erskine.

It will not be lost sight of that Cunningham's 'about 19th Oct. 1815' means that the MS. copy he was making in the back of *The Merry Muses* in 1826 was itself simply a fair copy of materials he had transcribed from Burns' originals, in the possession of I. Gracie, some ten years earlier. The Cunningham MS. begins on a leaf numbered 127/8 which replaces the (blank?) final leaf L4 of the printed work. Of the first song transcribed, "DAINTY DAVIE," the text will be found in the new Ferguson & Smith edition of *The Merry Muses*, Edinburgh, 1959, p. 74, 92, except for Burns' introductory paragraph and the 4th stanza:

P. 127–8: 'The following songs by Burns are extracted from a manuscript in his own handwriting. From their extreme indelicacy perhaps and other causes unkown to the Transcriber they have never appeared in print.

'The Introduction to the following song is in the Poets happiest manner, and truly characteristic of his biting severity against Fanaticism.

"The following Song was composed on the Revd. Mr Williamson's being pursued by the dragoons in the reign of Charles II. He took refuge in the Laird of Cherrytrees' house. Lady Cherrytrees put the *man* of God in bed with her daughter a girl of 18 years of age to hide him from the Men of Sin. But alas! the man of God forgot the Dragoons; and the Evil One got the better of him so far as to tempt him to produce to the young girl his

DAINTY DAVIE
Chorus
Leeze me on his curlie pow [&c.]

3. . . . An' splash gade out his gravie. — *Leeze*

4. He laid my back against a stane
   An' mony a thump he gae my wame
   An' weel I wot he ca'd it hame
   For he was my dainty Davie. — *Leeze*

5. But had I gowd, or had I lan' [&c . . .]"

'The Cherrytrees here spoken of is in Galloway & the late George Maxwell senr. of Carruchan a perfect oracle in such matters of Traditionary story assured the present minister of Girthan (1826) that the above story was perfectly true in the leading particulars.'

The dated paragraph preceding is in a darker ink and smaller writing, but it follows on in the text and appears to be contemporary with it. Its date has therefore been taken as that of the entire Cunningham MS.

P. 129: "SONG. *Tune:* The Quakers wife." Begins, "Come rede me dame," as in *The Merry Muses,* ed. 1959, p. 46, but there without notice of the tune. Variants: stanza 1, last line, "Nine inch will sair a Lady." Stanza 3/2–3, "An may it ne'er ken thrivin' . . . that gars me loup."

P. 130: "I'LL KISS THE WIFE SHE BADE ME." Begins, "Had I the wyte" (ed. 1959, p. 59, 73). Variants: "silly coof" (*for* 'silly cow' in 1959), "deny't" (*for* 'deny'), "Her ports grew ay the wider" (*for* 'they grew').

P. 131: "SONG. *Tune:* My Mither's ay glowrin' o'er me." The older words to this tune will be found in Allan Ramsay's *Tea-Table Miscellany,* 1724–27, and David Herd's *Ancient and Modern Scottish Ballads,* 1769–76, II. 118. Begins, "Come cowe me" (ed. 1959, p. 40, "BONIE MARY"). Stanza 3 is not identical with the 1959 text, giving for the first two lines the repeated "An' wasna Watty a blinker [*bis*]," and omitting the varied second line of ed. 1959.

P. 132: "JENNY MCGRAW." Text identical with ed. 1959, p. 124, but with Cunningham's note (which more aptly refers to "GODLY GIRZIE"):

'Jenny seems to have thought very like the poor lass who was once assailed with the stiff temptation by a young man on their way home from a Dumfries fair. She resisted long: at length, overcome by her seducer's perseverance, and perhaps too by her own "treacherous inclinations," she took her Bible out of her pocket and laid it under her head saying, "ye may do what ye like wi' my sinfu' body but I give my soul to the Lord." — This is asserted to have been sworn to before the Kirk session of Tinwald.' (Compare the song on this same theme in *Bishop Percy's Folio MS., c.* 1620, "OFF A PURITANE," ed. 1867, IV. 35.)

P. 133: "THE TROGGER." Text identical with ed. 1959, p. 75, but with Cunningham's note that this was written by Burns on a wager with his friend, Mr. John Lewars of Dumfries:

'One time Burns and his friend Mr. Lewars were going along Daltonbank on their way to Ecclefechan [*the Wigan, or Podunk, of Scotland.* — G.L.] Lewars offered to lay a wager with the Poet that he could not get a word to clink with Ecclefechan: Burns instantly composed this song to shew he could.'

P. 134: "MUIRLAND MEG. *Tune:* Eppie McNab." (As in ed. 1959, p. 60) Variant: end of stanza 3, "can (*for* 'an') ye play a wee." Cunningham notes:

'This song was written on Meg Hog, "Monkery Meg" as she was generally called, who kept a Baudy house at the Sands of Dumfries — she died in 1811 or 1812. [*In a smaller hand:*] a vera honest woman.'

P. 135–6 give a text not known to have been printed until now:

"WANTON WILLIE YIR WAME RINS OUT
Tune: Bonny Muir hen

1. O wanton Willie yir wame rins out
   O wanton Willie &c. —
   But ye'll get a needle an' I'll get a clout
   To clap on the hole that yir wame rins out.

2. O wanton Willie yir wame rins out
   O wanton Willie &c. —
   I'll haud up my pitcher to kep the spout
   That naething be tint when yir wame rins out.

3. O wanton Willie yir wame rins out
   O wanton Willie &c. —
   Just gie me a hotch an' I'll turn about
   An' cannily kep whan yir wame rins out."

A version of stanza 1 has survived in the Kirriemuir district as a children's rhyme (*Miscellanea of the Rymour Club*, 1906, I. 222).

P. 136: "KEN YE NA OUR LASS BESS." (As in ed. 1959, p. 145.) — P. 136–8 then continue with one of the texts expurgated, or rather imitated, by Cunningham in the second 'Aldine' edition of 1839, and of which the original has not before been printed:

"WAT YE WHAT MY MINNIE DID

[*Tune:*] auld moulie Maidenhead

1. O wat ye what my minnie did
   My minnie did my minnie did
   O wat ye what my minnie did
   My minnie did to me jo.

2. She pat me in a dark room
   A dark room a dark room
   She pat me in a dark room
   A styme I couldna see jo.

3. An' there cam' in a lang man
   A meikle man a strang man
   An' there cam' in a lang man
   He might hae worried me jo.

4. For he pou'd out a lang thing
   A meikle thing a strang thing
   For he pou'd out a lang thing
   Just like a stannin' tree jo.

5. An' I had but a wee thing
   A little thing a wee thing
   An' I had but a wee thing
   Just like a needle e'e jo.

6. But an I had wanted that
   Had wanted that had wanted that
   But an I had wanted that
   He might hae sticket me jo.

7. For he shot in his lang thing
   His meikle thing his strang thing
   For he shot in his lang thing
   Into my needle e'e jo.

8. But had it no come out again
   Come out again come out again
   But had it no come out again
   It might hae stay't for me jo. — "

If a subjective judgment may be allowed, this one song, most clearly of all twelve of the then-unpublished songs in the Cunningham MS., seems to bear the unmistakable mark of composition, rather than just collection, by Burns. Aside from its charm, and artful simplicity, it is written *from the woman's point of view,* a frequent device of Burns' in the *Muses* songs (and others) of which his paternity is unquestioned, as a study of them with this in mind will show, and one in which he almost invariably reaches his greatest psychological depth. (The song "THE MEIKLE DE'IL DAMN THIS C--T O' MINE," to the tune "To Daunton Me," in the first reprint of *The Merry Muses*, under the title *The Giblet Pye, c.* 1806, p. 103, seems similarly ascribable to Burns.) The cock-crows of phallic brag, not only in the songs but most famously in the letter to Robert Ainslie, 3 March 1788 (printed in the much-corrupted '1827' [*i.e.* 1872] edition of *The Merry Muses* and all its reprints to 1930), have always the air of over-protesting his masculinity. Burns' greatness in what he wrote of women was — precisely as with Shakespeare and his 'articulate heroines' — his remarkable identification with women and with their emotions, which is one of the crucial elements in the poetic temperament and one reason why it has often been confused with mere homosexuality.

P. 138–9: "DUNCAN GRAY." (As in ed. 1959, p. 98.) — P. 139–40 continue with another hitherto-unpublished song, the last one copied by Cunningham from the Gracie MS. in 1815, as noted earlier, and falsified in the second 'Aldine' edition of 1839:

"WHIRLIE-WHA

1. The last braw wedding that I was at
    Was on a Hallow day
 An' there was meikle meikle fun
    An' there was meikle play
 The bells they rang the auld wives sang
    An' to the kirk went they a'
 The bride's to bed wi' the silly bridegroom
    To play wi' his whirlie-wha. —

2. First she turn't her back to him
    An' syne she turn't her wame
 Lang she leuk't for kin'ness
    But kin'ness she gat nane. —
 At length she's ta'en him in her arms
    Flung him again' the wa'
 Says lie ye there ye fumblin devil
    Ye've lost yir whirlie-wha. —

3. O wae light on my kith an' kin
    They've done me meikle (harm) ill,

>   They've married me to an auld man
>   Fou sair again my will
>   But I'll dress mysel in my ribbons sae green
>   Nae lassie will be sae braw
>   An I'll hire a bonny young lad o' my ain
>   To play wi' his whirlie-wha."

Another version of this song is given in Peter Buchan's MS. collection, *Secret Songs of Silence* (1832), preserved as Harvard MS. 25241.9*, p. 80–81, beginning: 'There was a bridal in our town, Upon a holy day,' and giving every evidence of folk transmission. This adds a further stanza, falling between lines 4–5 of stanza 3 above:

>   [3a.]   Had I been married to ony young man,
>   Though never a sark ava',
>   He'd lovingly squeese me in his arms,
>   And play'd wi' th's whirleywha.
>
>   Now a' the lasses o' our town,
>   They bear me muckle envy,
>   But gin their case was bad as mine,
>   Their cheeks woul'd never dry.

Buchan also gives the following note: 'This song was written by Mary Hay, daughter of one of the Earls of Errol, after she was married to General Scott, from whom she eloped for want of - - - - -.' If this ascription of authorship may be taken seriously, it explains, at least in this case, the feminine point of view this song shares with so many of the erotic songs collected or written by Burns. I take the occasion to add here a still further example, which has never before been printed, and as to Burns' authorship of which there can be no question, though the pretence of its being an *extempore* production was one of Burns' usual 'arts' in presenting his work. (In the same way Burns sprang "SCOTS WHA HAE WI' WALLACE BLED" on his friend, John Syme, after a walk in the rain in August 1793, as having been composed impromptu during the thunderstorm.) The following song appears in a manuscript collection, made contemporaneously with the Cunningham MS., by George R. Kinloch, the most trustworthy Scottish folksong collector after Herd. The Kinloch MS., *Burlesque and Jocular Songs* (dated Edinburgh, 1827–29, on p. 167 and 170n, with a satirical title-page parodying that of Wedderburn's *Book of Gude and*

Godlie Ballatis), is now preserved as Harvard MS. 25242.12. It was smuggled out of Scotland, along with Peter Buchan's similarly 'high-kilted' *Secret Songs of Silence* (the word is Scott's), by the indefatigable Macmath, for Prof. Child's ballad researches, and was deposited in the Harvard Library in 1880 — along with Buchan's later — where it has never been paid the attention by ballad scholars that it deserves. It was disinterred only recently by Dr. William Montgomerie, for his admirable *Bibliography of Scottish Ballad Manuscripts, 1730–1825* (Ph.D. thesis, University of Edinburgh, 1954, unpublished), with first-line index of MSS. to 1900 [*n.b.*], f. 325–469, where it is analyzed as 'Kinloch III.' The Kinloch MS. ends with two songs by Burns, "A WICKED SONG" (*i.e.* "THE PATRIARCH," a Bible travesty, printed in the new edition of the *Muses*, 1959, p. 67), and "A MASONIC SONG," which has lain forgotten in this manuscript for a century and a half.

According to Kinloch, p. 269, the 'two Songs of Burns were communicated . . . by Robert Pitcairn Esq. W.S. who received them from the friend of Burns to whom they were sent.' The second of these songs, which has never been printed before, is preceded by the following note:

'Burns was called on for a song at a Mason Lodge, and wrote the following extempore & Sang it. A friend asked for a copy next day, when he sent,

A MASONIC SONG
By Robert Burns.

It happened on a winter night
And early in the season
Some body said my bonny lad
Was gone to be a Mason.
Fal de ral &c.

I cryed and wailed but nought availed
He put a forward face on
And did avow that he was now
A free accepted Mason.

Still doubting if the fact was true
He gave me demonstration
For out he drew before my view
The Jewels of a Mason.

The Jewels all baith great and small
  I viewed with admiration
When he set his siege and drew his gage
  I wondered at my mason.

His compass stride he laid it wide
  I thought I guessed the reason
But his mallet shaft it put me daft
  I longed to be a Mason.

Good plumets strong he downward hung
  A noble jolly brace on
And off a slant his broacher sent
  And drove it like a mason.

But the tempered steel began to fail
  Too soft for the occasion
It melted plain he drove so keen
  My galant noble Mason.

So pleased was I to see him ply
  The tools of his vocation
I beg'd for once he would dispense
  And make a Maid a mason.

Then round and round in mystic ground
  He took the middle station
And with halting pace he reached the place
  Where I was made a mason.

Then more and more the light did pour
  With bright Illumination
But when the grip he did me slip
  I gloried in my mason.

What farther past is here lock fast
  I'm under obligation
But fill to him up to the brim
  Can make a maid a mason.'

If not a masterpiece, this not bad for extempory (?) *vers de circonstance,* with the additional difficulty of working in — as adepts will already have observed — all the terms of the Masonic mysteries. The stanzaic pattern, and doubtless the air to which it was sung, are those of "THE FREE MASON'S SONG" in Allan Ramsay's *Tea-Table Miscellany,* ed. 1740, vol. IV, from which most of the (purposely bad) rhymes on 'Mason' are also taken. More striking is the subjectively feminine point of view from which the song is written, which, as noted above, is one of the most frequent, and rather surprising, of Burns' mannerisms in his erotic songs (as in "JOHN ANDERSON MY JO") and in a number of his most famous poems.

II

As THE FIRST person I showed the Cunningham transcripts to, in England, bowled me over by remarking casually, 'Never occurred to me that Burns was *hormoseksh'l,* y'know,' I should make clear at once that this is exactly what is not meant. Many of the secret-society and adolescent initiation rites of ancient Britain, as of the rest of the world, involve homoerotic mummery of an unmistakable but perfectly factitious nature. This has recently been photographed in Alan Lomax's superb documentary film in color, *Hoss Hoss,* on the Padstow horse mummers, and in various photo-documentaries of transvestist voodo rites in Haiti, not to mention the transvestist Mummers' Parades of Philadelphia, New Orleans, and the American Legion conventions. At least one of the Scottish secret societies in the 18th century is known to have accentuated this to an astonishing degree. This was not the Masons, to which Burns belonged, but the Beggar's Benison Society of Anstruther, Fife, the secret benediction alluded to in whose name being given away in Capt. Francis Grose's *Classical Dictionary of the Vulgar Tongue,* 1785, at BENISON: 'May prick nor purse never fail you.' (There is an additional metaphor in 'purse,' alluding to the scrotum, which has been lost in recent times. In one of the whores' insults to the medical students in the Dublin Nighttown scene that concludes section II of James Joyce's *Ulysses,* Paris, 1922, the second element of this by-now proverbial alliterative is varied as 'all prick and no pence.') It will be recollected that Burns warned his fellow Scots, in "On Captain Grose's Peregrinations" (in the *Weekly Miscellany,* Glasgow, 1790, No. 37, signed 'Thomas A. Linn') that they had best hide their secrets from Grose, or 'faith, he'll prent it!' The *Records,* and especially the *Supplement to the Records,* p. 13–20, of the Beggar's Benison, privately printed in Anstruther, 1892, on the dissolution of the Society, make fantastic reading on the whole question of homoerotic rituals, which are at least as ancient as the Knights Templar, if not actually derived from the Druids, of whose resistance to early Christianity these secret societies are supposedly survivals.

As is well known, personal and literary excellence always attracts imitation: sometimes frankly, in the appropriation of style or subject, down to and including plain plagiarism; sometimes inversely, in a complex ritual of pretended admiration overlayered with animosity (or pretended animosity, shot through with jealousy and admiration), in the form of parody or pastiche, especially when the effort is made — as often as not — to pass off such parodies as the authentic work of the greater writer being imitated, whose name is then signed to the imitation with perfect insouciance. Since even the Bible, as we know it, is grossly larded with pious frauds of this kind, the existing text of the Old Testament being a late rescension by the prophet Ezra and his scribes (about 432 B.C.; see *Ezra*, vii; *Nehemiah*, viii; 2 *Maccabees*, ii), with the wholesale intrusion of bogus 'Elohistic' dietary rules and genealogies, intended to authenticate the dietary and family privileges of the priestly group; there is nothing surprising in the similar falsification of writings ascribed to authors not even presumably divine, or divinely inspired. Modern French poetry, as a striking example, is peppered with crude parodies, not a few of which have somehow found their way into the officially collected works of their victims, for instance Mallarmé (the erotic farce-parody, "Les Lèvres roses," beginning 'Une négresse par le démon secouée,' first published in the *Nouveau Parnasse Satyrique du XIXe Siècle*, Kistemaeckers' edition of 1881, p. 165; possibly the work of Albert Glatigny).

Burns has also not been spared this type of bespattering, not only by ambivalent admirers trying simply to equal (!) his poetic attainments, but by intrusive poetaster-biographers, attempting to 'clarify' the details of his private and sexual life by means of pretended poetic avowals signed with the poet's name. An early example of this peculiar striving is cited below, at P. 170 of the Cunningham MS., item beginning 'By all on high, adoring Mortals know,' an obvious fake dating from 1821, for which even Cunningham carefully disclaims any responsibility, and intended to pierce the mystery of Burns' relations with "Clarinda" by means of a presumably autobiographical ejaculation in verse. Another such item is that which follows, transcribed recently by a leading Scottish folklorist 'from a photo-stat (also very grubby) in the possession of Edinburgh characters — workers in R. McEwan's brewery — whom [he] met in the Crown Bar, Lothian St.,' in November 1962:

ODE TAE A PENIS
by Robert Burns

Puir wee soft and flabby penis,
A wheen o' pleasure ye hae gien us.
An hour or twa ago, puir thing,
Ye made my lassie's gled hert sing,
For ye struck oot sae firm and prood
An' put Jean Armour in the mood.

She doted with the love ye gied,
An' lost wi' glee her maidenheid.
But noo, puir thing, ye look sae sad,
You're no use noo tae Rabbie lad.

And as I slowly puff my pipe
You look just like some wrinkled tripe.
But still ye did a guid night's work;
Ye did your duty, and didnae shirk.
She lay there, gigg'lin wi' pleasure;
Lie doon, and rest — ye've earned your leisure.

You're wabbit oot, an' soft as butter —
But think hoo ye made Jeannie splatter.
Ye squirmed just like a tremblin' jelly,
As ye went scuddin' up her belly.

Her comely thighs, her arse sae braw
    Did answer nature's ca'.
Fu' prood Ah wis o' hard-worked penis:
O' coorse ye jerked there weel atween us;
Ye gied yer a' tae satisfy
The urgent need o' Jean and I.

But noo my bonnie Jean's gane hame
Tae hing her head in sorry shame.
Ye ken best whit ye did her wrang —
Ah kept ye in for far too lang,
An noo I'll hae tae wait an' see
If Jean will hae her pregnancy.

Oh weel, we a' maun tak oor chances,
Let's saunter doon tae Poosie Nansy's,
An' when I've had a dram or twa
I'll let you pish again' the wa'.
Ye'll maybe pardon my abuses
An' realize ye've ither uses.

The facetious intention is of course clear, from the opening rhyme on 'penis' (more usually with 'Venus' in this type of folk-humor), not to mention the rhyme on 'pregnancy,' and that — also traditional — on 'jelly' and 'belly.' The twentieth-century slang ellipsis, 'in the mood,' in line 6, sufficiently demonstrates the real date of composition; being connected with, if not simply derived from, the popular or music-hall song of the 1930's, "I'm in the Mood — for *Love*." What is offensive is the insistent naming of Burns' common-law wife, four times over, in this context: an ungallantry difficult to accept even in the quasi-homosexual good fellowship of bar-room bards. It is to be observed how, among these — as the *envoi* above pointedly expresses it — the urinary activity finally replaces the sexual (the Porter's soliloquy, in *Macbeth,* on nose-painting versus lechery), and no further relationship need be had with the anxiety-ridden sexual sphere, except through this kind of fictitious keyhole peeping on the sex lives of the great and famous, and other parent surrogates. Compare also the similar address by the folk-poet to his penis, "Poor Old Dick," in *Immortalia,* 1927, p. 84, ending almost identically in sentiment: 'Henceforth you'll be my pisser, And I'll love you just the same.' In brief, no judgment is really possible, as to the "ODE TAE A PENIS", 'by Robert Burns,' preceding, except that passed by Prof. Child on one of Peter Buchan's chapbook rewritings of a traditional ballad, "Young Waters" (*The English and Scottish Popular Ballads,* 1882–98, No. 94), namely that 'it is a counterfeit of the lowest description. Nevertheless it is given in an appendix; for much the same reason that thieves are photographed' — or bad pennies nailed to counters.

It is understood of course that it is not the theme itself that makes the ascription to Burns improbable. Though phallic praise, or self-praise, is an unusual theme for any non-impotent or non-homosexual male, this theme does have an authentic tradition in Scotland, and may be assumed to have a defensive value against the cruel and castratory Calvinist Protestant ideas of sexual sin dominant in that country since the Reformation, and flouted in Burns' "THE FORNICATOR'S COURT" (*Muses,* ed. 1959, p. 171, also known as "LIBEL SUMMONS" and "THE COURT OF EQUITY"); and "THE FORNICATOR" (ed. 1959, p. 52), of which the latter is the only authentic statement in verse by Burns as to his own sex life, and notably reserved in comparison to the parody "ODE" above. A much earlier Scottish poet, the Clanranald bard Alexander Mac-Donald ("Alasdair MacMhaighstir Alasdair"), who served as an officer in Prince Charles' army in 1745–6, published an authentic poem to a 'Bod' — the usual Gaelic word for the penis, and now become a common British slang term for a person or 'guy' — in his collected poems in Gaelic, about 1751, a volume burned by the common hangman at Edinburgh, not for its bawdy poetry but for its Jacobite politics. There is a copy of this rare work in the Library of the University of Edinburgh. The Gaelic text follows, with a translation prepared by the Scottish folksong specialist, Hamish Henderson, and other experts at the School of Scottish Studies, to whom I am indebted in very many ways:

MOLADH AIR DEAGH-BHOD

Tha ball-ratha sinte riut
A choisinn míle buaigh,
Sar-bhod iallach, accuineach.
Rinn-gheur, sgaiteach, cruaigh,
Milleach, feitheach, feadanach,
Laidir, seasbach, buan.
Beodha, treorach, togarrach,
Nach diultadh bog no cruaigh.

Translation: 'PRAISE OF A GOOD PRICK. A member of good fortune is appended to you, that won a thousand victories. A prime article, well-thonged, well-accoutred, sharp-pointed, cleaving, hard, oily, sinewy, well-channelled, strong, steadfast, enduring, lively, full of stamina, high-spirited, and that wouldn't refuse action (be refused), soft or hard.' — Alasdair MacMhaighstir Alasdair (Alexander MacDonald), *Ais-Eirigh na Sean Chanoin,* The Resurrection of the Old Language, 1751.

In the *Japanese Peasant Songs,* compiled by John F. Embree, Philadelphia: American Folklore Society, 1944 (*Memoirs,* vol. 38), a work suffering in its sexual songs — of which there are many — from letter-expurgation, for instance at p. 65; a ten-stanza counting song in praise of the singer's own penis is given, p. 38–9, in both Japanese text and translation, each stanza turning on a new and admiring adjective or aspect of the bepraised penis. But both the Gaelic and Japanese examples, however, are hardly to be compared with the astonishing synonymy in admiration of the gaint Gargantua's penis by his childhood nurses, in Rabelais' *Gargantua & Pantagruel,* Bk. i, ch. xi; and the even more remarkable thesaurus of praise by Panurge, of Friar John's *couillon,* in Bk.

III, ch. xxvi, proceeding to 164 admiring adjectives in the French text, these being increased to 278 in the English translation by that most fantastic of Scots, Sir Thomas Urquhart of Cromarty. To even the score, of course, two chapters later, in a perfect crossing or 'flyting,' Friar John replies with 150 insulting adjectives as to Panurge's *couillon;* increased to no less than 435 in Urquhart's translation, beginning: 'Speak, thou jaded cod, faded cod, mouldy cod, musty cod, paltry cod,' &c. The scholiastic notes to Ozell's revision of Urquhart's Rabelais state that these lists are an 'obscene parody of the Roman liturgies,' which would set the form back many centuries, and place it as a survival or reversal of ancient religious outpourings of praise, which also of course exist in the Jewish and other liturgies, sometimes even in alphabetical form (as in the *Psalms,* cxix) for mnemonic purposes.

The alliterative form, drawing from the Anglo-Saxon poetic use of this device in wholesale fashion, is recollected as late as the 1690's, in that wonderful but seldom-consulted folklore source, *Scotch Presbyterian Eloquence Display'd,* by Gilbert Crockat and John Monroe, ed. Rotterdam, 1738, p. 143–4: 'One Mr. James Webster was admir'd lately at my Lord Arbuthnot his zealous Patron's Table for this Grace before Meat: "Out of the boundless, bankless, brimless, bottomless, shoreless Ocean of thy Goodness, we are daily foddered, filled, feasted, fatted;" and half an Hour's Discourse to the same Purpose.' This 'half an Hour's Discourse' being left unfortunately unrecorded, the champion certainly remains Sir Thomas Urquhart, though naturally more in the evident line of the alliterative and scatological 'flytings' in insult of the earlier Scottish bards, in particular the great "Flyting betwixt Polwart and Montgomery," printed in James Watson's *Choice Collection of Comic and Serious Scots Poems,* Edinburgh, 1706–11 (repr. Glasgow, 1869) III. 1–32, which is overlooked — or perhaps simply not dared to reprint — in the various Anthologies "of Invective and Abuse" in modern times.

No authentic poem or song by Burns quite in this line exists, though there are passages of phallic relevance in "NINE INCH WILL PLEASE A LADY" and "THE MOWDIEWARK" (ed. 1959, pp. 46 and 144), old songs collected and in part probably rewritten by Burns. The one actual statement on the theme that we have from his pen — unquestionably the most remarkable pæan ever written in praise of the poet's own penis — is in his letter to Robert Ainslie, of March 3rd, 1788, a letter unfortunately omitted from all editions of Burns' *Letters,* even that of Prof. Ferguson (1931; as also from his unexpurgated *Selected Letters,* 1953, in which compare p. 331), probably owing to the irrecoverability of the holograph manuscript. It is of this letter that one of Burns' greatest editors, William Ernest Henley, observed: 'The original must be read, or the reader will never wholly understand what manner of man the writer was.' The text is known only through its fortunate preservation in the otherwise entirely worthless and Anglicized Hotten edition of *The Merry Muses* of 1872 (falsely predated '1827'), and all its reprints; likewise in the American piracy (Philadelphia, about 1930) of McNaught's Burns Federation edition of 1911, in which the editor's pseudonym, "Vindex," signed to the Introduction, p. xxix, is changed to "Editor." As all these editions have now been forever superseded by the Smith & Ferguson *Muses* of 1959 (presently being reprinted), in which the Ainslie letter is not included, though space was somehow found therein for the excruciating music-hall obscœnum of the 1790's "The Plenipotentiary," in sixteen 8-line stanzas — taken from the Hotten edition! — the text of this very remarkable letter may be welcome here.

To Mr. Robert Ainslie, W.S., Edinburgh,
Mauchline, March 3d, 1788.

My dear Friend —

I am just returned from Mr. Miller's farm. My old friend whom I took with me was highly pleased with the bargain, and advised me to accept of it. He is the most intelligent, sensible farmer in the country, and his advice has staggered me a good deal. I have the two plans before me. I shall endeavour to balance them to the best of my judgment and fix on the most eligible. On the whole, if I find Mr. Miller in the same favourable disposition as when I saw him last, I shall in all probability turn farmer.

I have been through sore tribulations and under much buffetting of the Wicked One since I came to this country. Jean [Armour], I found banished like a martyr-forlorn, destitute and friendless. All for the good old cause. I have reconciled her to her fate. I have reconciled her to her mother. I have taken her a room. I have taken her to my arms. I have given her a mahogany bed. I have given her a guinea, and I have f - - - - d her till she rejoiced with joy unspeakable and full of glory. But, as I always am on every occasion, I have been prudent and cautious to an astonishing degree. I have swore her privately and solemnly never to attempt any claim on me as a husband, even though anybody should persuade her she had such a claim (which she had not), neither during my life nor after my death. She did all this like a good girl, and I took the opportunity of some dry horse litter, and gave her such a thundering scalade that electrified the very marrow of her bones. Oh, what a peacemaker is a guid weel-willy p - - - le! It is the mediator, the guarantee, the umpire, the bond of union, the solemn league and covenant, the plenipotentiary, the Aaron's rod, the Jacob's staff, the prophet Elisha's pot of oil, the Ahasuerus' sceptre, the sword of mercy, the philosopher's stone, the horn of plenty, the Tree of Life between Man and Woman.

I shall be in Edinburgh the middle of next week. My farming ideas I shall keep private till I see. I got a letter from Clarinda yesterday, and she tells me she has got no letter of mine but one. Tell her that I wrote to her from Glasgow, from Kilmarnock, from Mauchline, and yesterday from Cumnoch, as I returned from Dumfries. Indeed she is the only person in Edinburgh I have written to till to-day. How are your soul and body putting up? A little like man and wife, I suppose.

Your faithful friend,
R. B.

III

THE MATERIALS with which the Cunningham MS. proceeds, following the transcripts made from Burns' originals given to Banker James Gracie, were, as Cunningham says, 'coll'd from other sources.' This might be *culled, collected,* or *collated.* It does not actually matter, as they have almost all been printed in Henley & Henderson's 'Centenary' edition of Burns' *Poetry,* 1896–97, either from their original broadside or other printings, as with "FY LET US A' TO KIRKCUDBRIGHT" (MS. p. 141–6; 'Centenary,' II. 193–7) and "THE FIVE CARLINS" (MS. p. 147–51; 'Centenary,' II. 177–81), or from sources such as the Glendriddell MSS. (Cunningham MS. p. 152–3, 163–71; 'Centenary,' II. 244–74.) A number of these were printed by Cunningham, in falsified form, in his edition of Burns' *Works,* London, 1834, as Henley & Henderson note.

Whatever his irresponsibility in print, Cunningham unquestionably copied honestly enough the texts in his manuscript. This is proved by the comparison of his *Merry Muses* songs with those also appearing in Ferguson & Smith's edition of 1959, and the *vers de circonstance* appearing in Henley & Henderson, from unexceptionable sources. In his notes, however, Cunningham plainly romances. For instance, at MS. p. 153–4:

'[ON] A REPORT OF THOS. PAINE'S DEATH

> All pale and ghastly Tommy Paine
> Last friday went to hell
> The devil took him by the hand
> Says Tommy art thou well?
> He put him in a furnace hot
> And on him barr'd the door
> Lord how the devils lap and leugh
> To hear the bougre roar. — '

To this Cunningham prefixes the gratuitous statement that Burns wrote these verses 'while doing duty on guard at the little weigh house under the mid-Steeple Dumfries as a Volunteer.' This is in his smaller and darker hand, and was perhaps a later inspiration.

Similarly, on "HOLY WILLIE'S PRAYER," he notes (MS. p. 155): 'Holy Willie's real name was William Hamilton [*pencil correction in another hand:* Fisher]. He was found drowned in a ditch by the roadside into which he had stumbled "in drink" on his way home from a Mauchline fair, in the year 1806 or –7. *Sic pereat Gulielmus sacer.*' Cunningham is evidently trying to make a good story of it, the confusion of Willies — Hamilton instead of Fisher? — possibly misleading him. He does not give the text of the poem : 'as it is already in print I think it unnecessary to copy it in here.' He does give the prose introduction to it (MS. p. 154), 'copied from a MS. in Burns' own hand-writing.' This differs materially from the introduction given by Henley & Henderson, II. 321.

"Holy Willie was an old bachelor farmer and ruling Elder in the parish of Mauchline. He was so noted for his spiritual endowments particularly a gift of prayer that it was thought by most of the old women of the parish that he had set the devil the world and the *flesh* at compleat defiance. But alas Holy Willie was still but a man; and a glass

of good liquor and a bonny lass had to him always ir-
resistible charms. The occassion of the following was [&c.,
much as in Henley & Henderson, ending:] . . . The Pres-
bytery of Ayr had just given the iniquitous sentence and a
Mr. Aitken who was Procurator for Mr Hamilton had just
given Holy Willie in particular as he was at that time Pres-
bytery Elder a compleat drubbing when Holy Willie gave
his godly indignation vent as follows.''

P. 156–7: Burns' letter to Provost Robert Maxwell, 20 Dec.
1789, identically as in the *Letters*, ed. Ferguson, I. 377–8. Prof.
Ferguson omits here 42 (of the 44) lines of "THE CASE OF CON-
SCIENCE," included in this letter, printing them later in *The Merry
Muses*, ed. 1959, p. 37–9. Cunningham also does not transcribe
the text of the song. He gives a footnote identifying the "Mr.
Jeffrey" referred to in the letter as 'The Revd. Mr Andrew Jeffrey
then minister of Lochmaben [*several words obliterated*],' and
refers to his marginal additions to the version of the song printed
at p. 38–9 of the copy of *The Merry Muses* in which his MS. is
bound. He has there renumbered the seven printed stanzas 1, 2,
4, 5, 8, 9, 10, to make room for stanzas numbered 3, 6, 7, 8, and
11, which he supplies marginally, thus presenting a text almost
identical (except for the word "dunt" for 'runt' in stz. 6) with
that printed in the edition of 1959, from Burns' manuscript of the
same letter.

In the same way, at p. 9 ff. of the printed volume, "POOR BODIES
DO NOTHING BUT M-W," Cunningham has filled in the letter-dis-
guised name, "*Brunswick*'s great prince," and adds marginally
one extra stanza, beginning "On poor Stanislaus auld Kate laid
her paws" (not 'claws'), evidently from one of Burns' letters, as
printed (giving 6 of the 8 stanzas) in the *Letters*, ed. 1931, II. 250,
and — even more courageously in a popular edition — from the
letter to George Thomson, July 1794, in *Selected Letters*, ed.
Ferguson, 1953, p. 331–2, with Thomson's marginal 'What a
pity this is not publishable.' This missing stanza had been first
printed in *The Merry Muses* of *c.* 1800, and was reprinted in the
twin editions of 'Glasgow' and 'Dublin . . . Price Four Shillings'
(both without date, but printed about 1830, and both of 107
pages, 24to, though from different settings of type), as an addendum, on p. 102; being restored to its proper place in the text
in the edition of London, 1843, of 162 pages 24to. (Ashbee's copies
of these editions are preserved in the British Museum, Private

Case 31 *h* 24, 25, and 26, the Glasgow and London editions being unique. There is a further copy of the 'Dublin . . . Four Shillings' edition in the Hornel Library, Castle-Douglas, Kirkcudbright, which also possesses a unique copy of the enlarged edition of Dublin, 1832. This is the only other important collection — with the Murison Burns Collection, Dunfermline — of editions of *The Merry Muses,* and both these collections also contain copies of the fine-paper reprint of the 1843 edition, made about 1880, of 108 pages, 8vo.) "POOR BODIES" is now printed from Burns' MS. in the new edition of the *Muses,* 1959, p. 43, with a hitherto-unknown continuation in the same meter, p. 45; and was earlier printed from the same MS. by Clement Shorter, in 1916, as a pamphlet limited to 25 copies, under the title *A Suppressed Ballad by Robert Burns.* (Copy in the collection of Mr. Freeman Bass, London.)

Few of Cunningham's other marginalia in his printed copy are of textual importance, but some of his fillings-in of words dash-expurgated as printed are curiously different from what the modern Sassenach reader might expect. He fills in, for instance, at "ERROCK BRAE," p. 25:

> Yet still his [*pillie*] held the grip
> An' still his [*stanes*] hang,

'stanes' evidently to be pronounced as two syllables. In "FOR A' THAT" (Put butter in my Donald's brose), p. 28, he gives:

> His [*Ballocks bags*], baith side an' wide . . .
> A [*pillie*] like a rollin'-pin.

It is not clear what MS. authority, if any, he had for these insertions, and these two are given here only on the possibility that they represent something other than Cunningham's own vocabulary. All his improvements of this kind are, in any case, put seriously in doubt by some obvious errors, as in "OUR JOHN'S BRAK YESTREEN," p. 57 (a Scottish version of a widely collected European folk-riddle), where he supplies what is clearly the wrong word, in stanza 1, line 4, if it is to rhyme with 'rocks' in line 2. On p. 121, however, he seems to have forgotten the same word, and fills in "THE BUMPER," a skit on erotic heraldry, with 'two rampant [*stones*] as supporters we fix.' This is too much for the unknown later owner, to whom Cunningham's son, Peter, gave this copy, who has asterisked the line and written marginally: '2 r. *Pricks* you sawny!'

Cunningham also adds a few moralistic ejaculations of horror ('Gross baudry,' p. 47; 'filthy,' p. 49; 'Abominable,' p. 69), which seem rather hypocritical in that he did not stop reading if he were so scandalized. Possibly he felt it was his duty to Burns to go on. McNaught seems similarly torn two ways in his *Burns Chronicle* articles of 1894 and 1911. Cunningham also makes certain critical, not to say folkloristic remarks on some of the printed songs in his copy, such as that already quoted on "JENNY MCGRAW," p. 132. On "LANGOLEE" he remarks, p. 65: 'This plant grows to such extent in Ireland that it is a commonly received opinion that there are occasionally two saplings to be found on one stem. The story of "Pit in the tither ane" is too gross & too familiar to require repetition.' Unfortunately for folktale studies, it is no longer familiar at all; no Scottish version of the implied bi-penis story has ever been recovered. Similarly, on the tale in verse, "THE CRICKET AND CRAB-LOUSE," p. 72 (not in any other edition of *The Merry Muses*), he remarks: 'There is wit in this piece, but it is all coined in the devils mint.' This too is a well-known folktale, being included in the *Russian Secret Tales* [of Aleksandr Afanasyev, printed in Geneva about 1872], of which a French translation appears in vol. I of *Kryptádia* (Heilbronn, 1883) No. 7, and p. 293, with important comparative notes in Italian in vol. IV. 192–252.

P. 159–63: "BUY BRAW TROGGIN. *Tune:* Buy broom besoms." Begins, 'Wha will buy my Troggin, Fine Election Ware,' 12 stanzas and chorus. This is an extended political squib 'on a contested Election for the Stewartry of Kirkcudbright,' according to Cunningham. Under the title "BALLAD FOURTH : THE TROGGER," it is printed in Henley & Henderson's 'Centenary' edition, II. 201, among the ballads on Mr. Heron's election, 1795.

P. 163–5: "EPISTLE FROM ÆSOPUS TO MARIA." Cunningham states that Æsopus was 'Mr. Williamson the Player. He was Manager of the Dumfries Theatre for a considerable time. Miss Fontenelle was his first Actress & mistress.' Henley & Henderson, II. 66, 353, simply reproduce Cunningham's printed version of 1834, as they were unable to find any MS. text. Both printed versions omit the 3rd and 4th lines of the following excerpt from the MS.:

'What scandal called Maria's jaunty stagger
The ricket reeling of a crooked swagger?
What slander fram'd her seeming want of art
The flimsy wrapper of a rotten heart
Whose spleen even worse than Burns' venom [&c.]'

P. 170: A six-line effusion beginning, 'By all on high, adoring Mortals know!' with the rather hedging note by Cunningham: 'The following lines supposed to be by Burns are believed to have been written by him to Clarinda (*alioquin* Mrs McLehoise).' He adds: 'These Lines were handed about at the Anniversary Dinner in memory of Burns held at Dumfries, I believe, on the 25th January 1821, and were believed by all but particularly by Mr. Lewars the quondam friend and crony of the Poet, who was present, to be the genuine productions of the Poet.' To the contrary, they are a self-evident fake, possibly by Mr. Lewars himself, whose poetic interests have been noted earlier, at MS. p. 133, concerning the rhyme for Ecclefechan. The intention is clearly to prove something or other about Burns' private life, as the two last lines of doggerel show: 'Even shouldst thou, false, forswear the guilty tie, Thine and thine only, I must live and die.'

P. 171–3: Three *vers de circonstance*, apparently not printed in the 'Centenary' edition, as follows: "OLD THOMAS KIRKPATRICK BLACKSMITH" (begins, 'Amang a heap o' useless matters'). "ON ALEXANDER RICHMOND" (begins, 'Lord remember Singin' Sannock'). "THE POET BEING INVITED BY MR. F. SHORTT . . . TO DINNER" (begins, 'The King's most humble servant I'). These should be of interest to future editors of Burns.

P. 172–3: Two *vers de circonstance* which have not been printed before:

'ON COLONEL DEPEYSTER's giving the word half cock firelock, on a dull night of the Royal Dumfries Volunteers; before a splendid assemblage of Ladies.

Half cock says the Colonel
Brave Volunteers all
Full cock says the Ladies
Or nothing at all.'

'IMPROMPTU & REPROOF

'The Poet being one day at dinner with a number of Gentlemen at Terrawghtie near Dumfries felt much annoyed by a Gentleman present who was constantly dinning in their ears the name of some great man with whom he had lately dined or supt. The Poet's patience was at length fairly worn out when eying the Gasconader with a glance of withering contempt he bestowed upon him the following Poetic floorer:

O' Lordling acquaintance ne'er boast
Nor Duke that ye dined wi' yestreen
A Crab Louse is still but a Crab
Tho' perch'd on the Cunt o' a Queen.

The late James McClure Letter Carrier in Dumfries who was waiting on the Company & heard the above repeated it to Mr McRoberts the Schoolmaster who told it me.' The manuscript ends here.

IV

THE IMPORTANCE of the Cunningham MS. is not only in the four or five new texts by Burns that it uniquely presents, but also the offering in it of manuscript authority — even though at second hand — for the attribution to Burns of eleven songs that had appeared in the first edition of the *Merry Muses of Caledonia, c.* 1800, but of which more than half have never before been noted as Burns's, except by Cunningham himself, in the second Aldine edition of 1839, II. 155–59. There, however, he was reduced to printing forged openings and imitations of these songs, in obeisance to the wave of public prudery that engulphed England after the Regency, and stayed for a century. The new edition of *The Merry Muses* makes its only really serious mistake in referring repeatedly to Cunningham's forgeries of 1839 as 'Burns's fragmentary songs' (ed. 1959, p. 106, 110, 121–24), a *suggestio falsi* important to correct, as the forgeries are riotously bad, and have been rejected by all other editors of Burns without exception since 1839, especially by Henley & Henderson. What is even worse, the new editors of 1959 are led backwards from their first error to a second, and allege that the relevant songs printed in *The Merry Muses* are thus the 'originals,' presumably folk, of hypothetical Burns songs — *i.e.* of Cunningham's fakes! The real songs are accordingly grouped in Section III among "Old Songs Used by Burns for Polite Versions." Far from being 'old songs,' or 'folk originals' of Burns fragments, these texts in the *Muses* are almost indubitably original songs by Burns. As David Herd says, in his crusty way (B.M. Additional MS, 22,312, f. 74*v*), of Pinkerton's assimilating the younger poet Pennecuik to an earlier poet of the same name, "Tis pity the World were not undeceiv'd as to this matter, for Pinkerton has totally nail'd him in the head.'

The eleven *Muses* songs that may now, for the first time, be

certainly ascribed to Burns, on the authority of the Cunningham
MS., are the following. (The songs marked with an asterisk have
already been ascribed to Burns by earlier editors, in particular by
Scott Douglas, Henley & Henderson, and Hans Hecht, but on
subjective criteria only, which does honor to their flair for Burns.)
"COMIN' O'ER THE HILLS O' COUPAR", "DAINTY DAVIE" (ed. 1959, p.
74),* "DUNCAN GRAY",* "HAD I THE WYTE" (ed. 1959, p. 73),*
"JENNY MCGRAW", "KEN YE NA OUR LASS BESS", "O CAN YE LABOUR
LEA" (Aldine ed., II. 158, not noted in ed. 1959, p. 121), "THE
TROGGER",* "THERE CAM A CADGER", "WAD YE DO THAT," and "YE
HAE LIEN WRANG, LASSIE." To these should also be added "THE
PATRIARCH" (Kinloch MS., Harvard 25242.12, p. 263, entitled "A
WICKED SONG"),* of which Burns' original MS. was in existence as
late as the 1870's, when Scott Douglas examined it.

It will be observed that several of these attributions are not
made in the Cunningham MS. itself, but only in the group of forgeries supplied by Cunningham to the second Aldine edition in
1839. The MS. prototypes of these particular songs he apparently
did not transcribe into his copy of the *c.* 1825 edition of *The Merry
Muses* because they were already printed there. In two cases, as has
been shown, "POOR BODIES DO NAETHING BUT MOW" and "THE CASE
OF CONSCIENCE," he made corrections, and added six missing stanzas
from the original MS., in the margins of his printed copy, p. 10,
38–9. In the other cases it is a fair presumption that the printed
version was sufficiently exact, by comparison to his MS. prototype,
to be allowed to stand without correction. These are : "COMIN' O'ER
THE HILLS O' COUPAR" (*c.* 1825, p. 40), "O CAN YE LABOUR LEA" (p.
56), "THERE CAM A CADGER" (p. 60), "YE HAE LIEN WRANG, LASSIE"
(p. 36), and "WAD YE DO THAT" (p. 27), the opening of the last
being falsified in the Aldine edition, II. 156, from "Gudewife,
when your gudeman's frae hame," to 'Lass, when your mither is
frae hame,' which is a nice example of Cunningham's sly method
of misdirection. In all the others, the opening words are respected
even in the forgeries. Of one further song, "BROSE AND BUTTER" (*c.*
1825, p. 41), a manuscript in Burns' holograph is still extant, as
published in the new edition of *The Merry Muses*, 1959, p. 55,
thus making unnecessary any recourse to Cunningham's authority
for the text, though his troubling to forge an imitation of it, for
an edition of Burns' *Poetical Works* ('Aldine,' II. 155), makes its
folk origin, alleged by Prof. Ferguson, open to doubt.

The watertight division of editorial responsibility, in the new
1959 edition, between Prof. Ferguson for texts from Burns' holo

graph MSS., and Mr. Sydney Goodsir Smith (in collaboration with the late James Barke) for texts from print, has resulted — perhaps accidentally — in the playing down, and in one case the complete omission, of songs apparently first attributed to Burns by Scott Douglas in the margins of his unique copy of the first edition of c. 1800. The omitted song is "A LITTLE BLACK THING," margin of p. 122 (see the complete photostat of Lord Rosebery's unique copy, in the National Library of Scotland, at Edinburgh), to the same air, and on the same trick of spelling out its erotic words, as "MY GIRL SHE'S AIRY," now printed in the edition of 1959, p. 53, from Burns' holograph MS. Twelve of the sixteen songs attributed in whole or in part to Burns in the new edition, p. 65–84, are so attributed primarily on the authority of Scott Douglas' marginalia. That Henley & Henderson agree with him, in their 'Centenary' edition of 1897, is not — though set first each time — independent opinion, as Henley was supplied about 1893 with a MS. transcript by J. C. Ewing (see the second transcript made at the same time by Ewing, now preserved in the Murison Burns Collection, Dunfermline) of Scott Douglas' printed copy of the original *Merry Muses,* including all his marginal attributions, with a view to the preparation of a new edition that did not, however, appear in that form. It later appeared, almost complete, in the five volumes of *Merry Songs and Ballads,* 1895–97, edited by John S. Farmer, who was collaborating simultaneously with Henley on the equally unexpurgated *Slang and Its Analogues,* 1890–1909, in seven volumes.

It is worth observing that Scott Douglas' attributions often sound like those of a person who, as the saying goes, *knows something,* though he does not always document the source of his knowledge. It seems almost impossible that he was trusting solely to subjective or stylistic impressions. In one case (the introduction to "THE PATRIARCH") he states specifically that he was transcribing from Burns' 'original MS. possessed by Mr Roberts, Town-Clerk of Forfar,' a manuscript now lost. In other cases one is forced to conclude that he had available to him further texts in Burns' holograph that have also been lost or destroyed since. When, for instance, he pinpoints a single stanza of "BLYTH WILL AN' BESSIE'S WEDDING" (ed. 1959, p. 131, a song having much in common with the modern classic, "THE BALL O' KIRRIEMUIR"), the stanza beginning 'When e'enin' cam the town was thrang,' and pencils shortly by it, 'Burns's addendum;' or, in "ELLIBANKS" (ed. 1959, facsimile at p. 14, centre line in pencil), 'This is Burns's addition,' he is apparently drawing on something more than just intuition or internal evidence, but there is now no knowing what. In the same way, when he gives (original edition, p. 21, at the end of "THE PATRIARCH") a variant stanza of "HE TILL'T," not mentioned in the new edition, p. 156 :

> He till't and she till't, and a' to mak a laddie o't,
> The auld beld carl, Fell owre into the noddin' o't;

it is hard to agree with Mr. Smith, p. 28, that such variants are simply to be dismissed as the 'carryings-on' of an 'amateur versifier . . . playing himself.'

Prof. Ferguson's tendency, in the new edition, to call everything 'folk' that cannot be proved by extant MSS. to be by Burns, is really only a way of avoiding coming to grips with the problem of the texts, since Burns rewrote almost every folksong he ever collected, erotic or not. Prof. Ferguson has, in fact, shifted ground considerably, in the extreme conservativeness of his attributions in the new edition of 1959, from the position he announced in "Burns and *The Merry Muses*," in *Modern Language Notes*, 1951, LXVI. 473, where he observed that the exposure of the famous 'A very few of them are my own' in Burns' letter, probably of February 1792, to John M'Murdo (*Letters*, 1931, II. 222, redated), as a bumptious interpolation by Dr. James Currie, who first published this letter, makes it

> reasonable to infer that [Burns'] practice with bawdy songs was precisely the same as his practice with more decorous ones: when he had only traditional fragments to work with, he added lines and stanzas of his own which were consonant with the fragments. The student must therefore scrutinize with new alertness every bawdy lyric which survives in the poet's handwriting, or which contemporary opinion attributed to him. The pious defenders of the Burns legend can no longer brush these compositions aside as mere transcripts of folk songs. The burden of proof is shifted: unless the defenders can show that a given song was already known in Burns's day, we must assume that he wrote it.

In a surprising about-face, this is the exact opposite of the principle on which Prof. Ferguson has now edited his share of *The Merry Muses*, where, even when Burns' holograph MSS. still exist — as in the case of "BROSE AND BUTTER," and half a dozen others — he prefers to fall back on hypothetical folk origins, on no known evidence, calling Burns' MS. texts 'folksongs,' a 'recension [*n.b.*] of an old Scots song', 'an old song' (p. 60, on Duncan McNaught's undocumented authority, of which he complains, however, at p. 12), and twice 'probably traditional;' though only in the single case of "GREEN SLEEVES" can he himself show — as he requires above — 'that [the] given song was already well known in Burns's day.'

Prof. Ferguson divides the songs from Burns' MSS., insofar as these are still extant, into songs *by* Burns and songs simply collected by Burns, p. 55–62, but he does not anywhere indicate how the distinction was made. Apparently, those songs were grouped first, as indisputably *by* Burns, of which Burns himself had said so in the accompanying letters of transmission, and the rest, as follows, were lumped together after : "BROSE AND BUTTER", "AS I LOOKED O'ER YON CASTLE WA' " (under the variant title, "CUMNOCK PSALMS," given it by Burns), "GREEN GROW THE RASHES O" (the admitted 'recension,' p. 59, beginning "In sober hours I am a priest," not identical with the complete revision, p. 81, beginning 'O wat ye ought o' fisher Meg'), "MUIRLAND MEG", "TODLEN HAME" (which Burns states to have been written "By the late Mr McCulloch, of Ardwell — Galloway"), "WAP AND ROW", "THERE CAM A SOGER", "SING, UP WI'T, AILY" (p. 63, a stanza not present in the folk-version given by Herd, II. 121), and "GREEN SLEEVES."

Of only two of these, "CUMNOCK PSALMS" and "THERE CAM A SOGER" (*i.e.* "THE REELS O' BOGIE," given complete at p. 127 from the so-called '1827' [1872] edition, 'a very corrupt and anglicized text'), do Burns' letters actually say that they are "old," which does not by any means read out the possibility of his having rewritten them a bit, in accordance with his usual practice described above. "CUMNOCK PSALMS" in particular seems to bear the marks of Burns' rewriting, especially at the end. The original "REELS O' BOGIE" is printed from a much older MS. in James Maidment's *Ane Pleasant Garland,* 1835, as "CALD KAILL OF ABERDENE" (reprinted in John S. Farmer's *Merry Songs and Ballads,* 1895–97, V. 265), and shows striking differences, which are, however, possibly due to folk transmission. Only one single text in this group is, in fact, unmistakably from oral collection, "WAP AND ROW," which is accompanied in Burns' MS. by two bawdy phraseological memoranda, collected, according to his note, ed. 1959, p. 62, from one Tibbie Nairn and "a beggar woman in the Merse." Finally, in the case of two other of these songs, "BROSE AND BUTTER" and "MUIRLAND MEG," the Cunningham MS. offers new evidence that these texts are of Burns' own composition.

As his association with this first really scholarly edition of *The*

Merry Muses shows (McNaught's pseudonymous edition, [Kilmarnock : D. Brown & Co.] 1911, for the Burns Federation, is not textually to be trusted), Prof. Ferguson certainly cannot be suspected either of prudery or of any desire to purge the canon of Burns. What is so surprising about his unexpected recourse, now, to these 'folksong' attributions is not only that it flies in the face of his 1951 avaunt to precisely such attributions by the 'pious defenders of the Burns legend,' but that — utterly without reference to the folksong literature presumed to exist, but which does not exist — it contradicts so flatly the plain palæographic evidence of the Burns MSS., on which he is, with Prof. James Kinsley, editor of the forthcoming edition of Burns' poems for the Clarendon Press, the world's greatest authority. Even so, this is a good deal better than what was attempted in Dr. Robert D. Thornton's so-called 'scatological thesis' (Ph.D., Harvard), *Studies in Robert Burns and Scots Song*, 1949, in which Dr. Thornton — now author of *The Tuneful Flame: Songs of Robert Burns as he sang them* (University of Kansas, 74 pp.) — sets out to demonstrate that practically *none* of the bawdy songs that have been attributed to Burns are really his. This is a new and popular type of subjective criticism that has already been sweepingly applied by recent editors, and even more inappropriately, to such unlikely poets as the Earl of Rochester; whereby, after a sufficient exposure of the critic to the bawdy verses ascribed to his author — with special subventions for trips to Cambridge, Scotland, etc., to see even more such verses in MS. and rare print — they all turn out to be by someone else, or 'folk.' On subjective criteria, new and personal to the critic of course.

v

CUNNINGHAM's unique copy of the edition of *c.* 1825, into the back and margins of which he was transcribing from the MS. collection transmitted to James Gracie by Burns, is itself only a partial reprint of the original edition of the *Merry Muses of Caledonia, c.* 1800, and reprints only forty-five of the original's eighty-five songs (plus exactly the same number of new songs interpolated as were dropped). In a way it is unfortunate that it reprints *so many* as forty-five, for if it had contained less, Cunningham would perhaps have copied more MS. texts into it, to complete it, from the MS. collection made available to him by I. Gracie in 1815 — assuming, of course, that this contained more than the total of twenty-one songs apparently present. These are: the twelve transcribed by Cunningham (including three songs otherwise unknown), two which he perfected marginally in his printed copy, and seven others also in the printed copy and of which he forged imitations for the 'Aldine' edition along with the rest. Whether these twenty-one were all that the Gracie collection contained, or whether there were more, we shall never actually know unless Burns' MS. itself should be found, perhaps among the descendants of the Gracie family in Scotland or America, where the old Gracie Mansion is still the mayoral residence of the city of New York. The recent novel by Eric Linklater, *The Merry Muse,* apparently inspired by the new Edinburgh edition, takes off journalistically from the idea of the original MS. being miraculously found, stolen, recovered, disappearing again, etc. Unfortunately it is not so easy as all that. The only members of the Dumfries branch of the Gracie family that I have been able to find are Senhor Samuel de Souza Leão Gracie, of Botafogo, Rio de Janeiro, Brazilian Ambassador to the Court of St. James in 1952–55; and James Gracie Maddan, Esq:, formerly of West Malling, Kent. Mr. Maddan has many of the family documents, including the family Bible, but neither of these gentlemen possesses or knows anything of the whereabouts of the Burns MS. No contact has been made with the New York Gracie family, nor it is certain that this is of the Dumfries branch. It must also be borne in mind that many of Burns' erotic song MSS. are known positively to have been destroyed, in particular an important group — *possibly this very manuscript* — of which Scott Douglas records that a 'bonfire' was made, 'on broad moral ground,' by a Mr. Greenshields of Lesmahago. ('Kilmarnock' ed. 1871, II. 417.) The erotic MSS. of the modern poet, Pierre Louÿs, were saved only by a miracle from similar destruction in recent times, by the intervention of a shady bookseller, 'Dr.' Edmond Bernard, and many of them have been privately printed since the poet's death.

In attempting to reconstruct theoretically the Gracie MS. collection of Burns' *Merry Muses,* there are some basic mathematical considerations that must not be lost sight of. The fact that Cunningham did *not* transcribe into the back of his copy of the *c.* 1825 edition any of the many further songs appearing in the original edition, but not reprinted in that of *c.* 1825, seems to prove that they simply were not present in his prototype MS. The maximum possible contents of the Gracie collection could therefore have extended only to the forty-five *Muses* songs reprinted in the edition of *c.* 1825, plus the twelve not appearing there and transcribed by Cunningham. (These twelve include the three new songs, "WANTON WILLIE", "WAT YE WHAT MY MINNIE DID," and "WHIRLIE WHA," now printed for the first time in the present article, their titles — probably for no particular reason — all beginning with the letter w.) As twenty-one of this total of fifty-seven possible songs are accounted for in Cunningham's MS. as it now exists, and by the 'Aldine' edition forgeries, the maximum further contents of the prototype MS. in Burns' holograph could have been only thirty-six songs. This is all hypothetical of course. But, stated in this way, it shows that the Gracie MS. could not have been — even at its hypothetical maximum — and must not be construed as, the printer's 'copy' for the first edition of the *Merry Muses of Caledonia, c.* 1800, which, in any case, omits the three new songs.

This again tends to contradict the tradition, first circulated by Scott Douglas in 1877 (in his 'Library' edition of Burns, II. 47) in describing his unique copy, that the first edition of the *Merry Muses of Caledonia* was printed at Dumfries, simply because Burns died there. I suggest, below, that it was more likely published at Edinburgh, by the bookseller Peter Hill, who appears to have had access to a complete copy of the collection made in 1793. As a matter of fact, all that is certainly known about the first edition is that it has always been extraordinarily rare. Wordsworth has been quoted by Scott Douglas, in the appendix to J. Gibson Lockhart's *Life of Burns,* 1882, as to the 'utmost difficulty' already experienced in procuring even 'a slight perusal of the abominable pamphlet' in 1816 — ten years before Cunningham had to satisfy himself with correcting and completing a copy of the then-current edition of *c.* 1825. From a marginal note Cunningham makes in this copy, on p. 103, referring to one of the new songs in it, "THE MARRIAGE MORN": 'This is an English song, and to the best of my recollection was not in the older copies,' it is evident that he knew the original edition only by 'recollection' and did not have it open before him for collation of its contents.

For what it may be worth, the title-page of the first edition states only, very modestly, that the text had been 'selected for use of' — and therefore presumably by — 'the Crochallan Fencibles,' a convivial club *in Edinburgh.* The wording is peculiar, and seems to imply a much larger MS. collection than the eighty-five songs actually printed; but title-page puff need never be taken seriously and especially not in the 18th century, early or late. (The second edition, under the title *The Giblet Pye, c.* 1806 avers only that

'Some of' its songs 'are taken from the Original Manuscripts of R. Burns, never before published.' Whether the manuscripts were 'Original' or simply copies, the last half of the statement is certainly true, since this edition first prints a version of "FOR A' THAT," called "THE BONNIEST LASS" in ed. 1959, p. 69, which all critics agree is unquestionably by Burns, and which is, in that case, the closest he ever came to an apology or *tu quoque* for his erotic songs, in the pænultimate chorus on King Solomon: 'The smuttiest sang that e'er was sung, his Sang o' Sangs is a' that.' This edition of *c.* 1806 also first prints another very remarkable song, "THE MEIKLE DE'IL DAMN THIS C--T O' MINE," to the air "To Daunton Me," which I believe could be attributed to Burns on any criteria.)

Whoever the 'Crochallan Fencibles' editor of *c.* 1800 may have been, and whether or not he reduced the number of songs in the 'selecting' (omitting, perhaps, the three new songs now first printed?) it is easily within the limits of possibility that he could have added thirty newly-collected songs, partly folksongs and partly Burns originals from letters to Crochallan club members and others — for instance "COME COWE ME, MINNIE" and "ACT SEDERUNT O' THE SESSION" (ed. 1959, p. 40–42), both sent to Robert Cleghorn on 25 October 1793, and both printed in the original edition — thus bringing the hypothetical fifty-seven songs in Burns' collection (the figure arrived at in connection with the Gracie-Cunningham MS.) to the total of eighty-five songs and two variants in the printed edition. Burns' originals would, in any case, have been harder to obtain — though the *c.* 1806 editor managed it later — than collecting the supplementary folksongs. The amount of erotic folksong still circulating in Scotland, one hundred and sixty years later, is truly remarkable. As a case in point, a single amateur collector (not himself a Scot) was recently able to collect 'orally' over fifty erotic folksongs — including several of the *Muses* songs in folk transmission — in a single shire of Scotland and in only a few weeks' time; while a Scottish specialist, armed with a tape-recorder, was able to record almost half this number in the same locality, in a *single night,* on one 'roch reel.' (Both these collections will be printed in my own very large compilation, *The Ballad, Unexpurgated,* now being prepared for publication after twenty-five years of collecting.)

It would be difficult to say who the *c.* 1800 editor, and possible enlarger, of the Burns MS. collection might have been, though not beyond all conjecture. The only Scottish collectors of unexpurgated folksong anywhere near that period were David Herd, slightly before, and Kinloch, Buchan, Kirkpatrick Sharpe, and Maidment, two decades after. None of their periods of activity jibes correctly, and none of them was connected in any way with Burns, not even Herd, though one of the semi-erotic pieces in Herd's MSS. (I. 118, 233; and II. 71), "THE LINKIN' LADDIE," a two-stanza fragment of Child Ballad No. 241, "THE BARON O' LEYS" (Child, IV. 355), appears in Johnson's *Scots Musical Museum*, 1790, No. 237 (III. 246), having probably been made accessible to Burns — the real editor of the Museum, as is well known — by Stephen Clarke, the musical editor of the series, who was in contact with Herd. The same fragment appears verbatim in the original edition of the *Merry Muses* (ed. 1959, p. 152), and the appearance of this identical piece from the Herd MSS. in both the *Musical Museum* and the *Merry Muses* (as also "WAP AND ROW," *Muses*, ed. 1959, p. 62; *Musical Museum*, No. 457) is one of the strongest real links connecting Burns' own MSS. and the original edition of the *Muses*. It is also to be noted that no other known editor of Scottish folksong — and certainly not Herd — left erotic materials of anything like the graphic explicitness of those of Burns.

Prof. Ferguson makes a number of nominations as to the possible Crochallan editor, in the new edition of *The Merry Muses*, 1959, p. 16: 'in Dumfries, for instance, Colonel dePeyster or John M'Murdo; in Edinburgh, Charles Hay (later Lord Newton), or the poet's "facetious little friend," William Dunbar, or even Peter Hill.' As will appear in a moment, Peter Hill seems the most likely candidate. (A letter to the editor of the *North British Daily Mail*, Glasgow, 24 Aug. 1871, states at second hand that the editing was done by a group of 'young wags' in Edinburgh, which may simply be paraphrased from the title-page.) All of these men were friends of Burns, not folksong collectors, and it is to be observed that Prof. Ferguson is referring to someone working with Burns' own collection, 'from versions set down from memory, or from hasty transcriptions,' *i.e.* transcriptions made hastily during Burns' lifetime from the borrowed MS. collection — a collection that can, by the way, be copied out complete, in longhand, with a dip-pen (insofar as the first edition of *c.* 1800 may be considered a complete copy of it) in ten hours, or twelve at most. Which is probably exactly what happened. And which is not particularly hasty, either — representing hardly two days' work — when one considers that at Burns' first recorded lending of the MS. of which he worriedly, not to say pointedly, mentions that there was not

then "another copy of the Collection in the world," he allowed
John M'Murdo to have it for "five or six days," probably in February 1792. (*Merry Muses,* ed. 1959, p. 11.)

A year later, writing to George Thomson on 26 January 1793,
Burns specifically agreed that a copy be made, ceding, it should be
observed, to the insistence of a Very Important Person, Capt. the
Hon. Andrew Erskine (brother of Lord Kellie and a friend of
Boswell's — see their 'rollicking and preposterous' *Letters,* 1763,
'such as . . . only two young fools could publish'), one of Thomson's
other collaborators on the *Select Collection of Original Scotish
Airs,* who had written the words to some of the songs, even 'improving' some of Burns' words on occasion! He seems to have been
an amateur entertainer, in the tradition of the jovial Captains of
his time, such as Grose, Hewerdine, Morris, &c.; and his keeping
after Burns for material seems to have been intended not so much
to collect Burns' erotic songs, as to use them in a way that reminds
one of the similar and bogus amateur 'folksingers' of our own day.
Erskine wrote to Burns, as a postscript to a letter from Thomson,
20 January 1793:

> You kindly promised me, about a year ago, a collection of
> your unpublished productions, *religious* and amorous. I
> know from experiment how irksome it is to copy. If you
> will get any trusty person in Dumfries to write them over
> fair, I will give Peter Hill whatever money he asks for his
> trouble, and I certainly shall not betray your confidence.
> — I am, your hearty admirer, Andrew Erskine. (Quoted,
> by McNaught, in *Burns Chronicle,* 1894, III. 28; and in
> Burns' *Letters,* ed. Francis Allen, 1927, IV. 148.)

To this Burns answered, following protocol — which gives some
idea of what he thought about this reminder — as the last paragraph of his reply to Thomson:

> My most respectful Compl*ime*nts to the Hono*ura*ble Gen-
> tleman who favored me with a postscript in your last. — He
> shall hear from me & receive his M.S.S. soon. (*Letters,* ed.
> Ferguson, 1931, II. 149.)

After such a statement it seems absurd that any discussion need
be engaged in as to the source of the printer's 'copy' for an edition
printed 'for use of the Crochallan Fencibles,' even assuming that

it is necessarily true that the copy used was not Burns' own. Having remained hidden until 1814, the manuscript collection which James Gracie received from Burns could not have been that used by the printer, *c.* 1800, and it has already been demonstrated that this could also not have been the complete collection as printed. What became of the rest of the MS. remains a mystery, unless we assume that the thirty extra songs comprising this 'rest' were added *c.* 1800 by the Crochallan editor, with occasional enlargements as in "WAP AND ROW." The explanation of the three further, and hitherto unpublished, songs occurring in the final gift (if it was a gift) to Gracie, almost certainly in 1796, the year of the poet's death, would then simply be that these were among Burns' later compositions or collectings, and could thus not be copied 'over fair' by 'any trusty person in Dumfries' in 1793. What became of the complete MS. copy presumably made in 1793 is also not known, Capt. Erskine having commited suicide in September of that year. (See Burns' letter of 29 October 1793, lamenting Erskine's death.)

The passing of this copy through the hands of Peter Hill, the former 'Crochallan' Edinburgh bookseller, with whom Erskine offered to leave payment for the copyist — and who would thus be the person who actually received the copy — strongly suggests that Erskine's copy (or a further or supererogatory copy made from it before delivery, as was that made by J. C. Ewing a century later from Scott Douglas' unique printed copy) was precisely the one used as printer's copy for the edition of *c.* 1800, and that Peter Hill was its secret publisher and probable editor. The Crochallan Fencibles, as a group, must be credited with the deathless title by which the collection has come to be known, since no reference to this title, nor to any special title for the collection, occurs in any letter or other MS. of Burns's. (According to the recollection, however, of Capt. Murray of Kilmun, cited by Dr. James Adams in the *Burns Chronicle*, 1894, III. 104, there was a 'special compartment' in Burns' 'capacious pocket-book or wallet,' reserved for 'hastily stowed away "Walkers",' as he is said to have called them.) If the provenance suggested above for the printer's 'copy' for the original edition of *c.* 1800 be correct, as also the presumed supplying by the 'Crochallan' editor of thirty of the eighty-five songs there printed, no other *Muses* manuscript in Burns' holograph need ever have existed than the prototype copied for Erskine and given (?) at the last, with three additional songs, to James Gracie. In that case, the search for the long-lost text —

though evidently not the holograph manuscript — of Burns' *Merry Muses of Caledonia* may now be considered over, and its total contents recovered and printed. But that turns on an '*If.*'

VI

THE QUESTION as to whether the Gracie-Cunningham MS. collection was really 'presented' to Gracie as a gift is raised, in the preceding section, because there is something peculiar about the relation between Banker Gracie and Burns. As opposed to Buchan's erotic collection, *Secret Songs of Silence,* presented to a benefactor with an effusive letter of thanks (see the whole story in William Walker's *Peter Buchan,* 1915, p. 67–88, and *dépouillement* of the MS., p. 168–71), the MS. collection of sixteen or twenty bawdy songs — if not sixty — that Gracie received from Burns, was perhaps not quite so simple a matter as that of a helpful patron and a grateful bard. Yet one is loath to believe that it could have been, finally, a cash transaction, as was that of Buchan. The only two extant letters from Burns to Gracie make curious reading. The second, one week before the end, seems unfeignedly grateful, though it is not clear what offer Burns felt impelled to refuse. The first letter shows Gracie in the character of a hard man, evidently impatient to get on with the 'horning and caption' of a wretched debtor, while Burns, who had endorsed the debt, writes to him, conjecturally in April 1791 (*Letters,* ed. 1931, II. 72):

> Globe Inn, 8 o'clock P.M.
> Sir,
> I have yours anent Crombie's bill. Your forbearance has been very great. I did it to accomodate the thoughtless fellow. He asks till Wednesday week. If he fail, I pay it myself. In the meantime, if horning and caption be absolutely necessary, grip him by the neck, and welcome.

A further reference occurs in a letter to James Johnson, Aug. or Sept. 1795 (*Letters,* II. 313), asking that James Gracie, Bank of Scotland's Office, Dumfries, be added as subscriber to the *Scots Musical Museum.* Then, written at Brow, 13 July 1796 — Burns died on the 21st:

> My dear Sir,
> It would [be] doing high injustice to this place not to acknowledge that my rheumatisms have derived great bene-

fit from it already; but alas, my loss of appetite still continues. I shall not need your kind offer, *this week,* & I return
to town the begin*n*ing of next week it not being tide-week.
— I am detaining a man in a burning hurry — So God bless
you! (*Letters,* II. 329.)

There is a persistent tradition, cited by McNaught on the
authority of Prof. John Wilson ('Christopher North') , author of
an early appreciation, "The Genius and Character of Burns," 1843
(in *Works,* Glasgow, 1846, p. cxxx), that on Burns' deathbed,
'when "curst necessity" compelled him to implore the loan of
five pounds,' an unnamed 'miscreant, aware of his poverty, had
made him an offer of fifty pounds for a collection' — the manuscript of the *Merry Muses,* says McNaught — 'which he repelled
with the horror of remorse.' Gracie was in Dumfries, where Burns
died. He was offering money, or perhaps lodging, to Burns — at
least that is the implication of the "kind offer", "not . . . *this
week*", "God bless you!" (to a banker, after all) in the letter of
13 July 1796, one week from the date of Burns' death. And that
week he was refused, though, the day before, Burns had written
frantic letters to James Burness and to Thomson, imploring help
in meeting his tailor's bill. Eighteen years later, at Gracie's death,
his son found among his papers, and allowed Allan Cunningham
to copy in October 1815, a manuscript collection of at least sixteen
bawdy songs stated to have been received from Burns. No one else
ever received such a gift from Burns. Not one of his closest cor-
respondents, not even Cleghorn, ever received more than a few
songs, occasionally, and those always enclosed in personal letters.
Or the guarded loan of the lot, and then only for a few days. Or
simply the right to have the collection copied, as the Hon. Andrew
Erskine. Gracie was in no sense an intimate of Burns's. It is not
even known whether he was a benefactor. There are only the two
letters, an "EPIGRAM," the subscription to the *Museum* . . . and the
Cunningham MS. It looks very much as though the tradition is
true in its essentials; but perhaps there was no refusal with horror.
Or perhaps horror, and no refusal. We will never know. One almost wishes for the license of James Barke, in his fictional biography of Burns, to imagine the scene: the Banker, the dying poet,
the frightened widow — and the money.

There is another tradition too, or perhaps it is just part of
the same one (both come to us through McNaught in the same
passage, in *The Merry Muses,* ed. 1911, p. xvii), that Burns' widow

was induced to part with the manuscript 'on false pretences.' It now seems likely that Prof. Ferguson has misunderstood when he dates this tradition as necessarily referring to a period about four years later, at the time of the first printed edition. Most attempts to exploit or intimidate a young widow are made — like that on Petronius' Widow of Ephesus — before the husband's body is even cold. This is particularly true of the depredations on literary property and collections of all kinds (especially erotic ones, *bien entendu*) by dealers and fellow-collectors, who generally refer to any *other* dealers or collectors, who have made even greater haste and got to the widow before them, as 'vultures.' In the case of Burns, the real friends waited a decent interval: several months. Then, every scrap of manuscript in the poet's home in Dumfries was gathered together by Burns' friend, John Syme, as Prof. Ferguson notes, and sent to Dr. Currie in Liverpool. But that was in the winter of 1796/7. Long before then — and this is not hypothetical — Gracie had come into possession of the manuscript collection he got. Cunningham's copy of it, or of the part not reprinted about 1825, has remained to tell the tale, but it cannot tell everything.

One wonders, for instance, and in a sense rather different from Mr. Linklater's journalistic *The Merry Muse,* what became of Gracie's original manuscript. More than one of Burns' bawdy song MSS. are known to have been consigned in later years to what Prof. Ferguson refers to (p. 13, unaware, I am sure, that he is quoting Torquemada) as 'purification by fire.' Mr. Greenshields of Lesmahago has gone down to posterity for nothing more than having, 'on broad moral ground,' made 'a bonfire of them; — so here ends the matter.' (Quoted by Scott Douglas, 'Kilmarnock' ed. 1871, II. 417.) I suspect that these were the *Merry Muses* MSS. Little better could have been expected of the estimable Dr. Currie, had they fallen into his hands. As it is, he did his best to cover the trail, not stopping at forgery to do so; where Cunningham — bad, irresponsible Cunningham — stooped to exactly the same kind of forgery, to *leave* a trail. Whatever means Gracie used to get his manuscript, and Cunningham to apprise us of its existence, in a way we are in their debt.

THE MERRY MUSES AS FOLKLORE

I

THAT Robert Burns collected, and himself wrote, bawdy Scots songs is no longer in controversy, since the publication of his *Letters* and *Selected Letters,* both edited by Prof. De Lancey Ferguson (Oxford: Clarendon Press, 1931 and 1953). As there printed, the letters omit most of the bawdy songs that accompanied a not inconsiderable number of them, but Prof. Ferguson has now made amende, more than honorable, in the new edition of *The Merry Muses of Caledonia* (Edinburgh: Macdonald, 1959), edited in collaboration with Sydney Goodsir Smith, Esq; author of the best study of *The Merry Muses* ever published. This study appeared in *Arena* (London, 1950, No. 4), and was reprinted — with Burns' songs delicately letter-expurgated — in *Hudson Review* (New York, 1954, vol. VII). It is unfortunately not reprinted in the new edition of *The Merry Muses,* where it rightly belongs, its place being taken by a general introduction of lesser value by the late James Barke. Anyone interested in Burns' own part in *The Merry Muses* is particularly recommended to turn up Mr. Smith's article, which says a great deal more, and a great deal more racily, than can be said here.

The purpose of the present essay is to discuss *The Merry Muses of Caledonia* not as an incidental product of Burns' genius and patriotism, but as a printed source of Scottish and English folksong. From this point of view, all the editions are of interest, though Burns had nothing to do with any of them, the first edition appearing about 1800 (according to the watermark in the paper), some four years after his death. It is worth observing that of the eighty-five songs and fragments in this first edition, nearly half (35) were never again reprinted until 1895–97, a century after Burns' death, in the five volumes of the mysterious John

S. Farmer's *Merry Songs and Ballads;* and again in 1911 in an edition of *The Merry Muses* privately printed [in Kilmarnock, by D. Brown & Co.] for the Burns Federation, and edited by Duncan McNaught under the pseudonym 'Vindex.' In both these reprints the texts are somewhat incorrectly given, owing in part to the silent incorporation of variant readings made by William Scott Douglas, the great editor of Burns, in the margins of his copy of the original edition, which is the only one now known to exist. This copy is at present the property of Lord Rosebery, who graciously allowed a complete photographic copy to be made for purposes of the new Ferguson & Smith edition, and to be deposited in the National Library of Scotland, at Edinburgh.

The new edition of *The Merry Muses* of 1959 is not only superior in every way to the nearly thirty reprint editions that have preceded it, but also gives for the first time a number of hitherto-unknown erotic songs, poems, and fragments, either written or collected by Burns, and now published from his holograph letters and MSS. — the long-awaited pendant to Prof. Ferguson's edition of the *Letters* in 1931. To these new texts may be added an overlapping group (which cross-check in the overlapping part with Prof. Ferguson's) in the Cunningham MS., of which all trace had been lost since 1839, but which I had the good fortune to rediscover; just too late, unfortunately, for inclusion of its unpublished texts in the new edition of the *Muses*. The Cunningham MS. texts are therefore published in conjunction with, and preceding, the present essay. To save space, no duplication has been made of materials printed in the new edition of the *Muses*. It is, however, exactly these materials — duplicating each other from different MS. sources, with only the most minor verbal variants — that validate the Cunningham MS. in its entirety, and thus the entirely new texts in it, despite Cunningham's own rather dubious reputation as an editor. In any case, it is either that or jettisoning the new texts altogether, which would be a great pity, as it seems more than probable that they are by Burns.

There are a number of peculiarities about the 1959 edition of *The Merry Muses* that one would almost prefer to overlook. First and most prominent is the open warfare between its two editors: Prof. Ferguson pointedly disavows in several places all parts of the volume *except* the MS. transcripts and notes bearing his initials; Mr. Smith returns the compliment. As Prof. Ferguson's only crime, if crime it be, is that he tends to trust the paleographic evidence of Burns' own MSS. to any printed text — and even here

Dr. Currie and other forgers rise to confound the exact science of paleography — and as Mr. Barke, originally announced as one of the editors, is now dead and cannot share the blame, all must apparently fall on Mr. Smith. This is hardly fair. The resultant watertight division of the text into songs from MSS., songs from print, alien influences, &c. (there were *no* alien — *i.e.* Anglo-Irish — influences in the original edition, which is purely Scottish), has the effect of blurring any impression the reader might have of the original edition of *c.* 1800, which is now essentially reprinted by Ferguson & Smith, but in an entirely different order of the contents. Fortunately, a table of contents in the order of the original is given in McNaught's edition of 1911, and he also prints the more-or-less alphabetical Index (from the original edition, p. 123–28) in the *Burns Chronicle,* 1894, III. 36–7, though there high-mindedly expunged, with, for instance, 'The Marauder' replacing "THE FORNICATOR," 'How Can I Keep My Honour' (for "MAIDENHEAD") , 'Naething There' for "NAE HAIR ON'T," and so forth.

It would be disingenuous to overlook the somewhat prescientific, though terribly sincere, erotic fum-fuddling of Mr. James Barke's introduction to the new edition, to which Mr. Smith's superlative article on Burns and *The Merry Muses* was sacrificed. Mr. Barke 'places,' for example, the original "Ball o' Kirriemuir," which is at present the principal erotic ballad of Scotland, and is continuously being enlarged at the better taverns, as having authentically taken place at a harvest-home — near Kirriemuir, of course — about 1885, complete with circumstantial details of the aphrodisiacal rose-hips nettles scattered on the floor and being accidentally insinuated into the ladies' open-style or 'free trade' bloomers to start the Ball rolling! In point of fact, not only was a full text of the modern song printed ten years earlier than the date Mr. Barke gives for the incident, in *Forbidden Fruit: A Collection of Tales, &c., c.* 1875, p. 68 (which he was not, of course, required to know), but a prototype stanza of the same song will also be found in *The Merry Muses* itself, nearly a century earlier, in "BLYTH WILL AN' BESSIE'S WEDDIN'," the stanza beginning 'Tamie Tamson too was there . . .' where at least one of the editors might properly have been expected to notice it. Set back to 1785, instead of 1885, Mr. Barke's tale might well have ornamented his *The Wind That Shakes the Barley,* or any of the other volumes of his fictional biography of Burns. It is self-evidently out of place in a scholarly edition of Burns' most *difficult* volume. In fact, so is the whole introduction, though there can be no doubt that Barke was (and is) on the side of the angels, if only for his heart-rending account of a young red-headed barmaid half suffocated with embarrassment at one evilly-chosen dirty word flung at her by a drunk.

Aside, finally, from such errors in taste as including "The Plenipotentiary," about which more will be said later, the only quarrel one might seriously engage with the new edition would be on the question of ascriptions of authorship to Burns, which are not really within the province of the present essay. Some of these Mr. Smith seems to make on the authority of Scott Douglas' marginalia to his unique copy of the first edition; others on purely subjective criteria more clearly expressed in his article already mentioned. Mr. Smith is a Scots poet in his own right, and has obviously studied *The Merry Muses* profoundly. If subjective ascriptions of authorship may be allowed at all, those of Scott Douglas and of Sydney Goodsir Smith are as good or better than anyone else's on this aspect of Burns. It should be observed that the same problem exists not only in regard to the erotic *Muses* songs, but also as to the far greater number of songs that Burns collected from folk sources, and rewrote — *i.e.* expurgated — and then often enlarged with several original stanzas, for publication in James Johnson's *Scots Musical Museum,* 1787 *ff.,* and George Thomson's *Select Collection of Original Scotish Airs,* 1793 *ff.,* the projects that turned Burns' inspiration away from his own poetry and toward his national folksong for the last ten years of his life.

These *misch*-texts have been the despair of the greatest editors of Burns, including his most recent editor, Prof. James Kinsley, who has announced that he is collecting, for the forthcoming Clarendon Press edition of Burns' poems, all that 'survive in Burn's holograph whether they are certainly his work or not.' Such ascriptions must always be subjective in the case of the songs — failing any definite statement in Burns' letters — since it is obvious that even the existence of a given song in his holograph cannot tell us whether he himself wrote it, or how much of it he wrote if he originally collected it from folk sources. These problems are of greater moment to the study of Burns' art than to the study of folksong, to which Burns' contribution was in any case much complicated by his modernizing and rewriting of bawdy songs for his own pleasure, and his wholesale expurgations of them for Johnson's and Thomson's series. When lesser men have done, or have seemed to be doing, the same thing, they have been roundly denounced as forgers and fakers, in particular the Scottish collector, Peter Buchan, who seems to have been used as whipping-boy for Sir Walter Scott's exactly similar crimes. (See Scott's insufferable patronizing of Buchan, in his *Journal*, ed. 1890, II. 24, at date 23 Aug. 1827.) Buchan's vindication from the accusation of total forgery has long existed, though it is not well known, in Harry L. D. Ward's *Catalogue of Romances in the British Museum*, 1883, I. 528, in connection with Buchan's independent collecting of texts also existing in the then-unpublished *Percy Folio MS*. In the case of a great poet like Burns one would hesitate, of course, to apply such words as 'forgery,' and his revisions are to be gratefully accepted as what they are: the product of his genius influenced by folk materials.

II

BURNS first mentions his collecting of erotic Scots songs in various of his letters to which attention has been drawn by Mr. Smith, and earlier by McNaught in the two articles in the *Burns Chronicle* (for 1894 and 1911) serving in part as introduction to his 1911 edition of *The Merry Muses*. In a number of these letters Burns enclosed his current compositions in the genre, particularly his letters to Robert Cleghorn, co-member of the Crochallan Fencibles, a drinking and convivial club that met at Daunie Douglas' Tavern in Edinburgh, and for whose uses the original edition of the *Muses* is stated on its title-page to have been 'selected.' See especially the full texts of Burns' letters to James Hoy, 6 Nov. 1787; to Provost Robert Maxwell, 20 Dec. 1789; to Cleghorn, Oct. 1793, and at other dates; and to George Thomson, 4 Aug. 1795, and other dates. (*Letters,* ed. Ferguson, 1931, I. 136, 377; II. 213, 307.)

By 1793 Burns had at least once circulated his collection in its entirety, with tacit — and in another case explicit — permission to make a copy. Writing to John M'Murdo, in Dec. 1793, he says:

> I think I once mentioned something of a collection of Scots songs I have for some years been making; I send you a perusal of what I have got together. I could not conveniently spare them above five or six days, and five or six glances of them will probably more than suffice you. . .

There is not another copy of the collection in the world; and I should be sorry that any unfortunate negligence should deprive me of what has cost me a good deal of pains. (*Letters,* 1931, II. 222.)

At the point marked by the ellipsis above, the text of this letter has always been quoted as going on to say: 'A very few of them are my own.' This sentence has recently been disavowed by Prof. Ferguson, in David Daiches' *Robert Burns* (N.Y. 1950, p. 311, and in the *Burns Chronicle,* 1953), as a brazen interpolation by Burns' earliest editor, Dr. James Currie, intended to show that Burns was at least not author of the whole collection. However, until its exposure as a forgery, it has more particularly been used as evidence that Burns wrote at least *part.* This too was quite unnecessary, as he himself made no secret of it, saying in plain words of two syllables, in the letter to Provost Maxwell, for instance, 20 Dec. 1789:

> I shall betake myself to a subject ever fertile of themes, a Subject, the turtle-feast of the Sons of Satan, and the delicious secret Sugar-plumb of the Babes of Grace . . . in short, may it please Your Lordship, I intend to write BAUDY!
> (*Letters,* 1931, I. 377.)

The *Muses* song that follows, "THE CASE OF CONSCIENCE" (ed. 1959, p. 37), is not only forthrightly obscene, but sacrilegious and anticlerical into the bargain. Four years later, in the letter to Cleghorn accompanying Burns' new verses to the old chorus, "COME COWE ME, MINNIE" (ed. 1959, p. 40) , he begins:

> There is, there must be, some truth in original sin. —
> My violent propensity to B - - - dy convinces me of it. —
> Lack a day! if that species of Composition be the Sin against 'the Haly Ghaist', 'I am the most offending soul alive.' (*Letters,* II. 213.)

Another of these satirical introductions by Burns, to "A WICKED SONG" (*i.e.* "THE PATRIARCH," a Bible travesty), printed in the new edition of the *Muses,* has long circulated in manuscript. It appears as a MS. addendum in Scott Douglas' copy of the original edition, following after a MS. copy of "THE COURT OF EQUITY" (which had already been printed by James Maidment in 1823 as *The*

Fornicators Court). It also occurs in a much earlier manuscript, now at Harvard, George R. Kinloch's *Burlesque and Jocular Ballads and Songs* (dated Edinburgh, 1827–29, on pp. 167 and 170*n.*) at p. 263–66.

The circulation, similarly, of Burns' erotic song collection in manuscript, during his lifetime, among the members of a convivial Scottish society devoted to the drinking of hard liquor and the singing of bawdy songs — some of which were sent them, fresh from their composition or modernization by Burns, *via* Cleghorn — gives the necessary hint as to the origin of the printer's 'copy' for the posthumous first edition of *The Merry Muses of Caledonia*, about 1800. This edition is regularly stated, on no known evidence, to have been set up from Burns' own MS. collection; borrowed on false pretenses from his widow and never returned (as printer's copy seldom is). Prof. Ferguson has suggested, in his introduction to the new edition of 1959, that this could not have been the case; that the MS. may at that time have been — if it had not already been destroyed — in the possession of Dr. Currie, who would certainly never have assisted in publishing it. McNaught suggests, in the *Burns Chronicle* for 1911, that the MS. might perhaps have been 'filched' from Currie, but this seems unlikely. It is a curious fact that the *Muses* songs in Burns' holograph which have been cropping up now for a century (for instance a group sold at Sotheby's, 4 Dec. 1873, Nos. 1365–70, all apparently printed in the new edition) are almost invariably included in letters, and are seldom in any form that could be construed as sheets of a consecutive MS. or even of the 'special compartment' in Burns' 'capacious pocket-book or wallet,' reserved for 'hastily stowed away "Walkers",' as he is said to have called them, according to the recollection of Capt. Murray of Kilmun, cited by Dr. James Adams in the *Burns Chronicle*, 1894, III. 104.

One thing is certain: the songs in Burns' extant letters tally too well with the versions printed in the first edition of *The Merry Muses* to allow of any theory of independent folk-collection, and particularly not for Burns' own original songs of this kind. The first edition could therefore only have been set up from a MS. copy made by, and in the possession of, one of his earlier confidants, most probably one of the Crochallan Fencibles credited on the title-page as having 'selected' the text. For the same reason, the usual ascription of this first edition to Dumfries (simply because Burns' MSS. would have been there at his death) cannot be upheld. Edinburgh, where the Fencibles met, seems much more probable. The date, as aforesaid, is proved by the watermark in the paper, which gives '1799' on two leaves and '1800' on seven others in the Scott Douglas — Rosebery copy.

It is of course an open question whether or not the first edition included only the contents of Burns' own collection, or whether — aside from the 'selecting' — additions were made, perhaps from the Fencibles' later repertory, and from David Herd's MSS. This much at least can be said: the original edition of *The Merry Muses of Caledonia* of *c.* 1800 is entirely Scottish in all its songs, and is composed entirely of songs, without any admixture of unsung or unsingable poems. This is true of no other popular edition until the scholarly rehabilitation of Farmer and of McNaught at the end of the 19th century. All the popular chapbook editions, from *c.* 1806 to 1872 (predated '1827') add a very great deal of new material; occasionally folksong, occasionally even Scottish folksong, but just as often squibs, toasts, tales-in-verse, freespoken love poems such as those of Thomas Moore, plus a good many of the subliterary and subhumorous pornographic productions of professional entertainers of the period, such as George Alexander Stevens, 'Captains' Morris, Hewerdine, *et al.* This sort of bawdy poetry is of no particular quality, and of little interest to modern readers, even those looking for bawdry, who would naturally prefer something more modern, at least in idiom. It is also largely devoid of folkloristic interest, except as to the song and poem types, particularly the curious erotic puns of the "Toasts and Sentiments" of the Regency (in all editions after the first), and the jokes underlying the humorous tales-in-verse, which are otherwise generally doggerel.

III

THE CONTENTS of the authentic first edition of *The Merry Muses of Caledonia,* plus many previously unpublished songs and fragments from Burns' MSS., have now been made publicly available in the new Edinburgh, 1959, edition. In the pages now following, the attempt is made to analyze more particularly the special contents of folksong interest in the many chapbook revisions published as *The Merry Muses* during the 19th century. These have been examined only once, by McNaught in 1894, and then only summarily, to damn. Furthermore, as they exist only in unique copies, in the British Museum (Private Case), in two Scottish libraries, and in private collections in America, it would be very inconvenient for anyone later to try to reach or analyze all these editions again. This analysis is in line with the appeal I have made, in my bibliographical article on the best similar source for the 17th century, Playford & Durfey's *Pills to Purge Melancholy, 1699–1720* (in *Midwest Folklore*, 1959, IX. 89–102, at p. 92), for some *indexing* of the jungle of printed ballads, drolleries, folksong garlands, &c. earlier than 1850, still almost trackless except where Prof. Child and certain of his successors, such as Profs. Kittredge, Rollins, Belden, and Phillips Barry happen to have touched upon them. This is truly a crime, as the printed materials alone are enormous and rich absolutely beyond belief, not to mention the almost unexplored manuscript collections.

The first reprint of *The Merry Muses of Caledonia* appeared under the title, '*The Giblet Pye,* being the Heads, Tails, Legs, and Wings, of the Anacreontic songs of the celebrated R. Burns, G. A. Stevens, Rochester, T. L - - tle [Moore], and others, Some of which are taken from the Original Manuscripts of R. Burns, never before published. . . Shamborough: Printed by John Nox, and sold By the Booksellers.' There is no date, but the paper is watermarked 1806. (Unique copy: W. N. H. Harding Collection, Chicago.) It will be observed that Burns' name is here given for the first time. His name does not appear anywhere in the first edition of *c.* 1800, nor in any other edition until that of 1843, and then not on the title-page. Nevertheless, it must always have been an open secret after the publication of *The Giblet Pye,* as the bookseller's (?) addition of his name, in ink, to the title-page of the following edition will show. The first critical reference to Burns in connection with *The Merry Muses* was also made within the same decade, by Wordsworth, in 1816, as quoted by Scott Douglas in the appendix to J. Gibson Lockhart's *Life of Burns,* 1882. Says Wordsworth:

He must be a miserable judge of poetical compositions who can for a moment fancy that such low, tame, and loathsome ribaldry can possibly be the production of Burns. With the utmost difficulty we procured a slight perusal of the abominable pamphlet alluded to. The truth is . . . there is not one verse in that miscellany that ever was publicly acknowledged by Burns, nor is there above a single page that can be traced to his manuscript.

It is of course now certain that Wordsworth's 'truth' is untrue, and he is cited here only for his dating reference to the 'abominable pamphlet' and the difficulty already experienced in 1816 in procuring even a sight of it.

Although Wordsworth's is the first critical reference to the *Merry Muses* and to Burns' part in its composition — which he denies — the partial reprint as *The Giblet Pye*, ten years earlier, having already cited Burns' name on its title-page, the matter was in all probability already openly rumored in certain circles of British *bons vivants* at least. This can hardly be doubted, as it was clearly only in order to scotch such rumors that Wordsworth had sought out a copy of the original edition with the pains he describes. It should be observed, in any case, how hedged Wordsworth's denial is, hanky-pankying with such terms as 'publicly acknowledged by Burns' — as though any of his children would have been less his, had he not acknowledged them — and the arbitrary statement, now known to be quite erroneous, that 'not above a single page . . . can be traced to [Burns'] manuscript.' One sees there the *motive*, perhaps, behind the burning of these manuscripts for over a century now: to hide the evidence. Dozens of such pages have, however, survived, and have been traced in Prof. Ferguson's editions of Burns' *Letters*, and now of the *Muses*.

More pointed, and of course from the opposite point of view, are Byron's contemporary references, in his *Journal* and letters, as cited by McNaught :

> Allen has lent me a quantity of Burns's unpublished, and never to be published, letters. They are full of oaths [*sic*] and obscene songs. What an antithetical mind! Tenderness, roughness, delicacy, coarseness, sentiment, sensuality, soaring and grovelling, dirt and deity, all mixed up in one compound of poor clay.

This is probably the best typification of Burns' art ever put on paper. Byron repeats it, less well, in a letter to Bowles, this time not naming Burns, and calling the letters 'abominably gross and elaborately coarse' (the elegant chiasmus here shows that he is only striking a moral pose), and noting also that to them are often tacked 'some verses of the most hyperbolical obscenity.' The jolly hypocrisy of all these deplorings becomes obvious in the word 'treasure' in the opening line of Byron's next paraphrase of himself, in a letter to Hodgson, 14 December 1813:

Will you tell Drury I have a treasure for him — a whole
set of original Burns letters never published, nor to be
published; for they are full of fearful oaths and the most
nauseous songs — all humorous but coarse bawdry. However they are curiosities, and shew him quite in a new point
of view — the mixture, or rather contrast of tenderness,
delicacy, obscenity, and coarseness in the same mind is
wonderful.

What is evident here is that Byron was doing his best to publicize his find, two years or more before Wordsworth set out to
deny the rumors thus set in circulation, probably as much by
Byron as by the title-page ascription to Burns of some of these
same songs in the very rare *Giblet Pye* of 1806. It is also clear
that Byron did not understand the reason for this 'mixture' of
erotic songs, 'couched as postscripts to [Burns'] serious and sentimental letters' to his friend Robert Cleghorn, from whom they
doubtless had descended to Cleghorn's stepson, John Allen, librarian to Lord Holland, and an intimate friend of Byron's.

The statement in *The Giblet Pye* that some of its texts 'are
taken from the Original Manuscripts of R. Burns, never before
published,' is doubtless not literally true if, by this, Burns' holograph MSS. are to be understood. (The imprint is naturally fictitious, jesting at the expense of the reformer John Knox.) On the
other hand, at least one song by Burns is given — from *some* manuscript, now lost — which had not appeared in the edition of *c.*
1800 : the version of "FOR A' THAT" beginning 'The bonniest lass
that ye meet neist,' which contains, in the penultimate refrain on
King Solomon, the closest to an apology or *tu quoque* concerning his bawdy songs that Burns ever made:

> For a' that, and a' that,
> Tho' a preacher wise, and a' that,
> The smuttiest sang that e'er was sung
> His Sang o' Sangs is a' that.

The Giblet Pye is composed, as its title implies, of a mixture
of texts reprinted from the first edition of *The Merry Muses*,
and partly of English and other poems (twenty-one by G. A.
Stevens, three by 'T. L[it]tle,' *i.e.* Thomas Moore, toward the
end, &c.), mixed together in a one-to-one alternation, Scottish
and Stevens, for the first half of the volume, to p. 69, and about
six-to-six thereafter, like riffling together a deck of cards. It

adds the "Toasts and Sentiments" for the first time, at the end
of the volume, p. 135–6 (not the same toasts as those in later
editions), and the following songs of Scottish or other folk provenance that do not appear in the first edition. Some of these, though
there is no longer any knowing which, may very well have come
from manuscripts of Burns': "The Auld Moulie Maidenhead" (p.
87, not identical with the 6-stanza text, "HOW CAN I KEEP MY MAID-
ENHEAD," in *c.* 1800, p. 65), "The Philibegs" (p. 83, begins 'I
ay like to see the blue Bonnet'), "Key Hole" (p. 16, begins 'John
Thomason keekit in at the key-hole'), "Eppie McNab" (p. 87, on
which see J. C. Dick, *Notes on Scottish Songs*, 1908, p. 58), "The
bonniest lass that ye meet neist" (p. 124, by Burns, ed. 1959, p. 69),
and "The Meikle De'il Damn This C - - t O' Mine" (p. 103, begins
'When I was a lassie 'tween the rough and the bare,' very much
in Burns' style). One of the poems, entitled "The Toasts" (p.
116, begins 'Dinner o'er, and grace said'), includes a number of
erotic 'healths' or toasts worked into a rhymed text.

The next edition published, about 1825, is analyzed more
fully in connection with the Cunningham MS. in the preceding
essay. It uses for the first time the abbreviated title, '*The Merry
Muses:* A Choice Collection of Favourite Songs,' as opposed to
the original '*Merry Muses of Caledonia:* A Choice Collection of
Favourite Scots Songs, Ancient and Modern,' of *c.* 1800. The words
'Caledonia' and 'Scots' were now dropped to lend color to the
probably fictitious imprint, 'Dublin: Printed for the Booksellers.
Price Three Shillings.' (The original edition had no imprint
whatsoever.) The only copy now known is in the British Museum,
Private Case; though McNaught in 1894 described another copy,
now lost, lacking many of the pages in the body of the text. On
the title-page of the British Museum copy, someone — probably
a bookseller — has added in ink after the title, 'By Robert Burns,'
and after the price, '& 6.' The volume is 7½ inches high and
tolerably well printed, the largest and handsomest of all the 19th
century editions, most of which, including the original, are tiny
booklets about 5½ inches high and very poorly printed. It appears,
typographically, to date from about the 1820's, and this is made
certain by the MS. date '1826' on p. 128 of the British Museum
copy.

This 'Dublin . . . Three Shillings' edition of *c.* 1825 contains
forty-five songs that had already appeared in the original edition,
and twelve songs and poems reprinted from *The Giblet Pye*, including "John Thomason" (p. 96), "The bonniest lass" (p. 94),

and "The Toasts" in verse (p. 52). It adds a new group of prose "Sportsmens Toasts" (p. 126), and twenty-seven new songs and poems, of which fifteen were not reprinted in any later edition. Four of these were taken without acknowledgment from David Herd's *Ancient and Modern Scots Songs,* 1776, which is the first unexpurgated folksong collection of modern times, Herd having rejected Bishop Percy's kind offer to fake his texts, as he had already done for his own famous *Folio MS.* (The unpublished materials in Herd's collection, British Museum, Additional MSS., were later almost all printed by Prof. Hans Hecht in *Songs from David Herd's Manuscripts,* 1904, the principal exception being a mildly erotic Tinker ballad, tipped in backwards as the last leaf, which had existed as a broadside since 1616: *Roxburghe Ballads,* III. 230.) The texts reprinted from Herd in *c.* 1825 are "Barm", "Let Me In This Ae Night," "The Maid Gaed to the Mill," and "The Tailor came to clout the claise," of which only the last was among those reprinted later.

The drawing of these materials from Herd almost certainly indicates that this 'Dublin' edition was printed in Scotland. It must be admitted, though, that at least two items of Irish provenance (of which the first had appeared in *The Festival of Anacreon,* 1791) are also added: "Darby's Key to Una's Lock" (p. 65, a pendant to the 'blackguard Irish song called "Oonagh's Waterfall",' referred to by Burns in a letter to Thomson, Sept, 1794, and printed in *The Giblet Pye* as "Una's Lock," p. 99); and "Langolee" (begins, 'Ye botanists yield,' p. 64), which is displaced by a different "Langolee" in later editions, and is finally renamed "The Irish Root" in 1872. Both the "Langolee" texts are satires on the mountebank or medicine-show spiels, also existing in France at least since the early 17th century in the 'harangues' of the quack-salvers' clowns, Bruscambille, Tabarin, and Gautier-Garguille (all pseudonyms or clown-names), and themselves probably imported to France from Italy, and to Italy from the Levant in earlier centuries. Similar modern off-color satires on nostrum-sellers are the "Lydia Pinkham" song (printed in *Immortalia,* 1927), and "Professor John Glaister," to the tune of "Dumpledown Daisy," in the rare or unique British India army mimeographicum, *Camp Fire Songs and Verse* (Madras? *c.* 1939), in my own collection.

Only one real folksong is added in the *Merry Muses* of *c.* 1825, other than those from Herd, "The Lang Dow" (begins, 'Maggy lives at yon ha' head,' p. 75); and one, or perhaps two tales-in-verse, "The Female Porcupine" (p. 62), really just a pun, and

"The Cricket and Crab-Louse" (p. 69), on the profound and widely-dispersed folk motif of an insect — or sometimes the unborn child — lost inside the vagina and terrified by the intrusion of the penis, the fantasy underlying *Tristram Shandy* and Dianetics, now Scientology. (See also the Russian and Italian sources cited at p. 159 of the Cunningham MS.) There is also an interesting recitation with singing refrain, "The Courtships" (p. 77), in which 'A beautiful lady in fair London town' is wooed in exaggerated dialect by a comedy Frenchman, a 'Yorkshire Clown,' an Irishman, a Quaker — the highpoint of the humor in the piece — and last a 'jolly Jack Tar, who with Admiral Duncan [*d.* 1804] was enrich'd by the war.' This piece is followed by a similar rejection-song, "My Thing Is My Own" (begins, 'I, a tender young maid, have been courted by many,' p. 81), which is hardly more than a sophisticated version of a type of song still current in Scotland. In the Scottish songs, as in "The Courtships" here, the last comer, whom the girl finally accepts, is always the soldier, as here a sailor — and pointedly of the naval, not mercantile, fleet. The multilingual humor of "The Courtships," if not traceable to the Tower of Babel, is at least as old as the 16th century, in the character of Rabelais' Panurge, whose first encounter is in all languages, and another in sign-language only. (*Pantagruel,* 1532, Bk. II, chap. 9, 19.) It is also quite similar to Diderot's *Bijoux indiscrets,* 1748, chap. 47, where the vagina itself (*pudenda loquens* motif) is made to speak of its lovers in many languages, including a rather startling passage in English.

IV

ALL THE EDITIONS of *The Merry Muses* that follow, except for an Irish edition of 1832, are essentially the same in contents until McNaught's first scholarly edition in 1911. However, the actual wording of the texts suffered disastrous revision in the edition of 1872 (dated '1827'). The basic mid-19th century version exists in various forms, all probably printed in Scotland about 1830 and following. All are tiny chapbooks, all equally rare, with imprints: 'Dublin . . . Four Shillings,' 'Glasgow: Printed for the Booksellers,' 'Glasgow . . . Price 4s.' (with a cancel-title raising the price: 'London . . . Price 4s. 6d.'), and London, 1843. The last of these, one of the earliest giving a printed date, is a 24to of 162 pages, adding four new songs at the end, only one of which is erotic, "The Plenipotentiary." It was itself reprinted about 1880 on fine laid paper in 8vo size (108 pages). This edition of 1843 gives Burns' name for the first time since 1806, but only in the running-title, "Burns' Merry Muses," from p. 19 (beginning of signature B) to p. 160. The only known copies of these various chapbook printings of *The Merry Muses* are in the British Museum, Private Case; the Hornel Library, Castle-Douglas, Kirkcudbright; and the Murison Burns Collection, Dunfermline. No one of these libraries has them all. Only the Hornel Library has the edition with imprint, Dublin, 1832, which *may* actually have been printed in Dublin, as almost all of its twenty-three new texts are apparently of Irish provenance. (Contents listed by McNaught in the *Burns Chronicle,* 1894, and — somewhat less expurgated — in his 1911 edition of *The Merry Muses.*) What has erroneously been thought to be the one new Scottish song in the Dublin, 1832, edition is reprinted from another source (*The Pearl:* A Monthly journal of facetiæ, Feb. 1880) in *The Limerick,* Paris, 1953, p. 76–7: "They A' Do't, *Tune:* For A' That" (begins, 'The grit folk an' the puir do't'). This is a minor masterpiece and deserves further attention, though it is not identical except in title with the 1832 song, which is not Scottish at all.

The new redaction of about 1830 contains seventy-seven songs and poems, increasing to eighty-one in the edition of 1843. Of these, nearly half (38) are Scottish folksongs or songs by Burns that also appeared in the original edition of *c.* 1800. (The text of "Dainty Davy" given, beginning 'A loving couple met one day,' is not identical with the song of that name in the original edition.) Ten songs and poems are reprinted from *The Giblet Pye,* or in part from the edition of *c.* 1825. Of the twenty-nine new songs and poems, a great many more are of folkloristic and psychological interest than can be dealt with here, as can be seen even in the ruinous rewritings of their texts printed in the so-called '1827' edition (and all of its reprints), which was revised many years later from a copy of the edition of 1843.

The following new materials in the *c.* 1830 edition and its various chapbook reprintings are of special folksong interest. (NOTE: The page-reference given is that of the 'Glasgow' and 'Dublin . . . Four Shillings' editions of *c.* 1830, but will also match approximately the large-paper '1843' reprint of 108 pages.)

"The Reels of Bogie" (p. 10). Very similar to "Cald Kaill of Aberdene," printed from a much older MS. in James Maidment's *Ane Pleasant Garland,* 1835, and reprinted in John S. Farmer's *Merry Songs and Ballads,* 1897, v. 265. The tune "Cauld Kail in

Aberdeen" was one of Burns' favorites, and the stanzas set to it in the *Muses* of *c.* 1800, "GIE THE LASS HER FAIRIN'," with refrain, 'Hey for houghmagandie!' are ascribed to Burns in Scott Douglas' copy.

"The Mouse's Tail" (p. 42). This is one of the English folksongs particularly badly mangled in the '1827' edition, which gives an entirely false notion of its action, vocabulary, and sexual tone; accentuating, for instance, the motif of cuckoldry by means of a woman's ruse, until it becomes, rather, a sharing of the woman alternately by her husband and a young man, in a sort of trio orgy. This song has been collected recently in America, by Mr. Vance Randolph, in the original form.

"There was a pious parson" (p. 52, noted as to the tune, "Of Noble Race Was Shenkin"), in the limerick metre. This is descended from "There was a jovial butcher," printed in *The New Boghouse Miscellany, or A Companion for the Close-Stool,* 1761 (reissued with cancel-title as *The Wits' Miscellany,* 1762) p. 207–15, with a long burlesque 'criticism' in imitation of Cordonnier de St. Hyacinthe's *Chef-d'œuvre d'un inconnu,* La Haye, 1714, which mocked early 18th century pedantry by means of an enormously extended variorum edition of a simple nursery rhyme (similar, I am afraid, to what is being presented here). Two stanzas of "There was a jovial butcher" and a part of the critique are reprinted in *The Limerick,* Paris, 1953, p. 418, note 729, observing further that the limerick form is descended from the mad-song "Tom o' Bedlam," *c.* 1610, and is also similar to the form and scatological humor of "Sumer is icumen in," *c.* 1300. Several stanzas of the "Pious Parson" version of *c.* 1830 — which loses its interesting inter-*bloody*-ruptive last stanza as reprinted in 1843 and after — are still current in Scotland in the bawdy song, "The Hero Alexander," the Alexander referred to being the hero of the Scots' victory over the Norwegians, at Largs, in 1263. (See Allan Ramsay's *Tea-Table Miscellany,* 1724–27, note on "The Archer's March.")

"Green Leaves on the Green O" (p. 70). An earlier version appeared in Playford & Durfey's *Pills to Purge Melancholy,* ed. 1719, v. 13, as "The Trooper Watering his Nagg." This is sung by Mr. Ed McCurdy, on Elektra record 110, *When Dalliance Was in Flower* [1], New York, 1956, from the *Pills* text. A folk-transmitted version of the same song was recently, and may still be, current in America as "I Reckon You Know What I Mean," the title emphasizing the metaphoric or 'tease' nature of the song. This has been collected in various states, and in particular by Mr. Vance Randolph in his very remarkable *"Unprintable" Songs from the Ozarks,* 1949–54, vol. III, No. 4 (Library of Congress MS.), the most important collection of erotic folksong in English.

"As I Went Through London City" (p. 79, called "The Ride in London" in ed. 1872). A related song, "Jobson Brown, *Air: Brother-in-Law,*" appears in the bawdy Civil War songster, *The Rakish Rhymer* (New York, *c.* 1864; reprint, 'Lutetia,' 1917, p. 29), with the rationalization of the sadistic motif of sticking a cobbler's awl into a woman's body, that it is done only by accident, to mark the position of buried treasure found in a dream. This is perhaps intended as a modification — as also, sometimes, the tearing off of tree-leaves (in fact, hairs) in the dream, to wipe oneself — the most commonly encountered motif in marking dream-treasures of this kind being frankly the use of feces, that is to say anal-sadistic. The original song here is "The Cobler," in Allan Ramsay's *Tea-Table Miscellany,* vol. IV, 1740 (ed. 1871, II. 157–8), who commits suicide for love, using his 'awl that he had in the world,' with a final pun, naturally, on body and 'sole.' An expurgated modern version of the erotic form in *The Merry Muses* is printed as "Dublin City" in Burl Ives' *Favorite Folk Ballads* (N.Y., 1949), folio 2, p. 12, with the plaintive music, as a 'fragment given . . . by an Irish bartender, and reworked' by Ives. The text breaks down into 'nonsense'-numbering, by way of total expurgation, beginning with stanza 3, on the style of the Gypsy 'curse' or Jewish mock-prayer at Purim, consisting of gravely reciting numbers or the alphabet in all the mystery of Romany or Hebrew.

There are also a number of erotic folksong types in *The Merry Muses* of *c.* 1830 that continue to exist though the particular songs or poems exemplifying them here have not always survived in folk transmission. (Under caution, some idea of the types at least, though not of the authentic texts of the songs or poems involved, can be gained even from the '1827' edition of 1872, or any of its reprints, some of which do not bear the warning of that false date.)

One type that has *not* continued is that of the punning erotic toasts, though even these are occasionally encountered nowadays as violent and dysphemistic sexual brags, or in quatrain form with the punning or riddling element still present. In the *Merry Muses* of *c.* 1830 they are printed both in prose, at the end of the volume (not identical with the series in *c.* 1825), and worked into verse form in "A Sentimental Sprig" (p. 17), which replaces "The Toasts" of earlier editions. Extensive groups of these toasts had appeared in the erotic *Rambler's* and *Ranger's* magazines in the late 18th century, and some are reprinted in *The Covent Garden Jester,* 1785, p. 86–8. A rather contrived series dating from 1732 to 1820 is printed in the *Supplement to the Records of the Beggar's Benison and Merryland,* Anstruther, 1892, p. 17–23, taken from the minutes of the Scottish secret society mentioned earlier, with riddles, p. 27–31, 82–5, and proverbs, p. 86–8. Similar toasts are still used in the Scottish secret society, the Horseman's Word. See also John Dunlop's *The Philosophy of Artificial and Compulsory Drinking Usages in Great Britain,* 6th ed., 1839; likewise the delightful letter by John Keats (on the young man who offered the riddling toast, '*Mater omnium*'), printed in Grose's *Classical Dictionary of the Vulgar Tongue,* edition of 1931, at the 'plain English' equivalent; with others similar at "Beggar's Benison," "Best in Christendom," and "Monosyllable." The modern quatrain toasts of erotic nature are first seen in *Forbidden Fruit: A Collection of Tales, c.* 1875, at p. 39–43 (preceded by a group of erotic riddles), which includes almost all those still current, plus one of the old punning type, p. 76: 'Here's to the dark lane and the red entry, Ane gaes in, and twa stand sentry,' in which the relation to the older riddle-lore is clear.

The erotic tale-in-verse, an elegant poetic method of telling dirty jokes (on which see my article, "Rationale of the Dirty Joke," in *Neurotica,* New York, 1951, No. 9), was popularized by La Fontaine's *Contes et Nouvelles en vers* in the 1660's, and had seen its halcyon days in the 18th century in both England and France. It still crops up occasionally in English in modern times, for instance in the 1930's in New Haven, in the "Uther Capet" [Arthur Head] series of pamphlets, of which a full set does not seem to have been preserved even at Yale. The tale-in-verse is a type still very much present in the *Merry Muses* of *c.* 1830, particularly in "Lucy's and Kitty's Black Jocks," p. 12, the title being changed to the less understandable "Black *Jokes*" in all later editions except that of 'Dublin, 1832,' p. 27. The verse portion of the edition of *c.* 1825 had also ended, as it happens, with an incomplete text, accidentally omitting the verbal climax, and thus leaving the joke unexplained.

This poem is almost exactly translated from Vergier's earlier *conte-en-vers* in French, of which the text will most easily be found reprinted in *Contes en vers imités du Moyen de Parvenir* (Paris: Willem, 1874) p. 75. It is a sort of expurgated female-castration story, with the castratory act modified simply to shaving the woman's pubis, as a 'joke' or revenge, as also in what the editor of the collection just cited [Prosper Blanchemain] assumes to be the original tale. Two versions of this tale are given in Béroalde de Verville's *Moyen de Parvenir,* end of chap. 42, "Diette" (matching ed., 1870, I. 213), a great, mad, seminal collection of folktales retold, dating from the beginning of the 17th century. A modern fictional form of this standard neurotic idea of female castration, also presented simply as shaving, appears in *Neurotica,* 1949, No. 5: p. 17. Here, for the first time since Béroalde, no punch-line or other subterfuge of humor is engaged in, the neurotic or anti-fetichistic description of the mere act of shaving the woman's pubis appearing, as it were, bare.

As is clear, a tale-in-verse without its verbal climax or punch-line is, of course, nothing at all, being by definition only a joke versified. (As may also be seen rather clearly above, a joke in turn is seldom much more than an emotional or neurotic problem jested with.) It is important to note that it is exactly this final 'descent' from actions to *words* that differentiates the tale-in-verse from a true ballad or narrative song. Occasionally — not often — a versified joke will, in the contrary sense, 'rise' to become a ballad, by losing its punch-line and concerning itself more particularly with the action and generally humorous *mise-en-scène.* A good instance of this is the well-known "Sea Crab" song, turning on an almost open *vagina dentata* theme, with the crab dragged improbably from the seashore to the chamberpot to serve as the vaginal 'teeth.' This story, too, appears in the *Moyen de Parvenir,* chap. 49, "Advis," with verse imitation under the title "Le Cancre de Mer" by Blanchemain (using his pseudonym of "Sidredoulx") in the *Contes en vers imités du Moyen de Parvenir,* p. 99. It has been traced further, by Mr. Guthrie Meade — with a little expert help, uncredited — in *Midwest Folklore,* 1958, VIII. 91–100, at note 12, from a joking tale of Levantine origin recorded first in Italy by Sacchetti about 1400, to the Anglo-Scottish song in *Bishop Percy's Folio MS., c.* 1620, which still survives. The 19th century 'coal-hole' and 'cider-cellar,' later music-hall, singers much affected the tale-in-verse (whence its appearance in the various editions of *The Merry Muses*) because, having lost to a degree the audience's participation in the choruses, as in earlier tavern singing, the verbal climax — sometimes slowed down solemnly in the delivery, or even just a shouted pun or erotic homonym — now became the best way of insuring laughter or a round of applause at the end.

V

METAPHORIC folklore is almost always sexual, few other subjects requiring the concealment of so elaborate a rhetorical device. In folksong this also stems from the spontaneous and in part unconscious symbolism underlying certain poetic conventions, as that roses or almost any flower can represent the female genitals (as in the *Song of Songs;* also "My Wild Irish Rose," especially in its frank climactic line), and birds the male genitals (as in "Lesbia's Sparrow," Boccaccio's Nightingale, the Annunciation, &c.); that 'kiss' can refer to sexual intercourse (as in Burns' revision of "Comin' Thro' the Rye" and half a hundred modern popular songs), and 'dying' to the orgasm (as in Dryden's "The Extasy"). These simple symbols and others like them may be considered the normal content of the unconscious, especially in women; and poets and singers have always attempted to appeal to them through the indirect metaphors that would excite without startling the female audience, which is, as is well known, particularly susceptible to generalized sexual excitement by the unaccompanied male voice, and even more so by music. When the audience is male, a much more open use of metaphors is possible, and is in fact necessary, as the threshhold of sexual response to auditory excitement is much lower in men. In all the avian and mammalian species, it is the male that produces, not listens to, the mating song. When a metaphoric song or toast is presented before a male audience, it therefore becomes simply a game, not a seduction, and attempts to demonstrate in *tour-de-force* fashion how many changes can be rung on the rather limited theme, after all, of the sexual organs and acts. The direct appeal to the men's interest is also employed of using erotic metaphors alluding to, and thus pleasurably sexualizing, their daily work.

We have, in this way, in *The Giblet Pye* of *c.* 1806 (p. 112, also in *The Merry Muses* of *c.* 1825, p. 74), "The Deep Nine," a jesting poem on an Irish sailor of heroic proportions, interspersed with the sounding-lead cries of the sailor's profession, in which:

> By sounding half the girls in town
> Two inches soon were worn away.
> *Mark seven . . .*

And eventually,

> Who lately gave such matchless proofs
> Of length, and strength, and manly worth . . .
> His once-fam'd *deep nine* lifeless hung,
>   *Quarter less five.*

Similarly, in an earlier ballad, "The Fireship," *c.* 1690, preserved in the *Pepys Ballads* (ed. Rollins, 1931, VI. 153–5), the woman is elaborately described as a *ship,* and her sexual relations with the man in terms of a sea-battle, replete with ordnance-metaphors, &c., as also in the passage in English in Diderot's *Bijoux indiscrets,* chap. 47, already cited. This song continued to be sung as long as the sailing-ships lasted, and old-timers can still be encountered occasionally who can sing it. It is not identical with the song now called "The Fireship" ('A clean girl, a daycent girl, but one of the rakish kind'), but is the one variously called "While Strolling Through Norfolk", "Ratcliffe Highway," or "The Black Baller," and ends with the sailor admitting that though he has 'sailed with the Rooshians and Johnny Crapaud,' the young lady who bested him 'beat all the stink-pots o' the Heathen Chinee.'

In the rejection-song, "My Thing Is My Own," in *The Merry Muses* of *c.* 1825 (p. 81, discussed earlier), the girl rejects all her suitors in terms suited to their professions: the clerk's 'green bag and ink horn,' the music-master for his mishandling of her fiddle (another standard symbol, as in "DUNCAN MACLEERIE," in all editions of the *Muses*) , the tenant-in-tail, the tailor and his yard, &c. &c. The edition of *c.* 1825 couples two songs, "Venus and Love" and "The Tree of Life" (p. 99, 100), which do nothing but pun upon the idea of the vagina as a fountain and the penis as a tree, which are also among the commonest of symbols in folktales, myths, dreams, and even in the older and less expurgated genealogical charts. (In the later charts the stemma is made to grow out of the supine ancestor's chest, or even forehead; in the early Renaissance charts it is often frankly phallic.)

The 1830's editions of *The Merry Muses,* and all their reprints including that dated '1827,' add a whole new group of eroto-metaphoric songs, including "Jack of All Trades" (p. 101), "The Tenement" (p. 95, on the female body as a *house,* an idea touched upon several times in the *Song of Songs* and *Alice in Wonderland,* chap. 4, also in various prose obscœna, as in "Villa to Let," in *Forbidden Fruit, c.* 1875); and "The Citadel" (p. 45), this last being the description of a seduction in terms of a soldier

attacking an enemy fortress, in which not only all the usual 17th
and 18th century male ordnance-symbols and fireworks are used,
but also a rather unexpected waterworks defense. There is a very
similar poem or song in Sir Charles Hanbury Williams' *Foundling
Hospital for Wit,* nearly a century earlier, 1747, No. 5: p. 13, "A
Ballad on the Rape of Bergen-op-Zoom." The same 'sadistic concept of coitus,' as a death-struggle between the man and woman,
will also be observed in "AS I CAM O'ER THE CAIRNEY MOUNT," in
the original *Merry Muses* (ed. 1959, p. 113), though here it re-
vives the woman rather than kills her; in "The Fireship," mentioned above; and in the modern bar-room recitation, "Our Lil"
or "Lady Lil," first printed in *Immortalia: An Anthology,* 1927,
p. 8 (and there ascribed to Eugene Field), in which the mining-
camp schoolteacher, despite all her 'shunts and double-bunts, and
tricks' . . . commonly unknown, dies 'with her boots on' immediately after, and as a result of, Mexican Pete's sexual triumph
over her.

As has been noted earlier, in passing, the editor of the new
Merry Muses of Caledonia in 1959, Sydney Goodsir Smith, shortly
dismisses Scott Douglas' marginal variants in the unique copy of
the original edition of *c.* 1800, as the work of an 'amateur versifier,' and mere poetic 'carryings-on' (p. 28), with a reproduction,
at p. 14, of manuscript stanzas added marginally to Burns' version
of "ELLIBANKS" in the unique copy, though there is really nothing
to prove that these are strictly the editor's own efforts. Higher
on the same facsimiled page, a note by Scott Douglas observes
that the first sixteen lines of "ELLIBANKS" had been 'printed in a
Dublin collection, 1769,' a collection which has not been identified or traced, nor is this observation quoted in ed. 1959, p. 108.
Even more conscientiously, on the same page, Scott Douglas reverses the two refrain lines, without in any way changing their
wording — almost certainly in accordance with a manuscript text
being collated with the printed edition line by line. These visible
evidences of collation are far from suggesting that Scott Douglas'
marginalia are necessarily his own originals, though one would
not go so far as to ascribe them to Burns. One marginal addition
at p. 122, of particular folklore interest, "A Little Black Thing,"
has never been printed, though a very similar text of this folk-
mummery, later collected in Canada, is given in Arthur H.
Fauset's *Folklore from Nova Scotia* (1931) p. 133. Scott Douglas'
text begins, without title:

AIR "BLACK JOKE"

A little black thing on a cushion sat down
It was hairy without and toothless (but like velvet)
within   *With a fal, [&c.]*

A piper and two little drummers came there
And knocked at the door that was covered with hair
                    With a fal.

The piper went in and jigg'd it about
While the two little drummers kept ruffling without
                    With a fal.

The piper cam out, but not as he went in,
He had piped out his brains and was stripped of his skin
                    With a fal.

The piper had better been out o' the way
And not been so fond to play f — u — c — k
                    With a fal.

But pray who would not in the piper's place be
To enjoy such a pretty black c — u — n — t?
                    With a fal.

'Wisibly veak' as poetry, and not the height of adult humor
either, this is nevertheless exactly similar to Burns' "MY GIRL
SHE'S AIRY" (also to the air "Black Joke"), written during his
amour with Betty Paton, and copied into his Commonplace Book
in September 1784, but not printed in either the first or any of
the early editions of the *Merry Muses,* where it might be assumed to have inspired Scott Douglas. "MY GIRL SHE'S AIRY," as
now printed in the 1959 edition, p. 53, from Burns' holograph
MS., ends:

Her slender neck, her handsome waist
Her hair well buckl'd, her stays well lac'd,
Her taper white leg, with an et, and a, c,
    For her a, b, e, d, and her c, u, n, t,
    And Oh, for the joys of a long winter night!!!

Though certainly by Burns, this is also not very great shakes
as art-poetry, as will be observed. If "A Little Black Thing" is
by Scott Douglas, possibly he was inspired by Burns' Common-
place Book verses just quoted. Or perhaps — which seems less

probable — this is simply an accidental and parallel use of the folk-form of humor involving the spelling-out of bawdy words, either to arrive at a final rhyme (as here), or by way of disguise, as in the children's catch-phrases of farewell (which have been known to fool adults): 'See you when tea is ready!' and 'If you see Kate . . .' The metaphor on which the song turns, of the penis and testicles as a piper and two drummers, and, in particular, the *vagina dentata* reference in the second line (which Scott Douglas has crossed out and replaced with the less anxiety-laden and more anodyne 'but like velvet,' here in parentheses), are also clearly drawn from ancient folk ideas. Several 17th century poems exist, in both English and French, in which the similar metaphor is used of a hunter and his two dogs, the dogs waiting patiently by the side of the symbolic pond in which the hunter has gone swimming. A later Scottish toast in riddling form, very similar, has already been quoted from *Forbidden Fruit, c.* 1875: 'Ane gaes in, and twa stand sentry.' In just the same vein, an 18th century French epigram personifies the testicles as two disloyal serving-men who dance outside the prison where their master lies. Compare with this — though the metaphoric situation is quite different — the second stanza of "MADGIE CAM TO MY BED-STOCK," in the original *Merry Muses* (ed. 1959, p. 154), a stanza still surviving in variant form as a children's rhyme owing to the identification of sex with *food,* so common among children:

> C - - t it was the sowen pat,
> An' p - - - - e was the ladle;
> B - - - - ks were the serving-men
> That waited at the table.
> *Fal, lal, &c.*

VI

THE LAST folksong type of importance here is the parody or travesty. This is almost entirely absent from the editions of *The Merry Muses* earlier than 1830, though it had already enjoyed a long history in England, arriving from France in the mid-17th century with the travesties of Ovid, Virgil, and other classical authors, first by the 'joyeux cul-de-jatte,' Paul Scarron, in *Le Virgile travesti,* 1648, which created the form; then in English imitations by the Royalist wit, Dr. James Smith, in his anonymous *Loves of Hero and Leander,* 1651, and *Innovation of Penelope and Ulysses — A Mock-Poem,* 1658, both of these printed in various drollery collections. The notion of the travesty or 'mock' fell on fertile soil during the revolutionary period in England, not so much among the Puritan revolutionaries and Levellers as among the drollery-writing Royalist poets, of whom Dr. Smith was one of the most singular. It proceeded to such extremes as the Earl of Rochester's farce *Sodom, c.* 1668, satirizing in heroic verse the homosexual court of James I (not Charles II! as is erroneously stated by the editor of the only printed text now existing, L. S. van Römer, in *Kryptádia,* vol. IX, 1909); then to Thomas Duffett's horrible travesties of Shakespeare's *Tempest,* and the like, a form that continued in the theatre at least until Charlie Chaplin's movie burlesque of *Carmen* in 1915. Even Dryden's rewritings of Shakespeare at the period are nothing more than travesties, though not humorous, in the same sense that modern Hollywood 'revisions' of the Bible for million-dollar super-productions are generally burlesques, and profoundly sacrilegious to boot, without themselves in the slightest perceiving this fact.

The drolleries, up to and including that encyclopedia of drollery in six volumes, *Pills to Purge Melancholy,* 1699–1720, are filled with 'mocks' of their own best songs and most charming pastorals. One example is cited by Prof. V. de S. Pinto and Mr. A. E. Rodway, in their *Common Muse,* 1957, p. 8, noting the insistent anti-gallantry of much popular balladry, as when Marlowe's exquisite "Come live with me and be my love" was parodied as 'Come live with me and be my Whore.' No more striking example can be found in English literature than the mock, entitled simply "A Song," in *Pills to Purge Melancholy* (IV [ed. 1709] p. 261; reprinted with the music in ed. 1720, VI. 120), beginning, 'Underneath the Castle Wall, the Queen of Love sat mourning.' One would hardly think so harmless a beginning could offend anyone, yet the mock printed with it, as a second stanza, beginning 'Underneath the rotten Hedge, the Tinkers Wife sat shiting,' truly drips with a sort of insane anal-sadistic violence. This disease, or urge-to-defile — it can hardly be called anything else — is by no means solely English; a quite similar mock in French, entitled "Isaure," is printed in the *Anthologie scatologique* [edited by Gustave Brunet], 1862, p. 33, a supplement to the *Bibliotheca scatologica,* Paris, 1849, of Pierre Jannet, Payen, and Veinant.

The form here involves only a single bathetic collapse of tone at the end of each stanza, similar to a *sotto voce* mock used by American school-children in the 1920's, and perhaps still, where each verse of the inspirational songs the class was required to sing would be followed by the whispered phrase, 'In a night-shirt,' or the even more daring alternation of 'In the front' and 'In the back,' with an effect more or less droll depending on the song chosen: usually "From the Desert I Come to Thee," and "Annie Laurie," respectively. This trick, also, dates from the time of *Pills to Purge Melancholy*, 1719, v. 126, in which a harmless pastoral attributed to Sedley and appearing in its real form in *Comedians Tales, c.* 1730 (issued with cancel-title as *Spiller's Jests;* unique copy, Folger Library, Washington), at p. 83, beginning 'Young Corydon and Phillis, Sat in a lovely Grove,' is made to go off-color at the end of each stanza by the addition of the leering refrain — not present in *Comedians Tales* — 'And something else, but what I dare not [say].'

The false-revolutionary, or rather the abortive revolutionary urge to mock and defy, especially to mock and defy whatever is universally accepted as authoritative, classic, beautiful, true, and the like — as nowadays the questionable surrealist humor of soiling and defacing "Whistler's Mother," the Mona Lisa, and other Virgin-surrogates and masterpieces (if only with wise-guy captions), jazzing Schubert's "Trout" quintet, whooping it up for the Marquis de Sade and other anti-rational fads, Zen, science-fiction, &c. — died down in England during the relatively stable 18th century, with its reaffirmations of classicism and its pretentions of purifying and standardizing not only the language, by Dr. Johnson (in imitation of the dictionary of the French Académie), but even art, in Hogarth's *Analysis of Beauty*, 1753, which proposed to fix 'the fluctuating ideas of Taste.' After such absurdities of reactionism, it is not surprising that the travesties and parodies came back again, even stronger, during the new series of revolutions that ended the 18th century, even more trenchantly in Europe than in America, and that continued until the social concessions that halted the revolutionary ferment in England in the 1840's.

Against this background, the peculiar recrudescence of mocksongs, in the French *caveau* entertainments of the 1800's, and the coal-hole and cider-cellar songsters of England in the 1830's, and '40's, becomes more understandable. Béranger, the most popular song-writer of France, of whom Stevenson said that he was 'the only poet of modern times who could altogether have dispensed with printing,' was put on trial repeatedly for his 'orally transmitted' satires all through the 1820's, as William Hone in England had been put on trial in 1817 for his Biblical and satirical parodies of the Litany, the Catechism, and the Athanasian Creed (imitated from *The Foundling Hospital for Wit,* No. 1, of 1743). It was, of course, the political and not the religious sacrilege of Hone's parodies that was the real *gravamen criminis,* but this was never admitted, and when Hone demonstrated in a memoir (well worth consulting) that religious parody had freely existed in England for centuries, ending with Hanbury Williams' *Foundling Hospital for Wit,* over half a century earlier, he was released with public acclaim.

To return to our *Muses:* the 1830's edition of *The Merry Muses* is filled with burlesques — of "The Miller of Mansfield" (p. 31), of "Shepherds I Have Lost My Love" (p. 34, begins 'Shepherds I have got the clap,' which will give some idea of the formula), of "Corn Riggs Are Bonny" (p. 73), and of "Stella, Darling of the Muses" (p. 84), with a further group of sequels — what would nowadays be called toppers — to songs appearing in earlier editions. In the case of one of the Scottish songs in the original MUSES, "AS I CAM O'ER THE CAIRNEY MOUNT" (p. 24, here entitled "The Highland Laddie"), the original text is printed along with the 'burlesque' — as was the 'mock' in *Pills to Purge Melancholy,* 1720, VI. 120, already mentioned — so that the reader may not on any account fail to appreciate the parodist's art.

A relatively new form of burlesque is introduced in "David and Bathsheba" (p. 50), actually only a revival of Scarron's and Dr. James Smith's travesties of Virgil and Ovid a century and a half before. This is a Bible travesty, in a special sort of galumphing metre — 'Fair Báthshebá, if you'll be mine, I'll make you Queen of Palestine,' &c. — which is still commonly used nowadays for exactly the same kind of travesties, including many publicly published. In these latter, however, the Bible is not often parodied directly, but only by way of various quasi-religious grand operas, such as *Salomé* and *Thaïs.* (In the similar revision of Maugham's *Rain* for the motion-picture censorship, the sinning clergyman, of the book and play, trades his reversed collar for a string necktie, and becomes only an unspecified 'reformer.') It would be correct to say that "David and Bathsheba" is the one most successful piece in *The Merry Muses* of *c.* 1830, in the sense that it is the one still most widely imitated in popular poetry, both polite and obscene. The apparentage with many of the bawdy songs and sagas now current is very striking, especially as to the gallithumpian rhythm, from their opening lines on: 'In fourteen hundred ninety-two, A dago from I-taly,' ("Christopher Columbo"); 'He was wild and woolly and full of fleas,' ("The Bastard King of England"); and, at second hand from Rudyard Kipling, 'Hi ho, Kafoozelum, the harlot of Jerusalem,' as well as others which the reader can perhaps fill in for himself.

However unexpurgated these songs may become, a few lines later than the openings here quoted, they will not compare with the parodies that were sung nightly in the 'for gentlemen only' music-halls of the early mid-19th century in England. Nothing concerning this aspect of the music-hall songs will be found in Harold Scott's *The Early Doors: Origins of the Music Halls*, 1946, though he devotes several pages to the most outspoken of them: Offley's, The Coal Hole, and Cider Cellars, the last two owned by one William Rhodes, an actor-singer. The Coal Hole was most particularly famous for that apogee of all mocking and defying songs, "Samuel Hall," or "Damn Their Eyes!" (a parody of an older, and very serious, hanging-song and work-song "Captain Kidd," or "Chimney Sweep"), introduced there by G. W. Ross, and still going strong after a hundred years, but in versions now boozily over-accentuating the profanity to make up for the missing obscenity. Julian Sharman has described, in 1884, the genesis of his book, *A Cursory History of Swearing*, in a scene approaching a pandemonium of appreciation for the singing of this song, at a club of the 'best men' in London, all the members joining frenetically in the chorus of damn's.

Some of the obscene parodies sung in the early music halls are preserved in the now extraordinarily rare erotic songsters that were openly published in England at that time by William West, a theatrical printer, and by various competitors, and on at least one occasion reprinted in the United States, also quite openly, during the Civil War. As noted earlier, H. Spencer Ashbee, who formed the collection of editions of *The Merry Muses* now in the British Museum's Private Case, transcribes the inordinately long title of one of these song books — *The Blowen's Cabinet of Choice Songs*, which incorporates its tables of contents in its title — in his elegant series of erotic bibliographies (vol. I: *Index Librorum Prohibitorum*, 1877, p. 133–37, and 147), noting the 'truthful sketch' of these music halls in Thackeray's *The Newcomes*, chap. 1; and listing the titles of several dozens of these bawdy songsters. One other such title is transcribed in my exploratory article, "The Bawdy Song ... In Fact and In Print," which, heavily expurgated at its appearance in *Explorations*, University of Toronto, 1957, No. 7, is printed integrally here-following. One songster of perhaps special interest noted by Ashbee (in vol. III: *Catena Librorum Tacend-*

orum, 1885, p. 200), though this copy has not been preserved, is a bawdy Civil War songster, *The Rakish Rhymer,* New York, *c.* 1864, in which, playing no favorites, crapulously obscene parodies are printed of "Yankee Doodle", "The Star-Spangled Banner," and "Dixie," under the titles of "Yarhoo Doodle" (an anti-Union English importation), "The Joy of the Brave," and "Dixie's Land" (in the reprint, 'Lutetia' [Paris: Carrington], 1917, pp. 60, 100, 131), with several other songs in the comedy-German dialect that had by then become popular in America through the German soldiers fighting in the Civil War — a fact now generally forgotten. No copy of the original *Rakish Rhymer* of *c.* 1864 is known to exist; the reprint is in my own collection. An uniquely large further group of *fifty* of such songsters is preserved in the British Museum, C. 116 *a* 6–55.

One exception to the usual tone of these parodies is "Roy's Wife of Aldivalloch," of which the erotic text given in *The Rakish Rhymer* (ed. 1917, p. 117; with a similar Irish parody, "Tim Finigan Wakes," p. 90) is very much in the spirit of the older Scottish folksong. This has been traced by Dr. William Montgomerie, in the *Burns Chronicle,* 1959, p. 49–56, to the marriage of one John Roy, of Aldivalloch, to Isabel Stuart, on 21 Feb. 1727/8, in the parish of Cabrach, Banffshire. The bride, according to one version of the song, was 'bare saxteen,' and the groom 'thrice as auld,' on which beginning only a song of cuckoldry seems possible. The tune, "Ruffian's Rant," is compared by a contributor to *Notes & Queries* 1892, series 4, x. 38, to a 'well-recognised national air of Northern China,' referring as authority to 'Mr. Fleming's work on Chinese Tartary.' Whether the tune came from China to Scotland, or the reverse — *via* Buddhist or Presbyterian missionaries? — is not clear. This song, in any case, is the exception. Most of the mid-19th century parodies differ enormously from the bawdy continuations of the old folksongs (themselves not lily-pure) that Burns and others had attempted to write. By the 1840's the parodies had become not just bawdy but purposely nasty and dysphemistic, their idea of sex ranging from not-quite-healthy to gilravagingly diseased.

By some accident of taste, a horrible example of just the sort of song added to *The Merry Muses* at the worst period of its history has now again been made publicly available in the new edition of 1959, p. 162, "The Plenipotentiary" by Captain Morris, to the air "Shambuie" (in Ramsay), which is presumably segregated at the end of the 1959 volume among the 'alien' Muses, along with "Una's Lock," present on the similar grounds that Burns mentioned it in a letter to George Thomson (quoted later). "The Plenipotentiary" is an English piece; it first appeared in *The Merry Muses* in 1832 and was reprinted in 1843, stuck in at the end, probably as a filler, with three non-erotic items, "The Gipsey Girl", "Here's a Bumper to Her!" and "Fanny Is the Girl For Me." It dates from about the 1780's, when the actual Mohammedan envoy referred to was in the news, and there was much public humor in (what would be a century later) the *Police Gazettes* and *Pink 'Uns* of the time, concerning the presumed supervirility of Mohammedans in general and of the 'Plenipo' in particular. (Compare Bernard de La Monnoye's tale-in-verse, "Le Salamalec," nearly a century earlier.) The erotic *Ranger's Magazine* for Feb. 1795, I. 54–5, for instance, gives an illustration of the 'Bashaw' displaying to the flustered ladies of the court his monumental 'diplomatic ensign and its appendages,' which is also the subject of one of Gillray's most famous caricatures. At that time, any kind of bawdy song on the 'Plenipo' would have served as a topical tidbit, and Capt. Morris' poem was it. It will not compare, for either humor or *élan*, with the stupefying "Ballad of King Farouk," a British Army song, written on an almost identical inspiration in World War II, to the tune of the Egyptian national anthem, and printed with both courage and appropriateness in Hamish Henderson's *Ballads of World War II* (Glasgow, 1947).

The poem or song by Capt. Morris is not so much humorous as gruelling, as the briefest examination of it will show, with particular emphasis on the sadistic concept of coitus. The reason for its printing in the 1832 and 1843 editions of *The Merry Muses* — if not simply as a stuffer — is problematic. Its reprinting now, in a scholarly edition, in 1959, and at full length (sixteen 8-line stanzas), on the piffling excuse that Burns once mentioned it, is little short of a disaster. Fortunately, it cannot detract from the notable triumph for free speech of the year 1959, in which, of the only three indubitable masterpieces in the English language not allowed free public circulation — Burns' *Merry Muses of Caledonia*, Lawrence's *Lady Chatterley's Lover*, and Miller's *Tropic of Cancer* — two were openly published in a single year, with the third following immediately after.

VII

THE PERSON who, more than anyone else, was responsible for the petrifaction of *The Merry Muses*, originally collected and in part written by Burns, and edited posthumously for the convivial club of 'Crochallan Fencibles' to which he belonged, into the unpleasant and practically indefensible form in which it has principally been printed for nearly a century now, was John Camden Hotten. Hotten was a dubious publisher active during the Holywell Street period of almost-open publication of erotic books existing until the 1860's. He had one foot in reputable publishing as well — all erotica publishers do, in order to have something to show the police in explanation of their activity — and he is most particularly famous for having taken over Swinburne's *Poems and Ballads* shortly after publication, when the original publisher scuttled it out of fear of prosecution. A somewhat glozed account of Hotten's career prefaces D. M. Low's *A Century of Writers,* 1955, a centenary volume issued by Chatto & Windus (Hotten's successors), and including Swinburne's angry defense, "Obscenity in Books," from his *Notes on Poems and Reviews,* 1866.

As was usual until quite recently in England, Hotten was a bookseller as well as a publisher, and at least one of H. Spencer Ashbee's copies of *The Merry Muses* still bears in pencil the notation that it was bought from Hotten. In *A Last Scrap Book,* 1924, p. 5, George Saintsbury remembers with affection Hotten's bookshop, and his advertising of his erotica with the delicious catalogue-note, 'Very curious and disgusting.' By the 1870's Hotten was a dying man, and apparently failing in business as well. After having put out a handsome reprint of Dr. James Smith's *Musarum Deliciæ* (originally 1656) in 1870, he turned more and more to his secret publications and to his high-handed piracies of American books, which could not then be copyright in England. This sort of piracy continued until a very recent period — though in the opposite direction: British books being pirated in America — not only by fly-by-night publishers similar to Hotten, but by some of the largest. Mark Twain's letter to the newspapers expressing the whimsical desire to brain Hotten for one of his piracies-*cum*-forgeries (especially for the forged 'revisions'!) is well known. Not so well known is the anecdote, possibly true, told in Everleigh Nash's *I Liked the Life I Lived* (London, 1941) p. 112–14, of another of Hotten's American victims, Ambrose Bierce, rushing into Hotten's bedroom one morning to tirade him for some dubious publication, paid for with a 'dishonoured cheque,' only to learn that he had been mistaken for the undertaker, and that the man he was shouting at was dead.

Hotten's edition of *The Merry Muses* was one of the last books he ever issued or prepared for publication, and appeared in 1872 with the last two digits of the date cannily reversed. This false pre-dating, '1827,' also appears on most of the dozen (at least) British and American reprints of this edition, of which only the last, published 'by a Gentleman of London' in 1930, bothers to indi-cate its own real date. (Copies: Castle Douglas; and Houghton Library, Harvard.) The text, as has already been sufficiently indi-cated, was completely revised and ruinously 'improved' to suit the taste of the times in England, very probably by one of the hacks accustomed to preparing bawdy songs and parodies for the early music-halls, such as F. C. Perry, author of "The Wife's Randy Dream," Aaron Fry, author of "Yarhoo Doodle," a bawdy anti-Union song on slavery and the Civil War, as sung at the original Cider Cellars (*The Rakish Rhymer, c.* 1864, ed. 1917, p. 60), or the even more voluminous John Labern, of the original Coal Hole, several of whose bawdy song books are listed by Ashbee ("Pisanus Fraxi") in his *Index Librorum Prohibitorum,* 1877, p. 135.

The '1827' edition of *The Merry Muses* was based on a copy of the preceding edition, with imprint, London, 1843, as is shown by the including in both of "The Plenipotentiary" and the drop-ping in both of the last stanza of "The Pious Parson" (discussed earlier), possibly because this curious stanza is in the form of an erotic toast, already out of fashion by the 1840's, though the form still lingers on. It must be said, in fairness, that the Scottish texts of the '1827' edition are the part of the volume least revised and manhandled, though that is not saying much. The reason is that Hotten planned to add, and did add, Burns' name on the title-page, for the first time in any edition of the *Muses* since *The Giblet Pye,* about 1806, and the hack-editor was apparently told to leave the Scottish dialect pieces relatively 'unimproved.' Burns' un-deniable contributions to the volume are set first in the text, prin-cipally those songs in the early editions of the *Muses* that had also been printed in his openly-published works, such as "ANNA" and "THE RANTIN' DOG, THE DADDY O'T."

Fifteen such songs in the original edition of *c.* 1800 are listed by McNaught in the *Burns Chronicle,* 1894, but only half of these are actually published complete even in Scott Douglas' 'Kilmar-nock' and 'Library' editions of Burns, or in Henley & Henderson's 'Centenary' edition of 1896–97, which is the best. Only one of these songs, "WHA IS THAT AT MY BOWER DOOR" (ed. *c.* 1800, p. 119) — or rather the folksong on the night-visit that is its original — continues in living tradition, in the burlesque "Bollocky Bill the Sailor." This is best known now in the effete expurgation as

"*Barnacle* Bill," with text to match, from which it was hardly a
step to the utterly synthetic comic-strip and animated-cartoon
loblolly of "Popeye the Sailor Man." As with "Samuel Hall," these
expurgations invariably become the noisier and more violent, the
more the sex is drained out of them. Dialogue songs strikingly
similar to the authentic "Bollocky Bill" are known in other countries as well, mocking the lachrymose girl (singing) and her brutal
lover (angrily replying) at the night-visit. See in particular the
Polish text, with French translation, in *Kryptádia*, 1898, v. 233,
259; and compare the Serbian "Poskochnika," II. 284. An almost
identical dance song is also reported currently from Argentina. It
will be observed how the girl's slow and melancholy couplet
matches the languorous dance-motions 'proper' to girls, while the
men reply in a violent *staccato* of both words and dance. The
formal alternation in this way, in Hungarian music and dances, of
the sensuous *ritardando*, followed by a breakneck climax of speed
(the *lassu* and *friska*), is very well known, having been practically
travestied by Liszt and Brahms. It is unnecessary to underline the
symbolic sexual miming in all these.

To conclude the '1827' edition of the *Merry Muses*, a supplement is added printing for the first time Burns' remarkable letter
of phallic brag, to Robert Ainslie, 3 March 1788, which is omitted
from all editions of Burns' letters (and is therefore reprinted
earlier in the present volume), along with another letter concerning his marriage, addressed to James Johnson, 25 May 1788; plus
"THE COURT OF EQUITY," under the title "LIBEL SUMMONS," which
had already been privately printed by James Maidment in 1823 as
The Fornicators Court. Hotten, or his hack, comes back at several
points to Burns' contribution to the volume, particularly at "JOHN
ANDERSON, MY JO," which is given just before the letters, in a
misch-text from some unknown source — probably made to order
— combining the old form of the song, as seen in the printed text
of the edition of *c.* 1800, with Burns' additional stanzas (as indicated in Scott Douglas' marginalia to his copy of that edition).
The whole is then stated *not* to be by Burns, and his well-known
sentimental expurgation of it, about the aging lovers 'tottering
down' the hill of life hand in hand, to sleep 'thegither at the foot'
(or vice versa), is also printed; to show, as a small-type note explains, the ' "gold, pure and unalloyed" which Burns has substituted for utter grossness and dirt. Where, in the English language,
is there so pure and loveable a picture [&c.]'

McNaught, who shortly disposes of this, in his *Burns Chronicle* article of 1894, as some unknown penny-a-liner eructating his screed of cant, is nevertheless entirely taken in by the '1827' edition, as have been all the bibliographers of Burns since, and imagines it really to have been published at its stated date. He observes, however, that a falsely dated reprint of it had already appeared in Glasgow about 1880, and that others were being continuously produced. I have myself examined a full dozen of such reprints, most of them with the title-page date '1827' but others without; and some that confuse matters even worse with similarly false pre-datings and such mendacious imprints as 'Made in fac-simile of original edition: Privately Printed for Members of the Caledonian Society' (two printings, of 119 and 128 pages, with "David and Bathsheba" and "The Plenipotentiary" added to the first of these); or 'A verbatim reprint of the MDCCCXXVII edition, for myself and my friends.' The texts of all these productions generally follow that of Hotten's 1872 revision blindly, and further offer all manner of unimportant verbal variants, especially as to the system of dashes used in printing the sexual terms.

The only '1827' reprint of any folksong interest is undoubtedly the most shabbily-printed of them all (104 pages, sq.12mo), issued at an indeterminable date somewhere between 1890 and 1920, and evidently in Scotland, as it amateurishly adds one authentic Scottish song, "Comin' Thro' the Craigs o' Kyle," p. 101–2, at the very end, after "Libel Summons." This is a charming metaphoric piece about a 'bonnie lass, Smuggling whisky in a blether,' and has never been printed elsewhere. (Burns' expurgation is printed in Johnson's *Museum*, no. 328.) The only known copy of this edition is in the Murison Burns Collection, though it does not appear in its printed *Catalogue*, Dunfermline, 1953, p. 53. The only reprint of the *Merry Muses* of '1827' of historical or sociological interest is one published openly — for the first time before 1959 — in upstate New York (in Tonawanda, I believe), about 1910, with the printer's name and a stock-cut of an owl on the title-page. This must be very rare; I know of no copy but my own. As has been observed, most of the early editions of the *Merry Muses* — as of the majority of erotic books — survive only in unique copies. For the benefit of collectors it may be mentioned that the *real* fake of '1827,' published in 1872, is either the one in which the title-page initials have long swash forelegs (of xi, 125 pages; but not its cheap reprint, of 90 pages), or else the one with hollow white initials on square black blocks (vii, 124 pages), both measuring 6¼ x 4¾ inches, and both known only in unique copies in the Ashbee Bequest, Private Case, British Museum. All other fake editions are, *bien entendu,* fakes.

VIII

HOTTEN's edition of 1872 was apparently inspired by, and is in a way the diabolical punishment of, an article in the *London Spectator,* 19 August 1871, on Burns and Scott, specifically on 'coarseness and refinement' in Burns. (Compare "Vision and Vicissitude in Kafka", "Vivisection and Cross-section in Kierkegaard", "Impact and Hand-packed in Kropotkin," or anybody else beginning with a *K* — these buggers are never going to get to the *L*'s, I'm afraid — a type of critical cliché erroneously thought of as recent.) The article resulted in one of those lively newspaper correspondences, when there is no other news in midsummer, in the provincial press, particularly the Glasgow *North British Daily Mail* (22–31 August 1871), in which Burns' part in *The Merry Muses* was somewhat bandied about. This revived public interest, or at least so John Camden Hotten must have correctly guessed. The interest had of course much died down since the last previous edition, in 1843, which had boldly given Burns' name in the running-heads; and the awful disclosures as to its nature, by Burns' particular or signifying Nemesis, George Gilfillan, minister of the Steeple Kirk, Dundee, a reverend jackass who had actually written in *Hogg's Instructor* for 1847, No. 143, of the dying Burns:

> . . . he was desperate and at bay, vomiting forth obscenity, blasphemy, fierce ribaldry and invective . . . His eloquence, once so pure, even in its wildness and mirth, was now a hideous compost of filth and fire. Death never did a more merciful act than when he closed the most living lips that ever spake in Scotland — the lips of Robert Burns.

If that didn't instruct the Hoggs, I don't know what could. A partisan of Burns, Hugh Macdonald, objected to Gilfillan's attacks, to which Gilfillan replied by bringing to general public notice for the first time, in a letter printed in the *Glasgow Citizen,* 27 Dec. 1847, the whole subject of *The Merry Muses,* which had been until then a private matter of vest-pocket-sized booklets, secretly printed and intended to be concealed, and of tolerant

discussion at the Annual Anniversary Dinner in memory of Burns.
(Gilfillan's *Glasgow Citizen* letter is reprinted in the *Burns
Chronicle*, 1895, IV. 32–4, preceded by a curious article, "Deity or
Dirt?" by Dr. James Adams, discussing and lambasting the *Muses*
in part, as does his "Burns *versus* the 'Pot Boiler'," in 1894, III.
103–7.)

Having 'made' the edition of 1843 — of which it seems unlikely
that any copies remained unsold in Glasgow after January 1st,
1848 — Gilfillan did what he could for Hotten's edition, coming
back thirty years later to the horrendous subject that so attracted
him, in the "Life of Burns," dated 1878, appended to his masterpiece of overstuffed and pretentious typography, *The National
Burns*, 1879–80, Division III, page lxxxii (column 2):

> Chambers gives what is, we suppose, an accurate enough
> account of the way in which the collection came to see the
> light, after Burns' death, through the cupidity of a book-
> seller. He calls it a "mean-looking volume." This was true
> of the copy White [Robert White, of Newcastle] showed
> us; but we once saw, for a mere minute or two, a better
> got-up edition (not for sale, however), in two volumes,
> in the shop of the late Maurice Ogle, publisher, Glasgow.
> This miserable book may probably be still creeping, like
> the plague in Constantinople, in obscure regions of the
> country. But its very vileness prevents it from being nox-
> ious; it kindles no feeling but disgust, awakens no passion
> but anger, or rather grief — disgust at the volume itself, grief
> for the author . . . (Full text reprinted in *Burns Chronicle*,
> 1911, xx. 106–7.)

The Glasgow publisher on whom Gilfillan is here gallantly
blowing the gaff, he being safely dead, was actually Robert Ogle,
publisher and bookseller, who died at Edinburgh, 30 Jan. 1876, at
the age of 75. His father had the same name and occupation. The
firm name was 'Maurice Ogle & Co.,' whence Gilfillan's mistake.
The edition 'in two volumes,' otherwise unknown, of which we
have here the only hint as to its possible publisher, was the only
popular redaction that followed Hotten's, and is of particular
interest folkloristically. (There is perhaps some further hint in
that 'obscure regions of the country,' but this cannot now be traced
unless Newcastle, a famous chapbook center, is meant.) Only one
copy has survived, in the Murison Burns Collection, and this copy

is fitted with a brass lock, in operating condition, set into the front edge of the binding. Both 'volumes' are bound in one, being consecutively numbered though on different weights of paper; *The Merry Muses* is the second part, beginning on p. 83.

The title is '*Forbidden Fruit:* A Collection of Popular Tales by Popular Authors, including Meitor, Walker, Cæsar, Cowper, Turnor, Ryder, Wyper, Lover, Howitt, Burns. Also the Expurgated [*sic*] Poems of Robert Burns, known as Burns' Merry Muses. Copied from authentic M.S.S. The whole forming the most unique collection on an all-absorbing topic ever issued. Not for sale.' At the head is the caution: 'Not for Maids, Mothers, or Ministers' — in imitation of the caption in Hotten's edition, 'Not for Maids, Ministers, or Striplings' in the same position. No date is given, but from a satirical poem at p. 60, on Annie Besant's birth-control agitation and methods (which first attracted attention in 1874, the poem being later reprinted in *The Pearl*, 1879–80, after the sensation of the Bradlaugh-Besant trial for Knowlton's *Fruits of Philosophy*), it may be dated as no earlier than about 1875. Robert Ogle had continued publishing to quite an advanced age, and cannot be ruled out on that account. His finest book, a superb type-facsimile of James Watson's *Choice Collection of Comic and Serious Scots Poems,* 1706–11, had appeared in 1869, limited to 165 copies 'owing to its nature,' as booksellers' catalogues still say of it, and was the model for Hotten's *Musarum Deliciæ* of 1870 and the many other drollery and ballad-facsimile reprints that immediately followed, none of which are as fine.

Aside from the *Muses* section, of which the text is simply an abridged reprint of fifty items from Hotten's corrupted text, *Forbidden Fruit* includes a considerable group of otherwise unpublished Scottish and other erotic folksongs, some pornographic poems and stories, and several curious prose facetiæ, the one on names incorporated in the subtitle being a good example. It contains, as has already been mentioned, the earliest modern text of "The Ball of Kirriemuir," under the short title, "The Ball" (p. 68), as well as a version of the very ancient lying-song, "Three Old Whores" (p. 27, entitled "The Royal George," and connected with the British Army song, "The Captain's Wife," recently publicly published in T. E. Lawrence's *The Mint*), which is discussed in my article in Explorations, 1957, reprinted later. There is also an erotic counting-song, "Twelve Inches" (p. 32), still current and very popular in the United States in forms referring to both inches ("Inches One") and to the hours of a clock. None of these except

"There's Hair On't", "The Ball," and "Dainty Davie" (p. 38, the original folk version), has any relation to *The Merry Muses.*

The humorous prose obscœna of *Forbidden Fruit,* especially those playing on names, as on the title-page, are of particular folk-lore interest. Though they survive nowadays only as humor, they seem related to much older magical notions concerning names, numbering, the assuming of nicknames as a *rite de passage,* and the unpronounceable (taboo) appellations of kings and divinities as an apotropaic protection from exactly the 'harmfully' mocking perversion or misapplication of these names that is involved in this type of humor. ('Sticks and stones may break my bones, But *names* and faces never hurt me!') In much the same way, modern circus clowns are a merely *humorous* survival — through the Roman games whose name they still bear — of ancient transvestist, and earlier animal-miming priests; as the circus itself is a survival of their sacrifices, including the ritual baiting by animal 'trainers' (in Spain the killing) of the sacrificial animals.

These prose name-obscœna seem generally to be the *jeux d'esprit* of lawyers' clerks or law-students, as are also the mock parliamentarian speeches (the modern "Change the Name of Arkansaw!?") of which an early example appears in *The Foundling Hospital for Wit,* 1749, No. 6; in the same way that bawdy songs in France are still the prerogative of medical students and art-atelier assistants, as in Rabelais' time. The relation to the sacrilegious mock-sermons of the Feast of Fools is discussed in Isaac D'Israeli's *Curiosities of Literature,* ed. 1849, II. 165–6, 282–97, "Ancient and Modern Saturnalia." These orgies of personal and sexual liberty, centering around the Christmas — New Year's — Twelfth Night (Russian Christmas) period of license, at the mid-winter descent of the sun, for the three days 'in the tomb' curiously assimilated to Easter in Christianity, are common to all Western cultures and religions, as are also the public sexual rites intended to recapture and revive the dying sun. These rites now survive only in covert and much modified form: the mistletoe kissing-permission (under the *gui,* or sacred bough, of the Druids), and the winked-at sexual and verbal license of Mardi Gras and Purim, both of which 'feature' the mock-speeches here under discussion.

These liberties are also formalized in mock documents, permits, and even coins, such as those stamped and sold as souvenirs at the Abbaye des Conards (Lord of Misrule) celebrations as late as the 18th century in France. Versions are still common in the United States, sometimes in erotic 'spinner' (optical toy) form, a sort of quasi-magic in which the animal-totems of the competing political parties — figuring on both sides of the coin — are seen mounting each other when the coin is spun. Except for the almost-serious *Aresta Amorum* of the late medieval Courts of Love, as published by Martial d'Auvergne, the oldest collection of such fantasy documents is the mock-legal *Formulaire fort récréatif* of "Bredin le Cocu" (anagram of Benoît du Troncy, or more probably of Benoît Court, editor of the *Aresta Amorum*, its clear inspiration) in the late 16th century, which has recently been republished in Monaco, 1958. In the same way, the *Records of the Beggar's Benison*, the Scottish erotic society already mentioned, include its mock membership diploma in the form of a ship's license, dating from about 1765, with phallophoric decorations. (See also its *Supplement*, Anstruther, 1892, p. 17–31, 82–8, with erotic songs *passim*.) Licenses of this type are still sold in novelty shops in England and America, both in over-the-counter forms as "Fishermen's Lying Certificates" and "Henpecked Husbands' Fun Cards," etc., and in under-the-counter forms as "Farting Permits," "Muff-Divers' Diplomas," and the like. On the similar "Brevets" of the *Regiment de la Calotte,* '7726' (*i.e.* 1726), see D'Israeli, II. 296–7, and, less discreetly, 'Jean Hervez' [Raoul Vèze], *Les Sociétés d'Amour au XVIIIe. siècle,* 1906, p. 324–55, especially at p. 176–205, on the orgiastic Order of Felicity, with a glossary of their 'nautical' secret or metaphoric language (to be compared with Thomas Stretzer's eroto-metaphoric *Merryland,* published about the same period at Bath). An elegant collection of facsimiles of such "Brevets" and "Patentes" was published in the original folio size by Gay & Doucé in Bruxelles, 1881, as *Douze Facéties : Patente des Cocus, &c.* The Cuckolds' Patent is the only one *not* in facsimile, as an original copy could not then be discovered; but I have recently had the extraordinarily good fortune to find an actual example, dating from the late 18th century.

The most common literary expressions of these parody-formulas are the mock book-titles which are still extremely common in American folk-humor and can be collected by the dozens ("The Yellow Stream" by I. P. Freely; "Life of an African Princess" by Erasmus B. Black, and so forth), on the model of Rabelais' mock catalogue of the library of St. Victor, much imitated since. See, in particular, the materials gathered in the monograph on Rabelais' *Catalogue* by the "Bibliophile Jacob" [Paul Lacroix], 1862, and especially Renier Chalon's never-to-be-forgotten legpull, the Catalogue of the "Fortsas" auction of unique works (title and *the* item

no. 48 facsimiled in Edmund Pearson's *Books in Black or Red,*
1924, p. 32); to which may be added the satirical "Bibliothèque
de Mme de Montpensier" in Artus Thomas' *Description de l'Isle
des Hermaphrodites,* ed. 'Cologne,' 1724, p. 291–330; the "Catalogue des livres nouveaux de l'Imprimerie Souterraine," added to
Lettres Infernales, et Les Tisons, 'Aux Enfers,' 1760, p. 66 ff.; and
the mock catalogue, just a century later, of the library of 'Dr.
Rainbeau' (a friendly satire on the musicologist, Rimbault), copy
in the New York Public Library, Music Division.

The oldest example of this type of humor that I have been able
to discover, is the *Processus contra ser Catium Vinculum,* printed
about 1530, which I believe can be ascribed to the original 'maca-
ronic' humorist, Teofilo Folengo ("Merlin Cocciae"), as a work
of revenge against the head of the religious order from which he
had been expelled, who is named therein. This is presented as the
record of a mock law-case in Latin, with a truly remarkable phallic
ornament or seal, and with witnesses 'Ser Fottivinculo, Doña
Merda *eius filia,* Ser Cazzotinculo,' &c. The only existing copy is
bound with the similarly unique *Sonetti lussuriosi* of Aretino,
containing the fabulous original woodcuts after the drawings by
Giulio Romano engraved by Marcantonio Raimondi, a work which
had been lost for four hundred years, and was rediscovered only
in the late 1920's in Milan by the bibliographer Max Sander, who
describes his find in "Ein Aretinofund," *Zeitschrift für Bücher-
freunde,* 1929, N.F. XXI. 50–60.

IX

THE LATER history of *The Merry Muses* is perhaps more of
Burnsian than of folklore interest, but may be briefly sketched.
Scott Douglas' unique copy of the *Merry Muses of Caledonia,* of
c. 1800, came into the possession of the Glasgow book-collector,
W. Craibe Angus, who, before selling it — as bibliophiles are wont
— to another collector, R. T. Hamilton Bruce, arranged to have a
complete MS. copy made by James Cameron Ewing, the bibliographer of Burns, 'with the intention of having a new edition of
the book — edited by Mr. William Ernest Henley — privately
printed; that intention, however, was never carried out.' Ewing
made not one copy but two, as was only intelligent, of which his
own is now preserved in the Murison Burns Collection, with the
manuscript note just quoted. The other copy was sent to Henley,
as planned, who made minor use of it in connection with the

standard 'Centenary' edition of Burns' *Poetry* (1896–97) which he co-edited. Although Henley neither published the *Merry Muses* alone, nor included its songs — as he properly should have — in the 'Centenary' Burns, he did apparently make the Ewing transcript available to the mysterious John S. Farmer, with whom Henley was collaborating all through the 1890's on their monumental and thoroughly unexpurgated historical dictionary, *Slang and Its Analogues*, 1890–1909, in seven volumes and revised vol. 1 (incorporating Henley's additions, after his death). When the dictionary project was temporarily shelved for lack of funds in 1895, and again in 1897, in favor of the scholarly pot-boiler, *Merry Songs and Ballads*, 1895–97, in five volumes; Farmer was thus able to add, at the end of each volume of this work, a *bonne-bouche* of authentic texts from the original edition of the *Merry Muses*.

Again, later, in 1903, at some other unimaginable crisis, for cash to keep the slang dictionary going — then not only in sight of the good word 'Finis,' but with the revised volume 1 simultaneously under way — Farmer sent out private prospectuses, announcing a *manuscript issue* of fifty holograph copies to be made from the original text of the *Merry Muses*. It was in this prospectus that he dropped the hint as to the present location of the Scott Douglas copy, that made possible its rediscovery recently and its use in the new 1959 edition. How many copies were actually made of the 'manuscript issue' of 1903 is not known, but one of these copies — in a stiff clerical hand, not Farmer's — is now in the possession of Maurice Lindsay, Esq; in whose *Burns Encyclopædia*, London (why not Edinburgh?) 1959, at "Merry Muses," p. 167, this issue is discussed. It must be admitted that there is something a little *tacky* about Farmer's evident milking of the Ewing transcript for needed cash: it smacks somehow of trafficking. One is sorry to learn that it happened just that way — but that is the way it is with solving mysteries.

Neither Farmer's reprinting of the authentic texts in 1895–97, nor his MS. issue of 1903 was known to McNaught when he undertook the first critical edition of *The Merry Muses of Caledonia* in 1911, a work he had evidently been preparing since 1894. This was published privately for the Burns Federation [by D. Brown & Co., Kilmarnock], and limited to one hundred copies, according to the prospectus. McNaught's valuable *Burns Chronicle* articles of 1894 and 1911 — the latter ending with an advertisement for the new edition — were reprinted in major part as introduction, but now signed "Vindex," though the original articles were signed with the editor's real name. McNaught's own access to the unique printed copy of *c.* 1800 is not completely explained, but he certainly used it, as he follows the original order of the text, and incorporates into the 1911 edition almost all of Scott Douglas' marginalia (to the detriment of the original printed text). He was also the first person ever to describe the orginal edition fully, in the *Burns Chronicle* for 1894; Scott Douglas having referred to it precisely, but only very briefly, in his 'Library' edition of the *Works* of Burns (Edinburgh, 1877–79, II. 47; VI. 99–101).

McNaught's whole interest in the subject would seem to have risen from a study of the Scott Douglas copy about 1893, at the confused period when W. Craibe Angus was ceding it to R. T. Hamilton Bruce, from whom it passed to the then Prime Minister, Archibald Philip Primrose, the elder Lord Rosebery. Recognizing indeed the importance of this unique work, which had so narrowly escaped total destruction, as a monument of Scottish folksong, and relic of Burns, Lord Rosebery had the tattered pamphlet remounted page by page (with the loss of many of its page-numbers but none of the text), and enshrined in its present double binding-cum-box. It is perhaps only a curious coincidence, but the song or epigram, "SUPPER IS NA READY," in all editions of the *Muses,* is a good-humored if somewhat improper sally at the expense of a much earlier Lord Rosebery and his 'bonny lady;' a fact on which Allan Cunningham had already remarked, in 1826, in his manuscript analyzed earlier (MS., p. 13): 'The remarkable coincidence between this supposed Lady Roseberry's conduct and that of the true is really surprising.' The truth of the matter, which is somewhat more subtle, will appear later.

McNaught learned of Farmer's 1895–97 reprinting only after the 1911 edition was already off the press, and he adds an irritated "Note" concerning it on a special leaf tipped-in at p. 121, preceding "THE COURT OF EQUITY." This leaf does not appear in the American piratical reprint of the McNaught edition, made about 1930 in Philadelphia (no place or date of publication given; and of xxxi, 143 pages), which changes McNaught's signature to the introduction from "Vindex" to the even more anonymous "Editor," and throws in the Ainslie letter of 3 March 1788, also "The Plenipotentiary" (both from Hotten's '1827' edition of 1872), with a Scottish glossary for good measure. There are copies of this reprint in a number of American university libraries; the original of 1911 is far more rare. Filled with textual blunders as it is, McNaught's attempt was nevertheless deeply worth-while, and its introduction and notes were the first real clearing of the field, toward the rehabilitation of Burns' own *Merry Muses* collection.

It is worth remembering that neither McNaught's edition, nor the new critical edition of 1959, really reproduces the original text of *c.* 1800. The new edition, in particular, which is not in the original order, makes the pointless economy of saving ten pages (in a 175-page book), and jettisons the ten songs in the original *Muses* now available in standard editions of Burns — though in 1800 they seemed too erotic for all but private print — meanwhile valuably adding sixteen new texts discovered in manuscript. It is thus something both more, and less, than the much-needed reprint of the original. An actual *facsimile* edition of the *Merry Muses of Caledonia* of *c.* 1800, from the unique Rosebery copy, with all necessary editorial annotation relegated to an appendix, where it more properly belongs and might more usefully be consulted, still remains to be undertaken. One trusts that the stated copyright on the new edition of 1959 would not preclude the reprinting also of the newly-discovered texts, in a further appendix, from the manuscripts of a poet now dead for over a century and a half. The alarming precedent of the Boswell *Memoirs* case recently, however, leads one to fear the opposite.

It is by no means that the annotation of the two critical editions is not well done, and more than welcome — to the contrary! It is simply that such *apparatus criticus* inevitably overloads the text, and blurs any real impression of what the original work (or the original manuscript) must have been, not only textually and typographically but in the human sense as well. One finds more useful, in many ways, the more modest scholarship of facsimile presentation, followed by any necessary notes, in a matching appendix, as in the reprint of the equally rare and even more bawdy 'Antwerp,' 1680, edition of the *Poems on Several Occasions* of the Earl of Rochester, undertaken with extraordinary courage by the Princeton University Press in 1950. One is sorry to observe that the editor, Prof. James Thorpe, shows a courage somewhat more tempered, and almost succeeds in making a joke of the whole thing in his notes, by 'finding' that practically none of the poems and songs reprinted are by Rochester. In which case the *purpose* of the reprint becomes almost inexplicable. This is almost identical with McNaught's notion of 'vindicating' the memory of Burns, by rejecting the ascriptions of such great Burns editors as Scott Douglas, Henley & Henderson, and Hans Hecht; and accoutering his 1911 reprint of *The Merry Muses of Caledonia* with rather improbable headnotes intrusively identifying as 'An old song,' rather than as Burns's, all but hardly three of the songs. Were this really the case, there would have been very little point in his reprint at all, and the intended 'vindication,' as he says (in the opposite sense) of Hotten's edition, would be 'rather a slender pretext for hoisting such a sky-cleaving signboard.'

Aside from this visible and ambivalent attraction to, and pretended rejection of, the erotic materials involved; there is also the standard editorial habit of riding personal hobbies, and cultivating — usually for the purpose of furthering one's own career — new and daring theories as to a 'classic' text, in the humorless and obstreperous way already necessary to be satirized in the early 18th century, in Cordonnier de St.-Hyacinthe's deathless *Chef d'Oeuvre d'un Inconnu*. Most editors somehow cannot bear to let their text or author alone, and let his fame (or notoriety) ride unsaddled with theirs. The tail is always trying to wag the dog. I am speaking just as much of myself as of anyone else. For all the terrible shock it has been to a certain type of folklore editor, in particular (see Prof. A. P. Hudson's *Folksongs of Mississippi,* 1936, p. viii, quoting the original remark), the truest editorial vision was that of the incomparable George Lyman Kittredge, politely rejecting a very lengthy introduction to a comparatively short folksong collection, with a paraphrase of 2 *Maccabees,* ii. 32: 'The text is the thing.'

x

OUR CENTURY is now beginning to catch up with that of Burns in the freedom accorded bawdy song, at least for listening if not for singing — and print. Most of the best songs, musically, of the original *Merry Muses* have recently and very courageously been recorded for the phonograph, under the title *Songs from Robert Burns' Merry Muses of Caledonia* (Baton Rouge, Louisiana: Folk-Lyric Records, "Dionysus" label, D.1) . Superlatively sung by one of the finest modern interpreters of folksong, Ewan MacColl, this recording is based entirely on the unexpurgated Ferguson & Smith edition of 1959, and may therefore be considered entirely authentic as to its texts. The courage of its publishers, Mr. Harry Oster and Dr. Kenneth S. Goldstein, is worthy of the highest commendation. The same cannot be said for a somewhat earlier recording, chummily entitled *Bobby Burns' Merry Muses of Caledonia* (New York: Elektra 155), issued in 1958 with an ex-purgated wordbook illustrated, for some reason, with Japanese armorial crests, which gives some idea of the authenticity of the whole enterprise. On this earlier recording a number of thor-oughly expurgated texts, taken from the faked '1827' edition, are weakly performed by a Mr. Paul Clayton, to guitar accompani-ments credited to Mr. Fred Hellerman, and so absurdly maudlin, tuneless, and boneless, and in any case so flabbergastingly distant from anything conceivably connected with Scottish folksong, that it is impossible to discuss it, them, or anything about this record in any serious critical way. Everyone connected with it ought simply to be sent to Scotland (surely a new experience for them), and there driven into a bog.

As there has been quite an invasion, over the last seven or eight years, of similarly expurgated phonograph recordings of presumably bawdy songs, I ought perhaps to mention that these are in part my own fault, for prematurely announcing the pro-jected publication of a large collection of erotic folksong in Eng-lish, and ill-advisedly appealing to a number of successful radio 'folksingers' for unexpurgated texts. I do not, of course, accept the blame for the expurgation. Of this, the Clayton "Bobby Burns" record is a prime example, pricelessly remarking in its record-sleeve blurb: 'Of necessity certain four letter words had to be changed to other four letter words, but this was done without any bowdlerizing of the meaning or feeling.' As an example of doublethink this would be hard to beat. Typical of this Pick-wickian expurgation 'without any bowdlerizing' is, for instance, the substitution throughout of the word *cage* for *cunt*. Whether it is the 'meaning' or the 'feeling' here, that remains unchanged, would be hard to say. Briefly put, this whole piece of commer-cial claptrap is a disgrace, and its palsy-walsy exploitation of Burns' name is, in particular, an outrage. Most objectionable of all is its pusillanimous and farcically unresearched fobbing off on the public of textual pseudo-pornography and melodic pseudo-folksong which sound about as much like Burns' Merry Muse as a hermaphrodite in a bubble-bath.

Worse luck, it was just this indefensible "Bobby Burns" item that arrived in Scotland on the eve of the issue of the newer and courageously authentic disc sung by MacColl, and precipitated every kind of hostile and religio-patriotic criticism *except* for its sub-abysmal quality. The present and former heads of the world-wide Burns Federation (under whose imprint, *totidem*

litteris, the unexpurgated *Merry Muses* were published by Mc-
Naught as long ago as 1911, state for publication that they are
'very angry,' that 'Burns never wrote these songs,' and that 'A
record of these songs will be a slur on Burns and on Scotland.'
Well, that the Clayton-Hellerman-Elektra record is such a slur
is certain; but that any recording of the *Merry Muses* songs must
necessarily be a slur on the poet who collected and rewrote them,
and the country in which they were and (in part) still are sung,
is now amply disproved by this really splendid recording by Ewan
MacColl. One can quarrel with it, seriously, only as to its price:
obviously set excessively high at nine dollars to limit the audience, and to protect itself from any accusation of pandering to
the general public.

This recording is essentially a companion to MacColl's earlier
and equally fine *Songs of Robert Burns* (New York: Folkways
Records, FW. 8758), issued in 1959, and the effort has evidently
been made in the *Merry Muses* record to avoid too much overlapping of the tunes used. In both cases the texts have been learned
frankly from the printed editions and seldom from folk transmission — in which Burns' own songs will today only very exceptionally be found — and the airs, for the most part, from Johnson's *Scots Musical Museum,* on which Burns collaborated. One
cannot really do better than that, by way of authentic re-creation
of the old folksongs, by any modern singer. Also, and aside from
these melodies learned-from-book, some of the loveliest airs in
both the MacColl recordings come from his own family tradition,
both his parents being authentic folksingers themselves. Worth
particular note are the "Lea Rig" tune, used for "MY AIN KIND
DEARIE" in the *Merry Muses* recording, and the very similar and
absolutely superb "AY WAUKIN, O," given in the *Songs of Robert
Burns* recording. This short lament is one of the most perfect
achievements, in purity of phrasing and profound simplicity, of
any recorded folksong in any language.

Ewan MacColl's art in the unaccompanied singing of Scottish
folksong, and the fresh and virile emotion of his voice, are now
too well-known internationally to require any further eulogy
here. Most remarkable — and only too rare in folksinging — are
his perfect sustaining tone in the release of held notes, and the
unerring musicianship of his attack, always, without the help of
the usual noisy guitar or other accompaniments on which most
neo-folksingers nowadays rely, to remind them of the rhythm and
to cover errors of a half-tone or more in scooping up and down

looking for difficult intervals they have undertaken to hit. Mac-
Coll's singing is altogether one of the most moving experiences
available on folksong recordings today, when so much of what
is presented as 'revival' folksinging is so embarrassingly false.
His particular excellence is not so much in the ruddy-bloody, burly
and masculine rant, and the barrel-chested sexual brag expected
of men's songs in general, and of bawdy song in particular — and
in which MacColl can easily take cards-&-spades when he feels
like it — but in the poignant and emotional erotic songs *in the
character of the woman* so frequent in the poetry of Burns, and
so central and significant in the *Merry Muses of Caledonia,* where
every such feminine-identification song is — precisely for the reason
of that identification — to be supected of being Burns' own, or
importantly revised by his hand.

Burns' songs, from the point of view of the woman, even those
not overtly erotic, such as the polite version of "JOHN ANDERSON,
MY JO," are of the greatest significance in understanding his art;
and particularly those frankly sexual songs presented in the *Merry
Muses* in unexpurgated form, and with all the perfectly frank
'*he*-took-*me*' pronouns and anatomical details of a woman supposedly recounting her own emotions and experience. They are
clearly a real expression of human feeling, really felt, where the
noisy sexual self-adulation of the Ainslie letter (earlier reprinted)
is simply a man talking the way he knows men are supposed to
talk, but unfortunately giving away, to modern ears — especially
in the pawky and untypical caution of Burns' treatment of the
woman, in this letter — a whole hornet's nest of feelings of sexual
and social inferiority beneath. Burns' poems and songs in the
character of the woman cannot, of course, be held to be the
authentic expressions of the sexual psychology of women, but
rather the expression of that psychology as understood *by a man,*
and as only a poet and lover is able to identify with it. Within
these limitations, Burns' feminine-identification songs are among
the most penetrating statements of the erotic emotions of women
— as men believe them to be — that have ever been made. Compare
Shakespeare and the 'articulate heroines' of so many of his plays,
with whom he so clearly identifies himself, where the presumed
heroes are only vacillating and sub-virile sticks like Hamlet and
Romeo, yearning to be the noisily bawdy *alter ego* of a Mercutio.

Ewan MacColl is not the only singer of men's songs who rises
to greater heights when the song is of the woman's emotion, and
not of the man's sexual narrative and brag. The American singer,

Ed McCurdy, in his *When Dalliance Was in Flower* (Elektra 110), issued in 1956 and followed by a number of similarly-titled recordings, all taken in largest part from Playford & Durfey's *Pills to Purge Melancholy;* excellent as he is in the boisterous music-hall humor of the lusty songs of Casanova adventures among-the-milkmaids, invariably stamps his singing with a deeper sincerity when the song is to be sung tenderly and huskily, in the character of the woman herself. Quite aside from "AY WAUKIN, O," mentioned above, MacColl, in such songs, consistently strikes an extraordinary dark poignancy — in no way, of course, denied by the powerful virility of his voice — that makes one think of the magnificent brooding voices and laceratingly restrained emotionalism of two of the greatest women singers of our century, Kathleen Ferrier and Conchita Supervia; now, alas, to be heard only on phonograph recordings.

XI

RATHER THAN attempt to analyze in the foregoing essay, the contents of the original *Merry Muses of Caledonia* as folklore, it has seemed more useful to discuss in this way the lesser collections imitating its title; collections which remain even more difficult of access than the original, and which can now no longer hope to be covered or defended by Burns' great name. The text of the original edition being now publicly available since 1959, and essentially so since Farmer's *Merry Songs* publication in 1897 and McNaught's preliminary edition in 1911; it has seemed reasonable to defer its folklore annotation, which is more difficult and much more important, to a later occasion and perhaps to other researchers. A word must now be said, however, and perhaps more, owing to the booklet of unexpurgated texts and careful annotation by Kenneth S. Goldstein, which accompanies the remarkable phonograph recording just described. This is one of the most elaborate and valuable of such pamphlets that has yet been issued with a folksong recording, and it is well worth separate preservation (and library cataloguing, usually overlooked), not only as a partial or 'garland' edition of the *Merry Muses* — the 'penny merriments' of our own day, now that the broadside ballads have disappeared — but also for its provocative and thorough-going documentation, and the identification of the tunes involved.

As is usual with editors, Dr. Goldstein rides several hobbies here, in particular as to the complex textual relationship between Burns' collecting of folksongs and the Herd manuscript, somewhat earlier. The conclusion at which he arrives, several times indicated, is that of Alexander Keith (in *Burns and Folk-Songs,* 1922), that Burns and Herd were both independently 'tapping the same flow.' This is contrary to the position of so great an editor as Hans Hecht (in *Songs from David Herd's MSS.,* 1904, p. 319; compare also Henley & Henderson's 'Centenary' Burns, III. 452), and — if small things may be compared with great — my own. I consider it unquestionable that Burns had access to the materials of Herd's MSS., though it is equally probable that he did not know the real source of these materials, and would certainly have credited them had he known. Burns was not the man to steal another man's collection, or silently appropriate another man's research. The access to Herd's materials is very plain to see in "THE LINKIN' LADDIE" (a fragment of Child Ballad No. 241, "The Baron o' Leys"), which is copied verbatim from the Herd MS. I. 118, 233, and II. 71; not in Hecht) in both the *Scots Musical Museum* (1790, No. 237) and — though hardly erotic — in the *Merry Muses of Caledonia* (ed. 1959, p. 152). In the same way, "WAP AND ROW" — not taken from Herd — appears almost identically in the *Museum* (No. 457) and the *Merry Muses* (ed. 1959, p. 62). As I have tried to indicate in the closing section of the preceding essay, these two songs are, in fact, among the strongest links between Burns' *own* manuscripts and the original edition of the *Merry Muses of Caledonia.*

One solution to the difficulty, which would satisfy everyone, is simply to assume that Herd's manuscript materials were made available to Burns, along with much other manuscript folksong material, during his work on the *Scots Musical Museum,* by Stephen Clarke, musical editor of the *Museum,* who is known to have been in contact with Herd. Given the free-&-easy editorial manners of the time, it is not only not hard to believe, but almost certain, that Burns was not informed by Clarke, item by item, of the provenance of each of the texts he was supplied with for the purpose of revision, so that, as Hans Hecht sardonically puts it (p. 320) concerning the even more expurgated Thomson *Select Collection of Original Scotish Airs,* there would be 'nothing left in it to offend the morals of the Edinburgh West-end salons.'

Since, in the booklet referred to, Dr. Goldstein challenges the present writer — in a manner of speaking — as to the alleged French source of at least two of the *Merry Muses* songs now recorded for the phonograph, it may be useful to proceed here with a brief discussion of these curious French origins of certain of the Scottish folksongs in the original edition of the *Merry Muses*. One of these, "THE LASSIE GATH'RING NITS (Nuts)," is a rewriting — it is impossible to call it a 'parallel inspiration' — of a traditional French students' and children's song, "Fillarette," beginning nowadays, 'Un beau jour, Fillarette (larirete, lariret-te); Un beau jour, Fillarette, s'en allait couper les joncs.' The traditional air, which is far handsomer than that used for the Scottish version, is printed in Marie-Rose Clouzot's *La Clé des Chants* (1942) p. 122, under the variant title and first line, "Jeanneton, prend sa faucille."

In both the French and Scottish songs (see the *Merry Muses*, ed. 1959, p. 151), the young lady, whether Jeanneton or Fillarette, on her way to gather nuts (cut rushes), meets several enterprising young men, one of whom kisses her chastely, the second of whom begins to rumple up her clothing, and — both songs agree — 'what the third did to the lass, Is no put in this sang.' ('Ce que fit le quatrième n'est pas dit dans la chanson.') The French song also has a third young man, 'encor' moins sage,' who lays her down on the grass, or, in other versions, kisses her forehead, chin, or breast. The apparent loss of progress here, in kissing her forehead, is explained by the fact that '*front*,' forehead, is, in French folksongs of this type, the standard rhyming euphemism for '*con*.' (See the very important modern and historical collection, with the musical notation, under the title "Le Gai Chansonnier Français," [apparently by Gaston Pâris], which forms the first half of vol. III of *Kryptádia*, 1886, and is a model of combined 'library' and 'field' research.) The humorous moralities which then follow, in both songs, vary charmingly in accordance with the national characters of the two countries. In the Scottish version the poet ends, 'But the lassie wauken'd in a fright, And says, I hae sleept lang,' thus denying all conscious knowledge of, and sinful responsibility for, her seduction; while the French singer concludes — as to what the last young man did — with the classic satirical thrust against female sexual appetite: 'Si vous le saviez, Mesdames, Vous iriez couper les joncs!' (Note that the French text given here is not that printed by Mlle. Clouzot, but a variant collected from the singing of Paris students, 1953.)

The other song of French origin is, in a way, the most important text in the *Merry Muses*, though it is hardly a song at all, but an epigram in the style of Martial; as one may suspect that it was this epigram that was responsible for the preservation of the unique Scott Douglas copy of the original edition by the Rosebery family, who may very well have believed — though wrongly — that an ancestress of the family was satirized in "SUPPER IS NA READY" (*Merry Muses,* ed. 1959, p. 136), noted to be sung to the tune of "Clout the Cauldron":

> Rosebery to his lady says,
> "My hinnie and my succour,
> "O shall we do the thing you ken,
> Or shall we take our supper?"
> *Fal, lal, &c.*
>
> Wi' modest face, sae fu' o' grace,
> Replied the bonny lady:
> "My noble lord, do as you please,
> "But supper is na ready."
> *Fal, lal, &c.*

That is the entire text. Far from actually referring in any real way to Lady Rosebery, this two-stanza witticism is simply a translation, enlarged to eight lines, of a four-line *épigramme* at least two centuries older, appearing thus in the libertine collection of erotic poetry, *Le Cabinet Satyrique* in 1618 (ed. Poulet-Malassis, 1864, II. 215):

> Un mary frais dit à sa demoiselle:
> — Souperons-nous, ou ferons le deduict?
> — Faisons lequel qu'il vous plaira, dit-elle,
> Mais le souper n'est pas encore cuit.

This, in turn, is a reduction of a rather more interesting eight-line form, "Un mary fres, ancor an l'an é jour," (with the identical verbal climax), by Jacques Peletier of Le Mans, who died in 1582, and was co-compiler of one of the earliest French jestbooks of the 16th century. The whole epigram is, in fact, only an inflation of the colloquy or joke placed at the end. An even further inflation, in the 18th century *conte-en-vers* style (by Henri Pajon, d. 1776), will be found, along with Peletier's original, in Pierre Dufay's excellent compilation, *L'Enfer des Classiques* (1933 and reprints) pp. 41, 137, and 198; the Pajon version being entitled "La Femme complaisante." This was evidently considered a very good joke for two centuries or more.

In the oldest formally-presented European jestbook known to exist, the *Philogelos,* or Facetiæ of Hierocles and Philagrius, dating from about the 5th century A.D. (Greek text, ed. Eberhard, Berlin, 1869), the prototype folktale or joke appears as No. 244 of the section attributed to Philagrius : 'A young man said to his warm-blooded wife: "Wife, what shall we do? Shall we have breakfast, or devote ourselves to Aphrodite?" She replied: "As you prefer. We haven't a bite to eat".' Except for the change from breakfast to *supper,* the precise dry wit of the wife's reply has been preserved without change for over a thousand years. This jest is followed in the *Philogelos* by another, exactly matching, on the same theme, No. 245: 'A young man invited two lecherous old women to his house. He said to his servants: "Mix wine for one; and devote to Aphrodite whichever one prefers that." Both women spoke up: "We're not thirsty".' (Translations by Prof. Albert Rapp, in *Anecdota Scowah,* No. 3, San Francisco: Roxburghe Club, 1958, p. 24.) There can be no question that this is the origin of the jest, though the transmission of the poetic form of the 16th century French *épigramme* to Scotland is still something of a mystery.

The clear prototype of the Scottish text is that of the *Cabinet Satyrique* of 1618, but when it was brought to Scotland, or by whom translated, it is no longer possible to discover. The cultural relations between Scotland and France had been very close since the time of Mary Stuart (executed by Queen Elizabeth, with the connivance of her own Neronian son, James I., in 1587), who had become Queen of France at her first marriage with the short-lived François II. Other of the humorous folksongs of Scotland are, similarly, only folktales set to music, and of proximal French origin or descent, also probably since the 16th century. In particular, as has already been noted, "The Sea-Crab" (traced first in the *Percy Folio MS., Supplement: Loose and Humorous Songs,* ed. Furnivall, 1867), which still survives in both Scotland and America, and which is based on a folktale, probably Levantine, later passing to Italy, and first noted in France about 1590 in the *Serées* of Guillaume Bouchet, Serée vi, *ad fin.* (ed. 1873, II. 36), and the *Moyen de Parvenir* of Béroalde de Verville immediately after. Another such importation is the humorous Scottish ballad, "Get Up and Bar the Door" (Child No. 275), also surely of Levantine origin, via southern Europe, as traced by Reinhold Köhler, in Child, v. 96–98, ending with the French "Farce d'un Chauldronnier."

It is obvious that nothing can be really related, in song versions of such ancient tales and jokes, to real persons of modern times,

whether in the Rosebery family or any other. The substitution
of the name 'Rosebery' for 'Un mary frais' (a newlywed husband) in the opening line of the song here under discussion, is
simply the standard 'up-dating' tactic for old Joe Miller jokes,
by means of which ancient fabliaux and Arabian Nights tales
are refurbished and re-circulated, with the protagonists briefly
changed to current celebrities: such as Mr. Smith of the London
Times replacing Abu Hassan, or George Bernard Shaw and Isadora Duncan at a charity banquet (the 'genius child' story, which
has been traced to the Middle Ages), replacing Roland and Oliver
at their sexual brags at an Arthurian *table ronde;* or King Solomon and the Queen of Sheba at their legendary fencing in riddles,
by way of demonstrating their worth as lovers, a classic folklore
theme. Compare the beautiful, and openly erotic riddling-song,
"I Gave My Love a Cherry," which, as 'no one needs to be reminded,' is descended from "Captain Wedderburn's Courtship,"
and "A Noble Riddle Wisely Expounded" (Child Ballad, No. 1).

Throughout the *Merry Muses of Caledonia,* as in any other
such collection and from almost any country, one finds similar
instances of the modernizing and 'nationalizing' of ancient folklore themes, as well as of songs traceable many centuries earlier
in differing form and in other countries. In the essay reprinted
later, "The Bawdy Song," one very relevant example is given:
"A Talk of Ten Wives on their Husband's Ware," printed first
from the Porkington MS. (about 1460) in Furnivall's private edition of *Jyl of Breyntford's Testament,* 1871, Ballad Society, VIIA.
29–33. This song or poem is also known in a very early Dutch
version, from which the Scottish form was probably developed,
the latter appearing in the *Merry Muses* as "OUR JOHN'S BRAK
YESTREEN" (ed. 1959, p. 84). This Scottish version has been worn
down and abbreviated considerably, and the relative modernity
of the *Merry Muses* text is shown by the mere verbal climax, or
'punch-line' of the joking variety, with which it ends, as to the
penis being certainly not sinew but bone, 'For our John's it
brak yestreen, And the margh [marrow] ran down my thie.' This
again is probably directly from Béroalde de Verville's *Moyen de
Parvenir,* a work wonderfully suited to a certain classic type of
Scottish 'fantastick' such as Urquhart, the translator of Rabelais;
the same joke is given by Béroalde in chapter 63, "Exposition"
(ed. 1872, II. 47; and supplement of *Contes en vers,* 1874, p. 122,
"Os ou Nerf"). The similar story of the 'breaking of the egg' which
the foolish girl is made to believe has grown inside her, appears

in the *Merry Muses* as "KEN YE NA OUR LASS BESS" (ed. 1959, p. 145), though the joke element is completely missing from the song, which turns simply on the humor of the climactic metaphor of the young man's breaking the eggs, 'An the white's ran down her thie.' This continues to our own day in various joke forms, and in the children's rhyme or stanza sometimes appearing in "Christopher Columbo," beginning, 'She sprang aloft, her pants fell off, The villain still pursued her. . .', a stanza that perhaps more children than adults are able to finish.

It is worth observing that one of the questions discussed by the 'Twa neebor wives' — all that are left of the original 'Ten' — in "OUR JOHN'S BRAK YESTREEN," as to how the penis is able to stand by itself, gives the hint as to the riddling-origin and probable great age of the prototype theme here being overlayered on the old wives' "Talk." Riddles of this kind, with their sexual tone barely disguised by the translation, are ascribed to King Solomon in *Proverbs*, xxx. 15–29; but the riddling form or 'just-so story' was clearly considered out-of-date by the time of the Ezraic recension (5th century B.C.) in which the text now exists, and the riddles are given only in elegant rhetorical form as triads:

The horseleach hath two daughters, crying, Give, give. There are three things that are never satisfied, yea, four things that say not, It is enough:
  The grave; and the barren womb; the earth that is not filled with water; and the fire that saith not, It is enough. . .
  There be three things which are too wonderful for me, yea, four which I know not:
  The way of an eagle in the air; the way of a serpent upon a rock; the way of a ship in the midst of the sea; and the way of a man with a maid.

Of all of these, only the way of a ship in the midst of the sea is any closer to a solution than in the time of Solomon. (The deeper origin of the 'chicken without bones' of "I Gave My Love a Cherry" will similarly be found in *Ecclesiastes*, xi. 5.) These anatomical and animal riddles, such as that of Samson, in *Judges*, xiv, moving on to those of early scientific import — fire, water, ships, and so forth — obviously belong to the infancy of the human race, and are still regularly to be found among primitives and children, whose educational needs they still seem best to suit. One such anatomical riddle, or sociological jest on the giving in marriage, of which all trace has nearly been lost, and which may therefore be worth noting here, is alluded to in several of the *Merry Muses* songs. In "O GAT YE ME WI' NAETHING?" (ed. 1959, p. 79), the anatomical reference is the whole point of the song: that the girl's 'gude black c -- t' is all the 'tocher' (dowry) she has; but, even so, much too good 'When sic a scullion gat it.' In "HOW CAN I KEEP MY MAIDENHEAD?" (p. 119), the reference is very easy to miss, at this distance of time — though again the whole point of the song — in the line: 'But I'll do as my minnie did, For siller [silver] I'll hae nane, O, — I'll gie it to a bonie lad,' &c. In Burns' century the allusion was very clear, and his 'fat friend,' the antiquary Capt. Francis Grose, in *A Classical Dictionary of the Vulgar Tongue* (1785, a wonderful mine of folk-materials, as are also Grose's *Olio,* and satirical *Guide to Health*), gives at least two punning sorts of similar anatomical dowries, at "Rochester portion" ('Two torn smocks and what nature gave'), and "Cambridge fortune" ('A wind mill and a water mill: [Used to signify] a woman without any but personal endowments'); with a third and more brutal alliterative form added in the 2nd ed., 1788, at "Tetbury portion" ('A **** and a clap'). There is some clear connection here with the usage, imported earlier or at about the same period to the Northeastern United States, of repudiating all debts contracted by a woman before marriage, by marrying her naked, or 'in her shift,' to indicate that she had been taken without any dowry at all.

Burns makes purposeful reference to this usage, as the conclusion of "Tibbie Dunbar," written in 1789 for Johnson's *Museum,* III, No. 207, by way of supplying 'decent' if not very profound words for the jig-tune, "Jocky Magill" ("Johnny McGill"), to which, in the *Merry Muses,* "DUNCAN MACLEERIE" is set. "Tibbie Dunbar" (called "Sweet Tibbie Dunbar" in certain editions of Burns) ends with the singer rejecting all dowry, and offering to marry the girl he loves — 'for better for waur' — in her (petti-)coat or shift:

> I care na thy daddie, his lands and his money,
> I care na thy kin, sae high and sae lordly:
> But say thou wilt hae me for better for waur,
> And come in thy coatie, sweet Tibbie Dunbar.

Aside from these tracings backward in time, there are also the projections forward: to the modern survivals of the same folk materials. The survival of songs recorded in the *Merry Muses of Caledonia* is a large and difficult subject, which it would really be premature to attempt to cover here. More than one collector searching in Scotland today, and in particular the redoubtable Hamish Henderson, of the School of Scottish Studies — to whom the present essay owes a very great deal — has continued to find evidences of songs, both bawdy and polite, collected and rewritten by Burns or composed entirely by him, in living and authentic folk transmission. Evidences of this kind are not for me to present, but for the collectors of them. Let me limit myself, instead, to *Merry Muses* songs continuing to survive outside of Scotland as well.

There are more of these than would appear, such as "DUNCAN MACLEERIE" (ed. 1959, p. 142) which is perhaps even better known in modern Irish versions somewhat closer to the original model, and entitled "Brian O'Lynn" or "Tom Boleyn." Both strains derive of course from the scatological 16th century song, "Tam o' Lin," which is *not* identical with Child Ballad No. 39, of a "Tam Lin" who 'marries' the Queen of the Fairies (Venus and Tannhäuser), though the song turns equally on a strange magical element: the spoken or monosyllabic responses of the hero, very similar to those in "The Fause Knight Upon the Road" (Child No. 3; compare Rabelais, *Pantagruel*, Bk. v, chap. 28, the Semi-quaver Friar who answers only in monosyllables), and also, for that matter, in "Bollocky Bill the Sailor" as noted earlier. This last, in turn, is a modern survival of the songs of the night-visit, known not only in Western Europe but all over the world (see the *Song of Songs*, iii, and especially v. 2–8), and is closely related to "WHA IS THAT AT MY BOWER DOOR," in the original *Merry Muses* (*c.* 1800, p. 119), and in many editions of Burns since. The survival of a single burlesque line or trait from "KEN YE NA OUR LASS BESS" in "Christopher Columbo" has already been mentioned.

Of more serious interest is the survival of "THE YELLOW YELLOW YORLIN" (ed. 1959, p. 138) in the modern "Ball o' Yarn," or "Winding up her Little Ball o' Yarn," as observed by Mr. Vance Randolph in his remarkable Ozark manuscript collection. In its turn, "Ball o' Yarn" is now in the process of being forgotten (though given by Mr. Oscar Brand on one of his "Bawdy and Backroom" phonograph recordings, in *slightly* laundered form), and is being replaced by the college parody or continuation, "In Bohunkus, Tennessee," or the anti-gallant British "Oh, My Little Sister, Lily;" the air now used having become "In My Prison

Cell I Sit," or "Tramp, Tramp, Tramp, the Boys are Marching."
This is a long way from "THE YELLOW YELLOW YORLIN," but the
line of descent is rather clear.

Two surviving songs in the original *Merry Muses of Caledonia*
are especially worth historical attention. First, "THE JOLLY GAUGER"
(ed. 1959, p. 78), of which the MacColl recording, mentioned
earlier, opens on a rather singular dialectal pronunciation of the
title-hero, as 'gowjer,' which seems more Austrylian than Scottish.
As Sydney Goodsir Smith notes, crediting Henley & Henderson's
'Centenary' Burns, II. 297, this is certainly a parody of "The Jolly
Beggar" Child No. 279) regularly but probably falsely attributed
to James V. of Scotland. As is known, Prof. Child found his erotic
materials extremely painful, and suppressed them when he could,
as for instance in his wholesale expurgation of the Pepysian broadside congener of the present song, "The Pollitick Begger-Man,"
hopelessly cut to bits as given in Child, v. 113–14, which is unfortunately the only available printing. It is hardly to be expected,
therefore, that Child would observe that this song is still one of the
most popular and widespread of erotic folksongs, throughout the
English-speaking world, in two surviving strains.

One strain has become fused with the romantic "Rosemary
Lane" or "Home, Boys, Home" (known as "Bell-Bottom Trousers"
in the American college-version), and invariably includes the
cliché references to the pieces of silver or gold given to the seduced
girl 'to pay the nurse's fee' (Child, No. 279A, stanza 25). Note
the modern rationalized form in which this element is phrased:

"Take this, my darling, for the damage I have done;
You may have a daughter, or you may have a son," [&c.]

This is itself an interesting survival of the idea of the *Morgen-
gabe* as a monetary recompense for the sanguinary 'damage' of
defloration, or a guilt-offering connected with the more or less
conscious 'sadistic concept of coitus.'

The other form, which is far more obscene verbally, has been
assimilated to the Roxburghe ballad, "Room for a Jovial Tinker,"
reprinted in John S. Farmer's *Merry Songs and Ballads* (1895–97)
I. 41–48 — with a later form from *Merry Drollery* (1661) reprinted
at I. 142–47 — and in Pinto & Rodway's recent and snobbishly
entitled *The Common Muse* (1957) p. 279–81. In their erotic
supplement, present only in the high-priced edition, as issued in
England, Pinto & Rodway also give the very graphic modern
survival, "The Highland Tinker," p. 438, noting its relation to

the older form. Their version is not, however, one of those that shows the relation to "The Jolly Beggar." In the versions that do, the Tinker is introduced in swashbuckling lines parodying those of the Beggar and Gauger:

There was a Hieland tinker, and to London he did ride,
With sword and pistol in his hand, his bollix by his side.

As the chorus then explains, repetitively and even gloatingly, other parts of his 'ordnance metaphors' (as they are politely called nowadays) are 'swinging well below his knee,' in an uncircumcised fashion worthy of Brother John Henry, Paul Bunyan — an upstart in folklore, but folklore nevertheless — or any of the other heroic 'hard-men' of the great genealogy of Hercules, Samson, Achilles, Childe Roland, Lancelot, Rasputin, Tarzan, Superman, Little John (of the Robin Hood legends), L'il Abner, and so on; as described and explained in a little-known passage of John Aubrey's *Remaines of Gentilisme and Judaisme* (ed. Britten, 1881, p. 75–6, 152–54, 237–38), to which the late Huddie Ledbetter added the interesting information, in the Lomax's *Our Singing Country* (1941), p. 258–59, that John Henry and other hard-men are invariably 'double-jinted' as well. These are the usual physical stigmata of the folk-hero, and some similarly unrepressed sexual typification of the heroic Beggar-Gauger-Tinker is clearly implied in the lines modified to the not-altogether expurgated nonsense of a *dildo* refrain: 'With his fal de diddle de dal dal' (this is the '*fal, lal, &c.*' briefly noted throughout the *Merry Muses*), which is quoted by Child, No. 279Bb, stanza 1, from an Aberdeen slip-ballad of about 1800.

The one other principally surviving *Merry Muses* song — and here I am assuredly encroaching, because this principally survives in Scotland, and is sung elsewhere only in mock Scottish dialect, variously mispronounced — is the folk-epithalamium, or fantasy reminiscence of a folk-orgy at the winter or summer solstice, "BLYTH WILL AN' BESSIE'S WEDDING" (ed. 1959, p. 131). As already noted, this is the direct ancestor, and oldest known text, particularly in stanza 3, 'Tammie Tamson too was there, &c.,' which is exactly in the modern form, of the principal erotic ballad of modern Scotland, "The Ball o' Kirriemuir." As opposed to any statements made (for publication) by present or past heads of the Burns Federation, that the public recognition of the *Merry Muses'* existence and of their having been collected and in part written by Burns, would be a 'slur' on Scotland and on Scotland's greatest poet; it is very much to be doubted whether any male Scot alive today, above the age of twelve, has not at least once heard "The Ball o' Kirriemuir" sung, and joined in *at least* on the chorus. It is also a positive fact that numerous cultivated persons in Scotland today would consider their lives incomplete if they did not manage to add at least one outrageously obscene stanza, and orgiastic partners-all image, to the ever-growing canon of the "Ball o' Kirriemuir," which would already require a whole volume of any revised and enlarged edition of the Child Ballads, all to itself.

To the modern editorial conscience in the matter of folksong and folk-poetry, which was created by the irascible Ritson in his attacks on the 18th century proto-faker, Bishop Percy (no worse, really, than Allan Ramsay in Scotland, earlier), the most difficult part of Burns' activity to justify is neither where he got his materials, nor how immoral they may have been, but *what* he did with them. That his supernal art, and perfect 'ear' of the folk-poet he was, ornamented and improved every folksong he ever revised, is of course beyond all question. And even if this were not so, every folk-poet — even a bumbling chapbook printer like Buchan — has the right to, and does always revise and rewrite the historical materials he finds, whether or not he signs his name to the resultant product, as Burns seldom felt justified in doing. (One would prefer, also, that other people stop signing his name.) But from the simple viewpoint of the reliable transmission of folk-collected texts — a point of absolutely no interest whatsoever to either the folk or folk-poets, but only to 'library' researchers — one is driven almost to the heresy, sometimes, of wishing that Burns had just simply left his folksong texts as he found them, in the same way as did David Herd. This is particularly true as to the erotic folksongs, where, more often than not, there are no other historical texts of Burns' period than those he reshaped and revised in the *Merry Muses of Caledonia,* leaving the folk originals now unrecoverable forever.

XII

THE PSEUDONYM, "Vindex," assumed by Duncan McNaught in his 1911 edition of the *Merry Muses,* was in continuation of his perfectly correct insistence for over a decade, in the *Burns Chronicle* of which he was editor, that the chapbook editions of the *Merry Muses* during the whole preceding century, and especially the much-corrupted and endlessly reprinted '1827' edition, not only are travesties of the original edition, in part collected and written by Burns, but that they have done a great moral wrong to his memory. They are, in fact, still doing so, as noted earlier in connection with the Clayton "Bobby Burns" recording. The reissuing of the original *Muses* text seemed then, and is now, the best vindication possible, though McNaught's own editing goes a bit far in the direction of denying authorship of almost any of the pieces to Burns. (See Sydney Goodsir Smith's article in *Arena*, 1950, No. 4, reprinted in *Hudson Review*, 1954, on McNaught's excesses here.) The publishers, D. Brown & Co., who carefully refrain from giving their name anywhere on the book — though an obscure 'rolling-press' printer in upstate New York, at about the same time, did not hesitate to do so — go altogether too far in their prospectus, and practically turn the whole project into a hypocritical sham, with publishers' puff about 'the repeated request of the leading men of the Burns Cult' to reissue 'the m.s. collection made by Burns when engaged in the purification work which appeared in Johnson's and Thomson's publications.'

For the truth, after all, about Burns' 'purification work,' is that it was a failure, and that he threw away on it the poetic energies of the last ten years of a life that extended only to thirty-seven years in all, and of a creative life that extended only to twenty. Burns did not share the confusion, or hypocrisy, of the 'leading men of the Burns Cult' as to the value and purpose of what he was doing. Writing to George Thomson in Sept. 1794, he asks:

> Do you know, my dear Sir, a blackguard Irish song called "Oonagh's Waterfall." Our friend Cunningham sings it delightfully. The air is charming, & I have often regretted the want of decent verses to it that you may sing before Ladies . . . Do you know a droll Scots song, more famous for its humor than delicacy, called The grey goose and the gled? [*Muses*, c. 1800, p. 97, entitled "As I Look'd O'er Yon Castle Wa'," with a related stanza at p. 86, in "Wha the Deil Can Hinder the Wind to Blaw."] Mr. Clarke took down the notes, such as they are, at my request, which I shall give with some decenter verses to Johnson. — Mr. Clarke says that the tune is positively an old chant of the ROMISH CHURCH; which corroborates the old tradition, that at the Reformation, the Reformers burlesqued much of the old church Music with setting them to bawdy verses. As a farther proof, the common name for this song is, Cum-

nock Psalms. — As there can be no harm in transcribing a
stanza of a psalm, I shall give you two or three; possibly the
song is new to you. (*Selected Letters,* ed. Ferguson, 1953,
p. 333–6, noting Thomson's marginal, 'Delicate psalmody
indeed.')

This 'old tradition' as to the burlesquing of church music with
bawdy verses is not corroborated by any other record, and may
be one of Burns' little jokes — the whole context, and the reference
to psalmody, being obviously jocular. In point of fact, it is well
established that the main direction of parody was the other way
'round. William Chappell ends his great *Popular Music of the
Olden Time,* 1857, with the unequivocal statement that the folksingers could *never* have learned their melodies in church, because
there were no original melodies there to be had. The church
melodies, when they were popular, came from folksongs. At the
Reformation it was, to the contrary of what Burns remarks, precisely the old freespoken love-songs that were turned into psalms,
on a hint from Luther himself, as in the gauche and absurd 'sacred
contrefacts' of the Wedderburns' *Ane Compendious Booke of
Gude and Godlie Ballatis,* Edinburgh, 1567.
    The whole period was drenched in the anti-Renaissance at-
tempt to oust the pagan gods of Greece, newly appeared in Europe,
and the fescennine songs that were taken to be the very wiles of
Venus — and thus the sin of witchcraft and demonolatry — as in
the Rev. Thomas Brice's *Against filthy writing and such like delighting,* 1562, itself hardly more than a ballad (reprinted in
John Payne Collier's *Old Ballads,* Percy Society, 1840, I. 49–52;
and in H. L. Collmann's *Ballads & Broadsides,* Roxburghe Club,
1912, p. 36–7):

> What meane the rimes that run thus large
>   in every shop to sell?
> With wanton sound, and filthie sense,
>   me thinke it grees not well . . .
> Tel me is Christ, or Cupide Lord?
>   doth God or Venus reigne?

And so on for several pages in what appears to be a 'flyting' with
the earliest English collection of erotic poetry, *The Court of
Venus,* which may date as early as twenty years before, and of
which the Rev. Brice's parody, *The Courte of Venus moralized,*
was entered in the Stationers' Register in 1567 (I. 343).

Far from being the crotchet of a few excessively pious converts to Luther's reforms, this was one of the crucial points of attack on the old religion, especially in Scotland, and on the mariolatric remnants of sex worship that were then called 'witchcraft' — as Michelet so brilliantly demonstrated in *La Sorcière*, in 1862, and Dr. Margaret Murray after him. Thus, in the confessions tortured out of the victims in the Doctor Fian trial in North Berwick, 1590, we are told that the Devil himself had taught them how to play the reel 'uppon a small trumpe, called a Jewe's trumpe.' (See further in Montague Summers' *History of Witchcraft and Demonology*, 1926, p. 138–43.) George Sinclar even more circumstantially records, in *Satan's Invisible World Discovered*, Relation xxxv, 1671 (reprint, 1875), 'Anent some Prayers, Charms, and Avies, used in the *Highlands*":

As the Devil is originally the Author of *Charms*, and *Spells*, so is he the Author of several baudy Songs, which are sung [*i.e.* at the Witches' Sabbat]. A reverend Minister told me, that one who was the Devils Piper, a wizzard confest to him, that at a Ball of dancing, the Foul Spirit taught him a Baudy song to sing and play, as it were this night, and ere two days past all the Lads and Lasses of the town were lilting it throw the street. It were abomination to rehearse it.

Here, a good deal earlier than James Barke's hypothetical harvest-home of 'the 1880s,' we have the real origins of "The Ball o' Kirriemuir," in the orgiastic dances and sex festivals that extend as far back as human history, and of which the final surreptitious survivals were hounded to extinction under the name of the 'Witches' Sabbat.' Coming again into the half-light of publicity as the new and citified 'Buff-Ballers,' or naked orgiasts and dancers of Pepys' *Diary* (see also Grose's *Classical Dictionary of the Vulgar Tongue*, 2nd ed. 1788, at "Ballum Rancum"), and the similar clandestine theatre and orgy-groups of the same period in France, these continued in both countries until at least the time of the French Revolution, with sporadic survivals until as late as the 1930's in Paris and London, though finally almost entirely snowed under by the occult trappings. There is a fantastic history here still to be written, ending perhaps with the violent and flamboyant career, at the beginning of the 20th century, of the bogus-Scot, occultist, and bawdy poet, Aleister Crowley, about whom the last word has not yet been said.

It is on the basis of the sincere belief in the Devil's intervention in the singing (and evidently the creating) of bawdy
songs, or even just simple love-songs, that the Wedderburns'
'sacred contrefacts' were undertaken; and it is understandable that
they did not balk at a bit of patent absurdity here and there, most
famously in "Johne, cum kiss me now," as long as the good work
was accomplished, and Venus and the Devil (or are they identical?) were driven back into the 'navel of creation,' in Asia Minor,
whence they had emerged. This is what lies openly behind John
Wesley's oft-quoted remark — also attributed to the Rev. Rowland
Hill — that he could not see any reason 'why Satan should get all
the good tunes.' Luther's earlier remark, to the same effect, is
quoted as motto to Prof. Hans Hecht's *Songs from David Herd's
Manuscripts* (1904), though it was really intended more as a
reprimand to his own followers than to Satan's, whose songs are
typified only as beautiful and fine.

All Luther said, in his *Table-Talk*, was: 'How does it happen
that *in carnalibus* there are so many fine poems and beautiful
songs, while *in spiritualibus* we have only such rotten, cold things
(*faul, kalte Ding*)?' The answer, to any sensible person, would
seem to be to preserve the 'fine poems and beautiful songs,' and
to forget about the 'rotten, cold things.' But that is not the solution that was attempted. Luther was also not the first person to
have the propagandistic notion of 'sacred counterfeits,' which
preceded Christianity altogether; but his efforts in this direction,
and his influence, must be held responsible for having let loose
the avalanche of fake folksongs — counterfeited first for the church,
later for the theatre, in the 'ballad operas' of Durfey and the
1730's — that has been rolling over Europe ever since; and never
more coldly and rottenly than today, especially in the faked and
expurgated 'folksongs.'

In the same way that each religion drives out that preceding,
by assimilating all the old festivals to the new legends, the old
household and occupational demigods to the new saints, and so
forth; it is obvious that the popular old songs of preceding worships must become a necessary point of attack. Sectarian parodies
set to profane tunes, and even to the words of the old songs and
hymns themselves, had been undertaken by Catholic Christianity
as much as a thousand years earlier, and in particular on the eve
of the Protestant Reformation — that is to say, well before Luther's
activity began. This is discussed at some length in the introduction to Prof. Alex. F. Mitchell's reprint of the Wedderburns'

Compendious Booke of Gude and Godlie Ballatis, Edinburgh,
1897 (Scottish Text Society, vol. 39) pp. lii, lxi–lxiv, and cix–cxiii;
in the *Chansonnier Huguenot du XVe. Siècle,* 1870–71; and in
Charles Nisard's magistral *Des Chansons populaires chez les
anciens,* Paris, 1867, I. 451–4, "Chansons de Métiers," tracing the
practice to the early Christian heretics and propagandists, Arius,
Paul of Samosata, and Ephraim Syrus; and noting also that Apollinaris the Younger had gone so far in this direction, to drive
out the earlier Jewish worship, as to parody the *Psalms of David.*
Psalm ii. 12 has long since been suspected of being such a parody
or intrusion.

Even so late as the 18th and early 19th centuries, this practice
continued among the Scottish Protestants, particularly the Glassite
and Berean revivalists, as described by Prof. Mitchell, pp. lxii and
cxiii; also observing that 'In still more recent times Bishop Heber
did not disdain to set . . . his beautiful Epiphany hymn, "Bright-
est and best of the sons of the morning" . . . to the tune of the
Scottish song "Here awa', there awa', wanderin' Willie," picked
up by him during his visit to Sir Walter Scott.' Most surprising
of all is perhaps James Maidment's note, in his *Scotish Ballads,*
1868, II. 275 (silently taken in part from Stenhouse's "Illustrations" to the *Scots Musical Museum,* 1839, IIa. 187), of a 19th
century spiritualising not of a bawdy song but of a pagan!

> Geddes, in his *Saints' Recreation* [Edinburgh, 1683] had . . .
> one of his godly songs set to Cromlet's Lilt, the music of
> which will be found . . . in Thomson's *Orpheus Caledonius*
> . . . Not very many years ago, a gentleman who had gone
> to hear a celebrated Unitarian preacher in a church in the
> north, was rather startled by the congregation, after the
> sermon, finishing their worship by a spontaneous chorus to
> the tune of "Glorious Apollo."

The artless confusion between the religion of Apollo and
that, even, of Unitarianism, that gave this anecdote its savour a
hundred years ago, obviously lacks *zip* today, when a staid Brook-
lyn congregation can accept the theatrical hoking-up of their
Sunday worship with a cymbal-clash from the pulpit to open the
ball, ballet-versions of the Passion-play stories danced in tights,
etc. etc. — as, to be sure, David 'danced before the Lord with all
his might,' in a linen ephod (tights?) 2 *Samuel,* vi. 5–14, cymbals
included — on the muscular, show-biz principle that you gotta

blow 'em outa their seats, and that the main trouble with Christianity is that it's had 'too long a run.' (Photo-story, *Look* magazine, "New New York" issue, 1963.) Whatever this may be supposed really to mean, it sounds more like '*Mené, mené, tekál . . .*' If this is what it takes to spark the well-advertised 'return to religion' of the twentieth century, Burns' open anticlericalism and frank freemason appeals to 'Dame Nature,' instead of the bearded Jehovah, may cause far less blushes in the end.

For if one examines carefully what Burns was doing in *his* folksong 'contrefacts,' it becomes clear that, in spite of his freethinking, his recalcitrance to organized religion, his poetic mocking of psalms, kirks, ministers, pious hypocrites like Holy Willie and his female counterpart, "Godly Girzie" in the *Muses;* Burns was almost consciously carrying on the old work of driving the Devil out of Scottish folksong. Burns did not call what he was doing religion, he called it patriotism, as when he encouraged Johnson to forget about making money out of their volumes of folksongs, the *Scots Musical Museum,* and be 'a Patriot for the Music of your Country;' or when he himself refused any payment from Thomson for similar work, saying: 'In the honest enthusiasm with which I embark in your undertaking, to talk of money, wages, fee, hire, &c. would be downright Sodomy of Soul!' (*Letters,* 13 Nov. 1788, and 16 Sept. 1792.) Nevertheless, Burns did not for an instant imagine that he was simultaneously writing great poetry or even specially good songs. What he was doing, as he plainly says in his letters, was preserving the airs of the bawdy songs, and many others of course — a musical, rather than a poetic contribution principally — by adapting to them the '*random clink*' of 'a few lines, *smooth & pretty,*' as he modestly tells Thomson, in a letter of 8 Nov. 1792 (*Letters,* 1931, II. 129):

> If you mean, my dear Sir, that all the Songs of your Collection shall be Poetry of the first merit, I am afraid you will find difficulty in the undertaking more than you are aware of . . . For instance, in the air, My wife's a wanton wee thing [*Muses, c.* 1800, p. 116], if a few lines, *smooth & pretty,* can be adapted to it, it is all you can expect. — The following I made extempore to it; & though, on farther study I might give you something more profound, yet it might not suit the light-horse gallop of the air so well as this *random clink.*

Despite all glozing remarks to the contrary, as that in Hotten's edition of the *Muses* concerning "JOHN ANDERSON, MY JO," these expurgated versions are only very seldom among Burns' better songs. "SHE SAYS SHE LO'ES ME BEST OF A'," his expurgation of "Oonagh's Waterfall," is one of the best. But almost none of them will compare to the power and humor of either the bawdy folk originals, or Burns' own continuations of them in the same line, except on the grounds of singability before ladies — the dubious advantage offered by Burns in regards to "Oonagh's Waterfall," and first offered in his century in the preface to Allan Ramsay's *Tea-Table Miscellany,* at the very beginning of the genteel period so perfectly typified by Ramsay's title. A comparison, for instance, of "COMIN THRO' THE RYE" in the saccharine 'kissing' version now taught to school-children, with the glinting humor of the un-expurgated *Muses* version, will more than demonstrate what is meant, especially in the "Comin' thro' the grain" stanza probably interpolated by Burns, and (as Scott Douglas marginally notes) written with a diamond 'on the window of the Globe, Dumfries.' Again, Sydney Goodsir Smith, in many examples in full quotation, in his *Arena* article of 1950, brings eloquent evidence as to the difference. This much is sure, if all poetry and song had to be scaled down to what is presumably proper for school-children, that would very shortly mean the end of art, and possibly of song as well. We are nearly there. Burns' bawdy continuations, with his rebellious hand, of the *smooth & pretty* expurgations he was simul-taneously making with his dutiful hand, were obviously what his 'wildness and mirth,' remarked upon by Gilfillan, required of his poetic soul. Burns' bawdy songs expressed — and they are some of the best songs he ever wrote — the ambivalent resistance of what was really his art, against what he mistakenly thought was his religio-patriotic duty.

And yet, even here, Burns failed. Except for an occasional stanza, 'learnt from book,' neither his bawdy versions nor his ex-purgated ones have been accorded any wide folk acceptance. The Scots who still sing these songs sing the older forms by preference, and these were also the forms brought to Canada and the United States by the Scottish settlers. This is again a proof, if any were needed, of what has become a truism of folklore study: that printed texts have had very little effect on living folklore, and that their principal value is as historical evidence.

In the case of *The Merry Muses* it is just as well that this should be so. Burns' collection, and his own additions to it, formed only the nucleus of the printed work passed off under his name for over a century. On this nucleus was grafted, as has been shown, an equally large amount (three times renewed, and therefore three times as large) of extraneous matter, much of it far from 'Merry' and simply pornographic. In this kind of thing, the thread of the older folksong becomes difficult to search for and almost impossible to find. Not the sugary string of poetizing, of the pastoral and wayside-seduction type, effusively evident in the early 18th century literature, but the far older roistering humor concerning full-bodied men and full-fleshed women, with large sexual appetites and larger buttocks, of the kind that Chaucer and Dunbar had already handled centuries before. The tone of *The Merry Muses* changed radically after 1800, from a naked backwoods — or, rather, highlands — evocation of the sexual passion, with the accent on the humorous anatomy and accidents of that passion, to a kind of crank-turned and unpleasant obscenity that all Burns scholars and partisans have cried out in anguish at seeing attributed to Burns. Bawdy song in a mechanical century became a dirty, then a nasty thing, more particularly connected with the life of industrialized cities: with factories, counting-houses, brothels, music-halls, barrack-rooms, and the disjointed sexual sensibilities of men forced off the land, out of all contact with nature, and largely without normal relations with women or normal relations with anything else.

III

PROBLEMS OF EROTIC FOLKLORE

*L'humanité est outragée en moi et avec moi.
Nous ne devons ni dissimuler, ni oublier cette
indignation, qui est une des formes les plus
passionnées de l'amour.*

"GEORGE SAND"

MISCONCEPTIONS IN EROTIC FOLKLORE

I

THE COLLECTING of erotic folklore has only recently come to interest the world of folklore scholarship in the English-speaking countries. In Russia, Germany, France, and Italy, the material was collected and completely published long ago — between 1865 and 1914 at the latest — and is now not considered of any except historical interest. The compilers were in most cases the greatest folklorists of their respective cultures: Afanasyev, Krauss, Gaston Pâris, and Pitrè, among dozens of others. At least two very serious yearbook publications, *Anthropophytéia* (Leipzig, 1904–31), and *Kryptádia* (Paris, 1883–1911), were issued over a period of decades, running to some forty volumes, and solely devoted to the erotic folklore and folksong of all European languages, except English. Unfortunately, there are not ten complete sets of these publications, and their various *Beiwerke,* in any American or British public and university libraries; and of the few sets that do exist in these countries, the pages have in most cases not been cut. British and American folklorists, and especially folksong collectors, are now waking up to the existence of sex, two World Wars late, ill-prepared — being in general either too timid or too avid — and almost entirely ignorant of what has already been done, of how it was done, and, as a matter of fact, why it was done. No one can have any scientific idea of what sexual folklore is all about, of what to look for, or what any of it *means,* until the forty volumes just mentioned have been thoroughly explored. This is a very serious recommendation to the English-speaking folklorists, who are, to put it plainly, in the position of Johnny-come-latelys in this field. and looking for orientation.

The prudery that prevented erotic folklore from being collected or published in the first place, in the English-speaking world, has left a certain residual fuzziness as to why it is worth collecting now. The European collectors, especially those grouped around Prof. Friedrich S. Krauss in Vienna, editor of the yearbooks just mentioned, never for an instant made the slightest pretense. Erotic folklore is to be collected for the same reason that it is proliferated: because it is about sex. That is what makes it interesting both to the 'oral source' and to the collector — who is supposed to be a human being, with all the organs and impulses of a human being — that is what makes it socially valuable and historically important. Sex, and its folklore, are far more interesting, more valuable, and more important in every social and historical sense than, for instance, the balladry of murder, cruelty, torture, treachery, baby-killing, and so forth, which are the principal contents, to give only one familiar example, of the Child ballads; of which the almost total moral depravity, on all counts *except* that of sex, and fantastic unfitness for retailing to impressionable minds, has seldom been observed, owing to these particular ballads' lily-white purity as to sex.

What is more serious than the contradiction and the insincerity implicit here is the unspoken motive behind much of the present interest in the hitherto taboo sexual folklore. Anglo-American folklorists and folksong collectors are now hesitantly emerging from their parthenogenetic stage, not because of any significant liberalization of the famously antisexual Anglo-Saxon morality (that allows American postmasters, today, to stamp outgoing letters: REPORT OBSCENE MAIL TO YOUR POSTMASTER), but rather because of the unspoken and entirely erroneous belief that the 'vein' is just about worked out for every *other* kind of folklore. This basic misconception skews, and makes very equivocal, the entire show of interest.

The idea that there is a special kind of folklore that is sexual, as differentiated from all other kinds, is an optical illusion caused by the operation of a purely literary censorship. No such separation exists in fact. In the field, the sexual material is offered along with all the other material. It is not segregated into a special behind-the-barn session, or Jim Crow appendix, unless the attitude of the collector puts it there — generally by 'forgetting' to ask specifically for it, though never forgetting to ask for Child ballads. The sexual materials grow out of the ordinary life situation, and satisfy some of the most imperative and deep-seated fantasy needs of the informants. The more extraordinary or abnormal, therefore, the collecting or recording session is made, by the presence, by the personality, or by the sexual anxieties of the collector himself, the less likely that the informants' sexual materials will appear. That is a principal reason why they have been so uncommon in the past, in English, or have been collected only in caricatural form.

People who still sing today do not tend to discriminate very rigidly between their songs. They mix together the things that interest them, the love-songs with the work-songs, because that is the way they live. They work all day, and make love at night. It would seem to them absurd to separate the work-songs from the love-songs, except while they are working, and the relationship is even closer with the drinking-songs and ballads. Work-songs in particular are also eroticized by means of humorous metaphors, in which the men's work is described in sexual images and terms, as has been discussed at greater length in an earlier chapter, "*The Merry Muses* as Folklore," pt. v. The indiscriminate mixing of various types of songs and lore is not connected in any special way with sex. It is well known that singers will occasionally sandwich Child Ballads in among popular songs learned from the radio, or at any rate they used to. Now they don't sing much of either. They listen. That is the passivity of the century.

It would be a serious mistake to pretend, or to imagine, as newcomers in the field regularly try to do, that folklore and folksong have not been seriously damaged in the last half-century. The very powerful influences at work to destroy the spontaneity of folklore and folksong, and to replace them with bogus commercial artifacts, have perhaps been sufficiently discussed and lambasted. Whatever further cursing and swearing seem necessary, on a closer view of the hard-headed commercialists involved, will be reserved for a little *ritornello scherzando* toward the end, of which the title will give the reader sufficient warning.

Nevertheless, or perhaps for the very reason just mentioned, when people do sing today — especially young people — they are much more likely to fall back on sexual songs than on any other, and the tone is more insistently obscene than before. Meanwhile, the more normally erotic songs have disappeared in largest part, and those that are left tend to be very crude and hateful. One will therefore sometimes find various levels of repertory clear in the singers' minds, of songs that can and cannot be sung, especially not in the presence of members of the opposite sex — 'unless you know them very well.' This did not use to be the case. Anyone who collected before World War II knows this, and mixed repertories will still be found when collecting in such countries as Ireland and Scotland, and in areas where children and parents live together in close quarters, where the censoring of the spoken language and of the tales and folksongs the children hear would be absurd to undertake. Observe again, however, that the materials in these circumstances are seldom violently obscene: they simply take the sexual and scatological in their stride, as real folklore and folksong have always done, though you would not think so from the modern printed record.

Owing exactly to its recalcitrance to print, especially in English, and increasingly over the last two centuries, the last hunting-ground of authentic oral folklore and folksong is the obscene. This point has slowly been forcing itself upon the attention of the world of folklore scholarship, though some twenty-five years ago, when I began collecting specifically erotic folklore in English, on Prof. Krauss' plan, I could find no one in the university sphere to agree that this was in the slightest worth while. One or two *obiter dicta* had been dropped, in print — hardly more than in passing — as when Prof. A. K. Davis observed in 1928 that though 'the ballad is one of the last strongholds of ribaldry,' this is not something one 'would suspect from recent publications,' ("Some Problems of Ballad Publication," in *Musical Quarterly*, 1928, xiv. 283–96.) Nor, for that matter, from publications since. The truth of the matter has, however, made itself felt, owing to the damaged transmission now of most of the 'clean' folklore. Today, nothing but what is obscene that is left in English-language folklore, except children's lore, can be considered to exist authentically in oral tradition, and an important part of the children's lore is obscene as well. This has now even begun to have the opposite effect: of giving the sexual element an undue prominence in the eyes of recent collectors, but it is still just an optical illusion. They are used to seeing folklore through the small end of the telescope; now they are going to look at it through the big end. They are still in danger of getting the real scale wrong.

The only groups among whom an exceptionally high percentage of erotic folklore will regularly be found are adolescent males, especially soldiers, sailors, and high-school and college-students, or any other group of men — or women — such as prisoners, miners, or girls in boarding-schools, who are locked away from, or otherwise unable to achieve a normal sex life. It is natural that the percentage of erotic folklore will be higher among these groups, or at least that it will seem higher, because it expresses itself more urgently, and more openly in the monosexual situation, whether or not any collector is present. Even so, with a little more digging, the same soldiers and prisoners, college-boys and boarding-school girls, will be found to have an equally large amount of *non*-erotic folklore, equally well worth collecting, though certainly not so uncontaminated by non-oral elements from print and from the so-called entertainment arts. To phrase it simply, the sexual parts of folklore are sometimes larger — in proportion to folklore — than the sexual parts of the body are, in proportion to the body itself. But there is nobody whose folklore is all sexual.

If the erotic materials are to be asked for now and in future folklore collecting, or will at least be accepted when offered, as did not always use to be the case, they can still only come from people who have a great deal of other folklore too, 'authentic' or not, which is just as important to collect, though this part has of course never required any vindication. There are no special informants for sexual folklore. Barbers, hoboes, juvenile delinquents, and other groups who theoretically do nothing but 'talk smut,' are usually no better sources for erotic songs or jokes or riddles, than they are for any other kind of songs or jokes or riddles. One has only to ask for the others too. In the same way, some very nice old ladies (and the young ones even more so) will occasionally come out with some surprisingly bawdy songs — in among the other reminiscences of their youth, of course — but only if they can accept the collector *as a person,* and not as a stranger or city-slicker eager to commercialize their lore. People do not live in a vacuum, and they know now that folklore and folksong are not being collected by starry-eyed idealists; not often anyhow. Even though they may never have heard of the Unwritten Law, for advancement in the university world — 'Publish or Perish!' — they can at least be expected to recognize the crude commercial intent of a self-styled folklorist who descends upon them with three to five thousand dollars' worth of expensive high-fidelity recording equipment in a baby-blue station wagon. A few other hints for the recognition of the species will be given later.

Folksingers, and people who can tell stories well, are exceptionally sensitive to their audience. When they feel that the collector is too anxious, too exploitative ('He don't know nuthin' but gimme,' as I once heard this expressed), and especially when they feel that the collector is full of sexual inhibitions — whether these inhibitions express themselves by refusing everything that has to do with sex, or by refusing everything that doesn't — they tend to become very leery. They'd rather sing or talk about something other than sex. Or not at all. Collecting is a living situation: it is extremely easy to destroy the *ambiance*. There is a concert-pitch of tension and concentration on the part of the singers and tale-tellers, no matter how relaxed they may seem. It is necessary to take a very calm, even offhand, approach to the sexual material, or it cannot be collected at all. When the informant hesitates and is embarrassed, he or she must be encouraged and put at ease by the collector's casualness, and by the pretense — often it is only a pretense — of having heard it all before.

It is necessary to show a good deal of tact, to be able to sense how a collecting session is developing. And it is necessary, some-times, to know how to take 'No' for an answer. One can come back again to the subject, later. Life is long enough. The collector is, at best, an outsider and a guest, and the collecting activity is essentially only a disturbance, tending to falsify the real situation in which folklore and folksong are produced. That is one advan-tage, at least, of the tape-recording machine: it helps the collector to fade into the background. On the other hand, many singers who are perfectly willing to give what they call 'blue' songs or 'rough' songs, do not want to be recorded singing them. They will seldom call them 'dirty songs' except in contempt. Perhaps the language has changed a good deal since Shakespeare's time, but you will not hear anyone today say, with Falstaff: 'Come, sing me a bawdy song — make me merry.'

Finally, it is not true that women cannot collect erotic or scatological material from men, or vice versa, but the situation is likely to develop into something else. This isn't guaranteed, but it does sometimes happen (the same is true of selling vacuum cleaners), usually with no further effect than to increase the un-voiced tension between informant and collector. It depends largely, as stated, on the collector's own attitude, and tact, and to a surprising degree on the level of vocabulary used. The collector has to work at much the same level as the informant, or give up trying. This means both in approach and in vocabulary, though neither a yelping enthusiasm nor an unremitting stream of horse-guard profanity is either necessary or desirable. Only if the in-formant talks like a mule-skinner swears — which is seldom the case — is it ever necessary to attempt the same pyrotechnics, and even so he may be offended by the competition. It is well to bear in mind the story of Mark Twain's wife trying to cure him of profanity by reeling off a string of the oaths she had heard him use. 'My dear,' he is reported to have answered gravely, 'you know all the words; but you haven't got the tune.' The tune is everything. Singers and joke-tellers will not produce vital materials of any kind, and certainly not erotic material, if the collectors have the elevated air of being visitors from Mars, or of treating them like five-year-old children being taught to lisp pseudo-medical terminology when visitors are present: 'Daddy, I wish to uwinate.' They unconsciously take the position expressed some years ago by Prof. Allen Walker Read, in his very courageous work on folk-epigraphy, *Lexical Evidence, &c.* (Paris, 1935), that to 'pass up the well-established colloquial words of the language' in favor of neo-Latin euphemisms, is simply 'indicative of grave mental unhealth.' That is to say, without any neo-Latin, they think they're crazy.

One solution attempted in recent years has been to set the students in folklore courses to doing the collecting themselves, generally from informants of their own age and sex, on the 'jury of one's peers' principle. This does solve the problem of approach and vocabulary, and also produces a large amount of reduplicative material rapidly, but it tends heavily to overload the archives thus produced with college songs and tales. When the same students go out later into 'field' collecting, they are faced with the real problems just outlined, but the materials they may then bring back are far more interesting and uncommon. As is now well understood, the older folklore remains alive longest at the geographical periphery — in the far North, the deep South, and the outlying islands — and is replaced at the industrialized urban hub with newer materials of different *tone,* or with almost unrecognizable revampings of the old. Of nothing is this more true than of erotic folklore. It is very important not to make the mistake of the late Prof. Alfred Kinsey, who collected information by means of a formalized verbal questionnaire from five thousand northeastern American white college-boys (in major part), and then publicized the patterns discerned in their sexual habits as the sexual behavior of the 'Human' male. There are more human beings than white American college-boys. Even in America, it is perhaps those who are not in college, and not white, who have most of the authentic folklore today.

II

SEXUAL folklore almost always has the air of being humorous. Yet actually it concerns some of the most pressing fears and most destructive life problems of the people who tell the jokes and sing the songs. Their sexual humor is a sort of whistling in the dark, like Beaumarchais' Figaro, who 'laughs so that he may not cry.' They are projecting the endemic sexual fears, and problems, and defeats of their culture — in which there are very few victories for anyone — on certain standard comedy figures and situations, such as cuckoldry, seduction, impotence, homosexuality, castration, and disease, which are obviously not humorous at all. And they are almost always expressing their resistance to authority figures, such as parents, priests, and policemen, in stereotyped forms of sexual satire and scatological pranks and vocabulary. It is for these reasons that sexual folklore is generally retailed in a mood of exaggerated horseplay and fun. That mood cannot be created by giving a singer or joke-teller three drinks and a free cigarette (which is all the pay he usually ever gets, by the way; the rest of the profits, copyright, and so forth going to the collector), and then turning on a tape-recording machine, while the collector goes outside and sleeps, or pops into a control booth and makes faces at the singer. The collecting of folksong in the last century, in England and America, was done for the most part by retired clergymen and Sunday School music teachers, many of them women; and in Russia and France by democratic-minded noblemen. In this century it is being done by college professors, all of whom have to be referred to as "Doctor." No one can relax under those circumstances. The greatest collections of erotic material in the past were made in Scotland, not because the Scotch have more erotic folksongs than anyone else (though some say they do), but because the main Scottish collectors were hard-drinking, ordinary-seeming men like David Herd, George Kinloch, and Robert Burns, who were men-among-men and did not put on any 'side.' Those are the men who collect the best songs and folklore, of all kinds.

This brings up another, and very damaging, misconception as to folklore in general, and sexual folklore in particular. Folklore and folksong are now, for some reason, taken for granted as the perquisite of what might be called the old maids of the English departments in the universities — that is to say, those faculty members not specializing in Chaucer or Shakespeare — though folklore is evidently more properly the domain of the faculties of anthropology and psychology, where some formal training for the work would also probably be demanded. Folksong collecting is today the only anthropological specialty in the hands of largely untrained personnel and hobbyists. This is particularly evident in the pitiful reduplication and ignorance of most of the headnotes written since those of Child and his successor, George Lyman Kittredge, and of certain very exceptional scholars such as Phillips Barry, and Belden, Rollins, and MacKenzie. The rest of the published collections are of an insularity that passes belief — making almost no reference whatsoever to the tremendous European literature painfully indicated to them by Child and Kittredge, and more recently by Prof. Archer Taylor. They also betray only the most rudimentary historical sense, and that only occasionally, no song or ballad, no matter how ancient, ever being traced earlier than the American Civil War, or to the train wrecks, public hangings, and New Orleans' cribhouses of the 1900's, if that. Now that a few indexes have been published, in particular those of G. Malcolm Laws, one may hope for better: that is to say, Laws will be cited, or his research silently appropriated as a headnote, and all will be as before.

The problem of untrained hobbyist personnel, self-appointed to the work, is especially acute in the case of sexual folklore, for which nothing in the training of the average English teacher can be said particularly to fit him, or her, except perhaps the creation and promulgation of bawdy limericks — a type of folk poetry almost solely existing among the college group, professors and students alike. Bawdy limericks apparently represent for the educated group a sort of private revolt against the rules of prosody and propriety, at one and the same time, owing to the false accent with which most limericks begin, the improper geographical rhyme, and the gruellingly obscene subject matter, which is usually of a far more alembicated nastiness than folksong ever is. Concomitantly, however, the public pronouncements and printed publications of none of the members of an American college faculty — with or without tenure — have ever been, and it is difficult to believe that they are now suddenly to become, as free in the matter of sexual content as, for instance, the average paperback, for sale at the price of a chocolate soda in the campus drugstore.

The most profound misconception that exists about erotic folklore is that it deals with specially horrible stuff, that no decent person would want to know anything about; and that heaven would fall if it were printed. This idea is itself nothing but folklore. It is based, essentially, on a thorough ignorance of the extremely large literature that exists on sexual folklore — in the English language as in all others, except that in English one must dig a little harder to find it.

What does sexual folklore consist of? Its elements are the same as those of all other branches of folklore: language, lore (which includes customs, superstitions, proverbs, games and toys, initiations, and other primitive educational attempts), and the various oral arts in which people express their feelings about the subjects of sex and scatology: songs, tales, jokes, toasts, recitations, with all the mythic and emotional freight these oral arts must carry; and a small group of verbal entertainments, such as riddles, puns, proverbial comparisons, wellerisms and spoonerisms, along with a great deal of erotic slang coinage of a rather ephemeral kind. There are also certain materials confided at a folk level to written or other physical form: poems, manuscripts in verse or in prose (nowadays usually ascribed to Byron, Kipling, or some more recent bard), wall-epigraphs — both in public places and toilet rooms — printed and mimeographed 'novelties,' humorous erotic drawings and photographs of the sexual organs and acts; as well as erotic toys, ranging from little jointed creations out of matchsticks and broomstraws — made in prisons or by sailors — to watchcase automata in gold, inlaid with rubies and other precious stones to heighten the sexual parts. There are important private collections of these phallic and erotic toys in both America and Japan. (See in particular the materials illustrated in Krauss & Satow's *Japanisches Geschlechtsleben,* 1931; *Anthropophytéia,* Beiwerke: 1, in two volumes.)

At an earlier period in history such toys had an important religious significance in all countries, especially those toys of a movable, or winged and flying nature; and phallic survivals of this kind are still hawked to tourists at Herculaneum and Pompeii, as souvenirs, and in Mexico on All-Souls' Day (November 2nd), the latter in the form of a little dead Pharaoh in his coffin, who, by means of a hidden rubber-band, still represents the Resurrection of the flesh. Identical representations will be seen in the Egyptian tombs, with a totemic (matriarchal) bird fluttering down to drop a symbolized female genital on the erect organ of the supine male. The same toy, and the same idea, has also been encounted in the United States in the form of a little naked man in a barrel — also operated by a rubber-band — with the inscription running around the barrel in dog-Latin, '*Nil Illegitimi Carborundum!*' (Don't let the bastards wear you down!) In very much the same way, the circus slap-sticks and goosing-sticks of the comedy stage are an evident survival, descended now to the nursery forms of humor, of the ancient phallophoric street-processions of the Saturnalia, with the envoys of the gods, in the form of erotic 'madmen,' sexually

handling and presumably impregnating the barren women standing on the sidelines for that purpose. In the intermediate development, one sees the same phallically posing street-clowns of the
Italian *commedia dell'arte,* as in Callot's *Balli di Sfessania (c.*
1623). The 20th century form — the electrified goosing-stick of
American Legion paraders — naturally seems to the bystander
more crude, and openly sadistic, yet it is an even closer return to
the older form of the street-running 'madmen' of the Saturnalia, or
the priestly 'wolves' of the Lupercalia (February 15th), striking
women in the street with goatskin thongs to insure fertility and an
easy delivery in childbirth. In Catholic countries, such as France,
this is still celebrated, now assimilated to the Purification of the
Virgin, with bread (*'michettes'*) and cakes in the unabashed vulvar
form of split ovals decorated with lace and sugar, sold as *'pain
bénit,'* or holy bread. In Protestant countries this survives in the
even more elaborately symbolized eroticism of Valentine's Day,
with the sadistic tone of the flagellation with goatskin thongs
creeping back in the 'humorous' valentines, or anonymous hate-
cards, which have now practically driven out the early, lacier nineteenth-century forms concerned with love.

Also at the printed level there exists, in a very decadent and
outlawed state in Western civilization, a pornographic literature
intensively sought after by young people because it is the only
practical sexual education available to them. It is also of interest to
older men, and some few women, as a sexual substitute or excitant.
This has been discussed much more fully in the earlier chapter,
"Great Collectors of Erotica." Both of these interests are obviously
legitimate, but they have been made illegal, and this very illegality
has kept much of the erotic literature at a rather pure level of
what might be called quasi-oral circulation, being very often
hand-copied at inordinate length and circulated in manuscript or
typescript among adolescents. It is a literature which, in the
crippled and often pathological form caused entirely by its illegality,
it is easy to dislike and difficult to understand, as evidenced by the
recent stream of drivelling and rather-obviously gloating works
'explaining' the subject, cited in the earlier chapter, such as the
article "Unicorns at Play," in John Chandos' *To Deprave and
Corrupt...* (London: Souvenir [!] Press, 1962) p. 175–207, of which
the title, as opposed to what one might think, is simply a quotation from the British law as to obscene publications, which is one
of the principal laws crippling and abnormalizing this sort of folk-
literature in the West. In Eastern cultures where the sexual

education of the young is considered a religious duty, as in India and Japan, where 'pillow-books' of erotic postures in colored prints would be given to young brides, both the printed and the orally-transmitted erotic materials entirely lack the nasty and furtive tone, and pathological concentrations, of much of the similar material in the West.

The best-selling work in the field in English is over two hundred years old now, and, as Chandos observes, p. 183, is one of the few that 'evokes the name and appearance of sentimental love,' which is perhaps one of the reasons for its popularity. As it is not commonly known, and may be mentioned here, this work, *The Memoirs of a Woman of Pleasure* (1749, usually known as *Fanny Hill,* possibly a British pun on 'mons veneris') was first read aloud in manuscript by a relative of the author, John Cleland, to the Beggar's Benison Society, of Anstruther, Scotland, in 1737, twelve years before its printed publication. In other words, it began in oral circulation, as a formalized tale or recitation, and was connected with, or used as a preliminary to, the solemn rite of homosexual initiation and ritual examination for intercourse, described in the Records of the Society. Something of the same sort still survives today, at least at the verbal level of erotic toasts and brags, in various secret societies. Similar symbolically homosexual rites are also recollected on the eve of the Padstow 'Hoss' celebration in Britain.

When these initiations appear only in sadistic disguise, in boys' schools and fraternities, as described lividly in Calder Willingham's *End As a Man,* they are accepted with perfect calm by the public; though the degree to which these are taken, in pure sadism, in an important Texas 'military' college would probably bring them to an end if publicly known. This is very similar to the German students' face-slashing duels before World War I, but with the homosexual sadism directly frankly to the buttocks rather than 'displaced upward' to the cheeks. Neither, in any case, has ever really been considered wrong, but — rather — manly; whence Willingham's title. Compare the *osculo in ano* and other homosexual rites of the Templars, discussed at length in Richard Payne Knight's classic *Discourse on the Worship of Priapus,* 1865 (illustrated reprint, London: Skilton, 1952) p. 188–200, a key work on sexual folklore. When, as with the Templars, the homosexuality is enacted genitally, or oragenitally, instead of in the forms of duelling and flagellation, a scandal invariably ensues, as recently in one of the greatest universities of New York. This has already passed into folklore, with the offending fraternity of 'Betas' now being referred to as the 'Master Betas' (a joke earlier appearing in a very rare collection of bawdy American college songs, *Lyra Ebriosa,* 1930, where it is used as title to the fraternity snob song, better known as "In Bohunkus, Tennessee").

Doggerel pornographic rhymes, of similar initiational intent, are everywhere circulated among adolescent girls in manuscript form, as part of their secret education, under such titles as "The Story of a French Stenographer" or "The Love Alphabet," or even in long narrative texts similar to Cleland's, as "The Bride's Confession, or My Wedding Night." The literary form, or rather formula, is naturally very primitive, and does not seem ever to have changed — any more than has the subject-matter — since the time of the *Song of Songs* and similar Levantine epithalamia.

It is evident, or it should be evident, that all this material is already the property of 'the folk,' and has been for centuries, and that nothing is being kept from anyone except folklorists by refusing to allow it space in print in English. All the other civilized languages — and many uncivilized — have long since been covered thoroughly, in the Krauss volumes and series mentioned earlier and in certain lesser-known but equally thoroughgoing works such as those of Dr. Bernhard Stern (Stern-Szana) on the erotic life and folklore of Russia, Turkey, etc., and in many anthropological works since, which have simply refused to submit to the usual expurgation of English-language folklore. The idea of expurgating folklore and folksong in the English-speaking world dates from as early as the Protestant reformation in the 16th century, as has been discussed earlier, when the Wedderburns' *Compendious Booke of Gude and Godlie Ballatis* made a joke of Scotch Calvinist prudery forever, by attempting to replace the older love-songs with the more pious phrases of 'sacred contrefacts,' on the stated intention of driving the Devil out of folksong. Is the Devil gone? The Wedderburns' sacred counterfeits are gone, and Burns' polite expurgations live on principally only in print. The folksongs are still being sung, at least in Scotland.

This idea is extremely ancient. It is connected at every point where it appears in history with a stalking-horse of objection to impiety and obscenity, behind which is masked an attack on an earlier religion being replaced. In Scotland this was of course the Protestant attack, propagandizing on the model of Luther among the *menu peuple* by way of fake folklore, and directed against the older Catholic church and the Pope, who is referred to in the

Booke of Gude and Godlie Ballatis, in a highly satirical poem that
most of the modern editions expurgate, as 'The Paip, that Pagane
full of pryde,' going on to all the usual details about monks and
nuns, as in Boccaccio. This obviously has nothing to do with
'purifying' folksong, and is merely religious controversy and anti-
sexual propaganda warfare. As noted more fully above, at the end
of the preceding essay, the same activity had been engaged in, fifteen hundred years earlier, by the early Christians, in the attempt
to oust the earlier religions of Asia Minor. The older folksongs
of Harmonius, and even the *Psalms of David,* were revised into
hymns by Ephraim Syrus and Apollinaris the Younger; and these
in turn were expurgated or parodied even further by the heretic
and separationist sects of Arius and Paul of Samosata. Naturally,
once the earlier songs have been made to disappear, a whole folk-
myth grows up — especially among scholars — as to how horrible
and indecent they must have been. This is the alleged smell of
sulphur the Devil leaves behind, in the formal depositions of
people who don't want to go out on a limb and say they actually
saw the Devil making love to witches, with a scaly penis or hieratic
ampallang, at the Black Mass.

III

DURING THE great days of folklore collecting in Britain and
America — which are now definitely over, despite all wishful pretenses and the propaganda of the phonograph record business —
it was not possible to print in full the erotic material, and most
collectors therefore did not bother to transcribe it, or did so in a
very perfunctory way, in connection with the (praise God!) un-
censorable music, to which they then faked and published sentimental texts of their own concoction, the music also being doc-
tored, as is well known. The amateur collector, Alfred Williams,
who did not do any faking, mentions very honestly in his *Folk-
Songs of the Upper Thames* (London, 1923), that, instead, he
simply refused to collect what he knew he could not print. The
same was also done, but not so candidly, by the better trained and
therefore less pardonable British collectors, such as Cecil Sharp and
Sabine Baring-Gould, and by all American collectors almost without exception until about 1940, who have riotously faked and expurgated their sexual materials as published, and who are still
doing so. One striking example is the *Frank C. Brown Collection
of North Carolina Folklore* — the principal monument of Ameri-

can folklore collecting, with the exception of the journals — now in its seventh volume, under as many editors, all of whom have so far left it for the reviewers to observe that the materials are expurgated to the hilt. That is not an honorable way to collect or to publish folklore. The most that can be said for it is that it is an interesting hobby, like mounting cancelled postage stamps or dead butterflies in albums, or collecting one Child ballad in each county of the state of Virginia.

The work on the English-language sexual folklore all remains to be done. Not so much to collect it — though this is of course a continuing necessity — as to *publish* the existing manuscript collections, of which there are dozens gathering dust, some of these of extraordinary size. Several have already been lost, owing to the impossibility of publication in the past. Most particularly regrettable is the loss of a manuscript collection of American Negro songs made by the two best students and collectors of these songs in the 1920's. It is also of importance, now, to gather together the invaluable sidelights on origins and survivals of erotic folklore, to be found in the older and scattered printed sources such as the innumerable unexpurgated jestbooks published in English since about 1500 (on which see the essay, "Toward a Motif-Index of Erotic Humor," following); and in the slang and dialect dictionaries extraordinarily rich in folklore traces and materials, such as those of "B. E., Gent." (B. Edwards, 1699), and Capt. Francis Grose (1785, and enlarged editions, reprinted 1931); also Grose's *Olio,* 1792, and collection of quacks' advertisements, *A Guide to Health, Beauty, Riches, and Honour,* 1785, and his better-known *Provincial Glossary.* There is likewise a very great deal to be mined in the older antiquarian collections, especially in John Aubrey's *Remaines; Miscellanies;* and *Brief Lives;* now all completely available from his long-neglected manuscripts.

There are also similar modern collections, of which the only ones containing erotic materials in English are still those of rebellious amateurs, such as John Bellenden Ker's *Essay on the Archæology of Nursery Rhymes,* 1835–40, in four volumes (a lunatic work, but carefully recording many texts otherwise unknown); Vincent S. Lean's *Collectanea,* in five volumes; and, more recently, the privately issued "Supplements" of Indiana folklore and folksong by the retired ornithologist, W. L. McAtee, whose matching publications on erotic place-names and plant- and bird-names are an·unusual contribution. Prof. Allen Walker Read's already very rare *Lexical Evidence from Folk Epigraphy,* 1935, has been mentioned earlier, and is the only such collection published in English since *The Merry-Thought, or Bog-House Miscellany,* 1731, in four parts, of which very few copies of the fourth part are known to have survived. (Bodleian, and Harding Collection.)

What is necessary now is not only to study and republish all this material, but to publish it in some such form, and with some such historical commentary and interpretational insight, as to give its how & why, as well as its what-who-&-where; its *position* in the great stream of unwritten human history of which Michelet speaks in the opening words of *La Bible de l'Humanité* (1864) precisely a century ago:

> *L'humanité dépose incessament son âme en une Bible commune. Chaque grand peuple y écrit son verset . . . Il se trouve souvent que c'est le plus profond qu'on oublia d'écrire, la vie dont on vivait, agissait, respirait . . . A nous de les écrire, de retrouver leur âme, leur magnanime cœur dont tous les temps se nourriront.*

It is not enough, and it will never be enough, to publish raw collections of folk-tales and folk-materials, or hundredth reduplicative versions of overcollected song texts. What is necessary now, and long overdue, is to base publication deeply upon some meaningful and mature interpretation — socio-analytic, or psycho-analytic, or any other kind of analytic so long as it is analyzed — of what the material means, and meant to the people who have transmitted it; what it tells us about their unwritten 'verset' in human history; what it has left for us to understand about their otherwise unspoken and unrecorded lives and emotions, and most centrally about the emotion of physical love.

This is not a job for hobbyists and amateurs, nor for bumptious undergraduates batting out degrees. Their unquestionable courage, and they have it — the hobbyists generally have nothing more — cannot replace the hard work and laborious digging really necessary. It is an undertaking that will require long and far-ranging study, and patient research. One would be tempted to say that the study of sexual folklore is also certainly worthy of material and monetary support by the research foundations, but it is not likely ever to gain such support, for the simple reason that sexual folklore is *humorous,* at least in its form; and laughter is not allowed by the foundations. Also, it is not a subject that lends itself — except in the raw collecting phase — to the superficial teamspirit and anti-individuality of most of what passes nowadays as foundation-funded research.

The prime essential to work like this, and the one that is most often lacking, is *insight:* precisely what the 'measurement' or IBM approach pretends to supply, and cannot. That is what makes so nearly useless the great heavy tomes of, for instance, Frazer's *Golden Bough* and *Folk-lore in the Old Testament.* All those thousands of facts, and never any meaning! Or perhaps a meaning that has been small-mindedly hidden by an author afraid to take the jump, to say right out what he has understood, and what his materials have led him to realize; for fear of rumpling the feelings of the least considerable, though most vociferous, old-style religious fundamentalists, who want their literal Noah's Ark, three hundred cubits long, their literal Methusaleh, nine hundred and sixty-nine years old (*Genesis,* v. 27), and their world created (after Archbishop Ussher's *Annales,* 1650) on the first day of Autumn, 4004 B.C. In the exactly opposite sense, that is what makes almost supererogatory — after the brilliant basic insight of the author — all the three heavy volumes of documentation, and the so many thousand words of desperately contentious prose, of Robert Briffault's *The Mothers,* a stupendous work of research by one man alone and unaided, of which the mere bibliography, extending to *two hundred* quarto pages by itself, represents more profound study than goes into any ten of the usual folklore publications.

In pleading, a moment ago, for almost any kind of analysis of the collected materials, there was one kind of analysis that was not meant, and of which there has already been quite enough. That is the kind of thing being done by certain modern British amateur antiquarians, such as Mr. Eric Partridge, in his large slang dictionaries drawing so heavily (and with so little acknowledgement) on Farmer & Henley, and in *Shakespeare's Bawdy,* which is admittedly his own invention; as also by his followers or admirers, or parallel discoverers, Mr. James Reeves and Miss Margaret Dean-Smith. The pathos of these people's analysis of their sexual materials — which are blatantly the main thing they are interested in, though this is surely not wrong in itself — is not that their method is so hopelessly amateur, with *klang*-associations and wildcat etymologies blandly taking the place of any relevant research. What seems to be troubling them is, rather, a sort of pre-scientific or amateur Freudian nervousness, that there is PERHAPS some kind of recondite symbolism involved when the girl in Boccaccio's story goes to bed with her lover and wakes up with a nightingale in her hand, and they are very anxious not to miss it. They then proceed to stuff their books with mysterious winks and nods and nudges, about the erotic 'lingua franca of the folk,' which, though not quite of the same glorious delirium as Bellenden Ker's wholly invented 'early Dutch' prototypes of "Jack and Jill" and so on (see the example given in the Opies' *Oxford Dictionary of Nursery Rhymes,* 1951, p. 28), are nevertheless almost equally tiring after protracted exposure to them.

Only seldom do they seem able to rise to anything that, even as unconscious humor, is really worth the trouble, as in Mr. Partridge's magnificent howler — one of dozens — in *A Dictionary of the Underworld,* 1950, that the Yiddish word '*tochus*' refers to the testicles, because (quote): '*tockers* suggests *tick-tockers,* reminiscent of a clock pendulum, which swings.' As Hamlet says of the *mobled queen,* 'reminiscent' is good. I have tabulated several pages, in double column, of such fabulous information, all from the same folk-etymological source, in *American Speech,* 1951, vol. 26: p. 130–37; but paled before the job of tabulating the similar stuff in Partridge's *Shakespeare's Bawdy,* which also manages somehow to omit entirely Malvolio's 'These be her very *C's,* her *U's,* '*n*' her *T's,* and thus makes she her great *P's,*' in *Twelfth Night,* II.v. 88, a children's spelling-game plainly noted (for the first time, in two hundred years of Shakespeare criticism) in G. B. Harrison's 'Penguin' Shakespeare, 1937, p. 105. Compare also the perhaps relevant quotation in Partridge's edition of Grose, 1931, at "Nickumpoop, or nincumpoop": 'a foolish fellow, also one who never saw his wife's ****.'

In similar style, Mr. Reeves, who has learned a great deal of his technique from Mr. Partridge, puts his name at the head of the title of a book by Cecil Sharp (with Sharp's name somewhere at the bottom), in which he hacks together conflated and conglomerated texts from the Sharp MSS. — meticulously preserving the original punctuation, however — and informs the astonished folklore world that when Sharp records that the three milkmaids 'waiv-èd their milkpails to and fro,' this is a hidden reference to semen. Or spends thirteen pages discussing the 'dew' in the title of the "Foggy Foggy Dew," without appearing to be aware that the title is simply a corruption of "The Bugaboo," meaning demon or devil; thus leaving the fog just as thick as ever. This is perhaps analysis, but it is not the kind of analysis that is wanted now. Actually, it is nearer to the old witchcraft idea that sexual folklore is somehow 'mysteriously' obscene. To paraphrase Mark Twain on the "Sweet Singer of Michigan:" Sigmund Freud, if he could read it, would be glad he was dead.

IV

ONE FURTHER and very important point about expurgated folklore is this: it is guaranteed not to get anyone dismissed from his university job. The expurgation of folklore, or the simple refusal to collect it complete, is a sort of quiet dishonesty that makes printable books and articles out of what would otherwise be unpublished manuscripts. Even if there is no direct monetary profit in articles published in learned journals, and monographs published by university presses, they do tend to improve the compiler's standing. 'Unprintable' books — especially if they somehow get printed — are more than likely to jeopardize that standing. I do not think there is any misconception involved here, but the point has very little to do with folklore. It partakes, rather, of the ethical problem of the now vast and encroaching commercial miasma that Prof. Richard M. Dorson, writing over ten years ago in the *American Mercury*, has deathlessly called *fakelore*.

There is a profound moral contradiction here — not just for a bishop such as the protofaker, Thomas Percy, in the eighteenth century, or a clergyman such as Baring-Gould in the nineteenth, but for anyone — that forgery is all right, but that sex is all wrong. This is the identical contradiction that has brought folklore and folksong scholarship in the English-speaking world to the impasse implied in the present resolution, to examine, in 1960, the interesting subject of "Obscenity in Folk Literature," after 240 years of castrated publication of such literature, in England and America, beginning with the *Tea-Table Miscellany* of Allan Ramsay in 1724.

Fortunately, it does not matter in the slightest degree, to folklore and folksong, what is printed in commercial and university publications, and what is left out. This important fact, which people who live too much with books sometimes lose sight of, was very aptly expressed by Miss A. H. Gayton in the *Journal of American Folklore* in 1942, nailing a similar misconception:

> The idea that writing has affected European folklore attributes exaggerated importance to an almost irrelevant fact:

the fact that broadsides and songsters, collections of fables, etc., have perpetuated in print the products of a purely oral tradition, of an un-literate art. The printed record of folk-songs and folktales has been and is of importance, not so much to the folk themselves as to the folklorist investigating the nature and history of these cultural phenomena.

This means that scholarly publications are published for scholars. They have had, until recently, no other audience and no other real influence — particularly not on the folk. An anomalous situation has been created today by the phonograph recording, and the resultant avalanche of fake folksingers, and folk fakelorists, and other folk, all of them strictly out for the dollar, and feeding back to captive audiences the folksong and folklore which they hack together from the 'hard-back' compilations (of which they are now all great buyers and in some cases producers). What remains to be said about this infestation of hard characters and promoters — and *not* under the euphemism of 'revival singers' — will be found in the two closing essays of the present volume.

Nevertheless, whether the audience is a private one, of other folklorists, or must now include the phonograph-record purveyors — who are already complaining that the Sharp and Baring-Gould manuscripts turned out to be pretty tame when finally published (the record is called RAP-A-TAP-TAP: *English Folk Songs Miss Pringle Never Taught Us,* and is in truth abysmal stuff, dismally sung) — there is no real reason now why scholars should not take upon themselves the freedom to tell the same truth about folklore and folksong, in learned journals and university publications of rather limited circulation after all, that can be learned by anyone who will stop to listen to eleven-year-old schoolchildren on the street corners of Philadelphia, or anywhere else. Who is being protected by the self-imposed censorship? Usually the excuse is that it is for the protection of children — unless their name happens to be Lolita. Then aging gentlemen are incited to seduce them in best sellers. In the present case, the children are the ones who have the folklore. They entrust it to university professors, and then the professors have to protect each other from even suspecting that it exists. What would actually happen if this pusillanimous structure of falsification and absurdity were simply allowed to collapse?

We are treading here on the practical problem, not of obscenity as a moral transgression but as a tactical blunder; of practical people who do not intend to risk their jobs over what the present writer has heard referred to — in reference to himself — as 'a quixotic crusade for filth.' If that were the case, there would be no point whatsoever in discussing the possibility of liberalizing publication in the journals and so on. No such possibility would exist. Sex is now becoming a sort of bandwagon, since Kinsey, in line with the new and total American materialism, and people are jumping on. They can also easily be scared into jumping off, if their material position is endangered. There are no dirty words in Kinsey. It is all done with IBM machines, and the answers come out in graphs. No one can lose his job over that. But you cannot tidy up "The Bastard King of England" and "Christopher Columbo" with an IBM machine.

It is not a secret that the present writer is engaged in editing, for publication in France, a series of volumes intended to include the entire body of English-language folklore and folksong left out of the usual collections as 'unprintable.' This material was collected for twenty years singlehanded, but recently it has been possible to have the assistance of other collectors in Great Britain and the United States. Unfortunately, the fact of leaving out all these materials before means that they have to be put together all at once now. That makes the kind of volume no member of the Modern Language Association and the American Folklore Society seems to want to be associated with in print, though several members of both have been so very kind as to send some fabulous materials collected in their salad days.

If it had been possible for these materials to be published calmly, years ago, properly interspersed among the printed collections in which they belong — and that is the only intelligent and courageous way to do it in the future — this embarrassment would not now arise. The independent collector, Vance Randolph, who has shown more courage than all the rest of them put together since David Herd in 1769, was not allowed by the State Historical Society of Missouri, recently, to include his unparalleled erotic materials in the four volumes of his published *Ozark Folksongs*. The magnificent 'unprintable' collection he was left with has therefore remained simply an unpublishable manuscript in the Library of Congress and the Institute for Sex Research at Indiana University, with microfilm copies elsewhere. The so-called 'unprintable' folksongs and poems of the Randolph collection will now be published in connection with the series just mentioned. Dozens of other collectors have also sent material, but almost invariably with the proviso that they must never be mentioned, not even by their initials. Several have even had the candor to explain, almost in the same words, as did one fine old man, the late Josiah Combs: 'I collected these songs when I was a gay young blade. I am getting on in years now, and I cannot afford to jeopardize my position.' That tells the story.

As a matter of fact, the danger of 'jeopardizing one's position' is not as great as seems to be believed. Twenty years ago, a private scholar, James Masterson, in his *Tall Tales of Arkansas,* published several unexpurgated texts of the unabashedly obscene "Change the Name of Arkansaw!" speech, attributed to Mark Twain, in the notes to the chapter where they logically belonged, and in the ordinary way of publication. Heaven did not fall. Masterson did not lose his job. There is also no record that *PMLA* and the Oxford University Press had to go out of business because of De-Lancey Ferguson's transcripts of Burns' *Merry Muses* songs, or "Poor Bodies Do Naething But Mow," in Burns' *Selected Letters* — a popular edition (1953), page 331; nor for publishing Keats' *Letters* with the story of the young man who gave the superb toast, '*Mater omnium,*' being printed complete. It does not appear, further, that the American Folklore Society was dissolved for Arthur Huff Fauset's courageous collection of Negro tales and songs, *Folklore from Nova Scotia,* 1931 (in which will be found, for instance, p. 133, a survival of the strange erotic folk-mummery, "A Little Black Thing," printed in the earlier section here on the Cunningham MS.). Nor, for that matter, did the *Journal of American Folklore* have to cease publication because of Anna K. Stimson's "Cries of Defiance" in 1945, Waterman's article on obscenity in intellectual circles in 1949, or Dorson's folktale in 1951 about the man with an 'oversized organ,' who 'met his death when, asleep in an upper bunk, his outsized member fell over the side and the weight pulled poor Charlie crashing to the floor.' (I leave the motif-number, in the Thompson Index, for someone else to find.)

One must admit that the journal articles so far printed do not so much *present* folklore, as comment upon it, and deliver it up in neo-Latin paraphrases. The same is true of the present writer's study of castration jokes, in *Neurotica,* in 1951, as of almost all the remarkably freely-treated erotic material published in the psychological and anthropological journals and monographs, where folklore has always fared so much better than in the English departments, and where we learn quite clearly and unmistakably

all there is to know about the erotic doll-play of the Pilagi Indian children, etc., and without any mincing of words . . . but
the words used are not those of folk-speech, but of the psychiatric
jargon. On the other hand, as far as mere vocabulary is concerned,
no book more verbally obscene exists in the English language than
the 'Antwerp,' 1680, edition of the *Poems* of the Earl of Rochester,
yet this was republished by the Princeton University Press, ten
years ago, in exact facsimile, on paper watermarked — for some
reason — "Private Papers of Thomas Jefferson." Perhaps this was
intended as the Declaration of Independence of American university press publishing. In effect, that is what it was. These poems
by Rochester, Captain Radcliffe, and others, are by far the most
extreme examples of erotic poetry in English (or any other language), but no problem of any kind was aroused by their open
re-publication, by one of the most austere universities in the
country, except perhaps the problem of authorship. As is well
known, this is the new Shakespeare-Baconism in scholarly criticism: to study very carefully all of an author's bawdy poems and
manuscripts — especially Rochester's — going around the world
several times to see even more such bawdy poems and manuscripts
ascribed to him, and then republish them with the carefully hedged
statement that they're all by somebody else. On 'internal evidence'
of course. On the internal evidence of the new edition, at least,
Rochester's bawdy poems will doubtless one day be ascribed to
Thomas Jefferson.

People say, when you point out these logical contradictions
of the censorship of literature, folklore and art, that exceptions
are being made for great poets like Keats and Burns — even for
an important satirist like Rochester — exceptions that one cannot
expect to see made for 'silly jokes' and mere folk 'smut.' Yet what
is to be said then for James Joyce's *Ulysses,* also filled with 'silly'
folk-jokes and 'smutty' folktales, poems, and songs — even a Child
Ballad, No. 155, the anti-Semitic "Hugh of Lincoln and the
Jew's Daughter," complete with music (ed. 1922, p. 643–4), celebrating the principal English pogrom. It is true that we are a bit
hard-up for masterpieces in the twentieth century, and even eccentric works like Joyce's *Ulysses,* and the utterly raving *Fin-
negans Wake* (based on the title folksong) will have to do, since
we have no better; but could not some similar excuse, of Irish or
poetic madness, perhaps be stretched to cover folklore publication
as well? Meanwhile, any number of members of the English faculties in American universities, representing a good half of all the

folklorists in the country, can and sometimes do give Molly Bloom's erotic soliloquy, with which *Ulysses* ends, as optional reading to their eighteen-year-old students of both sexes. I believe a phonograph recording has even been made of it: very beautifully delivered too. And heaven does not fall.

Dean Herbert Halpert made this same point very explicitly in the *Journal of American Folklore* as long ago as 1941, in a review of Prof. Louis Chappell's *Folk-Songs of Roanoke and the Albemarle,* 1939, which is, with Fauset's *Folklore from Nova Scotia* mentioned earlier, the only unexpurgated folklore monograph as yet publicly published in the United States. Said Halpert:

> Worthy of note is the inclusion of the texts of several bawdy songs. Collectors have been as loath to publish "blackguard pieces" as folk singers are to sing them for strangers. We need more of these to round out our knowledge of the repertory and psychology of folk singers. Since most collections are pretty definitely not for popular consumption, there is no very real hindrance to the inclusion of "high-kilted" songs. We can take the chance of shocking a scholar who has read the 1776 edition of David Herd's *Ancient and Modern Scottish Songs* and knows the nurse's lines in *Romeo and Juliet.*

It should also be observed that university presses are not the only ones that exist, and that folklore study is not in any way required to be immolated on the shyness of the most reactionary or *arriéré* university press or learned journal point of view. There are commercial publishers too, some of them very brave and very enterprising, as the recent censorship history of D. H. Lawrence's *Lady Chatterley's Lover* and Miller's *Tropic of Cancer* has now proved. It would even appear that certain folklore compilers are already aware of the existence of other publishers than the university presses. There has certainly been a great deal of commercial publication — not to say commercialization — of folklore and folksong going on over the last twenty years, but not to avoid censorship. The contradiction that still exists, even among commercial publishers, as to what can go into scholarly works of essentially limited circulation, and what goes into popular novels of which a million copies are sold to housewives in the supermarkets, along with the soap-chips, has never been made so poignant to folklorists as in William M. Doerflinger's excellently researched but utterly expurgated collection of sea-chanteys, and the identical publisher's *Forever Amber,* put out at the same time.

There have been some notable cracks in the dike since the Princeton Rochester of 1950, which makes Henry Miller's *Tropics* seem rather mild by comparison; but again not principally in the folklore field. The finest sea-chantey collection since that of Doerflinger, Stan Hugill's *Shanties from the Seven Seas* (London & New York, 1961, with matching phonograph recording issued by "His Master's Voice," CLP 1524), which is not only the best and largest book ever written on the chanteys, but probably the best book that ever can be written now that chanteying has forever disappeared, is also thoroughly expurgated. I, for one, should perhaps not complain, since, as Mr. Hugill observes kindly in his preface, p. xv, he gave me the *real* versions of all the 'camouflaged verses' and incomplete songs scattered through his 600-page volume, in the hope that I will be able to publish them one day as he could not. This seems a very great pity. Meanwhile, sparked by the courage of Mr. Barney Rosset's unexpurgated Grove Press edition of *Lady Chatterley's Lover* in America, the same work appeared, equally unexpurgated, in England; while in America the identical publisher of Mr. Hugill's unfortunately bowdlerized chanteys issued on open sale the ancient Hindu erotic posturebook, the *Kama-Sutra* of Vatsyayana, never before publicly offered in England or America. As far as commercial publishers are concerned, erotic folklore and folksong still seem to be everybody's stepchild.

Two very clear advances have, however, finally been made in the two countries, toward the integral publication of erotic folklore and folksong, so long and so obviously overdue. One of the most conservative of the English Rochester scholars, Prof. V. de Sola Pinto, issued in 1957, with the collaboration of Mr. A. E. Rodway, a collection of broadside-ballad reprints and similar materials from unpublished manuscripts, curiously entitled *The Common Muse,* which includes — in an erotic appendix to the limited edition, reserved apparently for the non-'common' and non-folk élite here gone slumming — a small group of surviving off-color broadsides, and of orally-collected modern obscene ballads as well, by way of historical control. When re-issued in America, by a university book publisher of specialized audience, the erotic appendix was democratically included in all copies. Neither of the publishers went to jail, in either country, and Prof. de Sola Pinto and Mr. Rodway are both still at their teaching jobs. Of course, as is well known, whatever may be the hesitancies of English publishers, the atmosphere of intellectual freedom in British universities has long been very much in advance of the disturbingly conformist tendencies in the United States, where even the ostensibly *non*-conformist clubs on the campuses — for the purpose of drinking beer, reading 'science'-fiction, and making up bawdy limericks — all have their bye-laws, elections, rules and regulations.

Now finally, even in the United States, the possibility has been found, at the courageous insistence of Prof. Richard M. Dorson, editor, and Prof. MacEdward Leach, president of the American Folklore Society, to devote an entire issue of the *Journal of American Folklore* (July 1962, vol. 75: pp. 187–265) to a "Symposium on Obscenity in Folklore." This is a publication that marks an epoch in folklore studies in the English language, the only regrettable note being the absurd letter-expurgation, by means of hyphens, of all the so-called 'four-letter' words, including the apparently seven-letter word 'a - - - - e,' p. 250–51, which is almost too much of a goodygood thing. It should be observed that this was done solely on the printer's demand, none of the textual materials having suffered the slightest editorial tampering-with, except the present essay (there printed in part) and that only on the stated grounds of length. This essay, which was read *in absentia* by my friend, Mr. Jan Kindler, at the combined meeting of the Modern Language Association and the American Folklore Society, at Philadelphia, 28 December 1960, as part of the published "Symposium," is there reduced to less than one-third at the demand of the intended mediator of the symposium, Dr. John Greenway, who then could not appear.

This symposium was originally planned by two young American folklorists, who modestly took no credit for it, Dr. Tristram P. Coffin and Dr. Roger D. Abrahams. Dr. Abrahams' own contribution, on the American Negro erotic 'flytings' or contests-in--insult, "Playing the Dozens," is a preliminary chapter from his remarkable doctoral dissertation, *Negro Folklore from South Philadelphia: A Collection and Analysis* (Ph.D. thesis, University of Pennsylvania, 1961), issued in facsimile of the 400-page typescript in an edition limited unfortunately to only six copies! The submission and the acceptance of this dissertation for the Ph.D. degree is itself, as will be understood, even more epoch-making than the publication of the "Symposium" referred to, in the following year.

Nothing that can be compared with the absolute and unexpurgated courage of Dr. Abrahams' perfectly serious folklore study has ever before in history been offered to, and accepted by, a learned faculty and institution in the English-speaking world. In what is perhaps the only editorial aside to be found in the monumental *Bibliography of Sex Rites and Customs* (London, 1931) by Roger Goodland — the sole existing bibliography of sexual folklore, though from the very specialized 'phallic worship' point of view — in noting Dr. Edmund Buckley's *Phallicism in Japan* (Ph.D. thesis, University of Chicago, 1895), the bibliographer felt called upon to add: 'Probably the first serious study of any branch of phallicism to be presented to a university. The author is to be commended for his courage.' Dr. Abrahams' even more courageous work has been revised for projected open publication under the title *Deep Down in the Jungle*. One trusts this will be successfully achieved. If so, the scholarly precedent can be considered to exist, even more than in the *Journal of American Folklore* "Symposium on Obscenity in Folklore" of July 1962, and there should be no further problem as to the dignified publication of erotic folklore texts, of both songs, tales, etc., in the English language. But that remains to be seen. If, despite the liberty now accorded to fiction, the publication of erotic folklore still remains impossible or illegal in the English-speaking countries, nothing prevents its continuing publication abroad.

V

COMMERCIALIZATION of scholarship is now getting to be like prostitution in the 19th century poem: 'Every man turns away his face, and every man goes in.' Well, perhaps not every man, but quite a few. What has been so very strange, in the recent commercialization of folklore and folklore scholarship in the United States and England, is not the open desire for professional advancement and money motivating certain of the folklorists involved — which is perhaps only natural — but their inexplicable and unprofessional ignorance of the tremendous manuscript wealth of collected folklore, and folksong in particular, gathered by the greatest early reapers in the field, where nothing can be done today but to glean, and patiently waiting for publication. No one would care in the slightest if this publication were later commercialized (in any case, it cannot be prevented), as long as the dust were shaken off all these superlative manuscript and even phonographically-recorded collections lying dead and frozen in archives everywhere in the English-speaking world, and at least one full and unfalsified printing of them were made, before the usual radio-faking begins.

That folksong cannot any longer be collected, as once it could, is perfectly clear to everyone in the field. As already observed, this is far more true of the *non*-erotic than of erotic folklore. Perhaps the most unexpected misconception, therefore, in erotic folklore is that to which the preceding section of this essay may have seemed to be tending: the idea that the main thing waiting to be gathered and published today in the folklore field is the erotic folklore. To the contrary, that is the *smallest* part of what remains to be published, though doubtless the most interesting, and certainly the most humorous of all.

Folksong collecting in England and Scotland arrived at exactly the same impasse, or point of diminishing returns, and at exactly the same time, as collection in the United States — that is to say, on the eve of World War II — but it took cognizance of its intellectual responsibilities, and, by and large, did not jump off into the very dubious commercial exploitation of folksong in the 'entertainment arts' which has been going on since then in ruthless fashion in the United States, and to which some very big names have shamefully lent themselves. In an editorial in the *Journal of the English Folk Dance and Song Society,* in England, in 1938, Frank Howes made this very frank statement:

> Now that the actual collection of oral folk-song is for practical purposes completed in this country, the task that confronts students of folk-song is to sift the large quantity of material that has been preserved, and by comparative study to see how far its history can be written . . . the songs have been collected. If anyone wishes to acquire first-hand knowledge of folk-music now he must do it by research.

'Completed' is of course a big word. The idea that a bit of living folk-music might still be found, or that deeper studies than the textual and historical could certainly be made, perhaps did not occur to Howes, or may have seemed futile in the lack of surviving informants in England. However, there are still a surprising number of living informants left in the United States.

There is another major fact that Howes' editorial overlooks, or perhaps was too polite to mention; and that is, that although the collection of folksong in England may have been 'completed' by 1938, the publication of what had been collected most certainly had not. British university presses simply do not have the money at their disposal that is being thrown around pointlessly by university presses in the United States, as for instance when the volumes of the *Brown Collection of North Carolina Folklore* were printed on expensive glossy paper, though there is not a single half-tone cut requiring such paper in any volume so far. Nothing prevents American scholars from wangling publication grants and obtaining permission to edit and print the real and untampered-with British collections left behind by Cecil Sharp and by Sabine Baring-Gould in the Plymouth Public Library, and Alfred Williams at Swindon, Wiltshire; collections of which the conflated volumes by Mr. James Reeves are only a picked-over sample. It is of course essential that the scholar asking for permission *be* a scholar and not a hobbyist or recording-company scout, if permission is to be granted, as, thirty years ago, Hyder Rollins, the student of George Lyman Kittredge, was permitted to print at last the *Pepys Ballads* that had lain under lock and key in the Magdalene Library for over two centuries (and have still not been published complete).

If the collecting seems thin today, it was still remarkably rich in the 1900's, yet most of the British manuscript collections of that period are waiting mournfully to be published. If America has the money and Britain does not, the two countries are sisters in language and literature, after all, and are allowed to publish the monuments of each other's folk-culture. In the Harvard University Library alone there are at least two extraordinarily valuable older manuscripts — and probably more, such as the Rochester Miscellany of about 1680, MS. Eng. 636F — which any competent scholar could probably obtain permission to publish, if he can find a commercial publisher or arrange for a publication grant: the George R. Kinloch collection, and Peter Buchan's *Secret Songs of Silence,* both collections made in Scotland about 1830, and the pitiful story of the *Songs of Silence* manuscript told at length in William Walker's *Peter Buchan, and Other Papers* (1915). Neither of these, nor the Sharp, the Baring-Gould, the Alfred Williams and other similar collections, contain anything that would create the slightest moral stir nowadays if they were plainly and simply published complete, except a stir of admiration at their unquestionable value.

The same is true of the fine American collection left by John

A. Lomax to the Library of Congress and the University of Texas — and still largely uncatalogued — which *may* contain five or six bawdy song texts, but that is all. A hell of a collection of cowboy songs it would be if it didn't! The idea that all these magnificent unpublished manuscript collections of folksong, rotting in British and American libraries for fifty and a hundred and fifty years at a time, are filled to the gunwales with bawdy songs, and that is why they have never been published, is absolutely false, as half an hour's examination of any of them will show. It is merely a popular delusion, or tenet of the *pseudodoxia erotica* of the scholarly world, that is clung to because it is titillating to believe.

But beyond these, are even larger collections, as to which not the slightest breath of scandal as to 'high-kiltedness' has ever been bruited about, yet they have never been published either, and one is beginning to wonder whether they ever will. The Kidson collection in the Mitchell Library, Glasgow; the Percy Grainger collection in Melbourne (see Scholes' *Oxford Companion to Music,* 1938, p. 376), of which the collector's marriage could be celebrated 'in the Hollywood Bowl before an evening audience of over 20,000 people, for whose pleasure before and after the ceremony he conducted a Bridal Song composed by him for the occasion, and others of his works,' but whose folksong collections are preserved only in dinky little hektographed copies in purple ink, in chosen repository libraries. One is almost ready to stop after that, and throw up — throw up the sponge, I mean. And there are still the extraordinarily large North American collections, unpublished in the archives of women's colleges in the northeastern states; and the dozens of historical manuscript collections ranging as far back as the 17th century in Scotland, recently indexed to 1900, in a University of Edinburgh Ph.D. thesis in 1954, by Dr. William Montgomerie — a superlative index, and study, never yet printed, and by the only scholar today probably capable of preparing the long-awaited revision of the Child Ballad volumes, on the basis of the index to modernly-published texts by Dr. Tristram P. Coffin.

Above all, there is the superb collection made by Gavin Greig, and deposited in *ninety-three volumes* in the Aberdeen University Library, and in so beautifully clear and bold a handwriting that it would be perfectly feasible, and economically wise, to have it published simply by offset-facsimile of the manuscript itself. An index, by Mr. Patrick Shuldham-Shaw, has already been prepared. Any necessary editorial notes and further references could be added in set type at the end. This one time, in two and a half centuries — or at least since the *Scots Musical Museum* of James Johnson and Robert Burns, as re-edited by Stenhouse and Laing in the 1830's — an editor could perhaps deny himself the intrusiveness and ostentation of headnotes, and take a back-seat to the greatest folksong collector of modern times, and in the richest area for folksong by far.

One thing is certain. It is of the greatest importance now, that if, in any of these collections, including those of John A. Lomax, or in any further collections that may be made in the future, anyone happens to run into an erotic song, or tale, or joke, or riddle, rhyme, comparison, turn of phrase, bit of slang, or miscellaneous *obscœnum;* this should and must simply and calmly be printed right where it stands in the manuscript text, or logically falls in the editing of new material collected in the field — exactly as done by Fauset in 1931 — without the slightest special emphasis being placed upon it, or sign-pointers of horror and dismay, and without any more of this schoolmarmish paraphrasing and pussyfooting, or seven-letter 'four-letter' words. At all costs, such material should never again be left unprinted, in secret manuscript appendixes to the published work — waiting for somebody in France or elsewhere to come along and print it, like the Lady from Philadelphia in the *Peterkin Papers* — nor should it be printed up separately, either, for some presumed scholarly *élite,* in a sort of Jim Crow outhouse or hell-box, where it is a sitting duck for anyone who wants to shoot at it. Who could defend the Bible if all the erotic and sadistic passages were selected from it (as the Beggar's Benison Society planned to do, and Charles Bradlaugh and Annie Besant — surely on their inspiration — did do), and were printed up all together? It should not be necessary today to vindicate the right of Scottish, English, and American folklore and folksong to be published just as complete — and as they run — as are the folk-myths of the Semitic and nomadic tribes of Asia Minor in the 9th century B.C.

The manuscripts listed above are hardly more than the beginning, though they are obviously the place to begin, to protect these invaluable materials now only uniquely existing in single copies or microfilm. What about all the material that has already been collected in the form of phonograph recordings in the mere half a century since Edison and Berliner's inventions? Are folklore scholars really through with that? Or, truth to tell, have they even started on it? There are tons — literally and actually tons — of folksong and folklore texts and recordings made in the United States since 1900, by Lomax, Lummis, and Densmore, and endless others since, and more recently by the B.B.C.; not only in the English language, and in the Indian and Spanish languages too, but in all the languages of the world. Who has indexed these? Who has collected them? Who knows where they are, except for a handful of blues and jazz and hillbilly 'race' records that almost no one collected at all, for the twenty-five years when they were available for pennies, until the Negro cartoonist, E. Simms Campbell, in the mid-1930's, mentioned that they were perhaps worth collecting, in the pages of *Esquire* magazine? None of the commercial folk-recordings were originally preserved by repository libraries, owing to their not being mentioned by the copyright deposit law, nor will these libraries find anything but a scratchy and unlistenable remnant of them now. It is only thanks to the kid-enthusiasts for jazz and blues that a handful of the early shellac discs have been saved from total oblivion and reissued on long-playing records, to stock the new neon-lighted *discothèques,* and record-libraries of folklore and folksong foundations, that are only now beginning to come awake to the realization of what they let slip while concerning themselves for forty years with the theoretical 'communal improvisation' of folksongs in the eleventh century.

Just aside from the commercially-issued folksong discs, of the early period and of today, one would imagine that the greatest of care would be taken to index and make available to folklorists at least the great wealth of field-recordings deposited in national and university libraries. And one would imagine wrong. The Library of Congress, to take only the most striking example, is overflowing with recordings, specially made and left purposely by John A. Lomax, Vance Randolph, and many other collectors, not to mention the manuscripts and printed books. Who knows what all these endless and expensive archives contain? And those of the British Broadcasting Company, as well. Worse, who is even trying to use them? — except for commercial exploitation. At the present time, only one man in the United States, the independent researcher Edward Cray in Los Angeles, is trying to cope with the indexing of even the printed part of this monstrous mass of folksong material. He has no idea when he will be finished, and nobody knows, because he has only a minuscule amateur staff helping him — if he still has that. The original slips for this index of English-language folksongs were prepared by Prof.

Archer Taylor, and were shipped back and forth across the United States twice, looking for somebody damn fool enough to continue so thankless and monumental a job alone. Meanwhile, there are the ballad-syllabi of Dr. Laws and Dr. Coffin, and the headnotes to the Belden and Brown published collections. That is a great deal, but would any of the editors of these call it more than a beginning? The Scottish manuscripts, as observed, have now been indexed by Dr. Montgomerie and Mr. Shuldham-Shaw, but the printed literature of the British Isles since the 16th century has hardly been touched, except where Baring-Gould, or Child and Kittredge and a few of their students may have dipped into it for relevant notes. Even for the English literature of the 19th century alone, there is only the recent index or *Guide* by Miss Dean-Smith, which omits all the manuscripts and all the sea-chantey collections too, no one knows why. It certainly couldn't have been for lack of space: the whole thing doesn't run to a hundred pages, of which a large part is spent on antiquarian tracings which do not belong there, and on this amateurish nonsense about the erotic 'lingua franca' of the folk.

VI

DON'T GO AWAY satisfied, ladies and gentlemen; the show is only about to begin. The broadside ballad collections at Harvard and in the British Museum, at Oxford, Cambridge, and a dozen other libraries, which go back to the time of Henry VIII and are of the most staggering richness — not to say weight — not a fiftieth, not a hundredth of these ballads have ever been reprinted or studied except for one small corner, the Roxburghe and Pepys Ballads, and a few lesser collections, though fortunately these are among the oldest. Except for these reprint texts, almost none of this tremendous mass of collected broadside material has ever been catalogued, let alone indexed. The British Museum lumps it under the word "Collections," in brackets, in the Museum's printed catalogue, which is now in its second edition, though one would have thought there had been sufficient time for this work to be done since the first edition. A pitiful listing appears in *A.S.L.I.B.* for 1928, which is almost the only key to the whole field. The keepers at the Museum apologize for this listing, if you mention it, but they point out that they simply have not had time since 1928 to do any better. *They are too busy accessioning the new stuff as the collectors die.* That is the identical situation almost everywhere in the world. Practically the only fully indexed collections that exist are those of the American Antiquarian Society in Worcester, and the Massachusetts Historical Society, and these were indexed because, there, people sat down to do the work before the days of electronic hubble-ka-bubble, and high-speed super-duper photo-cell devices, by means of which whole staffs of bemused machine-tenders can now go skating around like water-bugs on a pond, getting nothing done.

The richest university in America, and probably in the world, Harvard, with $393,000,000 a year to spend (the second richest is Texas, with a mere 376), has also received some of the largesse of earlier collectors, such as the great Field collection recently. According to Dr. Laws' *American Balladry from British Broadsides,* 1957, p. 126, the Charles Welsh catalogue of the Harvard chapbooks and broadsides — which have been there from at least the time of Child and Kittredge, who are among the only scholars ever to have cited them — leaves 'thousands, largely uncatalogued, in the Houghton Library.' How many millions of dollars (per year) does it take to catalogue a thousand broadsides? And how many dollars would it take, today, to buy them? Same question as to Texas, and the John A. Lomax manuscript collection.

Nobody knows what has been collected. That is the plain truth. Nobody knows. Fortunes have been spent on collecting these ephemeral materials, over the last three centuries, while they could still be found — sometimes by impoverished scholars like Aubrey and Ritson, and gentlemen-collectors like Douce, who sacrificed themselves to leave a monument for the future study of folklore and folk-literature. But the future is too busy. Too sure that they are going to get the whole thing under control, 'one of these days,' on the great rich teat of government grants, by means of plastic and electronic doo-jiggers that will mindlessly sort out the sheep from the goats, and deliver the *meaning* of the whole operation on a neat little printed card. (Also your weight and horoscope.) Far from this situation being in any way new, it will all be found described over a century ago, in blistering style, in the "Anti-Dryasdust" introduction to Carlyle's *Oliver Cromwell.*

The folksong collectors have no time, because they are too busy collecting new texts — meanwhile complaining that these are 'corrupted and decayed' — or are counting the musical intervals of the tunes on their fingertips. The folklore scholars imagine that everything is all tied up because Prof. Stith Thompson's *Motif-Index* has indexed motifs. But that is not an index to texts, and it is not even a complete index of the motifs. 'Thousands' were purposely omitted at X700, as too obscene even to list. The bibliography of the *Anmerkungen* to Grimm's folktales, by Bolte & Polívka, is also not an index of tale-texts, but that is the place to begin the examination of the tremendous folktale literature of the past, instead of continuing hoeing hopelessly at some little corner of the present by means of materials collected *via* students' term-papers. One certainly wants the new material, but one is beginning to wonder what the value of this new material will really prove to be, when nothing is being done with it but to add it to the disorderly heap of the old. There are behind us two thousand years of folklore literature, at least, and the only real indexes that exist in English are the hopelessly antiquarian fumblings in the *Gentleman's Magazine* in the 18th century, in *Notes & Queries* in the 19th, and now, at a much higher level at last, the listings by Dr. Edson Richmond in the *Journal of American Folklore (Supplement)*, Dr. Charles Haywood's *Bibliography of North American Folklore and Folksong,* now in its second edition; and, as far as sexual folklore is concerned, the *Bibliography of Sex Rites and Customs* by Roger Goodland (1931) covering only the 'phallic worship' segment of the field.

Two unimportant but very typical examples: A man from Scranton — I know him well — spent two years writing letters trying to find the whereabouts of a remarkable article he had heard of, on the annunciatory folk-myth of "Animals Impregnated by the Wind," for a footnote on the survival of this myth in the modern 'doofus-bird' that eats nothing but red pepper and flies backwards. The article appeared in English, in *Isis,* published in Bruges, Belgium, in 1936, and was written by Dr. Conway Zirkle, of Philadelphia. Acres of diamonds! No index could turn it up. Ten years of useless inquiries could not uncover an even more recent and extended monograph of primary importance on the psychological analysis of the cult of the Mother-Goddess. That is erotic folklore too, though at a far different level than the jokes and little mythic beasts. Prof. E. O. James, author of the principal recent work on the Magna Mater, had never heard of it and does not cite it. Neither does G. Rattray Taylor, who covers some of the same material in *Sex in History,* 1953. By accident, the reference was discovered in an index-article by Dr. Weston LaBarre on "The Influence of Freud on Anthropology," in *American Imago,* 1958, a splendid coverage of a complex subject by the first American ever to publish an article on erotic folksong (in *Psychiatry,* 1939, vol. II). The article on the Mother-Goddess is by Dr. Edith Vowinckel-Weigert, and also appears, in English, in *Psychiatry,* 1938, vol. I. No folklore index or encyclopedia could turn these up. As a matter of fact, the most recent folklore encyclopedia or dictionary, published by Funk & Wagnalls, has itself never been supplied with its promised index, after more than ten years of waiting, and the original subscribers are beginning to wonder. . .

No one has studied, and no one has ever indexed, the enormous collections of drolleries, garlands, penny merriments, and chapbooks in British and American libraries, and especially not the fabulous wealth of the jestbooks in English, from Poggio in 1480 to the American Civil War of 1860, at least. A tiny segment — basically only the materials reprinted in the mid-19th century as *Shakespeare's Jestbooks,* in expurgated form — has alone been attempted, by Dr. Ernest Baughman (see Thompson's *Motif Index,* 1955, I. 38; also at Irwin, Neuman, and Marguerite).

For the English songbooks of the 17th and early 18th centuries, a beginning has been made, by Prof. Cyrus Day and Miss Eleanore Boswell Murrie, and a very fine beginning. But much similar index material remains unpublished in the Harding Collection. A few years ago, in *Midwest Folklore,* 1959, IX. 89–102, in a bibliographical note on *Pills to Purge Melancholy,* the last and largest of the drolleries, a very serious appeal was made on this subject. Nothing happened. Perhaps that was not the right place for the suggestion. Perhaps this is. Let it be said again: It would be of the greatest value to the study of English poetry and folksong, in their most fascinating period and aspect, if some fraction of the herd of nascent Ph.D.'s in English literature could be diverted from the usual stampede upon Chaucer, Milton, and Beowulf (see the *Cambridge Bibliography of English Literature, Supplement: 1940–1955,* vol. V, pages 130–45, and 225–37, covering fifteen years' publication only!) and turned to these vitally important indexing projects instead — the drolleries, the poetic miscellanies, the garlands, merriments, chapbooks, and especially the jestbooks, from the beginning to at least 1840 or 1860, when they were finally and completely expurgated and so died. As far as Chaucer and Milton and Beowulf are concerned, they have suffered enough.

One begins to lose courage. Not so much because of all there remains to do, but because of the crashing lack of interest in doing it, on the part of the professional class capable of doing it, and which one has a right to expect would use a part of its paid leisure in attempting to do it. Unless a stop is put to all this futilitarianism and reduplication, with endless piling up of undigested collection; and some significant start is made to indexing and *interpreting* what has been collected for so many centuries now, the time is very close when it will all just be thrown away. This is not a joke, this is not an overstatement; it is a very real and present danger, and just as real and present as the danger of all the same material being blown sky-high by the atom bomb, after which there will be nothing more to argue about. As to the material simply dropping away into the almost equal non-existence of desuetude and forgetfulness, that is exactly what is happening already, in a nice and polite and hopeless sort of way, with, for instance, the ninety-three volumes of the Gavin Greig collection, which have lain practically untouched in Aberdeen since 1925, as far as study or publication is concerned. Meanwhile, a whole new School of Scottish Studies — and may it flourish forever! — has been instituted to collect more. Next year they are going to microfilm the Greig collection. That is not exactly the same thing as publishing it, but it is perhaps a start.

For an eye-opener as to the way these things happen, one must read what Dr. Jan Schinhan, music editor of the *Brown Collection of North Carolina Folklore,* has to say — boiling mad — in the Preface to volume IV, 1957, p. xv–xvii, as to the miracle by which he was able to save the Brown phonograph-recordings for folksong scholarship, after they had been 'processed' at the Library of Congress. Without actually saying so, Dr. Schinhan puts his finger here on what is perhaps even worse than the letting of everything that has been collected fall into forgetfulness and decay; and that is the inhuman and anti-human strivings of the new generation of people into whose hands this heritage has fallen, to turn it all over — and their intellectual and moral responsibilities along with it — to new and glaringly imperfect electrical servo-mechanisms, obviously incapable of handling anything but its merest outer integument (and that, not always well), or of producing anything but exact numerical gibble-gabble in support of the vague or tendentious and even dishonest preconceptions fed into them. Meanwhile, the world is stifling in its records, as everyone knows. Paper! — and now phonograph-recordings and tapes — worse than the plague. While we sit kidding ourselves about the electronic Nirvana that awaits us.

We are dealing here with a very small corner of a very large problem — a problem that the world of humanistic scholarship, and the world at large, will have to solve, or go under. Folklorists are not going to be the last to go, like Lot in Sodom throwing out his wife and daughters and the dog, to the clamoring Sodomites, while he goes last. When other human values die, folklore dies. In fact, it is one of the first to go. One would imagine, perhaps, that raw self-interest would at least keep those other subjects indexed and analyzed and meaningfully studied that have more relation to the general health and welfare of whole national populations, than anything to which folklore can pretend. Again, one would be wrong. The greatest international index-project the world has ever seen, the most perfectly organized and executed opening-of-the-doors of a complicated and extraordinarily important human science, the *Index-Catalogue of the Army Medical Library,* in Washington, D.C., ceased publication in the middle of the alphabet some twenty years ago, during World War II, because some unknown Pentagon bigwig — not to be confused with the Caliph Umar who burned the Library of Alexandria — could not be made to understand its stupendous value. Nor has it been continued since. What about those hundreds of thousands or millions of index-cards from M to Z, the key to half the modern medical literature? That is not folklore that is at stake there; that is public health. Who cares? The Surgeon-General's *Index-Catalogue* is dead. One day they will bale up and microfilm the cards from M to Z — a conscience gesture — and that will be that. File & forget. Public health can be taken care of by sedative pills and coughdrops and cocainized soft-drinks, and the physicians can get their information from the four-color advertising handouts in their quasi-medical waiting-room magazines. What are the 93 volumes of the Gavin Greig manuscript, compared to intellectual atrocities like that? And what can mere reduplication on microfilm copies, and their boon-doggling and reshuffling in Hollerith hole-punching machine entertainments do, to make any of it available or meaningful? The original records are thrown away, the microfilms shrink or explode, and the case is closed. We are left with IBM 'findings.'

One moment more: Pitiful megalomaniacs, with radio-tubes in their heads, and grownup science-fiction kids, are sitting around today imagining that everything is going to be all right because the machines are going to do it all for them. Big Brother! Not only the indexing, but the interpreting too. Here is a quotation from a perfectly serious technical work, *Document Copying and Reproduction Techniques* by H. R. Verrey, London, 1958, page 186, discussing a new fine-grain microfilm, not guaranteed — any more than any other film — against scratches. (Oops! there goes volume 1!) This is a:

system of information storage which makes use of extreme reductions . . . [with] selection in the order of 50 milliseconds to any word in a 20 million bit store . . . The development of extremely fine-grain emulsions has enabled storage to be made at a density of a million bits per square millimetre, thus enabling a plate 3 x 5 in. to have a storage capacity of the human mind (10^{10} bits) or on plates occupying less than a cubic yard to contain all the information stored in the Library of Congress (10^{14} bits). These extreme reductions, however, permit both the handling and the searching of the medium to be done with a simple and compact device.

Isn't that great? It isn't that I doubt it for a minute: I'm sure it's true. I've even seen a publicity handout from a magazine I don't subscribe to, with a photo of a terribly pretty young girl holding up a yard of film-tape over a table full of envelopes, with the statement that the tape contains all the same information as the whole tableful of envelopes being sent to the subscribers. Of course, it doesn't say that they have even 10^8 (in plain English, a hundred million) subscribers, which is a *shade* under 10^{10}. Also, sucker-lists of addresses by the millions, or even the hundred millions, aren't too hard to put together, out of phone-books, professional directories, and the like, with little tin (electronic) dooflickers to mark the 'percentage pull,' or heavy buyers. There's one born every second, after all. But that is only a very specialized kind of 'information,' and mostly in the form of numbers at that.

Since people nowadays are all supposed to have numerical social-security numbers as well as names, I don't see why it wouldn't be a good idea simply to reduce all written language to a 25-number system (no w), and forget about names, words, ideas, and human beings altogether. This would take care of all languages, including the Slavonic, with a first or key-number indicating the language like a telephone exchange. The ideographs of Giles' Chinese dictionary are already numbered. (That takes care of the 'Yellow Peril.') At the folklore level, the 'polite' words could be those beginning with the Freudian feminine 2, 4 and 8; and the 'dirty' words those with the masculine 3, 6 and 9. Children in their cradles could be taught to lisp 16.5.5 and 16.15.15, instead of what they say now; and anything higher than 25.25.25 is automatically a four-letter word.

When the world gets overcrowded, and people have even less time (because they live longer), everything can be reduced even further, solely to five-letter words, for feeding more easily into the machine, on the style of telegraphic code-books: SCORB is 'I love you' (pronounced: 19.3.15.18.2); SCORC is 'Where is the bathroom?' SCORD, 'Can you lend me five bucks till payday?' and SCORF, 'When do we eat?' I believe that takes care of all the main human situations. That dirty jokes can be told in numbers-form is already the subject of a joke itself. This is known as IBLegman or Numerical Basic, and is copyright! Nobody can say 'I love you' in *Numbasic* without paying me fifteen cents (I mean 15¢). All other taxes are repealed. With that for a platform, I think I could run for president on a laundry-ticket. The whole thing can be run like the national lotteries or Irish Sweepstakes, with the payoff in low-number license plates, which are naturally swank. The Button, or secret and ineffable Jehovah-number of the whole thing, is half of the square root of five, plus 1/2 (AFAHE). Feed Fibonacci's number — the 'building-block of the universe' — backwards into the machine, and the world blows up. And 'go not to inquire for whom the bell tolls:' it tolls for you and me.

Meanwhile, and until the new number-Utopia arrives; when it comes to material of a more intellectual nature than the bank-code in bottle-bottomed numbers at the foot of a check, for photo-cell handling, the first thing one wants to know, as to the project of reducing the Library of Congress to 'less than a cubic yard' of microfilm (to shoot it to the Moon, of course), and before this vital neo-Conquistador project gets too far under way, is who is going to index and card-code all those 10^{14} (one hundred trillion) 'bits' of information in the great national library at Washington (also Leningrad, so make that two hundred trillion), *before* they can be fed into the machine — for purposes unknown, and about which one may, in any case, have one's private neo-humanistic suspicions.

Maybe the first thing we'd better search for, with that 'simple and compact device' are the thousands of folksong recordings, and the more than several such 'liberated' Japanese books, still not catalogued when last heard from, in among those 10^{14} bits of information in the Library of Congress; and which are therefore *not* going to be 'selected' at the rate of 20 million word-bits per 50 milliseconds or whatever it is, and are *not* going to be shoveled into the machine to come out on pretty tapes (gosh, that girl was pretty! that proves everything, doesn't it?) and are in fact never going to be found at all, until one of those non-simple, non-compact, non-predictable devices, also not made of cheese-crust and tin, known as a human being — with its low and contemptible 10^{10} bits of information in its head — will sit down quietly and catalogue them, or even read and index them, or maybe even think about them, possibly with a disorderly stub of pencil at its disposition and no electronic bazooka whatsoever.

This ridiculous mental garbage — very sinister in its way — about putting human minds on interchangeable 3 x 5" index-cards, and similar electromechanical piddle-diddling, is now the great new Nirvana of folklore and folksong studies too. This is a great deal more dangerous than the effluvium being wafted up from the Augean stables of commercialization from which, as remarked, 'every man turns away his face, and every man goes in.' There are of course a few old-style exceptions, but they are not the fakelore compilers nor yet the pennyaliner hacks doing record-sleeve jobs for the *semi*-authentic recording companies, that would like to blossom out into the big money by being a little less, dammitall, authentic.

One is accustomed to being told, when one has a decided point of view, that one's point of view is overstated and absurd. Why of course it is! What could be more absurd than the remarks preceding, on five-letter combinations replacing human beings, and no one caring enough to cry halt? Ridiculous — overstated — anything you please. And yet . . . The point has been reached, nowadays, where very serious American regional ballad collections are being published, and held up as models, such as the *Frank C. Brown Collection of North Carolina Folklore* (in seven volumes), with almost as much space devoted to the headnotes as to the texts, and these headnotes largely composed of nothing further than page-references, arranged by states, to other authors' similar regional collections. These, though seldom either quoted or analyzed, are nevertheless required to undergo the unsightly and unnecessary rebaptism of a scoliastic alphabet-soup aswim with such mnemonic monstrosities as FSUSA to represent Lomax, 1948; OASPS for Randolph, 1931; SSLKFS for Sharp, 1951; TBMWV for Cox, 1939; and over a hundred others on the same system, representing nothing more than the acrostics of the titles of these authors' books. The system being established, there is no shaking free of it, and solitary works by authors with the unmistakable names of Beck, Coffin and Cambiaire must be referred to instead in the indigestible goober-mouthfuls of SMLJ, BTBNA, and ETWVMB. All in full capitals throughout. Such cenotaphs of scholarly futilitarianism cannot be used except as indexes to each other, and will generally be found to lead one out — as with Barnum's 'Egress' — at exactly the same door where one went in, and particularly the FCBCNCFL, which may be referred to shortly as 'Brown.'

What is involved here is not in any way just the low comedy
of the original editor, the late Prof. Belden, picking up so pointless and unnecessary a system (probably from G. F. Northall's
English Folk-Rhymes, 1892, which employs a particularly outrageous two-letter reduction of this kind for all its sources); now
further repeated by most of the six later editors, and in Miss Dean-
Smith's *Guide to English Folk Song Collections* (1954) which de-
faces itself with WUP's and BGSWC's on every other page. What is
significant here, what is so sinister, is the dehumanization that
mentalities of this cold indexing-type seem to yearn for, and
squeeze down upon everyone else, while imagining themselves
to be teaching — or even studying — the humanities. Now it is
not I who am speaking, in the absurd overstatements of my (copyright) language, *Numbasic,* of SCORC and SCORF. Now it is other
people, being serious, to the tune of seven volumes so far, and
seven hundred or thousand if they have their way: FSUSA for
Lomax (both with five letters!) SSLKFS for Sharp (six letters for
five, this time!) OASPS, BTNBA, and BGSWC. *Run it through the
machine!* Everything must be reduced to letters, and everybody to
a number. Everything personal and meaningful must be rejected in
favor of the lowest-common denominator symbols that have
neither personality nor meaning, but that can so easily be manip-
ulated zombi-fashion, though the machine-tender drop dead on
the job.

Are we blind? Are we dead? Are we too dumb to shout No! No!
before they screw the coffin-lid down? It is not only in folklore
studies that index-mongers and card-filers, on government and
university grants, are busily draining out the soul and drilling the
cadaver of everything they touch. All around us human life and
art are being systematically rounded up, corralled, hog-tied and
castrated; the skin ticketed and folded away, and the bones numbered. Oh yes — admired, polished, even worshipped, like the
dead Osiris, but only if-and-when minus the genitals and the last
gasped breath of life. Then, and only then, the 'social scientists'
of folklore study, and the gooey sentimentalists (or efficiency
'experts') of five-letter indexes, motif-charts, sex-questionnaires,
advertising agencies, industrial psychology, public-opinion polls,
and the great international alphabet-soups of intellectual opportunists on salary, are able properly to handle the matter, and to
derive from it that illusory godhood of *control* that they are really
after. The index, the schema, the 'weighted' table and 'corrected'
graph, intended originally as dummy representations, as tools or
perhaps tongs to help grasp a complicated living reality, entirely

replace the reality. The spectrum analysis, the syllable count, tonal chart, and phrenological floor-map replace the poetic and artistic achievement, so crooned over and admired to begin with. The parts of the clock are hammered apart, tacked to a wooden panoply — like the art of the insane — and presented, not as something obviously non-operating and *not* a clock, but as something marvellously and 'scientifically' more.

Let's not be general. Let's be specific. Why SMLJ? Why SMLJ — when *Beck* requires no more than the same four letters to set down, and three less syllables to pronounce? Why SSLKFS (in six syllables) for the whole name, Cecil Sharp (in three)? ETWVMB for Célestin Pierre Cambiaire; BGSWG for Sabine Baring-Gould? Why are names like these, reeking with the real and crotchety human personalities of the people who bore them, to be crunched flat in the dehumanized gobbledygook of SMLJ, without even the excuse of saving breath, not to mention hole-space on the Hollerith machine? Or why not, at the very least, the dignified scientific minimum of a name or place and date, locating the human phenomenon or art expression being studied, in its human and historical context, outside of which it can neither be assessed nor understood, nor in fact have any real meaning at all.

For that matter, what about the submerged LJ's of Dr. Beck's so-abbreviated title, and all the others: the *Michigan Lumberjacks* that sang the *Songs* in his book back in 1941, about the big trees they chopped down on the Tittabawassee River? That is who and what is meant by SMLJ. Would you have guessed? Those are the sort of people that folksong has got to be collected from — college professors can't write it! — and that folklore studies and collections are supposed to be about. Real people, and some of them very tough. Not so easy to manipulate and control as SMLJ. Not so easy to depersonalize, to flatten out into numbered stanzas and faceless statistics, motif-tabulations and trait-charts; to be totted up, boiled down, pigeon-holed and reduced to green cardboard strips punched full of slots, or read directly into the vacuum tube from bottle-arsed printed numbers; cross-quizzed and questioned, and re-extruded from one machine to be remanipulated in another, and falsified, 'weighted' and 'corrected' (if they persist in telling the truth); and finally faked to a fare-thee-well with a plain stub of pencil for presentation as a meaningful 'finding' to the human beings, and concerning the human beings, from whom it has been abstracted, and who have so carefully been abstracted from it. The same people who are making this the future of folklore are making it the future of folk.

VII

THERE IS ONE more thing to say, and it is just as serious, though perhaps a great deal less important, than the logical contradictions and conclusions with which the reader has just been entertained. What is the reason for the present show of interest in the problems of collection, and the possibility now of publication, of erotic folklore and folksong in English? Is it really that free speech and the Spirit of '76 are beginning to boil up in the old arteriosclerotic veins (in the Pickwickian sense) of the very same collectors who for years have been chopping up their texts for publication — the way Baring-Gould and Cecil Sharp admitted they had done, and dozens of other collectors have also done but don't admit — and tossing the erotic fragments into their bottom drawers? To pull them out (or mostly not to pull them out, and to reply with insulting letters instead) when they get a twenty-year-later request for them from an unknown man in France. Are they really and truly tired of sitting around in the library, playing god with a blue pencil? Or is there something else, something unsuspected — not the overmastering need finally to blurt out the truth about folklore — that is involved?

The point was raised before, that whatever future there may be for folklore study in its recent marriage with psychoanalysis and socio-analysis, the suspicion has been growing, over the last twenty-five years that American ballad and folksong collecting is through, that there is nothing left to collect, or that the 'quality' of what can now be collected does not make it worthwhile. Why does this seem such a threat? To the degree that it is true — and there is more in it than many collectors care to admit — it simply means that the job of American folksong specialists, as in England and the rest of Europe long since, has now moved on to something more difficult: that the shotgun collecting phase has now to give way, and the indexing and actual study have got to begin. Collecting cannot be continued indefinitely simply by jumping off now into the erotic supplement or for-men-only outhouse. In any case, it is certain that the new erotic materials now being created, and the limping remnants of the old, available to current collecting, are not such as will lay much balm to the American folksong collectors' souls. And after that, what? There is no way out of it: the *study* of folksong must now begin, after decades of delay not shared by the study of folklore, which has gone on far in advance, in functional rather than mere formal analysis.

That no such study of English-language folksong has yet taken place, except in the rarefied atmospheres of the "communal improvisation" nonsense, will be found abundantly documented in Prof. D. K. Wilgus' *Anglo-American Folksong Scholarship*, since Child (Rutgers University Press, 1959), the first work in English ever to go so far as to state frankly, p. 237–9, that American folksong scholarship might really buckle down and deal with the erotic folksongs too — 'granting, of course, that the bawdy material is worthy of preservation and study.' Welcome as this somewhat tempered interest would be, it hardly needs to be reiterated here that American folklorists have something else to do first, and that they have not done it yet. Prof. Wilgus makes the same point with flabbergasting candor, when, on page 240, he finally arrives at the subject of his monograph — that is to say, Folksong Scholarship — the larger half of his 466 pages being necessarily spent on the recent history of field-collecting, which is hardly the same thing as scholarship; and on the 'communal improvisation' theory, which, as every schoolboy knows, has concerned itself since 1900 with such vital stuff as the "Equitabat Bovo" song of Kölbigk (11th century).

Prof. Wilgus remarks that a chapter which would attempt to treat of actual *studies* of folksong in Great Britain and the United States, might seem as ill-supplied with material as the famous essay on the snakes of Ireland. That is a good joke, all right, but where are the folksong studies? Difficult as it is to believe, Prof. Wilgus' work, finally, must content itself with offering, in justification of the word 'scholarship' in its title — as differentiated from the narrow patriotism of regional collecting — almost nothing further than two overlapping studies of a single Child ballad, "Edward," and one more recent study of another, "Heer Halewijn," alias "Lady Isabel and the Elf Knight." One would, as a matter of fact, have thought that Child had already said the last word and more on the latter ballad, in his note No. 4, the opening gong of his whole collection and keynote to its method of treatment, with *thirty-two* pages of headnote on bride-murdering in all times and climes — three-quarters of which have nothing whatsoever to do with the ballad — to introduce *five and one-half* pages of text. If, as Prof. Wilgus goes on to demonstrate, the only actual folksong scholarship now being expended on the fantastic amount of material collected in English over the four hundred years since 1566, is the technical analysis of the music [!] and that the study of this music is the 'incipit' of future folksong scholarship; is there not still something remaining to be done with the endless tons (not figuratively tons, but literally tons) of printed and recorded textual material on hand? If it comes to a choice — and it very well may — which does the world of folklore scholarship want: the texts or the tunes of the bawdy songs?

American folklore scholars would be deluding themselves in a very embarrassing way, if they imagined that their real field is so used up in all other directions, or the vein so thoroughly worked out, that they must now (to mix all possible metaphors) teach the old dog new tricks, and whoop it up weakly for what they think — in their heart of hearts — is 'pornography,' just as they once whooped it up for finding one Child Ballad in each county of the state of Virginia, or may still be doing. The salvation of folklore scholarship in the English-speaking world does not now really depend on spreading out — twenty, or perhaps fifty years too late — to the searching for, and the presumed (it is only the presumed) willingness now to publish, the erotic materials that were rejected, overlooked, or filed & forgotten, when they were available in fist-fuls, and from someone other than present-day undergraduates at students' beer-roasts and fraternity sings.

These Cassandra-like croakings are not based on any occult desire or hidden intent to drive off competition from the luxurious erotic field, which is not the present writer's private property and, God knows, is not luxurious either. To the contrary, the more the merrier! 'Come, sing me a bawdy song — make me merry.' Or, at least, send along a copy for review. One person cannot do everything, not even two or ten; but that is the way it has been shaping up, because almost everybody else in the scholarly field has been too busy — or too something — until now, and it is a pretty fair bet that they are going to continue to be. If a patriotic note will help, it should perhaps be underlined that the first collector of erotic folksongs who ever got his collection into print, outside of France, was not a Russian but a Scotsman: Robert Burns. Of course, he had to die to do it, and some of us are beginning to suspect that there may be no other way.

The final and most destructive misconception at large in the folklore and folksong field today is the dangerous idea that now that raw collecting has arrived at the point of diminishing returns, the mental strain of any necessary study and interpretation can best be taken care of automatically by the Big Brother of the vacuum tube, while the folklorist or folksong 'specialist' lallygags grace-fully with his prettier female students out in the hall. If there is one thing that is *not* wanted and not needed today, it is to set

Ph.D. candidates, and other half-paid slaves, to counting syllables, feminine rhymes, and the melodic intervals of one hundred and forty-one musical settings of a single and identical ballad (Lady Isabel being murdered a hundred and forty-one more times, that is); tabulating fourteen numbered 'traits' per folksong or tale, and an equal number of 'motifs,' each of which takes up fifteen pages of space in a learned journal (in very small type), and all of which is then to be juggled marvelously and mindlessly together so as to produce pseudoscientific 'findings;' on university money, if such is to be had. Everywhere a person looks, folklorists today are excitedly tabulating and measuring things, like the German rat-psychologists of the 1890's, and, you may be sure, with exactly the same results. The gas-chambers will open on the right. Measurement has exactly the same relation to the study of folklore that the measuring of prehistoric skulls has to the study of anthropology — that much and no more. The relics of the Pliocene age can usefully be studied by anthropometry. Is there nothing of more recent interest in folklore and folksong? The Nirvana, or rather the Eldorado, of folklore scholarship referred to earlier, is now becoming clear behind the cloudy mirages so artfully marked THINK. (And Doublethink.) It is the great peace of non-understanding that comes when scholars funk their responsibility to interpret in a human way the materials they have studied and collected; and, instead, pour their materials into adding-machine jukeboxes, and wait for the insights to slide out on a perforated tape into their palms.

The curse of folklore and folksong publication, as everyone knows, has been this endless doodling with the unimportant and nonsignificant paraphernalia of form — once the textual form, now the musical form — without any matching concentration on meaning and function; with no study, until barely yesterday, of *what the material means to the people who transmit it,* and not to the outsiders who collect it; what it tells us about their inner aspirations and their response to the lives they live. As far as sexual folklore is concerned, this complete overlooking of the essential, and concentration solely on the form, is tantamount to spending the entire wedding night examining the bride's trousseau.

When does the interpretation start? When does the curtain go up, on the meaning of the endless texts that have been collected? Who would discuss today the now utterly-exploded 'communal origins' theory, that has taken up the main part of the scholarly afflatus so far? The first forty years of useful collection from living

informants in North America were thrown away, at the scholarly
level, on a theory of so-called origins that hardly even hid the
aristocratic bias of the persons promulgating it, until one gallant
woman laid it low. No one in the university world could bear to
believe that art-products so fine as folksongs could possibly be
made up by folk-artists. And so, as the folksongs could not then
be shown to be decadent versions of art-poems by 'royal and
noble' authors, or at the very least by their court-poets, the only
possible solution seemed to be that folksongs were made up by
several dozen folk, or *Untermenschen,* all at once!

What is even more absurd and irresponsible is that the same
scholars, and their students and successors, after the same scant
forty years of fruitful collecting, from 1900 to 1940 — a major part
of which was further wasted in America not only on the 'communal
origins' theory with its open patrician bias, but, even more pointlessly, on reduplicative Child-ballad hunting — and having made
no psychological or sociological study whatsoever of the material
collected, and precious little historical and textual study either;
are now preparing to fritter away the rest of their brief hour upon
the stage in an equally futile sort of boondoggling with the musicological minutiæ of the tunes — Hollerith hole-punching machines in the university gymnasium, and all. That is the mountain
laboring and giving birth to a mighty small squeak of a mouse, no
matter how many volumes of handsome musical calligraphy it
may take.

With the recent and very striking exception of Alan Lomax's
Folk Songs of North America (New York, 1960), by and large, the
scholarly world of folksong study — folklore much less so — in both
England and America, has funked its intellectual responsibilities,
both as to what should be collected, sexually and otherwise, and
that it must be *interpreted,* functionally not formally, vis-à-vis
human beings and society. It has never actually got off the ground.
It has leapt, without ever studying or attempting to study the
human meaning of the songs themselves, from the Tweedledum
controversy over their unprovable 'origins,' to the Tweedledee
entertainments of 'tune families' and the 'melodic contour of
archetypes,' of which the 'inner core of identity' — Prof. Bertrand
Bronson's new *Ding am sich* — is to be determined by machinery.
Shortly phrased, the fuzzy anthropological-metaphysical obscur-
anticism of the eighteenth-century German and nineteenth-century Anglo-American university curricula, which produced the
'communal origins' theory — not to mention the various *other*

German racial theories that were produced — has now been re-vamped into a new inductive and permutational mysticism (in which the sum of the exploded parts is conceived to be not only the whole, but greater than the whole), and the electronic-mathe-matical gobbledygook by means of which the most dangerous anti-human and technocratic tendencies of the twentieth century are being peddled to itself as 'findings.'

Would it be pressing too far on the traditional license of this Feast of Fools celebration to observe that the study of folklore is not an American invention? It was begun in Europe — in Ovid's *Fasti* at the time of Christ, if not in the collecting of the Homeric legends by the *diacévastes* under Pisistratus, five centuries earlier. Folksong collections were being published in France, in Germany, and Scandinavia in the sixteenth century, in England in the sev-enteenth century, in Scotland in the eighteenth, and in Russia and finally in America in the nineteenth century. The greatest monu-ments of folklore collection in all European countries of importance were erected and practically complete by the 1860's, before Child had yet published even his preliminary volumes — based on their in-spiration — and decades before the first slave songs and children's songs were collected in the United States. Some of the most im-portant field-collecting had been done in Europe, as for instance by Herd before 1776, before there even *were* any United States. And European folklorists have not lost their lead. The leadership in folklore studies (on all subjects except sex, which is still rele-gated to frightened footnotes, as in the Stith Thompson *Motif-Index* at X700) still comes out of Finland and eastern Europe. Here is what one of the best folksong specialists in England today, A. L. Lloyd, had to say after coming back from a first hand observa-tion of how it is being done in Rumania:

> In eastern Europe they have a better balance on these things. They don't ignore the measurement side of folklore studies (in fact they're better than Bronson at it!) nor would they disregard mechanical aids where they're avail-able. But of course they don't stop there: they are much concerned with the life of the people they're dealing with — not only their economic and social life but their inner fantasy life too. As a consequence, they are able, for in-stance, to accept changing styles of folklore expression without consternation or dismay, and to make quite other judgments than merely esthetic ones, on the material.

It does not need demonstrating that the attraction of the pretentious futilitarianism of syllable-counting and tune-measuring, dealing as it does only with the textual form or the musical vehicle, and never with the actual subject matter, nor with the human needs this subject matter satisfies, is precisely that it is *meaningless,* and therefore — insofar as not 'jeopardizing one's position' is concerned — guaranteed safe. The sages of Swift's Lapúta made this sufficiently clear, in the 'thinking-machine' invented centuries before them by the religious utopian, Raymond Lully. Sages of this kind believe that their position is impregnable, because it is essentially a position of standing guard over nothing. Even so, they are wrong, as the future history of folklore and folksong study will show. Even when the subject matter is not 'safe,' as with Kinsey's sex studies, the preferred mechanical, mathematical, and manipulatory method of treatment betrays the futilitarian bias, and the *need to deal with human phenomena in a nonhuman way* (the so-called Finnish method in folklore), in plain words *to treat people as though they were things.* Thus the researcher is given the illusion of domination and control — of having reduced by machinery the inexact and unpredictable humanities, such as art, poetry, sex, and music, to an exact 'science,' which is then to be prostituted and commercialized in the market place, and in which the awaited next step is, of course, that the machinery itself should create as well as perform the music, sex, poetry, and art.

Sexual folklore is, with the lore of children, the only form of folklore still in uncontaminated and authentic folk transmission in the Western world. It has thumbed its nose for centuries at both censorship and print. It has proved unavailable to the enwhoring and embalming of commercialized 'popular culture.' It needs nothing and it wants nothing from pseudoscience and the process-cheese mashing of plastic brains. If real science cares to concern itself, at this very late date in England and America, with sexual folklore, it would do well to come with its mortarboard off, with clean hands, and with a sense of unwonted sacredness, in the presence of what is — for all its barbaric and sometimes dirty tatterdemalion — the central mystery and the central reality of life. And it would do well to take warning from the motto on Provençal sun-dials: 'Make your way — the hour is passing.'

FOLK LITERATURE AND FOLKLORE
With a Few Words on Science-Fiction

I

JOHN AUBREY who, more than anyone else, created the science of folklore in England, though the work of all the other great antiquaries, such as Camden, Selden, and Sir Thomas Browne saw print before Aubrey's was unearthed, has left, in his *Remaines of Gentilisme and Judaisme* (MS. 1686), a passage that offers a certain melancholy consolation to those who believe that the great old days of folklore, and of folklore collecting, did not come to an end until the decade after the First World War.

> It was a Custome (says Aubrey) for some people that were more curious than ordinary, to sitt all night in the church porch of their Parish on midsomer-eve . . . and they should see the apparitions of those that should die in the parish that yeare come and knock at the dore: and still in many places on St Johns night they make Fires, Bonfires, on ye Hills, &c.: but the Civil warres comeing on have putt all these Rites, or customes quite out fashion. Warres doe not only extinguish Religion & Lawes: but Superstition: & no suffimen is a greater fugator of Phantosmes, than gunpowder. (Lansdowne MS. 231; ed. Britten, 1881; Folk-Lore Society, IV. 26.)

As far as the fugating of Phantosmes is concerned, it is a simple enough syllogism that what gunpowder could do in the English Revolution of the 1640's, and, in the First World War, T.N.T. and Alfred Nobel's dynamite — on the profits of which we now have the embarrassing humor of the Nobel 'Peace' Prize — has surely been done even better in World War II by the atom bomb. But the fact of the matter is that the real destruction of folklore, in our own time, has best been implemented not by any such scientific insanities of

289

demolition, but by the more pervasive destructiveness of the 'practical-minded' popular education system for over a century now, and by the new servo-mechanisms and relaxational pleasure-machines (for a generation both working and playing less hard than ever before in history), during the last seventy years: motion pictures, phonograph and tape recordings, radio, television, and whatever similar devices of passive absorption may be coming next.

At the end of the preceding essay, allusion is made to the truism in folklore studies, now become clear, that 'The printed record of folksongs and folktales has been and is of importance, not so much to the folk themselves as to the folklorist investigating the nature and history of these cultural phenomena.' (A. H. Gayton, in *Journal of American Folklore*, 1942, LV. 122.) Apt as this is, it does not go far enough. The truth seems to be that not only is print useless to folklore except as an historical record, but that it has almost invariably had a deleterious effect on folklore, and particularly on folksong; consciously revising, formalizing, and even parodying and perverting its texts — as for political purposes, in the anti-Revolutionary drolleries — rather than simply transmitting them. In this, print is profoundly opposed to the folk-process of *consonant* and unconscious variation and selection, which moves in a slower and more glacial way, by means of which, though a given folksong may change most of its action and all of its wording *with the exception of the rhymes,* by the end of a century, and even the rhymes disappear in another century or so, the song 'itself' will remain recognizable and satisfactory to the people who sing it, at every point in its history. The printed revision — whether an expurgation or simply a modernization — does not have, and is particularly likely never to achieve, this cachet of folk-acceptance, owing to the overlayering and overwhelming of the real song by the newer personality of the reviser.

The entire print-linked development of folksong is in general downward: toward textual corruption, rather than preservation, toward cliché ornamentation, emotional repression and revision — under which head the usual expurgation is subsumed — and, most damaging of all, an unmistakable folkloristic falseness. This is sensed at once by the audience, and is resisted not so much in their refusing to accept it (to the contrary, they are anxious to accept it: they pursue it, and as willingly bought its particular doggerel in the broadsides of earlier centuries as in the newsprint garlands of 'popular songs' today); but rather in their inability to answer to it, or to sing it or even listen to it very long.

This willing acceptance of, in fact this anxious search for novelty, combined with the incapacity to love it or be satisfied by it very long, which is also typical of the mania of collecting and of the similar sexual Don Juanism. It is strikingly evident in all types of modern synthetic folklore: popular songs, invented holidays for commercial purposes (such as 'Father's Day'), topical jokes, 'quickie' gags and puns, ephemeral catch-phrases (like 'So's your old man!' and 'Your father's moustache!' also a hundred others — as opposed to proverbs, which are ageless), and especially in the coining of slang. *The principal characteristic of the fake-folkloristic product in all times is the extraordinary brevity of its period of public favor, as opposed to the equally extraordinary longevity and tenacity of real folklore.*

It is the fashion to excuse the commercial revamping and scholarly expurgation of folklore, to make saleable volumes or university reputations for hack compilers and their publishers, and the even more lucratively saleable songs, plays, musical comedies, phonograph recordings, and radio & television skits for the matching hacks of their respective trades, on the grounds that such works do, by some unexplained magic, somehow keep alive the folk-arts and folk-materials they are, in fact, slaughtering. I am far from agreeing that any of these stated ends are either desirable or real. Folklore does not depend, for its transmission, on any morganatic marriage with the university mind and university press, and certainly not on any cold-eyed enwhorement in the shyly self-confessed 'popular culture' brothels of Hollywood, Tin Pan Alley and Radio Row, and their apish imitations abroad — in Paris, London, Tokyo, Rome, and Berlin. Fake-folklore of this kind, such as cowboy pants, coonskin caps and bad jazz, now represents the one principal American cultural export product, with the possible exception of supermarkets and the pointless and insane architectural ostentation of skyscrapers.

The only tangible result, in the entertainment field at least, has been the creation of a kind of outrageously *kitsch* international homespun product, calculated to give the middle class (especially those of its members who like to congratulate themselves that they are something other than middle class) the pasty thrill of revivifying contact with plain sweaty folk and their virile naturalness and strength — somewhere, perhaps, among the natives of exotic Pennsylvania or Transylvania — while carefully avoiding any of the equally natural, but somehow distressing, sounds or odors rising from the exercise of that virility and the exudation of that sweat.

As far as the export product is concerned, this is simply a continuation of the Eldorado dream of the Spanish conquistadors, that became the *Rêve exotique* of America of the 18th-century Utopians, as studied by Gilbert Chinard in 1913; and it is not to be overlooked that the greatest romanticizer of this dream, Jean-Jacques Rousseau, had himself painted by Ramsay in the coonskin cap of the noble savages (of Québec) decades before the birth of the authentic Col. Davy Crockett. On the repellent methods used in the merchandising and exploiting of this particular fake-fad, among children in the British export market in 1956, see the Opies' furious description — complete with the prices charged — in *The Lore and Language of Schoolchildren* (Oxford, 1959, p. 118-20).

As to the endemic American product: aside, perhaps, from some fellowship in suffering between the European-American Jewish boys who wrote the tunes, and the southern Negro field- and dock-workers they purport to make sing, just what relationship is really to be found, even with a microscope, between that last and most inordinately rich vein of Negro folklore in the United States, and *Showboat* or *Porgy and Bess?* What relationship between the life of poverty and work and lust and songs of the last stronghold of white folklore in the deep south and the Ozarks, and such Broadway parodies as *Ruint, Tobacco Road* (the greatest theatrical success of the American stage since the even phonier *Uncle Tom's Cabin*), and the depraved hokum of Tennessee Williams' plays, or — the same with music — *Oklahoma!* and *Annie Get Your Gun?*

That part of folklore that can be printed, or broadcast, or dragged onstage nowadays, is the part that dies, or is long since dead and decayed. It is the other part — the part that does not easily unveil itself, that cannot be turned profitably to account for million-dollar musical superproductions, by political propagandists looking to be elected with a televised washboard band, by Tin Pan Alley poets *en mal d'inspiration,* nightclub 'folksingers' hard-up for material, jazz-historians, record-sleeve annotators, and English instructors in search of a Ph.D. — that is the part that lives, and will continue to live.

II

THE DEFINITE break between real folklore of popular acceptance, and the concocted and commercialized artifacts forced upon the public in the theatre and later the music-halls (now movies and television), actually occurred in England in the early 18th century, when the stylized and artificial Italian operas, with their highly-publicized castrated tenors, drove out the English ballad-operas. In these, with the exception of one the first of them, John Gay's *Beggar's Opera* in 1728, though the tunes were those of the old folksongs, the words — instead of the tenors — had been castrated, and their folk-basis caricatured and falsified, especially in the Scottish songs, on the model of Thomas Durfey's popular musical comedies nearly half a century before. The earlier interludes of folksong in English plays, as in those of Shakespeare and Jonson, and particularly in Heywood and Brome, had never involved any parodying of the texts sung on the stage.

The ballad- or folk-opera had been invented in Italy, in the wonderful fantasy of Orazio Vecchi's *Amfiparnasso*, about 1598 (which histories of the opera somehow overlook), turning entirely on the humor of the various folk-dialects, including Yiddish, in which the various singers un-understandingly address one another. The form persisted for a very long time in the comic street-theatre of Italy and France, but now survives only in the *zarzuelas* or street-operas of Spain, of which Rossini's *Barber of Seville* is the most famous operatic imitation. The transitory British ballad-opera fad of the 1730's followed directly on the heels of, and operated on the identical principles as the attempt by Allan Ramsay and the other 'ingenious young gentlemen' of Edinburgh credited in the Preface to the volumes of his *Tea-Table Miscellany* of 1724–29, to 'brush up' and expurgate the old folksongs for genteel presentation. Almost the entire third volume is devoted to the songs from Ramsay's own ballad-opera of 1725, *The Gentle Shepherd*, which probably inspired Gay.

Except in this essential matter of expurgation, Ramsay in turn had followed the example of the tremendously popular *Pills to Purge Melancholy,* repeatedly published from 1699 to 1720, the final edition under the nominal editorship of Durfey, whose musical-comedy songs are grouped as the first two volumes. (See my extended bibliographical note on this work and its real editor, Henry Playford, in *Midwest Folklore,* 1959, IX. 89–102; and the much better note by Prof. Cyrus Day, in *Review of English Studies,* 1932, VIII, No. 30.) Without knowing what they were doing, Durfey, Ramsay, and their imitators were effectively killing the nerve and destroying the folk-viability of the songs they faked and parodied; and this was also the fate of almost all their own synthetic folksongs and those that the ballad-operas attempted.

It is not necessary to trace here in detail the further history of the use of bogus folk-elements, generally as humor, on the musical stage, from the Georgian theatre-songs, re-edited by Frank Kidson and Alfred Moffat in 1901 (some of which have survived, such as "Sally in Our Alley" and "Black-Eyed Susan"), through the 19th century travesties by Offenbach and his imitators, W. S. Gilbert and Sir Arthur Sullivan, whose music — as is not generally realized — is often nothing more than a bold plagiarism of tunes from Mozart, Rossini, etc. (This is even true of his sacred music, his most famous hymn-tune, "Onward Christian Soldiers," being simply the opening of Beethoven's Violin Concerto, combined with a bit of "Rock of Ages.") The final, modern forms of so-called popular songs, as also those of the musical-comedy and grand-opera stage, are now glaringly stylized, artificialized, symbolized, commercialized, and 'refined' to the point of total imbecility and extinction, with both the action and the wording turning almost invariably on sexual frustration. Consider Tristan and Isolde *singing* — then of course *dying*, the usual symbol — their way through their Liebesnacht, as the "Merry Widow" of Franz Lehar (and a hundred Viennese-American imitations since) *dances* her way through hers; while Salomé, the bitch-Isolde of Oscar Wilde and Richard Strauss, grovels about on the stage with a decapitated head, in an equally symbolic but this time castratory and sadistic consummation, screaming in pidgin-French and German that she will 'kiss' it at last.

These claptrap commodities have increasingly brief lives — or increasingly limited snob audiences — as they appeal to less and less that is real or universal, or in any way meaningful and satisfying to the intended audience. The ephemeral fad or jingle or 'hit tune' must be replaced daily, because, at every level other than the temporary and superficial, the audience profoundly *hates* it and is frustrated by it, and repudiates it at the very moment of seeming to embrace it on four hundred thousand juke-boxes (and ten thousand more in Europe), and pouring wealth into its composer's lap. Things have changed greatly since a century ago, when Stephen Foster cribbed and copyrighted a Negro folksong in 1850, and collected royalties on it for years under the name of "The Camptown Races," with a similar plagiarism of the Scottish marching-song "To Daunton Me" (in Johnson's *Scots Musical Museum*, No. 182) as "Jeanie with the Light-Brown Hair." Merely to keep a 'popular song' popular nowadays for as much as a month requires, as is well known, that a fortune be disbursed privately in bribing disc-jockeys and other entertainers to plug it. In other words, it has to be stuffed down the public's craw by force-feeding, like a Strassburg goose, backed up with the collateral assistance of high-pressure publicity stunts and malarkey as to the performers' sex-lives, presumed virility, etc. — homosexual singers being favored currently instead of castrati.

One of the destructive elements that is commonly overlooked happens to be the next oldest, and also one of the most destructive, and that is that people no longer sing at their work. This is directly due to the factory system, and was already seriously undermining folksong by the beginning of the 19th century. Increasingly, after that date, folksongs could only be collected in what is called a 'pure' form, away from the industrialized cities; and the best modern collections are those that have been made as far away from the cities as possible, in such peripheral and undeveloped areas as the Ozarks, in Nova Scotia, and in the north of Scotland.

What is so heartrending and absurd is that now that people are forbidden to sing at their work, in factories and offices (and even in public bars!) the way blacksmiths and tailors and the cigarette-girls in *Carmen* were never forbidden, and yet worked very hard; the factory-owners and office-managers and their industrial psychologists have now found it expedient to pipe in canned music, which is then squirted in a refined *pianissimo* over the factory- and office-workers, on the milk-from-contented-cows principle. This has also been found useful in disguising the clamor, and parting the housewives more easily from their budgeted pennies, for useless plastic gewgaws and food substitutes, in the new supermarkets. In most cases, the musical material that is piped in has been vaguely imitated or sophisticated from folksongs, sometimes very ancient, and horribly travestied in the process, on the style of Ketelby's "In a Persian Market," or the unbearable *rubato* droolings in the Neapolitan style of the current crop of pelvic crooners.

As can be observed, this operates exactly on the principle of removing most of the natural elements from bread, in order to make it lily-white, and then 'enrichening' it with well-publicized vitamins by mixing in a white powder concocted of little more than the materials that have been removed. At a much higher price, of course. In just the same way, the British navy managed to destroy the sea songs of ancient lineage, by forbidding the men to sing chanteys at their work; ordering them about with a bosun's whistle instead. The songs of the 'wooden ships and iron men' are gone now. Now we have iron ships and wooden men, and they apparently don't do much singing.

How does folklore die? Half a block from the British Museum, near one of the best (and smallest) bookshops in London, there is an official sign, now some sixty years old, affixed to the Museum Chambers, Bury Place, just above eye-level, perpetuating in painted tin and in the most unmistakable fashion, the method whereby folklore is killed. The sign orders plainly as follows:

> The Metropolitan Borough of Holborn. — By-Law for the Suppression of Street Cries. — STREET SHOUTING. No person shall for the purpose of hawking, selling or advertising goods, call or shout in any street, so as to cause annoyance to the inhabitants of the neighbourhood. — PENALTY. Any person who shall so offend against the fore-going by-law shall be liable for every such offence to a fine not exceeding Forty Shillings. — The Common Seal of the Mayor, Aldermen & Councillors of the Met. Bor. of Holborn was thereto affixed this Twelfth day of October, One Thousand Nine Hundred and Four.

That is all, but it is enough, and was enough, to stop dead and forever one of the most ancient, most picturesque, and most appreciated types of folk-singing. Today, the street-cries of London are nothing but a memory, in old color-print books and in the wistful recordings for the phonograph by British madrigalist groups.

It is understood, of course, that the purpose of the ordinance was to protect the ears and nerves of city-dwellers from the noisy crying of merchandise in the streets, then considered a nuisance. But what was being accepted while the street-cries were being suppressed? Since the very same early 1900's, the automobile has made the same streets, and in all great Western cities similarly, entirely untenable — as far as noise is concerned — even to properly twentieth-century citizens with eardrums of solid brass. To withstand it, one must get into an automobile oneself, and screech and honk and outspeed all the other automobiles in the new Götterdämmerung of the Machine. Quite without overstatement, people go mad today from the overpowering traffic-noise on the Left and Right Bank quais, in Paris, that were once the quiet Mecca of all the world's book-lovers and scholars. One would be desperately grateful nowadays for the evocative cry, '*O! pio-paye!*' like a bird on the wing — however raucous, in among the traffic noise and stink — of even so much as one lonely fish-peddler, in these city streets now hygienically swept clean of song, of hurdy-gurdies and Barbary-organs, and of children dancing to their music. But it is not to be had. Instead of street-cries and songs, traceable almost as far back as human civilization (see *Psalms,* 69: 12), we have the 'popular songs' — that must be changed twice weekly, so popular are they — scraping mechanically from the juke-box or television machine at the corner bar, or even from portable transistor-radios toted competitively on the shoulders of the passers-by. That is how folklore dies.

Sixty thousand 'popular songs' are copyright every year in the United States alone. Sixty thousand! Who sings them? Who can sing sixty thousand songs — even in a lifetime? That, for every one of the few dozen songs that do 'take' in any year, then to fade; new fads and fakes will mushroom overnight to replace it, and be just as desperately embraced — for a passing moment, like Don Juan's thousand-and-three — is profoundly expressive of the audience's continual frustration and need. As with Leporello, who panders these thousand 'conquests' to Don Juan — that is to say, nine hundred and ninety-nine defeats, and the thousandth inevitably coming — the *business* of music-business would of course collapse if the public were allowed for an instant to be satisfied with the old favorites it really loves. Sir Philip Sidney confessed, (as he reports in his *Defence of Poesie,* 1595), he could not hear the old ballad of "Chevy Chase" chanted by a blind crowder without his blood being stirred as at the sound of a trumpet. Who today can endure the sentimental love-drool of a popular song of a decade or even a week ago? The 'built-in obsolescence' of the arts.

The purveyors of popular entertainments would be glad to peddle satisfaction instead of frustration if they could, but the censorship structure under which they operate does not allow them to do so. Also, as just noted, it would perhaps not be to their economic interest to do so. Meanwhile, the synthetic folk-art product does not and cannot satisfy, and therefore cannot often live long enough to roll up monster royalties for the copyright-owner in the fifty-six years allowed. The destructive element at work, which is part and parcel of the formula, and therefore inescapable, is well known. It is the faking and pulping process that all natural and normal instincts must submit to, both in their essence and in their artistic presentation, at the hands of the people who have now monopolized the principal access to paper, print, and public communications, from the triumph of religious and political censorship in the 16th century and of sex censorship in the mid-18th century — that is not when it started, that is when it was almost wholly achieved — to the preponderant rise of the newspapers and other 'mass media' in the century since the end of the Civil War.

What was a danger two hundred years ago, when there was only print (and the theatre) to contend with, has now become a total enslavement and a total obeisance of art and folklore, under the rolling-press and the motion-picture invented at opposite ends of the nineteenth century, and the radio-wave discovered early in the twentieth; each of these being immediately set to work — under the euphemisms of 'communication' and 'entertainment' — enwhoring itself as fast as it could. Each of these inventions was seen as a possible danger to privilege, even when finally restricted solely to 'entertainment,' and for that reason there was impressed upon them — and all of them now struggle uselessly beneath it (if they're really still struggling) — a total and codified and almost wholly inescapable censorship, sexual, economic, and political, in which the *lèse majesté* being monitored, twenty-four hours a day every day, is, in the West, more particularly that directed against advertising than against any king or dictator.

No one would deny today that this has destroyed folklore in print. It has also destroyed — which is perhaps a deeper damage and more important — the viability of most existing poetry, fictional literature, and visual art as well. The Eighth Art of the motion-picture, the only new art originated in three thousand years or more, is a staggering example, already rotted to the bone and far gone in sterility and perversion, except as to its technical and mechanical roccoco, before either it or its century was even fifty years old. Human beings now live longer than the arts they discover, and — let there be no mistake about it — there are not many arts still to be born, not even in the dangerous miscegenational marriage of human beings with machinery.

III

BEFORE THE triumph of the censorship, folklore abounded and was easy to record, from the time of the *Fasti* of Ovid, to the Scandinavian ballad collections of the 16th century, the tunebooks of Thomas Ravenscroft in Shakespeare's time, and the *Remaines* of John Aubrey in 1686. The latter, artless and unexpurgated as he left them, lay 'unprintable' in manuscript until 1881, along with his marvellously crotchety and informative *Brief Lives,* except for some bowdlerized extracts printed by D'Israeli and others. (*Curiosities of Literature,* ed. 1849, II. 268–70, not indexed.) There are at present three different editions of Aubrey's *Brief Lives,* of varying degrees of completeness. The biographical introduction by John Collier to his edition of 1931 is a masterpiece, perfectly in the style of Aubrey himself. One does not see much writing like that today. But in the sixteenth and seventeenth centuries — who will deny it? — literature and folksong were easy to write. Easy! The best of our folksongs, and most of the prose worth reading in English, all come down to us from then or earlier. And as to poetry, each century since has been covering its face in shame at the comparison.

Who can believe today that a mammoth committee of learned divines in 1600 could create together the long, sustained poetic song of the King James Bible, with no real poetry in any of the translations preceding, to help them, but Sternhold & Hopkins' translation of the *Psalms.* (This earlier translation of the "Psalter," which is in many ways more beautiful than that of the King James version, fortunately continues to be printed in the *Book of Common Prayer.*) As *literature,* the very printers then could write a better and more manly prose than professionals and professors can today. This remains true for all those halcyon two and a half centuries, from Caxton to Dunton and Curll. See the superb examples scattered throughout Dr. Clara Gebert's *Anthology of Elizabethan Dedications* (University of Pennsylvania, 1933), of which the closest one to everyone's hand is probably the piratical printer's preface to Shakespeare's *Troilus and Cressida,* 1608, "A Never Writer to an Ever Reader, News."

With the exception of the late V. F. Calverton in *Sex Expression in Literature* (1926), and, more recently, Prof. Gordon Rattray Taylor in *The Angel-Makers* (1958), no one has studied the literature and the society of the mid-18th century, not as the 'triumph of taste' that it is pretended to have been, but as the palpable collapse into false morality and flatulent prose that it was. At that period, the great age of literature had died in England, and the great age of scholarship was only beginning to emerge from the obfuscations of classical forgery and religious controversy. The control of literary fashions and literary ethics fell into the hands of a new, self-constituted group of arbiters and authorities such as Pope, Addison, and Johnson, all of whom were essentially hangers-on of the rich and noble — or tried their best to become so — and clearly thought of themselves as the patricians or dictators of literature, on the style of Aretino two centuries earlier. The principal difference was, that Aretino, though equally viperish and dishonest, was in no way a prude. The influence of Pope and Johnson is now hardly more than a footnote, as far as poetry and lexicography go, but they had — and they still have — an extraordinary influence on the then-nascent ideals of scholarship, not only as to what should be expressed, but even as to the ormolu pretentiousness of the 'proper' method of expressing it in print.

The attempt made, beginning in the 1720's, to 'purify' and formalize the English language, on the style of the Italian and French Academies and the dictionaries they undertook, had the effect, as everyone knows, of destroying the easy relation between the spoken and written language. By the 1750's, written English had been reduced to an artificial turgidity and sesquipedalian Latinity that would make the angels weep when comparing it (in the conversation of new arrivals in heaven) with the virile and racy prose of the centuries preceding, shared equally by both writing and speech.

This breaking apart of folk-speech and literature was not achieved without a good deal of resistance, both in England and on the continent, as evidenced in Swift's *Polite Conversation* (which was essentially on the 'purists' side, however), and in the *Dictionnaire néologique* of the Abbé Desfontaines slightly later. Writers as long before as Henri Estienne, Shakespeare, Cervantes, and Molière, had also considered it useful to get in a few satiric licks against the Euphuists, Gongorists, *précieuses,* and all the other names the type has gone by. But, in the eighteenth century, the Euphuist foppery was tricked out with a pseudo-scientific rationale — lacking only the calculating machines — and the *sous-entendu* of keeping the 'lower' classes in their place, and it swept the field.

These mock-patrician ideas and ideals as to 'levels' of language and so forth, were given their main impetus in England by Addison, and by Alexander Pope in *Peri Bathos, or On Sinking in Poetry,* and elsewhere. Pope also carried through his notions with the issuing of the first expurgated edition of Shakespeare, though the blame is usually wrongly laid on Dr. Bowdler a century later. These ideas were codified rapidly into the laws as to proper and improper publications, a legal position that British jurists had been anxious to find, since the collapse of the political and early sexual censorship during the 1640's Revolution. It is therefore from that period, from the late Restoration to the time of Pope, and from that period only, that dates the creation of a large subterranean and outlawed literature in English in which all sorts of semi-literary and folkloristic material — such as songs, bawdy poems, tales, jokes, toasts, and slang — found it necessary to take cover, though never had they been considered prejudicial before. One is stupefied to see the sort of thing that was damned and prohibited as 'low,' when the elephantine ideals of Johnsonian taste had finally triumphed: for one striking example, Goldsmith's utterly harmless comedy, *The Good-Natur'd Man,* on the basis of a single slang word one of the characters uses. This did not even have the excuse of prohibiting profanity or sacrilege, as in the backstage signs that could still be seen in American vaudeville theatres as late as the 1920's: 'The words HELL and DAMN, and the name of the Deity, are not to be used on this stage.' By our own time, of course, in the art-theatre the exact opposite had prevailed, as in G. B. Shaw's *Pygmalion,* puffed up into a *succès de scandale* because a girl smoked a cigarette on the stage and pronounced the British shibboleth-word 'bloody.' The similar success, even more recently, of the fake-folkloristic *God's Little Acre,* in theatre form, is equally well known; it having been put across strictly as hot stuff, under the combined title *Tobacco Road.*

The death of poetry has been too much lamented, since the turn of the present century, for it to be necessary to re-inter it here. I do not refer, of course, to the 'green armpit' or Beatnik excrescence school, which is doing better than ever in France and America, and has in fact largely taken over the whole field of poetry — almost invariably not in poetic form — ever since the way was laid open to the non-poets, a century ago, in Whitman's forced and false imitations of the cadenced prose of the King James Bible. This has been even more of a catastrophe in France than in the English-speaking world. In both cultures, poetry continued to hold its prestige, though decreasingly practised, until the First World War; and is now entirely dead, as also the related art of musical composition everywhere in the West.

The recherché nonsense of false poetry, since the time of Rimbaud at the very least, has brought every last vestige of the once-noble art of poetry to ridicule. The 'typographical' poetry of Marinetti and his Futurists and Dadaists, later the Surréalists, with their weak Anglo-American imitators and manifesto-pushers such as Wyndham Lewis, was itself already the end-point of ridicule, under the phoney priesthood of Guillaume Apollinaire at the

time of World War I. In case it were not, that end-point has certainly now been reached, in the ultimate razz: A. Beatnik, Esq;
the California computing machine of Mr. Robert Worthy, of the
Librascope division of General Precision, Inc., 'who' now writes
nonsense poetry — more in the style of "Jabberwocky" than the
Beatniks, truth to tell — at the rate of one six-line poem per
minute, by the kilometer or until turned off. The inventor has
no complaint to make (according to the staid London *Times,*
May 27, 1962, as reported from New York by Evelyn Irons) except
the machine's uncontrollable tendency toward obscenity. 'He's
terribly pornographic,' Mr. Worthy is reported as saying, 'and so
far we haven't been able to control this.' A similar machine, producing popular songs — words and music both — had already been
announced earlier, the identical gag but more of folkloristic than
the usual anti-intellectual interest. As the two arts of poetry and
music represent the warp & web, the essential fabric, of folksong,
it is obvious that with their passing — except at the level of reminiscence and concert performance and of ultra-modern bunkum
— viable folksong can now only with great difficulty be created, and
must restrict itself largely to topical and doggerel parodies set to
the older tunes.

The literary form of fiction, which has received a grotesque
overdevelopment since the 16th century, beginning with *Amadis
de Gaul* (1508), openly draws its popularity from the fantasy satisfactions available in the reader's or listener's identification with
fictional and, most often, quasi-erotic adventures. It is axiomatic,
therefore, that the fictional or tale form will show itself at its
greatest popularity in exactly those periods and those social organizations least capable of offering direct emotional and physical satisfactions to very large segments of the population. As corollary, it
will be precisely among these large disenfranchised segments of
the population — now rather unfairly subsumed under the head
of 'yearning shopgirls and frustrated housewives' — that fiction will
necessarily have its greatest audience. This is also the most ancient
history of the fictional or folktale form, and is the parabolic meaning of the legend of *Aesop's Fables* being told by a slave to his
master, as the only possible sort of oblique criticism of the social
structure allowed to him.

Compare similarly the story of David and Uriah's wife, represented to King David by the prophet Nathan in the parable of
the poor man and his 'one little ewe lamb' (2 *Samuel,* xii). Here,
however, the repressed intention finally bursts through at the end

of the story — as never in the similar Aesopic fictions as to lambs
and wolves — with the prophet Nathan's bold *de te fabula nar-
ratur:* 'Thou art the man!' The whole deeper meaning of the
story is also visible in the choice and sequence of the characters:
David the former giant-killer, who had delivered his people from
Goliath and the tyrant Saul, now become a tyrant in his turn, and
challenged by the new, but now merely verbal tyrannicide,
Nathan, using his parabolic fiction for slingshot. In the expanded
version of the same story, as "Naboth's Vineyard" (in 1 *Kings,* xxi,
and 2 *Kings,* ix, xxi), the king's theft of a vineyard is developed
into a whole internecine war, on the style of the legend of Helen
of Troy, with the evil Jezebel replacing Helen, or Uriah's wife.
Here it also becomes clear that the tyranny complained of is not
really the king's taking of the sexual property of his subjects, but
of their land, with the final and standard religio-sexual accusation
of having worshipped the idol Baal.

The lesser fictions, not able to arrogate to themselves divine
inspiration and protection, or the legendary canvas of national
history, hold naturally and more clearly to the smaller scale of
personal satisfactions rather than of social criticism, and regale
the listeners (and, since Gutenberg, the readers) with splendid
oral *feasts,* and with boldly heroic and sexual adventures of an
uncritical sort, dripping always with silver and gold. The criticism,
and dissatisfaction with society are hidden in the plain representation of these fantasy pleasures as a dreamed-of and delicious change
from miserable fact. Seen from this point of view, fictional literature is simply the modern formalization, since the introduction of
printing in the West, of the ancient folktale form. The principal
difference stems largely from the greater emphasis placed on individual worth and personal salvation since the rise of Protes-
tantism, as Max Weber and Tawney have brilliantly shown. The
fictions are now signed, though the author may quite consciously
have rewritten old folktales, as in the *Golden Ass* of Apuleius and
the *Satyricon* of Petronius, a thousand years before, and the French
conteurs later; and property-rights are claimed in the resultant
literary product, in the form of 'printer's privilege' or copyright,
and royalties are paid. Folklore becomes a business, in the sense
that the old wives, telling their folktales by the fireside as they
spun — or even the anonymous scribes of the Athenian tyrant,
Pisistratus, gathering the Homeric legends in the 5th century
B.C. — could never have conceived.

Nothing in printed fiction has ever had, and can ever expect to have, the continuing popularity and unfailing audience, not just for centuries but for millennia, of the great Levantine and Oriental folkmyths and folktale-collections such as the *Arabian Nights* and the East Indian *Ocean of Story*. Nor, technically, is there anything in the modern author-linked fiction that will not be found equally well done, if not better and with greater artistic economy, in the older folktales, not even in the 'short story' as re-developed by Gogol and Maupassant. The main modern development or difference, rising spectacularly from the over-emphatic individualism of the Protestant Reformation, is the terribly intellectualized introspection and conscience-searching, on the Dostoyevsky pattern, of almost all modern fiction and theatre of any pretention to literary art or quality. Needless to say, these self-torturing Romantic confessions, in fictional disguise, are not the most popular with the great general public, which still wants rapid sequence of adventures, and 'not too much *description*,' on the folktale pattern.

IV

As with the disaffection of the audience for folksongs, owing to the falsification of the product offered in that form in the ballad-operas and the various forms of popular theatre since (movies, radio, and t.v.), the neo-folktale in the form of the novel has also lost its millennial longevity and now operates limpingly under the law of fake-folklore enunciated above: of an extraordinary brevity of its period of public favor, as opposed to the equally extraordinary longevity and tenacity of real folklore. Again, as with 'popular songs' and ephemeral fads, this is diametrically opposed to the expected commercial advantage of the authors and promulgators of these songs and fads, in copyrighting, or otherwise attempting to maintain as their private property for purposes of gain, the items of intended folk popularity which they launch.

Blinded by their hoped-for gain, the authors and publishers of the novel have tossed their head proudly, over the last century, in despite of their audience — whom they erroneously imagine they are pleasing — and down has come the basket of eggs, and the planned chicken, cow, farm, fine marriage, and all. How many modern 'hard-back' novels can expect to last even six months before being swept up off the booksellers' tables, unsold, and sent back to the publisher for remaindering? (This was just as true of the 'three-deckers' a century ago.) And what is it that aborts them, over ninety percent, if not the audience's detestation of their falsity, as described above in connection with 'popular songs'? The audience for fiction today is recognized to be incapable not only of re-reading modern novels a dozen times (as were re-read the novels of former centuries, such as Cervantes' *Don Quixote,* before the form was destroyed — not created! — in English, in the repulsive artificiality of Richardson's *Pamela*); but even of getting through them barely once. There is no longer any pretense being made about this; it is frankly admitted in the very format of all pocket-reprints, journalism, fictional magazines, and other pulp-literature, of which neither the newsprint paper nor the rubberized binding is expected to hold up long enough to be re-read.

Since the middle of the 18th century and still in largest part today, all poetry and literature openly published in the English language (and much is still being printed, though little is written) is cut to the bone in any sexual sense, and faked to a finish. All writers know this, and none have been able to escape. The most awful examples are perhaps those of the theatre — now motion-pictures and t.v. — which died in England with Dryden in the seventeenth century, but still won't lay down. I have already detailed, in *Love & Death : A Study in Censorship* (1949), the one insane and obscene petcock of release — the substitution of a permitted sadism for the censored sexuality — in all the mass-produced literary forms today : the murder-mysteries, comic-books, bitch-heroine novels, and homosexual attacks on women by the 'heroes' of Ernest Hemingway, Mickey Spillane, and their more recent imitators and adulators. Nothing has changed, except for the worse, since World War II.

Owing almost solely to the crusading influence of James Joyce's *Ulysses* and D. H. Lawrence's *Lady Chatterley's Lover* — both printed abroad in the 1920's — and in particular to the courage of their publishers, the literary censorship has been relaxed to a degree in America and England, since the end of the 1950's, allowing some part of the freedom available for nearly a century to writers in France. Flaubert was among the last of French writers to suffer legal attack for his normal art, in *Madame Bovary,* and to take refuge in sadism and abnormality, in the wholesale horror of *Salammbô* in 1862 : immolation of children, crushing by elephants, mutilation of corpses, &c., for which only Sainte-Beuve had the courage to take him to task (in the *Nouveaux Lundis,* vol. IV) as complained of by Flaubert in an appendix. The new Anglo-American freedom is still nowhere near as great as that in France, where, for instance, Henry Miller's *Tropic of Cancer* (Paris, 1934) has long been published in open French translation along with the rest of his books, and has even created an imitative school of stream-of-consciousness realists and phoney autobiographers among the French writers themselves. These presumed imitators of Miller, who have forgotten Zola and Dujardin (and never knew Joyce),would be ashamed to admit that they are really imitators — as is of course Miller — of the wartime traitor and lunatic anti-Semite, Louis-Ferdinand Céline, now in the process of being rehabilitated and canonized, with the careful omission from the list of his works of his three most typical and central volumes: *Bagatelles pour un Massacre, Les Beaux Draps,* and *L'École des Cadavres,* of which the last is said to have given Hitler the idea of the death-camps.

The abnormalizing influence of over two centuries of sexual censorship in the Anglo-Saxon world, has not in any way been abated by the very limited or pet-poodle 'new freedom,' which also varies considerably in each of the fifty United States. The evil residue of the censorship is exactly this: that the new and partial literary freedom has immediately been seized upon and accepted strictly as the freedom to print and gloat over the most nauseating details of the sadistic and other sex-linked abnormalities, which had appeared originally in fiction specifically as an 'escape' from that censorship. The production of American and British novels, plays and movies, and of the derivative 'pop-culch' plastics and synthetics at the pulp level, has in this way been petrified in the forms of perversion and sadism originally undertaken by the authors to evade the censorship of sex, even though the necessity for such evasions has now in large part been lifted for 'literature' (*i.e.* novels, which are nowadays rather amusingly thought of as the entirety of literature!) though in *no sense* for the rest of the mass media of enormously greater circulation, such as radio and television.

This is an essential point of difference, which is the real subject of my entire monograph, *Love & Death: A Study in Censorship.* The real point I intended there to make was not that the sex-substituted sadism of modern fictional literature leaps to any critical eye, but that the same substitution of an allowed sadism for a prohibited sexuality in the folk literature and electrically-promulgated 'entertainment arts' of mass circulation can only result in the most dangerous and most sinister abnormalization of the whole psychic structure of future generations. It is of course not to be expected that anything this large can be changed by writing a pamphlet against it. We are the mice trying to decide who is going to bell the cat, only to discover that we are holding court in his lower jaw.

Sex-substituted sadism is still, and will doubtless remain for a very long time — unless the world successfully blows itself up; in which case nobody will really be sorry to see it go — the chosen evasion in all the literary and artistic forms of modern mass circulation. The young adults who form the audience today, and will tomorrow, have already been incurably infected as children with the *need* for this habit-forming perversion, via the comic-books of the 1940's and the television of the 1950's and since. The purely sadistic content of mass-appeal fiction and electrically broadcast spectacles is still incredibly high, and increases unremittingly, despite all wishful theories that it cannot possibly rise any higher, and that it will soon 'level off' to at least an approximate normality. No such levelling off has been observable over the last fifteen years, or is really expected. It is the opposite that is to be expected: an increasingly larger dose, and that is what continues to arrive. The massive sadistic concentration in the popular arts continues, not only in the endless commerce of murder-mysteries, best-selling war novels, miscellaneous horror-items, and psycho-'exposés,' where the expected brutality and killing or gruesomeness are the open and specific reason for buying or renting the book or seeing the movie or t.v. show, but also in the pseudo-historical form, now well-installed, of the bitch-heroine best-sellers, of which at least two — *The Burnished Blade* by Lawrence Schoonover, and *The Strange Woman* by Ben Ames Williams (I have simply tabulated the sadistic concentration of this latter, in *Neurotica,* 1949, No. 5, "Content of a Best-Seller") — specifically repeat the elephant and immolation horrors of Flaubert's *Salammbô,* with improvements.

All the social forces of presumed good will find themselves helpless in the face of these mechanically implemented and electrically promulgated perversions. No further gestures of resistance are made but the half-hearted parental, pedagogical, and religious attempts to prepare unenforced and unenforceable censorship lists and 'gradings' of a cultural diet which obviously cannot be controlled by any such hopeless measures and pious hopes, and which will doubtless eventually be completely scrapped — the tiny corner of good with the tremendous area of bad — and replaced by government-controlled art, about which the less said the better. One thing that might be said, without stepping on too many toes, is that history has proved that governments and dictatorships, no matter how benevolent, are not any more proof against supplying sadistic spectacles to the public, to keep it quiet, than are broadcasting companies. That is the lesson to be learned, no matter how big an idiot and idealist one may be as to the future of the world, from the gladiatorial games of Rome (and all the Roman colonies); and, closer to our own times, from the purposely-fomented pogroms of the Black Hundreds in Russia at the turn of the present century, intended to head off the gathering Revolution.

There has been some talk recently, at critical levels that are usually only too glad not to be critical of anything, that now that Lawrence's *Lady Chatterley's Lover* and Miller's *Tropic of Cancer* have been published openly in the United States, without causing the expected epidemic of rape and bastardy, certain American novelists and out-and-out literary degenerates, of the Marquis de Sade's type and avowed school, have taken advantage of this 'new freedom,' intended to allow honest literature to deal honestly with the facts of physical love, and have been peddling the most outrageous and revolting kind of fiction — anyhow, one hopes it's fiction — concentrating mostly on the seduction of children, homosexual sadism (usually now in Biblical scenarios or hoked-up historical form), and generally on the sexually repulsive and abnormal. This is so true that it is almost not worth mentioning anymore. But again, the point of sociological importance is not the activity of minor literary cliques and homosexual *chapelles* in Britain and America. These unimportant misfits are vowed to the mastering and destroying of the world, and always have been, in an endless genealogy from Machiavelli and the Jesuit apologists of his century, to Marinetti and Goebbels in our own. What is important is, rather, the leading into the identical channels — and often by the identical writers, in what they consider the 'mere' money-making or pot-boiling part of their activity — of the entire mass-production of popular fantasies and fake-folklore, for spoon feeding to whole national populations utterly without knowledge of, or control over, the literary and personal neuroses (or worse) of the persons supplying this perverted format for the private fantasy lives of the public. Fantasy lives that, as has already been noted, become all the more total and important for the individual in a mass-society, as his or her own congealed and disenfranchised position in that society becomes more and more massively clear.

American writers have so far proved incapable of responding to their new freedom except in the infantile stereotypes of *false revolt.* Of this, the most perfect examples so far have not been American, but French, in particular in the Surréalist goon-show (breathed upon only in the hushed tones of love, in the late Albert Camus' *L'Homme révolté,* 1951, p. 127, a hopelessly second-rate job on an important theme), which has also made of itself the main salesman and drum-beater not only for De Sade but for every other disorganized and meaningless fad and fake, feeding upon human and social decay, in particular the so-called 'non-objective' (that is to say, non-human and non-recognizable) modern art, as it is laughingly referred to. There being big money in this part of the popular-culture racket, American writers have not been allowed more than a look-in here, the field having long since been taken over by solid businessmen with the necessary capital behind them, exactly as with radio and the movies. American false-*révoltés* have been left to paddle their ultra-individualist canoes unimportantly out to sea, while the businessmen *entrepreneurs* move in. Typical is the case of the imported and caricatured French fad, as old as Gautier and Rimbaud, of the inverted-Sartrist beatniks — practically crucified in the usual anti-intellectual auto-da-fé, in various issues of the *New York Times Book Review,* (24 May 1959) and *Life* magazine (21 Sept. and 30 Nov. 1959), and since — who claim they are not 'involved' in the United States, but who voluptuously continue combing their anarchist beards (the true, and perhaps the only symbol of their revolt), and waiting to be tapped, like D'Annunzio or Malaparte, for the job of intellectual leadership.

I would emphasize again that what is important here is not the private but the public aspect of what I have referred to earlier, and see no reason to paraphrase, as the false-revolutionary, or rather the abortive revolutionary urge to mock and defy, especially to mock and defy whatever is universally accepted as authoritative, classic, beautiful, true, and the like — as nowadays the questionable surréalist humor of soiling and defacing "Whistler's Mother," the Mona Lisa, and other Virgin-surrogates and masterpieces (if only with wise-guy captions), jazzing Schubert's "Trout" quintet, whooping it up for the Marquis de Sade and other anti-rational fads, Zen, science-fiction, &c. Though this died down temporarily in the relatively stable 18th century, in its then contemporary forms — for it is not anything new, as the burlesque 'Academies' of Italy, as long ago as the early 16th century, demonstrate — the movement of false revolt has never been more bloated up into an all-pervading social and intellectual fetich than at present.

Among the 'art' novelists, as is particularly clear, this has also now been tricked out with a specifically abnormal sexuality, which is passed off on the audience, by means of perverted pornographic paperbacks issued in Paris, as sex. That is the one thing it most positively is not, and the perverted fake-sexual imitation — taken directly from the 'philosophic' pages of Sade's *120 Journées de Sodome,* now published in English in the same Paris paperback series — will eventually and certainly restore the censorship, and destroy the 'new freedom,' probably forever. The forces of literary and social reaction are not licked by their recent censorship reverses, nor are they sleeping. They are waiting; and meanwhile they are taking the perfectly logical position that 'the worse it gets, the better,' and the sooner it will be obviously desirable to the public at large to clamp down the censorship again.

The world has moved on, and would like to move on further. It is morally wrong, and profoundly foolish, for the precedent so laboriously gained, for normal love and sexual truth (at least in print) in the *Lady Chatterley's Lover* case, to be dipped in the dirt and thrown away, for the benefit of perverted littérateurs and their perversion. So anxious is a certain kind of intellectual, confused by the ideals of false revolt, to find perversion in everything, even where it does not exist, that one has even been treated to the astonishing spectacle of an 'exposé' article in a presumably avant-garde American magazine, *Eros,* No. 2 (1962), mysteriously 'demonstrating' that *Lady Chatterley's Lover* is not really about normal sex at all, but is a hidden or symbolic glorification of anal intercourse. This idea — which is false — is a British importation, needless to say, anal intercourse being something that the average public-school and university educated Britisher cannot get off the tip of his tongue. Even the presumed partisans of free speech in England and America cannot restrain the urge to throw this silly stone, which has about as much behind it as the similar Talmudic and exegetical interpretations of the Bible, attempting to demonstrate abstruse legal points (which the Bible neglects to mention); or the high comedy of Dr. Edmund Bergler's neo-Freudian efforts to prove that everybody in the world is a masochist.

Thus one finds, for instance, in Mr. Alec Craig's *The Banned Books of England* (2nd ed., 1962, p. 223, n. 18), the following gratuitous note by the author on the court trial of *Lady Chatterley's Lover* in England: 'The covert commendations of anal intercourse in the book were not explained by either side (see "Lawrence, Joyce and

Powys" by G. Wilson Knight in *Essays in Criticism* for October
1961, and *R. v. Penguin Books Ltd* by John Sparrow in *Encounter*
for February 1962).' After that, one can draw the curtain, though
it might be added that had Lawrence been suspected of recom-
mending anal intercourse with a handsome Greek or Italian boy,
and not with a woman, no one in English literary circles and
little-mags would ever have been so lacking in *esprit de corps* as
to 'expose' him.

The public or folk-group is being given both barrels by both
sides, and does not know which way to turn. It senses that it is
being led into the dark, and resists at all points the fantasy literary
provender or beverage being offered it. Yet it finds itself helplessly
coming back for more, at the same poisoned springs and mangers,
because it is demonstrably unable to live under the pressures of
civilization without some sort of private fantasy escape or recoil.
What is to be said, under these circumstances, for the presump-
tuous first fruits of the new literary freedom being offered: the
'slice of life' lust-murders in the writings of Mickey Spillane and
now even of so old a stager as Ben Hecht; not to mention, of
course, the motion picture hand-me-downs on the same theme,
tenderly extasiating over those bad boys (led astray by bad books,
oddly enough), Loeb and Leopold; or the similar 'tender' homosexual cannibalism of Tennessee Williams' recent masterpiece
(likewise the motion picture made from it by his friend, Gore
Vidal); the out-and-out psychotic hopheads of William Burroughs'
Naked Lunch (which lead one to wonder a bit about the real
future of calculating and 'thinking' machines); and, best publicized
of all, the 'witty' letch for 12-year-old girls described in Vladimir
Nabokov's best-seller — a perversion once thought of as solely
Russian, but now apparently in danger of becoming epidemic in
America as well, as a result of drinking too much Kentucky Vodka:
'The Vodka that will put *our* man on Venus first!'

All of these tasty delectations, and a few more, have been des-
pairingly satirized by an old-line literary critic, who knows well
that there isn't a damn thing he or anyone else can do about it
but try to laugh, Mr. Clifton Fadiman, in a remarkable article only
a few years ago, called "Party of One." This article is perhaps
most remarkable as, itself, an example of the 'new freedom,'
appearing as it did in a middle-class mass-circulation magazine,
Holiday (published in tandem with *The Saturday Evening Post*),
August 1959, p. 8–11, in among the travel advertisements, and
along with a full-page, four-color Bikini-clad nude (p. 71) worth

seeing not only for herself but in connection with the remarks elsewhere in the present volume, on beauty contests, which she illustrates, in a way beyond language, as no words of mine can do.

Mr. Fadiman refers casually, in his *Holiday* article, to such matters as fellation, hand-painted birth-control diaphragms, cantharides, homosexuality, voyeurism, excrement — in the literary sense, of course — Jack-the-Ripperism (surgically detailed, for some reason, as his opening paragraph, in what is called in short-story writing courses the 'narrative hook'), and unspecified 'sex freak waxworks,' which must be honeys after what *is* specified. All this, by the way, strictly as humor. In deference, however, to the message of the writers he is decribing, though hardly criticizing, whose 'foe is the normally sexed human being,' no normal or at least no ordinary sexual act whatever is mentioned, which could in any case hardly stand the comparison. To such a degree, that the critic himself is apparently finally convinced by what he thinks he is ridiculing, and records solemnly that, *per contra,* he found the unexpurgated *Lady Chatterley's Lover* 'so solemn and didactic in its use of "bad words" that it is hard to control one's laughter.'

This is again a demonstration, if one were needed, of that Gresham's Law of the intellect whereby bad art drives out good, and by means of which faked and diseased sex, and faked and diseased folk-literature and folklore are being passed off as the real thing, on a public profoundly desperate for the real end of the censorship, and its sick sequelæ, and of the falsity and disease it has created in the more than two hundred years of its reign. As Mr. Fadiman does not sum up, except humorously, perhaps I may be allowed to do so. Both the clique and 'art' novels today, whether written by presumably Angry Young Men (who Care), or by bearded beatniks (who don't), and — more importantly — the popular-art materials such as horror comic-books and t.v. serials and movies being produced by the same or similar writers, this time not for prestige but for money, all equally reek with the same social and sexual false revolt: the glorification, whether or not disguised as exposés, of perversion, homosexuality, a full palette of psychoses (latent and shock-'cured'), drug-addiction and other anti-rationalisms; as also pædophily, coprophily, vomitophily — I couldn't even find that one in the dictionary — and sadisms of every brand; ending inevitably in a total fæcal-explosion anti-everythingism . . . 'Come on, you Atom Bomb!'

V

THIS NIHILIST garbage had long ago reached America, not in any elevated literary avatar, but in the gross, pulp-paper, popular-art form of science-fiction, which is largely a retooling — to fit the overwhelming modern machine-based anxieties — of the earlier ghost stories and decadent-religious 'Gothic' tales of eerieness and dread. Almost nothing other than historical material, and that very superficial, exists on this subject. One exceptional piece is that by Maurice Richardson, in *Twentieth Century*, December 1959. The few relevant socio- and psychoanalytic writings, in particular Viktor Tausk's "On the Origin of the 'Influencing Machine' in Paranoia," are gathered in the "Machine" issue of *Neurotica* (1951) No. 8., with a prefatory note by the present writer.

The pessimistic tone and the fear of science, that so sharply distinguish science-fiction from the Utopias and imaginary voyages of earlier centuries — in which it was invariably assumed that the intellectually and scientifically operated Utopias discovered (such as Plato's) would be utopian indeed — was set very early by the anti-woman and pro-fæces misanthrope or misogyne, Swift, in *Gulliver's Travels* (1726) particularly in the section on the floating island of Lapúta; and in Sébastien Mercier's *L'An 2240* published in 1786. Another early pessimistic imaginary voyage, also into the future, is the "History of England in the Year 1931 . . . by Mrs. Midnight," in *The Nonpareil* (1757) p. 157–60, reprinted from *The Midwife, or Old Woman's Magazine,* of about 1750, and again reprinted in *The New Boghouse Miscellany* (1761) in which, owing to a 'mischievous habit of drinking gin,' the English have by 1931 become 'the most diminutive creatures upon earth,' and similar humorous touches. Finally, however, and in neo-Gothic fashion, the blame was laid squarely on science, at the turn of the 19th century in Mary Wollstonecraft Shelley's *Frankenstein,* a work written — it is perhaps interesting to recollect — for one of the literary competitions of the salon of the unvirile and neurasthenic Byron and Shelley, Mrs. Shelley's companions of choice. As is now known, her 'modern Prometheus,' Dr. Frankenstein, was punished for his temerity, in trying to snatch the fire of life from the gods (of electricity) for his Golem automaton, by becoming the model of the thousand and one 'mad scientists' who have followed him in the invariably woman-torturing operating chambers of science-fiction since.

This essential element in the nihilism of false revolt — the fear and hatred of science, ending in the frank anti-intellectual assaults in which popular American picture magazines, the French Surréalists, and the German Nazis meet — is taken to the extreme limits of *anti-Utopian* satire, far beyond anything prefigured by Swift, and leaving almost nothing but rehash for the later pulp popularizers such as Jules Verne and H. G. Wells; in Emile Souvestre's *Le Monde tel qu'il sera* (1846) with satirical fashion plates of future 'professional' styles, which, reproduced in *Harper's New Monthly Magazine,* in New York, 1856, were the earliest anticipatory illustrations published in America. But the absolutely ultimate word on the subjects of anti-science and anti-Utopia will be found in the two magnificently illustrated and excessively rare volumes of Albert Robida's *Le Vingtième Siècle* (1883–90, volume II being called *La Vie Electrique*), with an even rarer prophetic supplement on the War of the Twentieth Century, boldly cribbed by H. G. Wells. This 'humorous' precursor was republished in 1916, after the Germans had already taken the hint of poison gas from *Le Vingtième Siècle,* on Robida's stated inspiration. Altogether, Robida's work must be considered the most important and complete 'anticipation' ever published — particularly as to its antisocial effects — since almost all his exact pre-visions, in both his sardonic text and hilariously complex illustrations, of airplanes, helicopters, phonograph, television (to which he devotes several chapters, with a few perversions of the art not yet realized, not even 'subliminally'), test-tube babies, frogmen, and especially poison-gas and microbic warfare, have been assiduously turned into fact since World War I.

As will be realized, very little was left to explore, in the way of anti-science, by the time of the *Erewhon* of Samuel Butler, whose real significance in any such history is, rather, as the almost perfect example of total false revolt: not only against science, but against the even more obvious Oedipal father-figures, of Darwin and Darwinism (also Shakespeare and Homer), though his attack on his own father, *The Way of All Flesh,* which was his masterpiece, he never allowed to be published, and it appeared only after his death. This is a very standard pattern in false revolt.

The British and French precursors, of the 18th and 19th centuries, actually exhausted the intellectual content of science-fiction, and what has been printed since, mostly in pulp magazines of wide circulation, is only a popularized hack repetition for mass consumption. The precursors had also unintentionally succeeded in diverting the anti-clerical attack, so important in the intellectual baggage of the 19th century, into the anti-science attack of the popular science-fiction literature that replaced it, as the preferred mild or parlor-type verbal 'revolt' of adolescents, real and perennial. Pierre Malvezin having gone to jail for *La Bible farce* in 1881, his successor "Léo Taxil" found it politic to recant, and withdraw his own imitation, *La Bible amusante* (1882), entertaining himself thereafter with hoaxing the Catholic hierarchy as to a pretended Masonic 'pact with the Devil' enacted regularly in Charleston, with the American General Albert Pike 'performing the hierarchical functions' of the Evil One himself. It became evident, thereafter, to a certain kind of popular writer, that the white-coated scientist was a safer target, in a mass-circulated literature of 'revolt,' than the purple-robed priest whom he replaced in fantasy as the hated custodian of hieratic wisdom and temporal power — which the priest had been since ancient Egypt at least — and had essentially replaced in fact since the Rationalists and Encyclopedists of the century before. The only new element was to transmute the rational scientist, who had until then represented 'progress,' into a sort of obsessional King Charles' head of hatred and fear, for journalists and hack-writers to shoot at.

One of the most extraordinary and significant things about science-fiction is its almost total lack of sex, even of fake-sex — except, of course, in the 'mad scientists' operating-chambers particularly prominent in the movie versions. The reason for this is neither oversight nor external censorship, but the fact that the largest percentage of the audience for the *echt*-pulp science-fiction literature is composed of adolescent boys (who continue reading it even after they are grown up), who are terrified of women, sex, and pubic hair. These they identify with the *vagina dentata* image of the standard witch, or "Lena the Hyena," — the anti-beauty-contest winner — with a mouthful of protruding tusks, and stringy clutching hair; or, in the popular Edgar Rice Burroughs cosmogony, with the planet Venus, who is green, wet, female, fertile, grappling, and marshy, and altogether evil; as opposed to the proud, red, phallic, mountainous, sterile and scientific Mars. Even so, this whole configuration is hardly more than a minor aspect, sex being entirely rejected and lacking except at the symbolic level, and in the horror-types of science-fiction pulp, which are not the most popular.

Perhaps the only importantly sexual aspect of science-fiction, whether in its intellectual or pulp presentations, is in connection with the eugenic or test-tube baby, first proposed in humorous form by Robida. Just as the whole new form or folk-myth of science-fiction repeats the emotional charge of earlier religio-mystic fears of the dead, and so forth, but in scientific trappings; the eugenic or test-tube baby has become the modern focus of all the earlier, and almost mute resistance to — yet simultaneous acceptance of — the folk-myth of a Virgin Birth. This could express itself earlier only obliquely or sardonically, as in the folktale or joke of the old lady's confession to her religious adviser that she had 'never really been able to see the advantage over the other system.' At least a dozen revisions and reversals of this joke have been collected, over the last thirty years (and perhaps as many more have been missed) mostly in pictorial and cartoon form, turning on the reduplication of machines by sexo-mechanical acts, or the eugenic 'marriages of the future,' with a baby popping out of the machine when a coin is put into the vaguely symbolic slot. The science-fiction literature itself, however, remains almost entirely mute on the subject.

It should be observed that the whole 'eugenic' ideal was given its most particular development by the sexually-disturbed practical Utopians of the 19th century, especially Proudhon in France, and in the Oneida and similar religio-sexual Utopias in America attempting to formalize the erotic exploitation of whole harems of the young people of the opposite sex, for the benefit of the old men and women dominating the cult. As remarked in what is, on all counts, the most significant and seminal 20th century work of science-fiction — though never intended as that — J. B. S. Haldane's *Daedalus, or Science and the Future,* an address read to The Heretics, Cambridge, in 1923, and published in the following year (p. 41), the eugenic ideal of 'Marriage "by numbers," so to speak, was a comparatively novel idea when proposed by Plato 2,300 years ago, but it has already actually been practised in various places, notably among the subjects of the Jesuits in Paraguay. It is moreover likely, as we shall see, that the ends proposed by the eugenist will be attained in a very different manner.' Haldane then proceeds to show what this 'very different manner' might be, in a pretended history (p. 57–69) on the style of Mother Midnight's in the 1750's, written in the year 2073, and concerning the eugenic production of supermen in bottles — as depicted earlier by Robida — by parthenogenetic means. These means Haldane calls ectogenesis, ending with the further remark by the 'future historian' that: 'Had it not been for ectogenesis there can be little doubt that civilization would have collapsed within a measurable time owing to the greater fertility of the less desirable members of the population in almost all countries.' One need hardly be reminded who it was, and in what country, that took this eugenic bogey most seriously, and set out to 'purify the racial blood,' of such 'less desirable members of the population' as Gypsies, Jews, twins, and even all congenital cripples (except Goebbels).

Haldane's twelve-page *jeu d'esprit*, evidently perfectly serious under its mock-historical form, is the principal inspiration of Aldous Huxley's bitterly anti-Utopian *Brave New World*, which even makes use of Haldane's obiter dictum or joke about the probable basing of the religion of the future on such modern folk-heroes as Charles Bradlaugh and Annie Besant, the birth-control propagandists, but substituting Lenin and Ford. Huxley's book, in turn, was later used — along with the satirical Russian novel of the 1920's, *We* — in George Orwell's *1984*, of which the title-idea itself was also taken from the far more penetrating 'intra-atomic' war-with-the-Moon satire, on exactly the same style, of André Maurois' *1992*, published in 1929. It obviously is not hard to put together books on this total-plagiarism principle: what is hard is to make best-sellers out of them. When that is what they become, it is no longer their literary origins that are of importance, but the secret of their massive folk-appeal. That the appeal of all the writings just cited is in the bitter humor of their open pessimism and anti-scientific and anti-Utopian *parti pris* is, I think, very clear.

With the explosion over Hiroshima, the fears and doubts assailing science-fiction — or surging up to expression therein — have almost entirely disappeared, at least at the pulp level. The unabashedly optimistic kinds of science-fiction that have since remained popular in the pulps, on the formula tricks of time-travel and interplanetary trips, are at least as old as Bishops Godwin and Wilkins' and Cyrano de Bergerac's flights to the Moon in the 17th century, which also display the same striking lack of any expressed or rational motive that characterizes the actual flights now proposed. It is almost unnecessary to observe that no one ever goes to the Moon for purposes of neo-Conquistador domination, on any of these imaginary flights, but invariably for 'scientific' (once 'philosophic') exploration, on the style of the German 'ethnologists' in Africa before World War I, and the 'agricultural implement' arms-peddlers in the Orient since. The literature of the new interplanetary Conquistador dream is sharply opposed to any excessive thinking whatever, and especially to any brooding and melan-

choliac tone of anti-science or despair. The new science-fiction
enthusiasts are by no means pessimists or anti-scientists in the tradition of Robida and H. G. Wells. Their prophet is more particularly Jules Verne and his enormous Pollyanna output, gushing
with pro-scientificism on the style of *Tom Swift and his Mammoth
Cannon,* and other embarrassing symbolisms. They too reach for
the safety-catch of their automatics when they heard the word
'culture,' but *science* is sacred because it gets them to the Moon.

These are blatantly the wave-of-the-future wild west stories,
in which the raygat replaces the six-shooter, and the evil batrachian
monsters and vagina-dentata octopodes of the planet Venus (*ut
supra*) replace the Redskins as the 'inferior' race, or gooks, to be
liquidated at once so that the great work of civilization may go on.
They are then largely replaced by automata, servo-mechanisms,
test-tube baby-makers, and especially by thinking-machines, because the Master Race has no intention of doing any *work* — and
darn little raping and repopulating either. Thinking is of course
out of the question. Also, they must save all their strength for the
Great Work of extermination. (Anyone who thinks this is humorous must have a very short memory, *nicht Wahr?*) In the cowboy
movie the clean-thinking, hard-riding hero kisses his horse, to
avoid embarrassing the kiddies in the Saturday-afternoon audience; in the science-fiction movie or pulp he kisses the explosive
red tip of his rocket.

Just as the murder-mysteries *aficionados* once kept a few
mystery-writing college professors (even a Bible translator) on tap,
to lend an air of sober intellect or intellectual pastime to a literary
diet that is ninety-five percent bloodlust and lynch; the new slide-
rule-toting intelligentsia of the science-fiction pulps keep a few
sacred cows and brain-boys on the string, to lend color to their
deploring that the real meat-&-bone of science-fiction is and has
always been as stated above. There is also, of course, a parallel-
or side-literature in the vaguely hermaphroditic area between the
old ghost stories and the newer science-fiction, referred to as
'fantasy-fiction,' and solely composed of unspecified Gothic terror
and gruesomeness. To those who deplore the wild-west or raygat
type of paranoid science-fiction, with the 'earth-attacking blue
gloops exterminating the green bloops;' the 'fantasy' school of
horror and terror is thought of as more cultured. Its partisans flit
in the background of the new and more virile folk-literature of
science-fiction, of which they consider themselves to be the new
scientific élite, an outcast tribe of Des Essientes and Kerhanys, with

perfume organs, jazz marimbas, and bindings in human skin clut-
tering up their fantasy world, and the unmistakable offstage clank
of eighteenth-century Gothic chains and torture-chambers in the
diseased style of Horace Walpole and the Marquis de Sade.

The truth is that mass-extermination in the green bloop and
raygat horse-operas is too perfunctory and impersonal for these
real amateurs of science-fiction, who are also often its hack authors.
They find it crass. They prefer the closer and more intense and
more delicately unhealthy *delectatio morbosa* of the Marquis de
Sade (the hidden star of the locked-away other half of their collections), and touch upon science only in the endless variations on
Mary Wollstonecraft Shelley's 'mad scientist,' whose more recent
experiments, for some reason, generally involve the fellation-
fantasy of drinking blood, or the equally eugenic cross-breeding of
strapped-down young ladies with gorillas. Although the young
ladies are shown undressed in the pulp illustrations, and in the
horror-movies laboriously made on their pattern; the cross-breeding is apparently always achieved parthenogenetically — as far as
the text ever goes — the tortures, terror, and exactly indicated
surgical incisions of the raped and (symbolically?) spayed or castrated victim replacing the need for any more openly sexual scene.
The result, however, is exactly the same as in the crasser space-
operas and raygat exterminations : the creation of a Master Race
of supermen — half gorilla, of course. It all seems very familiar,
doesn't it; like a page out of the Nuremberg Trials.

As far as the merely fictional form is concerned, one need not
look very far to recognize, in these inevitable gorillas impossibly
raping slender young ladies out of all proportion to their size, the
bespectacled little readers' fantasy of themselves, or, rather, of
their unchained *Id,* something on the style of an anthropoid
Harpo Marx tearing uncontrolled through all the restrictions of
society, sanity, and even the law of gravity. The American science-
fiction writer of the early twentieth century, Edgar Rice Burroughs, is significantly less famous for his Mars stories, and their
pointlessly dualistic center-of-the-earth counterparts or rewritings,
than for his *Tarzan of the Apes,* an Oxford-educated neo-Rousseau,
or noble savage, who prefers to speak in the language of the apes
rather than English, and hates all human beings, especially black
ones. Burroughs thus offers an escape from civilization in every
direction — his form of 'revolt' — both forward in time, and backwards in history; as well as outward toward Mars and inward toward the center of the earth. It is obvious that the *direction* of the

escape does not matter, as long as the reader is offered the fantasy of
relief from civilization, its restraints and 'discontents.' As to the
gorilla-dream, there is a pictorial gloat on all the horror-stuff that
this immediately leads to, composed of stills from science-fiction,
werewolf, vampire, and similar sado-masochistic movies, Michel
Laclos' *Du Fantastique au cinéma*, published in Paris and cited
here solely for the record. A semi-slick compilation of the same
sort of material in magazine form, *The Monster*, Nos. 1 and 2,
was also issued during the 1950's in the United States by a Hollywood agent affectionately styling himself 'America's No. 1 Science-
Fiction Fan.'

The principal trouble with fleeing completely from civilization, or, in the science-fiction sense, casting civilization entirely
away by exterminating everyone else (the policy of Alfred Jarry's
unrepressed little king, *Ubu Roi*), is that it still leaves all the work
of the world to be done, and no one but oneself to do it, because
everyone has been exterminated except the *Uebermenschen* whose
fantasy this is. This problem has already been mentioned. Mrs.
Shelley's inspiration is resorted to again, and behind her the
ancient Jewish sorcerer's-apprentice legend of the Golem of
Prague, for the creation — not by means of the ineffable Name of
Jehovah, this time, but by the simultaneously occult and ration-
alistic star-stolen electro-magnetism or lightning of the 'gods'
(Prometheus, via Benjamin Franklin) — of whole sub-species of
machines or automata that will carry water, chop wood, mine coal,
cast iron, add up columns of figures, make love, THINK, and do
everything else that is just too much for the Master Race. As is
only too well known, this pasty delight in mechanical fantasies and
toys, and in the anti-human dream of crossing and equating them
with human beings (compare La Mettrie's *L'Homme machine*, in
1746), and finally of replacing human beings with the machines
of their own creating, has now slopped out over the edges of
science-fiction into fact, throughout the Western world, where it
has also its various fake-humanistic prophets, trying to gild the
pill with promises of servo-mechanism super-comfort; and even a
special artist, Boris Artzybasheff (whose mechanomorphic drawings
have been gathered in a recent volume), related to the Russian
novelist of the 1900's whose final solution, in *The Breaking Point*,
had been that everyone should commit suicide. This perhaps explains the quasi-human or simili-human machines' taking over.

It will be observed that the embracing of the Machine — in
fact, this suicide in its favor — is a strange ending for a literature or

an intellectual movement that takes its beginnings in the *fear* of science and presumably the fear of the Machine as well. All that has happened is the classic neurotic mechanism of the erotization of anxiety: the fear of an overmastering force has been transformed into an erotically-toned submission to it, and the desire (or so the individual convinces himself) to die ecstatically beneath it. Here, at the deepest level, one begins to understand the inevitable relationship, always trembling in the background, between science-fiction and the Nazi dream of the Master Race. I have indicated elsewhere, in "The Influencing Machine" (in *Neurotica*, 1951, No. 8, p. 37–8), the paranoid tone in so much of science-fiction, in which the guilt for the intended destruction of the world is somehow always to be cast on the destroyed — 'who were *preparing* to attack, but we got there first!' Briefly stated, the psychological dynamic is this: In the first step of the paranoid complex, the individual attempts to resolve his hatred of powerful father-figures, and ultimately of all authority-figures, by a false revolt against a whole series of such surrogate figures, but never against the real one. This ranges from the desire to assassinate all kings, presidents, Negroes, Jews, and so forth, to assaults (in literature) on the existence of Shakespeare or the law of gravity, and similar irrationalist or anti-scientific eccentricities.

When, however, this evasion or diversion of the problem begins to break down, the individual begins to project the guilt for the hatred that he feels upon the real or surrogate power-figure against whom it is actually directed, and who is then accused of hating or harming him. This is the crucial element in anti-Negroism, anti-Semitism, and all similar xenophobic ideas, usually with the not-even-hidden secret ascription of some physical sexual superiority or mental superiority to the hated group, or, rather, of some sexual or mental *plot* or attack against the paranoid individual, himself, such as harming his sexual organs or removing his brains by long distance prayers, charms, or — more modernly — electro-mechanical methods. In this way he arranges to believe that he was originally quite superior himself, sexually or mentally, but has been reduced to the hated group's 'inferiority' by means of their 'plot' or castrational rebellion against him, exactly identical of course with his own fantasy plot against the parental or authority figure, and usually indicating the fantasy form his attack would wish to take. See in particular the secret slave-revolt led by the cabin-boy in Melville's mysterious *Benito Cereno,* apparently a charade of fears of homosexual blackmail.

Before finally taking flight into these outright paranoid ideas
of his own private plots being turned against him by dark-skinned
'inferior' races, or mentally 'superior' races (coming from Mars), or
even by monsters that he has set loose, or machines that he has
created, now gone out of control and buzzing in his head or
belly; the deeply frightened individual — harassed by these unbearable extrojections of his fantasy guilt — may make one last
attempt to throw off completely all these ideas of hatred and rebellion that have taken him beyond his powers and are destroying
him. His hatred against his parents, authority, or the outer world
is turned self-accusingly against himself, as weak and paltry, and
he tries to make his peace with authority and the outer world, and
to love them again as a child. This final attempt, grotesque as it
may seem and abnormal as it is, protects the beleaguered individual from the final leap into madness and paranoia. He trans-
poses his hatreds into love; he identifies with, and now admires and
accepts, as a docile son, the overmastering power of the authority
figure, giving himself to it — homosexually, since power is conceived of as male — like a new Ganymede offering himself to the
Jupiter he cannot otherwise master.

Much more could be added to this rapid formulation, but there
is no need. One has only to read the literature of science-fiction,
some of which seems almost consciously to be parodying the Ganymede story, with Jupiter in the form of an eagle, seizing his
pædicon-victim by the back of the neck. The most touted of all
recent science-pulp stories, for instance, *Sinister Barrier* (1939) by
Eric Frank Russell — based on the suggestion by the anti-scientist
(and remarkable stylist) Charles Fort, that human beings are
'property' — is wholly of the influencing-machine type, with the
homosexual fears basic to paranoid delusions of persecution indicated in it by a simple reversal of oral intercourse: invisible and
unknowable creatures — the principal matter of the plot — sucking out the victims' 'emotions' through the back of the neck (dis-
placement of lower to upper, and front to back). 'Nelson's Column
broke at its base . . . fell and crushed three hundred. Emotion
welled to the heavens, bright, clear, thirst-quenching emotion!
. . . a homoburger awaiting the bite!'

The whole tone of the entire science-fiction literature in all
its forms — and, in the now classic critical cliché, it runs the gamut
from *a* to *b* — is that of a conscious readaptation to an assumably
infantile audience of the message of Nietzsche and of the *Manifeste
du Futurisme* (Milan, 1909) of the millionaire North African

proto-Fascist, F. T. Marinetti, in which the actual program of the twentieth century's 'Revolution of Nihilism' broke from cover, and was first openly expressed, without any of the Biblical parodying and Zoroastrian posing of Nietzsche. Paying for front-page ads in the French newspapers to publicize his message, which is itemized and explained with all the insane seriousness of another Dr. Mabuse; Marinetti planned to 'liberate' the world by means of fast sports-cars — probably the earliest clear personalization of the Machine — and *free verse,* which, to a European intellectual then, was expected to have all the affective charge of the similar rallying-cry, 'Free Silver,' at the same period in the United States. There is something terribly funny and yet unmistakably sinister about this millionaire crackpot, who demands in one breath: *'Boutez* [polite for *Foutez*] *donc le feu aux rayons des bibliothèques!'* in a world that now needs no libraries, and will Begin Again; and who ends with the open homosexual-warrior appeal to *'glorifier la guerre — seule hygiène du monde — le militarisme, le patriotisme, le geste destructeur des anarchistes, les belles Idées qui tuent* [!] *et le mépris de la femme.'* As the reader will probably have observed, this whole program was carefully put into execution — minus only the essential *free verse* — by Marinetti's friends and disciples, Mussolini and Hitler, of whom the former (who taught it to the latter) learned the whole thing at Marinetti's knee.

At the present time, science-fiction is in the ascendant, travelling on the coattails of atomic warfare — which it is its greatest pride to have foretold — and the intended conquest and civilization of the Moon and all the planets. (All except the Earth, that is, which is to be left in its present, relatively imperfect state.) Were the slightest assessment of the real or possible social value, as opposed to the propaganda value, of such projects to be made — which is apparently now almost treason to suggest, in any country — *before* they are 'classified' as vital to the public weal and defense, or even just as target practice for atomic war; it is precisely their foretelling and foreshadowing, for well over a century now, in the pre-psychotic and frankly anti-social imaginings of science-fiction literature and pulp, that would make the whole project of flying to the Moon more than suspect. Of course, as everyone has a private little list, in Gilbert & Sullivan style, of loved-ones and pests for whom a one-way ticket to the Moon is to be bought, on the very first space-liner out (not forgetting to take out a smashing big insurance policy on the said loved-one, at the airport slot-machine . . . just in case), there does not seem to be any hope of just leaving the Moon-travel projects in the lunatic literature in which they were found. In the human sense — and what other is there for us? — the most disastrous part of the whole thing is the evident impatience and anxiety to go and ruin things there, instead of staying and fixing them here. This is simply a part of the mute hatred of our own world, and the willingness to see it die.

This much, at least, has been found to be true in the literature of science-fiction, during the centuries it has been forming: that every new invention is seized upon by evil and imaginative men — not by nameless Demons of the Perverse, plaguing humanity, but by evil men — by the handle that will break it, and not by the handle that will turn it. To destroy civilization with it, if possible, and never and by no means to further civilization, except by getting as far away from it as can be conceived. This profound and ambivalent willingness *to see the world go up in flames,* and oneself along with it, is the measure of the disaffection of an ever-increasing portion of the world's population from the life that must now be lived on that world. As does every folk-literature, science-fiction allows a most penetrating insight into the fantasy life and emotional urgencies now hammering insanely in the temples of our collective mind and century. Continued only a bit further in the same direction, this will constitute the popular vote and agreement — thumbs down! — to the death-sentence, certainly not of the physical world, but of the world as we know it. This Earth lies in uneasy equilibrium between Venus and Mars, and not only in the simple Copernican sense. No rocket, no inner explosion of relativity or schizophrenia, can take us in both directions at once. The choice remains to be made.

VI

THESE BRIEF historical notes on science-fiction have been set in the unorthodox context of folklore — real and fake — to emphasize, as best I can, an important protective function of folklore which is being completely missed, not only by most modern folklorists; but often even by anthropologists, sociologists, and psychologically trained observers. The human spirit does not easily die: this is part of the simple biological heritage of all living things, the law of self-preservation, or the tendency of 'all things to continue to their end,' the Sibylline oracle's wisdom in Rabelais' *Pantagruel* (Bk. v, ch. 37). Every living organism, including both the human being and human society, has in it a certain protective force or strength, by which it attempts to heal any wounds made in its integument, and to right itself when its organic integrity and possibility of meaningful survival are attacked. This 'gyroscopic' force in the individual, as in society — to call it by the simplest mechano-metaphor to hand — takes its effective external form strictly in response to the external danger of invasion or attack. It can obviously succeed only to the degree that the individual or the society is able to deploy this protective force in forms and amounts capable of absorbing or overwhelming the attack. These are the truisms of individual biology: it is necessary also to appreciate their application to societies.

To the contrary of what might be imagined, when the methods of defense consciously available are evidently grossly inferior to the force of the attack, the individual does not often go valiantly forth to lose the battle, brandishing implements of warefare hopelessly outclassed. Instead, he returns upon himself, and either plays dead completely, thus evading the battle (as he hopes) by admitting that he is defeated; or else, and in addition, disappears privately into a fantasy world where he thinks of himself as motionlessly invisible to his assailant, and as preparing his later escape and even revenge.

The daydream, for that is in a sense what has just been described, is the secret treasury or crucial creative area of all such protective fantasies, whether these remain simply vague and private 'continued stories' into which the individual dips, as into a cookie-jar, to soothe or reward himself, as with sweets, when hurt or frustrated in fact; or whether they are formalized and expressed in private literary or artistic creations, stemming from the same source. It is also clear that the achieving of wide folk-acceptance, whether by such informal fantasies, in folktale or folksong form, or by signed artistic creations of which the author's identity is eventually lost through oral transmission, depends in the largest measure on the ability of the specific fantasy creation to embody and express the identical protective and expressional needs of the greatest number of people, who are themselves unable to tap, or have not succeeded in tapping in graspable form, their own identical emotional and fantasy needs.

Science-fiction represents today one of the most extraordinarily large and completely formalized fantasy escapes from the crushing power of the Machine and of the machine-world, now rolling like its ancient folk-representation, the Juggernaut, over all the older human values, which most of us feel are the only ones that are actually human. Science-fiction has therefore taken into itself a significant part of the affective strength in modern times of earlier forms of fantasy escape and fantasy revolt against such earlier menaces, to the essential human organization, as the prehistoric megalosaurians or the inundations of the late-glacial periods, recollected in the widely dispersed folk-myths of Floods, dragons, and the tyrannic giants and rulers of olden times.

One particular and centrally important 'protective' function served by science-fiction should be mentioned to close the subject here, and that is the evident protection it affords against conscious feelings of inferiority, and unconscious ideas of impotence and castration in the face of the threat of the Machine. It is generally believed that such Machine-fears have developed, in their specifically sexual form, only since the beginning of atomic war, with its publicized threat of human sterilization, at a time when Hitler Germany was engaging in the same activities surgically. The fact of the matter is that the whole complex of Machine-fears have been present, though of course less frankly stated, since the very beginning of the spontaneous resistance to the machine, by the Luddite machine-breakers of a former century. Consider, for instance, the American legend-song of "John Henry," the Negro 'hard-man' and hero who challenged the Machine, and died fighting the steam-hammer in a competition as to which could work the fastest digging the Big Bend Tunnel in the West Virginia Mountains, presumably about 1870. In a deeply-researched study by Prof. Louis W. Chappell, published in Jena, 1933, the whole origin of the ballad is traced, without any disguising of the sexual and symbolic undertones of both the hero and his personal legend, and, of course, the *mise en scène* of the great female tunnel to be dug.

The absolutely open sexual statement is first made in science-fiction, I believe, in George Weston's *His First Million Women* (New York, 1934), in which Comet "Z" sterilizes all the men in the world but one, who was down in a lead-mine — or up on the Eiffel Tower, as in the earlier *Crazy Ray* motion-picture — at the comet's passage. This fortunate fellow is then imprisoned, and is commandeered by all the governments of the world to undertake the earth's repopulation, by the wholesale methods of artificial insemination (despite the title). The atomic version of the same theme, Pat Frank's *Mr. Adam,* did not appear until over a decade later. Nothing remains to be demonstrated, by Freudian or other analytic methods, after fantasy statements so very clear.

Were this to be held to be simply some private fantasy or

neurosis on the part of the authors mentioned, one might cite the even more directly sexual expressions of the same theme, and at the folk level of oral, or rather 'novelty-print' circulation. These are the 'widely known drawings, such as the famous Rube-Goldberg-like do-it-yourself sex machine for girls,' noted by Mr. Frank A. Hoffmann in *American Journal of Folklore* (1962) vol. 75; p. 189. Some specific anatomical details as to the construction of this machine is given, with further reference to the erotic literature in which it had appeared over a century earlier — in Andréa de Nerciat's *Les Aphrodites* in particular — in *The Limerick* (Paris, 1953) p. 447–8, n. 1325, in a discussion of the 'Young man of Racine,' or 'named McLean,' credited with its invention. The striking reversal is here to be observed, in the folk-fantasy cartoon, that it is not the man who is replacing the machine, but the machine that is incomparably replacing the man. This theme is taken even further in the violently sadistic modern folk-ballad called "The Great Wheel," in which the machine eventually revenges the male — in the very process of replacing him — by tearing to bits the presumably 'unsatisfiable' woman for whose benefit it has been invented. (Compare *Proverbs*, xxx. 16, quoted in the preceding essay, "*The Merry Muses* as Folklore," pt. xi.)

In the entire folklore field, I do not know of anyone who has attempted to collect and analyze the cultural materials — even those perfectly respectable — in this very important and emerging area of twentieth-century folklore, with the exception of the American sociologist, Dr. John Del Torto, of San Francisco; and Prof. Marshall McLuhan, of Toronto, who puts his finger very neatly on the subject in calling it "The Folklore of Industrial Man" in his pictorial analysis of popular materials, largely taken from advertisements, *The Mechanical Bride* (1951). Dr. Del Torto's extraordinarily passionate exploratory blast, "The Human Machine," appeared in the "Machine" issue of *Neurotica*, 1951, No. 8, already mentioned, which also announced his larger study in preparation, *The Folklore of the Machine*, which one awaits with great anticipation.

Meanwhile, one can refer only to the excellent compilations of cartoon material, Hans Wettich's *Die Maschine in der Karikatur* (Berlin, 1916), Dr. Anton Klima's similar *Das Auto in der Karikatur* (1928), and the valuable issue of the German railroad journal, *Hanomag* (Hannover, 1922) devoted to *Die Lokomotive in Kunst, Witz und Karikatur*. A very striking cartoon of this kind — not reproduced in *Hanomag* — showing one locomotive raping another, while the top-hatted censor covers his eyes, was printed as the cover-illustration of *L'Assiette au Beurre,* No. 381, for 18 July 1908. There is, of course, a great deal more, both in textual and pictorial form, that remains to be collected and analyzed, in other literatures as well as the German. The one American work of this kind that comes to hand, John Durant's *Predictions* (1956) is distinguished only by its superficiality, but the illustrations are good. On the specific subject of the 'conquest' of the air and outer-space, one may consult, in particular, the pictorial history of the early balloons and airplanes by John Grand-Carteret, which includes a number of recent imitative caricatures of flying-machines even more complex and disturbing than those of the incomparable Robida.

There is also the entire, though very small, critical and bibliographical literature of the science-fiction field, written by its own enthusiasts, such as P.-G. Castex, *Le Conte Fantastique en France* (1951); Alfred Chapuis' *Les Automates dans les Oeuvres d'Imagination* (Neuchâtel, 1947); and the bibliography recently privately issued in Switzerland from the notes of the late Régis Messac, an early student of the 'scientific' murder-mystery as well. One of the most interesting elements of science-fiction, the fearsome and imaginary mechanical devices with which it has always been illustrated, has never been properly studied, nor does any anthology of this fantastic illustrative material — especially that appearing in the ephemeral science-fiction pulps — seem to exist. The earliest materials are to be found in the various illustrated histories of the airplane and balloon, which reproduce the early flying-machine fantasies of Leonardo da Vinci, Cyrano de Bergerac, Paltock's *Life and Adventures of Peter Wilkins* (1751) — the hero named for the earlier plagiarist of Bishop Godwin's and Dalgarno's anticipatory ideas — and the magnificently illustrated *Découverte Australe* of Rétif de La Bretonne. The study of these illustrations would well repay whoever would undertake it.

A rich vein also remains to be studied, and not in the humorous tone so far taken with it, to the exclusion of all others, in the illustrations for patents of crackpot inventions. There are at least two printed collections of these in English; the most remarkable is in French, Paul Gilson's *Les Folies Bourgeoises* (Monaco, 1957). Almost as rich are the various illustrated and textual histories of the water-closet, from Sir John Harington's *Metamorphosis of Ajax* to Chic Sale's *The Specialist.* There has been quite a fad for these in recent years in England, the most interesting both as to text and illustrations being the work of an architect, Lawrence Wright's *Clean and Decent* (1960), and the most mannered that of Reginald Reynolds. Illustrated collections of patented genito-urinary devices are the most hallucinatory of all such materials, but naturally the rarest. One not well known is *L'Acte Bref* (Paris, 1912) by "Doctor Brennus" [Roland Brévannès], which is simply a pretext for a catalogue appended, nearly as long as the author's 170-page text on premature ejaculation, of devices and books offered for sale. The key to the understanding of almost all this pre-psychotic illustrated material will be found in the Tausk article "On the Origin of the 'Influencing Machine' in Schizophrenia," already cited.

Finally, a whole literature also exists, not of humorous resistance to the Machine, but of gladsome lying down before it, as before its ancient mechanical and openly erotic forerunner, the Juggernaut, to be crushed. As first presented, this was usually expressed — and sometimes still is — as awe or admiration before the spontaneous beauty of line and mass (etc., etc.), and terrible power of the Machine, usually by people who have never noticed the same beauty in the macroscopic structure of a flower, or any awesomeness even about the Grand Canyon. An early work in this line, Hanns Guenther's photographic work, *Technische Schönheit* (Zürich, 1929) has had an endless progeny in the formula picture-magazines in all countries, of which the sex-*cum*-machine formula has been summed up in brief as: 'One ad, one bathing-beauty, one automobile, another ad.' And usually ending with some 'human-interest stuff,' about a dog. Perhaps the best expression of the adoration of the Machine in literary art — combatted, in this case, in "John Henry" style — is Eugene O'Neill's play-poem, *Dynamo.* In its religious or sociological form the same adoration is captured by Prof. McLuhan, who recollects that 'In the same way, austere Henry Adams, nostalgic for the twelfth-century Virgin of Chartres, unexpectedly found her at the St. Louis World's Fair in 1904. There, faced with a huge electric dynamo, he removed his hat and pronounced it the twentieth-century equivalent of the twelfth-century cult of the Virgin.' Prof. McLuhan may have overlooked the possibility that this was intended by Adams as irony, an art much practised at that period, as in Veblen's tongue-in-cheek *Theory of the Leisure Class,* of which the best part of the joke is that no one seems to have seen the joke at the time.

A few particular entries into the subject, from the point of view of ranking members of the cult, chortling in triumph (or pretending to regret) the ascendance of the Machine, will be found in Prof. Siegfried Giedion's *Mechanization Takes Command* (1948) with, as Dr. Del Torto's article remarks, 'its interesting illustrated chapter (pp. 230–245) on the mechanical slaughtering of pigs and the razor-blading of a woman's eye' — of which the relevance to 'mechanization' seems a bit strained; likewise the variously pro-and-anti humanistic writings of F. B. Gilbreth, Raymond Loewy (with Rube Goldberg illustrations), Buckminster Fuller, and Prof. Norbert Weiner. Of these, Weiner is by far the most significant, having written both the glorification of the 'thinking machine' in *Cybernetics* (1948), and a postscript, *The Human Use of Human Beings* (1950), expressing his sincere worriment that this will reduce men to the status of robots — while the machines THINK.

It is not possible in the space here available to present the materials necessary for an exploration of the deeper psychological elements at work in the cult of the Machine, in either its literary or its folk expressions. The one major element seems to be the yearning toward self-punishment and resultant forgiveness, for the sin of scientific presumption, which is thought of as a revolt against the Father-God, as in the myth of Prometheus. This is even more distinct in the parallel myth of Dædalus and Icarus, since here the father actually figures in the tragedy, though only in debilitated form, the real Father-God being evidently the Sun, who both is challenged by Icarus' flight, and deals out the ultimate punishment.

Science-fiction, with an anterior history of over a century and a half, has sprung into real prominence only since the creation of the atom bomb in 1945, with its implicit threat of wholesale human castration (sterilization) and death. Science-fiction attempts to control these and other castratory fears — specifically the fear of impotence in the face of the Machine — by a private literary manipulation of, and identification with, the hostile forces of science and mechanism. As could be expected, the murder-mystery and the western pulp, which attempted to solve with private lawlessness the sexual and economic anxieties of the Depression 1930's, are now being hastily retooled into science-fiction: machine fantasies to control the machine threat.

This 'identification with the aggressor' in science-fiction — whether produced by pulp hacks, college professors, military men, or all three rolled into one — is of particular significance in liberating the reader from his fear of the *Uebermaschine* and the *Ueber-*

mensch by the simple police-state formula: 'If you can't lick 'em, join 'em.' It also casts considerable light on the current, socially-implemented mechanization of man, on the unconscious satisfactions available to those who promulgate this mechanization, and on the release from anxiety held out as bait to those who succumb.

VII

MODERN FOLKLORISTS, by and large, are not attuned to the developing folklore of our own time. They tend to concern themselves almost entirely with collecting the vestiges of the past — as they find them, barely surviving, into the present — or else concern themselves totally with the past, in the form of its printed record. The excuse generally made, when any is thought necessary, is that the past is disappearing and that the present will remain, to be studied later on. This is obviously circular reasoning, and merely expresses the reluctance to deal with the difficult and emerging new forms, until they will be old — in barely surviving vestiges, as above. In any case, the problem is not really that of available effort, to be disposed economically: part on current collection, part on historical study, etc. The problem has now become much more broad, and is basically that of *recognition:* the folklore of our own century is being overlooked and left unrecognized, by almost the only group interested in dealing with it, owing to its increasing distance and external difference from the hitherto classic forms of folksongs, folktales, folkdances, and the like. We see before us the immediate possibility that these very three classic forms may largely disappear, on an international scale, except as the passively-absorbed televised entertainment of an audience of millions, performed by a numerically infinitesimal group of trained professional dancers, joke-tellers, and singers, probably numbering less already than one *per* one-hundred thousand persons composing the audience, if that. The same situation has already long since been achieved in what concerns competitive sports, which happen to be the one principal area of consciously surviving folk interest among the entire urban population of the world.

When, at the present time, the unprofessional folk-group itself attempts to dance, to sing, to recite poems, tell stories, or play games; the materials and the forms which it so employs, and which clearly involve all the available expressive and protective value that can be mustered by means of such folk materials and expressional forms, not only do not seem worthy of interest and study to the modern folklorist, but he finds himself standing back, refusing not only to collect the materials, but even to recognize them as folklore, and making purely esthetic assessments and rejections. For instance, that the 'Twist' is disgusting, either because it's too sexy, or else too repressed and not sexy enough (though it is identical in this ambivalent erotic tension, and repression of all physical contact, with Spanish Gypsy dancing); or that the 'popular songs' are too popular and too tuneless; that the jokes are too dirty, the poems too 'anodyne,' the limericks too horrible, the 'Little Willies' too sadistic, the ballads too bawdy, and the science-fiction too 'far out' to study. Even the played games of surviving folk interest — not to watch but to play: such as bowling, for instance, and the whole tremendous construct of *gambling*, legal and outlawed — are in no wise deemed worthy of folkloristic or sociological study, because they are not considered to compare with the intellectual superiority of, perhaps, chess, or with the earlier classic and phallic symbolisms of maypole dancing. Yet even the new stepchildren of both folklore and psychology, the 'industrial psychologists,' have begun to suspect, of bowling, that it has its uses in siphoning off the aggression of the employees against the boss; and, of gambling, that it represents the possibility of escape, by the private occultism or fetishism of 'luck,' from a calcified socio-economic situation in which the gambler's real chances of getting out of his social or economic pigeonhole are really almost nil.

Folklore is that which serves a certain function: the function of social or individual expression, appreciation, communication or control of particularly feared or valued aspects of the natural or civilized life being lived. Whatever serves this function is folklore. It is irrelevant whether it is of high or low quality from the esthetic standpoint of art — literary, pictorial, musical, and so forth. Folklore is art, and can be called art, or folk-art if one prefers, but that is essentially a terminological confusion of the matter owing to the introducing of subjective criteria of taste which will, in any case, change strikingly from one century, and even one generation, to the next. The highest forms of self-conscious art also cannot easily survive without broad and real folk-acceptance, since all art is, by definition, a form of stylized representation and communication. Where there is no communication, there is perilously close to no art, and certainly no folklore. Had Shakespeare's plays been of no interest to his contemporary audience, they would obviously never have been put on the stage, and might very well never have been printed. They have, since then, been almost as widely printed as the Bible; yet both works today remain largely unread, even if bought as a folk-gesture of obeisance to some cultural or religious ideal to which the buyer realizes himself to be either incapable of rising, or insufficiently trained to do so.

The external forms in which folklore expresses itself, and is communicated from one century to the next, whether by the so-called classic 'oral' means, or with occasional side-appearances in print, on the stage (an 'oral' form, certainly), and so forth, are not of essential importance as to the emotional or protective value of this folk material. They represent simply the formulas of its communication. These formulas change appreciably, over long periods of time, and it is necessary to be able to recognize the real undercurrent of folk-material and expression, no matter in what form it may present itself owing to the technical and historical irrelevancies of communication. When everyone sang, folksongs were a chosen vehicle of folk expression. Now that everyone reads — or at least *looks* — it is in what they are reading, or looking at, that that part of their folklore will somewhere be found which has been displaced from singing into reading or watching. It is almost irrelevant to observe that the forms being visually supplied to the public are now not being supplied because they are expected to satisfy the public, or folk-group, and to serve some useful purpose for them; but strictly in order to make money for the suppliers. Nay, further, it is perfectly well-known and is admitted that the generality of the bogus materials and meaningless forms now being supplied can hope for only the briefest fad popularity, and therefore only the briefest period of gain for the suppliers. The same is unfortunately true even when what is being supplied is, at least historically, 'authentic' folklore; but which, having lost its real viability owing to the activity of the purveyors of bogus replacements, can no longer really be revived. Thus it happens that the well-meaning classical folklore spectacles, pageants, songs, dances, organized folk-festivals, and similar — laboriously revived and hopefully re-injected into the population, as it is thought — seldom have the slightest chance of renewed viability, or hope of continuing survival, once the well-meaning (or even commercial) re-injection stops.

If this is true at the folk level, in the matter of real folklore versus the bogus *kitsch* of 'popular' songs and humor, as also of movies and t.v.; it is even more true at the snob or clique level, where the materials presented are insistently referred to as Art, with a capital *A*, even though they may essentially consist only of tittivated forms of folk-dance or miming and theatre, which are among the oldest folk-arts in the world. Where there is no popular appeal, the purveyors must make up for the narrowness of the snob or clique audience by increasing shamelessly the depth of the gouge taken out of the audience's purse. This is, for instance, the pumped-up situation with so-called modern art, music, and ballet, in which, more often than the public is allowed to realize — for fear of killing the bogus product completely — the real audience is composed of exactly *one* person, or rich patron, who not only pays all the bills, but can also be milked by middlemen and purveyors for fabulous and irrelevant ostentations, of no actual relation to the 'art' involved, such as putting up expensive build-ings as temples to the particular art, and driving up the price of any examples of it (if literary or pictorial) that may chance to appear on the auction-market.

It is of no importance. However thoroughly the suppliers of what passes as folklore and folk-art may be swindling the public — and that they *are* swindling the public is the main theme of the present essay — the public, or folk-group, tries to force its way mutely to some satisfaction in the end. The gyroscopic force inside the individual, to protect himself or herself from attrition and attack, and to continue an organized existence, makes it necessary, somehow or somewhere, to discover — in whatever hidden, crippled, symbolized, or (most often) endlessly reduplicated and inef-fectually small homeopathic doses — the protective and expressive human values that the individual must have, or die.

It is very difficult to keep this principle in view. People who, for instance, hate modern music and modern art (and there are many), cannot often bring themselves to realize or to admit that the monstrosities they detest do appear to satisfy, by their very disorganization and violence, the private urge to express, and personally to get hold of, the trigger-end — instead of always having to face the muzzle-end — of the same disorganization and violence of the world in which the listeners-to, and buyers-of, these 'arts' find themselves entrapped. What thus appears to be the fondling and possessing of something that is palpably (to those who hate it) ugly and disorganized and impossible to love, is therefore, in a deeper sense, the arming of oneself with precisely the weapon with which one is attacked: noise when one is attacked by noise, ugliness when one is attacked by ugliness, machines when one is attacked by the Machine. That this is practically a form of suicide — and the cure almost worse than the disease — is again irrelevant. What is involved is a unconscious survival of the very ancient rule of the duel: that the party who is challenged has the right to choose his weapons. To this must be added the extremely important psychological codicil: that *a person will generally choose to fight with the weapon of which he is most afraid.*

From the point of view of its protective value, *vis-à-vis* the specifically modern and mechanism-based attack on the integrity and meaningful survival of the individual, no modern form of folklore and folk-myth so strikingly expresses this functional and defensive attempt of the individual, in the absorbing of this type of mythic lore, as does science-fiction. It would be short-sighted to imagine, however, that this relatively new literary or sub-literary form is the only 'new' sort of folklore that will be formulated in the continuing history of the human race, or even in the close future. But at the moment no one is capable of guessing what these future forms will be, nor what relation, if any, they will have to those forms that have preceded, and that are thought of still as the only classic folklore forms. It will be sufficient, for the time being, if the attention of trained observers — and also a certain serious amount of thought and insight — are directed to these new and evolving forms of folklore, and to the unspoken needs they are intended to satisfy.

That special amalgam of the sciences of ethnology, history, sociology and psychology that is known as the study of folklore, has never required any sufficient training from the persons undertaking it. Were training really demanded, it is almost doubtful whether or not anyone could be found to qualify, on the basis of knowledge and competence in all the four specialties just enumerated. Any one of these is enough to require all the serious study of a lifetime or more. Meanwhile, it is of importance that the persons still concerning themselves, whether scientifically or in an amateur humanistic way, with this 'proper study of mankind,' not be led — as they have been led in the past — to a continuous and exclusive study of a Man who has disappeared, while overlooking the emerging Man who, whether we like him or no, is our contemporary, and is very possibly ourselves.

THE BAWDY SONG
In Fact and In Print

I

FEW AREAS of folklore have remained so uncontaminated by
vulgar gentility as has pure bawdry. This for the reason that the
bawdy songs, poems, jokes, proverbs, turns-of-phrase, and similar
lore in the folk-heritage of all nations, have had almost no recourse
to print, and, *en revanche,* print has had (except for the jokes)
almost no effect on them. Since the time of the attempted taming
of Scottish folk-minstrelsy into acceptably bowdlerized 'tea-table'
volumes by Allan Ramsay in the 1720's, to the final triumph of
tin-eared radio fakelore in the 1920's and since, no interested
person can have failed to notice that nothing authentically folk
can withstand the acid rot of prettification and faking in its
transmutation from fact into print. Of nothing is this more palpably true than of erotic folklore, of which the principal and
essential characteristic — the sexual parts — must disappear at
the censor's first snip.

In the scholarly world, which is that more particularly to be
considered here than the entertainment trades, the situation has
for over two centuries been much the same, except with a little
less noise: most of that also of a self-laudatory kind, in connection
with the expurgation proudly wreaked on the materials in both
the collecting and publishing. Where the undoctored originals have
been preserved by chance, and can be compared with the collectors' published volumes, the pathetic wishy-washiness and coy
expurgation of the latter, as opposed to the rough power and direct-
ness of the originals, makes for heart-rending reading. I do not
know of any exception other than Herd, from Percy's faked
Reliques in 1765, to the folksong manuscripts of Baring-Gould,
Cecil Sharp, and John A. Lomax, at the turn of the twentieth
century, every one of which gives mute evidence of the astonishing
irresponsibility of even the best of scholars and collectors when

it is merely a matter of expurgating a little folk-sex for publication, whether popular or scholarly. There is also generally some foppish pretention of improvement to be discerned — admitted or not — most often in the form of diddley-dumpty finger-counted re-arrangements of those wantonly irregular prosodic feet that are a principal characteristic of real folksong. In the past (and, at the popular level, right up to the present), there has never been any hesitation either, in cobbling together conflated texts out of the chopped-up, sexless, and often meaningless fragments with which these gentlemen then find themselves left.

What is the background of this impossible situation, which has created the falsified record of synthetic folksong which is neither scholarly enough for real scholars nor 'popular' enough to be accepted by the folk? Until the early 18th century, neither scholarship nor the entertainment trades concerned themselves often with folksong in English. The religious censorship considered such material definitely harmful, and put itself in the forefront of its parodying and expurgation; though the legal censorship did not consider popular art of this kind worthy of notice except on a political basis. The folksongs and broadside ballads were freely printed, as long as they did not meddle with politics, since the time of Henry VIII. No one ever dreamed that folksongs could damage the morals of the dairymaids who sang the original songs — and who are regularly seduced in them, suggesting an origin in fact — and to whom the broadsides' parodies of the songs were then sold by itinerant buskers, as in the well-known scene in *A Winter's Tale* iv. iii, in which only the elegant Perdita fore-warns the ballad-seller, Autolycus, 'that he use no scurrilous words in's tunes,' a warning patently intended as a jest or bull.

The folksongs of the sixteenth century in England were hand-somely collected in Ravenscroft's tune-books (now being re-printed), and in various manuscripts such as the Percy Folio and the Rawlinson poetic MSS., with the erotic songs indiscriminately mixed in, which was evidently the way the singers gave them and still do. Throughout the seventeeth century, folksongs and ballads continued to appear, without any notion of expurgation, in the drolleries and songbooks, intermixed with satirical songs and finally with the political parodies that so signally harmed the viability of the originals in appropriating their tunes, as had been attempted — but not so successfully achieved — by the earlier religious 'counterfeits.' After the Restoration, and in particular during the 1680's, it is unquestionable that bawdy song was

particularly in demand, as also the less popular but very similar
inspirations of erotic poetry, ranging from the romantic lovers'
sighs to the violently anti-gallant and obscene satires of the manuscript and printed literature circulating about the Earl of Roches
ter. The song collections continued unexpurgated, and in increasing size, right up to the final edition of Playford & Durfey's
Pills to Purge Melancholy, in 1719–20 (several times reprinted),
and *The Musical Miscellany,* ten years later, which is also in six
volumes and an equally valuable source, though it is extremely
rare and has never been reprinted. Anyone who cares to trace the
history of modern folksongs in English — whether erotic or otherwise — must begin work in the manuscripts, the drolleries, and
the songbooks of the sixteenth, seventeenth, and early eighteenth
centuries. The songbooks have been superbly indexed by Prof.
Cyrus Day and Miss Murrie, but the drolleries and the earlier
poetic manuscripts have not. There is a wonderfully valuable
project for somebody, based on the Harding MS. indexes.

After 1720, the expurgated and imitative folksongs began to
appear, edited in the first instance by Allan Ramsay and his 'ingenious young gentlemen' for the *Tea-Table Miscellany* published
by him in Edinburgh, and afterwards in the tittivated travesties
used in the ballad-operas, such as Ramsay's own *Gentle Shepherd;*
a genre which evolved into the curse of so-called 'popular songs'
today. As recently, at that date, as only a dozen years before,
there had appeared the entirely unexpurgated *Choice Collection
of Comic and Serious Scots Poems,* also published in Edinburgh,
by James Watson (1706–11, reprinted 1869, in a private edition
limited to 165 copies), which, though it contains little folksong,
includes at least one of the most superb madsongs, of folk-inspira-
tion, in the English language, "Halloo My Fancie," and the
touching lullaby, "Balow, My Boy," both of which appear earlier
in the Percy Folio; and, at the opening of Part III, the "Flyting
betwixt Polwart and Montgomery," an alliterative contest-in-
insult of a very ancient and obscene style. One may perhaps see
a survival of this form in the Negro-American "Dozens," as studied
by Dr. John Dollard in *American Imago* (1939) I. 3-24; and Dr.
Roger Abrahams in *Journal of American Folklore* (1962) vol.
75: p. 209-20, with relatively unexpurgated texts.

It is clear that, despite their Scottish patriotism, Ramsay and
his young men had already come under the alien English influence, rising from the Union of the two countries, which simply
meant of course the domination of Scotland by England; and that

the side that they were taking was very much that of the emerging middle-class and its repressive sexual ethic. The fate of the broadside ballads is an excellent example of this development. The broadsides had long been collected by educated fanciers of them, and were first reprinted in book form as early`as the 1580's by Anthony Munday, in his *Banquet of Daintie Conceits* (see George Daniel *Catalogue*, 1864, no. 1154), and even earlier by Clement Robinson in his *Handefull of Pleasant Delites,* a work which attempts to pass itself off as a collection of the love-sonnets then in vogue, though it does not contain a single one. For well over a century the broadsides continued to be collected, most famously by Pepys, though his was only one of many collections. When, however, formal collections of broadsides finally came to be reprinted, in the self-conscious 1720's the very first such collection, that attributed to Ambrose Phillips and David Mallet, was selected and published on the open expurgatory principle.

One of the most curious examples of that humorless Teutonic *Charlataneria eruditorum* satirized by Mencken, Rector of the University of Leipzig, in 1713, as by Sebastian Brant and Erasmus in their *Ship of Fools* and *Praise of Folly,* not to mention Rabelais in *Gargantua & Pantagruel,* centuries before, is the fact that the current and accepted mode of scholarly publication of folksongs was originally invented to parody the impertinent and intrusive pseudo-erudition of learned commentators in their annotations upon ancient poetry. The original application of these methods of satire against scholastic annotation and even falsification of the classics was, of course, Swift's *Battle of the Books* and *Tale of a Tub,* a method turned very soon thereafter to folklore with a brief and charming critical discussion, or *Comment upon the History of Tom Thumb,* by Dr. William Wagstaffe in 1711.

But the masterpiece in this line is assuredly *Le Chef d'Oeuvre d'un Inconnu,* by Hyacinthe Cordonnier (de Bélair), published in La Haye in 1714 under the pretended author's name of "Dr. Chrisostôme Mathanasius," with a superb satirical portrait showing the deeply furrowed brow of this great thinker, and his coat-of-arms — a bellows — with supporters, a jackass and peacock, symbolizing the union of vanity and stupidity. The real author's name appears nowhere in the book, as is only proper; nor, in fact, on any of his many other writings (he was, among others, part-translator of *Robinson Crusoe*), and even his usual pseudonym, "Paul de Saint-Hyacinthe de Thémiseuil," appears only in its initials set to a prefatory Latin poem in praise of the presumed author, Dr. Mathanasius, facing another such poem in Greek (actually in English, but printed in Greek letters), and still another in Hebrew (really in French), along with approbations, permissions, blurbs, &c., which take up a large part of the volume. This sort of turgidity was by no means new, especially as to the prefatory poems, and can be seen to advantage in the Shakespeare Folio of 1623, though most absurdly in English literature in Coryat's *Crudities* even earlier, and in the works of William Cartwright, the detractor of Shakespeare.

This entire edifice is constructed with purposeful topheaviness on a little forty-line folksong — the *Chef d'Oeuvre* in question — on the night-visit of Colin to his beloved's bed, which is surrounded with one hundred and fifty pages of introduction, and eight hundred pages of notes (in its final edition). Upon this rather slender scenario of song, in which Colin's beloved continually warns him, '*Si mon Papa vous entend, Morte je suis,*' is raised a truly magnificent volume of commentary, line by line, with every reference traced and chased to antiquity and beyond; and even — to top the joke — in the last and best edition, published in Paris, 1807, in two volumes, at his own expense, by P.-X. Leschevin, Commissioner of Gunpowder and Saltpeter at Dijon (this part is not a joke), with further and more complete commentaries upon the commentaries — of real bibliographical value, it should be noted.

To avoid any imputation of ungratefulness, the engraved frontispiece of the second part or volume is the portrait of the 'oral source' of the text, the housemaid, shown with the very cup of coffee she was carrying when Dr. Mathanasius heard her singing "L'Autre jour Colin malade." Most editions also give an engraved folding-plate of the music and several perfectly irrelevant archæological finds. As this is hardly enough properly to 'commentate' any folksong text, there are also four indexes, of books and manuscripts cited, authors praised, and authors not praised (whose replies are therefore printed as well), also demigods and devils referred to in the commentary; plus innumerable supplements on every subject conceivably connected with anything previously mentioned (including the archæological discoveries, measured and illustrated, and the Preface to *Don Quixote* in Spanish), and, as aforesaid, notes, *notes*, NOTES to everything, line by line. The final edition of 1807 extends to 1,079 pages in all, and its notes proceed four times through the alphabet from *a* to *iiii*, all based on the forty-line folksong of lovesick Colin and his night-visit.

One would imagine, after such a beginning — imitated in all the languages of Europe, from Alexander Pope's *Peri Bathos, or The Art of Sinking in Poetry,* by "Martin Scriblerus," and Oliver Goldsmith's notes on *Mother Goose,* to the *Vermakelyke Slaatuintjes,* or delights of cabbage-garden verses, of the Dutch humanist, Egbert Schonck of Nijmegen, in 1775, with the text covering one sixth of each page, the rest being devoted to the detailed commentary — that no one would ever undertake thereafter to lavish, in all seriousness, upon any folksong, the inexpendable wealth of hilarious scholarship here poured upon one. But that would be counting without the innate humorlessness of the scholiastic mind.

Before the ink was even dry on Cordonnier's *Chef d'Oeuvre d'un Inconnu* (which went through nine editions itself, not counting the imitations), two very serious-minded gentlemen in Great Britain, Ambrose Phillips, with, it is believed, the assistance of David Mallet, set out to give the world *A Collection of Old Ballads, &c.* (London, 1723–25, in three volumes; reprinted *c.* 1870), in which not only the text was selected on a thoroughly expurgatory basis, as aforesaid, but was further improved with elegant copperplate engravings intended to edify the reader, instead of the crude woodcuts traditional to the broadside format — as still in the Mexican *corridos* — intended to entertain him. Also, and most importantly, the scholarly custom was therein begun, in all seriousness, not of annotating the ballads on the style of Dr. Mathanasius, which would have been bad enough, but of even more certainly spoiling the reader's pleasure in the ballads by preceding each of them with long antiquarian headnotes, 'historical, critical, or humorous,' in which the editors display their erudition, and often their ignorance, as has been standard ever since.

II

ONE UNDERSTANDS that, whatever may happen in the marketplaces of literature, and in the knock-down-&-drag-out business of mass entertainment, there remains always a devoted group of antiquarians and scholars, creeping painstakingly in and about the ivied halls and dusty libraries of institutions of learning; and that in their hands, at least, folksong and folk-traditions are handled with due gentleness and respect, and embalmed with all the footnoted care of the scholarly tradition, even if, as just observed, this tradition is sometimes taken humorlessly far.

Unfortunately, the case is otherwise. It may be shortly said that the entire history of folksong publication in the English language is one of falsification and expurgation for the last two hundred years, and that it has invariably disguised its forgeries and dishonesties behind mealy-mouthed prefatory brags of sexual purity. This is not only true of the earliest popular and *soi-disant* scholarly collections published to compete with *Pills to Purge Melancholy* in the 1720's — the Phillips-Mallet *Collection of Old Ballads* in 1723, and Ramsay's *Tea-Table Miscellany* in 1724 — but of even the most recent as well, from the most scientific, the *Frank C. Brown Collection of North Carolina Folklore* (in seven volumes, under as many editors), to the most shabby and mock-scientific by ignorant and incompetent amateur antiquarians, not to mention the mere popular compilations for the new mass market. Not only the precise style of the *Chef d'Oeuvre d'un Inconnu* became and has remained the norm, and the ideal, of ballad and folksong publication, then and ever since; but — and obviously to the far greater damage of the historical record — the sexual expurgation and falsification engaged in, whether openly or silently, in most of the regional and occupational folksong and ballad collections published over these two centuries, has had the effect of making most of them into waste paper before they were even finished printing.

On the other hand, it is very important to remember that this has not had any effect on folksong. Only on the printed collections. The songs themselves have not been lost, or, if they have, it has not been solely because of their sexuality. They have merely escaped the attention, until now, of certain collectors of folksong in the English-speaking world. There is of course a process of attrition and change, and various profoundly damaging sociological obstacles are now preventing the transmission of authentic folksong and folklore, as discussed in the preceding essay. It is also a fact that the sexual songs are among the longest lived, partly because they tend to have the best tunes — as both Luther and Wesley complained — but just as essentially because they mean a great deal to the people who sing them, probably a great deal more than the songs about Robin Hood, Captain Kidd, Jesse James, and other criminals, glozed over as these may be with all the bogus historical glamour of Merrie England and the Wild West.

Only in the English-speaking world today do reputable folklore scholars and folksong 'specialists' still lend themselves to the shabby concealments of falsification and expurgation. In the eighteenth century this had already become standard, most of the collectors in England vying with each other noisily as to who could expurgate most; and that is the anachronistic ethic to this day of the traditional or 'Child Ballad' collectors and scholars. One can hardly do more than quote a few examples from the very long tradition here, beginning with Allan Ramsay, who announced in the ninth edition of the *Tea-Table Miscellany* in 1731:

> In my compositions and collections, I have kept out all smut and ribaldry, that the modest voice and ear of the fair singer might meet with no affront.

The same proud boast, rephrased, will be found in the whole series of folksong compilations following, as cited in Henry A. Burd's biography of Joseph Ritson, who created the modern scholarly ethic in his indignant attacks on the protofaker, Bishop Percy, and the falsified edition of the *Percy Folio MS.* issued in 1765 as the *Reliques* of English popular poetry. One might begin with the plagiarist, Thomson, whose *Orpheus Caledonius* pirated Ramsay (though with a bit less expurgation), Benjamin Wakefield's *Warbling Muses,* Edward Capell's *Prolusions* (1760, in which 'A regard to the beauty of his page, and no other consideration,' induced this editor — almost alone of all — to renounce the ostentation of headnotes, leaving a simple blank in their stead), John Aitkin's *Essays on Song Writing,* and finally Ritson's own *Select Collection of English Songs* in 1783, which, though it did not actually falsify a single word, is just as solicitous as Ramsay, half a century earlier, in the underlying process of selection, to exclude:

> Every composition, however celebrated, or however excellent of which the slightest expression, or the most distant allusion could have tinged the cheek of delicacy, or offended the purity of the chastest ear.

It would probably be considered too psychoanalytic to observe that all these gentlemen seemed to be laboring under the mistaken impression that the chastity of women is principally affronted by means of the *ear,* and were very concerned about not doing so. In point of fact, this is an ancient folk-idea as well, as is very clearly expressed in the miracle of the Annunciation.

Thirty years after Ritson's *Select Collection,* Dr. Bowdler's expurgated Shakespeare and Gibbon made him a byword of ridicule among the few stalwart souls still left to object, yet it was hardly more than the ultimate extension — silently continued in our own day in most 'students' Shakespeares and Herricks — of a movement that had already castrated every English poet *but* Shakespeare by 1783, and Alexander Pope had already started that. Folklore collectors today, who apparently understand the scholarly ethic created by Ritson in his attacks on Bishop Percy's falsifications two hundred years ago, and who speak and write contemptuously of Percy's *Reliques,* will and do still sit down today at their typewriters, to fake for publication their field-collected texts of songs, folktales, proverbs, and the like (and even officiously attempt to assist in this same way with texts collected by other people, and submitted to them for 'editing'), exactly as did Percy and later Peter Buchan with a quill pen; yet think nothing of this transpicuous dishonesty, because the 'only' parts they are cutting out and smoothing over are the sexual parts.

One of the most regrettable and absurd aspects of the whole matter is that, simultaneously, in the publication of the far less interesting and less important broadside ballads, which are seldom traditional and even less often poetry — being generally the worst of doggerel — there has not been any expurgation at all, even in the English-speaking world, for over a hundred years! Under the eagle-eye and uncompromising scholarship of Dr. Frederick Furnivall, broadside ballad reprints have been faithful down to the last comma, since 1868, at which date Prof. Francis J. Child withdrew from the publication of the *Percy Folio Supplement,* owing to Furnivall's insistence on publishing it unexpurgated and complete. Nevertheless, the ballad reprints are and were published by exactly the same societies, and sometimes by the same university presses or commercial publishers who are still printing the faked and expurgated regional and occupational collections. How is that to be explained?

One explanation offered, perhaps sardonically, is that the *old spelling* of the broadside ballads hides the impropriety, as in Chaucer and in the Child Ballad of "Crow and Pye" (No. 111), which was in any case then omitted from the Sargent-Kittredge 'students' edition of Child. The old spelling is not it. One of the best collections of the sea chanteys, that of Mr. William Doerflinger, was published in the United States in 1951, one hundred percent expurgated, from *un*expurgated recordings made in a sailors' rest home, by Dr. Mary Barnicle among others. Aside from several dozen songs visibly curtailed of their most essential lines (with three discreet little dots . . . for cenotaph), in only one case is there even the traditional Elizabethan *etc.* to suggest that something is missing: in "Ratcliffe Highway," p. 115. In a single ballad, "The *Ebenezer*," p. 201, the expected rhyme gives the only hint as to what was omitted, in the way of a traditional comparison:

> Our bread was tough as any brass
> And our meat was as salt as Lot's wife's . . .

It would have been pretty daring, now wouldn't it, to have given the rhyme? The publisher of the volume in question was the same who was simultaneously publishing the famous bitch-heroine best-seller, *Forever Amber,* with almost no holds barred. *Forever Amber* is not in the old spelling either.

The explantion is simply this: Folksong publication, especially in America, had no one of Furnivall's courage and intransigeance to follow. Instead, it has followed Prof. Child, and has therefore irretrievably and unnecessarily crippled itself; nor will the texts that were censored and rejected then, be found today. Furnivall was not a man who would allow the slightest tergiversation with the scholarly ethic, in which he *believed,* and which was not something by means of which he made his living — to abandon if it would put that living in danger. That is all there is to the problem, then and now, Furnivall left the *Oxford English Dictionary,* of which he was the originator, when the boys'-school principal who was made its editor insisted upon expurgating it; nor did Furnivall return later when the final editors made fools of themselves, and a joke of their earlier cowardice, by sneaking the omitted words all back in again, under the old spelling (*n.b.*), at Chaucer's and Andrew Marvell's 'quaint,' and 'windfucker.' (For reasons unknown, 'cock' had not been omitted, nor any of the scatological terms.)

Prof. Child took a very different tack from Furnivall, and, as noted above, withdrew from the editorship of the *Percy Folio* — of which the publication had been undertaken at his request, after a century of withholding by the Percy family to avoid exposure — when Furnivall refused to expurgate it. Furnivall therefore had to publish the final volume of the *Percy Folio* himself, the other editors, Child and Hales, having refused to allow the use of their names on this supplementary volume of "Loose and Humorous Songs." (A later reprint, by the De La More Press, in 1905, cleverly splits up the text into four volume also, but the fourth volume does not include the "Loose and Humorous Songs"!) The whole idea of a separate group or supplement, incidentally, does not stem in any way from the *Folio Manuscript* itself, but was an improvement added originally by Percy, who marked all the sexual songs for omission, by means of three cautionary crosses, while he was hacking together the collection of fakes of the rest of the text, which he issued as the *Reliques*.

Prof. Child's withdrawal from the resulting "Loose and Humorous" volume sufficiently indicates the attitude of mind that led or forced him to omit from the five volumes of his own great *English and Scottish Popular Ballads* (Boston, 1882–98) all ballads offending the then-prevailing standards of decency, in Boston; even the ancient and humorous "Sea Crab" ballad, of the existence of which he could hardly have been unconscious since the oldest text in English is that in the *Percy Folio Manuscript*. Despite certain complaints he made, as for instance in headnoting "The Keach i' the Creel" (No. 281, v. 122) that 'No one looks for decorum in pieces of this description, but a passage in this ballad, which need not be particularized, is brutal and shameless almost beyond example;' the fact of the matter is that Child simply asterisked out the passages he did not care to print, as in "The Knight and Shepherd's Daughter" (No. 110; II. 464, 471 ff.), in "The Jolly Beggar" (No. 279; v. 112–13, particularly regrettable since the Pepys Ballad expurgated here — though Child says, v. 109n., he cannot omit 'all ribaldry' like Ramsay — is not included in the presumably complete edition of Pepys' collection by Hyder Rollins), and, for that matter, on the last page Child ever published, "The Trooper and Maid" No. 299; v. 307).

Acting on these sufficiently broad hints, the 'students' edition of the Child Ballads, abridged by Helen Child Sargent with the assistance of Child's greatest student and only successor, George Lyman Kittredge — who obviously knew better, but was trapped — meticulously omits even the few remaining humorous or pastoral ballads that might conceivably have proved too 'high-kilted' (the word is Sir Walter Scott's, quoted by Kittredge in Child, v. 398) for the nascent Ph.D.'s in English literature, of 1904. Since that time, and with infinitesimal exceptions, the entire modern ballad and folksong literature in the English language, now in the principal half century of its publication, has been totally expurgated, except for one stupefying theme now to be considered.

With all the diplomacy and understanding in the world, a person begins to get a little bit impatient. And one asks oneself: What is it, then, that *can* be printed without disgracing an American folklorist, without shaming his wife and mother, or — which is really the plain truth of it, nowadays at least — without getting him fired, as feared, from his university job? Well, what has been printed? Anyone who cares to examine the five volumes of Prof. Child's stupendously researched *English and Scottish Popular Ballads* — the monument and cynosure of Anglo-American folksong scholarship — from the analytic point of view, just this once, will be struck not so much by what has been left out in the way of sex (and scatology, which seems to have been left in, as in "Kinge and Miller," No. 273, Appendix III; vol. v. 84–87), as by what has been left in, in the way of sadism. The idea seems to be, exactly as with Bishop Percy and his three cautionary crosses, on the one hand, and howling forgeries on the other, that murder and treachery are regrettable, no doubt, but are folklore and are to be left in; but that sex is too awful to print without an apology, and so had better be left out.

Child's influence has stunted and stultified ballad collecting in more directions than just that of bawdry, and as this influence has never been challenged — except to the degree that it has now become a bit difficult to collect in the field the ballads he chose as 'traditional' — it is not to be expected that its underlying preconceptions, on the ethical level, would be noticed at all. The obvious result has been not only the rejection of field-collected erotic ballads, but also the fact that simply as a problem in library boondoggling, or scholarly documentation, the bawdy ballad has not yet been adequately handled — or, in fact, handled at all — by those most competent to do so. Child's lead in explicitly omitting and expurgating this whole aspect of the ballad, which is certainly one of the most important in any literary, musical, or simply human sense, has been followed by all his progeny almost without exception. Since 1900 there have been, according to one count, over six hundred ballad and song collections (popular and scholarly) publicly published in English, not one of them without almost-total sexual expurgation.

There is a macabre contradiction here which, as I have already devoted a hundred-page pamphlet to attacking it as it expresses itself in far broader areas of popular culture, it seems worthwhile only to touch upon now. And that is that it is only *sex* which these scholarly and semi-scholarly gentry find it necessary to expurgate from their endless subsidized volumes on the folksongs and ballads of every profession, every country, every state, province, and territory, every ethnic group, every mountain-range, river, stream, brook, creek, and dried-out waddy in which only the sparest-ribbed of hungry cows can be persuaded to stumble and munch that dubiously folk fodder later to be regurgitated for their Ph.D. theses, their Sunday afternoon crumpet-bashes to entertain the ladies' clubs, their midnight 'folksong' bars complete with brand-new guitar or genuwine hillbilly dulcimer. *No sex!*

However — hangings? local murders? love-betrayals? cruel and unusual humiliations? piracy, mutiny, shipwreck . . . torture and cannibalism too, if you please? railroad wrecks *ad naus.*, with every scream and gurgle of the dying? All your stomach will bear, and sometimes a good deal more. But — no sex. After which, the primest specimens are then strung together and published, with the music, and long bibliographical headnotes referring solely to other collections of similar innocuous stuff, and otherwise threshing nothing but old straw, as the 601st and 602nd volumes since Child, on university money if such is to be obtained.

In at least one case this concentration on sadistic folk-material is so self-evident, that some inspired or perverted reader (hard to know which) has gone to the trouble of listing inside the front cover of the copy in the New York University Library all the more deliciously gruesome items, on a one-, two-, and three-asterisk marking system, according to the amount and quality of the grue. The work is Hyder Rollins' *Pepysian Garland,* in which is gathered what Prof. Rollins felt to be the flower of the Pepys Collection at Cambridge, leaving unwary buyers to pay for the rest (since the *Garland* materials are all omitted) in the dozen dry volumes then published by Harvard as *The Pepys Ballads,* and subsequently remaindered as unsaleable. These stall-ballads of the 16th and 17th centuries, with their woodcut-illustrated horrors, hangings, and other attractive marvels, were the combined murder-mysteries and comic-books of Pepys' time. For a discussion of the similar — God knows the far greater — substitution of an allowed sadism for a censored sexuality in the murder-mysteries, comic-books, etc., of our time, I may refer the reader to my own rigorously understated discussion in *Love & Death: A Study in Censorship* (New York: Breaking Point, 1949).

Nowhere in the entire ballad literature is this substitution of an allowed sadism for a censored sexuality more strikingly displayed than in Prof. Child's own five volumes. Anyone who will examine these three hundred and five ballads with this point in

mind, will immediately be overwhelmed, beginning at No. 4, with
the killings, the drownings, the stabbings, the poisonings (with
all the subsequent agony, down to that of the pet dog, for comedy
relief: in "Lord Randal," No. 12J and following), the decapi-
tations, the burnings alive ("Lady Maisry," No. 65), the hearts torn
out and eaten, with the magistral note, No. 269, telling and re-
telling this horrible story back through ten languages and several
dialects, to Boccaccio and Guilhem de Cabestan; the bodies of
dead women — down to the knucklebones and teeth and tongue —
turned into musical instruments by way of 'buffoonery' (No. 10A,
"The Twa Sisters." 1. 121); the absolute Walpurgisnacht of killing and maiming of children, or burying them alive, in "Leesome
Brand," No. 15; "The Cruel Mother," No. 20, *et passim;* not to
overlook the ancient pogrom-fodder of "Hugh of Lincoln," No.
155, which is for some reason the one ballad still picked to teach
children in American public schools; and "Lamkin," No. 93D,
with the false nurse who:

> . . . rammed the silver bolt up the baby's nose,
> Till the blood it came trinkling down the baby's fine clothes;

the studied gruesomeness and perversion of the "The Three
Ravens," No. 26 — which might easily have been written by one
of the literary gangsters of the 'new freedom,' in an earlier rein-
carnation — where a pregnant doe, 'As great with yong as she
might goe,' lifts up the bloody head of a dead knight to kiss his
wounds (to be compared with the entirely gratuitous details into
which Prof. Child enters as to the perverted Peter the Great slob-
bering over the decapitated head of "Mary Hamilton," No. 173);
and — just to have begun with — the plain ordinary lust-murders
of the Jack-the-Ripper type, retold in song, in "Babylon," No. 14,
and "Lady Isabel and the Elf-Knight," No. 4, which, as earlier
observed, is the opening gong of the whole collection and keynote
to its method of treatment, with thirty-two pages of headnote on
bride-murdering in all times & climes — three-quarters of which
have nothing whatsoever to do with the ballad — to introduce five-
and-one-half pages of text.

There is, of course, not one whit of doubt that the folk concentration on these terrible themes implies and involves an equally
terrible anxiety — and guilt — but neither Prof. Child nor any
of his successors seem often to have shared it. They do not even
seem to be aware that some of this stuff on which they lavish their
years of scholarly attention and critical appraise (as when Child

observes at No. 291 that 'the last two stanzas are unusually successful' in describing the blood and pieces of skin and flesh of a man
torn apart by four horses and dripping on the rushes), can be
assessed as something other than 'traditional.' Nor do they inquire,
nor have they ever inquired, why, if all this, and to such a degree,
and to an amount never before crowded within the pages of any
one work except perhaps the Bible, and with such a fine German-
university drone bass of page-references to those unquoted and
unquotable Scandinavian congeners and cognates, where even
more blood is spilt and licked up, and more bodies hacked to bits
and eaten (if they are anything like No. 269), but of which our sadly
abridged Anglo-Scottish balladry has deprived us — or, rather,
would have deprived us, but for our scholarly labors with Child —
why the simple normality of sexual intercourse has got to be
apologized for and deprecated, or silently left out every time.

These concentrations have by no means come to an end in the
presumed liberation of the 'revival' folksong movement of recent
years. One has instead seen exactly the same thing operating, but
in the entertainment context, with — even among the so-called
leftwing singers who created the revival, since the 1930's — war
ballads, industrial ballads, and so forth, but those of not too insistent a social consciousness: just men killed 'fightin' the steamham-
mer' (where the sexual element dares hardly surge up except in
symbols), or under the lash of 'Black Betty,' the prison-camp whip.
Among the neo-folksingers making no pretention to liberalism, not
even these subterfuges are engaged in, and the concentration is,
among other matters, on great disasters such as breaking dams,
train-wrecks and sinking ships, which are, in fact, the last subjects
on which authentic folk-ballads in the *corrido* style have been
written in modern times in English, ending just before World War
I with "The Wreck of the Old '97" and "The Sinking of the
Titanic." Finally, and most prominently, there are of course the
ballads of crime, treachery and atrocity, which take place principally in the Scottish highlands and the Western badlands, so it
would be practically unpatriotic to object; and the plain murder-
ballads, especially those in which the victims are women, while the
homey and friendly singer gloats in anticipation over his victim's
terror, almost in an aside: 'Pretty Polly, I was diggin' on your
grave the best part o' last night.'

Far from representing any excesses of recent singer-enter-
tainers, these are also the concentrations of all the regional and
industrial folksong collections published, or, rather, appear to be

their concentration since the sex-ballads have been rejected and omitted, exactly in the tradition of Prof. Child. This is even the case in the secondary works, such as indexes, that have stemmed from the Child Ballad canon, as for instance — and this is far from the only instance that could be given — Dr. Laws' syllabus of modern folk-ballads from broadsides, which cannot find any better way to demonstrate "Ballad Recomposition" than by giving *in extenso* (the only such presentation in the work) eighteen pages of texts and treatment, complete with stemma of relationships, of a single ballad — none other than "Pretty Polly," as above — in which a young man murders the girl he is tired of, who goes down on her knees before him and begs, 'Johnny dear dont murder me for I am big with child.' The rest is a little too rough to quote here.

The reason why it has been possible for all this truly repulsive sadism and perversion to be printed by university presses, where nobody has cared to call attention to it until now, is partly that it is mixed in with the small amount of normal sexual material and humor that leavens the mass, and keeps people from observing what is really the principal content — no matter how many IBM machines they may strain all the 'themes' and 'traits' and 'motifs' through. The time has perhaps now come to make use of somewhat of the same astuteness, but going in the opposite direction. It is time to mix in a little bit of normality — a bit of normal eroticism and healthy scatological humor, even if this involves the desperate courage of rhyming 'brass' with 'arse' — right along with the murder and perversion, in order to *get away* with the crime of dealing with what is normal instead of what is abnormal and sadistic. Naturally, one does not want to go so narrow-mindedly far as to say that the murder and perversion are the part that ought to be considered 'unprintable.' That wouldn't be free speech. Free speech means plenty of murder and blood and perversion, but no sex. Or no sex, unless one is willing to fight it to the Supreme Court, if necessary; separately — like *Lady Chatterley's Lover* — in every one of the fifty states, and England.

It is almost time to stop apologizing for sex. And begging for fair play for sexual intercourse, as though it were no worse, really, than murder. As far as bawdy ballads and erotic folklore generally are concerned, they simply cannot be compared to the anti-social and anti-human bent of the non-bawdy and non-erotic kind, by and large. Omitting from the discussion the outhouse epigraphs and obscene limericks — of which the latter are in any case the folklore almost solely of the college group, students and teachers alike

— no person can produce, in any language, any erotic ballad or song concerning homosexual cannibalism or lust-murder or any of the rest of it. The closest one can come to it are some symbolic deaths, as in "The Great Wheel," based on sex-hatred and the sadistic concept of coitus. As a matter of fact, in twenty-five years of collecting, I have encountered only three sea-songs that even mention homosexuality at all. And no cannibalism. For cannibalism you will have to go to the ballad of "The Eaten Heart," in the Child Ballads and elsewhere, and to the high humor of "Little Billee" in the *Bab Ballads*.

Erotic ballads and songs are supposed to amuse normal people, and express their emotions, or even excite them. Is that wrong? Murdering pregnant women by beating them over the head with gate-posts does not amuse normal people: it turns their stomachs, or makes them reach for a gun. It will not be found in any collection of erotic ballads and songs, or any other kind of erotic folklore, in any language. It will be found only in ballads like "The Gosport Tragedy" and "The Wexford Girl," in the lily-pure pages of university press syllabi, and in the joyously unconscious record of the first full-length study of the genre, Olive Woolley Burt's *American Murder Ballads* (1958). That is a great title. There is a book they put in a cage in Russia, and show to folklore students as an example of American culture.

But finally, if all these things can be published — in and out of the universities — and nobody turns a hair; can it possibly be true, can grown men and women, even in the universities, bring themselves fearfully to believe, that "Blow the Candle Out" is too erotic, "The Ram of Darby" too ruttish, "The Ball of Kirriemuir" too orgiastic, "The Red Light Saloon" too alcoholic, "Christopher Columbo" too adventurous, "The Bastard King of England" too illegitimate, and "Bollocky Bill the Sailor" too testicular to print?

III

CONTRARY to what might be imagined, the principal difficulty in finally coming to grips with the history and development of bawdy song in English folklore, over the last two centuries, stems rather from the excessively large amount of recent material available, than from any lack. What is lacking is the historical record. Although, at the level of open and ordinary publication, Playford & Durfey's *Pills to Purge Melancholy* (1719–20) and *The*

Musical Miscellany (1729–31) marked the end of the bawdy song in print, the main effect of this withdrawal of the advantages of publication from erotic folk materials in English was simply to restrict such materials, by and large, to the oral transmission and the purely folk level, at which they are in any case far more certain of survival. In addition, as will be seen, certain very broad literary traces do exist, and these have become all the more precious now that the oral transmission even of erotic folklore and folksong in English is beginning to be damaged, to a serious degree, by the competition of the synthetic and commercial popular arts which have already almost entirely killed off all the non-erotic forms of folklore.

It is one of the paradoxes of communication that paper and glass, which are among the most fragile of human inventions, long outlast the monuments of metal and stone, and can far more surely be entrusted with the transmission of human history and knowledge. How much is left of the Sphinx, and what Champollion could discover her riddle just from the evidence of the stones? Where is the Colossus of Rhodes, of 'triple and eternal brass,' and what would we know of it except for the record of brittle papyrus rolls? No less than four photographic works have recently appeared, in as many years, by Anand, Fouchet, Golish, and Daniélou, attempting to explain the monumental erotic sculptures of the love-temples and caves of ancient India. Who could have imagined, when erecting them, that these would ever be thought hard to understand? The paradox is therefore this, that architecture does last a fair while — as centuries go — but that the transmission of *meaning* requires something more fragile and perishable, something more human.

The superiority of paper is, of course, the ease of reproduction and the superior safety of broad dispersal available to the written word. Only one thing, apparently, lasts even longer than the written word, and that is the spoken word: folklore, myths, legends, oral traditions, customs, songs — in a word, that phylogenic part of the history of the human race that the individual attempts to remember and to repeat. Over the last two centuries, however, folklore has become even more perishable than paper, and even paper can now seldom be trusted with it. Immediately on the final driving underground of erotic folklore, in England and Scotland, in the 1730's, or rather its falling back then to almost entirely oral transmission, the false and derivative forms of the same material, in the theatre and in satirical poetry, swelled up to unlimited proportions to replace it. Our present position is no more than a hectic continuation of that, and in an unbroken line.

This is a development that had already begun significantly, nearly a century before, in the Royalist drolleries, many of which contain almost nothing but political parodies — though largely of an erotic or obscene nature. As one striking example, *The Rump* (1662, type-facsimile c. 1872) in two volumes, which had earlier appeared as *Ratts Rhimed to Death, or The Rump-Parliament Hang'd up in the Shambles* (1660), and was reprinted again as *A Collection of Loyal Songs* in 1731, at what was the crisis of the popularity of the political form. Most of the drollery literature of the seventeenth century is mined with this concentration on political and art-poetry — so far as its usefulness as a folk-song source is concerned — and few of the drollery collections will be found to contain any high percentage of folksongs except *Wit and Drollery* (1661, and 1682) and *The New Academy of Complements* (1669, unique copy in the Folger-Shakespeare Library, Washington; reprinted 1671 and 1713). This unusual work has the unmistakable air of attempting to pass itself off as a properly elegant and artistic drollery, though it is really 'only' a collection of folksongs — following the section of models for love-letters — anonymously compiled 'By the most refined Witts of this Age' for the newly-established publisher, Samuel Speed. The relatively large amount of authentic folk material in *Pills to Purge Melancholy,* in 1719–20, is simply due to the great size of the collection in this final edition in six volumes. The actual percentage of folk song in it is not particularly high. Like all late drolleries the work is mostly devoted to art-poems of a more or less erotic nature, and to the theatre parodies of the part-editor, Durfey, and others. This theatre form still exists, in the so-called musical comedies or light-operas in most European cultures, and has from the beginning proved to be the principal enemy of authentic folksong.

It cannot be over-emphasized that what was happening here was not, essentially, an attempt to *expurgate* folksong or folklore, but rather an attempt to *replace* it by the signed and personal compositions of theatre-writers such as Durfey, and publisher-compilers such as Allan Ramsay, whose intention it was to advance themselves — in a personal and pecuniary sense, and at the expense of folklore, evidently — but without any conscious notion of the deeper immorality of what they were doing. Both Durfey and Ramsay engaged equally in expurgation, and both of them (especially Durfey) in a particularly uncharming allusive or nicey-nasty

way that became worse and worse as their century wore on. Their
expurgation was not based on any real moral preconception, except
in a superficial and external way, and was visibly for the purpose
of making their commercial productions palatable to the contemporary audience. Without being in the least cynical, it may
be assumed that had the early-18th century audience shown itself
to prefer bawdy, as it had at the height of the Restoration in
poetry, forty years before, in the 1680's; both Ramsay and Durfey
would probably then have written and published bawdry to suit.
In point of fact, Durfey had done exactly that, at the beginning of
his career in the time of Charles II, and it is mainly his later productions that show the unpleasantly 'knowing' allusiveness most
obvious in "A Dialogue Sung by a Boy and Girl, suppos'd a
Brother and Sister" (in *The Comical History of Don Quixote*,
Part III, 1696), reprinted in *Pills*, 1719, II. 143–4.

When this reverse side of the shotten fabric of expurgation is
examined, it becomes clear that the destruction of folklore and
folksong did not so much rise directly from any socially-demanded
expurgation of the theatre parodies and paraphrases, as from the
parodists' personal intent, which was to replace anonymous folk-
materials — the 'property' of everyone — with the signed and ex-
ploitable productions of self-advancing *entrepreneurs* in both the
theatre and print. We fall here into the whole deepest marasmus of
the emaciation and destruction of folklore, which is seen to be
simply a result of the broad social over-development of *the notion
of private personal worth and position, rather than identification
with the human group.* The glorification of the individual, and of
his 'vertical motility' on the social scale — irrespective of the morality or immorality of the means whereby that glorification and that
'upward' motility are achieved — is closely connected, as is now
well understood, with the increasing power and self-idealization
of the middle-class in the century and a half between the English
and French Revolutions, and of the Protestant or personal-salva-
tion ideals, rather than Catholic religious background, of that class
in the Germanic north, in Switzerland, Holland, Scotland, and
England; centering crucially about the opening of the eighteenth
century.

This subject is very large, and has been handled in classic
fashion by Max Weber (as popularized in English by Tawney). Its
important relation to the literary scene is best exposed in Victor
F. Calverton's *Sex Expression in Literature*, a work now too much
overlooked; and, less well handled, in the more recent 'matrist-

patrist' formulations of G. Rattray Taylor. This question will be returned to again, in the final essay of the present volume, "Who Owns Folklore?" in examining the really disastrous proportions to which has been bloated up, in very recent times, this class-related insistence upon exceptional personal worth and artistic *property,* especially by business enterprisers in the 'entertainment arts' who are patently not artists at all.

The literature of the drolleries, continuing halfway through the eighteenth century, is covered in part in Arthur E. Case's *Bibliography of English Poetical Miscellanies: 1521–1750* (Oxford, 1935), a work importantly enlarged in the listing by Norman Ault in the *Cambridge Bibliography of English Literature* (1940) II. 173–256, which is further based on the holdings of the great W. N. H. Harding collection, in Chicago, Ill. The parallel literature of the *English Song-Books, 1651–1702* — involving much of the same poetry and songs as the drolleries, but in volumes also printing the music — has been magnificently covered by Prof. Cyrus Day and Miss Eleanore Boswell Murrie (Oxford, 1940). Their model volume also includes a first-line index of all the songs in all editions of *Pills to Purge Melancholy,* and of the more than two hundred other song-books covered: some four thousand songs in all. This is a key work in the study of English folksong, and should most certainly be continued at least to 1750 (if not 1850!) by other researchers, a project for which Mr. Harding has apparently prepared much unpublished manuscript material.

The burlesque and satirical poetry, of the first half of the eighteenth century has been covered in part by the work of Prof. Richmond Bond, and a further and fuller bibliography of the subject is announced in preparation by David Foxon, Esq; of the British Museum. It may be observed that there is still a serious gap to fill, between the materials covered by Case and Day & Murrie on the one hand, and Prof. Bond on the other, particularly for the satirical poetry of the second half of the seventeenth century, the period of Butler's *Hudibras* and *Dildoïdes,* and of the Earl of Rochester, his protégés and imitators, and the erotic materials published under his name, which are in large part certainly his work. One of the most significant items in this literature — which continued, of course, well into the 1820's — is *The Found-ling Hospital for Wit,* of 1743–49, anonymously edited by Sir Charles Hanbury Williams, in which, along with a certain amount of folk-balladry and folk-humor only slightly transposed, the whole turning of erotic poetry and folksong parody, in England, to the uses of political satire was finally achieved, and has, in fact, re-mained almost static there, as far as publicly seen, to the present day.

We are far, today, from being the first to have observed the debasing and destroying of folksong and folklore by substitute products of lesser authenticity. As long ago as Shakespeare's time, the young antiquary, Thomas Ravenscroft, set out — at the age of seventeen — to preserve the old folksongs, and rounds and catches of the time of Henry VIII, which he felt were already in danger of loss. (Ravenscroft's songbooks, *Pammelia*, 1609, and its supple-ment, *Deuteromelia*, are now republished by the American Folk-lore Society.) Yet nothing, either in the theatre or in the art-poetry of Shakespeare's time, represented as yet any clear attack on the folksongs. A number of these will, for instance, be found in their complete and apparently traditional form, as sung on the stage by the main comedian in Thomas Heywood's play, *The Rape of Lucrece* in 1608 (enlarged 1638; excellently re-edited by Allan Holaday, University of Illinois, 1950). Other folksongs appear, on any jovial pretext, in a perfectly typical jestbook or rogue-biog-raphy, *The Pinder of Wakefield* . . . 'A Pill fit to purge Melancholy in this drooping age' (1632; edited by E. A. Horsman, Liverpool University Press, 1950). This work transmits certain much older folksongs such as "Tom a Lin," and "A Cobbler would a-wooing ride," the latter being a version of the sixteenth-century "Hogyn" (in Richard Hill's *Common-place Book*, MS. *c.* 1536; ed. Dyboski, Early English Text Society, 1908, Extra Series, vol. 101: song no. 94), which turns on the same scatological 'sell' or catch used earlier in Chaucer's "Miller's Tale."

What was being done casually by the stage comedians and jest-book and drollery compilers of the seventeenth century, in the way of collecting folksongs from living singers, and retailing these songs in literary or sub-literary productions; and had been done purposely, in musical-antiquarian fashion, by Ravenscroft; finally came again to be considered a worthwhile pursuit in the eighteenth century. It is generally but quite erroneously construed that the revival of interest in England, in the folk-poetry (and folksong) of earlier centuries resulted from the publication of Thomas Percy's *Reliques of Ancient English Poetry,* in 1765; and, in Scotland, from the later publications of Robert Burns and Sir Walter Scott. The fact of the matter is the reverse. It was the al-ready very appreciable interest in folk-poetry and ballads that led Percy to 'revise' for publication the early seventeenth-century

Folio Manuscript that he had the wit to save, as it was being taken, leaf by leaf, to light the fire in the house of a friend; as, later, Tischendorf found an even worse fate overtaking the leaves of the *Codex Sinaiticus,* one of the oldest known texts of the Bible, in a monastery on Mount Sinai itself.

In the same way, in Scotland, the antiquarian interest in the older folk-balladry — an interest long preceding that in England — had already been expressed in its most important early publication, James Watson's *Choice Collection of Comic and Serious Scots Poems* (1706–11, 3 vols.; reprinted 1869), issued in a forthright and unexpurgated fashion nearly a century before the activity of Burns and Scott, an activity based largely on revisions and modifications by the poet and novelist-antiquarian themselves. The whole early history of the antiquarian folksong 'movement,' not only in Scotland and England, but also in the Scandinavian countries in which it really began over a century earlier — and from which many of the oldest of the ballads had been transported via Dutch Friesland and Scotland to England — will be found masterfully recorded in S. B. Hustvedt's *Ballad Criticism in Scandinavia and Great Britain* (New York, 1916), a work long out-of-print and even forgotten, but of capital interest to folklore study.

The true originator of the modern movement in the English-speaking world for the collecting of folksong, not from old manuscripts, nor from printed broadside ballads — which were only infrequently folksong at all — nor yet for purposes of popularization, or of enlarging one's own singing repertory; but from the 'mouth of the folk,' and with a clear and purposeful realization of the historical value of such collecting; was David Herd, in Scotland, whose collections were published anonymously as *Ancient and Modern Scottish Songs,* in 1769 (enlarged edition 1776; reprinted 1869 and 1870). Herd's work is signally free from expurgation, even at a period when this had already become the vogue, not only among popular compilers and revisers, but even among the best of scholars, such as Ritson, as earlier discussed. The various materials that Herd did not publish have almost all been printed since, by Prof. Hans Hecht, as *Songs from David Herd's Manuscripts* (1904), a work in which the point is several times made — as also in Henley & Henderson's 'Centenary' edition of Burns' poetry, earlier — that Herd's manuscripts had certainly in part been used by Burns in his work on revising Scottish folksongs for the *Scots Musical Museum,* but just as certainly without knowledge of their source. This controversial point has already been dealt with, at the end of the essay, "*The Merry Muses* as Folklore," all of which is of relevance here, as to the undisguised expurgation of the folk-materials by Burns.

Enough has also been said, in the same essay and in that preceding it, on Burns' *Merry Muses of Caledonia* (not published until about 1800, four years after the poet's death), from some of which eighty-five texts — in part his own, and in part folk-collected — Burns' art and patriotism were able to distil, and considered it desirable to distil, handsome, if politely expurgated versions, for publication in James Johnson's *Scots Musical Museum* (1787–1803) and George Thomson's more elegant *Select Collection of Original Scotish Airs* (1793 *ff*.) The measure of Burns' success is — for better or for worse — "Comin' Thro' the Rye," which remains well-loved and classic with the expurgation of hardly more than one stanza and one word: into 'kiss,' on the style of modern bawdy jokes being culled for radio transmogrification under the rule of thumb, 'Can you do it with *kissing?*'

The most curious aspect of Burns' method of procedure is his substitution, on occasion, of patriotic geography for erotic detail, as in the song "Andrew an' his Cuttie Gun," of which the chorus is given thus in *The Merry Muses:*

> Blythe, blythe, blythe was she,
> Blythe was she but and ben,
> An' weel she lo'ed it in her nieve,
> But better when it slippit in.

In Burns' published version the last two lines become:

> Blythe was she by the banks of Earn
> And blythe in Glenturit glen.

The full-fisted original makes clear what it is that one senses so false and forced about these all-too-many 'blythes.' Several further examples of this kind of impact of print on bawdy song — or, rather, lack of impact — will be found in Sydney Goodsir Smith's remarkable article on Burns and *The Merry Muses*, in *Arena* (London, 1950, No. 4; reprinted with expurgations in *Hudson Review*, New York, 1954, vol. VII), which was unfortunately not used to introduce the important new reprint of *The Merry Muses* (1959) edited by Mr. Smith and Prof. DeLancey Ferguson.

Mr. Oscar Brand, whose further contribution to bawdy song will be given deserved credit below, notes two elegant examples of Burns' own expurgation, in an article "In Defense of Bawdy Ballads" (in *Modern Man*, Skokie, Illinois, January 1957, p. 52); Burns 'popularising a sedate version of "Green Grow the Rashes," while other Scotsmen still sang:

> Green grow the rashes, O,
> Green grow the rashes, O,
> The sweetest bed that e'er I got
> Was the bellies o' the lasses, O.

While "John Anderson, My Jo" . . . used far more robust language than the tender rewrite [by Burns] we sing today:

> See that you grip me fast, John,
> Until that I cry, Oh;
> Your back shall crack, ere I cry, Slack,
> John Anderson, my jo.'

(The end of the third line here is actually given as 'or I do that,' in the original *Merry Muses;* the inner rhyme suggesting a later hand.) It is almost cruel to compare any stanza of the original with Burns' 'tender rewrite,' referred to, as to the old lovers who have climbed the hill of life together, and:

> Now we maun totter down, John,
> And hand in hand we'll go;
> And sleep thegither at the foot,
> John Anderson, my jo.

The fact is that, in this case, Burns' expurgation — he was not proud of these; he did them out of what he thought was his duty to Scottish folksong — turns on a symbolization or partialization of one of the most striking stanzas of the original, on the husband's advancing impotence, which is still present in the form now alive in folk transmission in Scotland:

> John Anderson, my jo, John,
> When first that ye began,
> Ye had as good a tail-tree
> As ony ither man;
> But now its waxen wan, John,
> And wrinkles to and fro;
> [I've t]wa gae-ups for ae gae-down,
> [John] Anderson, my jo.

With what other expurgation the Scots collectors before Burns tormented their materials — from Watson and Ramsay (though surely not Herd), to Sir Walter Scott and others since — will probably only be known on the completion of Mr. Hamish Henderson's broad project, already well advanced, at the School of Scottish Studies, University of Edinburgh, of recording for publication the entire body of modern Scottish folksong; while refusing, as Mr. Henderson says in the Foreword to his *Ballads of World War II* (Glasgow, 1947), 'to insult these ballads by bowdlerising them.'

The tolerance really accorded bawdy song in Scotland, behind the centuries of Presbyterian fulmination against it, is made very clear in a preachment reported from some time in the 1690's, in *Scotch Presbyterian Eloquence Display'd*, anonymously edited by Gilbert Crockat and John Monroe (Rotterdam, 1738) p. 134:

> Mr. Kirton, in *October* last, preaching on Hymns, and Spiritual Songs, told the People, "There be four kinds of Songs, Profane Songs, Malignant, Allowable, and Spiritual Songs. Prophane Songs, *My Mother sent me to the Well, She had better gone her self, For what I got I dare not tell, But Kind* Robin *loves me.* Malignant Songs, such as *He, Ho,* Gillicrankie, *And the King enjoys his own again;* against which I have not much to say. *Thirdly,* Allowable Songs, like *Once I lay with another Man's Wife.* Ye may be allowed Sirs to sing this, but I do not say, you are allowed to do this, for that's a great deal of Danger indeed. *Lastly,* Spiritual Songs, which are the Psalms of *David.*"

The quotation here kindly recorded by Mr. Kirton is the only fragment still surviving of the old text of "Kind Robin Loves Me," one of an important group of Scottish songs expressing the daughter's resistance to, and defiance of, the mother's control of her sexual activities, as, most strikingly, in "My Mither's Ay Glowran' O'er Me," in Ramsay's *Tea-Table Miscellany* (ed. 1871, I. 63–4; and compare p. 103–5). The polite form of "Kind Robin" is given by Herd (ed. 1869) I. 311. The song "(When) Once I Lay with Another Man's Wife," parodied in *The Beggar's Opera,* was either based on a play on words, or has since been so disguised, as it survives in the form of a toast, still sometimes heard:

> Here's to the happiest hours of my life,
> Spent in the arms of another man's wife —
>   My Mother!

After which, little more need be said as to the Oedipal strivings, in the strict Freudian sense, involved in these songs and jests.

IV

No DEFINITION of the words 'erotic,' or 'bawdy,' so far as they are connected with folklore, literature, and art — or even, for that matter, the meaninglessly meticulous alliteration of the legal formula as to literature that is 'lewd, lustful, lascivious, indecent or obscene' — has any real meaning except in relation to some definite historical period. It is simply a truism now, after the lifetime spent fighting for this one point by the late Theodore Schroeder, that the conception of 'obscenity' is entirely fluid and subjective, both historically and geographically, and connects itself to quite different areas of the human body, and of human activity, in differing places and times. All that seems to remain constant is the ambivalent feeling, of attraction and fear, that invests whatever is agreed, in any given culture, to be obscene.

The black-letter ballads, beloved of young maidens of the sixteenth century, as in Shakespeare's Autolycus scene, in the *Winter's Tale,* iv. iii. 180–292, and in Ben Jonson's similar Nightingale scene, less well known; had become almost too 'coarse,' too 'offensive,' too 'rank' to bear reprinting in the *Shirburn Ballads,* edited in 1907 — at the height of the so-called 'Naughty Naughts' — by Andrew Clark, editor-expurgator also of Aubrey's *Brief Lives.* In the same way and time, many of the charming English country lovesongs of the nineteenth century, of the "Seeds of Love" type, appeared wholly unprintable to such collectors as the Rev. Sabine Baring-Gould and Cecil Sharp, as also to some of their executors since.

Sharp himself apologized on at least one occasion for his expurgations, and his rewritings of collected texts in an unfolk style of poesy, as in "Dabbling in the Dew." Most of his rewritings he later withdrew, and returned to the original wording, but the expurgations were allowed to stand. Of these he remarks, in the preface to *Folk-Songs from Somerset* (1904, with the Rev. Charles L. Marson): 'In a few instances the sentiment of the song has been softened, because the conventions of our less delicate and more dishonest time demand such treatment, but indication has been given, and we plead compulsion and not desire in these alterations.' A few of these expurgated texts have since been published integrally, in *The Idiom of the People* (1958, edited by James

Reeves). But in a large number of cases even these were in a sense
disguised by Sharp's principal concern being with the tunes rather
than the texts, and his taking down only enough of the text — the
opening stanzas usually — to get the tune, when the text seemed
evidently too erotic for him to print; as for instance "The Crab-
Fish," collected from a woman singer, almost at the end of his
career in 1921 (MS., p. 4873).

This basic concern with the tunes, and with the possibility of
publication (identical with that of the parallel collector, Alfred
Williams, to be quoted below) has, sardonically, also proved a
mirage, as a large or the largest part of his manuscript *Tune
Books* remains unpublished. It is singular to observe that in spite
of almost the cult that has formed around Sharp's memory, including a fine brick memorial building in London, and all that, especially in what concerns folk-dancing rather than singing; no one of
his cult has come forward to publish, or to find funds to publish
the totality of the some five thousand tunes he had collected by
1921, probably the largest body of field-collected folksong ever
made by one collector in England or America, and of which only
a fraction appears in his famous printed volumes. (The manuscripts of both words and music are preserved at Clare College,
Cambridge; with copies at Harvard and elsewhere.) Yet it is
Sharp's twenty-three volumes of manuscript *Tune Books* that are
his memorial, as the fine brick building is not.

The Rev. Baring-Gould was a completely different sort of person and a special case: a rigid and brutal man, of the type of
Charles Dickens, under his country-parson exterior, as his cruel
novels show. Sharp, who collaborated with him, after breaking
with Marson, makes the extremely significant remark, as to Baring-
Gould's expurgations, quoted in the biography, *Cecil Sharp,* by
A. H. Fox Strangways and Maud Karpeles (1933) p. 54, that after
Baring-Gould 'had altered or added to the original words' of a
song, 'as often happened because they were "outway rude" or
fragmentary [*rude* is a British euphemism for obscene], he was
apt to forget that his alterations were not part of the real song.'
Long experience in collecting, from living singers, erotic texts of
which only very polite versions can be found in modern print, has
demonstrated, I feel, that Sharp has here caught on the wing the
whole *modus operandi* of the one most serious deterioration of
the historical record of folksong by prudish and popularizing collectors, who either cannot remember or cannot admit that what
they are printing is faked.

One has the impression, as the centuries' progress is examined in the English-speaking world, that one is dealing with people who are more and more easily shocked, because they more and more want and need to be shocked; who conceal more and more, because they have deeper and deeper feelings of sin about what they are concealing, and who are therefore easily titillated and excited by the exposure of less and less — an ankle, an armpit, or some other peripheral area — but would be entirely overwhelmed by the noon-day exposure of the biologically desired middle. Far from becoming more 'pure' in this fashion, they evidently become more neurotically excitable, with a continuous erotic nervousness or awareness immanent at all times, and symbolized or suspected in everything they see or hear. The threshhold of their response to what they consider erotic thus drops lower and lower — where in normal and natural people it becomes higher and higher, and more difficult to arouse — until finally almost some nothing-at-all will drive the neurotically shockable into a frenzy of combined censoriousness and prurience.

In the British Isles, Scotland and Ireland retained longest a certain freedom — at both the folk-level and, in Scotland, at that of scholarly recording — in connection with the folksongs of the sexual passion. This freedom is and was, nevertheless, very much connected with social level or social class. It has often been observed that the real character of any historical period, and thus the control of its whole morality (both real and façade) is a reflection of that of the social class dominating the particular historical period, and of the goals and preconceptions of that class. When, for purposes of entertainment, folklore and folksong were dragged upon the public stage in Great Britain, in the travesty-Scotch dialect of Thomas Durfey's musical comedies, and in the ballad-operas of the early eighteenth century, or — not in England this time, but in Scotland — as the poet Burns was put on exhibition as a kind of clodhopper curiosity for the elegant Edinburgh soirées of the winter season, 1786/7; what was allowed to be presented before the public was inevitably nothing but a genteel and emasculated caricature (in the case of Burns, self-emasculated), largely composed of the presumably amusing linguistic and cosmetic irrelevancies of backwoods accents, large shoes — i.e. cowdung stained — and an even larger figleaf. The specific case of the figleaving of Robert Burns has here been studied most carefully, not only because it is a most striking example of the willingness of the victim to submit to the process, on one mental justification

or another; but also because it is the one historical case in which
we have almost totally available both the glozed and expurgated
product, and the real folk-materials and private artistic productions, in *The Merry Muses of Caledonia,* on which the expurgations were based.

There operates also, in Scotland (as elsewhere), a most important sociological law, which, though examples of it are not
difficult to observe, I do not recollect having seen formulated
in print. And that is *the petrifying but protective influence of
great military defeats on those nations which have nevertheless
managed to survive these defeats.* As the Scots are themselves the
first to recognize, the whole cultural and political life of Scotland
is still attuned, basically, to no later historical period than the
mid- or late eighteenth century, except in the neo-Marxist atmosphere of Glasgow and the industrial area, which has entirely leapt
the nineteenth century, into the present, owing to the challenge
of the industrial blight. Cultured Scotsmen today still brood over
their defeat by England — under the flattering pretense of 'Union'
of the two kingdoms — in the early and mid-eighteenth century,
and refuse still to put its banknotes in their pocket, preferring to
print their own. In exactly the same way, Southerners in the
United States can still be found yearning for the ante-bellum
South of the 1850's, which only their grandparents knew. Thus
also the Japanese, who inhabit after nightfall, in their theatres
(those theatres not devoted to imitative pelvic crooners and the
Twist), the feudal world that disappeared, also in the 1850's,
before the gunboats of Commodore Perry. Irishmen still bemoan
Cromwell's atrocities and the Battle of the Boyne in the seventeenth century; Armenians still sullenly remember the wave after
wave striking upon them, at the crossroads of the world, in the
west-moving centuries of Tamerlane and the Hun; Jews — *væ
victis!* — who have already forgotten Hitler, still bewail the destruction of their Temple and their land in the first century of
this era.

All these proud peoples have been traumatized, during all the
centuries of their more recent history, by the great military defeats
upon which their national power was broken. *The whole aspect
of their culture has in every case been petrified in the form and
image of the moment of that defeat.* Yet, far from being harmed by
this immobilization of their development, it is that immobilization
that has preserved them as national and cultural entities. They
have outlived, or hope to outlive, their traditional oppressors —

most of whom have already disappeared from the stage of history, as the 'defeated' peoples have not — but they are still angry, still aggrieved, still bursting with the pride of their separateness, and would not throw off if they could their proud distinctness and brooding cultural petrifaction. To the degree that this is not true, these peoples are visibly about to die, or to disappear without trace, and of set intent, into the technically and militarily superior cultures of the victors and oppressors, whom they can no longer hope to lick and are therefore going to join.

Between the group that is anxious to join and to 'modernize,' and the larger national entity that still resists, and that senses, in modernization, the final defeat against which it has so long held out; there is of course a war to the death. One cannot take sides; one need not takes sides. It is not out of any inner evil that the joiners find themselves forced to join, but by the tremendous pressures of advancing time and technology, striking harder against those under the direct pressure of the technology than those who, because of their geographical location or continued relation to the soil, are still able to hold out. Seen from this viewpoint, the relevance of this struggle to folklore and to folksong is extremely clear. For it is by clinging to their insularity, to their private cultural folklore and folk-religion, to their myths and legends, and especially to their dialect speech and songs, that all these 'defeated' peoples know well that they have best and solely protected themselves from destruction and disappearance in the past, and hope to protect themselves still. For exactly the same reason, the victor nations fight the folklore, the folk-habits and even foods, the language and the religion of the defeated, and are impatient to see all such 'peculiarities' disappear and be assimilated under the wave of 'progress' and modernization, however little these latter may respond to any human need, even in the victors themselves.

v

THE TERRIBLE difference between the erotic folksongs of the soil, and those of industrial cities, army barracks, and other unnatural human displacements, has already been observed in the closing paragraphs of the earlier chapter on *"The Merry Muses* as Folklore." It is not necessary to repeat here the distinction there made. At the very moment that the best Scottish folksong antiquaries, such as Charles Kirkpatrick Sharpe, James Maidment, and George R. Kinloch, and the somewhat less reliable chapbook printer and ballad-collector Peter Buchan, were following on after Herd and Burns in the serious collecting of the folksong of their country; the whole tone of English folksong (though not Scottish) was beginning to change, moving outward slowly, in its new difference, from the great human over-agglomerations of the principal industrial and commercial cities such as London.

The Scottish antiquaries of the early nineteenth century preferred to follow the lead of Burns and Sir Walter Scott only in part, and did not importantly rewrite or revise their collected materials, except for Buchan, who was and remained a naïve ballad-printer and had unfortunately none of the necessary background of the scholarly collector as which he attempted to pass himself off. It is also clear that Buchan's notions of folksong 'editing' and revision were simply those of the preceding century, and were disoriented in just the same way as, and by the great example of, Bishop Percy and Sir Walter Scott. The real scholars of the period do not appear to have expurgated the texts printed in their collections. But they refrained from fighting the public's moral pose, and grouped the 'high-kilted' ballads, as Scott had warningly called them, in small and privately issued supplementary volumes. These were obviously modelled on Burns' *Merry Muses of Caledonia,* which had been published in just this way, after his death, by the members of the Edinburgh drinking-club, the Crochallan Fencibles, for whose entertainment the collection had in part been made; and who also put their name on its title-page, and probably gave it its deathless title as well.

Thus were published, in anonymous editions limited to thirty or sixty copies, Kirkpatrick Sharpe's *A Ballad Book* (Edinburgh, 1823, re-edited by David Laing, 1880; and, much less well, by Goldsmid, 1883 and 1891), and James Maidment's *A North Countrie Garland* (1824; reprinted by Goldsmid, 1884 and 1891); likewise *A Packet of Pestilential Pasquils* [1868?] a thirty-page supplement to Maidment's larger collection of historical satires, *A Book of Scottish Pasquils.* The same compiler's privately issued *Ane Pleasant Garland of Sweet Scented Flowers* (1835) was 'selected from a Manuscript volume of Miscellaneous Papers preserved in the Library of the Faculty of Advocates.' This rare volumelet has never been reprinted, and its texts are more particularly of satirical poetry than folksong. Nevertheless, it includes some important folksong texts, such as "Cald Kaill of Aberdene" (of which two similar texts are given by Herd, ed. 1869, II. 205, and Supplement p. 52; and another as "The Reels o' Bogie" in

late editions of *The Merry Muses,* ed. 1959, p. 127); as well as
others further reprinted from this source in John S. Farmer's
Merry Songs and Ballads (1895–97) vols. I and V. Farmer's volumes,
which also include almost the entire text of the original *Merry
Muses,* from the unique Scott Douglas copy, show evident signs of
haste and even padding in this case, *Ane Pleasant Garland* being
erroneously attributed to the editing of Kirkpatrick Sharpe, instead of to Maidment, and even the title being wrongly given as
'Garden.' The texts are, however, correctly reprinted. It is fortunate, too, that Maidment issued *Ane Pleasant Garland* when
he did, since the manuscript volume from which it was excerpted
can no longer be found in the Advocates' Library, now the National Library of Scotland, at Edinburgh.

George R. Kinloch's anonymous *The Ballad Book* (1827, reprinted by Goldsmid, 1885), was intended in the same way as a
supplement to his formally published *Ancient Scottish Ballads,* in
the same year; and an even further and somewhat more bawdy
supplement was never published at all. This is preserved in manuscript, at Harvard, under the title *Burlesque and Jocular Ballads
and Songs* (1829), with a mock title-page also inserted, evidently
intended for publication, parodying that of the Wedderburns'
Gude and Godlie Ballatis of the sixteenth century. Also at Harvard
is now preserved the manuscript of Peter Buchan's erotic supplement to his *Ancient Ballads and Songs of the North of Scotland*
(1828, reprinted 1875), under the title *Secret Songs of Silence*
(1832), of which the sad peregrinations and full contents are recorded in William Walker's life of Buchan. The Kinloch and
Buchan manuscripts should certainly be published, though the
latter does of course contain an unknown proportion of Buchan's
own compositions in the genre, as a surviving letter to him from
Laing makes clear.

Many moderately erotic folksongs are nevertheless preserved
in Buchan's *Secret Songs of Silence* that cannot elsewhere be
found, though they are certainly not his originals. For example,
"The Lea Rig," of which the older texts pose quite a problem, as
noted by Hans Hecht in *Songs from David Herd's Manuscripts*
(1904) p. 281–2, a problem complicated even further by the text,
"My Ain Kind Dearie," given only as to the *tune* of "The Lea
Rig," in the *Merry Muses* (ed. 1959, p. 102). Buchan's text here
is one exception to the interesting peculiarity that nothing in the
various antiquarian collections just discussed — whether openly or
privately printed — will be found to be as erotic verbally as *The*

Merry Muses of Caledonia. Buchan's text begins rather abruptly, 'Excuse me now my dearest dear,' with a curious reference to 'the waur horse' (which Buchan told Motherwell was the title of the original song, that he had learned from his great-grandmother, though Hecht refers to it briefly as 'a modern vamp'), and continues, quite probably authentically:

> The laddie and the lassie
>   Gaed out to gather prinkle, O;
> The laddie's breeks were riven,
>   The lassie saw his p[in]tle, O.
> How dare ye be sae baul, sir?
>   An' you my father's cottar, O,
> As to put in your lang thing
>   For [Where] I lat out my water, O?

After that came silence, a silence that lasted at the scholarly or even the would-be scholarly level for over a century. Nothing was any longer printed, in either Scotland or England, of the slightest pretention to unexpurgatedness or completeness, in the way of folklore or folksong compilations (except of Roman and Greek antiquities), and, what is even more distressing, nothing seems even to have been collected — though remaining unpublished — with any attempt whatsoever to be complete, if this would involve accepting or recording erotic materials. One has the impression that since nothing of this kind could be successfully published, nothing was collected, and that it was as simple as that.

One of the last of the old-style collectors in England, working as recently as World War I, Alfred Williams, tells artlessly in his *Folk-Songs of the Upper Thames* (1923) p. 16, that 'more than once, on being told an indelicate song,' he 'had great difficulty in persuading the rustic . . . informant, that I could not show the piece, and therefore I should not write it. "But why not?" I have been asked. "There was nothing wrong with that." Neither was there, really . . . The unsophisticated villagers feel hurt at the decision and often discover considerable embarrassment.' As a model of how *not* to collect folksong, I do not think that could be bettered, and Williams has the honesty to add that he felt like 'something of a hypocrite' on such occasions, especially when he considered that even 'where the songs were professedly bad, this much might be said of them — they were so honestly. That is to say, they were simple, open, and natural. They were morally immoral, if I may say so, and not cunningly suggestive and damn-

ably hypocritical, as are some of the modern music-hall pieces.'
Nevertheless, as he could not 'show' them, or print them, he did
not take them down anyhow; though, in making the collection at
all, his 'chief concern,' as his Preface notes, was 'to have the words
before they had completely disappeared by reason of the death
of the singers — chiefly the most aged of the villagers, male and
female.' These statements of Williams' are quoted at length,
though they leave much still to be elucidated (perhaps by the
study of his manuscripts, left to the Public Library of Swindon,
Wiltshire), because they represent the only frank statement of the
expurgatory principle on which folksong collecting in the English
language has operated, in an increasingly exclusive way, for over
two centuries.

Already, at the beginning of the nineteenth century, with the
drying up of integral collection, for private issue, by the Scottish
collectors, the folklorists (then still called antiquarians) found
themselves effectively driven off by the expurgatory principles
avowed by Ramsay and all his popular successors, as by Percy,
Burns, and Scott. All interest in the subject of folksong had to be
redirected into the one 'safe' area left — the *music* of the folksongs.
In precisely this way, under repressive governments and absolute
monarchies in the past, when the having of almost any idea on
any subject was *per se* dangerous, a great flowering invariably took
place instead in such studies as mathematics, logic, and other
'tool-making' activities of the human mind — the tools being
made for other and later thinkers and researchers, in less repressed
countries and periods, actually to use. The newly developing
musical antiquarians of the late-eighteenth and early-nineteenth
centuries thus had the perfect escape (which is today being bloated
up to a presumed importance never even imagined before) of concerning themselves solely with the music of the folksongs, to the
practical exclusion of any interest in the words, whether erotic or
not.

Thus, of the greatest of the English musical-antiquarians of
the nineteenth century, Percy Dearmer bitterly remarks (in *The
Oxford Book of Carols*, 1928, p. xv): 'in 1855–9 William Chappell
published his two volumes of the old music [*Popular Music of the
Olden Time*], but he ignored the living folk-song, alas, when it
was still abundant.' Though Dearmer does not of course mention
this fact, the historical texts Chappell gives, mostly from broadside
ballads and the old drolleries, are also thoroughly expurgated, the
refined words, replacing others, being set off by warning quotation-

marks, intended at least to alert serious readers that all is not as it seems. Even more hopeless, however, was the point of view taken by Chappell's scholarly successor, Prof. H. Ellis Wooldridge, in his re-edition of the work, in 1893, under the title *Old English Popular Music;* who threw out of the text even the few living folk-songs that had accidentally been included in the earlier edition by Chappell, on the priceless grounds that they 'rest on no better authority than tradition' (vol. II, p. x), as though the ancient 'documentary evidence' he preferred to draw upon — then out-fitting it, of course, with four-part harmonizations by himself and Sir George Macfarren! — had not itself been derived, in the first place, from 'no better authority than tradition.'

Despite Wooldridge's strictures (and it remains to be seen what change of viewpoint, if any, will be developed in the new edition of Chappell's original work, now announced), the living folk-tunes continued to be collected by a few of the field collectors, in par-ticular Baring-Gould, Cecil Sharp, and Frank Kidson (in his *Tra-ditional Tunes,* Oxford, 1891). However, all the even semi-erotic texts collected by these gentlemen, and their musical successors, in particular by Cecil Sharp, were either thoroughly expurgated or left unpublished in manuscript until only a few years ago. Now that they have in part been published — except for the great Kidson collection, preserved or embalmed at Glasgow — one is stupefied at the profound harmlessness and mildness of the texts Baring-Gould thought it necessary to falsify, and Sharp to refrain from publishing at all.

Almost the only area in which, throughout the nineteenth century, any thorough collecting of both texts and music could be ventured, in Great Britain, was that of the carols, on the lead of the ancient-text scholar, Thomas Wright, since these could in general be trusted to be models of sexual propriety. Even here, however, it is only the modern form of which this is strictly true; as may be seen in the 'impious' folk-carols of Burgundy, col-lected, or possibly written by the folk-poet, the elder Piron, and published by his lifelong friend, the great French antiquarian and bibliographer, Bernard de La Monnoye, in the early eighteenth century, at a time when British ballad and folksong study was still searching for historical 'justification' and points of departure.

The hidden reason for this century-long recoiling from the integral study and collection of folksong in England, continuing to the present day, is of course not discussed in the writings or biographies of Baring-Gould and Cecil Sharp, nor yet in Dearmer's carefully reserved historical sketch, cited above, prefacing an essentially religious carol collection. The reason is this: What were considered to be the folksongs of 'common people' in England, were found — in the country districts — to involve a liberal admixture of erotic material, as described by Alfred Williams, and seemed therefore undesirable to deal with except as to the music and its historical origins. In the cities, the only material that presented itself was even more distressing, being almost totally of gross or bawdy nature, except where it derived from the murder- and horror-featuring broadside ballads (an appreciable number of which were bawdy as well), as the day of the broadside ballad drew to its end, and the day of the music-halls developed. Two very typical, but very proper, collections of the ballads of the decadent period are W. H. Logan's *A Pedlar's Pack of Ballads and Songs* (Edinburgh, 1869), and John Ashton's excellent *Modern Street Ballads* (1888) in which latter a not-altogether expurgated version is given, as "Humours of Bartlemy Fair," p. 111–15, of a parody side-show recitation still current in its bawdy form under the title "The Hamburg Show," or "Larry, Turn the Crank" (in *Immortalia,* 1927, p. 153).

A few somewhat more daring items are given in a work of limited edition published at about the same time, *The Curiosities of Street Literature* (1871) anonymously compiled by Charles Hindley; for example, the mock-uneducated letter, "Pretty Maids Beware!!!" reprinted from Hindley as the final item — in the openly issued edition, p. 375 — of Pinto & Rodway's *The Common Muse* (London, 1957). In this latter work, the most important contribution is the final group of unexpurgated broadsides, many of them of the later period, forming the 'de luxe' edition's Appendices, p. 378-439, from the hitherto unexplored Bodleian and Nottingham collections, for example "Black Thing," p. 402–3. A similar item, in the more elaborate symbolic form, turning on metaphors taken from the farm labor of mowing grass, is "Buxom Lass!" printed in facsimile of the actual broadside in the Baring-Gould collection, British Museum, in *The Everlasting Circle,* a selection of texts from the manuscript collections of Baring-Gould, and the later collectors, Hammond, and Gardiner. As edited by James Reeves (London, 1960), this volume is outfitted with a long editorial introduction handling the question of erotic symbolism in folksong in a very amateur way, under the mysterious denomination of the 'lingua franca' of the folk; and also omits the music collected with the texts.

Cecil Sharp, who was no broadside specialist, and who appears to have been influenced by Baring-Gould in what he says of them, gives evidence of the frequent bawdry of the broadside ballads during their late development in the eighteenth and nineteenth centuries by attempting to cast on them the responsibility for the bawdry of folksong in general. His biographers, A. H. Fox Strangways and Maud Karpeles, observe (*Cecil Sharp,* 1933, p. 51) that in the case of the admitted bowdlerizing of Sharp's *Folk-Songs from Somerset,* 'some alteration was inevitable . . . the sentiment is sometimes outspoken, or actually obscene. When the sentiment was of that nature, it was Sharp's opinion that the song was of individual, not communal, origin, and that this individual was often the ballad-maker who hawked the songs about round the country. (He was to be seen with his long printed sheets, and to be heard crooning rather than singing, in Bermondsey, thirty years ago [1903].) This view gains support from the fact that in the Appalachians where the broadsides did not exist, sentiment of that kind is not known in the songs.' Since, of course, a good deal of such 'obscene' sentiment *was* collected in the Appalachians at almost the same time, by the parallel American collectors Josiah Combs, and L. W. Chappell, the probable explanation is that the mountain singers did not feel able to give bawdy songs to Sharp, who was accompanied throughout by Miss Karpeles as amanuensis, the two of them having to be put up — as their backwoods hosts were on occasion made to understand (p. 172) — in separate rooms. This was certainly only proper, but erotic materials cannot often be collected under such strained circumstances, however much the collectors may congratulate themselves on having put the singers at their ease.

The principal influence driving out the folksongs was not the broadsides, but was and is the competition of the fake folksongs of the music-halls. The English music-halls have been studied only in a very superficial way, and without any proper reference to their antecedents in England, let alone to their main development in France, during the eighteenth century, in particular in the Café du Caveau, with its staff of bawdy and satirical songwriters, and the special publications of its erotic songs, as in *Les Muses du Foyer de l'Opéra* (1783), and Thévenot de Morande's *Correspondence de Madame Gourdan* ('Londres,' 1784; reprinted Bruxelles, 1866, and 1883). Though, from the time of Allan Ramsay's *Tea-Table Miscellany* (1724) and onward, nothing could be issued in the openly-published ballad and folksong collections in England

and Scotland but, in the way of sexual songs, mediocre caricatures and milksop modifications; an entire subterranean literature was developing in parallel fashion, of the men's songs of a satirical and bawdy kind, as sung in their private political and drinking clubs since at least the time of the English Revolution a century before, and probably immemorially earlier.

VI

MEN'S PRIVATE drinking clubs, particularly those that were really private and could give spectacles in which naked female dancers or actresses appeared, were derived in a direct fashion from the French orgy-groups of the late sixteenth and seventeenth centuries, which were themselves survivals of the Templar and other 'witch-craft' or anti-Christian groups. The movement had apparently been brought to England by the libertine courtiers of the libertine Charles II, such as the Earl of Rochester, on Charles' return to England from his continental exile, at the Restoration; the first English group being recorded by Pepys as the "Ballers," later "Buff-Ballers" (according to Grose in 1785), for presentation before whom Rochester's *Sodom* was presumably written. One of the main such groups, the "Cosmopolite," headed and protected by the Duc d'Aiguillon in France, along with its erotic poetry and (probably) song publications from the society's private press, has been discussed in an earlier chapter here, "Great Collectors of Erotica." The most purely erotic club in England in the mid-eighteenth century was perhaps the "Hell-fire Club," or "Society of the Monks of Medmenham Abbey," founded about 1755, and protected by Francis Dashwood, Baron Le Despencer, on whose estate was the secret orgiastic 'Abbey.'

Other societies, such as the Freemasons, and in particular the "Beggar's Benison" in Scotland (also mentioned by Grose in a veiled fashion), had ostensible initiatory and anti-religious intent, as well as a large repertoire of erotic songs and toasts; setting these, in a very direct fashion, in the older tradition of the Templars. Another, the "Wig Club" is amusingly described in the series of capital articles by David Foxon, "Libertine Literature in England, 1660–1745," in *The Book Collector* (London, Spring 1963, p. 34, n. 27) along with the "Beggar's Benison," which is very correctly called a 'phallic club,' to pair it with 'its offshoot the Wig Club — the wig (perhaps more accurately a merkin) was said to have been made from the pubic hair of Charles II's mistresses, and was added to by all new members.' Both are described further in Louis C. Jones' *The Clubs of the Georgian Rakes* (New York, 1942), and 'between them,' Mr. Foxon adds, 'their members included George IV, four dukes, seventy-three peers and law lords of Scotland, thirty baronets and two bishops.' To research like that, one must certainly tip one's lid!

The songs of these clubs form one of the main nuclei of the developing erotic literature of the eighteenth and nineteenth centuries in Great Britain, and in this cadre one begins to understand the appearance of Burns' *Merry Muses of Caledonia* under the auspices of an Edinburgh drinking-club, the "Crochallan Fencibles," whose name itself was intended as a mock on the volunteer military organizations of Britain during the French Revolutionary period. (The first reprint of the *Merry Muses,* under the title *The Giblet Pye,* about 1806, surviving only in the unique copy in the Harding Collection, was almost certainly privately printed for some similar and very limited group.) Long before, however, the bawdy songs and toasts of the drinking clubs were being published by the original 'men's magazines' of the 1780's and thereabouts, in volumes side-issued for the subscribers to these magazines in certain cases, under such titles as *The Buck's Delight* (1783, copy in the Bodleian, *Phi* collection), the *Covent Garden Repository* (named for the fashionable prostitutes' quarter of London), the *Ranger's* and *Rambler's* jestbooks and songsters — these being the two main bawdy magazines of the period — and, in particular, *The Frisky Songster* (two copies known: Kinsey, and Harding Collection). On the legal condemnation of this work, which went through several editions, see G. Chitty's *A Practical Treatise on the Criminal Law* (2nd ed. 1826) II. 42–3. Compare also *The Frisky Muse,* 'Humbly dedicated to the Choice Spirits of the Age, by Rigdum Funidos, Their Ballad Maker in Ordinary and Composer Extraordinary' (London: For the Author, 1749), a work of 56 pages, octavo, noted by Rose-Reade, *Registrum Librorum Eroticorum* (1936) no. 1849, but very unfortunately without any location given, as, from its date, this would appear to be the earliest work of its kind in English, after the termination of the drolleries in *Pills to Purge Melancholy,* in 1720. A similar collection, *The Muse in Good Humour* has been mentioned in an earlier chapter.

This tradition of forthright bawdy song in men's drinking groups has a very ancient history which will be discussed somewhat more in detail later, and to which allusion has already been made, in the reference to *Psalms,* 69: 12, 'They that sat in the gate spoke against me, and I was the song of the drunkards.' As Chappell remarks (ed. 1859, II. 411), this was quoted by Archbishop Laud about 1640, at the beginning of the English Revolution, when 'The most scurrilous libels were affixed to the walls in every quarter of the town; ballads, of which he was the subject, were composed and sung in the streets; and pictures, in which he was exhibited in the most undignified postures, were publicly displayed. The ale-houses teemed with songs in which he was held up to derision.' There, certainly, is the completely expressed development in England — where it had already of course been going on for centuries, among the strolling minstrels at noble banquets and mere ale-house parties, well lubricated with liquor and song, as the early prohibitions against the singing of satirical songs at the time of Henry VIII, especially in Scotland, make clear.

Perfectly clear, too, is Falstaff's threat, in *1 Henry IV,* II. ii. 42 (about 1600): 'An' I have not Ballads made on you all, and sung to filthy tunes, let a cup of Sacke be my poyson.' By 'filthy tunes' he is referring, to be sure, to their musical rather than moral quality. As toper and good-companion, Falstaff's love of bawdy song is made one of his leading characteristics, and is finally his friend's epitaph as well, when Shallow is remember to have plagiarized the tunes the carman whistled, 'And sware they were his fancies and goodnights.' (The cart-drivers' whistling in this way to their horses and bullocks still survives in Argentina, where the chorus, for instance, of one of the most beautiful *tangos canción* recorded by the late Carlos Gardel, "La Madrugada" (Sunrise), is given in whistling, interrupted by warning cries to the bullocks, 'Ay, la blanca!' South American folk music, both vocal and instrumental, has made the transition to the citified approximations of phonograph-recordings and nightclub renditions with exceptional success and a heaping measure of the original authenticity.)

The sixteenth and especially the seventeenth centuries in England were the golden age of popular singing there, and any number of references demonstrating this could be culled, such as that of Pepys inquiring as to the musical abilities of his servants on engaging them. It was exactly the 'gunpowder' of the English Civil War, after 1640, as Aubrey notes, that turned the bawdy and satirical songs of the ale-houses to the specific purposes of political satire, which had earlier been the form of musical satire most particularly forbidden. The drolleries are, in largest part, the record of these Royalist satires against the Puritans — *The Rump* contains nothing whatever except such satires — who are of course accused of every possible sexual crime, nameable and nameless, as with horses, dogs, and nuns; and of scatological misadventures arising inevitably from their presumed cowardice in the face of the Royalist gunfire. These satires competed seriously for space, with the love-songs, even in the printed songbooks; and finally drove them almost entirely out of the poetic miscellany volumes by the mid-eighteenth century, as in *The Foundling Hospital for Wit* (1743–49). The political forms were by then being written by purposely subsidized wits and songwriters, with special 'mughouses' being set up by the time of the British Georges for their singing, as had long since been the case in France with the *Mazarinades* and the similar poetic libels against Cardinal Richelieu. The enormous French satirical collection of the early eighteenth century, the thirty-five manuscript volumes of the *Recueil de Maurepas,* overflows with such productions, of which all those actually obscene are gathered in six volumes published by Gay in Bruxelles ('Leyde'), in 1865. The eighteenth-century society of the "Calotte" similarly devoted itself in France to circulating these rhymed satires.

The earlier private topicality, of the kind implied in Falstaff's threat, setting private parodic satires to known tunes, has survived until quite recent times, generally in work songs, and particularly in the sea-chanteys and soldiers' marching songs, with stanzas directed against specially disliked officers, or all civilians in general. Seldom, however, are such songs now based on real incidents, but have become merely generalized complaints or handlings of standard or purported situations, as in the Civil War song, "No Balls At All," set to the rhythm of a topical satire against excesses in women's clothing, "Nothing To Wear," by Wm. Allen Butler; and the modern Scottish "The Ball o' Kirriemuir," in the style of earlier folk-epithalamia appearing in *Pills to Purge Melancholy* and the *Merry Muses of Caledonia,* in which one may assume that real people and erotic incidents at real country weddings were at least thought to be recorded. Except in the medical faculties of the universities, one sees few examples in modern times of good-humored private satirical songs of this kind, such as that recorded in the French jestbook, *Contes à Rire* (c. 1668; ed. 1881, p. 67) in a brief tale entitled "*Affront fait à un amant avaricieux,*" in which the avaricious lover is kicked downstairs by the young lady whom he has been night-visiting, when he kisses her chastely in her bed on the grounds that it is too expensive to bring up children! The jestbook goes on: '*Cette agréable rencontre étant venue à la connaissance de tous les villages d'alentour, on en fit une chanson et ce jeune badaud fut tellement moqué qu'il n'osait plus se trouver avec ses égaux.*'

Topical songs and especially poems do still exist, but they no longer are to be heard in such number as before World War I, as is remarked in Orson Welles' motion picture romanticizing that period, *Citizen Kane,* where, at a stag-dinner, with satirical sculptures in ice-cakes and girl-dancers galore (with whom the guests jump up to dance), the newspaper publisher remarks deprecatingly, when asked if it isn't true that there is a song about him, that people will write a song about you if you do nothing but 'buy a bag of peanuts.' Most of the topical songs and ballads surviving even from the time of World War I are those commemorating great disasters (as still in the Mexican broadside ballads or *corridos),* as for instance "The Wreck of the Old 97" and "The Sinking of the Titanic," of which the first has an erotic parody and the second an erotic Negro version on the folk-hero "Shine." Most other such songs surviving, or even now being written, are entirely on political and military personages, as in the humorously scatological song — on the purported use of patriotic ladies' 'chamber-lye' to make gunpowder, and the erotic results arising therefrom — known during the Civil War as "John Haroldson," and revised during World War I with the change simply of the satirized general's name to "Von Hindenburg" (printed in *Immortalia,* 1927, p. 101, still entitled "Chamber-Lye"). The original Civil War version had been printed earlier in a rare contemporary booklet under the title *The Lay of John Haroldson,* probably in Philadelphia. (Copy: New York Public, 3*, and others located by the Union Catalogue, Library of Congress.) The violently satirical ballad of British soldiers in Egypt during World War II, "King Farouk," courageously printed by Hamish Henderson in 1947 in *Ballads of World War II,* is perhaps the latest known authentic survival of the form and one of the most outspoken.

In *A Journey through England in 1724* (quoted by Chappell, II. 624, he requoting from Malcolm's *Manners and Customs,* p. 532, as I must also do, having no access to the original), the mughouses of London later featuring satirical political songs are described, where and by means of which the citizens, after the fatigue of the day is over in their shops and on the Exchange, unbend their thoughts before they go to bed. But the most diverting or amusing of all were the mug-house clubs in Long Acre, Cheapside, &c. where gentlemen, lawyers, and tradesmen, used to meet in a great room, seldom under a hundred.

They had a president, who sate in an armed chair some steps higher than the rest of the company, to keep the whole room in order. A harp played all the time at the lower end of the room; and every now and then one or other of the company rose and entertained the rest with a song, and (by the by) some were good masters. Here was nothing drank but ale, and every gentleman had his separate mug . . . and every one retired when he pleased, as from a coffee-house.

Though this sounds like nothing other than a very late survival of the Welsh minstrel era — the harp continuously playing, and the 'president' in his armed chair seem very significant — the mug-houses, at some point in their development during the reign of the early Georges, clearly became the temples of political satire and bawdy song for the city-dwellers. These are certainly the clubs whose repertories of most acclaimed bawdy songs and toasts (an important part of the activity being the drinking of healths from one table to another) are recorded in the erotic songsters of the century from 1750 to 1850 and slightly after. The featured singers of these mug-houses or clubs generally seemed to have styled themselves 'Captain' (on which see 2 *Henry IV*, II. iv. 126), and may very well have been professional soldiers, as for instance Capt. Morris, whose obscene song, "The Great Plenipotentiary" is included in all late editions of the *Merry Muses*, though very much an English song, and not Scottish, and of a tone and inspiration utterly different from the erotic folksongs collected by Burns.

The official promulgation of sobriety and prudery in England from the 1830's on, with the avowed intention of repressing the revolutionary spirit of the time among working people and others, drove the bawdy singers underground, as the fertility rites of ancient worships had been driven underground earlier as 'witchcraft,' and the last resistance to Christianity as the 'buggerlie' heresy of the Knights Templar. From the London grog-shop cellars and Dublin coal-holes — now imitating the French Café du Caveau, far more than the almost courtly mug-houses of a

century before — there were issued, up through the 1870's, a whole
float of brashly titled and execrably printed "Cockolorum Songsters," "Coal-Hole Companions," and "Bang-Up Reciters" ('A
most indescribable collection of some of the most Delicious, Ama-
tory, Luscious, Lecherous, Frisky, Funny,' and never equalled
Recitations, Ever written, never before printed, and to be had
in no other Publication . . . with a Rummy Batch of Funny
Condrums [sic]. The whole written by a "Regular Teazer".')
There is no satisfactory list of these publications, and the only
important collection of them was broken up at the George Daniel
sale in 1864. As noted in the first essay in the present volume,
end of pt. III, Ashbee's *Index Librorum Prohibitorum* (1877, and
reprints) I. 133–37, gives a list of nearly fifty such bawdy sextodecimo songsters, along with the inordinately long title of one
of these, *The Blowen's Cabinet of Choice Songs,* of which practically the whole table of contents is repeated in the title, liberally
interspersed with exclamation points. Though most of the fifty
songsters Ashbee cites have not survived, a similar group of fifty
other songsters of the same period is preserved in the British
Museum (not in the Private Case).

Let it be understood clearly that the bawdy songs of the 'cider-
cellars' and 'coal-holes' — which became the modern music-halls
— are not, except accidentally, folksong, nor do they make pleasant
reading. They are generally anecdotes of erotic or scatological
adventure or misadventure, told in doggerel verse (and to heaven
knows what tunes!) and are most closely related to the older
French form of the *conte-en-vers,* fully discussed in a later chapter, "Toward a Motif-Index of Erotic Humor." It was songs of
this type that were used to pad out the various editions of Burns'
Merry Muses of Caledonia all through the nineteenth century,
under the curtailed title of *The Merry Muses,* not one of which
gives the original Scottish songs in major part. The most particularly 'music-hall-ized' editions are those of Dublin, 1832, and
that dated '1827' (very often reprinted), which was actually issued
in London in 1872, by the erotica-publisher Hotten, and had unquestionably been revised by a music-hall songwriter in the worst
possible taste of the genre.

The tone of the erotic music-hall songs at this period was
utterly vulgar and absolutely open; the 'cunningly suggestive and
damnably hypocritical . . . modern music-hall pieces' of the
time of the First World War, as described by Alfred Williams,
had not as yet become necessary — a suggestiveness long-since

achieved, in any case, in such songs by Durfey as that in the character of a brother and sister cited earlier (*Pills to Purge Melancholy,* II. 143–4), from his *Comical Don Quixote* of 1696. The tone of 'cider-cellar' songs can only be described as repulsive, varying from a merely endless stupidity in doggerel rhyme to a purposely nasty and dysphemistic sexual brutality, intended to shock and revolt, and doing exactly that. One can almost sympathize with the recoiling of the British antiquarians — as folklorists continued to be called during the century when this stuff was the erotic 'folksong' of the London nights, and of Dublin even more so — into a perfervid study of the musical manuscripts and religious carols of earlier centuries. It is not to be imagined, either, that the antiquaries worth their salt were too unworldly, or too covered with library dust, not to know what was going on about them, or what was being sung nightly in the early music-halls, any more than a modern folklorist worth his salt can afford not to know what is being sung today over the radio, no matter how painful.

One of the most riotous of the ballad scholars, so far as the ambivalent interest in, and horror of, his erotic materials is concerned, was the Rev. J. Woodfall Ebsworth, to whom the editing of the main British broadside-ballad reprint fell, when its first editor, William Chappell, decided he was too old to go on with the *Roxburghe Ballads,* in part owing to having learned that the issuing society, under the direction of the monolithic Frederick Furnivall, insisted that the text be respected, *ruat cœlum,* and that no expurgation would be allowed. In a private reprint, at the same period, of one of the bawdiest of the older drolleries, *Choyce Drollery* (repr. 1876, with erotic Supplement), Ebsworth valiantly attempts to justify his inclusion of some of the erotic pieces — in a special "Supplement," which is usually missing, and was probably seriously underprinted — by means of the following very interesting allusion, not only to the erotic nature of the music-hall entertainment, but to the formal survival into the 1850's ('twenty years ago') of exactly the mug-house organization of the 1720's, its baronial 'president' become a mock 'judge':

A song follows, beginning "There were three birds that built very low" . . . it is degraded from position here; for substantial reasons, and (with a few others, afterwards to be specified), given separately. Nothing but the absolute necessity of making this a genuine Antiquarian Reprint, worthy of the confidence of all mature students of our

Early Literature, compels the Editor to admit such prurient
and imbecile pieces at all. They are tokens of a debased
taste that would be inconceivable, did we not remember
that, not more than twenty years ago, crowds of MP.s,
Lawyers, and Baronets listened with applause, and encored
tumultuously, songs far more objectionable than these (if
possible) in London Music Halls, and Supper Rooms.
Those who recollect what R[oss] sang (such as "The Lock
of Hair" [probably "Oonagh's Waterfall, or The lock
that scattered Oonagh's p-ss," as Burns titles it, in a letter
to Thompson of September 1794, calling it 'a blackguard
Irish song,' *Merry Muses*, ed. 1959, p. 166, reprinted from
the '1827' edition of music-hall provenance], "My name it
is Sam Hall, Chimbley Sweep," &c.), and what "Judge
N - - -" said at his Jury Court, need not be astonished at
anything which was sung or written in the days of the
Commonwealth and at the Restoration. A few words we
suppress into dots . . . (p. 229–30.)

As with the similar songs of the university students, and
especially the medical faculty, soon to be discussed, one almost
suspects in such songs and recitations an intention similar to that
of the *ordeals* of earlier periods, still surviving in the sexual and
sadistic initiations, and initiatory sacrilegious acts, similar to those
of the Templars, of modern college-students, field and factory
workers, and the like. The purpose of these is, perfectly openly,
to force the candidate to be as horrible as possible, and to spit
(at the very least) upon everything he truly loves and respects —
such as love, family, and religion — and to embrace and wallow
in everything he truly hates and finds disgusting, whether it be
the kissing of another man (or the demon-cat Baphomet's anus),
or the engaging in blindfold and pretended self-castratory acts, or
the swallowing down of mock-scatological messes. In almost the
same way, in the students' songs and limericks, and in these early
music-hall songs, as in those of the yearly convention clubs in
America today, it is as if the singers were forcing themselves on,
and being egged-on as well by their screaming and applauding
audience, to say the most horrible things possible or imaginable,
and thus to show their courage and 'virility,' as well as that of the
audience in being able to listen. The identical purpose or formula
is strikingly evident in the fare now offered in special nightclubs
by the new American 'sick-comedians,' in the one authentic record,

so far, of this type of ordeal-entertainment: the "Lenny Bruce" issue of the liberal newspaper, *The Realist* (New York, June 1963), p. 28–31, self-styled 'the magazine of the lunatic fringe.'

In his *Cursory History of Swearing* (1884) Julian Sharman describes in a preliminary page, 9–10, the genesis of his book, in a night at the "Scuffler's Club" — probably not its real name: the Savage Club may have been that intended — the meeting-place of the 'best men' in London, where a version of the profane hanging-song also mentioned by Ebsworth, "Samuel Hall," a descendant of "Chimbley Sweep," and earlier of "Captain Kidd . . . When he Sailed," brings down the house. (The anterior history of this song has been studied by Prof. Bertrand Bronson, in *Western Folklore*, [*California Folklore Quarterly*], 1942, I. 47–64, and was splendidly traced earlier by Miss Anne G. Gilchrist, in *Journal of the English Folk Dance Society*, 1938, III. 167–70.)

But what seemed most to invigorate the spirits of the Scufflers was a song that had been demanded more than once during the evening and was at length only given after extreme pressure on the part of the audience. We do not know the name of the song; we are not certain we should recollect the tune; but we are positive of the words, such of them at least as formed the refrain of the melody. In every stanza there was held up to reprobation some unpopular type. The severer virtues were no less mercilesssly handled [*n.b.*], while all authority of the more invidious kind, from that of the beak to that of the exciseman, was subjected to the same unceremonious treatment. Every versicle — well do we remember it — concluded with the exordium, "Damn their eyes!" Never can we forget the rapturous reception that was accorded this piece of harmony. The men literally shrieked with delight. "Damn their eyes!"—they grasped convulsively at tumblers and decanters and banged them on the table. "Damn their eyes!" — they hurrahed, they shouted, they raved, they swore. "Damn their eyes!" they bestrode chairs and benches, as they might have bestridden hobby-horses, and tournamented about the room. Was this then the pæan or war-song of the Scuffler's Club?

As with the morning light we came to reflect upon the midnight orgie, we felt we had opened a chapter in a strange history. . .

VII

Meanwhile, a new group in England and America had under-taken the preservation and creation of obscene songs and poems: the university students, particularly those of the medical faculty, whose penchant of this kind goes back several hundred years at least, to the Latin jestbooks and facetiæ of the early seventeenth century — a hundred years earlier, too, in the burlesque academies and Aretinesque school of Italy, and in France as well if Rabelais' Panurge is evidence. The older bawdy-song clubs of non-university men did not die all at once, and are not, in fact, dead. But they have been largely replaced by loosely organized clubs made up principally of men — sometimes women as well —connected with the universities, and retaining, or said to retain, manuscript song-books in which each succeeding generation enters its repertoire. I have never succeeded in seeing such a book, but they are reliably reported from both Cambridges (in England and Massachusetts), from Oxford and from Yale. As the young men mustered into the army, especially as officers, and now in the air-force, are in large part taken from the universities, they carry their repertoire of bawdy songs with them for the 'beer-roasts' and drinking-and-whoring furloughs common to both the university and to armed-service life, where young men are grouped closely together with-out any sufficient access to women.

With the soldiers' songs one finds oneself on the most ancient historical groundwork underlying the whole subject of erotic song. Also, and very fortunately, the whole of the early historical material has been masterfully gathered in the brief and little-known treatise, "Sur l'Origine de la Liberté qu'avoient les Soldats Romains de dire des Vers Satyriques contre ceux qui triomph-oient," by the Abbé Augustin Nadal, added as a supplement to his *Histoire des Vestales* (Paris, 1725) p. 332–86, the subject having been suggested to him by the Abbé Renaudot. (Copy: Ohio State University, Coll. G.L.) Nadal made a very full search of the Greek and Latin writers, the best materials recorded being those of Denis of Halicarnassus, Bk. VII, "On the Games of the Circus;" Titus Livius, "On the Triumph of Cneius Manlius Volso," victor over the Gauls (Bk. 39), also Bk. 50, chap. 4; Dion Cassius "On Nico-medes" (Bk. 43); and Pliny's well-known passage on the satirical songs against Julius Caesar by his soldiers, accusing him of having fed them nothing but cabbages (Bk. VIII, chap. 19). Also Martial's *Epigrams,* II. 4, and another on the triumph of the Emperor

Domitian ('Festa coronatus . . .'), which plainly states that 'The soldier, crowned with laurels, marching among the laurel-covered horses, will divert himself with all the railleries permitted during so great a Feast.'

Even more interesting are the traces of far older liberties, of which the soldiers' satirical songs are evidently only a development, such as the famous harangue of Curion the elder, against Caesar, quoted by Suetonius, accusing him of homosexuality, as 'the husband of all women and the wife of all men' (*omnium mulierum virum & omnium virorum mulierem*). Most particularly clear behind these liberties of criticism and insult, which still survive as the prerogatives of members of parliamentary bodies in many Western nations, are the Feast of Fools celebrations — not then so called, of course — specifically at the Saturnalia, at the return of the sun at the winter solstice, or Christmas, when insults by slaves against their masters, and female slaves against their mistresses, were briefly allowed. In very recent times, the owner-editor of *Time* and *Life* magazines, Mr. Henry Luce, is said to have reinstated or to have intended to reinstate this custom, at Christmas, as a relaxation of any possible year-long tension between the editors and the corps of anonymous journalists forming the staff.

It is important to observe, at the deepest and farthest level, the repetitive castratory myth behind the original 'festival of revolt' at the Saturnalia, in the castrating and killing of each of the father-gods in turn by his son: Uranus by Chronos or Saturn, and Saturn by Jupiter. This is again repeated at the human level in the legends of Laïus and Oedipus, and in that of the castrating of Noah by his son Ham, when drunk with wine (Talmud *Sanhedrin*, 70a), later modified in the parallel story of Lot and his daughters, to the father's incestuous seduction when made drunk for the purpose, at a similar re-peopling of the world after a cataclysm. As is well known, Freud has made another form of this primal legend, especially as to the son's replacing the killed-and-eaten or castrated father in his mother's bed — an essential feature of the legends, as is the mother's favoring and saving the hated boy-child — the point of departure of his great speculative essays, *Totem and Tabu* and *Moses and Monotheism*.

The same story is not only repeated in that of Moses hidden in the bulrushes by his mother from the omen-warned Pharaoh, the father's omen being common to almost all these legends; but also in that of Moses' own firstborn son, Gershom, circumcised by his mother Zipporah — a most remarkable trait, and referring clearly to the matriarchal Egyptian bird-goddess — in order to avert divine attack (*Exodus,* 2: 21–2, and 4: 24–6). Compare the similar night-frights and attacks upon the third and final patriarch, Jacob, in *Genesis,* 28: 10–17, and especially 32: 24–6, in which he is wounded by the divine messenger 'in the hollow of his thigh,' when he proves too powerful to be vanquished in any other way. Of all these legends, that of Chronos has lasted the longest, as he still survives in popular iconology as 'Father Time' or the 'Old Year,' with his significant sickle or scythe (the attribute of Chronos), always struggling against, yet always being ousted by, the be-diapered infant of the 'New Year.' It is hardly to be doubted that these are the basic ideas of revolt, dating from the infancy of human civilization, commemorated in the Saturnalia and Feast of Fools, and in the mocking songs and satires to which they have given rise.

During the transitional period, the similar Jewish customs assimilated to the Spring festival of Purim have retained an unbroken line of transmission. It has often been observed that the *Book of Esther,* on which the festival of Purim is based, does not mention anywhere the name of the Jewish Jehovah, and is only accepted into the canon of the Old Testament for secular uses. As the names of the two main characters in the story imply, it is almost certainly derived from the much more ancient worship of Marduk (Mordecai) and Ishtar, and turns specifically on the salvation of her people by the 'female-hero' Esther. The *Book of Esther* also opens with a royal orgy lasting exactly six months (a reference to the changing seasons), at which Queen Vashti, who is simultaneously holding a similar feast for her vassal-women, is ordered to appear — naked, according to the usual interpretation — 'to shew the people and the princes her beauty,' at the men's feast. This she refuses to do, and is therefore repudiated by the king for fear that, if her deed 'shall come abroad unto all women . . . they shall despise their husbands in their eyes.' (*Esther,* 1: 10–22.) This refusal of the orgiastic liberty of the festival specifically and only to the queen, resulting in the ordinance by the king, 'into every province . . . and to every people after their language, that every man should bear rule in his own house,' is an unmistakable legendary formulation of the far anterior struggle between original matriarchy and the patriarchy that replaced it, and it is significant that Esther, though also a queen, subordinates her power to the salvation of her patriarchal people.

The similarity of the whole Esther legend to that of the opening or frame-story of the *Arabian Nights,* of which the corpus of Levantine folktales was developed in the same geographical area some fifteen hundred years after the date ascribed to the *Book of Esther,* has long been remarked by orientalists. (See: *Encyclopædia Britannica,* 11th ed., 1911.) But the implications of this parallel, both as to the legend and to the folktale-frame of the *Arabian Nights,* have not yet been frankly accepted.

It will be understood, of course, that the Abbé Nadal is not the source of the preceding considerations, except as to the Latin and Greek authors cited. The only Biblical reference he allows himself, in what he clearly feels to be a rather improper context, is nevertheless of particular interest: the satirical songs during the military triumph of the unknown champion, David, over Goliath, in *1 Samuel,* 18: 6–7: 'And it came to pass . . . when David returned from the slaughter of the Philistines, that the women came out of all the cities of Israel, singing and dancing, to meet king Saul, with tabrets, with joy, and with instruments of musick. And the women answered one another [*n.b.*] as they played, and said, Saul hath slain his thousands — and David his ten thousands. And Saul was very wroth . . . ' It is from this incident of the women's satirical song against Saul, and in David's favor, that the feud arose between the old king and the young champion who finally supplanted him. What is perhaps most interesting in the citation is that it is the women who sing, and not the men. In the same way, Miriam's song of triumph over the Egyptians, in *Exodus,* 15: 20, is also accompanied by 'timbrels and dances' of all the women, but it is only one stanza (or responsory) in length, obviously implying that the preceding nineteen stanzas, taken and put into the mouth of the 'slow-tongued' Moses (see *Exodus,* 4:10), but beginning with the identical stanza, are really the song that Miriam sang.

The point here is not one of Biblical history, but of the history of song, and particularly of satirical and military song. The essential point is this: when the women sing, it is clearly their proper and expected activity, to welcome — erotically, of course — the returning soldiers; but when the soldiers sing, it is an extraordinary or festively-permitted activity which, appearing only later historically, has presumably been taken or learned from the women, and may therefore be assumed to have been thought of as having religious status or magical power.

What this religious or magical power was, is finally to be seen

in the larger subject of the whole origin of comedy, in the Baccha-
nalia and the street-running and *insulting* comedians (we have
them still) of religious processions and funerals, later of military
triumphs. Their activities, as for instance at the Lupercalia, were
openly phallic mimings of mock-rape, intended to symbolize, if
not to cause, human fertility and 'resurrection.' From these
nympholept street-comedians and musicians have developed all
formal comedy and theatre on the one hand, and formal dance
or ballet on the other. These begin with the Atellane comedies
of Greece, and the Exodia or humorous intermissions, called
'jigs' in Shakespeare's time and 'vaudeville' and 'burlesque' in our
own, which are at the present time the prevailing pattern or form
of mass-broadcast humorous entertainment. The basic citation is
that from Aristotle: 'Tragedy owes it origin to the dithyrambs
chanted in honor of Bacchus, and Comedy to the obscene songs
which, authorized by custom and by law, were long chanted in
many of the cities of Greece.' Aristotle does not mention why,
nor discuss the sacred or magical purposes implied in their being
so authorized.

In an even more specific sense, the obscene songs of the soldiers, which they were allowed — nay encouraged — to compose
and sing against their victorious generals, turning on the parsi-
mony, sexual habits, mishaps, and even cowardice of these victors,
could only have had one possible reason. This is the profound
folk-belief implied in turning away any compliment (especially
toward one's children) with some deprecating remark as to the
worthlessness of the thing or person complimented. This of course
is still very common: 'A poor thing, but mine own.' The purpose
of such songs, and such deprecations, was and is evidently apotropaic, being intended to ward off the evil-eye or *'guigne'* ('jinx,' or
sidewise glance of the envious) dangerously present at all moments
of happiness or of success and victory. ('Knock on wood!') This
is believed by all primitive peoples, and many not so primitive,
owing to the presumed jealousy of demons at all *rites de passage*
— especially those demons or 'bad fairies' that one has forgotten to
invite to the christening or other festivities — and to the ghosts of
the departed; and also, which is even less difficult to observe, to
the obvious hatred and mute curses of the defeated, especially
when they are being led with yokes around their necks under
Arches of Triumph.

Very many such apotropaic obscene and scatological ceremonies exist in the folklore of the world, such as that of 'shitting

on money' (politely 'spitting' on it) when receiving any large sum; and the many sexually-symbolic acts connected with money, such as the breaking of the bride's held-out platter, with silver coins, for the honor of the first 'dance' or 'kiss;' or the enforced gifts of money to be dropped into a woman's newly-bought purse (which is generally chosen by the woman to represent unconsciously her own physical sexual estimation of herself or of her vagina) in order to 'uncross' or 'unhex' the virginal curse of its newness. Another form, no longer surviving except in the approximations of club and fraternity initiations, is that of the ancient mock-payments to seigneurial lords of a yearly rent composed of no money at all if one could offer instead 'a leap, a cough, and a fart,' on Christmas Day. The 'Merry Tenure' of Baldwin *le Pettour,* in Suffolk, held by these means, is noted in Camden's *Britannia* (3rd ed., 1753, p. 444), and quoted with an amusing gloss in Reginald Reynolds' *Cleanliness and Godliness* (London, 1943, p. 182). Something of the same kind is clearly alluded to in the illustrations of the mock processions, with bellows and puffing cherubs depicted on the banners carried, at the Dijon Feast of Fools, as shown in Du Tilliot's *Mémoires* on this subject (Lausanne, 1751), especially in plate 6, and the openly erotic 'elephant-walk,' or mimed *soixante-neuf,* in plate 7, which still survives among circus comedians and as a children's game in many countries. The intention is in all cases not actually, or not so much, to humiliate either person, as to ward off the danger of the evil-eye, considered to be specially present at all such moments of good fortune.

Soldiers, exposed continuously by their profession to sudden death, are a prime group using this sort of superstitious averting of supernatural danger by means of obscene songs, initiations, and other ceremonies; quite aside from the minor occult risks they run owing to the hatred of the defeated (waving flags docilely as the parade goes by, nowadays, or even running out to kiss the victors). The same is perhaps even more true of sailors, especially in the days before steam, when they were entirely at the mercy of the elements and of natural forces beyond any but token control. Exposed to danger at all times by reason of their trade, the sailors sang songs that have always been notably obscene, for which reason they have also only appeared in pitifully expurgated form as usually printed. The psychological point is also very clear that the riotous obscenity of these songs also gives expression to the anger — in psycho-analytic terms the 'anal sadism' — of these men, deprived of all possibility of natural sex lives for long periods, during the fullest years of their virile strength; very hard worked, and in continuous danger and fear.

The similar or attempted sexual privation of students, as well as their being generally of the mustering age or class, is one of their closest points of contact with the life of the soldier. It was during the middle ages that the semi-professional class of students first came into existence in Europe — hybrid creatures leading a careless life somewhere on the margin between the status of clergy and laity, and spending most of their spare time and money on prostitutes (or else being simply their pimps), if Villon's picture of the life is true, which it is hardly possible to doubt. Sometimes grouped in the colleges, sometimes wandering as the goliard poets and musician-entertainers and mountebanks from whom the modern theatre has in large measure developed since the Reformation, these 'bummler' students are the forerunners of the modern singers, in France, of the 'Chansons de Salles de Garde.' There is nothing specially French about either this student profession, nor the joyous obscenity of its songs, and similar student-singers were to be found, and will still be found, in all the Germanic and Anglo-Saxon universities, not to mention those of Italy and the Hispanic countries. A good deal of fine illustrative material on the wandering scholar-singers of former times is given in Max Bauer's *Sittengeschichte des deutschen Studententums* (Dresden, *c.* 1930). The professional student of this kind is, in any case, of Oriental and Levantine origin as an institution, and came to Europe only in the middle ages as a result of the influence on Europe of Græco-Arab and Judæo-Arab learning, and the organization of its schools of medicine, law and philosophy in Italy and the Italian islands, Southern France, and Spain, during the centuries of the Arab Conquest, preceding the Crusades.

Other métiers besides that of soldier, sailor, and student have also their special songs, with the usual obscenity that is inevitable and expected when men are brought together without any women present. This obscenity is also noisily welcomed in certain situations where there *are* women, as may be seen in the rare little *Chansonnier du Bordel* of about 1833, and the many similar British collections of convivial and whore-house songs of the end of the eighteenth century, already discussed. It is to one of these other professions that the honor must go, of having first published the erotic songs and poems of its group (if the songs of prostitution be omitted from the discussion). This was the profession of typographer-printers, whose erotic folk-poems or poetic obscœna are preserved in a tiny pamphlet, called simply *La Typographie*, without place or date of publication, but which is clearly a ten-page supplement, and in matching format, to the *Dictionnaire de la Langue Verte Typographique* (with a supplement of 'Songs due to the Typographical Muse'), a slang dictionary edited by Eugène Boutmy, a professional French proof-reader of Russian origin, as issued by the erotica-publisher Isidore Liseux in 1878. The little supplement is mostly composed of songs in double-entendre in which the terms of typography are used in such a way as to give a sexual meaning in the context of the poems: a non-sexual form of the same metaphoric *jeux-de-mots* of printers is Benjamin Franklin's well-known epitaph upon himself. This sort of verbal entertainment is very old, and is most particularly common in songs making use of the terminology of war, with gunnery, cannons, and even bows-&-arrows and swords, obviously suggesting an origin of the form in the obscene songs of soldiers. (Compare the erotic scene turning on musical metaphors, in Shakespeare's *Taming of the Shrew*, III. i. 36–80.)

The first scientific publication of the French soldiers' songs, of an unexpurgated kind — in fact, the first scientific publication of the obscene songs of any nation — occupies most of volume III of *Kryptádia: Recueil de documents pour servir à l'étude des traditions populaires* (Heilbronn, 1886). The songs are traced when possible to the popular songbooks of the early sixteenth century in France — the earliest that exist — and the musical notation is also given in many cases. The editor of this first and model scientific collection of erotic folksong was the leading specialist in the older French folksongs, Gaston Pâris, though his name does not appear on the work. All the contributors to *Kryptádia* (which also contains some remarkable Welsh and Gaelic material) were agreed to retain their anonymity, until the principal editor, Prof. F. S. Krauss of Vienna, began the publication of the parallel but much larger series, *Anthropophytéia*, at the turn of the twentieth century.

Slightly before, and for the first time, the erotic songs of the French medical profession at last appeared in print, in an anonymous pamphlet issued by Unsinger (Liseux' usual printer) dated 1883, and containing only nine songs. The only known copy is preserved in the Library of the Faculty of Medicine of the University of Paris. It is specifically to such songs of the medical students or 'carabins' that the title of "Chansons de Salles de Garde" is given, though soldiers equally have guard-rooms — and similar songs. The identical songs of the medical students are shared, at least in France, and French-speaking Belgium and Switzerland, by students in other faculties as well, particularly art-students, and art-atelier assistants, a profession now almost extinct after hundreds of years of reflected glory in the 'schools' and ateliers of the master-painters of Italy and France.

How little the pamphlet of 1883 just described, with its nine songs, was representative of the real and tremendous float of erotic songs of the French students of medicine and art, can only be seen by comparing it with the very next publication of the same kind, which appeared — entirely without any other predecessor but this slender pamphlet — in the years 1912 and 1913, amateurishly and laboriously printed (the first volume is dated 1911 on the title-page, with a "Point Final" at the end, in 1912, complaining of the printing delay), probably somewhere in the provinces, under the title: *Anthologie Hospitalière & Latinesque: Recueil de Chansons de Salle de garde, anciennes et nouvelles, entre-lardées de Chansons du Quartier Latin, Fables, Sonnets, Charades, Elucubrations diverses, etc... Réunies par* Courtepaille. Paris, chez Bichat-porte-à-droite, 1911 (and 1913). The second volume has an "Avant-Propos" signed Taupin, obviously by a physician. The Bichat indicated in the imprint is of course the great French anatomist, Xavier Bichat, who died prematurely young in the United States in 1802, and who is the patron-saint of French medical students.

This work is very rare, and no repository copy is known in any public or university library in France or Britain, though a devoted collector has caused sets to be deposited — after nearly twenty years of searching for them — in various public and university libraries in the United States. Aside from its folkloristic songs and art-poems of the medical and humorous sort, the *Anthologie Hospitalière & Latinesque* includes an excessively large number of original medical and erotic poems, many of them of very mediocre quality, in particular those signed "Hébé," the pseudonym of the editor-publisher, whose initials were, in effect, E.B., and who, though certainly an excellent and industrious compiler, was by no means capable of producing viable 'folklore' at will, as none of the folksong compilers except Burns ever has, though many have tried. Folklore and folksong, as everyone knows, are wayward mistresses, and it is difficult indeed to know which art-song will become folksong — or why! — and which art-poem, of no seeming difference from any other of similar subject, will circulate orally and in painstaking manuscript copies, made and 'improved' by the folk, sometimes for centuries.

The further reprintings and fortunes of this key *Anthologie Hospitalière,* and of its mysterious compiler, the pharmacist-bookseller, 'Dr.' Edmond Bernard, are discussed at some length in my introduction (in French translation) to a one-volume abridgement of its contents — and that volume very narrow — published under the title *Les Chansons de Salle de Garde* (Paris: Cercle du Livre Précieux, 1962). Though the contents are not expurgated, the illustrations are, and in an outrageous way which I very much deplore. I am not responsible for the choice of either. This edition also includes a more or less complete bibliography of the some two dozen collections of these students'-songs in French, under many such different titles as *3 Orfèvres à la Saint-Éloi;* but almost all of these are nothing more than even briefer abridgments of Bernard's original *Anthologie* of 1912–13.

One very exceptional French collection that should be mentioned presents excellently the modern erotic songs of the French sailors, under the title, *Chansons de la Voile,* "*sans voiles,*" presented as by one "Jean-Marie Le Bihor, pour les amis du gaillard d'avant, Dunkerque," in 1935; but actually a supplement to the volume of expurgated sailors' songs published by the same author (Capt. Armand Hayet) in preceding years, *Chansons de Bord.* Two other collections of erotic sailors'-songs in French also exist, but Hayet-LeBihor's volume is clearly the best. This is similar to the format used by the earlier Scottish collectors, of grouping their 'unpublishable' erotic materials in supplementary privately-issued volumes of matching format to their publicly-issued collections. The only printed collection of English-language sailors' songs and chanteys of the 'unpublishable' kind is a small square volume with a lock set into the fore-edge of all its pages (in the only copy now known: Kinsey Institute), entitled *A Collection of Sea Songs and Ditties,* 'from the stores of Dave E. Jones.' This is American in origin, and was printed about 1928 or 1930, containing 48 pages. It has been attributed to either Frank Shay, or to David W. Bone, author of *Capstan Bars* (1931), on what grounds I do not know, with the implication that it is the erotic supplement to the publicly-issued chantey-collection of one or the other. Two further such collections do exist in English, but have not yet been published: the *Jones-Conklin Manuscript* (Folksong Archive, Indiana University), a collection of song-texts, about one-third erotic, mostly copied from broadsides of about 1825, and largely on subjects relating to the navy and the sea, which is being edited for publication by Dr. Kenneth S. Goldstein; and the supplement to Stan Hugill's superlative *Shanties from the Seven Seas* (London, 1961), which is discussed elsewhere in the present volume.

XI

THOUGH the largest part of the literature of actually erotic folk-song and balladry put on printed record during the last hundred years, in the English language, is that of the college groups, combined with that of the armed forces as earlier observed; none of this song material ever appeared in print until about 1927, in the collection *Immortalia*, probably edited by T. R. Smith (editor also of *Poetica Erotica,* from which certain pieces are reprinted), and privately printed in New York. None, that is, except for a bare handful of songs in the erotic magazine, *The Pearl* (1879–80, several times reprinted) and its sequels, *The Boudoir* and *The Cremorne* ('1851,' really 1882); and in Prof. Krauss' yearbook of erotic folklore, *Anthropophytéia* (1910–11) VII. 375, and VIII. 374, in which these few pages of British Army songs and jests, collected in India by a contributor signing himself "Dr. Susruta," are the entirety of the English-language materials in this ten-volume set and its further volumes of "Beiwerke" and "Beihefte."

Even the songs in *The Pearl*, etc., can hardly be considered 'folk,' but are mostly erotic and flagellational doggerel of the music-hall type, including a large group of limericks. A volume does exist, of similar songs and poems, stemming from the English universities, under the title *Cythera's Hymnal, or Flakes from the Foreskin,* under the obviously false imprint, 'Oxford: Printed at the University Press, for the Society for Promoting Useful Knowledge' (really London, 1870), and it must be admitted that this is one of the least pleasant and least readable such volumes that has ever been printed. Ashbee's *Index Librorum Prohibitorum* (1877, and reprints) I. 185–7, which describes it carefully, adds the brief but exact critical appreciation in French — apparently by the Belgian philologist and bibliographer, Octave Delepierre — '*Il est fâcheux que l'auteur (ou les compilateurs) ait donné tant de place à des morceaux d'un genre sale et désagréable,*' which says worlds for the difference between the songs in *Cythera's Hymnal* and those of erotic folksong as it really is. The whole collection reeks with the spirit, earlier discussed, of an *ordeal,* particularly for the reader. As is also true in many limericks, initiations, etc., the whole idea seems to be a striving to appear as 'sale et désagréable' as possible, by way of showing one's courage — 'Harder to be bad than to be good!' — virility, modernity, rebelliousness, and the like.

At least two of the university men who compiled *Cythera's Hymnal* have been identified: Capt. Edward Sellon, an erotic novelist of the 1860's, about whom Ashbee gives many details; and George Augustus Sala, a war-correspondent and private author of flagellational books (the inner connection need hardly be underlined). Sala is also author of *Harlequin Prince Cherrytop*, an erotic playlet or farce of a certain folklore interest, being largely composed of bawdy jokes and rather primitive catches and 'sells' (on which latter see *The Limerick*, 1953, p. 451, n. 1384, quoting Pope). This work has already passed into 'educated folklore' under the fabled title of *The Sod's Opera*, attributed naturally to Gilbert & Sullivan, and in the British Army recitation "King of the Goddam Isles." Nothing that is really folksong — even college folksong — will be found in *Cythera's Hymnal* except a version or parody of "No, John, No," or "The Spanish Merchant's Daughter." A few erotic folksongs, in music-hall revisions, do appear in the interestingly written pornographicum, *Randiana, or Excitable Tales* (1884), described as the final item in Ashbee's *Catena*, in particular a song beginning 'As Mary, dear Mary, one day was a-lying;' but the text is entirely spoiled by the writer's artistic assonances and variations in the repeats, a very common and unfolk music-hall trick.

One out-of-place item, accidentally reprinted during World War I, is likewise composed only of a set of music-hall pornographica in verse, though it does have a certain historical interest, as to the Civil War. This is *The Rakish Rhymer, or Fancy man's Own Songster and Reciter* (New York, c. 1864) of which no copy is now known to exist, but which was reissued in Paris in 1917, under the rubric 'Lutetia,' by the erotica-publisher Paul Ferdinando ("Charles Carrington") with the idea of catching the shillings of at least a few officers among the notably bawdy-singing English soldiers. But the contents were by then so old-fashioned, and in any case so out-of-keeping with the real soldiers' songs of either Britain or America, that it seems hard to believe it sold at all well. The only copy I know of, even of this reprint, is my own. A number of important folk-texts are nevertheless preserved in it, among its Civil War parodies earlier mentioned, principally a few in dialect humor — Irish, Scots, German-American, etc. — of the type of "Roy's Wife of Aldivalloch", "Dot Leetle Fur Cap" (still circulated as a Christmas novelty-card in America: this text not appearing in *The Rakish Rhymer,* but in another pornographicum of the period), and "Tim Finigan Wakes."

Altogether this means that there is really no printed record of erotic folksong in English, of either the college or army group or any other, between the 1820's volumes of the Scottish collectors, and the year 1927, except of the most fragmentary kind. Also, none of the great unpublished folksong collections in English, described in the chapter preceding, "Misconceptions in Erotic Folklore," contains any significant proportion of erotic folksong, except of the very mildest or most symbolized sort, all of which could long since have been published had anyone cared to deal seriously with these great manuscript collections.

A feeble echo of what must have been American college singing, in the law-schools, of the same kind and period as that of Sharman's "Scuffler's Club," quoted earlier, is recorded in Philip Hamburger's "The Great Judge" (in *Life,* 4 Nov. 1946; reprinted in his *The Oblong Blur,* 1949, p. 25), where Judge Learned Hand, famous for his liberal decisions in sex-literature cases in the 1930's that paved the way for the 'new freedom,' is described as being 'prevailed upon to sing a ribald song of the sea, entitled *The Cabin Boy,*' on a visit to Chief Justice Oliver Wendell Holmes. 'When they left Holmes [who 'relished his repertoire'], Hand turned to [Felix] Frankfurter and said, "I fear the old man thinks I am a mere vaudevillian".' The shortest known version of this ballad, in the limerick metre, begins:

> The good ship's name was *Venus,*
> Her mast a towering penis,
>   Her figure-head
>   A whore in bed —
> A pretty sight, by Jesus! . . .

It continues almost endlessly, working the "The Good Ship *Venus"* all the way from Australia to Liverpool, with the crew catching 'the syph in Teneriffe,' and every other possible geographical rhyme and sexual misadventure, including those of the captain's daughters and the ship dog. The rest of the 'repertoire' referred to remains unknown.

The Latin students' songs and epigrams were printed for the last time in *Medulla facetiarum* (Stuttgart, 1863); the greatest of the Neo-Latin erotica, Nicolas Chorier's *Dialogues of Luisa Sigea,* being similarly reprinted for the last time (by Weigel in Leipzig) as late as 1913, under the pseudonymous title of Joannis Meursii *Elegantiae Latini Sermonis,* for the German university audience. The students' songs in Germany were thereafter largely replaced by the scatological quintains of "Frau Wirtin," the students' land-lady, in the vulgar tongue; as, in Scotland, by the adding of new quatrains to the national framework of "The Ball o' Kirriemuir," and, in England and America, by bawdy limericks. It is signifi-cant, I think, that two of the only three university bawdy-song societies reliably reported in America over the last fifteen years are devoted strictly to the bawdy limerick, a subject to be dealt with more fully in the chapter following.

Beginning with the publication of *Immortalia* about 1927, a rapidly increasing group of American publications of erotic folk-songs, jokes, and obscœna of the 'novelty' kind, made an appear-ance, necessarily private and unfortunately rather amateur. All these publications, private as they may have been, stemmed from the growing liberalization of the Anglo-American moral scene as a result of World War I. The liberalization of book and magazine publishing is only one of many aspects of this development, though the one that will perhaps leave the clearest historical record. Many of these publications are more particularly concerned with jokes, etc., than with songs and poems — which there appear only inciden-tally — and are therefore dealt with more fully in the later chapter, "Toward a Motif-Index of Erotic Humor." In particular *Anecdota Americana* ('Boston' series, I and II), *The Book of a Thousand Laughs, Cleopatra's Scrapbook,* and *Bibliotheque Erotique* (in two volumes), all dating from about 1928–29. The specialized limerick collections comprise the largest part of this literature, as listed in the bibliography to *The Limerick* (1953). An imitation of *Immor-talia,* entitled *Poems, Ballads, and Parodies,* with imprint, 'Benares — Paris, 1923,' was issued probably in Detroit about 1928, and contains a number of texts not to be found elsewhere.

At the scholarly level, the attempt was also made to extend the growing liberalization of publishing to scholarly folksong collec-tions, in Arthur H. Fauset's *Folklore from Nova Scotia* (Memoirs of the American Folklore Society, vol. 25, 1931), which contains several very interesting unexpurgated song and tale texts, in-cluded without special comment in their logical place. The same attempt is apparent, to a lesser degree, in Louis W. Chappell's *Folk-Songs of Roanoke and the Albemarle* (Morgantown, W.Va.,

1939), though most of Prof. Chappell's unexpurgated collectings still remain unpublished in his files, as is also the case with the field-collected materials of a large number of other modern American ballad collectors. In any case, the lead of Fauset's and Chappell's courageous publications has not been followed by any of the other Anglo-American ballad scholars or collectors, and only at the present time is the attempt being again considered.

A most interesting private publication of the combined college and World War I songs, of American men, is *Lyra Ebriosa,* 'Being certain narrative ballads of vulgar or popular character and illustrative of the manners of the times,' issued in a Southern seaboard state in 1930, which contains only 31 pages, including the text of Mark Twain's "*1601.*" (Only known repository copy: University of Kentucky.) Yet even the few soldier songs recorded here make quite pathetic any comparison with the thoroughly expurgated *Songs and Slang of the British Soldier, 1914–1918,* edited and published by John Brophy and Eric Partridge (London, 1930; enlarged ed. 1931). Partridge's further contribution on the same subject, "From Two Angles," in *A Martial Medley* (London, 1931) p. 59–102, under the pseudonym, "Corrie Denison," is slightly less expurgated, and gives further texts. The real record of the British soldiers' songs is hardly more than caricatured in these publications.

An authentic and unexpurgated collection of the British soldiers' songs finally appeared just at the beginning of World War II, probably during the 'phoney War' period of late 1939 or 1940, as certain political references in the text make clear, in particular an anti-Nazi parody of "Jabberwocky." This mimeographed publication of 78 folio sheets, under the cover-title *Camp-Fire Songs and Verse,* 'Collected by a well known Cavalry Regiment,' was issued in India, probably in or near Madras, which is mentioned several times. The collection is notable for its very full texts, and the extremely large repertoire it presents. This is one of the essential documents in the modern history of erotic folksong in English, and it is fortunate that a copy has survived. This copy was brought back to England, a decade later, by a British jurist, and was very kindly ceded to me, at a price set purposely low — since it is beyond price — by an English bookseller knowing of my study in the field, and to whom I wish to express my gratitude. Here, finally, one has the record of the bawdy songs the British soldiers really sang in World War I, and unquestionably since the late nineteenth century. A bare handful of matching British armed-forces' ballads of World War II are given in the private supple-

ment to Pinto & Rodway's *The Common Muse* (1957) p. 434-9.
The far more important record of Hamish Henderson's *Ballads of
World War II* (Glasgow, 1947) has already been mentioned.

Mimeographed songbooks like the British India *Camp-Fire
Songs* became the rule during World War II, particularly among
the Canadian and American airforces, and still continue to be
issued. They are of course an unsanctioned activity, privately
undertaken by the men. I have had the good fortune to be able
to collect copies of quite a number of these — though by no means
all. There is no real point in listing all the known titles here. They
begin in date with *North Atlantic Squadron* (Gander Bay, Newfoundland, 1944), and *Songs of the Airedales in the Pacific*
(Australia, 1944). A very interesting example, of which the only
known copy is preserved at Harvard, is *Aloha Jigpoha,* appearing
just after World War II, in Honolulu, 1945, and including both
the political songs as well as the bawdy-song repertoire of officers
trained at Boulder, Colorado, for service against Japan. Quite a
few of these mimeographed airforce songbooks developed out of
the Korean War. The most considerable are *Death Rattlers* (Ma-
rine Air Corps, Korea, 1952?) and a very large collection extending
to 121 hektographed quarto leaves, with a 30-page further supplement in thermographic copy of the typescript, *The Fighter Pilots
Hymn Book,* compiled by Capt. William J. Starr (Cannon Airforce
Base, New Mexico, 1958), limited to one hundred copies. This is
the only such American collection signed by the compiler.

A further courageous aspect of all these airforce collections
is the inclusion not only of the usual bragging songs of expected
victory and *esprit de corps,* but also the brooding songs — far less
well publicized — of expected death; the singers not being afraid
to exteriorize and express their fear. A number of these pessimistic
songs will be found in the openly published but very expurgated
collection, *Air Forces Airs,* edited by William Wallrich (New York,
1957). The World War I songs of John J. Niles' *Songs My Mother
Never Taught Me* (New York, 1929) and E. A. Dolph's *Sound Off!*
(1927); and of World War II in Eric Posselt's two collections,
Give Out! (New York, 1943; repr. 1944), and *G.I. Songs* (1944,
under the name of "Edgar Palmer"), similarly contain little more
than expurgated texts. The same is true of the two (possibly three)
gift or souvenir volumes, edited by Melbert B. Cary, Jr., at the
Press of the Woolly Whale, New York, 1930-35, of the principal
Army song of World War I, *Mademoiselle from Armentières* (the
earlier British song, "Three German Officers Crossed the Rhine,"

a parody of Uhland's necrophilic "The Landlady's Daughter.")
Another volume of the same title, and similarly expurgated contents, edited by J. T. Winterich (Peter Pauper Press, 1953), was
obviously intended entirely as a reminiscence, since "Mademoiselle
from Armentières" was hardly sung at all during World War II.

   During the late 1950's, in Tokyo, a reprint of *Immortalia*
— originally a fine large quarto — was issued in small duodecimo
size by a Japanese offset-printing firm for sale to American soldiers
and tourists, as by the "Karman Society," and with compiler's
name given as "Arthur Mackay," probably a pseudonym. The
original edition of 1927 gives no compiler's name, and has been
more reliably attributed to T. R. Smith, compiler also of *Poetica
Erotica,* an anthology (often reprinted) of erotic art-poetry in
English. As with Carrington's reprinting of a Civil War songster
during World War I, in Paris; this Japanese reprint of *Immortalia*
is a good example of the hopeless and unconscious anachronism of
a certain kind of chapbook publishing activity — especially common as to jestbooks and dreambooks, formerly the songbooks' only
real competitors in the popular field. The songs in *Immortalia* are,
by and large, not in any way those of World War II or the Korean
War, and are also occasionally badly revised and poetized by the
compiler, who goes so far, for instance, as to print the parody side-
show spiel or recitation, "The Hamburg Show" ("Larry, Turn the
Crank") p. 153, in broken lines, as though it were in verse.

   A more recent enlargement of *Immortalia,* under the title of
Folk Poems and Ballads ('Mexico City, 1945,' really U.S., 1948),
suffers disastrously from the editor's amateur equipment and ear,
with the usual editorial mania for silently 'improving' his materials, and some peculiarly truculent anti-religious asides which
nearly sent him to jail. A similarly faked collection of British
songs and poems, partly of Army provenance, appeared in Paris,
1956, as "Count Palmiro Vicarrion's" *Book of Bawdy Ballads,* its
principal interest being that it is the first printed presentation of
British material of this type since the closing down of the erotic
magazine, *The Pearl,* and its continuations as *The Cremorne,* etc.,
about 1883. This *Book of Bawdy Ballads,* which was hacked together in a great hurry to preëmpt the field — as shown by
the unfinished musical notations attempted — is of course put
entirely in the shade by the British India collection of about 1940,
Camp-Fire Songs and Verse, mentioned above. The pseudonymous
"Vicarrion" is identified, in recent catalogues of the British bookseller Bernard Stone, as the internationally famous Liverpool poet,

Mr. Christopher Logue, whose own signed volumes of Angry Young Man (British beatnik) poetry have been compared by *Time* magazine to the *Song of Songs*. I would not go quite so far.

IX

THE BAWDY sea-chanteys, which, like the soldiers' songs and for the same reasons, tended to be far rougher and more detailed in their eroticism than the bawdy songs of country origin, have now disappeared along with the wooden ships on which they were sung. Some had of course simply been land-songs taken out to sea, especially those not used in chanteying, but for singing 'before the mast' in the sailors' off-hours, though with significantly altered texts. As noted earlier, only one brief group of the authentic un-expurgated chanteys and 'forebitters' has ever been printed at all, in the little *Collection of Sea Songs and Ditties* 'from the stores of Dave E. Jones,' mentioned above, a tiny, canvas-bound booklet, printed without place or date (but in the U.S. about 1928 or 1930), with a hole punched through each page and the covers to accommodate a padlock. The one known copy of this booklet has now disappeared, but I was fortunately able to make a complete copy of it before its disappearance, in 1944. Through the kindness of one of the last of the British shantymen, Mr. Stan Hugill, a manuscript group of British chanteys, dating from the 1920's, has also been recovered. Except for this manuscript collection and the "Jones" booklet, the bawdy chanteys would soon be as entirely lost in print as they have become in fact; and it would be impossible, in future times, actually to assess or understand their erotic content from the absolutely terrified hints and dark implications (as about 'hog-eye') in all the printed chantey collections. The best recent opportunity to take a frank stand, and remedy the matter, was very regrettably missed when unexpurgated recordings were made, in an American sailors' home, for use in Mr. William Doerflinger's *Shantymen and Shanty-boys* (1951), but, as published in this volume, the American sailing-man's and seaboard-logger's life and song are presented as being chastely, almost virginally devoid of sex.

In the same way, the unexpurgated soldiers' songs of World War I and II — not to mention those earlier, and now forever unrecoverable — have been preserved only in the few private mimeographica earlier mentioned, made in outlying airforce bases in Newfoundland, Australia, the Hawaiian Islands, Guam, etc.;

the one honorable exception among the printed volumes being Hamish Henderson's *Ballads of World War II* (1947), largely of Scottish provenance, and interestingly intermixed with political songs, as in the American mimeographed collection *Aloha Jigpoha*. It seems hardly necessary to say that the official and semi-official song books of both wars, and the many namby-pamby 'songs of men' collections intended to cash in on the wars (a charming thought, isn't it?) were repositories only of the most unsung and unsingable patriotic cant and pantywaist naughtiness. Why soldiers are expected to kill and be killed in real earnest, but to make love only in simpering U.S.O. euphemisms of the 'roll me over and do it again' variety, is hard to understand. In any case, there seems to have been a bit of progress between the two wars, as in the recollection of World War I in England, in Norman Hancock's "War from the Ranks," in *A Martial Medley* (1931) p. 145, observing that the standard fare at the soldiers' clubs then had been 'Prayers, hymns, and a plate of rice and prunes for tuppence. Gives yer the belly ache, dont it?'

Privately published collections of bawdy songs do exist, in all these genres, as has been seen, and several important modern manuscripts. However, the printed volumes are all so excessively rare or unique, and so almost completely unknown, that it has seemed worthwhile to give references to them, and some short *aperçu*, at least of what they contain, which will have to serve the generality of readers. Few of even the most relatively modern works cited will be found in any public or university library anywhere, and anyone who aspires actually to collect these volumes will have to be outfitted with more luck and money than I had when I was Prof. Kinsey's bibliographer for over two years, with unlimited discretion to buy books in just this field.

The college songs themselves, which one would imagine to be the one set of materials that could have been preserved, if only in manuscript, in the universities, do so exist; but until recently these have been collected only in the private guest-books and manuscript repertoire of the fraternities and 'houses,' especially in the older colleges of England and America. These have also, on occasion, caused trouble to the students, and have been detroyed in part. On the turning back to the colleges of men in the American armed forces, the army mimeographica of World War II have continued as mimeographed collections of the bawdy college songs, heavily skewed in the direction of limericks — which are now *sung* — including the new science-fiction limericks.

One curious transitional collection was *Unexpurgated*, issued in Los Angeles, 1943, as by the 'Bidet Press,' and reissued without title as by the 'Open Box Press' ("Edited by R. Schloch, Ph.D."), of which no copies are now known except in private hands, among science-fiction enthusiasts, as it happens. This is largely a collection of limericks, but including also 'class-conscious' bawdy ballads of the socialist ultra-left: a good example of the 'revolt' even against revolt. A mimeographed collection made by students at the California Institute of Technology, about 1960, *Songs of Raunch and Ill-Repute*, made the tactical error of giving the student publishers' correct address, and this work was seized and in large part destroyed. The révolté young men of Cal-Tech have now no permitted public way of expressing their deeper emotions on these subjects except their annual half-naked mudfight, an interesting anal sadistic spectacle, without even the pretext of a football being struggled over to explain it, of which photographs appear regularly in the national picture-magazines. But no bawdy songs, please! As the president of an entirely different North American university explained — on the dignified attempt being made to publish materials on exactly the subject of bawdy song — 'I'll sweep the floor with any bloody son of a bitch who commits any God-damned breach of taste around here.'

Nevertheless, the college songs and other erotic folklore of the campus are being collected at the present time, in a serious way, for the folklore archives of various American universities, by the fairly simple expedient of setting the students themselves to bringing in this material from their own fraternities and 'beer-busts,' also sororities; and sometimes presenting it in term papers. This successfully brings a large amount of somewhat reduplicative material to hand rather quickly, and it is regrettable that this could not be done long before. It is also not yet known what can or will be published of these collections, which are clearly a formalized development of the 'house' and fraternity private repertoire books. Where trained folklorists are involved in this collecting, a very high level of perceptiveness in both the collecting and interpretation is possible, as in Dr. Roger Abrahams' epochal thesis, *Negro Folklore from South Philadelphia* (1961), discussed in an earlier chapter.

In the case of certain professions, such as cowboys and hoboes, it is no longer possible to go back now and collect the songs that were rejected or overlooked when these were far more common than they are now. Nothing but expurgated texts, absurdly romanticized in exactly the fake lines replacing those expurgated, have been printed in any of the various cowboy-song volumes, such as that of the late Prof. John A. Lomax, though a few untampered originals are still preserved among his Texas manuscripts. Only one unexpurgated cowboy ballad seems to have been recorded for the phonograph, in the private 'party-record' presentation common toward the end of 78-rpm period of the 1940's (though very few of the songs on such private recordings are actual folksongs, being mostly nightclub or neo-music-hall hoke). This is the almost unbearably long and detailed "Castration of Strawberry Roan," which may be compared — by those who can endure the subject-matter — to the broadside and drollery ballad, "The Gelding of the Devil," which is of course derived from the folktale 'Le Diable de Papefiguière" in Rabelais' *Pantagruel,* Bk. IV, chap. 45–7, later versified by La Fontaine.

The hobo and tramp songs, which are of great folklore interest, being almost the last expression of the semi-professional wandering class at least as old as the dissolution of the monasteries and alms-houses under Henry VIII, appear only in forms so expurgated as to be mere caricatures, in Godfrey Irwin's *American Tramp and Underworld Slang* (London, 1931), and George Milburn's *The Hobo's Hornbook* (New York, 1930), of which the latter offers one of the most fabulously complete and complex expurgating systems of asterisks, hyphens, dashes and dots, that has ever seen print. The Gypsy songs, which are parallel in part, are now fortunately being collected without expurgation in Scotland, where they still principally survive.

Many of the modern sagas of high erotic adventure, such as "Christopher Columbo" (of which the history is traced in Walter Klinefelter's *Preface to an Unprintable Opus,* by "Pedro Pococampo," Portland, Maine, 1942, limited to seventy-five copies), "The Bastard King of England," and "Our Lil," about which more still remains to be said, all take their backgrounds from the life of sailors, cowboys, bush-rangers, hoboes, and so forth, but must be carefully distinguished from the authentic productions, or even favorite songs, of real sailors, cowboys, etc., which the songs above-cited are not. Most of these songs — and many of them are not songs at all, but simply poems and recitations — cannot be traced earlier than the 1890's, and it is also usual to find them fitted out with bogus attributions to such authors as Jack London, Robert Service, Rudyard Kipling (never forgetting to add, 'Yes, and it cost 'im the poet-lariatship too!') and Eugene Field; just as, earlier, Robert Burns, and more modernly A. P. Herbert or even G. B. Shaw and Noel Coward! — all almost certainly false, expect in the case of Eugene Field.

In this wilderness of professional silence and amateur irresponsibility, it is hoped to publish soon a very large and broadly typical collection of bawdy songs and poems in English, gathered from all classes and professions, and from the entire English-speaking world, traced to their earliest texts in preceding centuries where possible, and suitably annotated, as the second publication in the series, "Les Hautes Études," in which *The Limerick* (Paris, 1953) forms volume I, and of which I have the honor to be editor. Another very important collection, repositoried in manuscript in at least two public and university libraries in the United States, is that made solely in the Ozark Mountains of Arkansas and Missouri by Mr. Vance Randolph, and these materials are also to be issued in the same series. Mr. Randolph's collection includes not only "Unprintable Songs," but also large and valuable selections of the obscene folk-rhymes of children — a prime transmitting and retaining group, always — also riddles, toilet-epigraphs, folk-sayings, etc., gathered and presented in the best tradition of the volumes of sexual ethnology and folklore published by Prof. Friedrich S. Krauss, as *Kryptádia* and *Anthropophytéia* (with all their 'bei'-series and 'bei'-volumes) from 1883 to 1931. The Randolph "Unprintable" manuscript not only includes the musical notation of all the songs, but is supported by a series of nearly one thousand phonographic recordings, deposited in the Folksong Division of the Library of Congress. It is altogether a fascinating and remarkable supplement to his many published volumes of Ozark folklore, and deserves and demands publication, though this has evidently been impossible until now in America.

The contamination of folksong by well-meaning expurgation and — even worse — by pretentious 'poetical' editing, is worth more space than can be given to it here; nor is the major part of its damage limited in any special way to erotic folksong. As far as the erotic collections are concerned, the rule of thumb seems to be that the better the printing of the presumably 'bawdy song' or 'songs of men' volumes, the less likely they are to contain anything bawdy or authentic; while the amateurish and smearily-produced mimeographed folios (always of very limited editions, in fact) will generally be found to contain the real texts. The most thorough-going example of this sad contradiction that one has recently seen is the contribution to the subject by the Canadian singer, Oscar Brand, a professional radio and recording entertainer, under the title *Bawdy Songs and Backroom Ballads,* handsomely printed and presented in New York, 1960. In this large and colorful volume the texts are not only as ruthlessly expurgated as might be imagined, but seem also to have been revised and modernized with the intention of making them more 'entertaining.' This is the classic and even innocent intention of all folklore revisers, who cannot be made to understand that they are doing damage no matter how well they mean.

This particular volume is a continuation of Mr. Brand's earlier series of phonograph recordings of the same title (Audio-Fidelity 906, 1806 and following), numbering five or more in all, issued since 1955. Mr. Brand sings well, according to popular standards, also accompanies himself — sometimes dubbing himself in as a second guitar and voice, to give the listener full measure — and the only really grating note is the demanded expurgation, rising to some kind of reverse climax in the presentation of the Civil War parody "No Balls at All" as "No *Hips* at All," and in the verbal broken-field running of the final verse given for "The Little Ball of Yarn," which achieves the true pinnacle or *ne plus ultra* of any expurgator-reviser's art. This is really a pity, because Mr. Brand has made a definite bid to dominate the field, and evidently has had the unexpurgated materials before his eyes, though he has yet to put anything authentically 'bawdy' into either his recordings or books except the tunes.

The truth of the matter is that this type of expurgation and revision has been going on continuously for many centuries, and more particularly in the hands of the entertainer-singers now again attracting public attention in the 'folksong' field, than in the hands of scholars or scholarly collectors, however uncourageous. It is even a part of the activity of real folksingers, in all periods, who continuously change and modify their texts, and even their tunes, though often they are unconscious of so doing, and will deny it if asked. Yet nothing is more positive than that the texts, at least, have been continuously changing during the centuries of their transmission, until often nothing remains but the original rhymes, if that. The underlying cause here is the nature of the original activity in the creation of a folksong, or any other song, which is first and foremost the poetic creation of the *words* of the chant, rhyme, lyric or narrative poem, which then becomes the song when fitted to music — very often to music taken at second hand.

Every ballad and song is essentially only a poem set to music. This seems merely a truism, and is stated far better in Kittredge's 'The text is the thing.' Yet, were it to be recollected, there would be far less confusion than there is at present over the fact that *the basic activity of folksong is not that of the musician but that of the poet* — folk poet or formal poet as the case may be. The music is the vehicle, and no more than that, and is not the primary element except in folk-music, such as dance tunes, not connected with singing. The music is of course a vehicle of great emotional value, and is also of use in inspiring the form of later additions to the song, and in its mnemonic recollection and transmission. But it is nevertheless only a vehicle, and often simply borrowed from some other or older song, a point worth insisting upon.

This subordinance of the music has been badly lost sight of by recent scholars, in part owing to the musical emphasis and predisposition of folksong scholarship since the time of Chappell and of Sharp, for well over a century now. An excessive interest in the music of folksong, as distinguished from the words, has also been bloated up owing, on the one hand, to the avoidance by these means of any concern with the basic erotic tone and texts of so much of folksong, and, on the other, to an evasion by these means of the inevitable implication of the present diminishing returns in field collecting: namely, that it is now time to *study* folksong, instead of simply collecting it. That certainly does not mean to continue studying nothing but its music. The musicological approach, as a primary interest in the study of folksong, has always been a mere blind, or blind alley. This is perhaps the opposite of the error of the formal poet or popular or scholarly collector, assuming too great an importance for his own silent poetic 'improvements' of field-collected texts, in the style of Bishop Percy and Sir Walter Scott; but it is an error just as well.

It cannot be doubted that the historical development of poetry, as a *formal* art, is later in time than that of primitive folksong. For it is not in the cold, technical formalizations and conventions of poetry that the essence of the poetic art resides, but rather in the original word-handling part and in everything implied in the word inspiration. The later concentration on techniques and codified forms is more commonly the activity of orators and philologists who are not poets at all (as in Aristotle's *Rhetoric* and *Poetics*), or of dilettante poets unsure of their inspiration, who are generally only in the field for its secondary advantages such as its use in pleasing and attracting women. A word more should be said about this last point.

Erotic poetry, especially in the form of song, is extremely ancient. It was considered by the Greeks to be a special form of the poetic art, with its own muse, Erato — she with the lyre — indicating the intimate relation to music. This relation is always sensed, as to erotic poetry in particular, and is clearly admitted by the repressive religious objection to all music other than that used in worship, and even there with the prohibition of certain too 'sensual' instruments and 'lascivious' modes. Shakespeare takes the opposite and natural point of view of the lover, in the opening line of *Twelfth Night:* 'If Musicke be the food of Love, play on.'

The only other forms of poetry thought worthy of muses by the Greeks were lyric and heroic poetry (that is to say, songs and ballads, but on themes other than erotic), and these were understood to be derivative. They could hardly have preceded love poetry, or rather love song, which is, after all, not unique to the human species or even to the mammalian order. The love-calls and sexual displays of any number of male animals and birds, even insects — some of which, lacking vocal cords, perform their love-music with their feet or wings to attract the female — and particularly the spasmodic cries and bodily motions and swayings of the rutting period and heat period in animals of both sexes, imply a long pre-history of erotic song and of erotic dance, as integral parts of the sexual approach of living creatures, long preceding the appearance of human life on earth. This is also true of other arts, in some of which, such as architecture and aerial navigation, the insects (for example dragonflies) are still immeasurably superior to man. Probably the most specifically human development in the sphere of poetry and song has been in its later enlargement from a total concern with the erotic domain, to include the more recent and derivative lyric and heroic themes, respresenting respectively the presumed interests of women and of men.

The citations earlier made, from the Abbé Nadal and from scriptural texts, tend very strongly to show that song was first developed into a formal art in human cultures (including responsory singing) not by the males, out of their rutting- or war-cries, but by female poets and singers. As is generally admitted nowaday, on the basis of the work of Briffault, the present patriarchal system arose from a seizing of power from a world-wide and more natural matriarchy preceding. In the taking over of power from the female group, all their religious and honorific trappings and activities were also taken over by the men, especially by the priestly class, or stated to have always been theirs — as in the example of the "Song of Miriam," already noted — the women later being rigidly excluded from these very activities. The triumphal songs of the soldiers are clearly among these ultimately usurped activities, and it is their satirical bent, rather than the earlier noble tone of thanksgiving (as in harvest ceremonies) that seems particularly to have developed in the hands of men. It is thus the *triambos,* or fig-leaf mask carried by the comic and phallic satirical street-performers in the festival of Bacchus, that gives its name, according to Nadal, to the 'triumph' itself (quoting Zonare, Tome II, "On Diocletian").

By the time of the *Greek Anthology* and the Latin *Priapeia,* the whole tone of love poetry, and of poetry in general, had become signally intermixed with that of satire, and, as in the *Priapeia* and Martial's *Epigrams,* a satire specifically obscene. Here again, one can be almost sure that a usurpation has taken place, and a profound and damaging change of accent — the forerunner and type of the modern parodic 'improvement.' The satirical priapic poems (which have become the modern bawdy songs of men), hung on the phallic 'god of gardens,' and threatening with pedication anyone who steals the crops or disturbs the garden, just as Shakespeare's epitaph threatens with damnation anyone who moves his bones, are open parodies of the women's sincerely erotic *ex votos* earlier hung on the same statues and in the same groves and gardens, but for a far different reason, under matriarchal and sex-worshipping religions; and which still continue — variously disguised, but still as *ex votos* of fertility — in the churches of the patriarchal and sex-hating religions that have come later. Even if the grunts of Adam, when he delved, are now to be understood as socially conscious work- or war-songs; Eve, when she spun, has never sung of anything but pregnancy, children, and love.

X

WHAT DO plain people sing when they sing bawdy? And what is it that is so bloody frightening about it all, that no publicly published ballad volume in English has ever yet been able to include more than a few hints or well-expurgated verses? The country people of England whose songs could still be collected by Cecil Sharp, Alfred Williams, and others about the turn of the century — though they never published any of the few even mildly sexual songs they collected — and the highland singers of the southern United States, whose songs have been collected so strenuously since about 1910, do sing or did sing a not-very extensive group of traditional ballads in which the young man goes to bed with his young woman, or makes love to her in the open, on the grass, with more or less (usually less) erotic detail, and often with airs and verses of great beauty. There are also a large number of country songs of sexual humor and satire, or misadventure, inevitably a bit more crude than the love songs. These two groups of materials represent the largest proportion of the sexual songs still unpublished in the great manuscript collections referred to several times above; and they demand publication, and that the centuries of their history be traced.

These country songs of country people are of a sexual naturalness and simplicity which actually places them beyond all criticism. They are precious part of the heritage of folk-art in the English language. Songs of this sort have not been dealt with at any length in the present essay, first because they cannot truly be called 'bawdy,' and are certainly not in any sense obscene. They need to be dealt with from a quite different approach, in an entirely different context, and probably by other researchers than myself. Secondly, this is too large a subject to be handled here as it deserves. Whole volumes could and must be devoted to the publication and interpretation of the folk love-songs of the English language, and the matching songs of humor and satire, from late medieval to modern times. And there are also other languages.

This much seems clear already. The great consonant pattern of country life — and its immeasurable superiority over industrial or commercial city life, for the human individual — is the entering of the human being into a close relation with the real and tremendous rhythm of life, death, and resurrection that is the underlying pattern of the agricultural, or pastoral and natural life. In this life of nature, as opposed sharply to the life of city-culture, the key reality, or mystery, or act of faith, and the principal possibility of *change* that the human being is able to enact, in the great procession of time and the seasons, rises in monolithic fashion from the sexuality and fertility of nature: from the sowing and expected fertility of seeds, with their flowers and fruits; of animals and birds, and of human beings. Without embracing this central reality — wholly, and without laziness or prudery — no real relationship can be made or expected with nature, with agriculture, or the keeping of animals and flocks. Everything connected with the life of country people rises from this attempt to enter into consonance with the stream of nature, of time, and the elements; fighting and changing these just enough to make human life possible. The folklore, the science, the religion, and the songs of people living this life are filled, in a sincerely accepted way, with the profound sexual tonality, both open and symbolized, that is basic to its fabric. The sexuality and fertility of the human being becomes his or her principal feature, as it is in biological fact, and the prime concern of the husbandman. He sees it, he accepts it, and he celebrates it in his folklore and song, precisely as he accepts the same immanent sexuality of every other part of his life, with the superb simplicity of Shakespeare's *Antony and Cleopatra*, II. ii. 242: 'He plough'd her, and she cropt.'

Two English country love songs of unknown date, famous in particular for their beauty, are "The Bugaboo," often somewhat meaninglessly called "The Foggy Foggy Dew;" and "The Boatsman," usually known as "Blow the Candle Out" and sung to a tune very similar to that of "The Lincolnshire Poacher":

> Your father and your mother
> In yonder room do lie,
> Embracin' one another,
> So why not you and I?
>
> Embracin' one another
> Without no fear nor doubt,
> So roll me in your arms, my dear,
> And blow the candle out.

Or the song may be a proud and artless brag by the young man, entering boldly into the anatomical details he cannot get out of his mind, as in the modern parody of "The Ash Grove," one of the loveliest of Welsh airs, with the glorying chorus:

> I've seen it, I've seen it,
> I've *been* in betwee-ee-een it —
> The hair on her dicky di-do
> Hung down to her knee!

Or the lament of the maid betrayed, as in that most often collected of all such songs, "Rosemary Lane," now better know in its nautical and false-nautical versions as "Home, Boys, Home," and "Bell-Botton Trousers":

> Once I was a serving-maid, down in Drury Lane,
> My master used to beat me, my mistress did the same,
> Till along came a sailor, with buttons on his knee,
> And that was the beginning of all my miseree.

The necessary censorship under which ballad collections have been inevitably prepared for publication, even the collections of the notably bawdy sea-chanteys, have made it impossible for them ever yet to record the rare verse of wonderfully graphic detail which follows the usual verse where this poor girl, who

> . . . like a foolish maid, thinkin' it no harm,
> Crept in bed beside him for to keep the sailor warm.

> She had no lovin' husband for to save her from his spell,
> She had no kind young sister, did our sorry little Nell,
> And very soon she'd dropped her drawers and let him sheet
>   it home;
> He rammed it up until she felt it tickle her backbone.

Yet this nautical version appeared only a few years ago, cut down to nothing more than exactly this stanza, in a minor British literary review — and heaven did not fall. It should be mentioned, also, for the record, that there is a fairly unexpurgated version in one of the two publicly-published collections that have come closest to freedom, L. W. Chappell's *Folk-Songs of Roanoke and the Albemarle* (1939, p. 60, a fragment entitled "The Boy Child," and compare also "Jackie Rover," at p. 87).

This is not the place, nor is there here the space, for a categorized analysis of all the themes and sorts of bawdy song, even those benefitting from the clearest and most orthodox folk transmission. It does seem worth noting, however, that in the many variations on the theme of husband and wife who do not get along, violence and profanity can be expected to replace any sexual libretto, and that is what generally happens. This is the case in the only three humorous sexual songs of modern survival that Child's famous collection records at all — "Our Goodman", "Get Up and Bar the Door," and "The Farmer's Curst Wife" — and it would appear to be strictly because of this substitution of

sexual hatred for sexual intercourse that an exception was made
for them. (Child, Nos. 274, 275, and 278.) All of these, in any
case, are given in versions far milder than those sung by university
students at the turn of the century, when Child or his assistants
could certainly have collected them had they tried. The uncen-
sored and 'unselected' versions are still widely current, "Our
Goodman" under the title "The John B. Stetson Pisspot" and
many others.

One further exception, "The Old Woman of Slapsadam, or
The Wife of Kelso," remains unpublished among Child's manuscripts at Harvard. This appears to be a version of "Johnny Sands,"
the song that starts the fight on the raft in Mark Twain's *Life
on the Mississippi*, in which the adulterous wife gives poison to
her husband, in order to blind him, and then offers to help him
commit suicide in his despair. An Irish version, "Eggs and Mar-
rowbones," beginning 'There was an oul' woman in our town,'
is handsomely rendered by the Canadian singer, Tom Kines, on
his recording *Of Maids and Mistresses* (Elektra 137, issued in
1957), noting that he 'took this charming version down from
the singing of a parish priest in a small fishing village in County
Antrim, North Ireland. (See other references in G. Malcolm
Laws, *American Balladry from British Broadsides*, 1957, No.
Q 2–3, p. 274–5.)

As has already been observed, Child completely omits any
text of, or reference to, the song having the longest unbroken
genealogy of any bawdy song in English, "Good Morning Mister
Fisherman," or "John Henry and the Crab" (as it is now generally
called), though a version dating from about 1620, under the title
"The Sea Crabb," is given in the "Loose and Humorous" supplement to the *Percy Folio Manuscript*, of which Child was one
of the editors and the prime mover in its ultimate scholarly
publication. The identical story is also found as a prose-tale in
various French jest-collections of the late sixteenth and early
seventeenth centuries, and in earlier Italian as well as Levantine
sources, always ending with the *vagina dentata* element of the
sea-crab simultaneously clutching the pubis of the wife and the
nose of her husband. The song retained this element at least
until 1927, as printed in *Immortalia*, p. 58–9, though it has disappeared from all versions collected (to my knowledge) in recent
years. "The Sea Crab" is a bawdy folksong that can stand as a
sample of many, both as to the sort of themes and treatment
employed, and for its evident appeal to the transmitting audience

in various cultures, over the centuries of its existence. A number of texts are printed, but very poorly analyzed on the Finnish trait-and-motif tabulation method — a cold and thoroughly inhuman approach of unproved value — by Mr. Guthrie Meade, in *Midwest Folklore* (1958) VIII. 91–100, with historical tracings lumped into a final note, taken mainly from Stith Thompson and Wesselski without proper credit given. If this is a sample of the sort of handling and analysis of erotic folksong being taught to folk-lorists in training today, the future of any such study looks mighty glum indeed.

Also omitted by Child is any version of the oldest surviving erotic folksong in English, "A Talk of Ten Wives on their Husbands' Ware," though this too had already been published by Furnivall, from Ormsby-Gore's Porkington MS (about 1460), in *Jyl of Breyntford's Testament* (Ballad Society, volume 7a, 1871, pp. 6, 29–33). This remarkable bragging- or lying-song which is probably connected with the similar French prose *Évangiles des Quenouilles*, or 'old wives' decameron' of the fifteenth century (in Jannet's Elzévirienne edition, Paris 1855), is the more remarkable in that it is still very widely sung today, but in a transformation in which the 'wives' lie about their own sexual organs' incredible size, and not that of their husbands', beginning:

> Three old whores from Canada
> Were drinking brandy wine,
> And their whole conversation was:
> Your cunt's no bigger than mine.
>
> You're a liar, says the first,
> For mine's as big as the sea;
> The ships sail in and the ships sail out,
> And they never bother me, &c.

Variants collected in New York, Cleveland, Newfoundland, Vancouver, the South Pacific, and England, from 1939 to 1955, all with a very dysphemistic chorus, change the locale sometimes to Baltimore or Mexico, and the wine to cherry; but Canada and brandy are the favorites. "Our John's Brak Yestreen," in Burns' *Merry Muses of Caledonia* (c. 1800, ed. 1959, p. 84), in which the neighbour wives discuss the problem as to whether their hus-bands' penises are of sinew or bone, rather clearly stands at the point of change between the ancient "Talk of Ten Wives" and

the modern "Three Old Whores," or "The Whoorey Crew."
Burns' text begins in a form very similar to the modern:

> Twa neebor wives sat i' the sun,
> A twynin' at their rocks,
> An' they an argument began,
> An' a' the plea was c - - ks.

Gerrit Kalff in his thesis, *Het Lied in de Middeleeuwen*
(1908) gives an eighteenth-century Dutch version entitled "Wens-
liedje" (Wishing-Song), bridging the gap between the Porkington MS. form, and the modern song, with even closer verbal
similarities, but the cognate English form has never been recovered. Kalff's eighteenth-century transitional text begins, oddly
enough (in translation): 'Seven little wives fine, Sat on an evening
drinking Brandywine . . .' It may also be observed that 'old
whore' — aways pronounced colloquially with the 'o' as a long
'u,' in both languages — is a Dutch term for any bad-tempered
or nagging woman, not necessarily a prostitute; suggesting that
this element too may have been derived from a Dutch text, via the
presumed lost English form. The date of this posited but lost
form is probably in the seventeenth century, at the latest, as with
the similar songs of Dutch provenance — and in that language —
sung on the stage in Thomas Heywood's *Rape of Lucrece* (1608)
by a comedian assumed to have played in continental European
companies earlier. It is curious to observe that the chorus of
the modern song generally ends with the shouted 'I'm one of the
whoorey (*or* jovial) crew!' suggesting a relation to the song "The
Jovial Beggars" or "The Jovial Crew" (in Chappell, ed. 1893,
II. 52), or even to the play, *A Jovial Crew,* in 1641 (printed in
1652), by Richard Brome, whose similar *The Northern Lass*
(1632) had been one of the very first of the English 'ballad operas'
based on the use of appropriated folksongs and folk backgrounds,
as is also the case with the *Masque of the Gypsies Metamorphos'd*
(1621) by Ben Jonson, whose servant and friend Brome had been.

VIII

THE SEXUAL FOLKLORE of children is by no means the most difficult to collect, but it is the most difficult to make certain folklorists realize has been authentically collected from children.
If the collecting of erotic folklore and folksong always requires
tact, the collection of children's lore of this kind requires in-

finite tact. The children know very well that grown-ups do not generally approve of this part of their play, and private-initiatory activity, and are not easily persuaded that it will be accepted without moral shock, and — what is more important — without reprisals later, on the part of parents or teachers. The folklorist in this case must take sides against authority, and become a member of the quasi-secret community of the child. Or else, such examples of the sexual folklore of children that can be collected can only be those which fall accidentally or punitively into the teachers' hands. It is obvious that this is not a satisfactory way of collecting folk material, of any age-group. The same problem exists with prison-lore.

Among the items of erotic folklore of children that come most often into their elders' and teachers' hands in this way are those profiting least by oral transmission, which have to be circulated in written form, owing in part to their length. There are, in this way, a number of long, handwritten doggerel folk-poems — 'by Lord Byron' — describing a wedding night or a simple seduction, but replete with intensely erotic details, which circulate mostly among adolescent girls, and occasionally among boys (who generally prefer real initiations, or at least pictures, in cellar-clubs gloryingly if secretly styled "The Cherry-Hawks," or similar). These poems, short stories, or "Love Alphabets," and so forth, clearly serve to complete the children's sex education, in a way that the various pious "How To Make Love Though Married" handbooks do not and cannot, and which the "What Every Young Girl Should Know" breviaries of earlier decades would have died rather than try. The best known of these crude but clearly necessary folk-pornographica, *The Diary of a Young Stenographer* (sometimes "... *French* Stenographer"), has been printed sub-rosa at least twice since the 1920's, in one case in a small volume by itself, and has been collected continuously in handwritten and typed copies, touchingly misspelt, since that time. A privately-issued phonograph record has also been made of it, during the 'party-record' period of the 1940's or '50's, spoken by a young woman. It is very doubtful, however, that the current manuscript copies stem from any printed or phonographic version — these being of great rarity — but rather from each other. They are kept by this method in the same age-group at all times, as are the many orally-transmitted obscene rhymes and quatrains of younger children, of which those of the past have appeared only in the eccentric four-volume collection, *An Essay on the Archæology of Our Popu-*

lar Phrases and Nursery Rhymes (London & Andover, 1835–40), by John Bellenden Ker. As opposed to the usual rule of continuous shortening of such songs and poems ("Our Lil," for instance — attributed to Eugene Field — is now being collected as hardly more than a four-line toast or epitaph; she who was a two-page tale), the "Young Stenographer's" diary seems to get longer and more detailed all the time.

Whoever writes them originally, it is easier to see in these poems an evocation of the passionate young girl *as the young man or boy would like to imagine her,* than it is to conceive of them as an actual expression of young girls' fantasies, though they are unquestionably that as well. It is certain that these poems and rhymed obscœna are handcopied or typewritten, and circulated among themselves by adolescent girls in America and England today, just as thirty-five years ago when the collections, largely composed of such items, *Cleopatra's Scrapbook* and *Bibliotheque Erotique* (both American) were printed. That is a generation ago, or more. Another generation before, and in another culture, we have the evidence of Dr. Albert Moll, in *The Sexual Life of the Child* (English translation, London, 1912, p. 262–3), that sexual folklore of an identical kind circulated among German children as well:

> Erotic and obscene books and pictures . . . obtain a wide currency in schools, in part as printed pornographica, and in part passed from hand to hand in the written form. Thus, from a number of girls' schools come reports of the circulation of thoroughly obscene writings among girls from twelve to fourteen years of age. Especial favourites are descriptions of the wedding-night, mostly in manuscript form; also an obscene version of the story of Faust and Gretchen; and quite a number of other improper poems pass from hand to hand in girls' schools. In boys' schools, the circulating matter consists rather of obscene printed books and pictures . . . Obscene photographs are found even in girls' schools.

The survival of recitations of this kind among adults, even in the abbreviated form of toasts and epigrams (almost always quatrains) is also not strictly a part of folksong, but of folk-poetry, and will be discussed in the chapter following. There is nevertheless a certain amount of change between the genres, most strikingly

in the case of limericks — also to be dealt with in the chapter
following — which are now very commonly sung, with a chorus
between 'stanzas,' in the style of the "The Ball o' Kirriemuir."
Probably the best-known erotic rhymed recitation in America over
the last thirty-five years or more is "Our Lil," which is a presumed
eyewitness narrative of a contest in sexual intercourse between a
mining-camp prostitute — 'the best our camp produced' (formerly
a school-teacher, 'before she came West') — and 'Greaser Pete,'
whose penis of fantastic size, when measured 'from thar, to *thar*,'
finally kills the woman at the end of the poem, in the standard
sadistic concept of coitus. There is a British imitation, "Eskimo
Nell," which heightens considerably all the unpleasant aspects of
the original, the woman being finally simply killed with a gun,
replacing the impotent penis: an even clearer example of the same
concept.

"Our Lil" is usually recited with considerable dramatic emphasis, though at the same time kept rolling out in an insistent
rhythm, probably a rather ancient style of delivery. Certain standard gestures are also connected with it, particularly that of spitting hypothetical tobacco juice into a far-off spittoon between
stanzas (or, rather, at significant pauses, with a drawn-out *'Wal
. . .'*), and of measuring with the two hands at the boasting line,
'from thar — to *thar!*' An elegant woodcut 'of the old school,' by
John Held Jr. is printed in Frank Shay's *More Pious Friends and
Drunken Companions* (1928) p. 141, showing wasp-waisted Lil
or Nell displaying her striped stockings to four white-bearded
but appreciative miners, against a backdrop of timberlined
mountain-tops, but no text is ventured. A frighteningly expurgated version is given in Milburn's *Hobo's Hornbook* (1930) p.
140, the only publicly-published approximation.

Though at present strictly a rhymed recitation, "Our Lil" has
folksong antecedents of a much older and more 'polite' kind,
which are in many cases the only sort of pre-history still dis-
cernible behind modern erotic songs, in the lack of any record of
collected texts over the intervening centuries. The parallels thus
drawn are therefore only parallels, yet often very illuminating
at least at the symbolic level. According to Chappell (*Popular
Music of the Olden Time,* 1859, II. 559), 'Oldys, in his MS. additions to Langbaine, says, "In a collection of Poems, called *Folly
in Print, or a Book of Rhimes,* 8vo, 1667, p. 107, there is a ballad
called 'The Northern Lass.' She was the Fair Maid of Doncaster,
named Betty Maddox; who, when an hundred horsemen woo'd

her, she conditioned, that he who could dance her down, she would marry; but she wearied them all, and they left her a maid for her pains".' There is also another song on the redoubtable Miss Maddox, entitled "The Day Starre of the North," in *Folly in Print*.

In the headnotes to Child No. 64, "Fair Janet," in which, exceptionally, Prof. Child expresses some consciousness of the 'unspeakably ferocious features of the Norse and German ballads' that he describes (II. 102–3), the underlying idea here is traced to an ordeal-by-dancing in various Scandinavian and Breton ballads, in which the woman must *dance down* endless partners as a proof of her chastity, that is to say, as a proof that she is not in a state of weakness after childbirth, and also that her breasts cannot be made to spurt milk, no matter how badly they are manhandled. (With this ugly 'trait' compare my *Love & Death*, 1949, p. 68.) The singular fancy of the lady's skin melting like snow, present in the ballad of "The Northern Lass," just mentioned, is curiously duplicated in the first Breton ballad cited by Child, in which the woman swears — in addition to the rest of the ordeal — that she 'hopes she may melt like butter if ever she had daughter or son.' This evidently stems from the terrible 'oath of cursing,' to test the chastity of the wife of any jealous husband, in *Numbers,* 5: 21, the details of which will be found there and not here.

A Scottish ballad is later given by Child at No. 220, "The Bonny Lass of Anglesey," from David Herd's *Ancient and Modern Scottish Songs* (2nd ed. 1776) II. 231, noting a very similar Danish ballad, in both of which a woman tires out fifteen lords who must dance with her on a wager of marriage. The test-of-chastity element is entirely absent here, except as it is implied in the whole thing being a preliminary to the proposed marriage. Child admits that he does not know 'what to make of' this "Bonny Lass of Anglesey," nor does he observe the relation either to his own No. 64, "Fair Janet," or to the "Fair Maid of Doncaster" a century before. We are of course accustomed to the operatic substitution of *singing* for sexual intercourse, as in what are presumably the 'erotic' scenes of Wagner's *Tristan und Isolde, The Merry Widow,* and a score of lesser operettas, all of whose eroticism is consummated strictly in song. That *dancing* can similarly symbolize — or even replace — sexual intercourse, is not only implied throughout *The Merry Widow,* but has been made abundantly clear at the practical level by the various dance-crazes over the centuries (and especially since the turn of the present century, with the "Bunny Hug," the "Turkey Trot," the "Maxixe" and

"Tango," the "Shimmy," etc., ending of course with the "Twist"),
and particularly by the religious and moralistic opposition to each
and every one of these dances since the sixteenth century, if not
before, grouping them with bawdy folksong as part & parcel of the
'worship of the Devil.'

"Our Lil" partakes of the same symbolism, but in reverse. That
is to say, her ballad or recitation has *re*-replaced the dancing of
the "Fair Maid of Doncaster" and similar ladies, by the implied
and symbolized sexual intercourse. This cannot, of course, be
proved, yet this approach seems in many ways meaningful. Also,
it offers the only possible spoor for the study of certain main
themes of erotic folksong, where the centuries of expurgation and
refusal of texts have crippled any serious research, for lack of
historical materials. As will be seen, when it is possible finally to
publish the collections and tracings of modern bawdy songs that
have been made for this purpose, very few such songs can be
traced to earlier centuries than the seventeenth, though this does
not by any means exclude the possibility that many more bawdy
songs — of appearance entirely modern — would really prove to be
much older, were the record complete. A speculative approach is
the only one possible here. This is no more than is also true of, for
instance, Child's anti-clerical Anglo-Scottish ballad No. 276, "The
Friar in the Well," and the 'remote source' he suggests for its
central incident of the Entrapped Lovers — not extravagantly,
either, as he points out — in the collection of Persian folktales
somewhat similar to the *Arabian Nights,* the *Tuti Nameh,* or Tales
of a Parrot, of Nakhshabi; as also in the *Ocean of Story.* It has long
since passed out of the domain of controversy that the sources of
folklore and folksong are very deep in the individual and very
remote in history, and that they must be sought where they will be
found, which is not always where one might expect.

XII

IT IS SELF-EVIDENT, on any examination, that modern bawdy songs
turn on the identical themes, and sometimes on the identical tunes
found in the old drolleries and songbooks, and it is fantastic that
they have been considered until now too frightening somehow for
public record. There is also the howling absurdity, always unconscious, of all these professional and professorial *collectionneurs
enragés* of folksong, over the last six or eight decades especially,

trying so desperately hard to keep from contaminating the people who sing . . . with their own songs. Would governments really collapse, and banks fail; would philanthropic foundations really withdraw their support from provincial universities (I am given to believe they would), if some simple soul just plainly recorded the rollicking Tinker ballad of ancient genealogy, that begins — in petrified rhymes now centuries old:

> The lady of the manor was a-dressing for the ball,
> When she spied a Hieland tinker lashing piss against the wall,
> With his great big kidney-cracker, and balls the size of three,
> And half a yard of foreskin hanging well below his knee!
>
> *Hanging down! Swinging free!*
> *With a half a yard of foreskin hanging well below his knee!*

These songs are amusing, these songs are honest and un-ashamed, and the best of them have nothing leering or crapulous about them. They are as natural as the acts they describe, and they are not about anything that is a mystery to anybody above the age of twelve, any more than are the mountains of kotex-boxes displayed on drugstore counters. But they do have a tremendous vitality that upsets the narrow bookish mind, and wholly flab-bergasts any editor who finds a verse missing and realizes he could never in the world get up the *echt* folk zip to fake it.

An example, among hundreds that could be given. The principal modern British anti-gallant or anti-family songs, in the style of the 'mocks' or parodies appearing in the drolleries, are the Scottish gypsy song "My Father Was Hanged for Sheep-Stealing" (a 'mock' on "My Bonnie"), known in America as "My God How the Money Rolls In;" and another called "Piccadilly," sung to the same rambling tune as "Ball o' Yarn" ("Road to the Isles" or "Tramp, Tramp, Tramp"?) itself 'mocked' in the American college parody, "In Bohunkus, Tennessee," which begins with very similar anti-family lines. The first stanza of "Piccadilly" is well known, and often collected:

> Oh my little sister, Lily,
> Is a whore in Piccadilly,
> And my mother is another in the Strand,
> And my father hawks his arsell
> Round the Elephant & Carstle —
> We're the *finest* fuckin' family in the land!

Known to be a fragment, this remained impossible to complete for decades, at the level of honest field-collecting, and one would be interested to know which popular or scholarly editor thinks he could have written or supplied the second stanza, discovered at last:

> Oh my little sister, Heather,
> Has a maidenhead of leather,
> And she's married to the leader of the band.
> On their wedding-night, the sod,
> (*Spoken:*) Didn't know what to DO, by god!
> So he just reached up and broke it with his hand.

That has 'music-hall' written all over it, with even the specific reference to the leader of the band, who is given his line to say. Yet it has lived, and will live for quite a while. One wonders whether the same is true of the dismal scatological recitation or chant called "A Letter from Home," beginning 'Home presents a doleful picture, Dark and gloomy as the tomb . . .', dirtying every member of the reciter's family with some unhumorous disease or disaster, and moving on pitilessly to the perfectly worthless scatological explosion or collapse of the punch-line: 'Mine's a cheerful occupation, Cracking ice for grandpa's piles.' There is such a thing as *style,* even in hating one's family, and bawdy song has that style in bucketsful.

In the impossibility of giving full and frank quotations, it has hitherto been difficult to demonstrate the very marked national differences in bawdy song, as between England and America, or Ireland and Scotland, though this is not its least interesting aspect. Perhaps the most typical of the recent American songs is "The Great Wheel," a gruesome story chanted solemnly to the hymn-tune "Oh Master, Let Me Walk With Thee," in which the husband of the woman who 'never could ever be satisfied,' builds a gigantic mechanical succedaneum for her, with all sorts of obvious Detroit-style flivver attachments, which most certainly does satisfy:

> But this is the case of the biter bit,
> There wasn't no method of stopping it —

and this whole sorcerer's-apprentice tale ends dreadfully in a fecal explosion, which can most conveniently be described in psychoanalytic terms as an anal-sadistic substitute orgasm, in which the machines avenges its impotent creator by tearing the woman to bits. Although this is one of the ballads most frequently collected at present in America, only its opening verse has ever been observed elsewhere: scrawled on the wall of a dressing-booth in a public bathhouse in Edinburgh, in January 1957, 'in a childish hand.'

For, to the contrary, the essential and typical Scottish bawdy song or formula-ballad of modern times is the folk-epithalamium "The Ball o' Kirriemuir," deriving from the drinking song, "We're Gayly Yet," in Herd (ed. 1869 II. 121), and "Blyth Will an' Bessie's Wedding" (to the tune of "Roy's Wife of Aldivalloch," also a satirical marriage-song) given in Burns' *Merry Muses of Caledonia* before 1796 (ed. 1959, p. 131); the modern form first appearing in *Forbidden Fruit* (Glasgow? *c.* 1875). As currently collected, both in Scotland and America, the dialect pronunciation is insisted upon, and the text begins:

Oh the Ball, the Ball, the Ball o' Kirriemuir,
Where your wife and my wife were fooked upon the floor.

Here one begins to understand the fear many people have of bawdy song, and the tremendous release from conventional trammels and restrictions — on a fantasy basis, of course — that it offers to others. A song like this outrages, from its very first verse on, all the presumable prejudices of monogamic morality. From the epics and romances of chivalry, through the endless modern plays and novels yearning with ill-concealed pleasure over adultery (and murder), one sees of course an unbroken line of veiled resistance against these principal civilized tabooes — often including those concerned with property, and incest, as well. But in "The Ball o' Kirriemuir" it comes right out into the open. And not just for the funny, cuckoldy man next door, either, but for the singer and listener too: 'Where your wife and my wife . . .'

So many stanzas are being continuously added to this song in Scotland that it has become practically an epic itself. Or rather, the original song has been used as a formula or framework — similar to that of the limerick in England and America, and the 'Frau Wirtin' quintain in Germany — on which all poetic resistance to social and religious authority is pegged, as with the Scuffler's Club song earlier. "The Ball o' Kirriemuir" is not so much anti-gallant or anti-family, as a total and formula rejection of all the restraints of Western anti-sexual morality. It clearly represents a sort of verbal or fantasy Saturnalia for city-dwellers, no longer on the occasion of a country-wedding — as in the text collected and enlarged by Burns — but at a generalized and non-historic 'Ball of dancing,' a folk entertainment long under religious attack in Scotland over the centuries, as a survival of the so-called 'witches' sabbat' or reminiscence of pre-Christian sex worship, which is probably the truth.

In all its version and additions "The Ball o' Kirriemuir" describes — and with what sly and perfect hits, off all possible local characters — a sort of imaginary village sexual free-for-all that has the earmarks of a fantasy- or folk-recollection (if the term may be allowed) of the most ancient kind of communal marriage, if not of sacred rites of public coitus. One observes too that the same total or pan-sexual fantasy of revolt is also found in the non-Protestant culture of France, in many of the *salle de garde* songs such as "Les Trois Orfèvres" and "Le Plaisir des Dieux." Lest the historical implications here suggested seem simply a bit of overstrained antiquarianism, it might similarly be mentioned that the well-known ballad of "The Darby Ram" or "The Old Tup," which has never yet been published in unexpurgated form, is clearly related to the totemistic ram-dancers of England, descending from a period long preceding modern history; yet who, dressed or disguised in the animal's skin, were still dancing recently enough to be taken cognizance of in the 1890's, in Joseph Wright's *English Dialect Dictionary* (Supplement volume) under "Derby ram." In the song, after the mammoth ram has at last been slaughtered, in a deluge of blood, and the totemistic feast celebrated, the singer ends with a pretense of mocking the 'silly' exaggerations of his own song:

> It took all the boys in Darby Town
> To haul away his bones,
> It took all the girls in Darby Town
> To roll away his stones. (*Chorus.*)

> The man that owned this mighty ram
> Was 'counted very rich,
> But the one that made this silly song
> Was a dirty son-of-a-bitch.

This version was collected as sung by Senator H. H. Smith, at Hindman, Knott County, Kentucky, about 1910, and was very kindly supplied by the late Josiah Combs, who unfortunately could not include it in his thesis, *Folk-Songs du Midi des États-Unis* (Paris, 1925), which does, however, contain a number of very interesting borderline songs, such as that of "The Old Wife," p. 155 — recorded two centuries earlier, in Scotland, in Ramsay's *Tea-Table Miscellany* (ed. 1871, I. 103) — whose daughters make her break her teeth chewing on a bullet, rather than let her have a 'stout young man, To furnish [her] with spruncin'.' Prof. Combs added that George Washington is said to have sung "The Darby Ram" to the children of Chief Justice Ellsworth, 'but probably not this version!' Another curious animal-song, noted fragmentarily in the Pennsylvania hills before 1900, according to the recollection of Col. Shoemaker, is "On Goat Hill," now extant only in parodies such as "Up at Yale," or "In Mobile," in which latter also survive a number of strange animal exaggerations, such as flying cows, and bulls that are milked, 'Because babies must be fed — In Mobile!'

The few bawdy Irish songs collected are difficult to generalize from, except that they have a particularly droll wit, as in the mock-archæological "Old Irish French-Letter," recently collected. Most of them seem to be bawdy parodies or 'mocks,' as that on "Tim Finnegan's Wake," though it is equally possible that the bawdy form is here the original, as is also true of Irish street-song, "Brian O'Linn," of sixteenth-century origin. These parodies are naturally set to the old tunes, and sometimes even older tunes — almost always very lovely — which leads to some rather startling contrasts. For instance, the most gruellingly unpleasant song of the more than eleven hundred songs and poems I have collected, is probably "Brinzi O'Flynn" (also known as "Tumble Lynn" or "Tom Boleyn," both being parodies, or rather continuations of "Brian O'Linn," but with an entirely different tune). Yet this purposely dysphemistic song, which also contains one of the only references to oral sexuality ever noted in a folk-*song* in English, has the most beautiful minor-key air imaginable — like angels singing.

Another example of this evident use of much more ancient tunes is Durfey's "Tom and Doll," or "No, John, No," printed in *Pills to Purge Melancholy* (ed. 1719, II. 26–8) and beautifully sung by Mr. Ed McCurdy on the first of his *When Dalliance Was in Flower* recordings (Elektra 110) as issued in 1956. Here the long-sustained octet stanzas have unmistakably a religious air. (Compare the modern form, "The Spanish Merchant's Daughter," collected by Cecil Sharp in Somerset, reprinted in Percy Buck's *The Oxford Song Book,* 1916, I. 147.) A similar case, among the French *salle-de-garde* songs, is "Les Filles de Camaret," which almost all French students of both sexes know, and which is merely a bawdy modern parody of an obviously very old *complainte,* of heavenly beauty. The crude words do not in any way touch the beauty of this melody, as anyone who has heard it sung — or heard the set of *salle-de-garde* recordings recently issued under the title *Bacchus* — can testify. I have found the same melody, with words not identical with "Les Filles de Camaret," in a mid-eighteenth century manuscript collection of erotic songs, *Recueil de vaude-villes gaillards,* the text naïvely erotic in 'ordnance metaphors' so ancient as to involve the bow-and-arrow!

A cautionary note: It is generally believed that many or most bawdy songs are nothing but uncouth parodies of older and 'better' songs. Despite the exceptional examples frankly given in the preceding paragraphs, the weight of the evidence is that the sexual versions came first, and that their unassailably popular tunes were assimilated, by the despairing religious opponents of such songs — particularly in the sixteenth century, at the time of the Reformation — to sacred or at least innocuous themes, a practice continued by theatre revisers and by religious antiquarians and scholarly collectors well into our own century. The reappearance time after time of the original themes, in re-parodied sexual form is, in a very deep way, the measure of their satisfaction of inexpugnable human yearnings, and their expression of — with hunger — the most powerful human need.

In the days when priests ordained ritual public coitus at dawn, at the winter solstice, under the mistletoe-laden boughs of sacred trees, to bring back the dying sun from fearfully remembered glacial night; in those days there was no need of bawdy song, yet that was perhaps its heyday. The remnant that we have of it is strange and misshapen, more often monstrous and repellent — as the world it mirrors becomes monstrous and repellent — than simple and unashamed as it once was, in the days of the *Song of Songs.* Even so, there is more honesty and nobility — and immeasurably more life — in even the worst bawdy songs than in the ephemeral slubberdegullion of so-called popular songs. That the sexual impulse is, and involves, a sacrament as profound as that of any religious formula, is hardly to be sensed in the tepid love-droolings and pæans to frustration of modern popular song; yet it remains, immanent and unmistakable, in the power and surge of bawdy song in all languages, for all its uncouth humor and savage trappings. It is of that power, and not of that uncouthness, that people are afraid. The bawdy song is surely the only remaining kind of song in English that can seriously be called 'folk.' In the world as it has become, the bawdy song is also the only clear, and even elevated, yea-saying to the sexual reality and its outcast worship, nowhere else any longer nakedly expressed.

THE LIMERICK
A History in Brief

I

KNOWN TO everyone, but its paternity admitted by very few, the bawdy limerick has held its place now, for exactly a century, as the chosen vehicle of cultivated, if unrepressed, sexual humor in the English language. As almost nothing that has been written about the limerick can be taken seriously — which is perhaps only fitting — a few words may not be out of place here, as to its real history, its origins, and its century of triumph, by way of celebrating the centenary of that triumph.

The limerick is, and was originally, an indecent verse-form. The 'clean' sort of limerick is an obvious palliation, its content insipid, its rhyming artificially ingenious, its whole pervaded with a frustrated nonsense that vents itself typically in explosive and aggressive violence. There are, certainly, aggressive bawdy limericks too, but they are not in the majority. Except as the maidenly delight and silly delectation of a few elderly gentlemen, such as the late Langford Reed, and several still living who might as well remain nameless, the clean limerick has never been of the slightest real interest to anyone, since the end of its brief fad in the 1860's. Nor has this fad ever been successfully revived by the periodic advertising contests, exciting amateur versifiers to hack together clean limericks by the tens of thousands. It should be observed in this connection, and despite the continuous devaluation of any monetary sum over the sixty years past, that were a prize to be offered here of £3 a week *for life,* as has been given for a limerick last line, in a British cigarette contest in 1907, the present writer could seriously demand and safely expect that thousands of unpoetic amateurs in Great Britain and the United States would slap themselves silly for the next six months or two years, trying to compose seven-line stanzas in spondaic hexameter — alternating with amphibrachs and amphimacers, if I felt like being cruel —

all seven lines to rhyme solely with the words *silver, swollen, spoilt,* and *sylph* (none of which have rhymes). Needless to say, the winning entry and all seventeen thousand losing entries would immediately and forever be forgotten, except by their authors, the moment the winner would be announced. Viable folk-poetry, and folk-poetic forms, cannot be created by any such cash-on-the-barrelhead methods.

The original limerick fad was accidentally created by the reprinting in London, in 1863, of Edward Lear's *Book of Nonsense,* a volume of very tepidly humorous limericks, illustrated by the author, that had first appeared nearly twenty years before, in 1846, without any extraordinary success. Inspired by the reprint however, *Punch,* the humorous English magazine, seized upon the form. The same was done in America by a minor writer and sedulous-ape, Charles Godfrey Leland, who later also embarrassingly imitated Carroll's *Alice in Wonderland* — illustrations, typography and all — in *Johnnykin and the Goblins* (1877). Leland's anonymous imitation of Lear was called *Ye Book of Copperheads,* and was published by Leypoldt in Philadelphia in 1863. It is entirely satirical, all its limericks being directed against the Northern 'copperhead' defeatists, and the anti-Lincoln agitations during the Civil War. In the same year there had also appeared a set of "Nursery Rhymes for the Army," in Wilkes' *Spirit of the Times,* in New York; twenty-three limericks signed L.L.D., initials that may possibly represent Leland's name with the vowels omitted.

Almost immediately after, a much more widely circulated imitation appeared, this time acknowledging Lear's inspiration in the title, *The New Book of Nonsense,* and issued in Philadelphia in 1864 to be sold for the profit of the Sanitary Commission, the Red Cross of the Civil War. With that, the limerick fad was launched in America, though always under the name of 'nonsense rhymes' or 'nursery rhymes' until the 1890's, when, for the first time, the name *limerick* seems to have been applied to the form. The name is of unknown origin, having been appropriated from that of the town in Ireland for reasons never really explained, possibly from a now-forgotten chorus, 'Won't you come up to Limerick?'

Other imitations came thick and fast after the Sanitary Commission volume of 1864: *Ye Book of Bubbles* (which took even the "Ye" of its title from Leland), *Inklings for Thinklings,* and at least one other proposed *Nonsense Book* illustrated by the children's artist, Susan Hale. The fatuousness into which the form immediately fell, without the excitements of the Civil War to get its teeth into, is pathetically betrayed in a letter from Miss Hale, as to her final volume of the sort, remarking: 'Mrs. Billy Weld . . . provides, collects and invents the rhymes, and I draw the pictures right off into a nice long-shaped blank book. I have got 22 done, and they go off very fast, much quicker than the Nursery Rhymes for the fair, for the rhymes are only fool stuff . . .'

Punch was similarly running 'fool stuff' in the 1860's, and might have gone on forever except that the fad of the clean limerick was suddenly brought to an end — owing to a disconcerting number of bawdy and sacrilegious limericks being submitted anonymously, among the entries to *Punch*'s first big geographical-limerick contest. According to tradition, the leaders of this anti-fad, and authors of all the best early dirty limericks, which immediately began to circulate orally of course, were a group of college wits and clubmen, notably the poet Swinburne; an army officer, Capt. Edward Sellon, and the war-correspondent, George Augustus Sala, all three of whom are known to have written much other sub-rosa poetry and erotic prose, mostly flagellational. *Punch* closed down its geographical contest with a slam, and the clean-limerick fad fell dead. It had lasted hardly five years, a great deal longer than most fads. Since that time, the clean limerick has lived on fitfully only as the last resource of newspaper poets (especially about the 1900's) hard-up for witty fillers, as a useful framework for humorous artists to hang their drawings on, and, as aforesaid, as advertising-contest pap from time to time. As for the public at large — that is to say, the authentic folklore-transmitting group — the only real popularity of the limerick during the entire century of its modern existence, since the end of the Civil War, has been wholly and solely in the bawdy form.

Before continuing with the further history of the limerick, which looks as though it will continue for quite a while yet, what about its pre-history? It has been tiresomely repeated, and is even partly true, that Lear took the form of his 'nonsense rhymes' from several illustrated children's books of the early 1820's: *Anecdotes and Adventures of Fifteen Gentlemen,* attributed to one R. S. Sharpe, and *The History of Sixteen Wonderful Old Women* of a competing publisher. (There was also a *Fifteen Young Ladies* collection too.) Actually, these 1820's limericks are far better than Lear's, and the drawings — probably by Robert Cruikshank — incomparably better. The specific rhyme known to have inspired

Lear is the following, reproduced with its amusing illustration in the Opies' *Oxford Dictionary of Nursery Rhymes,* at "Tobago:"

> There was a sick man of Tobago
> Liv'd long on rice-gruel and sago;
> But at last, to his bliss,
> The physician said this —
> "To a roast leg of mutton you may go."

The illustration shows him attacking the leg of mutton, which looks more like a ham, with a carving-fork and knife and a blissful expression.

Lear's imitation of this form, as is well known, invariably drops back, from the simple but dramatic resolution of the action in the final line, to the namby-pamby repetition of the first line — very weak, even for nonsense verse — made to do double duty as the last line as well, possibly with some tremendously unimportant change in the adjective rung in by way of climax. Lear also curiously betrayed, in many of his limericks, an unsurmountable private fear of public disgrace (the only passions of his life being, unfortunately, for cats and handsome Greek boys), in the continuous importation into his couplets of the Mrs. Grundy of public opinion, in the horrendous and ever-present *They:* 'When they said, "Why is that?" he fell in his hat, That frightened old man of Corfu,' and so on. The whole thing, and most particularly the echoic last line, represents a clear failure of nerve, an inability to take the obvious and final jump, and to resolve even the stated nursery situation in some satisfactory way. This is the neurotic problem at the root of all 'nonsense,' and is — as much with Lewis Carroll as with Lear — the secret or Sense of Nonsense.

II

THE PRE-HISTORY of the limerick is remarkably easy to trace. It is necessary only to recognize, as modern developments not really essential to the limerick pattern, the anapestic form or foot (two short syllables and a long) in which it has become familiar, as well as the falsely stressed 'There *was* . . .' in the opening line, which is a century older than Lear in any case. The earliest limericks will be found in nursery rhymes, or something very much like them, as far back as the fourteenth century. To avoid controversy, I do not insist that "Sumer is i-cumen in" (about 1300), the oldest popular song in the English language, is in the limerick form, but a rather good case can be made for its stanzaic portion at least, and the possibility ought not be overlooked. In modernized spelling:

> Ewè bleateth after lamb,
> Low'th after calvè coo;
>   Bullock starteth,
>   Buckè farteth —
> Merry sing cuck*oo*!

With all that has been written about "Sumer is i-cumen in" — and it has taken almost a library of learned annotation to vindicate even the simple barnyard humor of the buck's crepitation at the highest note and melodic climax of the song — no suggestion has ever yet been made as to just what its prosodic form may be; and where, and when, and whether any verses similar to it may be found, in any language.

In their excellent manual, *The Making of Verse,* in 1934, Robert Swann and Frank Sidgwick have discovered another early animal limerick (and that it is a limerick they clearly state) in the British Museum's Harleian Manuscript 7322, dating from the end of the fourteenth century:

> The lion is wondirliche strong,
> & ful of wiles of wo;
>   & wether he pleye
>   other take his preye,
> he can not do bot slo (*slay*).

This is followed in the manuscript by similar warning rhymes, as to dragons and bears, but not in the limerick metre. A century and a half then pass without any record of this engaging form. It reappears suddenly, in the late sixteenth century, in the mad-songs of the half-naked wandering beggars, turned out to mump their livelihood after 1536, at the dissolution of the religious almonries under Henry VIII. The greatest of the mumpers' songs is "Mad Tom," or "Tom o' Bedlam," first recorded in Giles Earle's manuscript music-book about 1615, though probably decades old by then, and in the limerick metre throughout:

> From the hagg & hungry Goblin,
> That into raggs would rend yee,
>   & the spirit that stand's
>   by the naked man,

in the booke of moones defend yee . . .
Of thirty bare years have I
twice twenty bin enragèd,
  & of forty bin
    three tymes fifteene
in durance soundlie cagèd,

On the lordlie loftes of Bedlam
with stubble softe & dainty,
  brave braceletts strong,
    sweet whips ding dong
with wholsome hunger plenty . . .

    That is nonsense too, but of a different kind than Lear's. This superb poem of "Tom o' Bedlam," of which hardly more than the beginning is given above, has been made the subject of an entire quarto monograph, in the impeccable scholarship of Jack Lindsay, under the title *Loving Mad Tom,* published at the author's own Fanfrolico Press in 1927 (which is getting to be the only way to do things anymore), and giving samples of the endless variants rung, in the same metre, throughout the seventeenth century, in praise of tobacco, in dispraise of women, in mockery of the Puritans, and for the benefit of other 'wandering professions' besides that of madman: tinkers, blind beggars, jovial peddlers, oakermen, and simple drunkards — a whole anthology of superlative balladry, all in the limerick metre of "Tom o' Bedlam." Later, in its turn, "Tom o' Bedlam" also inspired the one greatest mad-song of the English language, "Halloo my fancy," written in part by Col. William Cleland, uncle of the author of *Fanny Hill.* ("Halloo my fancy" is given complete, along with "Tom o' Bedlam," in Charles Williams' *New Book of English Verse,* 1935, where both will well repay the trouble of looking them up. The original texts are in the *Percy Folio Manuscript,* about 1620; and Watson's early Scottish collection, in 1706–11. A humorous imitation of "Halloo my fancy," called "The Shiftlesse Student," has not formerly been noted: it appears in Sir John Mennis' & Dr. James Smith's *Wit and Drollery,* 1661, p. 223–26.)

    Formal poets never have scorned the possibilities of the madmen's song and limerick metre. On this pattern, Edgar, in Shakespeare's *King Lear,* disguised as 'poore Tom,' chants his spell to the rhythm of "Tom o' Bedlam," beginning: 'Swithold footed thrice the old, He met the night mare and her nine fold . . . And aroint thee, witch, aroint thee!' At least three other songs by Shakespeare are also in the limerick form: "And let me the cannakin clinke, clinke," in *Othello;* Stephano's sea-song in *The Tempest,* "For she had a tongue with a tang" (attempting the innovation of a double-couplet, never followed up); and Ophelia's touching mad-song, in *Hamlet,* IV.v, "His beard was white as snow." As will be observed, two of Shakespeare's songs are mad-songs, and two drinking songs; implying that he felt the form was too 'popular' or too simple to be used seriously. Yet the possibilities of the same metre, for 'pure' or lyric poetry, were brilliantly explored by the rival school of Ben Jonson, in Jonson's own *Masque of The Gypsies Metamorphos'd,* "The faery beame uppon you," and most particularly by his protegé, great ugly Robert Herrick, who even attempted a love song in the limerick stanza, the exquisite "Night-piece, to Julia," first published in his *Hesperides* in 1648, though undoubtedly written long before:

> Her Eyes the Glow-worme lend thee,
> The Shooting Starres attend thee:
>   And the elves alsó
>   Whose little eyes glow
> Like the sparks of fire, befriend thee . . .

The rest is not given here, to leave the pleasure and the discovery of this jewel, to whoever does not know it, who will look it up. It should be mentioned that its relation to "Tom o' Bedlam" was first noted by Miss Ethel Seaton in the *London Mercury* in 1923, to which journal is owed all the modern interest in the song, already in danger of being forgotten again, despite its rediscovery and reprinting, almost complete, at the article "Tom o' Bedlams," in Disraeli's *Curiosities of Literature* (ed. 1849, II. 343–9). So many examples of these predecessors of the limerick, mostly in the iambic foot, could be quoted from the great outpouring of English humorous and folk poetry in the seventeenth century, especially in the satirical drollery collections of the Restoration, that one despairs of trying, short of having the space of a whole book to quote them in. For a very full, but by no means complete, selection, the reader is referred again to Jack Lindsay's elegant monograph, *Loving Mad Tom* (1927), with which one can disagree only as to the accustomed balderdash of Mr. Robert Graves, in his Foreword; and the excessive caution of Lindsay's inquiry (p. 75) whether it be not 'fanciful to see something of a lingering memory or a chance re-invention of the stanzaic effect in the limerick of our contemporary coversation, in which is crystallised so much brilliant obscenity.'

Let me end this very brief survey, with one of the most technically unexceptionable seventeenth-century limericks, the first in which all the modern peculiarities of the form appear: "*Mondayes Work . . .* To the tune of *I owe my hostesse money*," in the *Roxburghe Ballads*. Published in broadside ballad form before 1640, this is a perfect modern limerick — anapestic metre (here and there), proper names setting the rhyme of the stanzas, and all:

> Good morow, neighbour Gamble,
> Come let you and I goe ramble:
>   Last night I was shot
>   Through the braines with a pot
> And now my stomacke doth wamble . . .
>
> Gramarcy, neighbour Jinkin
> I see thou lovest no shrinking,
>   And I, for my part
>   From thee will not start:
> Come fill us a little more drinke in.

The rhyme here, as a matter of fact, is rather close to that of the modern bawdy limerick about the fellow named Perkin, whose gherkin was sherkin' his ferkin'; not to mention Skinner and Tupper, who took the young lady to supper. A parallel inspiration or 'chance re-invention,' to be sure.

Before another century had passed, the limerick form, now fully achieved in all its particulars, had so often been turned to the uses and abuses of satire, in poems and songs of drinking, wenching, and other 'low professions,' that no one, not even Herrick, could have saved it as a lyric form, and Shakespeare's refusal to take it seriously was vindicated. Eventually the rhythm 'fell' — probably still carried by the wandering bedlam beggars, the ancestors of our own hoboes and tramps — to the dialect songs of Scotland and Ireland, as in "Katy's Answer" to the young Laird, in Ramsay's *Tea-Table Miscellany* of 1724 (ed. 1871, I. 63):

> My mither's ay glowran o'er me,
> Tho' she did the same before me:
>   I canna get leave
>   To look to my loove,
> Or else she'll be like to devour me. . .

Certain of the peculiarities, picked up along the way, turned even the dialect form to dialect satire, particularly the use of a proper name (improperly, of course, according to the rules of all poetry but humorous) in calling forth the rhyme. 'Neighbour Jinkin,' just noted, seems to deserve some part of the blame here, as the commonest tune used for the dialect satire songs in the limerick rhythm mentions him (in the anti-Welsh form of his name) in the opening line: "Of noble race was Shenkin." The same rhythm and tune are later used in a violently erotic piece, "The Pious Parson," in all editions of *The Merry Muses* after 1830, still surviving in Britain as "The Hero Alexander."

Finally the limerick metre was abandoned altogether to the uses of nonsense and nursery rhymes — the classic decay and descent of much folklore, of which the last traces often survive only in children's rhymes and games. It is among the nursery rhymes, since the early eighteenth century at least, that the limerick form will mainly be found, as in "Hickory dickory dock", "Dance a baby, diddy," and many others that he who seeks will find. So typical of the nursery was it eventually felt to be, that its form was used by mid-century in a mock-critical piece, "To the Critics and Poets," reprinted in *The New Boghouse Miscellany, or A Companion for the Close-Stool* in 1761, p. 207, and burlesquing the pompous flatulence of the learned commentators of the day. This particular vein of satire had been first mined in Swift's *Tale of a Tub,* and Dr. William Wagstaffe's *Comment upon the History of Tom Thumb* in 1711, and by Hyacinthe Cordonnier, in his *Chef d'Oeuvre d'un Inconnu* (1714) and its many imitations, which one would have thought had finished off the commentators and their excesses forever; but are, instead, themselves forgotten, while the commentators go endlessly on.

The poem of the anonymous Boghouse poet is entitled —

On Jollity: An Ode, or Song, or both.

I.

There was a jovial butcher,
He liv'd at Northern-fall-gate,
   He kept a stall
   At Leadenhall,
And got drunk at the boy at Aldgate.

II.

He ran down Hounsditch reeling,
At Bedlam he was frighted,
   He in Moorfields
   Besh--t his heels
And at Hoxton he was wipèd.

The commentary that follows, which goes on for pages precisely in the mock-serious style later used by Norman Douglas in handling bawdy limericks, notes carefully, for example, how, in the second stanza, 'The geography of the places where the action happened is strictly observed.' This is almost identical with Douglas' note, as to the logical order of events in the equally scatological misadventure of the lady named Skinner (or Pinner), 'who dreamt that her lover was in her.' It is also worth observing that, though proper names had already been set as rhymes in the limerick form, in "Mondayes Work" — concerning neighbors Gamble and Jinkin — the present example, "On Jollity," from the *New Boghouse Miscellany* of 1761, is the earliest 'geographical' limerick yet discovered (first appearing in *The Midwife, or Old Woman's Magazine,* about 1750, as reprinted also in *The Non-pareil,* 1757, p. 165–70), and has certainly enough place-names, false rhymes, and even an opening 'There was . . .', to satisfy any historian.

III

So MUCH for the history of the limerick before Lear, which has here obviously been only briefly sketched. Sufficient has been shown, however, to justify the opening statement that the limerick is, and was originally, an indecent verse-form. For anyone who cares to trace it further back than the unrepressed buckè of "Sumer is i-cumen in," the field is wide open. But history, as everyone knows, is only half the story. The other half, and the harder part, is what is nowadays called the psychological element: earlier the 'soul,' or spirit of the thing. Fortunately for any such profound study, all the materials are still in existence for the examination of the erotic content of the limerick, since its revival as a popular art form, and its elevation from the nursery, owing to the efforts of *Punch,* Leland, and the nameless poets of the 1860's.

All the materials, or perhaps lacking only one early document, chastely entitled *A New Book of Nonsense* (London, 1868), and extending to only twelve pages. This is the earliest collection of erotic limericks known to have existed, though no sure trace of this brochure has survived except a bare reference to its title, in the important Campbell-Reddie manuscript bibliography of nineteenth-century erotica (II. 175). Almost immediately after, however, there appeared the much larger collection of bawdy and sacrilegious verse, *Cythera's Hymnal,* with the mock imprint

'Oxford: Printed at the University Press, for the Society for Promoting Useful Knowledge,' 1870; which collection gives at the end a group of fifty-one erotic limericks, headed "Nursery Rhymes," which, since they cover almost exactly an equivalent dozen pages, lead one to believe that the lost *New Book of Nonsense* of 1868 was perhaps only a preprint of these pages.

Cythera's Hymnal is known, through the revelations of the bibliographer of erotica, H. Spencer Ashbee ("Pisanus Fraxi"), to have been the joint production of Capt. Edward Sellon, author of numerous erotic novels, and a study of Hindu eroticism, who died a suicide in 1866; and the journalist, George Augustus Sala, assisted by several other Oxford men. The same authors also paid their respects to the classic erotic and satirical poet, Martial — their obvious inspiration, as he had been for Herrick — in an *Index Expurgatorius Martialis,* published at the same time, and translating *only* those bawdy epigrams of Martial usually omitted from college pony-translations. Most of the poems of *Cythera's Hymnal* are howling and even revolting parodies, Sellon's "Chordee" (a parody of "Excelsior") being the least objectionable. From the viewpoint of the social critic, the most interesting piece is a satire on the noble do-gooders of the nineteenth century, out preaching a hypocritical gospel of sexual repression among the children of the poor. This is set to the infectious rhythm of the nursery rhyme or song, 'There was a little man, And he wooed a little maid, And he said, Little maid, will you wed, wed, wed?' printed for Walpole at the Strawberry Hill Press in 1764 as the work of Sir Charles Sedley, the Restoration wit, and thus setting the 'There *was* . . .' formula-opening well into the preceding century, though here not in the limerick form.

This particular parody is reprinted, with a new group of sixty-five bawdy limericks, in the extraordinary erotic magazine, *The Pearl,* which ran for eighteen consecutive monthly issues in 1879–80, and has been reprinted at least three times, most recently in New York, about 1933, though even the reprints are now very difficult to find. *The Pearl,* like *Cythera's Hymnal,* is largely composed, on the poetry side, of long narrative poems on flagellation, excruciating for anyone to try to read who does not share this typically Anglo-Saxon and German perversion. Most of these poems may be suspected of coming from the pen of Sala, a man whose secret biography is waiting to be written. The hundred and twenty limericks included, in all, in these two sources, and in the continuation of *The Pearl* as *The Cremorne,* falsely dated '1851,' include a large proportion of the bawdy limericks still in oral circulation in both England and America, and these must be considered the classics or old favorites of the genre. Evidently their main circulation, in both their own century and this, was by word-of-mouth, in the classic folklore fashion, and certainly not via the very rare secret publications, of limited circulation, in which they were committed to print.

I would not care to fall into the modern mania of counting and measuring the themes and motifs of the hundred and twenty limericks here cited, and the perhaps hundred and fifty more that make up the total 'float' or repertoire of orally-circulated modern limericks — the only ones that can be agreed to be socially indicative and significant. Much less would I care to try sliding them through the sucking-and-blowing apertures of a calculating machine, in order to discover the leading 'traits' or themes with which they are concerned, even assuming that anything meaningful could be learned in any such way. As the card-punching and sampling system has, so far, guessed wrong in all the political elections on which it has been tried; I do not think any serious folklorist would care to trust it with the significance of bawdy limericks.

Even without too much measuring, however, it is clear that, in a preponderant way, most bawdy limericks are concerned with the unconscious or unwilling *humor* of the sexual impulse: its organs, its attitudes, and misadventures. The form being unrepressed, by definition, no holds seem to be barred on the hostility expressed. The same is true of clean limericks and the even more sadistic "Little Willies," but it is curious how much of this sexual hostility in the erotic forms is self-turned against the poet or protagonist, the hapless hero with whose disasters and insufficiencies the limerick poet so clearly identifies himself. There can be no question that this is a sort of whistling in the dark, for the people who make up the bawdy limericks, and who nowadays even sing them; attempting, as it were, to laugh away their sexual fears and impotencies — real and imaginary — in short satirical doggerel efforts of elaborate rhyme, in which, be it said once and for all, *woman* is the usual butt of the satire, as is true of almost all drinking songs.

In the only serious psychological study ever made of limericks, by Prof. Weston LaBarre, in the journal *Psychiatry* in 1939, they are called simply 'drinking songs,' and the important point is made that limericks are written and retailed only by the educated group: a group apparently perfectly attuned to the special impropriety of the limerick, both prosodic and moral. As the *Journal of American Folklore* has recently been so very kind as to allow me to remark, in its epochal "Symposium on Obscenity in Folklore" (July 1962), bawdy limericks apparently represent for the educated group a sort of private revolt against the rules of prosody and propriety, at one and the same time, a revolt that almost no other social class cares to share. Limericks are not only the folklore almost solely of the educated, but are almost their only folklore, with the exception of jokes and tales — including a large number credulously believed to be true — and a limited repertoire of bawdy and sentimental songs.

Limericks are not liked by, nor commonly to be collected among, workingmen, farm-hands, cowboys, sailors, and other classic oral sources — 'as yodelling tipplers are called by philologists' (Sydney Goodsir Smith). Many non-college and non-whitecollar people who have no objection to bawdy, will neither recite limericks nor listen to them unless they are sung. Except for the basic subject-matter, non-college people simply do not find it easy to understand where the humor is supposed to reside, in all the trick geographical rhyming and other purely formal and intellectual ornamentation of the limerick. It seems transpicuously clear that the daring prosodic revolt of the falsely stressed 'There *was . . .*' and the even falser geographical rhyme of the typical limerick, do titillate persons who have been educated to believe that these are poetically 'wrong,' but no one else. The epigrammatic quality of the limerick, which it shares with its formal ancestors of the *Greek Anthology* and the *Priapeia,* and among the Roman satirists such as Martial, also makes it unsuitable for non-college folk, who far prefer the larger developmental and adventurous possibilities of the longer ballad form.

Since World War II, and a bit earlier, an attempted democratization has been taking place, in the possibility of singing the limerick instead of declaiming or reciting it, or simply collecting and transmitting examples in manuscript or typewritten form (now also on tape-recordings). Limericks can now be heard sung in the convivial company of college fraternities (and sometimes sororities), the drinking-clubs of army and air officers, and so forth; but even there the groups involved are usually drawn from the educated classes. Quite a number of limerick collections have in recent years been mimeographed and privately circulated by such college and armed-service groups, nothing 'new' ever appear-

ing in these mimeographica except the science-fiction limericks
of recent vintage. The pages of limericks given are now clearly
thought of as a single object or song, with a chorus indicated.
As sung, the limericks are chanted *seriatim* by various members
of the group, to the tune, usually, of the venereal-disease song,
"The Spanish Nobillio" or "Gay Caballerò" (much worn down
musically in the transmission), each singer electing himself or
herself to come forward with a remembered or presumably ex-
temporarily invented limerick, which thus becomes part of the
'song' being communally improvised by the group in classic folksong fashion, and never twice the same. The stanzas are separated,
and the singers allowed to catch breath, take a drink, or furbish
up their inspiration, by a chorus or challenge sung by the whole
audience:

> That . . was . . a very nice song,
> Sing us another one —
> Just like the other one —
> Sing us another one, do!

In America, the chorus or connective verse has become more
recently, to the tune of "Cielito lindo":

> Aye, yi, yi-yi! —
> In China they never eat chili;
> So sing me (here's to) the next verse,
> Much worse than the last verse,
> And waltz me around again, Willie!

The intention here is openly to encourage the next singer to an
even 'worse verse' — no longer merely 'another one, just like the
other one' — as everyone becomes slightly more intoxicated, in
part by the singing, and a great deal less repressed. The British
connecting chorus is the most interesting of all:

> Now hear, all ye dukes and ye duchesses,
> Take heed of my warning, I say,
> Be sure that you owns all you touches-es,
> Or I'll land you in Botany Bay!

These choruses are naturally sung in as many different ways
as there are different singers, so it will be of no use writing to
me in care of the publisher to say that the above wordings of the
chorus are 'wrong,' a word which has, after all, no real meaning
folkloristically. One man's wit is another man's poison. Of course,

additional *verses* in the limerick form would be far from un-
welcome — as also songs and poems — but should perhaps be transmitted by homing-pigeon, St. Bernard dog, or some other uncommon carrier, as they might very well turn out to be illegal in the
mails.

IV

ONE OF THE elements in the limerick that has tended to further
its formalized presentation in private drinking-clubs, in the colleges and elsewhere, is the greater ease of its recollection, in quintain form, than that of the long ballads preferred by folksingers.
This epigrammatic or witty quality is common, as well, to the
similar form popular among German students, the "Frau Wirtin"
quintains, and the erotic quatrain or "Vierzeiler" of even wider
popularity in the German-speaking countries. (See the collections
in E. K. Blümml's *Futilitates* and *Das Spittelberg,* cited elsewhere.) The historical original of this formalized presentation
is the erotic toast, about which little if anything has ever been
written. This type of toast — 'Gentlemen, I give you (*or,* Here's
to) . . .' followed by some prose or rhymed typification of the
person or institution to be drunk to by all — had its greatest
development in the mug-house clubs of Great Britain throughout
the eighteenth century. Various collections of these toasts will
be found printed in the erotic songsters and jestbooks of the
time, continuing well into the nineteenth century in all the
editions (except the first) of *The Merry Muses.* The toast is now
almost extinct in England, being reduced to the mere muttered
formula, 'Cheers!' and the curious 'Mud in your eye!' in America,
a scatological or equestrian survival.

The real popularity of the erotic toast much diminished after
1830, when, for instance, the *Merry Muses* song in the limerick
metre, "The Pious Parson," was printed in thirteen stanzas, the
last being a toast to the hero of the song: 'Then here's a health
to the parson, We'll drink him when we're mellow, &c.' In the
editions of 1843 and after (as in that of 1872, dated '1827'), this
final stanza is silently dropped, the fashion of toasting being already out of fashion. It has survived in minor form in the army
everywhere, and in Scotland, where a farm-workers' secret society
still in existence offers erotic toasts or brags very similar to those
in the *Records of the Beggar's Bension Society,* of Anstruther, in
Scotland, from the 1730's to the 1890's, when the society was dis-

solved. Minor groups of toasts in quatrain form, usually beginning 'Here's to . . . ' or 'Give me . . .', are printed in the *Book
of a Thousand Laughs* (about 1928) and other American obscœna
collections of that period. Dr. Roger Abrahams has also shown
their continued existence, in a survival of the British eighteenth
century form, in the erotic lore of modern American Negroes,
which retains other forms and even certain vocabulary of older
British provenance.

There being no new thing under the sun, as remarked upon
by *Ecclesiastes,* i. 9; under every layer of folklore another deeper
layer will be found, going as far back and as deep down as anyone
can trace. Behind the erotic toasts, in prose and verse, lies a much
earlier form in which the verbal ordeal — of being as violently
obscene as possible, in the wording of the toast, as in the Scottish
forms — is an actual scatological or scatophagous ordeal as well.
The externalized oral sadism still visible in such American toasts
as that beginning, 'Here's to Mag, the dirty bitch, With clap and
syph and the seven-year's-itch . . .' was, in the more ancient
form, turned against the person giving the toast; and it is sometimes still obvious that the giving of such a toast is an ordeal
for him. When the ordeal is not in verbal form, but is physically
some scatophagous, or flagellatory, or auto-castratory initiation
ceremonial, it is even more obvious who the victim is, who is sometimes also blindfolded and prepared as a sacrifice.

The earliest traceable forms here are those connected with
late-medieval religious, or rather anti-religious rites, in such ordeal
forms as stabbing a crucified dummy-figure, or spitting upon or
otherwise defiling holy relics of the religion that the initiate is
thus defying and rejecting. Even behind these lie the totemic-
feast survivals hypothesized by Freud, and which are the only
explanation yet offered for the demanded or alleged use of sacrificial blood in so many of these ordeals, both religious (such
as circumcision, and other religious forms too obvious to mention) and irreligious, as in the so-called 'black mass.' The authentic
vestiges here are fully explored in the supplement to Richard
Payne Knight's *Discourse on the Worship of Priapus* (ed. 1894;
illustrated reprint, London, 1952, pp. 185–206, and 246–7, citing
Michelet's *La Sorcière*), the best source in English on the trial of
the Knights Templar and the 'monstrous' accusations made against
them. According to Ashbee (*Index Librorum Prohibitorum,* p. 9),
this supplementary essay is by the great English antiquary, Thomas
Wright, assisted by Sir James Tennent, and Mr. George Witt.

Further details as to the accusations of this type against the Templars are given in Ashbee's *Centuria* (p. xxxvii, n. 48) from Sir William Dugdale's *Monasticon Anglicanum* (1718) p. 181. These citations are purposely given here, rather than quoting the material, as it is strong stuff that should be studied in its own context.

By Shakespeare's time the ordeal of the Templars, or other primitive fraternities, become the ordeal of the toast, had entirely lost its religious or anti-religious connections, and was strictly a self-imposed asseveration or expression of his overpowering emotions by the lover. In this way Hamlet, at Ophelia's grave, challenges Laërtes: 'Come, show me what thou'lt doe. Woo't weepe? Woo't fight? Woo't teare thy self? Woo't drinke up *Esile*, eate a Crocodile? Ile doo't.' The key is the *Esile*, or vinegar, to be drunk; hardly more than a polite allusion to the mad lover's self-imposed ordeal of drinking off the contents of a woman's chamber-pot as a proof of his love. The same idea spontaneously occurs in all times and cultures in male masochists. It appears in open form in the toast "Here's to Mag," already mentioned, and also seems to be present in the repugnant images of the chorus of "Three Old Whores" or "The Whoorey Crew," which there is reason to believe is a survival of a very old song. An even more unpleasant form of the lover's ordeal — very common in folktale and folksong as the "Legend of Sir Gawain" — is the marrying of a repulsive hag, who turns into a beautiful princess at the consummatory 'kiss.' One of the most striking examples is the Danish and Scottish ballad of "Kempy Kay" (Child, No. 33; and compare the much modified "Kemp Owyne," No. 34, still sufficiently repulsive), in which, in Kinloch's version, the bride-to-be, known as the Fu'some Fug, is thus described in one of the milder stanzas:

> She rampit out, and she rampit in,
> She rampit but and ben;
> The tittles and tattles that hang frae her tail
> Wad muck an acre o' land.

In both parts of Shakespeare's *Henry IV* there is of course a good deal about drinking, and drinking customs, in support of the character of Falstaff as a great drinker of sack; nor does Shakespeare overlook to mention the important custom here under consideration, which Falstaff describes in the character of the fine gallant and wit, loved by the prince, because he 'drinkes off Candle ends for Flap-dragons, and rides the wilde-Mare with the

Boyes, and jumpes upon Joyn'd-stooles, and sweares with a good grace.' (2 *Henry IV*, II. iv.) With this should be compared the quotation in the preceding chapter, as to the singing of "Samuel Hall" at the London "Scuffler's Club" in the 1880's, including the jumping on joint-stools and tournamenting them about the hall, and of course the swearing 'with a good grace' at the choruses of the song.

As will be understood, the Flapdragon of the lighted candle-end was to be drunk off while *burning,* and this ancient ordeal still survives as a forfeit at the children's ancient ghost-mummeries of Hallowe'en, in the form of 'bobbing for apples;' not to mention the fire-eaters, sword-swallowers, and snake-charmers of carnivals. By the time of Swift, the Flapdragon had become a 'Snapdragon,' by the usual process of folk-etymology, as described in *The Tale of a Tub* (1704) Sect. XI: 'He bore a strange kind of Appetite to Snap-dragon, and to the livid Snuffs of a burning Candle, which he would catch and swallow with an Agility, wonderful to conceive,' being thereupon lighted up from the inside, exactly like the Jack-o'-lantern skull of Hallowe'en.

Grose, in his *Classical Dictionary of the Vulgar Tongue* (1785) gives a few of the verbal toasts, to which the ancient ordeal had by then become limited, though it should be remembered that the 'mug' in many of the eighteenth-century mug-houses was frankly a chamber-pot. He gives, for instance, at "Best": 'To the best in Christendom, i.e. the best **** in Christendom, a health formerly much in vogue.' Differently and somewhat more nobly worded, this is the identical toast '*Mater omnium*' given in Buxton Forman's edition of Keats' *Letters,* along with the amusing philological discussion to which it gave rise. The ordeal element is still very prominent in Keats' anecdote, in that the 'young fool' who has offered this toast only in its discreet Latin, is then 'egged on' to give the toast in plain English instead. A 'crossing' of toasts, or competition in obscene rhymed toasts, is given in *The Book of a Thousand Laughs,* as between two rival congressmen of Iowa and Maine; reprinted in *The Limerick* (1953) p. 416, n. 708, with a matching example, in scatological prose, from *The Pearl,* No. 1 (1879), as "The Rival Toasts," rising from the rivalry between the American and British navies. It is this violent and dysphemistic form of toast — as a sort of brag or oath — which has mainly survived.

One final return to perhaps the earliest form, or *Mater omnium,* which, whether given in verbal or enacted fashion, unmistakably implies the very ancient worship of the female sexual organs. In its most recent survival, the modified challenge of the drinking of Eisel-vinegar or the candle-end Flapdragon returns to the much more frank original. This is the commonly-encountered folktale — persistently told as a true anecdote — of any one of a number of famous actresses, the 'toasts' of the 1890's, who is erotically 'toasted' by her harem of polyandrous admirers as she sits naked in a tub of champagne; the dénouement being that, when the drinks are measured out of the tub, a pint more is discovered than the number of pints of champagne used. One is close there, in the history of the toast, to both the beginning and the end.

V

THE NOTE struck earlier, in the British limerick chorus, of absurd and out-of-place resistance to non-existent authority figures, such as the 'dukes and duchesses' who are boldly warned off the (sexual) property of the singer, is the crucial element in the psychological structure of all limericks, as in most erotic and satirical poetry whatever its metrical pattern may be. Authority figures can be almost anything or anyone, depending on the background of the poet or singer: some people hate royalty, some people hate bishops, monks and ministers, or policemen. There are people who write books against the law of gravity (which they hate simply because it's referred to as a 'law'), or to prove that Einstein was wrong, or that Shakespeare was written *by another man of the same name,* as Mark Twain put it. I knew a man once who would become furious over printed signs in public places that did not begin with the word 'Please. . . .' Few people can admit that they are fighting non-existent authority figures, as they seldom fought the parents who are the real authority figures that they are still seething about, and who, in the present case, appear in the limericks they write or quote disguised as kings, dukes, and bishops.

The main focus of resistance and hostility in limericks tends to circulate in this way about perfectly mythical figures of royalty and nobility, such as the petrified image of poor mad George III hidden in American folklore since 1776 under the stereotyped heading of the hated 'Englishman' or superior snob. Resistance to the clergy comes only second in limericks, and would probably long since have faded, with the now utterly uninteresting religious controversies stirred up a century ago by Darwin and Bishop Colenso; were it not for the geographical necessities of the limerick rhyme, which have perpetuated in certain favorite limericks such otherwise unknown and irrelevant dignitaries as the Bishops of Twickenham, Woking, and Chichester, of whom the last is practically dragged in by the seat of his britches only in order to get another part of that garment somehow involved in a florid rhyming scheme concerning a young lady whose charms had already 'made all the saints in their niches stir.' It is obvious that the ordinary cowboy, miner, field-hand or workingman will not go for effete and over-intellectual stuff like that, in either Britain or America. The workingman, in such a mood, much prefers singing "The One-Eyed Riley" or " 'Twas on the Good Ship *Venus*" or "The Bastard King of England" or "The Crab Fish," when he does any singing at all, or is *allowed* to sing — even polite songs — in his public bar (where the juke-box or television machine suffers from no such restriction). Whatever he may sing in the way of bawdry, the uneducated singer inevitably prefers the more active and adventurous ballad form, giving room for a more phallic, and less pettily linguistic, sexuality.

One of the clearest deficiencies of the limerick, preventing it from ever achieving broad folk-acceptance, and keeping it class-linked to the basically non-singing educated group, is the lack of a really good limerick tune. Almost anything is acceptable in the way of words, to both singers and audiences alike — though obviously not to poets — if the tune makes some basic appeal. If proof were required of this, one need only consider the unconscionable drivel set as words nowadays to so-called 'popular' songs, whose popularity is shorter-lived than a sick pup, in part because the tunes are so awful too.

The limerick has nothing to compare with the folksongs, as to music, and simply cannot compete. The "Gay Caballero" tune, generally used, is hopelessly weak, and melodically very circumscribed. It takes quite a deal of alcohol to be able to listen to twenty limericks in succession sung to its tune, no matter how loud the audience shouts out the connecting chorus, and begs for 'another one.' The few efforts that have been made to work up a new limerick tune have never been followed, mostly because they are not worth following; for instance that attempted in W. R. Titterton's over-manly *Drinking Songs* (1928), which is also outfitted with a *tooralooloo* refrain, and an echoic repeat of the final line. ('Please don't shoot the pianist — he is doing his best.')

By far the best limerick tune is that of Sir Arthur Sullivan, in *The Sorcerer,* I believe, for the sorcerer's limerick song, beginning, 'My name is John Wellington Wells.' But this too has never been used, outside the Gilbert & Sullivan operetta. Its only influence seems to have been on the late Aleister Crowley, who luxuriated in the reputation of being 'the worst man in the world' — an undeserved distinction which he did his best to keep going by writing obscene and insulting limericks against all his friends, among other entertainments. Among the last that Crowley ever wrote is this poetic 'signature,' parodied directly from Gilbert, but given here because it indicates the correct pronunciation of Crowley's own name, which people usually get wrong, while claiming nevertheless to have gone on Black Masses with him (in their youth):

> My name it is Aleister Crowley,
> I'm a master of Magick unholy,
> Of philtres and pentacles,
> Covens, conventicles;
> Of basil, nepenthe, and moly.

Another group of seventeen limericks by Crowley, almost all about intercourse with birds, is noted frankly at the end: 'Above all written straight off under the influence of cocaine in the early hours of the morning on 11 Oct. 1920, at the Villa Santa Barbara, Cefalu, Sicily,' with the penultimate note: '6.15 a.m. I'll shave.' They say that narcissistic details like this show the inner workings of a poet's mind, but I wonder.

The final question as to the limerick is that implied in Crowley's signed example: who are the authors of bawdy limericks? It is understood that most limericks entertain only their authors, and, whatever attempts may be made to circulate them, never achieve folklore status at all. But what of the others, that everyone knows — who writes them? Some of the original authors, when the form was new, and classics were being cast in the hot mould of Victorian anti-clericalism, have been mentioned above, in particular Swinburne, to whom what must be Limerick No. 1 in any collection has always been ascribed, the charmingly normal idyll, in extravagant rhyme, as to the young couple of Aberystwyth, 'who united the organs they kissed with,' moving on finally — in lay-analytic terms — from the oral to the genital stage at last. Other known limerick authors of Swinburne's time and circle were Dante Gabriel Rossetti (who obviously had to write them, if only to get the 'languid love for lilies' of his published poetry out of his system), and the university humorist, A. C. Hilton, whose parody of Swinburne, "The Octopus," is the funniest and most lethal example of the parodist's art in English. Of course, *which* limericks were written by which poets is the part most difficult to discover.

On the other hand, one is wise not to be taken in by the facile attributions of everything bawdy to everyone temporarily in the news. Nothing is sadder than to see the hoary attributions of bawdy folksongs to poets who never in the world wrote them, especially Lord Byron, changing faithlessly to new and equally positive attributions, as new writers come into vogue; these also soon to be replaced in their turn by others as the 'secret authors.' Thus one has recently seen Sala's bawdy farce, *Harlequin Prince Cherrytop* attributed in print to Gilbert & Sullivan (!) under the title *The Sod's Opera;* and "The Bastard King of England," which once used to be fathered off on Kipling, later attributed to Robert W. Service, the sourdough poet of the Alaska gold-rush; then to A. P. Herbert, Member of Parliament; and, most recently — perish the thought! — to Noël Coward. It is the same with attributions of bawdy limericks to Tennyson, Woodrow Wilson, and who-not: one must ask to see the documentary proofs, or to speak to the person who is supposed to have heard the putative poet recite his verse. Or else, as with the great Sea Monster of Loch Ness, the case must be left 'unproved.'

Occasionally the matter is entirely reversed. *Everybody* wants to be the father, and instead of being unable to discover the author, one is embarrassed with an excessive richness of rival claimants. Of one particular item, probably of the 1930's,

> Have you heard about Magda Lupescu,
> Who came to Rumania's rescue?
> It's a wonderful thing
> To be under a king —
> Is democracy better, I esk you?

it is necessary sadly to admit that the present writer has personally encountered not one, but three separate and distinct 'authors' of this rhyme, one of whom — of Teutonic origin and fresh off the boat — could hardly pronounce any further words of the English language than this one limerick and his claim to authorship.

The bawdy limerick has now quieted down a good deal, from the days when it was an outcast thing, as evidenced in the remarkable letter on the mystery of its *name,* written by Dr. Murray, editor of the *Oxford English Dictionary,* to *Notes & Queries* in 1898, strongly objecting to its use in referring to innocent nonsense rhymes. It may be observed, as to the name 'limerick,' that the bawdy examples in *Cythera's Hymnal* and *The Pearl,* in the 1870's, and finally in *The Cremorne* ('1851,' really 1882), are invariably given under the rubric of "Nursery Rhymes." This pinpoints the coinage of the name 'limerick' as at some time between 1882 and 1898, possibly in the columns of the sporting newspaper, *The Pink 'Un* (a sort of British *Police Gazette;* both being imitations of earlier French risqué journals on colored pulp, such as *Le Piron*), to which Murray's indignant letter seems to allude, if not to *Pick-Me-Up,* or *Judy.*

The shelving away of the bawdy limerick now, almost as classic, is largely due to the collection published in Florence in 1928 by the Scottish antiquarian and novelist, Norman Douglas, who is the only person ever to have had the courage to sign a bawdy limerick collection with his real name. *Some Limericks,* as Douglas' volume is modestly called, is not particularly large, containing only sixty-eight limericks, of which few can have been original with him, though one may suspect his improving hand in many. In his introduction, which is a masterpiece of dry humor, Douglas seems seriously to imply that he had also made a collection of English swear words — and had 'caught the old ones in the nick of time' — at the period when he was also compiling the 'breathless catalogue' of his classic study (which he had to publish himself) of *London Street Games,* in 1913–16, with their titles so reminiscent of the similar list of old dances in the rediscovered manuscript fragments of Rabelais' *Pantagruel,* Bk. v, chap. xxi (given only in the English translation by Samuel Putnam). If the collection of swear words was not just one of Douglas' leg-pulls, which it does not seem to have been, it is a great pity it has not survived. Julian Sharman's perfectly titled *Cursory History of Swearing* (1884) does exist, and a more recent study by Prof. Burges Johnson, along with a curious manuscript collection on the subject, preserved at Princeton; but these are not worth what a study at the hands of a master like Douglas would have been, as evidenced by the brief sample of his intended introduction, printed in that of *Some Limericks.*

If sheer size were any criterion, Douglas' work would be far overshadowed — which it most certainly is not — by a more definitive collection, *The Limerick,* published in Paris, 1953, a heavy tome of over five hundred pages, giving nearly eighteen hundred bawdy limericks, good, bad, and indifferent, without critical evaluation or psychological study, but with a certain amount of historical annotation and folklore parallels. This reprints all formerly published bawdy limericks, and more than double that number of unpublished examples, arriving at 'the largest collection of limericks ever published, erotic or otherwise.' An Addenda of several hundred further examples has been accumulated since that time, in part from the private mimeographica of college students in the United States, and should eventually be published. Meanwhile, a pamphlet plagiarism — if folklore can ever be said to be plagiarized — was issued in Paris in 1955, by "Count Palmiro Vicarrion," magnanimously offering the tourist public a selection of two hundred limericks, taken and ruthlessly 'improved' from *The Limerick.* A similar *'Bagman's'* volume is issued in Milan.

Douglas' collection is nothing so pedestrian. His annotations, which have made the fame of his book, and are in part responsible for the continued popularity of the limerick form, are strictly in the mock-serious style of Dr. Wagstaffe on *Tom Thumb,* Oliver Goldsmith's annotations to *Mother Goose,* and "To the Critics and Poets," earlier mentioned, as well as the many similar *jeux d'esprit* in the eighteenth century. There is even a Geographical Index, similar to that of Cordonnier's *Chef d'Oeuvre d'un Inconnu,* tabulating with great seriousness all the sexual and scatological minutiæ of the limerick adventures described. Since the original publication of *Some Limericks,* privately in Florence in 1928, there have been many piratical reprints (all listed in *The Limerick,* bibliography, pp. xiii, 361–69). One in particular is disguised under the title, *From Bed to Worse,* printed secretly in Wiesbaden, in 1945, by 'some members of the Army of Occupation in Germany,' as its title-page states; forgetting, however, to mention Douglas at all. (Copy: Yale.)

A number of slavish imitations, not of Douglas' collection but of his manner of annotation in mock-serious style, have also been laboriously assembled and constructed, in manuscript and in print, most of them infinitely lacking in the wit of Douglas. The most glaring example is the preface to the "Vicarrion" collection, mentioned above, which is almost difficult to credit, in its flat imitation and grovelling unhumorousness, confusing the mere use of dirty words and surréalist non-sequiturs with the art of bawdy humor. An equally bathetic plagiarism of Douglas was issued in Switzerland in 1944, under the title *A Collection of Limericks,* by one "Nosti," a would-be humorist somewhat imperfectly acquainted with the English language, and having the temerity not only to steal most of Douglas' text and notes, but to attempt to improve on and paraphrase the latter in broken English. The book is fortunately very rare.

The American critic, Mr. Clifton Fadiman, writing on the limerick form in *Any Number Can Play,* would deny that even Douglas' own notes have any wit about them, and states coldly that 'the book on the whole is a bore that makes its strongest appeal to the phoney Bohemian temperament.' This sounds like treason in the ranks, but the true explanation is probably that Mr. Fadiman likes — and I suspect writes — those god-awful 'clerihews,' which are some kind of poetico-prosaic morphodites that only their inventors could love; so perhaps his testimony should be written off as biassed. All clerihews being perfervidly clean, they are all signed and of known authorship, something on the style of the epigraphs one observes in public lavatories: 'I came, I seen, I SAW!!' as found by Dr. Allen Walker Read (*Lexical Evidence from Folk Epigraphy,* Paris, 1935, p. 18) in Timpanogos Cave, northern Utah. This sort of thing is vowed to the swift forgetfulness of a coat of paint, and is folklore only by courtesy. Far different are the anonymous gems of real folk-poetry and epigraphy, scrawled in diamond on the glasses and windows of old English taverns, as recorded in *The Merry-Thought, or The Glass-Window and Bog-House Miscellany* of 1731, in four parts. (Copy: Oxford, with incomplete copies at Harvard, and British Museum, P.C.)

Since World War II, whole clubs have been organized for the perpetuation of bawdy limericks, and their public annotation, inevitably in the style of Dr. Wagstaffe and Norman Douglas, and particularly on the West Coast and in Chicago, as the American Limerick Society, the Fifth-Line Society, and others. This is an outgrowth of the similar college fraternity and army bawdy-song societies and informal 'beer busts,' with their manuscript collections, discussed in the preceding essay. One wishes one could somehow convince the college professors, advertising photographers, librarians, and science-fiction enthusiasts, who seem to make up most of the membership of these limerick clubs, that Norman Douglas has now had enough adulation and imitation, and please to lay off.

The only really interesting continuation of Douglas' little jest so far — and even there the notes are the least successful part — is *That Immoral Garland,* an original manuscript by the American poet and translator (worth any twenty others today), C. F. MacIntyre, which includes over a hundred of this poet's original bawdy limericks, of which he is justly proud; not one of which begins with the inactive 'There *was* . . .' but leaps incontinently into the action of the piece from the very first line on. This attempt to free the limerick from the trammels of its wasted line — still thrown away on the meaningless affectation of an 'improper' geographical rhyme, as Lear threw away *both* the first and last lines on the same — is the only real improvement in the limerick form in over two centuries. Were it to be continued successfully, this might give the limerick a new lease on life. As it stands, the only other new element in modern limericks is purely one of content, imported by an enthusiast group utterly collegiate in background, which is now also concerning itself with the concoction of bawdy limericks: the science-fiction fan club kids, both adolescent and superannuated. Of their output it can only be said that if the organ-deficiencies and melancholy accidents of normally bawdy limericks sometimes make depressing reading, the same *in mathematical symbols,* and involving complicated quasi-sexual intercourse with mechanical contraptions and with the blue gleeps and green bleeps of the planets Mars and Venus, is truly too sad to endure.

What remains to be said? The future. Have limericks a future? Yes, certainly they have a future, and a livelier present than those damn clerihews! Only in English, of course, though imitations of the clean form do exist abroad, oddly enough only in Dutch. As Brander Matthews long ago observed, the limerick is the only original verse form of the English language. It apparently also intends to stay that way. One suspects that the limerick of the future will be hopelessly similar to the limerick of the past, and will change merely externally, in the technology and terminology of the horrible castratory accidents over which it all too often gloats. Even so, it would be manifestly unfair to deny to any class, even the educated class, the right to create and circulate whatever folklore and folksong it is capable of, however weakly verbal and uselessly formal the more virile classes might find this folklore to be. The egghead is getting it from all sides: I do not feel his limerick should be taken away from him, or that he should be forced to sing it — just to prove he's one of 'the Boyes,' which he

isn't — when, really, he would much prefer to be sitting placidly
in the library annotating his limericks with parallel texts from
Martial, the *Priapeia,* and the *Greek Anthology;* and never get out
and *do* any of the boldly bawdy things mentioned in these limerick
fantasies at all.

To avoid the accusation of having cravenly evaded giving any
real limericks, in all the dusty library-annotation that has gone
before, let me end this essay and open the brawl — as to my
errors, 'tone,' and so on — by quoting at least one limerick, which
is not only authentically erotic, in its mild way, and does not begin with the false and wasted accent of 'There *was* . . .', but has
also the remarkable peculiarity of being the favorite limerick of
quite a few women, most of whom otherwise loathe limericks (in
which they generally figure both as villain and victim), for the
same reason that calves hate cookbooks:

> For the tenth time, dull Daphnis, said Chloë,
> You have told me my bosom is snowy;
>   You've made much fine verse on
>   Each part of my person,
> Now *do* something — there's a good boy!

TOWARD A MOTIF-INDEX
OF EROTIC HUMOR

I

As IS WELL KNOWN, the *Motif-Index of Folk-Literature*
by Prof. Stith Thompson, in both its original edition (1932–36)
and later revision (1955–58), and the further motif-indexes based
on the Thompson system, rigorously omit — or appear to omit —
all classification of motifs in erotic and scatologic humor, allotting
to this subject the number X700–799, "Humor Concerning Sex,"
but leaving these blank, with the following note:

> Thousands of obscene motifs in which there is no point
> except the obscenity itself might logically come at this
> point, but they are entirely beyond the scope of the present
> work. They form a literature to themselves, with its own
> periodicals and collections. In view of the possibility that
> it might become desirable to classify these motifs and place
> them within the present index, space has been left . . . for
> such motifs.

D. P. Rotunda, in reprinting this note in his *Motif-Index of
the Italian Novella in Prose* (Bloomington, 1942) adds the somewhat restive codicil: 'I quote this note from Professor Thompson
. . . upon whose classification this Index is based. I agree that
some line must be drawn, although some may question its allocation, and I leave the space free' (p. 214, n. 1). The question of
allocation is evidently difficult. Another culture than our own
might prefer to include the obscene motifs and omit the hundreds
of descriptions of horrible murders and sadistic mutilations at
the sigla Q400, "Kinds of Punishment," and "S.—Unnatural
Cruelty", "Revolting Murders or Mutilations", "Abandoned or
Murdered Children," in the work of both Thompson and
Rotunda, in which motifs there is certainly no point except the

454

sadism itself. As I have made this particular cultural contradiction and intellectual blind spot the subject of an independent
work, *Love & Death: A Study in Censorship* (New York, 1949),
there seems no point in pursuing it further here.

In any case, it is obvious that the Rotunda index, and also
the parent index by Thompson, do actually include a large number of motifs of sexual humor and scatological import, scattered
under ambiguous headings such as "Clever Verbal Retorts"
(J1250), "Gullible Fools" (J2300), "Illicit Sexual Relations"
(T400), "Humor of Discomfiture" (X0-99), and the like. In point
of fact, the Italian *novelle,* and likewise the French fabliaux, the
Arabian Nights, and so forth could not be motif-indexed at all
if "Humor Concerning Sex" were really omitted, as this is one
of the principal themes of the genre. Rotunda therefore gives,
for instance — but in almost every case under the *other* or non-
obscene heading — such motifs as "Man made to believe that he is
pregnant" (J2321, from Boccaccio, Day IX. 3), which is still a
well-known joke in America, a monkey being palmed off on the
dupe as his excretory 'child'; 'Impotent suitor rejected — Woman
says they could not smooth out their quarrels' (J1367), also
still told in English, though probably by way of the French *conte-
en-vers* "La Paix du Ménage"; various *pudenda loquens* tales
(at H451 and D1610.6), and a whole series of bawdy jokes at
J1742-49, with one at X612, "Christian dupes Jews into revering
his excreta" (cited to Sacchetti, No. 24, in the 15th century),
of which there is a much softened modern reversal in which a
Jewish trickster persuades a Russian cossack (or Irish policeman)
to get *gefüllte-Fisch* heads, 'to give him brains.'

This possibility, on the one hand, of rejecting obscene jokes
with moral horror at X700, while bringing them back in disguise
at dozens of other numbers, makes clear one of the deepest
deficiencies of any classification scheme: the inevitable subjective-
ness of approach by the indexer. For almost any given tale can
be indexed in at least two ways, depending upon the formal element chosen, the point of view taken, or even, for that matter,
the protagonist with whom the indexer consciously or unconsciously identifies. What is the subject, or proper 'motif-indexing,'
of the following widely distributed tale or joke, which I have
collected orally some twenty times in the United States between
1935 and 1953: *A Jewish rabbi temporarily replaces a Catholic
priest in the confessional, and deals out identical penances to the
women who present themselves for absolution; telling the last*

*woman (who has sinned only once) to say three paternosters and
put three dollars in the poor-box, and the church will owe her
two more acts of intercourse.* Owing to the persistent emphasis on
money in the mock penances given, this story can be understood —
and I have so collected it at various times — as satirizing either the
rabbi's presumed excessive interest in money (thus anti-Jewish);
the confessional's presumed simoniacal interest in money and sex
(thus anti-Catholic); or all religions generally, as evidenced in
the whole burlesque *mise-en-scène* of the story and the usual
explosive obscenity of the punch line or verbal climax, an essential
feature of *jokes* as differentiated from *tales.*

Depending upon the point of view taken, this story can also
be motif-indexed, on the Thompson scheme, under at least five
different headings: as an "Absurd Misunderstanding" (J1823,
"Misunderstanding of church customs causes inappropriate action"); "Jokes Concerning Jews" (X610); "Confession of Sins"
(V20, see Rotunda's V29.4, "Sodomist makes sport of confession");
"Illicit Sexual Relations" (T40, *cf.* Rotunda's T463.1, "Sodomist
forces confessor to absolve him"); or, classified strictly from the
operative point of view, by the sexual nexus on which the story
turns — that essential element without which it cannot exist — the
actual subject must be considered "Sexual Sins Punished" (Q240).
The approach through the formal aspect, however, concentrating
on the humorous treatment of this subject matter, would require
a sixth classification, under the nonexistent X700.

What this demonstrates is that any classification system such
as the Thompson *Motif-Index* could be redone from start to
finish in any one of several completely different ways, depending
only on the indexer's subjective approach to, and understanding
and evaluation of, his materials. In most cases this depends
basically on the *method of grasping reality* (and, in the present
case, the special sense of humor) typical of the indexer's particular
culture. Each such system would therefore be just as valid, and
precisely as useful, as any other of equal size, depending only
on the fullness of its cross-index volume. (That of the Thompson
Index, as now revised, is particularly fine.) The same is also true
of any other pair of all-embracing classification systems, whether
of ideas, such as Roget's *Thesaurus,* and the recent attempts of
Mortimer Adler; of living organisms, as in the Linnæan and Al-
drovandian systems; of human actions, in the *Shulchan Aruch*
and the confessorial manuals; or of 'everything in the world,'

as in the subject classification printed in the index volume to the *Encylopædia Britannica* (11th edition, 1911), and the Dewey Decimal library system, of which the latter is being continuously enlarged and desperately revised to this day, but will never and can never be 'complete.' The classification systems commonly proliferated by out-and-out psychotic personalities are just as likely to be of equal fullness, complexity, and probable validity. An excellent example is *La Science Unique* (Paris, 1953), of Emilio Molina Martinez. Cruden's Bible *Concordance,* which 'cost the compiler his sanity,' should also be cited, though cause and effect have probably been confused here. At least one such work, the Marquis de Sade's *120 Journées de Sodome,* motif-indexing all possible tortures and cruelties, compares astonishingly with the sections Q400 and S of the Thompson Index, mentioned earlier, which are, as a matter of fact, grossly inferior — in point of completeness — to Sade's parallel classification.

The real value of any 'motif' or 'trait' index does not stem from any inherent superiority of its particular cultural bias or point of view, but simply from the arbitrary acceptance of that point of view by the largest possible number of later researchers; thus, ideally, making it possible to confront and compare, at one and only one prearranged point of reference or rendezvous, the largest number of parallel items from various cultures and literatures, and thus making possible also the study of their similarities, their differences, their history and probable migrations, and a stab at understanding the secret of their longevity and human appeal. Unfortunately, this is not what has happened. The most important single work of motif-indexing so far published since that of Rotunda on the novella, the index to the entire corpus of the *Arabian Nights* in *Thèmes et Motifs des "Mille et Une Nuits,"* by Nikita Elisséeff (Beyrouth, Syria: Imprimerie Catholique, 1949), which does not follow the Thompson system, is — though certainly not for that reason — not mentioned nor in any way taken cognizance of in the new, revised edition of the Thompson *Motif-Index* in 1958. Evidently, the dream of international cooperation in folkloristic science, FF fellowship, &c., is still somewhat remote, and only by the merciful accident of being alerted to the existence of Elisséeff's work, through the inexhaustible erudition and up-to-dateness of Prof. Archer Taylor, was an American researcher recently saved the terrible embarrassment, and waste of years, of *re*-indexing the motifs of the *Arabian Nights*.

II. THE LITERATURE OF EROTIC HUMOR

BEFORE PROCEEDING to any preliminary attempt at a Motif-Index of Erotic Humor, to fill the gap in the Thompson classification at X700 — though from a psychological rather than a formal point of view—it may be of real use to other researchers to outline briefly the existing literature of erotic and scatologic humor on which such a motif-index is to be based, and in which the historical materials for any larger development of it must be sought.

It is true as stated in Thompson's note of rejection quoted above, that the 'obscene motifs . . . form a literature to themselves, with its own periodicals and collections,' but this has only become true during the last hundred years, and then only in certain cultures: specifically Russia, Germany, and the English-speaking world. Before about 1840 to 1860, and in all countries — as now still in France—the erotic and scatologic jokes were seldom or never omitted from, or separated in, the joke and tale collections. It seems more than probable that they were even considered the most piquant and entertaining part of those collections, as they still are today — particularly in those cultures where they are most taboo. In the others, as in France, Denmark, Japan, and in many primitive cultures, sexual humor is taken for granted, orally or in print, with hardly a second glance or disapprobatory reflexion, as a part of humor and of life as normal as any other, or more so.

Printed jestbooks are the principal exception to the rule, enunciated by Miss A. H. Gayton in 1942, and already referred to, that 'The printed record of folksongs and folktales has been and is of importance not so much to the folk themselves as to the folklorist investigating the nature and history of these cultural phenomena.' Printed joke collections are now, and have apparently always been, eagerly sought, bought, and memorized by professional and semi-professional entertainers, and their contents have thus been continually 'fed back' to the orally-transmitting audience, for at least the 500 years since the introduction of printing in Europe. The evidence also indicates that such printed (earlier manuscript) collections have not only been of seminal importance, as just described, but that their transmission partakes more particularly of the literary conventions of *signed* and theoretically unchanging texts, than of the anonymity and fluidity traditional to folklore. This is by no means a recent development. The earliest secular tale collections still extant — and the religious

legends even more so, being actually sacrosanct as to their texts —
as for instance the Homeric legends, the Aesopic and Milesian
fables, the tales embodied in the Talmud, in the *Golden Ass* of
Apuleius, in the *Amorous Epistles* of Aristænetus (4th A.D.), and
the later *Jests* of Hierocles, exist only in the form of rigidly transmitted literary texts, almost all of presumably known authorship,
though Homer and Aesop are unquestionably collective editorial
identities.

Evidently these collections were not original with their presumable authors, but were gathered in the first instance from
oral transmisssion, doubtless with a bit of literary retouching, as
is still always the case. But, as confided first to manuscript, then
to print, these particular collections have nevertheless had their
primary influence on the disseminating audience, for some 2,000
years now, in rigid literary form. There is no reason to believe
that they were not as eagerly sought, and memorized in their main
lines from manuscript copies, by the professional speakers and
jesters of their time, as the later *exempla* of Alfonsi-Sephardi and
others were memorized by medieval preachers. Anyone who has
been present at the creation of a Hollywood or radio humor skit —
with the materials drawn from steel filing-cabinets filled with
jokes and 'situations' clipped and pasted on filing-cards from
print — will understand that the method has never changed. Compare the details of technique of the modern Michigan rabbi, a
'noted raconteur,' who 'owned several collections of Jewish jokes
and kept a regular file of usable stories for his public addresses,'
cited by Richard M. Dorson in *Studies in Biblical and Jewish
Folklore* (Bloomington, 1960) p. 113. If there is a difference here
from the method of Rabbi Mosheh Sephardi, converted under
the name of Petrus Alfonsi — in honor of his godfather at baptism,
the King of Spain — and author under that name of the most
famous medieval collection of Latin *exempla,* this difference
would be hard to state. The same reliance on manuscript is more
than probable, also, of the extraordinarily large Levantine collections of the Middle Ages, the *Ocean of Story* and the *Arabian
Nights,* which are far larger than a tale-teller can easily memorize,
and of which, in any case, we know precisely nothing except via
the manuscript texts recovered. The particularly popular story
of Aladdin and his lamp, for instance, was lost from sight except
in the French adaptation of Antoine Galland for nearly 200 years,
and was generally believed by scholars to be his own invention,
until the identical manuscript text of the *Nights* used by Gal-

land was accidentally rediscovered by Zotenberg in the 1880's.

Jestbooks for popular consumption appeared in Europe soon after the introduction of printing, and were repeatedly issued, in cheap and relatively large editions, from that time on. Their popularity is as great today, at least in France, as it ever was. The *Facetiæ* of Poggio in Italy (*d.* 1459), and of Bebel in Germany (1514, completely translated into German, and magnificently edited with comparative notes and apparatus by Wesselski in 1907), the *Baliverneries, ou Contes nouveaux d'Eutrapel* of Noël du Fail (1548) and *Nouvelles récréations et joyeux devis* of Bonaventure des Périers and Jacques Peletier (1558) in France — exactly a century after the death of Poggio — were the first jestbooks in their respective countries, and created the modern form. That the original audience intended was the educated cleric and preacher, as in the *exempla* earlier, is made clear by the presentation of their (collected) jokes, by Poggio and Bebel, in Latin. The first modern jestbook in the 'vulgar tongue' happens to have been the first English jestbook, which was not the *Hundred Mery Tales* in the early sixteenth century, as usually stated, but Caxton's much earlier incunabular edition of Aesop, with a supplement of jests from Poggio and Alfonsi, among them one illustrated with a charming and naïve erotic woodcut showing the lovers hidden in a tree, the first erotic illustration printed in England and one of the first printed anywhere. (It is omitted from Jacobs' nineteenth-century reprint of Caxton's Aesop.)

Far from being special or separate 'obscene . . . collections,' as might be understood from Thompson's note, the riotously unexpurgated jestbooks of these early types were the *only* ones that existed at all, until barely a century ago. The sexual and scatological jokes appear in the jestbooks absolutely without differentiation, interspersed liberally among all the other jokes, and in very high percentage it should be observed. Until late in the eighteenth century — and then, basically, only in England and Germany—no sexual expurgation was even dreamed of in almost any popular joke collection, in any language. All changes demanded and condemnations made were, in every known case, for purposes of religious and political, rather than sexual censorship, though striking under a moralistic screen, *bien entendu,* as is still the method of the religious and political censor. This is equally true of the tale collections published concurrently, in particular Boccaccio's *Decameron* and the rest of the Italian *novelle,* in which the Levantine tales, brought from the Near East to southern Europe, passed into popular currency first in Italy and Spain, then in France through the derivative *Cent Nouvelles Nouvelles* and the fabliaux, and in such random groups as the tales embodied in Rabelais' *Gargantua & Pantagruel* (1535, listed in L'Aulnaye's early nineteenth-cenutry editions of Rabelais, which also contain the *Erotica Verba,* the earliest known erotic slang dictionary), in Henri Estienne's *Apologie pour Hérodote* (1566, splendidly edited by Ristelhuber, 1879), and in the *Moyen de Parvenir* of Béroalde de Verville (1610, the tales indexed in the best modern editions [by Prosper Blanchemain], 1870–72, and Charles Royer, 1896).

Cryptic and crotchety as it is, practically unreadable and utterly without influence (except on Sterne and Joyce) in its imitation of Rabelais, the *Moyen de Parvenir* marks a most important date in the literature of European folktales and humor: the virtual end of the tale collections, except in reprints, with only Basile's *Pentamerone* following; and the beginning of the reign of the joke. Or, rather, the *breaking apart* of the earlier folktales into, on the one hand, the quick verbal humor and riposte of the Poggian joke or *facezia* — the favorite of the strolling jesters and goliards such as Tyl Eulenspiegel in Germany, the mountebank street-comedians, Bruscambille, Tabarin, and Gaultier-Garguille in France, and the theatrical comedians in England — and, on the other hand, the redirection of the large developmental possibilities of the tale or *novella,* possibilities brilliantly prefigured a thousand years earlier in the *Golden Ass* of Apuleius and the *Satyricon* of Petronius into the novel, a form already widely popular for over a century in *Amadis de Gaul* (1508) and the other overblown romances of chivalry on the ancient style of *Daphnis and Chloë,* as satirized by Cervantes. Royer and Courbet ("C. E. Roybet") have trenchantly expressed this change from tales to jokes in their introduction (1873) to the *Serées* of Guillaume Bouchet, a sort of lesser contemporary of Montaigne, or early whimsical essayist and joke interlarder of the Charles Lamb or Southey type. The *Moyen de Parvenir* in 1610, says "Roybet," is the:

> expression dernière et parfaite du conte français . . . La nouvelle, qui jusque là avait gardé sa physionomie, son allure & ses proportions particulières, se transforme subitement. Condensée en quelques mots par des esprits satiriques peu soucieux des détails inutiles, elle devient l'anecdote moderne, rapide & aiguë comme une flèche; puis,

d'autre part, agrandie par les écrivains à la mode, elle s'élève au roman de cour.

One of the most striking characteristics of the jestbooks, their wholesale and inveterate copying from one another, has often been observed, but without ever drawing the clear inference that these collections — which derive mainly from one another, and seldom from coeval folk sources — are not so much being alimented by folk sources as constituting, themselves, a main source of the jokes in oral transmission. As to their copying from one another, that is only one intermediate step in their migrations: from one mouth to another, one book to another, one land to another. Almost the entire French literature and poetry of the crucial sixteenth century stem from Italy, just as the English literature and poetry of the sixteenth and seventeenth centuries take their inspiration from France (only occasionally directly from Italy, via translations, as in Shakespeare's sources). Of nothing is this more true than of the popular or sub-literary art of humorous tales and jokes, arriving in Italy and Spain in the first place from and during the centuries of the Arab conquest. That is the main bridge for western European folktales and jokes, and any such tale or joke that can be traced at all will generally be found to follow backward this same itinerary: through France, to Italy (or Spain), and thence to the Levant. The Slavonic and Germanic tales do not even make this Western detour, but pass directly up through Asia Minor, via Turkey and Greece, to eastern Europe. This answers the question, tiresomely reiterated, 'Who invents jokes?' Jokes are not invented; they are evolved. And they arrive to us from other countries and older civilizations, by way of oral and printed infiltrations over a period of centuries, and along certain massive and rather well delimited cultural highways.

Of particular interest, in this connection, are the tales and jests — all erotic — embodied in the well-known sixteenth-century Arabic manual of sex technique, *The Perfumed Garden* of al-Nafzawi, which has been translated into French and various other Western languages since 1850; and in the *Contes licencieux de Constantinople et de l'Asie Mineure* (1906), edited by Jean Nicolaidès, as the first volume in a series to be discussed more fully below. In this volume will be found over a dozen Levantine versions of bawdy jokes being told today in England and America, such as No. 39, "La Femme qui en a un à louer," known in France since the early seventeenth century in the form of a mock-legal "Baïl faict par une jeune femme de son con," and in the U.S. currently, as concerning Speedy Pedro, the Mexican marvel of rapidity. Also worth consulting is *La Fleur lascive orientale* ('Oxford' [Bruxelles], 1882, a rare English translation being later privately issued [by Smithers in Sheffield] as by the "Erotika Biblion Society"), a collection of Near-Eastern and Oriental tales translated anonymously by J. A. Decourdemanche, translator also of the in part erotic *Sottisier* (Turin, 1878) of the Turkish jester, Nasr-Eddin Hodja, later edited definitively by Wesselski in 1911. Among the tales included in *La Fleur lascive orientale* is the "Night of al-Kader," the erotic 'three wishes' tale from the *Arabian Nights,* of which Decourdemanche interestingly notes that 'a story of this kind will also be found in the Babylonian Talmud, which would refer it at least to the 8th century of our era.' I have been unable to trace this Talmudic reference and would appreciate any information concerning it. This tale is still very widely circulated throughout Europe and America, with various twists or 'gimmicks' concerning a monkey's paw (the W. W. Jacobs story), egg-beaters, and the like. Were it possible to trace the tale, it would very likely be found to be much older than the Talmud, as it is clearly of didactic intent, pointing to the moral — a main tenet of much more ancient Greek religious ethics — that the gods know what is best for us, and that any attempt to force special gifts from them, as by prayer or magic, will inevitably upset the laws of nature and bring disaster.

Having lost contact with the Near-Eastern sources, until Galland's *Arabian Nights* translation a century later, and the Levantine and native inspiration of the tale collections having come virtually to an end with Basile's *Pentamerone* in 1636, the European jestbooks of the seventeenth century and since, in all languages, were able to proceed to almost nothing further than a continuous and slavish copying and plagiarizing of one another, and this is still the case. Their whole development and decadence is very similar to that of the dreambooks, the jestbooks' only real competitor in the chapbook field. Freud has observed that the European dreambooks — which are still being published, with lottery-number interpretations — are only 'pitiful plagiarisms' of their now-forgotten Oriental prototypes, of a sort so ancient as to be alluded to in the Old Testament stories of Joseph and Daniel, both of whose fortunes arose from successfully interpreting dreams and visions where the book-learned mages of the kings had ignominiously failed.

It might come as a surprise to observe the date of the last more or less original joke collection of Europe, until the beginnings of modern folktale collection 'from the mouth of the folk,' as by the brothers Grimm. The last conscientious jestbook editor, who was something other than a mere plagiarist, was Antoine Le Metel, sieur d'Ouville, whose *Contes aux heures perdues*, published first in 1644, became the storehouse rifled by all later compilers, both in French and in the derivative collections translated abroad, especially in English. A simple piracy of D'Ouville, under the title *Récréations Françoises*, or *Nouveaux* [!] *Contes à Rire*, went through more than twenty-five editions from 1658 on, for over a century, and is probably the most widely circulated jestbook ever published. A selection, unfortunately brief, from D'Ouville's original collection, was edited under the title *L'Élite des Contes*, in 1876, with important comparative notes and tracings by Ristelhuber, whose earlier abridged edition of Poggio is also very valuably annotated. No joke collection of any originality, in either French or English, was published after that of D'Ouville in 1644, until the scientific and erotic collections from folk transmission, issued by Afanasyev, Pitrè, Krauss, and others, in the last third of the nineteenth century; and the more recent popular compilations in French, of Perceau, Geiger, Ramond, and especially "Curnonsky" and his imitators, since the mid-1920's. This represents nearly three centuries of conspicuous inoriginality, plagiarism, and drought.

The jestbook compilers of the late seventeenth and eighteenth centuries never thought, for some reason, to look for native materials in any serious ways, but were satisfied simply to retell all the old stories, refurbishing them with the names of current personalities, and of popular actresses and comedians. This is still the rule in most of the hackwork jokebooks being published today, and was already standard by the time of Mottley's *Joe Miller's Jests,* in 1739, in which most of the stories are ascribed irrelevantly to contemporary political and theatrical personalities, such as Joe Miller himself; as also in the two earlier jestbooks (the second recently discovered by Evan Esar) from which Mottley's work is almost totally cribbed. These, in turn, were likewise credited on their title pages to the popular comedians Spiller and Polly Peachum, who of course had no more to do with their compilation than do the comedians credited today with editing the usual ghostwritten jokebooks.

A particularly illuminating example of this method of up-dating old jokes is given by Jerah Johnson in the *Journal of American Folklore,* (1960) vol. 73: p. 248, and compare p. 250. A story now generally attributed to George Bernard Shaw — and the dancer, Isadora Duncan, though the writer cited politely omitted to mention her — is identified as occurring in an Old French *roman* of 1319; and Johnson notes that 'the motif of this anecdote is not included in the Stith Thompson *Index.*' A similar example, possibly even older, is the *Arabian Nights* story "How Abu Hassan brake Wind," commonly told today about Mr. Smith of the London *Times,* who was exiled to India for having told an improper riddle at a banquet, and returned twenty years later, a military hero, to tell the identical improper riddle at the banquet given in his honor. A polite version also exists in which a young boy is sent to prison 'for breathing heavily on a glass case in the British Museum.' He returns after forty years' imprisonment, a shaky old man, to breathe his defiant last breath on the very same case! These are, of course, not the identical *Arabian Nights* story, but derivatives showing now only tale-type relationships, though of an extremely close kind, as in the use of bodily exhalations in the last example. The original Abu Hassan version or transgression is preserved and improved — *i.e.,* evolves further — in the eighteenth-century French tale, "Berthe, ou le Pet heureux," in which the turning of the accident to good fortune (as with Major-General Smith, formerly of the London *Times)* was apparently first introduced. It is retold intermediately in Aubrey's *Brief Lives,* in the late seventeenth century, with no other change than to transform Abu Hassan into a courtier of Queen Elizabeth's, Edward de Vere, Earl of Oxford, who spends seven years in proud disgrace in Italy after a gastric lapse at court. In this form, which Aubrey tells as historical fact, the tale is now first fitted out as a joke, with a sardonic punch-line or verbal climax put into the mouth of the Queen: 'My lord, I had forgot the Fart.' Mark Twain's famous *1601, or Tudor Conversation,* turns on an identical scene in the presence of Queen Elizabeth, as recounted by a mythical Aubrey or Pepys.

It is to be observed that, as retold by the late eighteenth-century erotic poet, Vincent Lombard de Langres, in *Berthe, ou le Pet mémorable* (1807, with other *contes-en-vers*), the subtitle refers to the tale as an 'anecdote of the ninth century,' suggesting a fabliau origin, which I have not been able to trace. Another such fabliau, rewritten in the eighteenth century, is the anonymous *Nocrion, conte Allobroge* (1747), reprinted Bruxelles: Gay &

Doucé, 1881, with comparative notes by the singular antiquary, Jamet the Younger, whose manuscript annotations, or *Stromates*, in the Arsenal Library, Paris, still remain to be explored and published for their folklore interest. "Nocrion" is based on the *pudenda loquens* fabliau of Garin, "Le Chevalier qui faisoit parler les cons et les culs," which also inspired Diderot's *Les Bijoux indiscrets.* Gay's bibliography observes (ed. Lemonnyer, I. 377) that an anecdote similar to that of "Berthe" is given in the notes by Paulin Pâris to his edition of the *Historiettes* of Tallemant des Réaux, a collection of biographical anecdotes, very much on the style of Aubrey's *Brief Lives,* which has been generally overlooked as a folktale source.

In stating that the turning of the unfortunate fart to good fortune is first introduced in the eighteenth century, in the tale of "Berthe," I am perhaps overlooking not only its untraced ninth-century source, which would be even earlier than Abu Hassan; but also a curious trait in the story as told by Aubrey, or, rather, in the true history of the nobleman to whom he assimilates this tale, Edward de Vere, Earl of Oxford, of whom Aubrey tells us that this 'great earle . . . spent fourty thousand pounds *per annum* in seaven yeares travell,' and 'lived at Florence in more grandeur than the duke of Tuscany,' that is to say, exactly during the years of his self-enforced exile. One has the impression that it was this report of fantastic opulence and expenditure, during his period abroad, that attracted to the Earl of Oxford this very folktale, and thus the trait of eventual wealth or good fortune always existing therein, on the proverbial principle that 'shitten luck is good luck.' An extremely large amount of folk-material could be collected on this subject, particularly as to the identity of *gold* with excrement. See, as a beginning, the Thompson index-volume, VI. 260–61, and especially the tale of the marking of a dreamed-of 'treasure' by these means, at X31.

Owing to the extraordinary increase in chapbook publishing facilities in the seventeenth and eighteenth centuries, the paradoxical position was quickly reached where the native or 'original' folk content of the jestbooks had most conspicuously dried up and was lacking, at exactly the period of their heaviest printing and greatest circulation, from about 1700 to 1820. This is very similar to the present disaffected position in the popular arts, where, at the very moment of the greatest technological possibility of mass circulation, in print, movies, television, and so forth, the materials so circulated are of an almost total folk falsity where-ever they touch, or purport to touch, upon folklore, folksong, and the like. This situation has been developing generally since the parodying of folksongs in the ballad-operas of the 1730's, if not since much earlier with the 'sacred contrefacts' or religious parodies set to folk tunes at the very beginning of the Protestant Reformation, as has been discussed at length earlier. The influence of the later jestbooks must, in the same way, be assessed as in large measure bogus or fakeloristic — to use the term that has now 'passed into the language' — pumping tired and undesired jokes into a disgruntled audience that would really have preferred something native and 'new.'

Not until the wild West humor of the American almanacs of the 1850's, and slightly earlier, and the frontier journalism of the John Phoenix and Mark Twain types, was this 'new' element rediscovered: the ancient art of telling tales and spinning whoppers in a droll and leisurely fashion. But by then it was impossible to re-inject this element into the jokebooks, which continued to retail all the ancient chestnuts without any but unimportant dialect or costume changes, as for instance the burnt-cork blackface of the bogus 'Nigger' minstrels; while the Twains, the Nasbys, and the other authentic native humorists had to make their careers in journalism and on the lecture platform (now radio) instead. The almost total disaffection of the audience came rapidly, after the expurgation of the jestbooks in the Anglo-Saxon culture in about the 1830's, on the wave of moralistic reaction and repression preceding and attempting to avert the revolutions of the 1840's. The expurgated jokes thereafter to be found in the English-language jokebooks and chapbook series (such as those of Wehman and the Ottenheimers until World War I, and Haldeman-Julius and Shomer until World War II) and in the dreary joke columns of humorous journals of the period, such as *Punch,* later *Life,* the *Literary Digest,* and the college-humor magazines, have become increasingly different — not only in matter but in form — from the older tales and jokes. The folk nerve has been almost completely cut. Page after page and at machine-gun speed, these publications shoot out their hopeless puns and 'one-liners,' with less and less emphasis on art in the telling, or in fact on almost any verbal art; and with more and deeper reliance on improbable and even maniacal situations (the modern 'sick' and 'bop' jokes), on the accompanying illustration — which finally becomes everything, as in the comic books and *The New Yorker* — on hostile repartee and the 'quickie' format, and most of all on the

brief and unsatisfying climactic pleasure of the verbal explosion
or punch-line. Visibly dying, this sort of shrill and counterfeit
slapstick is almost unrecognizable as the reliques or effluvia of
folktales.

For the record, it would be desirable to give here some brief
bibliographical reference to the literature of the jestbooks, but
unfortunately almost no serious study of them has ever been published, possibly owing to the evident contradiction in terms such
study would imply. The best thing in the *Studies in Jocular
Literature* of W. Carew Hazlitt is its title, while the deeply
knowledgeable tale-tracers, such as Clouston, and, on the continent, Köhler, Pitrè, Ristelhuber, and Wesselski, never confided
to print any general discussion of the jestbook literature they
knew so intimately. Essentially, all that exists is the excellent title-
list of English-language jestbooks to 1660, in the *Cambridge Bibliography of English Literature*, vol. II, taken in part from, and
supplemented by, the list to 1800 in Bohn's edition of Lowndes'
Bibliographer's Manual, p. 1200–1208, at "Jest Books;" and two
capital articles by Schulz, *Die englischen Schwankbücher*, in
Palaestra (1912) vol. 117; and F. P. Wilson, "The English Jestbooks of the Sixteenth and Early Seventeenth Centuries," in
Huntington Library Quarterly (1939) II. 121–58, with which all
further research must start. I have prepared a supplementary list,
covering the whole period since Caxton and continuing to 1840,
which more than doubles the number of raw titles on hand. I
would be glad to turn this over to anyone who wishes to continue
with a formal bibliography of the English-language jestbooks,
a formidable job that would require protracted access at least to
the very rich holdings in the British Museum and in the Douce
Collection at Oxford. The materials for such a bibliography are
not available in the United States. At least two of the very finest
collections — those of George Daniel, and more recently Hoe —
were disgracefully allowed to be broken up by booksellers and
at auction.

For French jestbooks there is also no real bibliography, and
the best listings will be found in various private collectors' catalogues of the early nineteenth century, particularly that of Viollet-
Leduc (1847, reissued in 1859), and in the *Bibliographie des
Ouvrages relatifs à l'Amour*, by 'le Comte d'I***' [Jules Gay],
in the 2nd edition, 1864, only; the later and much fuller editions
being unfortunately alphabetical instead of subject-arranged. The
same is true of the great *Bibliotheca Germanorum Erotica et*

Curiosa by Hugo Hayn and Alfred Gotendorf (1912–14), with its important but very scarce ninth volume supplement by Paul Englisch (1929). These volumes cover the German jestbooks from their beginnings — and of course very much else — with extreme thoroughness, but again without much grouping or indexing by subject. This is also the case in the illustrated bibliographical volumes II and IV of the *Bilder-Lexikon der Erotik* [edited by Leo Schidrowitz], 1928–31, a stupefying work that almost any folklorist must approach wearing dark glasses. A reprint, with a new supplement announced, is now in process of publication in Hamburg. The *Bilder-Lexikon der Erotik* is an absolute mine of ethnological materials on erotic and scatologic themes, both pictorially and textually, and swamps, not to say dwarfs, all comparison with the American *Encyclopedia of Sexual Behavior,* edited by Drs. Albert Ellis & Albert Abarbanel (New York, 1961), and the recent and sickly imitative *Sexologia-Lexikon* edited by M. Giuseppe Lo Duca in Paris, of which the whole editorial slant is a visible gloating over the sadistic and castratory entries.

An analytic study of motifs in a brief selection of early English jestbooks has been prepared in recent years, by Prof. E. W. Baughman (Indiana University Ph.D. dissertation), and a similar project on German jestbooks is announced at the University of California in Berkeley, but neither of these has as yet been published. A group of model tale-tracings appear in *Journal of American Folklore* (1960) vol. 73: p. 248–51, in particular by Jerah Johnson, and Jan Brunvand, so elegantly and thoroughly done that one trusts these represent light-hearted samples of larger work in progress. Less broadly, perhaps, but very importantly, a project of indexing motifs in French Renaissance tale-collections is announced in the Thompson *Motif-Index,* 1955, I. 26, by a group of researchers at the University of South Carolina: in particular Cecilia P. Irwin's "Summaries of the Stories of Béroalde de Verville's *Moyen de Parvenir,*" M.A. thesis, unpublished, 1953; and Sarah C. Pinkney's analysis of tales in the *Heptameron* of Marguerite of Navarre. Stith Thompson makes, however, the plain statement, I. 17 — concerning the fabliaux — that 'A motif-index of the whole corpus of fabliaux has been examined for additional entries. Fabliaux with obscenity as the only point have been excluded, though good [?] jests with risqué elements are retained.' This is obviously only a repetition of the principle, already cited, at X700, somewhat paraphrased, and even a bit modified, if one understands correctly what a 'good' jest 'with risqué elements' may be. But it is also obvious that the work has to be done all over. In the same way, one of the most important early French tale collections, the *Cent Nouvelles Nouvelles,* attributed to Antoine de La Sale, seems to have been covered only in part by the Thompson *Motif-Index,* while Rabelais is not even mentioned in its list of sources. See, however, the very striking group of tales, scattered through *Gargantua & Pantagruel* (1535 ff.), fortunately all listed in the best of the early critical editions of Rabelais, by Stanislas de L'Aulnaye (Paris, 1823) III. 667–8, an edition also containing important folklore and folkspeech materials in the "Erotica Verba" and "Rabelæsiana," III. 431–666. The same materials are reprinted in various one-volume editions published in the 1830's.

III.   THE CONTE-EN-VERS

THE SCIENTIFIC study of folktales, and collection of folk humor, are actually far older than the brothers Grimm and the turn of the nineteenth century, to which this new science is usually referred. The aristocratic collectors of folksong in the Scandinavian countries as early as 1590, such as A. S. Vedel, historiographer to the King of Denmark, and the noblewomen, Karen Brahe and Mette Gjöe (on whom see S. B. Hustvedt's *Ballad Criticism in Scandinavia and Great Britain,* New York, 1916 pp. 28–30), were closely matched in France by the seventeenth- and eighteenth-century scholars and aristocrats whose pleasure it was to learn folktales from their cooks and coachmen and other 'oral sources,' and to dress these stories up in the cultured doggerel of the *conte-en-vers,* after the popularizing of this form by La Fontaine in his *Nouvelles en vers tirée* [sic] *de Bocace et de l'Arioste* in 1664 (postdated 1665, facsimile edition 1935). By the 1740's, the 'mucker pose' among the French nobility — what would nowadays be called the 'pop-culch kick' — had proceeded to such lengths as the publication of pretended chapbooks, such as *Les Écosseuses, ou Les Oeufs de Pasques,* and its supplement on the feast of St. Jean ('Troyes,' 1742), put together for a lark by a group of noblemen and women, headed by the Comte de Caylus, Moncrif, and the Abbé Grécourt, with the professional last touches set to the work by the slang poet and humorist, Joseph Vadé (over a century before Mark Twain, George Ade, and so on, who are thought of as the inventors of the slang humor form). To this libertine group is also due the publication, on the private press of the Duc d'Aiguillon, at Vérets in Touraine, of a large collection of erotic folktales cast in the *conte-en-vers* form under the title *Recueil de pièces choisies par le Cosmopolite* ('À Anconne, chez Uriel Bandant,' 1735; reprinted 'Leyde,' 1865), which includes the Italian text of the similar *Dubbij amorosi* attributed to Aretino, and dating almost a century and a half earlier than La Fontaine. I would also attribute to the same group, and in particular to the littérateurs Moncrif and Grécourt (*d.*1743), the editing and publication of the equally rare and clearly supplementary *Les Muses en belle Humeur* ('Villefranche,' 1742), which is the first collection of consciously 'improper' folksongs ever made. Both these works, and the extremely interesting issuing group, have been discussed more fully in a preceding chapter, "Great Collectors of Erotica," pt. v.

Throughout the eighteenth, and until surprisingly late in the nineteenth century, the *conte-en-vers* was the favorite form of poetic expression in French society, and was attempted by practically everyone. It has never been as popular in English, though Pope's imitations of Chaucer, and other early eighteenth-century British materials worth examining are cast in this form; in particular Hall-Stevenson's *Crazy Tales,* and the *Select Poems on Several Occasions* (*c.* 1730) of Thomas Hamilton, Earl of Haddington, often reprinted, a valuable Scottish tale source. As has seldom been recognized, a large number of traditional Anglo-Scottish songs and ballads of a humorous kind are also simply *contes-en-vers* set to music, such as "The Keach i' the Creel" (Child No. 281, with important additional references in Rotunda, K1211, noting that 'Allusions to this motif are numberless in the Renaissance as well as in the Middle Ages'); "The Crab Fish" (omitted by Child, though the oldest English text, based on a joke in the *Serées* of Bouchet and of much older Italian and Levantine provenance, appears in the *Percy Folio MS., c.* 1620, edited by him); "Supper isna Ready" in all editions of Burns' *Merry Muses of Caledonia* (*c.*1800), a translation — despite all appearances — of a sixteenth-century French epigram, "Un mary frais;" and "The Barrin' o' the Door" (Child No. 275), which is still told today, in America, in at least two joke forms more closely related to the Italian *novella* on which it is based. The joke, which concerns dishwashing, has important similarities to the ensorcellment tale-type of the Arabian Nights "City of Brass," also Barbarossa and his frozen army, and "The Sleeping Beauty," who can be awakened only by a 'kiss' in polite versions, as in this Child ballad; but

compare the *Pentamerone's* full-blooded farcical version, in which
everyone in the house, including the furniture, dishes, and chamber-pot, are magically impregnated by this 'kiss.'

At all periods, and in both the French and English *conte-en-*
vers, the subject chosen was almost invariably erotic; and the
whole form, and in particular its creation and transmission only
among the eduated classes, compares interestingly to the bawdy
limerick popular for over a century now (1860–1960) among the
educated, and particularly in the university world, in the English-
speaking countries. The particular appeal of the *conte-en-vers*
evidently arose from the 'low' subject matter — in the social, as
much as the moral sense of the term — combined titillatingly
with the most elegant possible turn of expression and erotic
equivocation. The *conte-en-vers* has also its briefer counterpart,
the *épigramme,* from which it clearly developed, and of which
the key collection for folkloristic purposes is *La Légende Joyeuse*
('A Londres' [Paris?] 1749–51) in three volumes, the text being
entirely engraved. Only two complete sets of the original edition
have been located: in the Private Case of the British Museum
(the volumes separated at 29 *b* 57, and 30 *b* 44), and my own copy.
Fortunately, there is a later reprint under the same title, and the
first hundred *épigrammes* are also reprinted, with naïve erotic
engravings, as *Le Cabinet de Lampsaque* ('A Paphos,' 1784). Two
similar collections, more or less accessible in nineteenth-century
reprints, are *Le Joujou des Demoiselles,* of about 1750 (reprinted,
'Larnaca: Giov. della Rosa' [Bruxelles: Gay & Doucé, *c.*1880]),
and F.-F. Nogaret's *Les Épices de Vénus* (1787), a supplement to
his paraphrase of Aretino's Sonnets, as *L'Arétin françois.* The
latter is reprinted in volume ii, 1867, of Jules Gay's (*Choix de*)
Pièces désopilantes, dédié aux Pantagruélistes, almost the entire
volume consisting of *contes-en-vers* and *épigrammes,* in part also
taken from Nogaret's further, but rather mild, collection, *Le Fond*
du Sac. Even the reprints here cited are extremely difficult to
find, but are worth the effort. The transmission of erotic folktales and jokes, across the eighteenth century, cannot be studied
without them.

Behind the *épigramme* lie the *Dubbij amorosi,* attributed to
Aretino (reprinted in the *Recueil du Cosmopolite,* as noted earlier), which are given in the curious form of 'Cases of Conscience,'
with their 'Resolutions.' These are not so much intended as
raillery of the confessional — as might appear at first sight (and
is, in fact, the main target of the illustrations of the *Cabinet de*

Lampsaque, later on) — but are more likely survivals of the mock or legalistic argumentations of the late medieval Courts of Love, of the twelfth century, which, as gathered by Martial d'Auvergne, were also first published in the early sixteenth century, with even further legalistic notes by the French jurist Benoît Court. The erotic arguments of the Courts of Love — of which the most famous is, perhaps: Whether or not a woman may refuse herself to her lover on the grounds of being married to someone else? — are themselves evidently modelled on the logical hair-splitting of the Judæo-Arabic philosophers and Talmudists so signally in-fluencing European forms of thought during the centuries of the Arab conquest and the Crusades. Whatever their ultimate gen-ealogy, the *contes-en-vers* and *épigrammes,* as finally evolved, differ strikingly from the classic literary epigram or *vers-de société,* as understood for instance by the Latin satirist Martial, in their use invariably of a *joke* — by preference bawdy — as subject; where the epigrams of Martial, and earlier of the *Greek Anthology,* had turned on purely original and poetic inspirations: droll, satirical, and obscene, as often as not, but never basically jokes, nor folk-tales retold.

The only real difference between the search for brief tales and 'original' native jokes, to turn into *contes-en-vers,* in the eighteenth century in France and Britain, and the search — by members of the same noble and literary classes — for folktales in general, in the early nineteenth century, was simply and only the format in which the recovered materials were presented. The collected folktale reset as a *conte-en-vers* was credited, by himself, to the society poet. The collected folktales, presented undoctored, though in the folklorists' own prose — thus allowing a bit of exercise to their talents — were credited to the folk. The *conte-en-vers* is therefore the real connecting link between the earlier folktale col-lections and the modern scientific collections, and is the real reposi-tory of the native and original humorous material for nearly two centuries (1650–1850), where little of an original nature and almost nothing native will be found in the jestbooks. The entire literature of the *conte-en-vers,* whether dated from the burlesque and Are-tinesque academies of the 1530's in Italy, or from La Fontaine's *contes,* 'tirée de Bocace' as he perfectly frankly admits, in the 1660's, or even, for that matter, from the exactly similar method of the folktale-based fabliaux centuries before, represents in sum an exceptionally large repertory of jokes and tales, purposely *sought from the folk* at a period when the jestbooks were already forgetful or contemptuous of folk sources, and far gone in sterile mutual plagiarism, seldom straying beyond the basic collection made by the early patrician collector, D'Ouville, in the leisure of his *heures perdues,* before 1644.

As with the jestbooks, the *conte-en-vers* has never been seriously studied, certainly not from a folkloristic point of view; and no bibliography exists other than what is to be found in the private catalogues of the Viollet-Leduc, Pixerécourt, Nodier, Solar, Cigongne, and similar 19th-century collections, and in Gay's *Bibliographie de Ouvrages relatifs à l'Amour,* as above. The most important *conteurs,* from the point of view of folk materials and unexpurgated content, are, far and away, the Abbé Grécourt, Alexis Piron (author of *La Métromanie, ou le Poëte,* 1738), and Jean-Baptiste Rousseau — not be confused with Jean-Jacques! One tale, reprinted in all editions of Piron's *Oeuvres badines,* which is still often collected in English, is that which he presents as "Le Placet": *A nobleman, to whom a petition is submitted by a pretty young girl, will not stay to read it but seduces her forthwith, only to find — on finally reading her 'placet' — that it is a complaint against a doctor who was not able to cure her of venereal disease.* This same story is retold by François de Neufchâteau, as "La Consultation épineuse," with the nobleman modified to a mere lawyer, and the crashing venereal disease climax softened to the girl's sobbing continuously that the man she is complaining of had done 'that and more, and more, and more' — to wit, he had started all over, which the lawyer finds himself unable to do. Neufchâteau's version has in turn been reprinted in *Le Parnasse Hippocratique* of "Docteur Minime" (ed. 1896), omitting the poet's name and in various other sly ways palming off the *consultation* referred to as medical rather than legal. As collected in America in recent years, the story is invariably told about a priest in confession, with the 'more, and more' or 'worse, and worse' element taken precisely from Neufchâteau, but returning to the venereal disease *dénouement* of Piron.

This is again a very good example of the difficulty of teasing out the really essential or pivotal point of any joke, a difficulty often due to the changes in protagonist undergone during the transmission and migrations of the joke. It is obvious that this tale, as nowadays told and collected in America, could and probably would be motif-indexed under Thompson's system at V20, "Confession of Sins," owing to the recent and irrelevant turn of its being cast in anti-clerical and anti-confessional form. It is equally obvious that it does not really belong there. Even if indexed not by personnel, but by the particular form of the climax collected, the Piron 'original' and the Neufchâteau modification of this identical tale might easily be widely separated under the Thompson system, at Q240, "Sexual Sins Punished," for the first, and possibly J1367, "Impotent Suitor Rejected," for the second. From the operative point of view, of the nexus on which the story unchangingly turns, the real subject is seen to gravitate around the sudden climactic surprise or reversal, so essential to many jokes, and to be most closely related to Thompson X0-99, "Humor of Discomfiture." From the same position, *all* of the Thompson sigla, X200-599, "Humor of Social Classes," and X600-699, "Humor Concerning Races or Nations," and much of P400, "Trades and Professions," ought probably to be withdrawn, and reclassified by the operative element, instead of the largely irrelevant and fluid personnel of nations, classes, and professions.

One particularly valuable result of the historical and geographical method in dealing with jokes — as opposed to the shotgun multiplication of motif-listings from various sources and disparate cultures — is the light it sheds and the assistance it very often provides, as in the preceding example, in integrating and tracing the real or *pivotal* motif, and separating this from the merely confusing background elements of personnel, punch-lines, and other adventitious trappings and 'gimmicks' forming part of the tellers' private art, which are transmitted by the audience in good faith as somehow essential to the tale itself. This is the identical problem, or mystery, of the transmission of folksongs, in which every singer clings to, and generally imagines he is repeating, his version of a song word-for-word and note-for-note as he learned it — this being the only 'right' version — yet every version is different.

IV. FOLKLORISTIC COLLECTIONS

THE CONTE-EN-VERS disappeared as a literary form by the end of the nineteenth century, the anonymous *Contes Gaulois* and *Après-Soupers* 1883) of L. Jaybert, and the *Fanfreluches* of Prosper Blanchemain (under the pseudonym "Épiphane Sidredoulx") being among the last, and these are purposely archaizing in both title and form. The best of Blanchemain's are given in a supplement (1874) to his edition of the *Moyen de Parvenir,* along with earlier *contes-en-vers* in imitation of Béroalde's prose tales, such as those of the great proto-folklorist, Bernard de La Monnoye, in the late seventeenth century, collector — though not author — of the 'impious' folk-carols of Burgundy in 1701, and discoverer (in vol. IV of his edition of the *Ménagiana,* 1715) of that most fantastic and naïvely obscene of all folktale collections and facetiæ, *La Cazzaria* (1530) of Antonio Vignale, of the Academy of the "Intronati" or Dunderheads of Siena, of which both French and German translations have been published in recent years. (A riotous English translation, by the late Samuel Putnam, has circulated in manuscript since about 1935, but has never been printed. The original work is discussed by Putnam at some length in the excellent, but already nearly forgotten, *Encyclopaedia Sexualis,* edited by Victor Robinson, New York, 1936, pp. 491–492.) Though dead, the *conte-en-vers* has occasionally been resuscitated in the twentieth century, most curiously perhaps in the "Uther Capet" pamphlets, issued in New Haven in the early 1930's by the dean of Yale University booksellers, Arthur Head, and based in classic fashion on improper jokes of the period. No complete series of these pamphlets seems to have been preserved, even at Yale, nor of the parallel series of facetious art-poems, such as the *Tit-illations* of the painter Waldo Peirce.

The last serious presentation of folk jokes in the *conte-en-vers* form was *Les Pantagruéliques: Contes du Pays Rémois* (1854, doubled in size in the final edition, 1871) by the folklorist, J.-V.-F. Liber, whose intention, in his *Pantagruéliques,* appears to have been, in some measure, to make polite fun of the excessively expurgated collection of tales of the same 'Pays Rémois' made by a noble amateur collector, the Comte de Chevigné, a decade earlier. The same idea seems in part to have motivated Aleksandr N. Afanasyev, the greatest Russian folklorist of the nineteenth century, in undertaking to publish privately at his own expense, about 1872 in Geneva — 'sans bruit, dans une retraite éloignée des agitations du monde, là où n'a pas encore pénétré la main sacrilège de quelque censeur,' as his introduction pointedly observes — a supplement to his standard collection, *Narodnye russkie skazki (Popular Russian Tales,* 1855–64), under the title *Russkiya zavetniya skazki (Russian Secret Tales).* This posthumous supplement is not included in the government-sponsored reprint of Afanasyev's main work in the 1930's, though some guarded discussion of it will be found in Y. M. Sokolov's *Russian Folklore* (New York, 1950), pages 75 and 477, erroneously giving the title — one can almost hear the stenographer misunderstanding the translator's accent! — as Russian *Sacred* Tales.

The scientific collection and presentation of erotic folk material came of age, in a single bound, in Afanasyev's *Russian Secret Tales*. The stories are presented in prose dialogue, as they were collected, with a minimum of rewriting or literary titivation of the connective text, citing a few variants and parallels (as to Homer and Boccaccio), and without any attempt to expurgate or disguise the occasional obscene vocabulary by veiling this in the elegant Latin periphrases still deemed necessary to this day in both psychological and folklore journals in English. Typical of the Anglo-Saxon response to Afanasyev's courage was the meeching notice of it by W. R. Ralston, curator of Slavonic literature in the British Museum, who remarks gratuitously in his *Russian Folktales* (ed. 1873), p. xi: 'There is one other recent collection of *Skazkas,* that published last year at Geneva under the title of *Russkiya Zavetnuiya Skazki.* But upon its contents I have not found it necessary to draw.' (Oddly enough, the copy here noticed by Ralston is not to be found in the British Museum, the only copy of the original Russian text now known in the West being that preserved in the "Enfer," No. 1436, of the Bibliothèque Nationale.) Less hidebound folklorists on the continent were not slow to recognize, in Afanasyev's supplement, the way out of the imbalance and sterility into which the censorship of their own collections was inevitably leading them, as it was later to lead Anglo-American folklore study, and to undertake the dignified publication of their presumably 'unprintable' materials on the same plan.

In 1883, two ranking specialists in south Slavic folklore, Isidor Kopernicky and Friedrich S. Krauss, in collaboration with the leading French and Italian folklorists, Gaidoz, Carnoy, Gaston Pâris, and Giuseppe Pitrè, undertook the publication, in Heilbronn, Germany, of a yearbook of erotic folklore, *Kryptádia* (*Secret Things*), limited to 210 copies, the number later being reduced to 175. The first volume comprised a translation of Afanasyev's Russian text into French (with a few parallels in German), and a selection of Norwegian and Picard folktales, the latter group collected by E.-Henry Carnoy as a supplement to his *Littérature orale de la Picardie* (1883), and later much enlarged as volumes x–xi of *Kryptádia* in 1907. It was felt necessary, at that time, for all the editors and contributors to retain their anonymity, and only after their deaths were two of the editors' names divulged: that of Kopernicky, by Krauss in his later general folklore journal, *Am Ur-quell* (*Der Urquell,* 1898, ii, 233–239), and of Gaston Pâris, by the later publisher of *Kryptádia,* H. Welter in Paris, in a note to vol. x, dated December 1906. The names of the other editors and contributors, given above, are here noted for the first time.

By a singular accident, the erudite ex-priest and bibliophile publisher, Isidore Liseux (who paid for his uncommercial ideals by dying of starvation and cold on a pallet in the back of his bookstore in Paris, in the winter of 1894), unaware of the translation in *Kryptádia*, re-translated Afanasyev's text into French, and published this in 1891. Liseux's translation, which is much the better, has been reprinted several times — most recently by Kellinckx in Bruxelles, 1957 — and an English translation was also made from it for the erotica publisher "Charles Carrington" (Paul Ferdinando), Paris, 1897, under the title *Stories from the Folk-lore of Russia*. This English translation is an uncommonly scarce book, and could usefully be reprinted by facsimile at the present time. None of the existing editions mentions Afanasyev's name, nor, unfortunately do they reprint the extended comparative tracings of parallels to these Russian tales in other folk literatures, written in Italian, apparently by Pitrè, and given in *Kryptádia*, IV, 192–256 (as a supplement to the brief notes in vol. I, 291–292), a documentation of the first importance. As with the *Arabian Nights* touch of leaving one jewel-encrusted window unfinished in the palace which is constructed overnight by the genie — all the treasures of the king's realm proving insufficient to finish even this one window — it is instructive to observe how very little can be added today to this extraordinary documentation, published in 1888 when no motif-indexes, tables of tale types, and so forth existed. 'There were giants in those days.' (*Genesis*, vi. 4.)

The very clear and important introduction in French, to both Afanasyev's collection and to volume I of *Kryptádia* itself, on the position and value of erotic folklore, are reprinted in full, in more available form, in the well-known erotic bibliography series of "Pisanus Fraxi" (H. Spencer Ashbee), in vol. III, *Catena Librorum Tacendorum* (1885), pages 360–368, and may conveniently be consulted in the recent and courageous facsimile reprints of Ashbee's volumes, London, 1960, and New York, 1962. Important groups of erotic folktales from almost all the main European cultures — except English — are given, on the same plan, in the even larger yearbook series of erotic folklore, edited singlehandedly by Krauss from 1900 on, under the title *Anthropophytéia* (*Sexual Relations of Mankind*), in ten massive quarto volumes, with several side-series of "Beiwerke" and "Beihefte," the latter devoted specially to reprints of the older jestbooks. The "Beiwerke" are monographs, each on the sexual folklore of a single culture, ending in 1931 with a remarkable two-volume illustrated study of Japanese sexual life and folklore, by Krauss in collaboration with Tamio Satow, whose contribution was translated from the original manuscript in English, arranged in encyclopedia-form, now unfortunately lost. By far the most important series of folktales published in any of Krauss's yearbooks are volumes III and V of the "Beiwerke" to *Anthropophytéia*, entitled *Das Geschlechtsleben des Ukrainischen Bauernvolkes* (1909–12) by P. Tarasevskyi and V. Hnatjuk, giving the astonishing total of 719 erotic tales and related materials, in both the Ukranian text and German translation, with notes and parallels. This is an invaluable supplement to Afanasyev's earlier collection, as also to the even rarer Russian work, partly in verse, *Mejzdu Druziami* (*Among Friends,* vols. I–II; Cargad [Constantinople], *c.* 1870). The only copy — volume I only — is preserved in the "Enfer" of the Bibliothèque Nationale in Paris. Nothing to compare with these nearly forty volumes in all, edited by Krauss, exists at the present time in print in the English language, nor can any serious comparative study of erotic folklore or humor be made without access to, and intensive employment of, the materials there recorded.

A minor series, imitating and usefully continuing the twelve volmes of *Kryptádia,* are the *Contributions au Folklore Érotique,* in four volumes, issued in Kleinbronn and Paris (1906–09) by M. Gustave Ficker — an excellent example of 'name-fatality,' or names that control one's career, as Aubrey has termed it. All the volumes are collections of folktales, the first from Constantinople (discussed earlier); the others from Alsace, Aquitaine, and Picardy, these last three being issued under pseudonyms. Facing the title page of volume IV, and in Dr. Henry Labonne's *Le Sixième Livre de Rabelais,* also issued by Ficker (1910), page 98, eight further volumes are announced, to contain 'contes licencieux' collected in Corsica, Catalonia, Béarn, Bray, and Austria, as well as supplementary tales, and erotic proverbs, riddles, and folk-poetry and speech of Picardy and Aquitaine; but, unfortunately, nothing beyond volume IV was ever issued, and, as all the authors' names (except that of Nicolaidès) seem to have been pseudonyms, the collected materials have never been recovered.

Despite the extraordinarily great volume of erotic publication, undercover in England and semi-publicly in France, during the nineteenth century, almost no erotic jestbooks were published in either country to supplement the moribund openly-published sort. One exception is *Tom Brown's Jests,* a more or less erotic — or, rather, simply *not* expurgated — early eighteenth-century item, of the kind then usual in England, reprinted verbatim in the United States, 'For the Booksellers,' just before the Civil War, a century later! This is an extreme example of the plagiarism, and thoughtless anachronism, typical of jestbook publishers. Mottley's *Joe Miller's Jests* was also reissued, in unexpurgated facsimile of the 1739 original, by the British erotica publisher, John Camden Hotten, about 1865, but in this case in a consciously archaizing way. A decade later, the erotic magazine, *The Pearl,* issued in London by "D. Cameron" in 1879–80 in eighteen monthly parts, as also its several continuations such as *The Boudoir* and *The Cremorne,* included erotic joke columns to match the polite similar columns in the humorous magazines of the time (the influence driving out the jestbooks), and a number of erotic jests and tales can usefully be found in these rare publications. (Two continental reprints of *The Pearl* were made in the 1890's, and another — confusing the date lines on the first six issues — in New York, about 1932.)

In France, at about the same period, few jestbooks appeared, despite the many more or less scholarly reprints of the old tale collections (one collection, issued periodically in the 1890's, *Les Joyeuses Histoires de nos Pères,* does not pretend to be anything but popular), and the popularity of the emerging literary form of the folktales, thinned out by means of background descriptions, 'additional dialogue,' and other verbiage, into pretended short stories, as in Voltaire's *Zadig,* Balzac's *Contes Drolatiques* (1832), and Anatole France's imitations of these, right down the scale to Armand Silvestre's pamphlet series, *Les Joyeusetés,* about 1900. The illustrated humor magazines, as noted above, were also doing a great deal to kill the jestbooks, and in France this was made even easier by the relative freedom from sexual censorship (only!) of the magazines.

One jestbook of actually erotic contents, *Histoires d'hommes et de dames* (1913), with erotic frontispiece by Lobel-Riche, is mentioned by its anonymous compiler, Louis Perceau, in his *Bibliographie du roman érotique* (1930). No other copy than my own can at present be located. Aside from the 'histoires,' this work also contains sections of erotic riddles, 'heights,' and charades, of which the last are in the complicated French form, 'à tiroirs,' and are not known to have been published elsewhere. Perceau was interested from the very beginning of his career in erotic folk-humor, on the style of the ancient *Bigarrures du Seigneur des Accords* of Estienne Tabourot (mentioned below), a work which clearly influenced him greatly. His first published book, under the pseudonym "Jacques Oncial," *Le Trésor des Equivoques* ('Gelatopolis' [Paris: Sansot], 1909), is a collection of erotic spoonerisms, a form to which he also returned in his last book, *La Redoute des Contrepéteries,* which has been kept in print and importantly supplemented, since Perceau's death, by the publisher Briffaut, and has been further supplemented in an interesting technical work on the same humorous subject, by M. Luc Étienne (Perrin). Perceau's early erotic works are uncommonly scarce. Of the *Trésor,* no copy is known in any repository library, except that of Ohio State University.

One other exceptional jestbook, or collection of facetiæ, purely scatological in this case: the popularity of the famous "Pétomane" at the Paris Expositions led to the publication of a collection of anecdotes and jokes entirely on this theme, *Le Peteur Universel,* issued as a chapbook, without publisher's name but by the textbook firm Garnier, in 1901. It should be observed that in Germany and Austria erotic jokebooks continued to be printed undercover in some number, until World War I, as they had been throughout the nineteenth century, beginning immediately after the expurgation of the publicly-published kind. More recently these have been replaced by collections of the "Frau Wirtin" verse, or *Das Wirtshaus an der Lahn,* improper and generally scatological tales-of-my-landlady, in quintain form, resembling the English-language limerick. On this correlation, see *The Limerick* (Paris, 1953) p. 468, n. 1730, referring further to an excellent article on the subject by F. L. Wells, in *American Imago* (1951) VIII. 93.

Aside from the formalized "Frau Wirtin" verse, the German language has an exceptionally large fund of erotic quatrains or 'Vierzeiler,' in its various dialects. Some of these will be found in the volumes of *Kryptádia* and *Anthropophytéia,* already discussed, and there are other dialectal groups in what is essentially the main work on erotic folksong and folktales in German, *Futilitates: Beiträge zur volkskundlichen Erotik,* in four volumes, edited by E. K. Blümml & Josef Polsterer (Latzenhofer), and privately issued by Dr. R. Ludwig Verlag, in Vienna, in 1908. This is a remarkable and excessively rare work, as is also Blümml's earlier collection, with music, *Erotische Volkslieder aus Deutsch-Oesterreich* (Wien, 1906), dedicated to Prof. Krauss. Another collection of 'Vierzeiler,' in this case of the red-light or prostitution district of Vienna, is *Der*

Spittelberg und seine Lieder (Wien: Privatdruck, 1924), credited to the two erudite collectors, "K. Giglleithner & B. Litschauer," who are, however, none other Blümml, in this case in collaboration with the great Austrian erotica-collector, Gustav Gugitz.

Though very little attention is being paid here to German materials, since they will be found fully recorded bibliographically in the Hayn-Gotendorf-Englisch *Bibliotheca Germanorum Erotica et Curiosa* (1912–29) in nine volumes, and in Dr. Paul Englisch's supplementary study, *Das Skatologische Element in Literatur, Kunst, und Volksleben* (Stuttgart, 1928); one special type of German jokes worthy of notice are the 'Lotzelech,' or Viennese Jewish jokes. Of these, at least one wholly erotic collection exists: *Tausendundein (Neue) Lotzelech für Herren* (Pressburg: H. Hartleb, *c.* 1895), Bd. 1, this being apparently all that was published, and containing 171 jokes. Another 'Lotzelech' collection, Avrom Reitzer's *Solem Aléchem* (2te Auflage, Wien & Leipzig: Deubler, *c.* 1900), contains only rather mild examples, despite the magnificently promising subtitle: '*Nix für Kinder:* E Waggon feiner, rescher, saftiger Lozelech, Schmonzes takef pickfeiner Schmüs für ünsere Leit.' A far more graphic collection, even rarer, of which I possess a copy, is '*Lacht zum Bescheissen!* Eine ausgewählte Sammlung erotischer Vorträge, Gedichte, Anekdoten, &c., für Freunde ausgelassener Fröhlichkeit. New-York und Philadelphia (Bei A. R. Schlecker),' [Germany, *c.* 1900], on execrable pulp-paper. This contains jokes, poems, 'heights,' riddles, and so forth, exactly in the miscellany style imported to America, unquestionably by printers of German or 'Pennsylvania Dutch' origin, in the undercover midwest collections noted later, such as that of "O. U. Schweinickle" in the late 1920's.

The renaissance of popular — as differentiated from scientific — joke collections from folkloristic sources began in France in the mid-1920's, spreading almost immediately to the United States, on the success of two collections of Jewish jokes, edited under the title *Histoires Juives* (1923–25) by Raymond Geiger. Almost immediately thereafter appeared a sort of southern French continuation or response, the *Histoires Marseillaises* (1925) of Édouard Ramond, tales in which the protagonists are invariably the French meridional types, "Marius and Olive," as, in Irish-American jokes, "Pat and Mike," or, in the jokes of middle Europe, "Mikosch and Strakosch." (A rare collection of modern erotic jokes and other humor in German — including 'heights' and similar burlesque queries — is entirely concerned with these two folk heroes, both of whom, though *schnorrers,* address each other consistently as "Baron": *Allerlei saftige und seltene Mikosch-Anekdoten,* 3te Auflage, Pressburg, 1892.) A number of other French collectors also took a hand. The most important were the well-known gourmand, cookbook editor, and after-dinner speaker, "Curnonsky" (Edmond Sailland), and J.-Wladimir Bienstock, the translator of Tolstoi, who collaborated on an extended series of popular collections of jokes. Each of these contains, in the limited edition 'hors commerce' on fine paper, a supplement of the more verbally erotic jokes, though those in the open text are themselves of a liberty which cannot but surprise Anglo-American readers. The titles of the "Curnonsky"-Bienstock series, appearing between 1924 and 1928, are: *Le Bonheur du Jour, Le Livre du Chevet, Le Magasin de Frivolités, Par le Trou de la Serrure, T.S.V.P., Le Wagon des Fumeurs,* and two volumes of droll errors clipped from newspapers, *Le Musée des Erreurs,* a form not relevant here. Having changed publishers for a final volume some years later (*Histoires de Tous et de Personne,* 1934), and the new publisher not agreeing to the double-edition method, the final erotic collection of the "Curnonsky" series appeared privately in two small volumes as *Histoires Aérodynamiques* ('Marseille,' 1935), some copies entitled *Petites Histoires de Rire.* These volumes are as interesting as they are rare, though they appear to be in part a reprint or plagiarism of the *Histoires Raides* (1929) attributed to Louis Perceau, which is the only collection of erotic jokes — with the exception of *Anecdota Americana,* II ('Boston,' 1934) — illustrated with frankly erotic drawings.

Simultaneously with the success of the Geiger, Ramond, and "Curnonsky" series, a large number of imitative collections, drawn from the native jokes of the various provinces of France, were issued centering about the year 1930 (including a few edited by "Curnonsky," or Ramond, in competition with himself, under other pseudonyms). These have continued since the end of World War II, until the present time, though in far less number. Some forty or more volumes appeared in ten years, between the two World Wars, probably the largest group of jestbooks ever published during any equivalent number of years, except in England about 1800 as seen in the Douce collection of chapbooks preserved at Oxford.

Some of the confusion as to the modern French jestbooks, which have never either been studied or collected seriously, rises in part from their reduplicative titles — though this is the one feature on which the mutually-plagiarizing compilers do expend what originality they can muster — but even more from the compilers' use of pseudonyms, especially in the very large series issued by the publishing houses, Quignon, and Les Éditions de Paris (earlier, 'de France'). Édouard Ramond, in particular, seems to have had recourse to pseudonyms in his later volumes, for a reason with which one can sympathize, and should frankly record, for all the aid & comfort it may give the opponents of erotic humor and erotic folklore — and such do exist! As expressed, with ill-concealed gloating, in Abbé Louis Bethléem's supplement to the Roman Catholic Index, *Romans à lire et romans à proscrire* (11th ed., 1932) p. 176, Ramond, who 'had published three volumes of scatology and pornography'— *i.e.* his joke-collections — and 'was director of the commercial services of the [French] National Museums . . . was condemned in court in 1930 for having embezzled several hundred thousand francs.' His later volumes were thus issued under the polite screen of pseudonymity. The only serious discussion of Ramond's case is that of Camille Mauclair [Faust], in his bitter attack on fake modern art, *La Farce de l'Art Vivant,* vol. ii: *Les Métèques contre l'Art Français* (1930) chap. xxiv, "Leur Aveu," owing to the notion, then current, that Ramond was being thrown as scapegoat to Mauclair's only-too-well founded attack.

I have made an almost complete collection of modern French jestbooks — actual completeness being evidently impossible in dealing with ephemeral literature — and have caused a large group of duplicates to be deposited in the Schmulowitz collection of wit and humor, in the San Francisco Public Library, one of the best such collections in the United States and the only one containing any extended series of the unexpurgated modern French jestbooks. Two recent items, one of them entitled *250 Histoires pour vous mettre en train!* by "Maurice Saint-Amour" (Paris: Éditions Rabelais, 1959), have returned to the separate presentation of the more erotic jokes in a supplementary 'Carnet Rose' on pink paper, supplied on demand. This is also true of one other 'Carnet Rose' collection, *Pour Adultes Seulement* (Éditions Rabelais, 1955) 223 pages in all — an expurgated and abridged edition likewise existing, of only 128 pages — edited by Robert de Gicey. The same compiler is also thought to have been editor of one of the latest collections published, *Histoires Parisiennes* (Éditions de Paris, 1960), not to be confused with a less interesting collection of the same title published about 1930. The 1960 work is of an almost total freedom as to sexual content, and in it will be found literally dozens of erotic jokes also known currently in the English-speaking world. For the first time, however, it seems possible that the direction of transfer has changed, and that a number of these stories have migrated, on the wave of Coca-Cola and other aspects of American culture, from the United States to France.

v. English and American Erotic Humor

ENGLISH-LANGUAGE erotic humor ceased to appear in print, except in the approximations of the illustrated magazines, since the 1880's. Only one or two eccentric or off-trail items seem to have appeared until well after the renaissance of the jokebook genre in France, as for instance the jokes unexpectedly interspersed in *The Confessions of Nemesis Hunt* (1902, 3 vols.), a particularly rare erotic autobiography written by a woman; in *All About Monte Carlo and Roulette,* by "O. Plucky" (1913), giving a few broad jokes in the style of the illustrated sporting magazine, *The Pink 'Un* (the British *Police Gazette*), and in a rare and ephemeral joke collection of the World War I period, issued in 1918 by "Carrington" (who also reissued in 1917 an equally rare erotic songster of the American Civil War, *The Rakish Rhymer*), entitled *Some Yarns,* of which the only known copy is preserved in the library of the Institute for Sex Research, at Bloomington, Indiana. In 1926–27 there were also published in Nice, France, in the English language, two pamphlet volumes of erotic jokes and other facetiæ, under the title *Tropical Tales,* by "Kimbo," the pseudonym apparently of Bradley Gilman, whose somewhat amateur *Clinic on the Comic* (1926), issued simultaneously in Nice, is preserved in the Library of Congress.

The open reappearance of erotic humor in print in the English-speaking countries was inspired by the very important and seminal *Anecdota Americana* ('Boston: Humphrey Adams' [New York, 1927]), compiled by Joseph Fliesler, an American advertising man of Hungarian origin, at that time national publicity director of UFA Films. A second volume, not edited by Fliesler, was issued in 1934, also under the rubric 'Boston: Humphrey Adams,' and an expurgated version of the original collection was issued by Samuel Roth in 1933, reprinted 1934, and revised as *The New Anecdota Americana* in 1944. The Roth expurgation is often confused with the original, to which, however, it bears little similarity except in the title. It is an unimportant collection, including much of the sort of semi-erotic humorous material being openly published in the rowdy humor magazines issued by college students since the 1920's, and professionally published for them as listed below. The original Fliesler collection is of a far more valuable sort. It is not, of course, totally original, stemming in part from Geiger's *Histoires Juives* (with the Jewish backgrounds and dialect changed to American Negro, in several cases); but contains sufficient examples from oral collection to show the broad lines of relation between American erotic humor and that of Europe. Fliesler is himself a raconteur in the great European style of the itinerant Jewish jesters or *bodchonim* of the nineteenth century — similar to the professional Levantine tellers of the *Arabian Nights* — among whom might also be mentioned, without in any way forcing the analogy, Krauss, Harry Hershfield, and many other notable raconteurs. (See the interesting discussion of Jewish teller-types in Dorson's selection of tales recorded on tape, in *Studies in Biblical and Jewish Folklore,* 1960, cited earlier.) Jewish taletellers have always been of great importance in the migration of jokes, owing to their own extensive migrations, and to the evident comforting and survival value of humor among oppressed peoples, as also among the Armenians and the Scotch. The professional Jewish jester type, transplanted to the United States at the turn of the twentieth century, has for over fifty years now importantly impressed its characteristics and its unexpurgated repertory — with obvious changes, as from Yiddish to Negro dialect — upon the professional entertainment field, first in vaudeville and the burlesque theatre, later in motion pictures and radio, now in television and the night clubs, or entertainment restaurants on the French style, which have entirely replaced vaudeville and burlesque.

A word must be said on the semi-erotic professional humor magazines of the United States since the 1920's, such as *Hot Dog!, Jim Jam Jems,* Captain Billy's *Whiz Bang* and *Smokehouse Monthly,* and the fabulous tabloid newspaper of the 1930's, *Broadway Brevities* (of which my own almost-complete set, based on Earl Emmons' collection, is the only one preserved, with a group of duplicates in the Institute for Sex Research Library). Aside from the college humor magazines, which still often attempt a few unrepressed jokes on the same lines, there are the more recent professional publications such as the Kansas City *Laff Magazine,* the joke columns in the various men's magazines on the style of *Esquire* and *Playboy* (compare the much older British

Pink 'Un, mentioned earlier), and the series edited by J. M. Elgart — originally reprinted from a trucking firm's intramural magazine — entitled *Over Sexteen,* of which seven volumes had appeared by 1960, not counting the imitations entitled *Sexations,* and similar items. These publicly issued collections, of which many others exist beyond those cited here, are of a highly inauthentic slickness, and most of the sex is in their titles and pictorial illustration. They nevertheless contain materials of value on present-day erotic humor, buried among the puns and cartoons, and usually also disguised in elegant semi-erotic paraphrases. This is occasionally taken to the length, especially in the men's magazines, of making whole short stories, on the style of Balzac's *Contes Drolatiques,* out of what are essentially only bawdy jokes. A well-known example is the story "Entrance Fee," in Alexander Woollcott's *While Rome Burns,* which earned for Woollcott the bogus attribution of a curious collection of story-length jokes on this style, published by Samuel Roth ("Norman Lockridge") under the title *Waggish Tales of the Czechs* in 1947, a collection that shows its utter contempt for the audience by having the ostensible 'Czechs' speak, on occasion, in a rich Negro comic dialect.

A more authentic, and far less slick and professional group of semi-private publications has also existed in America since the late 1920's, in the form of erotic miscellanies, apparently of German inspiration via the American midwest, where they are published by job printers in out-of-the-way places such as Wheeling, West Virginia; or Detroit, and mixing together jokes, erotic storiettes, ambiguously worded letters, doggerel pornographica, and topical obscœna such as mock speeches by public figures, parodies of book titles, liquor and cigarette brand-names, and similar 'novelty' material, some of it pictorial. Miscellanies of this sort date from the seventeenth century in England, and ultimately from the *Bigarrures du Seigneur des Accords* of Estienne Tabourot in the late sixteenth century, on which were modelled the "Fancies and Fantasticks" of *Wits Recreations* (1640), reprinted with *Musarum Deliciæ* in 1817 and 1874. Two important eighteenth-century examples are *The Foundling Hospital for Wit* (1743–49) edited by Sir Charles Hanbury Williams, and *The New Boghouse Miscellany, or A Companion for the Close-Stool* (1761), reissued with the title expurgated to *The Wit's Miscellany* in 1762. Compare: *Papers for the W.C.,* printed on toilet paper, in Leipzig, *c.* 1876 (of which no copy is now known), also *Sitting Pretty: The Bathroom Companion,* by H. S. Reyem, and *Poems for the John,* both the latter

published in the United States, 1960. Aside from the pure scatologica, the earliest modern erotic examples are *The Sugar of Life*
(1854), unique copy in my own collection; and *Forbidden Fruit:
A Collection of Tales* (Glasgow? *c.* 1875), also unique, preserved
in the Murison Burns Collection, Dunfermline. The erotic magazine, *The Pearl* (1879–80), and its sequels, are also essentially of
this type.

The modern American group begins with an unpublished
manuscript, *A Treasury of Erotic and Facetious Memorabilia*,
made in the United States about 1910 (which may be the work of
the Chicago newspaperman and erotic glossarist, Henry N. Cary),
of which the original is now preserved in the library of the Kinsey
Institute. At least three such collections were actually printed in
the late 1920's: *Cleopatra's Scrapbook* ('Blue Grass, Kentucky,'
1928); *The Book of a Thousand Laughs* by "O. U. Schweinickle"
[Wheeling, W. Va., 1928], dated by its plagiarizing a whole group
of jokes from Fliesler's *Anecdota Americana*, and actually partly
in the German-American or 'Pennsylvania Dutch' dialect; and,
the largest, including stories, jokes, obscœna, and a good deal of
doggerel verse, probably by the compiler, entitled *Bibliotheque
Erotique* ('London' [Detroit], 1929) in two volumes, photo-
illustrated, which was reissued in twelve parts as "Library
L'Amour" (*sic*) about 1930. A mimeographed miscellany, *Smile
and the World Smiles With You*, was issued on Guam, 1948, and
several times reprinted by 1952 for the American soldier audience,
but no complete copy seems to have been preserved. Also semi-
privately, there have been William Curran's *Clean Dirt* (Buffalo,
1938); *The Farmer's Daughter*, a midwestern American collection
of jokes; *Locker Room Humor* and *Bar Room Tales*, companion
volumes, issued without publisher's name in Canada, 1958–61.
Artlessly presented, and without too much intrusive professional
slicking-up, these modern jestbooks and miscellanies derive largely
from authentic oral and folk transmission, and are well worth
collecting and study before they become impossibly rare, as most
of them are already. It is also more than probable that many others
have been lost without trace, as has been the case, not with a few
but with most of the similar erotic songsters of the nineteenth
century, now known only through reference to their bare titles
in the Ashbee bibliography, as discussed in an earlier chapter.

Only about 1930, for the first time in the English language,
was the attempt made to deal with erotic humor in a scientific
fashion, in an exceptionally scarce work privately issued in New

York under the title *The Way of a Virgin* (not to be confused with an unimportant pornographicum, *The Way of a Man with a Maid*, published about 1923 in Paris). In this work a number of humorous tales are traced to earlier European tale collections, in a serious way, and it is to be regretted that the promised second volume was never published and that the author has never been positively identified. The work has been attributed, however, to the American scholar, Raymond Thompson. In 1939, Dr. Weston La Barre published, in the journal *Psychiatry* (Washington, D.C.), II, 203–212, the first open study of this kind, based on a collection of erotic limericks and other verse, under the title "The Psycho-pathology of Drinking Songs," and dealing with the psychological content and appeal of this type of erotic humor. Not until ten years later was this lead followed, in Richard A. Waterman's "The Role of Obscenity in the Folk Tales of the 'Intellectual' Stratum of Our Society," in *Journal of American Folklore* (1949) vol. 52: p. 162–5, of which it may be remarked that the quotation-marks might just as correctly have been left off 'intellectual' and put around 'obscenity' instead. One is surprised, in fact, to find this accidental concession to vulgar brain-baiting in a learned journal, pointed up by the use of the hygienic or semantic tongs of quota-tion-marks.

Whatever may have been lost at earlier periods, in the way of manuscript collections of erotic folktales never printed, or printed collections of which no copy has been preserved, it has been pos-sible recently to have some insight into the large amount of such material collected, apparently at all times, both in an amateur way — along with ballads, erotic slang, toilet epigraphs and the like — and by professional entertainers for expurgated or semi-expurgated joke telling in public. I have myself examined, and have been allowed to copy completely, at least a dozen such collec-tions made in the United States and England between 1935 and 1950, some of these extending to hundreds of examples, either written out in full with various flowers of the collectors' rhetoric intermixed, or with only the punch-lines briefly noted. My own collection of orally transmitted tales of the same period is also quite large, though I have in no case been able to transcribe the tellers' exact wording. More recently a few stabs at such collection have been made, by other collectors, by means of tape-recordings, which have the enormous advantage of preserving not only the tellers' original wording, but also the nuances of humorous shad-ing and inflection (though, of course, these latter are again lost in transcribing for print). As erotic folktales do not die, and are among the most tenacious and authentic in oral circulation, this is a very rich area for future collecting by means of tape recording. A certain amount of such collection has already been done, I believe, in Scotland.

One outstanding collection (not recorded) with which the present history comes to a close, is that made by the independent Ozark folklorist, Vance Randolph, since about 1920, and included by him in his 'unprintable' manuscript collection (1954, preserved in the Library of Congress and at the Institute for Sex Research, Indiana University), catalogued as Item 6, *Pissing in the Snow, and Other Ozark Folktales.* This collection is — as with everything else in the Randolph manuscript — the most important yet presented in the English language, though it numbers only one hundred tales. One out-of-place item, No. 69, "Senator Johnson's Great Speech," is also included. This is a version of "Change the name of Arkansaw!" which has been attributed to Mark Twain, a type of mock parliamentarian speech of which a prototype appears in *The Foundling Hospital for Wit* (1749) VI , 22, "Speech without Doors, in Answer to a supposed Speech Within," the mock speech here being given by the groom of a member of Parliament to an audience of his peers. A similar burlesque, in this case erotic, common in America and nowadays usually ascribed to Lady Astor, has been known in France since the mid-nineteenth-century agitations of the feminists. (A note on the grotesque 'novelty' medals struck in France, similarly in mockery of the parliamentary pretentions of the early feminists, stemming of course from the French Revolution, will be found where one would hardly be likely to look for it: in *Aloysia Sygea et Nicolas Chorier,* by M. P. Allut (Lyon, 1862) p. 5, 63–4, a privately issued and very sober vindication of the early Spanish woman writer, Luisa Sigea of Toledo, from the good-humored ascription to her, on the part of Nicholas Chorier in the 17th century, of his elegant work in Latin on erotic technique, entitled *The Dialogues of Luisa Sigea.* Later editions ascribe it, equally good-humoredly, to the highly moral Dutch philologist, Johannes Meursius.)

Among the most interesting tales in the Randolph collection are No. 16, "It Didn't Cost Him Nothing," an ensorcellment story of the "Barrin' o' the Door" type, likewise rationalized as a wager; No. 41, "Tacking on Her Maidenhead" (derived from Béroalde de Verville); and especially the stories containing animal elements, which are generally the most ancient in origin, in particular No.

21, "The Half-Wit and the Eel," a *vagina dentata* story rationalized as of a serpent 'lost' in the woman's body; and No. 6, "Betsey and the Mole Skin," in which it is the penis which is outfitted with an animal head and 'sharp teeth sticking out in front,' as in some of the oldest known depictions of the Devil, such as that of the Tarot cards in the Leber collection at Rouen, and, as humor, in the illustrated *Songes drolatiques de Pantagruel* (1545). One story, collected practically everywhere in Europe, is No. 23, "The New Hired Man," which takes elements from Boccaccio's name-tale, "Putting the Devil in Hell" (Day III. 10), but turns principally on the trickster who pretends that his own name is obscene. A version of this appears in *Russian Secret Tales*, No. 72, "Les Noms étranges," which Afanasyev observes to be 'une plaisanterie du type de celle d'Ulysse chez Polyphême, prenant le nom de Outis.' This would refer the tale type to the Homeric legends, gathered in, but much older than, the fifth century B.C., making this probably one of the oldest recorded joke types in the world, and connected of course with even more ancient ideas of name magic.

Particularly to be remarked in the Randolph collection is the fact that practically all of his one hundred tales, outfitted though most of them are with punch-lines, do not stop at this verbal climax, but continue on with some homey moralizing or droll observation, often a paragraph in length. This brings the whole body of Ozark joke-telling, as here recorded, more closely in line with the tradition of the earlier tales than of modern jokes, which almost invariably rush headlong to their verbal climax, and stop abruptly there, in tableau, as though all the actors — and particularly the 'butt' — have been destroyed by this explosive climax, and no further existence for any of them except the protagonist (and then only if he is of a named type) can be imagined. Randolph says nothing as to this point, but closes his introduction simply with the following statement — more honest than most:

A few of the items in this book were recorded phonographically, and transcribed from the playback. But in most cases I made notes in pencil as the narrator spoke, and typed the story a few hours later. Not one of my tales is a verbatim transcript, but they are all pretty close to the mark. They are not literary adaptations or reworkings. I have not combined different versions, or used material from more than one informant in the same text. I just set down each story as accurately as possible, and let it go at that.

The present writer began the publication, in 1951, of a classification index of erotic humor more or less that envisaged by Thompson in the note to his *Motif-Index,* quoted earlier, at X700, but based on psychological elements rather than on form and on identification by protagonists — the groundwork of the Thompson system. Only a single main section was published, as a sample, covering *castration themes,* in an article entitled "Rationale of the Dirty Joke," in the lay psychiatric and literary magazine, *Neurotica,* No. 9 (New York, 1951), pages 49–64. There the classification headings or motifs are stated informally, as the subjects of the consecutive paragraphs; the main subsections "Vagina Dentata", "Castration", "Circumcision", and "Overcompensation" being indicated, and the folktales-told-as-fact being grouped separately from those admittedly jokes. The material is presented with both running commentary and abbreviated italic texts for all the tales and jokes, a format modeled on that of Freud's *Wit and Its Relation to the Unconscious.* Though no further sections have yet been published, the entire system was prepared in manuscript form on the same plan, based on a collection of some 2,000 modern jokes and tales, with comparative and historical tracings; and trade publication by a scientific publishing firm in the United States was intended. The indefinite delay of publication, and the very many requests received since that time for access to *a.* the classification index, and *b.* the file of jokes on which it is based, suggest that this preliminary report may be of service to folklorists. The motif-index itself will be available, as the framework of the complete collection to be entitled *Rationale of the Dirty Joke,* when it is possible to publish this volume.

It is agreed that the whole development and inner coherence of any such motif-index must be self-sustaining and self-explaining, to allow of publication without any tale texts. In the present case, however, it does not seem altogether wise to offer the motif-index without the supporting materials on which it is based, and, without which, so difficult a subject-matter — and, in particular its historical and psychological analysis — cannot easily be brought into systematic form. Meanwhile, the single chapter already printed will demonstrate the approach used, and, I think, its superiority to any more skeletal form.

This preliminary essay has been intended to indicate source materials in various European languages, but only for the purpose of tracing historically items in collections of jokes of recent currency in the English language. Any attempt to create a motif-index for the entire literature of erotic humor, since its beginnings (?) and in all countries, is evidently too vast and would be too optimistic at the present time, though every effort should be made to trace the English-language materials as far back through their earlier migrations and transformations as possible. Criticisms and additions will be gratefully received, as to the bibliographical materials presented, and toward the further collection of joke texts. It is requested that all proposed additions be documented by the actual texts from printed jestbooks (in whatever language), or from oral collection. In the case of orally-collected texts, the place and date — at least the approximate *year* — of provenance seem essential. This request for supporting texts is not intended as a covert fishing for jokes, but to avoid the necessity of access to rare printed works, and field-collecting in distant locations, not actually available to the present writer.

FOLKSONGS, FAKELORE, AND CASH

I

ONE OF THE most encouraging signs in the present development of the folksong fad is the overcrowding of the field. This will inevitably result — in fact, some say it has resulted already — in the driving out of a sizeable group of folklore fakers, johnny-come-latelys, city-billies, folkniks, folksongers, and other opportunists who have been attracted by the tales of a quick buck, plenty of beer, girls, and public acclaim, supposedly the reward of taking four lessons on that well-known endemic North American folk-instrument, the Spanish guitar, and memorizing a couple of Child ballads and semi-bawdy music hall songs such as "She Wuz Pore But She Wuz Honest" and "Lord Randal My Son."

To give some idea of how the wind is blowing, and this absolutely *sans blague,* I was told in the early summer of 1960 by an American folksong specialist (a folksong specialist is any member of the English or anthropology faculties of a state college who is not specializing in Shakespeare), that of twenty students signed up for the summer seminar on folksong he had undertaken to teach, only four did *not* intend to try — before fall — to get jobs singing the songs they were studying, either in 'folksong bars' (as though there were some other kind of bar!) or in the form of commercial 'folksong recordings' of their own rendition of these songs. Why he was surprised is hard to say, since he had himself made a similar recording, several summers before: one of the worst and most wooden ever put on the market. As most of these specialists are right this minute assuring the more malleable undergraduate eggheads committed to their care that 'anyone who can talk can sing,' and that 'folksinging should be done without any expression whatsoever,' (*style,* as Alan Lomax has complained, in *Sing Out!* Summer, 1959, is apparently beyond the comprehension of both the fake-singers and their teachers alike), it is clear that the future of phoney-baloney folksinging is rosy indeed. Except, as aforesaid, that it is getting a bit crowded with all those *other* phonies, who are not our friends and whose LP's we must never plug.

This development of folk-arts into commercialized fakes is now getting to be standard. Not to mention yoyo tops and Hawaiian hula-hoops (the sex education of little girls of yesteryear), this is the path that jazz trod over twenty years ago — some say longer, with the white 'jazz-singers' of the 1920's — and the handwriting is on the wall. It devolves upon those of us who really care about folksong, and who, without excessive jealousy or proprietary pique, can admit to having cared about or collected folksong somewhat longer than the two months of a summer seminar — in my own case twenty-five years — to work out a few rules of thumb, or retch-guards, whereby we can avoid wasting our time and patience on folksongers and their fakelore, or spending the small amounts of money we have left (what with all this competition) on buying up the flood of new funny-books and records stuffed with the worthless imitation folk-junk they are peddling.

What are the distinguishing characteristics of fake folk-singers, and folk fakelorists, and phoney fakers and similar folk — if you see what I'm trying to get at — and how can the ordinary folklorist, or member of the audience, not really interested in cashing in on, or being swindled by, this new racket, tell the true from the false?

FIRST: The fake folksinger has learned all his songs 'from his old grandma,' or from an 'eighty-three-year-old shepherd in Hipboot County, Montana.' No folksonger has ever been in the New York Public Library or British Museum, or knows where these institutions will be found. They have never read a book or gone past third grade in school (to hear them tell it), so all their crud can be trusted as positively and authentically 'folk-transmitted.' They also tend to wear woollen shirts, and to shave off their hair and grow beards. This proves they are just folks and real authentic, being indistinguishable tonsorially from overfed corporals of the Prussian Light Cavalry regiments of 1871. How much more authentic can an American folksinger get? Contrariwise, your old-style mountain singer dresses in plain pants or overhauls (no sandals or beard), and *has some other job besides folksinging*. This is an important point. He is also likely to have a few printed slip-ballets somewheres around the house, or even a tattered copy of Ramsay's *Tea-Table Miscellany* or Burns' *Complete Songs*, like as not, and to be proud to admit he has learned a lot from it. This explains how it can happen (as it happened to me just last spring) that a real, authentic, internationally-appearing folksonger can sing you a fine old Scottish song about the interesting doings of a young man and a girl, learned 'from his old father in Snohomish County' — this told to you in all confidence as background for an intended tape-recording — the same song being nothing other than a word-for-word memorizing of a ballad printed in Herd's collection in 1776, the music likewise being memorized from print. There is nothing new about this. Also, the least part of the fraud is generally the unavowed memorized text and tune. The Rev. Sabine Baring-Gould — himself the most outrageous folksong-faker since Bishop Thomas Percy — was entirely taken in by (if he did not himself compose) the ten stanzas of doggerel, beginning and attempting to 'explain' the well-known "Gypsy Laddie" (Child Ballad No. 200), given him by an 'illiterate hedger' who had naturally 'inherited his songs by oral tradition from his grandfather;' and spent the rest of his life visibly miffed when Prof. Child dismissed this politely as a 'little romance.'

The rule is, therefore: real folksingers are intelligent people with an amount of shrewd common sense and dramatic flair, who do their best to learn good ballads from the best sources they can find — printed or otherwise — and who sing unaccompanied, or to an accordion, banjo, or something equally distressing to listen to. Folkniks, *per contra,* are homey, uneducated bums (when they are not teaching college), who never read a folksong book in their life, it says here, but who can and do accompany themselves with all the lushest and most applause-worthy chords of the six-string guitar. Mixolydian, of course.

SECOND: The early folksongers of the 1930's in the United States, who created the present folksong fad, used to add unionizing last stanzas to the cowboy songs and work songs in which they specialized, all about that One Big Union that tames the loco steer and will give us Clean City Government and paper-towels in the factory toilet. This is now looked upon as smacking of political *parti-pris* . . . unless the song happens to be "Bublitchki" or "Polushko Polie," sung in pidgin-Russian as learned in an adult-education kindergarten course, in which case it is simply the singer's plain patriotic duty and will help put *our*-man-on-Venus-first. The resulting catholicity of the neo-folksinger's repertory is little short of breathtaking, and sometimes stomach-turning as well, to all but cast-iron digestions. No one would today be surprised to hear, sung by one and the same singer, on one program: a tasty assortment of Child ballads (especially the ones about gruesome murders), a Palestinian children's round, sung with a strong Ashkenazi accent, and an Argentine tango-canción memorized from an old Carlos Gardel record of the 1930's; this followed — after a suitable break for folkloristic *café express* and selling copies of the folknik's latest records and book — with Burns' expurgated version of "John Anderson My Jo," the well-known sentimental stinker about the married couple tottering down the hill of life, to sleep 'thegither' at its foot, but no sex except in the high priced edition, limited — as it says right on it — to doctors, dentists, ministers of the gospel, pediatricians, pederasts, criminologists, *folklorists* above the age of four, and Associate-Professors of Applied Rape at the Jersey City Institute of U-Drive-It Aeronautics. The program then closes with "I Gave My Love a Cherry," in a suggestive version, a Japanese boatmen's song in Japanese (a bid for the Zen-beatniks in the audience, also in sandals, to keep the applause going later), and "Go Down Moses" scatted on the new electronic ukelele-dulcimer with cross-chords from "Salty Dog" and "Upright Organ Blues," for a smash finish in the colored people's supplement or outhouse. This may sound exaggerated, but I have before my typewriter a single issue of an insiders' folksong mag of recent date serving up a far more indigestible banquet of musical delight; and am refraining from citing the real programs of real concerts I have heard, only to avoid losing a few lifelong friends whom I will lose anyhow. As to the scat versions, I can testify to having been treated recently to a scatted "Silent Night, Holy Night," recorded by a Negro spirituals quartet, as member of a captive-audience on the bus from Vence to Nice on a perishingly hot July afternoon. Abraham Lincoln, if he could have heard it, would be glad he was dead. (This line is still stolen from Mark Twain, on the *Sweet Singer of Michigan.*)

The rule therefore is: a real folksinger sings about what he knows about and cares about, and sticks to one country and its history — his own. Within the limits of a bit of diversity in his repertory, a few humorous songs being mixed in with the feuding ballads, the keynote of the real folksingers' material is *consonance.* The folksonger is after the exact opposite: dissonance, and he prides himself (and just as often herself) on treating the audience to cutey-cute contrasts and a false-rebellion Cook's tour of sensation sucking and musical exotica, lacking only the bird-calls and zither-harp, but that will come. Folksongers are patriotic for everywhere and everything, and lack utterly that mean, distrustful attitude toward furriners so typical of real folksingers. If you re-mark upon this, you are given privately to understand that the folksongers are going to make everybody in the world love every-body else in the world by means of folksongs, folk dances, and the Pen-Pal Club. It is as simple as that. But phrased somewhat less in the 'little-man' or populist soft-focus democrackering the folk-songer pretends to serve, what he is really doing is goosing his jaded and dead-passive audience with the unusual songs and virile strength and sweat of unknown and 'undesirable' populations in all the quaintly exotic (read: gook) countries of the world, pre-cisely as with jazz. This makes it unnecessary to do anything else about it; and besides, one is beat, man, beat. Otherwise, why bother going around sucking up other peoples' virile strength?

THIRD: The kind of folklore faker who publishes books or writes sleeve-notes for other people's LP sleeve-jobs, rather than take a chance and sing in public himself, is difficult at first sight to distinguish from the ordinary flatulent college-professor. This confusion is carefully cultivated by the faker or phudnick (a phudnick is a nudnick with a Ph.D.), who generally styles him-self 'Dr.' on his printed stationery — or in connection with what-ever mail-order lecture-bureau he may be running — years before he gets his Ph.D., if he ever gets it. Real college-professors, on the other hand, hate to be called 'Dr.' and will generally pass, out of sheer gratitude, any flunker who refers to them familiarly as 'Doc.' A little alertness (especially on the part of the research founda-tions) will usually serve to distinguish the authentic professor from the folklore phudnick, even though both of them are likely to give out, on occasion, with the identical lecture on "The Origins of Jazz: Part I, Its Invention by Lord Francis Bacon and Jelly Roll Morton in 1892," with blackboard demonstrations à la Jules Feiffer, accompanied by scratchy old 78 rpm's (on the Bruns-wick label).

Most college-professors — I refer to those who do not have tenure: those who do have tenure are sometimes too busy get-ting their hands on the girl-students to bother with anything else until a very advanced age — have actually been exposed to some academic polish, and it generally shows. The folklore-fakers, no matter how big a library may make them honorary librarian, always seem to have difficulty getting the volumes of Child right-side-up in front of them, and one sometimes wonders who ghosted their Ph.D. theses. It will be observed that the phudnicks, who pretend to know something, but don't, are the exact contra-positive of the folksongers who pretend to know nothing and do. They meet on their sleeve-notes, which are exercises in ignorance and pretention, with an average error of plus-or-minus one hundred years in any printed date ventured, and are peppered with profoundly knowing references (at second hand) to Captain Billy's *Whiz Bang* and the *Fabliaux des Quenouilles* in the fifteenth century — whatever that may be. However, Kit Marlowe, Tom Durfey, and Bobby Burns are always referred to knowingly by the nicknames they never used, and a very flattering photograph of the fakelorist will also appear on the record-sleeve, right above that of the singer (shown caressing his guitars) if possible.

The books these gentry hack together are always superbly footnoted — *if* they happen to be reprinting for the umpteenth time texts already studied by George Lyman Kittredge or some more recent scholar or indexer, whose research is then simply appropriated wholesale and his name omitted, by some elaborate accident, from the notes in the back of the book. (The two most remarkable examples of this accident in modern times are both due to a single folk-scholar, Mr. N. M. Penzer, who not only omits from the bibliography of his edition of *The Ocean of Story* the original edition by Tawney which he is reprinting, bloated with footnotes; but who similarly omitted from the fantastically complete bibliography of his edition of the *Pentamerone* of Giambattista Basile any mention of the actual Italian text, by Benedetto Croce, from which he was translating!) Also in the back of the book the truth is usually told, in small type, about the faked and conglomerated texts — heavily expurgated too, but that isn't mentioned — which appear in the body of the book under some such *suggestio falsi,* of provenance, as 'Sung by Elizabeth Dowdington, at Stoke-Poges, April 17, 1905.' Seventeen stanzas, of which only the 1st, 11th, and 14th were actually sung by Miss Dowdington, the rest being taken in part from an undated broadside found wrapped around a codfish ball in Stockholm (this is of course a remnant of the secret codfish-worship or erotic *'hubble-ka-bubble'* of the folk, as is also the students' song, "One Fish-Ball," never however collected at Stockholm); and in part cobbled together from various other fragments, revised and rearranged by the fakelorist himself 'for the sake of coherence.' Miss Dowdington's tune is also transposed into the key of six sharps, instead of *C*, and arranged for four-part singing, so that the tonic or finalis will slip more easily into the various sucking-and-blowing apertures of the automatic tune-analyzer set up in the university basement. This is, of course, all in the good cause of bringing folksong to the folk (who would *never* have any if the fakelorists didn't help them), but, under the circumstances, that exact provenance, 'Stoke-Poges, April 17, 1905,' sort of sticks in one's craw when paraded as honest scholarship.

Before turning this unpleasant page of our modern non-Theophrastan character-book, one practical warning should be added. Failing any supply of prefabricated page-references, or other conveniently readymade work, modern fakelorists turn by preference to the unpublished manuscripts of earlier collectors, which they have found in out-of-the-way libraries, and which they then swindle the trusting backwoods librarians or land-poor relatives into sending them in microfilm, to 'edit down,' as this type of faker brashly puts it. This trick was invented by Allan Ramsay (the Bannatyne MS.) and Bishop Thomas Percy, the first and worst of the folklore-fakers, respectively, in the eighteenth century. Modern fakers are generally 'editing down' about fifteen suckers' manuscripts at any one time, the editing consisting mainly of finding fly-by-night publishers to print it from typewriting by the cheapest possible photo-chemical process, and arranging for the royalties to be payable strictly to them (the fakelorists), with tuppence a year conscience-money to the victim's starving widow. Or none at all, if the stuff can somehow be proved to be in public domain, because part of it was printed in the "Letters to the Editor" column of the Buchan *Bullcalf* in 1899. All the people on these con-men's sucker-lists are meanwhile continuously worked off against each other as sources of swonk and attractive bits of useless but recondite information, as possible helps in swinging a Fulbright award for that 'year in the field' abroad from which they return absolutely insufferable, whereas they were only repellent before), and as leads to further unpublished manuscripts. The resultant volumes in every case to be published under some such title as *"The Everliving Idiot,* Edited by JOHN CREEPE (in big type), from the manuscripts of ohwhatthehellwhocares (in small type) Francis J. Child."

FOURTH: One trait common to both fakelorist and folksonger nowadays is that both of them are cruelly loaded down with *machinery.* Your old-style folklore collector used to require the perhaps obvious but relatively inexpensive equipment of —

    1 pencil-stub,
    1 used envelope (turned inside-out),
    1 pair eye-glasses, for library work,
    1 pair heavy shoes for tramping around finding 'oral sources,'
    $5, for buying liquor to get them singing when found.

By means of apparatus like this, and perhaps slightly larger disbursements for liquor (or tobacco), were collected all the great folksong compilations of Europe since 1590, and later Britain and America, until 1910; as by David Herd, Robert Burns, Cecil Sharp, and Gavin Greig, to mention only a few of the greatest. What has been collected since that time with disc and tape recordings has made a very profitable industry, but has added precious little to the essential body of recovered texts or music in folksong. Nine-tenths of what has been mechanically recorded is reduplicative regional futilitarianism, and its value can be measured only in cash. Being so much more expensive than the old pencil-stub method, it is the mechanical recording technique *itself* that has created the folkniks, by tempting them to cash in on their investment in equipment. It is therefore a fact — and despite the so obvious and opposing fact, that folksingers die when folksongers are born — that the real business of the neo-folklorists, who are really just recording-company scouts, is to make saleable folksong recordings, of greater or less authenticity, and to peddle them, as a small but cushy corner of the entertainment industry.

As such, they go out now to every corner of the English-speaking world and abroad, as the German musical ethnologists invaded Africa and Asia in the 1910's, heavy laden with high-priced hifi recording-traps, and will look at you with heartbreak engraven on their face if some thoughtless 'native' sings a note before the folknik can get to the trigger — I mean push-button — of his expensive equipment, which weighs up to half a ton and requires a truck to carry it. Back in the processing studio, which has been outfitted with the even larger available capital of the real brains behind the act, the record-publishing company, or the army-inspired university and its 'human engineering' lab; even larger and fancier machines batter at the helpless tape suspected of containing a length of folksong. After which, if intended for commercial issue (and when isn't it?) the song is revised, re-written, orchestrated for jazz-band, and resung by the record-publisher's pet folksonger, male, female, or demi-caractère, all of whom are thus relieved of any necessity of paying a royalty to the original singer. In addition, and perhaps the better to disguise the steal, various types of Hollywood gunk and other background noises are further dubbed in, including washboard obbligatos, church-bells (on the New Religious revival), and sepulchrous echo for that 'three-dimensional sound' so easy to sell. But this is only the beginning. The mechanical folklore armamentarium will include soon, if it does not already, the new musical-interval counter, or IBM plastic brain, which will automatically separate the music-hall tunes from the Child ballads while the folklorist sleeps, by nuggeting out their 'inner core of musical identity,' and which can also be used — with only one small $28,400 attachment — for brainwashing Japanese spies (disguised as musical ethnologists), and eavesdropping on possible Messages from Outer Space while waiting for the war to start, after which the same machine will have certain other uses.

A heavy coating of this sort of folklore machinery, or bug-armor, sprayed over with a businesslike willingness to *use* the country people, factory-hands, etc., who are giving their folksong and art in perfect good faith, covers most specimens of the newly-hatched genus of insect parasites, *folkloreoptera,* from head to toe. It is especially marked on their mottled baby-blue station wagons, with pointy-bubs in front and fish-fins in back, guaranteed to scare the living bejesus out of the simple denizens of North Scotland, Southern Italy, farthest China, and Arabia Deserta, who are to be encouraged by the roving folknik or wayfaring wide-boy to sing some authentic ditty — without any self-consciousness, naturally — into the double-track stereophonic tape-recorder mounted on the delicate lavender roof of the station wagon, and specially outfitted by our own double-jointed scientists (working under water) with the new duo-Crotchworthy playback chamber, twenty-four floating-grease spoolwinders, machined at 100° F. to within a tolerance of .00,009″, and keyed to the now standard (but authentic) hifi-fooklore R.I.C.H. curve, which is somehow guaranteed to make little Mozarts out of people who have until now even hated singing in the bathtub. All by machinery, of course.

NOTE: The spellings in the preceding specifications have all been carefully checked with the paragraph of TECHNICAL INFORMATION printed on the back of the record-sleeve, which shows a semi-nude Yemenite belly-dancer, wearing only a veil, on the front.

(Wotsamatter, it's folklore, ain't it?) This sleeve, or sucker-trap, envelops the eventual $5.95 phonograph record issued when the roving folknik gets back from his concert-*cum*-recording trip, and puts everything under immediate and lifelong copyright for himself and heirs, on the basis of a simple payment of two bucks and the cheap lithoprint pamphlet of words-&-music slipped into the sleeve.

If the folknik's trip happens to have been paid for by a government grant, for noble international aims, &c., the copyright on all folklore swag brought back is *still* his — especially if the movie- and juke-box rights are worth anything — and the noble aims, international brotherhood of man, &c., can go to hell. Of more importance to all concerned is the incontrovertible fact, insisted upon by the record-sleeve, that the recording, as issued, has been manufactured from the finest Drecklon-Merdex chopped plastic (molded in hot suet), and the tapes remonitored strictly on the neo-R.I.C.H. curve, which is even richer than the old one — in high frequencies that only a dog can hear, and suffer from, that is — using none but the very newest Hitlerfunken microphones and Dollarfresser cutting-heads, made by Our German Friends in retooled gas-chambers, admittedly, but they have Know-How. Needless to say, the lesser breeds without the Know-How — the North Scots, Southern Italians, Deserted Arabs, &c., — who have been doing all the folksinging, will receive as their share: folk-all.

The final identifying rule is therefore this — and it has no exceptions. All folkniks, folksongers, folklore-fakers, fakelore-compilers (in twelve-volume series, and no end in sight), as also jazz-historians and Friends of the Downtrodden Negro Singer, have one characteristic in common, and by it they can invariably be told from the real thing: *They are all out for the money,* plus a goodly bit of cheap public attention and acclaim. Most of them have no other job than the hoked-up 'folklore' they are peddling, and would not take any other job, which might require some further effort than is required to exploit and debase the unpaid art-production of country people, factory-hands, itinerant singers (if there are any left, God help them), and the historic folk-arts to be found in 'public domain' in public libraries. Folk-fakers will not sing, record, or print one bloody word or note without a brassbound contract for a cut of the box-office take. Furthermore, unless they can pretend to be the artists themselves, *their artists are never paid,* except grudgingly, in damaged and returned copies of their own recordings, which are not released to them until several years after the possibility of any sales competing with those of the folk-faker or his record-publisher is past.

The above unfailing stigmata are not only the most infallible characteristics of the breed, but also the most peculiar thing about them, since they are so completely at variance with the whole soul and character of folklore. Real folksingers, and for that matter real folk, whether they can carry a note or not, *will* occasionally give forth with a song, or tell a joke, spin a tale, crack a riddle, or cut a caper at a local dance or beer-joint, just on the basis of good spirits, or having had a couple of drinks, or trying to please a pretty girl, or all three combined; without requiring cash payment and a 56-year copyright made out to them in advance. This is not even considered praiseworthy or peculiar of them, but simply the way it is done — the way folklore is (to coin a phrase) orally transmitted.

Folklore has been going on for centuries, and folklore collecting at least since the time of the *Fasti* of Ovid, two thousand years ago. But with all these quick-buck experts lousing up the field with their snivelling tricks, bogus *expertise,* and transparent pretenses for over two decades now, to the point where nobody can stand the smell from several thousand miles away, folklore is probably going to be a dead-letter soon. That is why they are all in such a terrific hurry to get in on the act before they are dry behind the ears, to bring out their (?) books, to book their concerts, to put out their records, or rather the records they call their own, composed of other people's songs and generally other people's singing, and all-in-all to get that share of the cash which they are positive is theirs by right, before the bubble bursts.

A constructive suggestion: I am in favor of a new law, punishing with one year at hard labor the singing of any folksong (two years if in a foreign language), or the playing of any folksong record; with the death-penalty for second offenders. This *might* — though it seems doubtful — cause some hardship to the one or two leftover octogenarians who learned their folksongs in an honest way from broadsides, and not from their 'old father in Hohokus.' But mostly it would rid the scene of this new infestation of entertainment-industry leeches and lice, whose repulsive and infected doings I have endeavored, with the utmost of restraint, to distinguish above from folklore and folksong.

WHO OWNS FOLKLORE?

I

THE CRISIS in folksong studies, which has arrived unheralded and, like the larger part of the iceberg, dangerously unperceived, centers around the disorganizing influence of the recent realization, by some, that folklore is worth money. Not very much money, admittedly, but just enough to blur the serious moral question involved in collecting and accepting the folksongs and folklore of largely unpaid informants and then copyrighting this material in the collector's name. This has been going on quietly since the turn of the century, but its significance has only dawned on folklorists recently, as it has become increasingly possible to to sell the collected folklore, in the form of highly-paid articles in national magazines, high-priced commercial omnium-gatherums of greater or lesser authenticity, printed and reprinted over a period of decades from electrolytic plates; and now phonograph records and radio, television, and motion-picture pop hit tunes.

This has created a small bonanza, especially for folksong collectors of an opportunistic bent, now that the so-called 'folksong revival,' which is little more than the commercial exploitation of folksong on records and in concerts, is in full swing. It has also created an unpleasant situation for other collectors, by increasing the tension and the unvoiced pullyhawlying between informants and collectors — who are inevitably outsiders and sometimes intruders. Amateur and sporadic collectors are generally unconscious of both the tension and the problem, but over the course of years of broad collecting it does and must result in serious lacunæ in collected repertory. The present writer was recently frankly told by an exceptional singer, an American Negro sailor singing informally in a Paris bar, who broke off in the middle of the transcription of a song: 'Ah, hell, that's about all fer tonight: I'm just sittin' here cuttin' my throat singin' fer beer an' cigarettes. By the time I git back to Nashville you're gonna have my song on a big record in the stores for five dollars.' His prophecy happens to have been wrong — the present writer has never made or issued a commercial recording, and never will — but the remark must be taken as expressive of what the singer knew, from the experience of his race if not of himself, was a fair probability as to the folksong he was giving away 'for cigarettes.'

This situation is not exactly new. Its unpleasantness rises from the realization of the monetary profits now newly involved. When Robert Burns and Sir Walter Scott, and other lesser men, collected folksongs and revised these songs into art productions of inferior value, folkloristically, to the originals; they were at least working — in the case of Burns, absolutely refusing all payment as 'downright Sodomy of Soul!' (letter to George Thomson, 16 Sept. 1792) — from a sense of national patriotism. That is no longer the case, however much the flag may be waved in the book-titles resulting, and George Washington on a horse, or bandaged Yankee Doodle with drum and fife, come marching down the dust-jacket.

There is also an increasing tendency to make whole books out of what turns out to be, when the footnotes are carefully studied, the repertory of sometimes one single informant or hardy more. This also is not new. George R. Kinloch's anonymous *The Ballad Book* (Edinburgh, 1827), a sort of humorous and erotic supplement to his major work, *Ancient Scottish Ballads*, almost solely represents the repertory of one singer, 'Mussel-Mouth'd Charlie,' nowhere mentioned in the volume itself, though this may have been in deference to the somewhat clandestine nature of the whole supplement. More recently, Dr. Norman Cazden's *Abelard Folk Song Book*, in 1958, also divided into two sections for the non-erotic and the mildly erotic songs ("Oh Dear, What Can the Matter Be?" among the latter), leans very heavily on the repertory of one singer, the late George Edwards, a Catskill lumberman, noted by Dr. Cazden in his acknowledgments and introduction as having supplied, 'by far,' the 'largest number of our songs and ballads.' What is meant here by the word 'our' is not clear. The copyright is issued to the publisher, Abelard-Schuman, with no mention of Mr. Edwards or his heirs.

What does this mean in legal fact? To avoid any air of personal bias, I will take an example from my own collecting, in this case at about fourth hand. In Alan Lomax's new and very remarkable *The Folk Songs of North America* (London, 1960), of which I have expressed my extremely high opinion for its courageous analytic and functional interpretations, in a review in the *Journal of American Folklore,* 1961; a text is given of "Frankie and Albert" (in expurgated form, under an abbreviated title, and with music not collected with the text), credited to me. I obtained this song in the form of an *un*expurgated pencil manuscript by a Negro pianist and singer, the late Palmer Jones, who stated that he had been taught to sing it by the exonerated murderess, Frankie Baker, herself, in the early 1900's. The manuscript — laboriously handwritten in 1927, when I was ten years old and can therefore hardly take much credit for it — was given to me by the late Robert Carlton Brown, who got it from Hilaire Hiler, for whose father Palmer Jones had originally written it out. The legal rights in that text — which is one of the best ever collected, and most authentic ever printed — now no longer belong to the presumed composer, Frankie Baker, nor to Palmer Jones, nor to the Hiler family, the Brown family, nor to me. These rights have now passed automatically to Alan Lomax, through the fact of publication, by the copyright notice printed in his new book. Speaking hypothetically, neither the ultimate informant nor any of the transmitting owners, nor any of their family or heirs, have any longer the legal right — and except by courtesy are not allowed — to print the words of this song as now for the first time printed in Alan Lomax's book, nor to sing or play them to any tune whatsoever for profit, over the radio, on television, or in a motion-picture, nor to record them for commercial issue on discs. A text of this exceedingly popular native American ballad has already been used in a hit play (thirty years ago), in at least one motion picture, and in an animated cartoon, *Rootetytoot,* built entirely around it; and it could easily again come to have commercial value. But the present text has legally passed out of the heritages of all the anterior informants and owners of the manuscript — *and out of the legal heritage of all the people of the United States and the world* — into the legal heritage and private property of the copyright owner and his family for the next fifty-six years, through the simple fact of printing the symbol © on the back of a title-page.

None of this is as hypothetical as it may seem, since precisely the situation envisaged here has actually occurred, and could occur again in connection with many of the hundreds of songs printed in Lomax's book for the first time, or reprinted in it from other sources; and with even greater mathematical probability in

connection with the thousands of songs, folktales, and the like,
that have entered into copyright and become the private property
of other collectors over the last fifty years. The song as to
which it actually did occur is "Tom Dula" (Dulac), and the problem could easily be aggravated if the 'bitch-heroine' motion picture for which the passionate story behind this song practically
yearns — fully detailed by Lomax and in the *Brown Collection,* ii.
703-08 — should be undertaken by Hollywood. This song, reprinted in the new Lomax volume, was first printed in the earlier
Lomax collection, *Folk Song U.S.A.,* in 1947, there credited as
'Used by permission of Frank Warner,' though the volume itself
was copyrighted in the name of the Lomaxes. When this song became a hit-tune in America recently, the copyright on the 1947
volume gave valuable rights to the Lomaxes, involving sizable
monetary payment, apparently equal to those of the collector-
singer, Frank Warner. This is perhaps the law, but is it fair? Also,
is it fair to the 'oral sources' from whom all folksong and folklore
is collected, who stand, generally unpaid, behind the copyrighting collectors and 'revival' singers, but who seldom — never, to
this writer's actual knowledge, except in this one case — are considered even for an instant when the time comes to divide up the
cash profits?

In a letter published in *Sing Out!* (New York, Oct. 1960), the
late Aunt Molly Jackson, a deeply authentic folk singer and poet,
voiced her dying protest against this sort of appropriation of her
own freely-given art by pawky collectors. She writes:

> I am eighty years old now. I live all alone. I am a widow
> . . . Barely existing along on the old-age pension. Nobody
> seems to pay me any attention. Only the folk song collectors
> that want me to teach them the songs I learned from my
> Kentucky ancestors 75 years ago. But if I ask them where
> I can get a few pennies for the songs I teach them, they just
> don't know. Since I left my home in Kentucky in 1931, I
> have had my songs that I composed translated in 5 different
> languages and records made out of my songs but I have
> never received one cent from anyone.

The Scottish collector, Peter Buchan, in the early nineteenth
century, at whom everyone nowadays seems to think it necessary
to throw a stone, was one of the few folksong collectors ever to
have the honesty and generosity, or even the simple practical in-

telligence, to put his main informant *on salary* for several years. More recently, a few handouts have been given to ageing Negro musicians, shipwrecked in northern cities, by writers of the ever-saleable "Histories of Jazz" and other journalistic piffle, but this is only a drop in the bucket when compared to the amounts of money paid to the same writers for even a single snappy article on the subject in a 'men's magazine' or other national publication, which can run from hundreds into thousands of dollars, not counting the later royalties when a group of such articles are gathered and republished as a book.

The competition at the present time for saleable folklore and folksong items might surprise folklorists who have not recently set their feet outside the halls of academe, and into the hills of benzedrine, on Madison Avenue, and in Tin Pan Alley and Holly-wood. The methods currently being used to snag, to concoct, and to peddle such items, even by highly reputable firms, are astonishing in the extreme. Particularly surprising are the two recent volumes, appearing with the name of Mr. James Reeves at the head of their title-pages and copyrighted in his name, comprising transcripts from the Cecil Sharp manuscripts, conflated to a fare-thee-well by Mr. Reeves — but respecting the original *punctuation!* — and without any mention of the music simultaneously presented in the manuscripts for each song; as also from the similar manuscripts of Baring-Gould, H. E. D. Hammond, and others. The names of Sharp, Baring-Gould, and the others are simply *spurlos versenkt* (except fleetingly at the bottom of the title-pages and somewhere in the introduction), and the material is copyrighted internationally by, and to that degree now belongs to, Mr. Reeves. The English Folk Dance and Song Society, in whose possession some of these MSS. now are, is unaware — according to correspondence with them recently on precisely this subject — of the actual operation of the copyright law in these matters. Mr. Reeves now evinces an interest in the similar manuscript materials of the late Alfred Williams, preserved in the public library of Swindon, Wiltshire, and used only in part in that collector's *Folk Songs of the Upper Thames* in 1923. It remains to be seen, if these are similarly published, not only who gets top billing on the title-page, but whether the materials are to be copyrighted in the name of the collector's family, of the people of England through the Corporation of the Borough of Swindon, or — as has been the fate of the folksongs of the Sharp and Baring-Gould manuscripts — of Mr. James Reeves.

These publications have sold very well, both in England and America, and a phonograph recording from the same selection of the underlying MSS. has recently been issued, almost anonymously, in London, at two guineas postpaid-foreign. What is particularly distressing is that the materials thus printed and recorded are *not* fakelore. They are folklore of the best and most authentic kind — except for Reeves' conflated texts and kindergarten maunderings as to the 'lingua franca' of erotic folk-symbolism (which he misses in the case of "The Nightingale," however, an example classic since the time of Boccaccio). The transmogrification of the centuries-old heritage of folksong and folklore into the private property of copyright is more serious and more sinister, when enacted upon folk materials of primary value, such as those collected by Sharp, than would be the case if this were just one more of the endless commercial series and sets, now upon us in full force, entitled "Cavalcade of Pennsylvania Folk-Prosody" (Vol. XVI), or some such high-sounding *patriotard* bunkum, at $6.95 per volume, issued by fly-by-night offset printers at vest-pocket addresses, affectionately known to themselves as "The Psychoslopical Press, Ltd.," or similar, and battening on the fact that the accession-librarians of five thousand American college and public libraries apparently have standing orders to buy anything with the crucial words, 'bibliography,' 'encyclopedia,' or 'folk' — *folk* anything — in the title. If the supply runs temporarily dry of second-rate compilers who need the advertising for their professional careers that such publication adds up to, there seems always to be be a sufficient number of bibliographical or folklore classics, out of copyright, or calculated to *go* out of copyright before the offset republication (unless piracy is the correct term) is finished printing. In one recent and particularly outrageous case, this was clearly calculated to the exact month, and this of perhaps the greatest classic of them all: the five volumes of the Child Ballads.

At a much higher level there are questions opened out, by this whole subject, too difficult perhaps to be answered here, but they are eminently worth raising if only because they have seldom been frankly phrased and never faced. A curious note is struck by the 'warning' — so described — at the end of the introduction to Alan Lomax's *Folk Songs of North America,* cited earlier: 'warning is hereby given that *most of the songs in this volume are protected by copyright*' (author's italics). Much of the material here sign-boarded as private property, under the copyright law, for twenty-eight or fifty-six years, was apparently collected by Lomax and his father, in part on funds allotted by the United States government during the mildly socialistic government spending and pump-priming of the 1930's, with the intention of saving *for the American people* some authentic vestiges of its fast-disappearing folklore, and with the implied further intention of ploughing or feeding this material back, through eventual publication, to the children of the people who had contributed it free. Free. The Lomax's books are by no means the only ones that have found themselves in this highly equivocal situation, in which public funds and scholarship awards have the air of having been expended to create private property and private gain in the folklore field. It is well known that government publications are not and cannot be copyrighted, and that anyone has the right to reprint or otherwise use them as desired. Until all folklore publications are issued on some such non-copyright, or government-retained copyright basis, Anglo-American folklorists are in the position of people unintentionally touching pitch, and they are going to be defiled. That pitch is money, and the tar-brush with which it is being applied is the curious idea that the lore *of the folk* somehow becomes the property of folklorists by the simple act of printing it. The higher the pitch rises in the barrel — and the more money that swirls somehow within reach, by the accident of hit-tune or motion-picture profits — the dirtier folklorists are going to find themselves forever bedaubed.

In a recent Supplement (April, 1960) to the *Journal of American Folklore*, p. 12, the Chairman of the Committee on Copyright Law makes the following recommendation: 'As of immediate practical concern members of AFS are advised to see that their publishers are members of ASCAP. This alert and efficient organization protects the property rights of its members.' The letter 'C' in the abbreviation ASCAP stands for 'composers,' for whose protection — and that of their publishers — this organization was created. On the basis of what moral or legal right is this arrogation of 'property rights' to be assimilated to collectors, who are practically sworn, by the ethics of folklore and folksong scholarship, not to compose a single line of the material they print? We are a long way, one hopes, from the century of John Gay's *Beggar's Opera*, and the dozens of imitation ballad-operas that followed, cynically enriching 'composers' and impresarios on the basis of fakeloristic parodies set to folk-tunes; or even, for that matter, from Stephen C. Foster, a century ago, copyrighting the Negro folk-tune, "The Camptown Races." As is not well known, "Jeanie

With the Light-Brown Hair" is also a pirated folk-tune, being nothing other than the Scottish marching song, "To Daunton Me," in Johnson's *Musical Museum*, 1790, No. 182. Many similar examples could also, of course, be cited since.

II

THE UNDERWORLD of folksong exploitation includes a few batrachian grapplings and regurgitations in the dark, of which even the most retired Ivory Tower folklorists are now becoming unwillingly and accidentally aware. For instance, if the singers or editors of 'folk' or 'popular' recordings are willing to print their names in parentheses after the title of each song, as 'arrangers,' they are paid a penny more or two cents more per song per record sold, adding up sometimes to hundred of dollars extra (beyond the original fee) when the royalties are totted up after the full period of sale is over. This convention — no one knows whether it has any viable legal status — creates for the singers or 'editors' a sort of synthetic property-right, in the musical arrangement and revised wording, when the material used is evidently centuries old, out of copyright, or otherwise in public domain.

The professional folksong people themselves are beginning to bridle at the dishonesty and repulsiveness of the practices which are putting over the so-called folksong revival, in which, for example, ten thousand paid attendances were totalled in a single weekend of the monster "Newport Folk Festival" (New York *Times,* June 27, 1960, as reported by Robert Shelton), at which folk festival however, the actual percentage of 'ethnic' — *i.e.* authentic — folk music to commercialized fake-folk bunkum was precisely 'twenty or so minutes . . . against fifteen hours of commercial music heard.' (Israel G. Young, in *Sing Out!* October, 1960.) Young also briefly reviews Alan Lomax's new American folksong collection, mentioned above, of which he remarks — tromping down flatfootedly on the pedal — that 'The only sour note occurs when we are warned that our heritage, so movingly described, is entirely copyrighted.'

In the same issue of the same insiders' folksinging magazine (along with a protest by the present writer somewhat less polite than this one, and here preceding), and in the earlier issue of February, 1960, two further insiders, Irwin Silber, editor of *Sing Out!* and Bill Eitman, describe the whole fantastic and repellent situation and its quasi-legal basis, and sum up the grass-roots revolt against it, in two articles on "Folk Songs and Copyrights" and "Copyrights and Collectors." These are astonishing documents, which would open the eyes of folksong specialists who may not be aware of what is really going on today outside the university world. The authors appeal to the 'honesty and integrity' of the neo-folksingers, while documenting in the most extraordinary and desperate fashion the utter abandon of both these qualities by the commercial collectors and singers to whom they are appealing, whose revamping and signing of folksongs — not to mention plain theft, in cases where the folk composer is actually known — and whose copyrighting practices and spurious claims of authorship are summed up flatly as the 'looting of the public domain.'

Some of the controversy stirred up by these articles is probably hypocritical. Not the attempted replies — these are sincere enough, though of course they restrict themselves to complaining about the 'tone' of the attack (especially my own), since no one would venture to deny that the facts are as stated. The hypocrisy, oddly enough, is in part on the side of the angels. In a way, what is bothering the professional folksongers of the 'revival' is not any outrage to their moral fibre by the practices of the copyrighters, but the evident fact that a certain number of the early-comers — especially Lomax, and others all too easy to identify — have sewed things up so tight that the newcomers are almost unable to whip up copyrightable repertory for their own output of recordings and books. It is time, and more than time, for the world of folklore scholarship to take a position in this controversy. Not only because it is the folklorists' own collections that are, in part, being rifled, but because it is the folklore and folksong of their own countries and people that are being prostituted, solely for the profit of the more opportunistic members of the publishing and entertainment industries.

Among the more recent spurious claims of folksong authorship — backed up by granted copyrights, be it understood, in the case of printed books — are such farcical absurdities as the sixteenth- and seventeenth-century British folksongs, "Go from My Window" and "Two Maidens Went Milking," claimed as 'written by Burl Ives' (this and all the following cited by Irwin Silber); the eighteenth-century "Blow Ye Winds of the Morning," currently claimed by the Kingston Trio; "Michael, Row the Boat Ashore" and "Drill, Ye Tarriers," credited as having been written by The Weavers; "Who's Gonna [!] Shoe Your Pretty Little Foot?" and "Michael, Row the Boat Ashore" (bis), also claimed by The Skifflers; "Swing Low, Sweet Chariot," by The Tarriers; "Auld

Lang Syne," claimed in Herbert Haufrecht's recent collection, *Folk Sing,* under the *noms-de-guerre* of the non-existent Jessie Cavanaugh and Arnold Stanton; and — stopping at nothing, apparently — the crediting of popular singer, Jimmie Rodgers, with the authorship of "Waltzing Matilda", "Froggy Went a-Courtin'," and "Lord Randall." The meaning of this nonsense is simply that, without such printed and broadcast claims, certain royalties set by the revised copyright law of 1909 at two cents per phonograph record manufactured could not legally be demanded by the singers, and these gentry apparently do not mind claiming to have written "Go from My Window", "Auld Lang Syne," and "Lord Randall" if they can receive two cents (per record) for doing so.

The end point has now been reached, not in America but in France, where the Breton national anthem, *"Bro Goz ma Zadou"* (Land of My Fathers), has been claimed and successfully copyrighted by private individuals, who, however, to show that their hearts are in the right place, have agreed to allow the song to be sung in public without payment of royalties on certain national holidays. Far from appreciating this *gentillesse,* the Bretons — who are by far the most fiery of French patriots — have preferred to take a lesson from the copyrighters' own book, and refuse to pay any royalties whatsoever, which they conceive in any case to be far less than the copyrighters deserve. (Local opinion is about equally divided between tar & feathers and hanging.) They have instead taken advantage of the language they speak in common with the Welsh, and have adopted since 1955 the Welsh version of this song, "Land of My Fathers," abrogating the copyright on the Breton version by using the slightly more martial rhythm of the Welsh, and changing the title, in impeccable riposte, to *"Bro Goz hon Tadou"* (Land of *Our* Fathers). They are now able to sing their own national anthem without paying anything to anybody, though the case has yet to be tried in the courts. The contests still being held in Brittany — as in Wales — for folkloric airs composed for dancing and processions, now pointedly end their announcement with this eloquent "Nota Important," as printed in *Ar Soner* ("The Minstrel"), Lorient, June, 1960, p. 11: '*Les airs retenus ne pourront être déposés* [copyrighted] *en aucun pays, ils feront partie du patrimoine public breton. La propriété de l'auteur sera morale.*'

It is to be hoped that British and American folklorists will take warning from the Breton experience, and this signal example of mad-dog commercial initiative, before some other 'folk-

singer' of equal crust, using it as precedent, decides to copyright
the rest of the available national anthems with, of course, revised
wording, hot-jazz orchestration, close harmony, omission of passages or sentiments in inconveniently high register (such as 'Send
her victorious' or 'Whose broad stripes and bright stars,' perhaps),
and other now-standard copyrightable improvements.

But that is only one side of the story. The other side appears
when, on occasion, the copyrighting singers and editors, and their
book and record publishers, are apprised by their competitors'
lawyers that they have unwittingly made use of some century-old
folksong that some other artiste has already latched onto, via
'arrangement' or other publication in book form or as sheet music
(of which latter unbelievable thousands have been copyrighted
every year now for over a century). Then, over goes the switch,
and they suddenly become desperate to prove, *mirabile dictu,*
that is is just an old folksong, don't you know, and really belongs
to all of us, as sons of Adam, Abraham Lincoln, My Country 'Tis
of Thee, the Little Man, and other populist shibboleths of similar
cut.

Thus it happens that a year does not go by that surprised
folksong collectors do not receive S.O.S. letters — in my own case
cablegrams — and special pleas through friends-of-friends, asking
how much money would be considered a proper fee to prove the
'p.d.' (public domain) status of some such ancient folksong as
"A Dainty Ducke" (in the *Percy Folio MS.,* circa 1620), *"Amo,
Amas,* I Love a Lass," or "Bollocky Bill the Sailor" — in polite
renditions, to be sure, as Robert Carlton Brown once remarked,
entitled "Testicular William the Nautical Gentleman," or something of the kind. When the amount of money offered simply for
page-references like these is considered (in round hundreds of
dollars, that is), one begins to have a rough idea of the real stakes
the record publishers and their 'folksingers' are actually playing
for. This is the company in which academic folklorists are now
finding themselves, possibly without knowing how they got there,
simply because of too rigorous a concern with their highly pre-
sumptive 'property rights' in folklore and folksong, gained on the
basis of printing field-collected folk materials with a copyright
notice.

Not to put too fine a point to it, in the fifty years that have
passed since the revised copyright law of 1909, almost the entire
body of British — and particularly American — folksong, and
much of the parallel folklore, has passed from the mouth of the

folk into the pants pockets of folklore promoters, and even a few folklorists, insofar as profiting, or attempting to profit, from printed publication, public performance, phonograph-record distribution, and possible motion-picture and broadcasting rights are concerned. The folklorists are now, apparently, looking for even further protection of 'property rights' in material that has become theirs only by the operation of something that looks bad and smells worse, and that lies — morally if not legally – about halfway between squatter-sovereignty and hijacking.

III

THE LATE Louise Pound who, as is well known, was the David to the Goliath of the 'communal origins' theory largely responsible for the strangling of modern ballad-study, proposed, as the final and crucial test of folksong — to distinguish it from the art-poem from which it generally takes its rise — that folksong must come to us in anonymous form and 'have lost all sense of authorship and provenance.' (*American Ballads and Songs,* 1922, p. xiii.) It is worth adding or comparing to this the important point made in a similar context by the Russian folklorist, Y. M. Sokolov:

> Anonymity is not a kind of distinguishing mark of folklore, in comparison with written literature. To secure for themselves, for their own name, the works of their personal creative genius has become the practice of the majority of peoples only since the beginning of the epoch of capitalism. In the epoch of feudalism the authors of written literary works, and also the authors of works in the field of the . . . arts (architecture, sculpture, painting), often did not aspire to perpetuate their own names. (*Russian Folklore,* New York: Macmillan, 1950, p. 11.)

The important exceptions to this statement are principally in the periods preceding feudalism, from which have come down to us, through their own intentional effort, the 'immortality' of the monarchs responsible for such monuments as the pyramids and the Taj Mahal, as well as the names of the real or presumed authors and editors (as in the case of the Old Testament) of particular collections of the ancient poetry, folk-legend, and religious literature of various cultures. Before these, however, as in the art-masterpieces of the prehistoric caves, and concomitantly, there are also tremendous periods of anonymity for all art, written or representational, all of which has therefore come down to us solely under the responsibility of the peoples of the creating cultures.

It is specifically the striving not only to sign and demand personal recognition for one's own art-products as private property down to the most insignificant items and details (such as initialled lamp-shades, and signed tablecloths and kerchiefs), and in this way to demonstrate one's personal worth in a society increasingly dedicated to 'vertical motility' on the social scale; but even, and in the same way, to sign and demand personal recognition for folklore and folk-art, and thus to make off with the profits and applause accruing, that has brought about the virtual destruction of real popular culture in our own time. The purposeful attempts in this direction, particularly over the last two centuries, have been most marked among the *entrepreneurs* of the European and American theatre and entertainment world, for the evident reason that the cash profits have been greatest in this particular avenue of the appropriation of folklore. The crisis has developed over a period of a century now, specifically in the music-halls and popular theatre of England and France since the 1850's, and in their massive development before our eyes into movies, radio, and television today.

The Man That Corrupted Hadleyburg in all this has been the application of electrical energy to folklore, which never needed electricity, the phonograph, radio, t.v., movies, etc., for its dissemination, and is being ruthlessly caricatured and destroyed by these 'communication' techniques, that strengthen the sending power of folklore, perhaps, but at the inevitable cost of fatally reducing its authentic folklore charge, now already below zero, to a minus quantity. It is now becoming increasingly clear that the enormous technological expansion of the possible audience for a single picture or spoken word in the twentieth century, from thousands to 'captive' millions, is actually in the process of destroying meaningful public communication. Every technological expansion and instantaneity has necessarily been countered by an equally and increasingly gigantic and pervasive censorship — social and political, as well as sexual — whose business it is to muzzle and neutralize and oversimplify in advance, to the intended vanishing-point of meaninglessness and vacuity, every word, every picture, even every symbol, emitted by these giant methods of 'communication' upon their stupefied audiences of simultaneous millions.

We have arrived in the western world at a point in the perversion of popular culture where not only print can do nothing for
the transmission of folklore except to harm (or embalm) it, but
where even the tremendous technological triumphs of simultaneous mass communication have proved incapable of competing
with actual folk-transmission, or of doing its job. This is so far
from being merely paradoxical that already in World War II,
when the propaganda services of all the countries involved were
given a message that it was considered really essential to make
the 'enemy' believe, this was never confided to the mendacious
press-releases and propaganda broadcasts that even the biggest
fools on both sides knew enough to discount two hundred percent — especially when presented under the euphemism of news
'comment' or impartial 'analysis.' Instead, such messages were
syringed privately into public consciousness by back-alley methods, like a poisoned enema, by means of instigated rumors and
word of mouth; that is to say, by the classic methods of ordinary
folk-transmission, but now magniloquently referred to — as thus
perverted — under the designation of 'white' propaganda, the usual
kind being presumably black. One is reminded of the 'divinity
fudge' cooked up on chafing-dishes in girls' schools, which avoids
the unappetizing color of the real thing, though retaining its
flavor, by being concocted entirely without chocolate. Public confidence in this propaganda fudge, of whatever color, has, in any
case, deteriorated unspeakably further after two World Wars.

The same methods are of course being kept active in peace-
time in the open and hidden advertisements of the absurdly
overrated 'mass-media,' which are at the present time entirely
divorced from the real or natural interests and folk-character of
their audience, except insofar as they concern themselves with
sports. The rest of the output of these 'media' — from newspapers
to t.v. and all the rest of it — is without exception undesired and
undesirable, and must be force-fed to recalcitrant, if not entirely
captive, audiences, by means of shocker publicity tricks and habit-
forming perversions such as sadistic spectacles (as in Rome, and
doubtless for the same reason), and, finally, by means of plain
cash baits. That the threatened next step is to make use of the
paranoid and hypnotic persuasions of 'subliminal perception'
techniques — hardly necessary to resort to if anyone really wanted
the product — need surprise no one. I would suggest, after that,
a kind of 24-hour-a-day compulsory government radio, playing
through the fillings in people's teeth, with no legal way of turn

ing it off. *All advertisements.* Motto: 'It beats as it sleeps as it cleans.' One hour a week, on Sunday, an international brotherhood broadcast about the 'common man,' with folksongs, accompanied by organ music, and masticated juicily by picked teams of those failed politicians or ethical-society pulpit-caressers who seem to make up the bulk of the professional and international lovers-of-mankind — on yearly salary.

The public *loathes* the mass-media, which it has never to the slightest degree trusted since the days of the moon hoaxes and newspaper canards of the nineteenth century at least, and by which it understands perfectly well that it is being simultaneously enslaved and defrauded. One fake-folkloristic detail that is the ultimate and perfect typification of the entire swindle: consider the bogus folk-festival of the yearly national 'beauty contest,' in which the only parts of the young lady contestants' private anatomy that remain hidden under *cache-sexe* Bikinis, composed of two postage-stamps and a cork, are precisely the parts the audience is dying to see. That is not the kind of beauty contest that started the Homeric Wars.

Oversold and overextended into impotence in their relations with the public, the only real concern of the mass-media — and more particularly of the advertising agency bright-boys hidden behind the scenes — is that the well-hoaxed advertisers, who are paying the piper, should not be allowed ever to realize that it is simply a schoolboy fraud or leg-pull; that exactly as many pairs of shoes will be worn, and loaves of bread eaten, without any advertising whatsoever — though evidently not as many Rolls-Royces, yachts, hi-fi television combines, and vacuum-sealed tins of top-shell terrapin, quails' fingernails, and peacocks' pukings, as advertised in the snobbier comic magazines. Furthermore, and in plain English, that the whole stage-décor scientificism of the setup, intended to validate the astronomical fees charged — the phoney polls, the 'weighted' samplings, the rigged popularity indexes, nay even the magnificent 'national cross-sections' of daytime t.v. watchers apparently home on the dole, quizzed by batteries of dirty-nailed lobbygows over Hitler-style tapped telephones, and processed 'electronically' by white-coated business machine tenders (who THINK) — is nothing more than a colossal and expensive fake, of which the cost is naturally passed along to the public, hidden in the box-top price.

The replacement of the arts of literature and the stage, since the First World War, by movies, radio, television, disc- and tape-recordings, and other mechanical substitutes and succedanea for the living experience still in the womb of Time, has operated principally as a mass premium for mass illiteracy and passivity, and has had the effect, owing to the monumental and reduplicative censorships under which it staggers, not of making human communication more easy, more broad and instantaneous — as advertised — but of making it *impossible,* except for sexless and synthetic art, sadistic entertainments, and falsified information that no rational person wants to see broadcast at all. The devastating effect on the audience has been all the more marked in that this mass drowning in hokum and bunkum is in a terrible way the exact opposite of the real and vital emotional involvement with one's environment that the human being needs — in meaningful work, in believable art and authentic folk-expression, that one recognizes as belonging and true — as a bulwark for the individual, and one of the few remaining, to protect the ability to generate real and human emotions, against utter estrangement and collapse in an increasingly mechanized world.

That the responses of this newly killed, and therefore dead-passive, audience to bogus entertainment, and its saturation with the accompanying drone-bass of mendacious advertising and news, can possibly be sampled by hole-punching machines 'manned' by push-button scientists need not particularly be wondered at. Nor that the dregs of music, poetry and art that captive audiences can be forced to absorb (not to mention the official propaganda and other pap) will soon be, if they are not already, mechanically extruded by permutational ticker-tapes and vacuum-tube machines that THINK — an obvious necessity in civilizations that don't. But that such cultural offal should be referred to as *folklore* is, of course, outrageous. One would prefer that it continue to rejoice in the self-applied denomination of 'science.' When every human emotion or folk expression must be broken on the wheel beforehand, as the *sine qua non* of public performance, and forcibly reduced to the simultaneously watered-down and jazzed-up fakelore and kitsch, until nothing remains but pre-fabricated human process cheese, wafted over with a garlic belch about the 'common man,' it seems almost unnecessary to observe that what passes for folklore and folksong — and of this *folk* — cannot possibly be anything under these circumstances but the most pitiful travesty.

Of course, no one wants to prevent, or would try to prevent the folk from singing their own songs privately or telling their own jokes — that is to say, if they can get a word or a song in edgewise, among their silently absorptive duties as captive audience. (Making their own bread, or planting their own corn, in twelfth-story apartments — with or without all the folk rites appertaining — is obviously more difficult, though doubtless permitted.) As a matter of fact, the type of 'for the folk' anthologies, of which the Lomax volumes are the principal current examples, are specifically intended to give back to the folk their own songs, which they would of course, never, never have without the paid ministrations of wandering folklore collectors. They can sing the songs all right, and even 'learn 'em from book.' Thus the mad scramble to publish such books, which amateur street-corner skifflers are even encouraged to buy. But heaven help anybody that tries to sing a printed song or tell a printed folktale for money! The money to be made out of folklore (and we are now learning to our surprise just how much money there seems to be), belongs to the *owners* of folklore. And the owners of folklore — God bless us all — now turn out to be the folklorists who collect and print it, generally on government and university grants; but who did not create it, who are, as a matter of fact, forbidden by the rules of the game even to try to create it, and who — one ventures to say — bloodywell cannot create it.

La Clé des Champs
Valbonne (A.M.) France

INDEX

INDEX

ACKNOWLEDGMENTS

IT IS MY privilege to acknowledge here the kind permission to print manuscript and other materials in the collections of the Department of Printed Books, British Museum; the Houghton Library, Harvard University; the Hornel Library, Castle-Douglas, Kirkcudbright; the Murison Burns Collection, Dunfermline Public Library; and the School of Scottish Studies, University of Edinburgh; and in the private collections of the Rt. Hon. the Earl of Rosebery, and Mr. W. N. H. Harding, Chicago.

I must also acknowledge the prior publication of certain of the essays reprinted here — in all cases in much enlarged or unexpurgated form as now printed: "Pisanus Fraxi" in *Bibliography of Prohibited Books*, New York, 1962; "The Horn Book" in *American Aphrodite*, No. 9, 1953; "Misconceptions in Erotic Folklore" and "Toward a Motif-Index of Erotic Humor" in *Journal of American Folklore*, vol. 75, July 1962; "The Bawdy Song" in *Explorations*, No. 7, 1957; "Folksongs, Fakelore and Cash" in *Sing Out!* October, 1960; and "Who Owns Folklore?" in *Western Folklore*, vol. 21, January 1962; to all of which my thanks are due for permission to reprint.

G. LEGMAN